THE LETTERS OF

RALPH WALDO EMERSON

THE LETTERS OF
RALPH WALDO
EMERSON

EDITED BY

ELEANOR M. TILTON

VOLUME EIGHT 1845–1859

NEW YORK
COLUMBIA UNIVERSITY PRESS

The publisher gratefully acknowledges
support toward publication given by the
National Endowment for the Humanities.

COLUMBIA UNIVERSITY PRESS
New York   Oxford
Copyright © 1991 Columbia University Press
All rights reserved

LIBRARY OF CONGRESS CATALOGING-IN-PUBLICATION DATA
(Revised for Vol. 8)

Emerson, Ralph Waldo, 1803–1882.
The letters of Ralph Waldo Emerson . . .

Vol. 8. edited by Eleanor M. Tilton.
1. Emerson, Ralph Waldo, 1803–1882—Correspondence.
2. Authors, American—19th century—Correspondence.
I. Rusk, L. (Ralph Leslie), b. 1888.
II. Tilton, Eleanor M. (Eleanor Marguerite), 1913–   .
III. Title.
PS1631.A4 1939   39–12289
ISBN 0–231–07516–2

Casebound editions of Columbia University Press books are Smyth-sewn
and printed on permanent and durable acid-free paper

PRINTED IN THE UNITED STATES OF AMERICA

c 10 9 8 7 6 5 4 3 2 1

THE LETTERS OF
RALPH WALDO EMERSON
1845–1859

1845

To Caroline Sturgis, Boston? January ? 1845[1]

I am sorry to be so slow in sending these letters you wished to see, but for an idle man I have /been/ pressed & surprised with affairs & company for many days in succession, and now that I come to collect them I miss the letter from T. C. on Tennyson which I lent to Mrs /S./ Ripley,[2] I suppose, & which is not yet restored. This last letter of Louise interests me much more than anything before from her, it is so sad, yet so sincere & delicate in its tone. I see that it does not authorize me in any inquiry after her present [d]welling[3] & state.

To Samuel Joseph May, Concord, January 13, 1845

[Enclosed with the letter of the same date to Samuel E. Sewall, below.]

To Samuel E. Sewall, Concord, January 13, 1845[4]

Concord, Jan 13, 1845

Samuel Sewall, Esq.
Dear Sir,

Enclosed I send an open letter to Mr May giving an account of the transaction in relation to the Cogswell estate, as far as I am informed.[5] If

1. MS in the Tappan papers, Houghton Library, MH; ph. in NNC; p. [4] addressed: Miss Caroline Sturgis. The note is endorsed 1845. The Carlyle letter referred to is that of August 5, 1844 (Slater, pp. 361–364). The first letter from Louise Weston after that date is of December 3, 1844, dated from Boston (the next letter is of April 29, 1845, and is dated from Augusta, Maine); this note then must be later than December 3, 1844. Replying on February 4, 1845, to Emerson's letter of February 1, 1845, below, Caroline Sturgis says she has seen Louise Weston; this note then must be earlier than February 4. Finally, Caroline's letter of February 4 has in it a direct comment upon Giles Waldo's letter to Emerson of December 27, 1844. Since this note of Emerson's did not go through the mail and covered a packet of letters, I conjecture that it was written in Boston.

2. Sarah Bradford Ripley is likely.

3. A corner of the leaf is torn here.

4. The MS has not been located; text from Truman Nelson, "Emerson Letter Gives Insight to Purchase of Wayside as Alcott Home," *The Concord Free Press*, January 20, 1967, p. 1. I correct the spelling "Sewell," not an error Emerson is likely to have made.

5. Emerson with Samuel J. May and Samuel E. Sewall, trustees for Abba May Alcott, were buying the Cogswell property: Emerson purchasing eight acres of land and May and

you please, you will read it before sending it. I hoped Mr. Cogswell would have given you your deed, but he brought it to me. I therefore borrowed the money, $850.00 of the Concord Bank for a few days saying to the President that probably on Thursday next,[6] as I shall be in Boston on that day, I might be enabled to pay him. I will call on Wednesday or Thursday in relation to it.

Yours Respectfully,
R. W. Emerson

To Horatio Cogswell, Concord, January 26, 1845

[In the MS Account Book for 1845–1849, p. [7], under the date January 26, 1845, is recorded the payment of $6.00 "by cheque in letter" to Horatio Cogswell. It is not clear from entries on pp. [2], [3], and [4] whether this money is additional to expenses already recorded in connection with the purchase of the Cogswell property.]

To Samuel Gray Ward, Concord, January 31, 1845[7]

Concord, 31 January

My dear friend,
   I hope the City looks friendly & domestic to her sometime son, and not reproachful & too mindful of his wanderings. Tis a good goblin, and

---

Sewall purchasing one acre with house and outbuildings. Horatio Cogswell had apparently brought to Emerson both deeds. Cogswell had already sold the property to Washington C. Allen (deed recorded with Middlesex County Registrar on September 18, 1844; MS vol. 447, p. 497) who appears as grantor on both Emerson's deed (Jan. 15, MS vol. 454, p. 445) and that of Mrs. Alcott's trustees (Jan. 10, MS vol. 454, p. 447).

   Emerson financed these purchases by borrowing from Daniel Shattuck, president of the Concord bank, for five days the necessary $850. He contributed also $6.00 for "Cogswell's expenses" and paid the lawyer Nathan Brooks a dollar for the transfer of the insurance policy to Samuel E. Sewall and Samuel J. May, Mrs. Alcott's trustees. Brooks acted also in the transfer of the purchase money to Sewall and May (MS Account Book, p. [4], entry dated only "Jan," but falling between entries dated January 13 and 18). An entry in the MS Account Book for 1845-1849, pp. [2] and [4] under the covering date January 8, 1845, records Sewall's payment to Emerson of $857.20. On p. [3] of the Account Book record, Emerson records his payment of $500.00 to Cogswell for eight acres of land as well as the payment of the $850.00 and $6.00 (his share of $12.00) for the expenses and 50 cents (his share of the $1.00 for the transfer of the insurance policy). This entry is under the covering date January 11.

   Both deeds are drawn so as to protect Mrs. Alcott from Bronson Alcott's fecklessness, whether she chose "to occupy and enjoy the premises with her family free and clear from all claims of said Amos and his creditors" or the trustees chose to rent the property or sell it on her written order. This is the property known as the Wayside which was subsequently sold to Hawthorne.

   6. The text has "Next" here; Emerson could not have intended a capital "N" here.

   7. MS in the Ward papers, Houghton Library, MH; ph. in NNC; p. [4] addressed: Saml. G. Ward. at house of T. W. Ward, Esq | Park Street | Boston. The letter is endorsed 1845

the most devout lovers of nature will find the Exchange, the Tremont House & the Concert Room tolerable in February. The woods of Berkshire (a week ago all cased in diamond) the frozen lakes and skies a little too pure must reckon themselves happy if a fortnight hence they preserve the least charm for your imagination. Indeed what a maceration & self-immolation in these children of art & civility to have lent their grace to those rocks & Wildernesses so long! I praise & admire you, though you should never see the Saddleback mountain again.[8] Well, I long to hear the tale of your horrible sufferings in savage life, and shall hurry to town before the charm of your escape is worn off. I pray you offer my best congratulations to Anna on this glad occasion.

Ever yours,
R. W. E.

To Caroline Sturgis, Concord, February 1, 1845[9]

Concord, 1 February, 1845.

I was in town on Thursday, & met William Tappan, and we took a long walk over the Mill Dam[10] towards Brookline. I proposed to bring him to your house, but he intimated a design to go there by himself, so I

---

and the stationery is the same Emerson had used for his letter of December 2, 1844, and would use for the letter below of March 13. The Wards had come down from Lenox on January 30. The matter of the letter would be puzzling if it were not for a letter in a similar half-jesting vein from Charles Sedgwick to Ward of February 2, 1845 (Ward papers, Houghton Library). Both Emerson and Sedgwick write as if Ward were leaving the Berkshire Hills for good, but Sedgwick begs him not to be tempted by the fleshpots of the city, and Emerson congratulates him on quitting savage rural life; both letters are extravagant in style. The Wards had taken up country life in May 1844; in August, Ward proposed to buy farm land and in September he had made part of the purchase (letters in Ward papers, MHi: May 15, 1844, Thomas Wren Ward to his partner Joshua Bates; August 22 and September 17, Samuel Gray Ward to his father Thomas Wren Ward). Since there was nothing flighty about Samuel Gray Ward, whose father described him as "prudent, industrious, and a great happiness to me" (letter to Bates cited), Emerson's letter is, I think, like that of Sedgwick, a somewhat labored joke. And since I can find nothing specific for which Mrs. Ward might on this date be congratulated, I take it as an allusion to her assumed sophistication as a woman of fashion who has returned to the world to which presumably she belongs. Again a letter of Sedgwick's strikes the same note; writing Ward on February 23 (Sunday, but misdated 24 by Sedgwick), he says he has heard of "your wife's dissipating" and dancing until two in the morning.

8. Mt. Greylock, the highest mountain in the Berkshires, is in the northwest corner of Massachusetts; it was known also as Saddleback in the nineteenth century.

9. MS in the Tappan papers, Houghton Library, MH; ph. in NNC; p. [4] addressed: Miss Caroline Sturgis. The letter did not go through the mails; it apparently accompanied the returned volume of Fourier. Emerson's MS Account Book for 1845-1849, p. [9] shows a payment to Adams's Express of .66 under the date February 1.

10. January 30. For the Mill Dam in Boston, see Walter Muir Whitehill, *Boston: A Topographical History* (Cambridge: Belknap Press, 1959), pp. 90–93, 100–101.

contented ⟨he⟩ myself with carr/y/ing him to the corner of Winthrop
Place, & indicating to him your house. Did he come? He thought he
should go to New York in the P.m. & presently return hither to spend
perhaps the rest of the Winter. So you shall be sure to see him if you will.
I liked him well enough—Is not that astonishing after seeing him three
times? He has not the genius of Charles K. N.[11] nor the vigour of my
Iroquois friend,[12] but is far more agreeable company than either.

I have read through this volume of Fourier with surprising ease
considering what courage it cost to begin. It is well worth reading. Here
is another French Revolution, which, however brilliant & astonishing,
can never make any progress out of French territory. It is a French mind
speaking to French minds, and when it arrives among the Saxons will be
sure to find many a/n/ ⟨Nels⟩ incorrigible Nelson & Wellington. It repeats
precisely the old French dream of regenerating men by skilful disposition of circumstances. There are so many French men in every country
(such as Brisbane, Ripley, Dana,[13] in ours,) that this will ride & prosper

11. Charles K. Newcomb.
12. The Iroquois friend is certainly Thoreau.
13. Albert Brisbane, George Ripley, and Charles Dana. In 1842 and 1843 Emerson had
found Albert Brisbane only too eager to convert him to Fourierism (*Letters*, 3:30, 38, 146);
see also Emerson's "Fourierism and the Socialists," *The Dial* (July 1842), 3:86–96, and below,
April 20, to J. S. Dwight. In his MS Journal V, Emerson writes: "Fourier is a French mind,
destitute of course of the moral element. Brisbane, his American disciple, is also a French
mind. The important query is *what will women say to the Theory?*"[a] (*JMN*, 9:100). The journal
passage quoted above concludes with "Certainly not Brisbane but Channing must propose it
to them." Someone has added in pencil "jr" after Channing's name, but Emerson plainly
means William Henry Channing.
[a]Caroline Sturgis' reply offers one answer to the question:
"Still seizing everything in the claws of morality, dear Waldo? Why may we not live like
grasshoppers? Must we be so good? Planets and Potatoes, seas & soapbubbles, all things are
made for man, and how can we be lost? I cannot understand the thirst for excellence—I
have no taste for it but follow the winds wherever they blow, while all wise people shake
their heads and cry out to me, 'Take care, my dear, the devil is close behind you.'
"Why not wish Fourier to make the finest arrangements possible!—we must eat our
dinners every day, why not eat them in the best way? Music & mathematic, science, wit,
economy, all things demand it except love, for that can find a home everywhere: but let us
give love its noblest instruments and see to what it will attain. Fourier is not French in his
system, only in his inferences. What can be more magnificent for this world than his table of
periods, what more true for all worlds than that 'les attractions sont proportionelles au
destineés.' God has no aspirations, no renunciations, ⟨why⟩roses & nightingales have none,
why should we. only to be at home!—that is so good; ⟨P⟩but we all put on great-coats &
travel about in stage-coaches—nobody knows where. Everything is for me—why should I
renounce anything? If I cannot have what I must have in this world why not go to another
—can man or angel make objection. If a man must be patriotic and stay where he is born let
him have a great heart—there is no renunciation in that. And then too the divine rises &
says, 'You have sinned—Repent & be forgiven.' & to this no answer can be made but that
here we must stay and take our part with Irish & Ethiopians, villains & slaves. Since it is so,
why not bring order into this Chaos as soon as possible. Will it be too easy to be good; shall
we be so refined that love & beauty will not still be above us? Can any outward arrangement

like a poem of Voltaire, for a time; but whenever it comes across an English mind, like W. H. Channing and finds any reception, I fear it will prove a disaster /to him/, so certain it is that he will recoil. What a misfortune that our English blood is loaded with that black melancholy

---

supersede the laws of individual being? Now ⟨we⟩our ⟨are⟩barks are stranded upon the shore or puddled about in inland lakes from which there is but a narrow outlet;—would it not be better to be borne along on a wide stream where with *vigorous* arm we could row to every island & wild-flower that should attract us? Would there be any moralist if all were in harmony with all; do ⟨energy⟩puritans sit with keen grey eyes around the angels with their heavenly harps. Let us learn the scales here & tune our instruments for the great symphonies.

"But there is something in this morality,—manliness is it—which I do not rightly apprehend. I am always so happy because joy seems upon the very threshold, or unhappy because it is so far away, that I am like one tossed upon the sea,—now plunged in dark hollows, now riding the high waves. Thus is it with all women however they may seek to veil their weakness in incessant gossip, bread-making, and literary manias, except a few who have retired upon their sorrows. Is it because we cannot look straight-forward like men, or that men do not need to love. Only to join my hands and place them in another's would be happiness. Why is it that men do not believe in love? The⟨y⟩ few who seem to do so, mistake passion or philanthropy for ⟨lo⟩it—they do not see that love is the Open Sesame of the Universe. They seize hammer & spear and go about striking and piercing: they burst open the gates of life, the shattered gates fall upon them and they lose that which they would find.

"It may be that G. W. only 'flies from love' because he has no one to love him.[b] Friends are nothing: only to be in love is the desire. If a woman should love him he would no longer wish to be left alone, for then he would know that all could be forgiven, that he would be loved for himself, not for his qualities. He is too delicate a nature to deal with men only: if once his heart could be satisfied he would again meet them frankly. This, of a stranger, what right have I to say?—but he sends his love to all whom you love. I should not say friends are nothing, it is good for me that you are my friend. This becomes always more real, while almost everything else becomes every day more unreal. The most splendid systems cannot equal one friend, but must we not accept these systems also, for they will help us find the balance in ourselves.

"You are eager for Fourier as the Caliph was to hear every night the tales of the genii, & so I will send you the second vol. I can borrow Frank Shaw's for myself as I have almost finished it. ⟨Also I send the one for⟩ Shall I give you the one for Sampson Reed some day in Boston?

"Your bird of Paradise lights upon the earth, I believe. I did not see him.

"Your friend
"Caroline."

"Feby 4th 1845.

"Is not Margaret growing too good?—I cannot write to her, I am so wicked. Ellery and I fire pistols at each other occasionally. He says he is very unhappy but there is some pleasure in saying it. I went to see Louisa Weston—she entered the door while I was on the steps & I knew it was ⟨her⟩she by her expression—she sent word she was very much engaged—so much for intrusion. I hope you will always be a good father confessor for all these young ladies & gentlemen and will let me see the confessions, for I am your sister & a silent one. Sometimes I can interpret them better than you; that is because you do not like to admit possibilities—all must be absolute with you, but I know very well that there is something besides blue sky in the Universe. I wish these people who go into caves would let me love them; we could go about together and gather flowers, but they think you like nothing but diamonds & feel friendless while you are their friend—Friendless in being loved above themselves or not all. Dear Waldo, Good night."

[b]G. W. is Giles Waldo; his letter of December 27, 1844 is quoted; the bird of Paradise is William Tappan; Margaret is of course Margaret Fuller and Ellery, Ellery Channing.

savage element of morals, whilst the light hearted Gauls have no such impediment. But I appreciate the genius of this new Napoleon, so able, so equal, so full of resources, & so just in his criticism on /existing/ society, though the critique loses some of its point in New-England. I wish you to send me another volume immediately, if you can spare one. If we were permitted to make experiments, I would enlist for five years under this gay oriflamme. But there is an immense presumption against every experiment in morals. We must not overstep our sphere or system to gratify hopes & wishes which as such decorate our days like rainbows but could only be realized by violence. In all Arcadia it is against the law to crush butterflies. Do not imagine that I forget the loneliness & privation of women, of those who are the boast & excellency of the sex,—I regard it as a postponed good which puts the gods in their debt, and not as a mean fast which can be broken at the first tavern. How many things are there not, my dear friend, which dear friends cannot say to each other; but the wise world will answer all questions at last. Let it tell you how heartily I am yours. Can you soon lend me this volume of Fourier again for Sampson Reed the Swedenborgian who asks for it?

To William Aspinwall Tappan, Concord, February 2, 1845 [14]

My dear friend,

It was fully my intention early this evening to have written you a letter, as I had something at heart to say. But another has taken the hour I meant for you, & I have only to ask at present your care for these enclosures. With much regard, with much expectation,

Your friend,
R. W. E.

Concord 2 Feb.

14. MS in the Sophia Smith Collection, MNS; ph. in NNC; p. [4] addressed: William A. Tappan | Care of Lewis Tappan, Esq. | New York. | The year is written with a different pen; it is certainly correct; the note is written just as Tappan is leaving Boston; see February 1, above. There is an ink note on the address leaf that is apparently written by the donor or very likely the donor's mother; it lists other letters in the collection including one from "George ⟨i.e. Giles⟩ Waldo" and one from "my M[other?]" referring possibly to a letter by Ellen Tappan to her paternal grandfather Lewis Tappan (misdescribed as to William Sturgis, the child's maternal grandfather).

To Edward Jarvis, Concord, February 5, 1845[15]

Concord, Feb. 5, 1845

My dear Sir,

I have been hoping to hear from you for some weeks whether you would come to our Lyceum on the first or second Wednesday of this month; for so I think we left it,—that you should choose between those two days & inform me. Our necessity has meantime filled up the first of the two evenings, as we expect Dr Palfrey tonight. Will you come next Wednesday? If so, and I hope you will let it be so, please to inform me by mail. I regret that I shall not be in town on that Evening.[16]

Yours, with great regard,
R. W. Emerson.

Dr Edward Jarvis.

To William Henry Furness, Concord, February 7, 1845[17]

Concord, 7 February, 1845

My dear friend,

I will do something, so help me the Muses! for the Diadem; but a more invita Minerva than that of my experience is not between the Delaware & the Merrimac rivers.[18] However I have been spirited up lately from several sides to collect my verses, and in all the medley or motley, something may turn up that I can send. I have written to Carlyle by the Cambria, reciting to him Mr Carey's good intentions, & my concurrence with the same, and that Mr Carey comes to us like a deus ex machina,[19] to save us in these last days from all pirates. I told him of the design of the picture, and urged his compliance with the request to sit. I have not heard from him for two months.—

I have not sent any advertisement such as was agreed, to signify

15. MS in the Barrett Collection, Alderman Library, ViU; ph. in NNC; without address leaf. Listed in *Letters*, 3:277, from auction catalogue; Rusk notes that Jarvis' lecture for the Concord Lyceum on "Health," was given on February 12.
16. See December 6, 1844, for correction of Charvat's schedule of 1845 lectures; Emerson was in Dover, New Hampshire, on February 12.
17. MS in the Furness papers, Van Pelt Library, PU; ph. in NNC; p. [4] addressed: Rev. William H. Furness. Philadelphia Pa.; postmarked at Concord, February 7; printed in *Records*, p. [35]; listed in *Letters*, 3:278.
18. Cicero's proverb meaning contrary to the bent of his genius; i.e., Emerson finds his muse reluctant, but he did contribute three poems to *The Diadem* for 1846 (BAL, 5206, 1363): "Loss and Gain," "A Fable," "The Fore-Runners." See May 9 below. Emerson's *Poems* was published at the close of the following year.
19. *Ars Poetica*, 1. 385.

Carlyle's approbation of the new edition, as I suppose you may not want
it yet. But I will not be wanting in my part to so good a design.[20]

Ever yours affectionately,

R. Waldo Emerson.

William H. Furness.

To Caroline Sturgis, Concord? February? *c.* 8? 1845[21]

Well I have nothing to answer at present to this spirited defence of
Fourier but will keep it before me. Yet the moral sentiment always nerves
us: the indulgence always effeminates: and from Sparta down to Boston
—but the sermon is a long one—you shall not have it from me. I am
quite of the other persuasion. Only I have heard traditions from poets &
spirits, seen them in pictures & statues, gazed at them in dear faces &
manners which I cannot keep entirely out of my head, and which taught
another doctrine than this Frenchman. and just for taste & for beauty,
which should rest on strength, I should think things would go better in
an austerer society—and the roads would be safer.

I am somewhat puritanical in my way of living, you will think; but I
am not in my theory: yet if I should calculate like these French people, I
should say, let me be the only libertine in a restrained society, to reach
the heaven of Epicurus. In a libertine society, all falls abroad to grossness
—it is the universal thaw & dissolution of things.[22] And that seems to me
the open tendency of these gay arrangements. Perhaps I slander the
divine man, the beginner of the new French Revolution, which we will
hope will end better than the others, but afar off this smells furiously of
the guillotine. I will not fail to examine this new book you have sent me,
though at first look, it seems not so easy to read as the last.

It was very kind of you to go to see Louise W.;[23] and very kind is the

20. Carey and Hart's one-volume edition of *Critical and Miscellaneous Essays* (*BAL*, 5205).
See Slater, p. [374], where Emerson outlines Carey and Hart's proposal and quotes a letter
from Furness (not in *Records*).
21. MS in Houghton Library, MH; ph. in NNC; p. [4] addressed: Miss Caroline Sturgis
—| Care of Wm. Sturgis, Esq. Boston. Since this letter, endorsed "Feb. 1845," is clearly a
reply to Miss Sturgis' letter of February 4, see February 1 above, it cannot be much later
than February 10 even allowing for Miss Sturgis' habit of putting off the mailing of her
letters. He returns this volume of Fourier on March 2, see below.
22. In MS Journal W, p. 23, Emerson writes: "Fourier, in his talk about women, seems
one of those salacious old men who are full of the most ridiculous superstitions on this
matter. In their head it is the universal rutting season. Any body who has lived with women
will know how false & prurient this is; how serious nature always is; how chaste is their
organization, & how lawful a class of people women are" (*JMN*, 9:191).
23. Louise Weston. See Miss Sturgis' letter quoted with February 1 above.

comment on G. W.[24] I am afraid I have not written him the best answer: I must send him another. Where are my letters and those you were to lend me? Here are more papers. I prize the whole of your letter.

W.

To Benjamin Rodman, Concord, February 8? 1845

[Emerson would surely have replied to Benjamin Rodman's letter of February 7, 1845 (RWEMA), inviting Emerson to be his guest if he accepts Thomas A. Greene's invitation to lecture in New Bedford in March. He had refused Greene in a letter of February 7. Rodman's letter, however, provides information: the subject of Emerson's lecture in Fall River on January 7 was "Napoleon."]

To Giles Waldo, Concord, February? ? 1845

[See above February 8? to Caroline Sturgis, where a letter to Waldo is clearly indicated and a second letter proposed. I let this entry stand for both.]

To Daniel Martindale, Concord, February ? 1845

[The minutes for the March 4 meeting of the Peithologian Society of Wesleyan University report a letter from Emerson; see Kenneth W. Cameron, "Emerson at Wesleyan University," *ESQ*, 11 (II Q, 1958), pp. 56–57.]

To T. Sewall Lancaster, Concord, February 14, 1845[25]

Concord, Feb. 14, 1845

T. Sewall Lancaster Cor. Secy.
Gloucester Lyceum
Dear Sir,

I will not again refuse the friendly invitation which has already come to me once or twice heretofore from your Lyceum, but will hold myself engaged to you for Thursday Evening March 6th,—as that is one of the days you propose.

Yours respectfully,
R. W. Emerson.

---

24. Giles Waldo. See Miss Sturgis' letter quoted with February 1 above.

25. MS in the Rare Book Department, PP; ph. in NNC; p [4] addressed: T. Sewall Lancaster. | Gloucester | Mass | ; postmarked at Concord; the date is blurred but appears to be that of the letter. The letter was inserted in an edition of *The Complete Works of Edgar Allan Poe*, Extra-Illustrated by Thomas W. Lawson, New York and London, G. P. Putnam's Sons, 1909. It appeared with the passage on Emerson in "A Chapter on Autography," 18:160–161. The manuscript has now been removed from the book.

To Caroline Sturgis, Concord, February 14? 1845[26]

Sam Ward came to see me on Monday & spent a night here.[27] I was
never so much impressed by the finished beauty of that person. He was
a picture to look at as he sat, and his conversation was the most solid,
graceful, well informed, and elevated by his just sentiment. What sincere
refinement! What a master in life! for his talk for the most part was of
his new purchased farm, of the house & buildings he is to raise, of his
village neighbors, and of Massachusetts & American politics. I compared
this man, who is a performance, with others who seem to me only
prayers. How easily he rejects things he does not want, and never has a
weak look or word. He recommends by his facility & fluency in it the
existing world of society and Alcott & Fourier will find it the harder to
batter it down. I found myself much warped from my own perpendicular
and grown avaricious overnight of money & lands, after hearing this fine
seigneur discourse so captivatingly of chateaus, gardens, & collections of
art. He brought with him his translations of Goethe's pieces on Art & left
with me the one called the "Collector" and the next day I found the
images of Ward & of the "Collector" perpetually blending themselves.

26. MS in the Tappan papers, Houghton Library, MH; ph. in NNC; This is a single
sheet, torn at the fold; the second leaf was evidently torn away before the letter, possibly
incomplete, was sent to Cabot; the note "send J E C" appears at the foot of p. [2]. Printed
from Cabot's copy in *Letters*, 3:278–279, with Cabot's misleading elision marks at the beginning of the letter. That the leaf torn away is the second leaf and not the first is evident from
the paper manufacturer's stamp.

27. Ward's visit to Emerson had to be in February, for the Wards did not arrive in
Boston from Lenox until January 30, and before March 3, Ward took his wife to New York
to leave her for treatments from Margaret Fuller's mesmerist. These termini are established
by a letter of February 2 to Ward from Charles and Elizabeth Sedgwick who report having
heard that the Wards "got through" (there had been a storm) on Thursday; Charles Sedgwick himself had been in Boston the last week in January, returning to Lenox just in time to
bid the Wards good-bye (Charles Sedgwick to Thomas Wren Ward); see also Emerson's note
of welcome of January 31 above. By February 28, Mrs. Sedgwick writes her daughter
(Catherine Sedgwick Minott) that she hears the Wards are going to New York; on March 3
she writes a relative in New York: "I suppose you have our dear friends the Wards with you
now." Ward had returned alone to Boston by March 10, but as Emerson's letter of March 13
below shows Emerson did not see him that week. (The Sedgwick letters cited are in MHi, the
first two in the Ward papers; the others in the Dwight-Sedgwick papers.)

Of the four Mondays in February, the first seems unlikely; moreover, if the visit had
been made then, Emerson would have mentioned it in his reply to Caroline Sturgis'/letter of
February 4; see February 8 above. The 24th of February is ruled out because Emerson was
in town that day (see March 2 below and Miss Sturgis' letter of February 24). Of the other
two Mondays, neither is ruled out by Emerson's February lecture engagements (see December 6, 1844, above for correction of Charvat). The journal entry describing Ward's visit is
undated (*JMN*, 9:132). I assign Ward's visit to February 10 and the letter to the 14th,
although dates (17, 21) in the following week are not ruled out.

He is like Goethe & Madame de Stael of that class of persons who should never die: they are so felicitously adapted to this world that it seems as if they must lose by being transferred to any other.

To WILLIAM ASPINWALL TAPPAN, CONCORD, FEBRUARY 26, 1845 [28]

Concord, Feby 26, 1845

Do you not wish to go to Middlebury College with me next July to attend the Commencement. I am to deliver a speech to the Literary Societies there, on the 22 July. Vermont will be then in full leaf, and you who know the place will be the best guide. If I could know that you would go, it would help me when I came to write for them. [29] But whatever we get at the journey's end, we are pretty sure of good speech on the journey: speech is nowhere else so exculpable.

To CHANDLER ROBBINS, CONCORD, MARCH 2, 1845 [30]

Concord, March 2d, 1845

My dear Sir,

Had I remembered any piece of mine which seemed to have a special fitness for your purpose, I should have made an opportunity, amidst a press of petty affairs, to name it; but none occurring to me, I have left the selection to your and my good fortune. It would have given me pleasure, could I have known of the occasion earlier, and *if the Muse had been willing,* to have recalled for poetry those earlier days—many anxious, many pleasant, all thoughtful days, which I spent in the service of the Second Church. I stood a few weeks ago at the foot of the new tower,

28. MS in the Sophia Smith Collection, MNS; ph. in NNC. This unsigned note is a single sheet addressed on the verso: William A. Tappan, | Care of Lewis Tappan, Esq. | New York |; it is twice stamped at a Broad Street express office, the name illegible.

29. See February 2 above to Tappan and February 1 to Caroline Sturgis. He had certainly in January attempted to effect a meeting between Tappan and Caroline Sturgis. Since he would invite Caroline also to hear his Middlebury address, he may be suspected of match-making. But see August 17 for Emerson's disappointment in Tappan's failure to keep an engagement to meet him on the boat.

30. No MS has been located, text from Chandler Robbins, *Our Pastor's Offering* (Boston: printed by George Coolidge, 1845), p. 34; listed *Letters,* 3:279.

Emerson's letter is not very clear, and we do not have Robbins' letter to him. In the work itself, three poems appear to be credited to Emerson: Edward Bliss Emerson's "The Last Farewell," without title immediately following this letter; "Woodnotes I" which is Emerson's and "My Thoughts" which is Christopher Cranch's. All texts follow *The Dial.* Other poems by Cranch appear in the work; all appeared in *The Dial.*

and gazed up at its stately mass and proportions with great satisfaction. I hope it will confer new benefit every day as long as it shall stand.[31]

Yours, with great regard,

R. W. Emerson

To Caroline Sturgis, Concord? March 2, 1845[32]

Sunday 2 March

We are eager to draw our friends close to us & get the most we can from them at once, so little faith we have in the permanence of this pretty dream.[33] (But it will be as easy to blow another bubble as this, and the raw material of the rainbows was only a little soap & water.) Yet to carry friendship to its height & grandeur seems almost to indispensably require a second existence. Our life is scarcely long enough for its proof & tempering. A friend carried through some crisis with our consciousness & counsel does not particularly encourage us; but when the originality of his choice takes him out of our sympathy & even out of our neighborhood & circumstance, he may acquire claims on our reverence & on our intellect which must be paid in a new world. Sometimes also it seems as if no one could thank the great but himself: there will be a little misapprehension of his act in the best friend. But whilst I believe that virtue is thus great & savage, I am always prompted to succour it with praise, and can hardly hold my tongue from saying to a generous mind, 'persevere.' These are two parts of friendship, & the third is the desire of perpetual presence & society.

It is full of mysteries, it is full of fate. Our daemons or genii have obviously more to do with it than the measure-loving intellect, and what most of all fascinates me in my friend is not permanently in him, but

31. See *JMN*, 9:78, for Emerson's note of the razing of the Second Church (March 11, 1844) and his address of March 10. See p. 119 for the cost of the new building he here refers to. The book was to be sold at a Fair to raise money for furnishings for the Church.

32. MS in the Tappan papers, Houghton Library, MH; ph. in NNC; p. [4] addressed: Miss Caroline Sturgis. The letter is endorsed 1845; March 2 fell on a Sunday that year, and the reference to the second volume of Fourier makes the year certain; see February 1 and 8? above.

33. This letter is a metaphysical reply to Caroline Sturgis' plain declaration: "Do not find a place for me in Concord for I do not wish to come there. I do not like to refuse anything and I must refuse to see people there . . . Ellery and I must look for our farms in heaven" (a.l.s., Tappan papers, Houghton Library). Caroline's letter is without date, but the last paragraph is headed "Monday, eveg," and the postmark is Boston, February 26: that is Wednesday; the allusion to Ellery's hope of a farm provides the year; see below, April 30, for Channing's purchase of "twenty" acres in Concord. In her undated reply, she acknowledges the return of the Fourier.

comes & goes, a light that plays about his head, but does not always dip so low as into his eyes.

Is it not so, my dear friend, you who are always more valuable to me? But I did not take this sheet to write sentences on friendship, but to beg you to send me another volume of the Frenchman, instead of this, which I have not read much of.

W.

To James Munroe & Co., Concord? March 6? 1845

[In a letter of March 7, 1845, Munroe & Co. lays down the terms for the proposed publication of Samuel G. Ward's translation of Goethe's *Zur Farbenlehre* and presents the "estimate" of costs as requested; on the first leaf appears a note signed by Ward and dated March 10; Ward accepts the terms. It is not clear that Munroe is replying to a letter from Emerson or to a verbal request. Ward's note on the letter shows that Emerson must have returned the letter to the publisher. See, below, letter of the 13th to Ward, which shows that Emerson had visited the publisher's office on the 12th and learned that Ward had called there. I let this entry stand for the possibility of two letters to Munroe & Co.]

To Wendell Phillips, Boston? March 6, 1845 [34]

My dear Sir,

I am sorry if it annoy you, but excuse you the Concord Lyceum will not but awaits with erect ears the truth concerning Texas.

Yours in haste
R W Emerson, Curator

6 March

34. MS in the Feinberg Collection, MiD; ph. in NNC; single leaf; printed in Charles Hamilton's Catalogue 26, lot 116, 1958, and, from that, by Cameron, *ESQ* (4th Q, 1958), 13:37. The handwriting of this note is unlike Emerson's normal hand; he is certainly not using a familiar pen. The paper is a scrap torn from a larger sheet. Emerson is clearly writing in haste; there is no address. The note may have been delivered by hand.

The MS records of the Concord Lyceum (CFPL) show that on March 5, it was voted to invite Phillips to address the Lyceum, whereupon two curators resigned, Emerson and Thoreau being elected to replace them (*Letters,* 3:279). Phillips appeared to lecture on slavery on March 11. Since normally lecture dates could be adjusted, the firmness of this note seems to suit the occasion. See letter (defective) to Samuel Gray Ward of March 12 below.

To Francis Alexander, Concord, March 12, 1845?[35]

Concord, 12 March

Francis Alexander, Esq.

Dear Sir,

I am sorry to say that though I have not at any time forgotten your request since it was made, I have yet met with no opportunity of procuring exact information respecting the Minns Farm in Lincoln. My neighbors estimate it variously as containing from 170 to 200 acres, and say that it has been in the market for some years past, offered at about $10,000. I have heard from one person that the proprietor does not at present wish to sell it. I learn however that George Minns, Esq., a lawyer in Court Street, is a brother of the late owner, & can give you any information respecting it. Mrs Minns, his sister in law, now resides on it.

Yours with great reg[ard],[36]

R. W. Emerson.

---

35. MS in the Barrett Collection, Alderman Library, ViU; ph. in NNC; p. [4] addressed: Francis Alexander, Esq. | Boston. | ; postmarked at Concord March 13. According to the *Vital Records of Lincoln, Massachusetts to the Year 1850,* Constant F. Minns died in 1841. Three *[sic]* years after his death, the records show a child born to his widow Frances Ann Minns. No Minns appears thereafter in the *Records.* The letter then is likely to be later than 1844 if only to allow for "some years past." It has to be earlier than 1853 when the painter Francis Alexander went to Europe (not returning until 1869) and when George Minns moved from 23 Court Street to 20 Old State House. The date assigned remains uncertain, for the *terminus ad quem* cannot be closed in. Except for a small portion sold to the Fitchburg railroad in 1844 (deed dated November 15), this property (194 acres and 21 square rods) was not sold until November 14, 1862 (Middlesex County Registry of Deeds, MS vol. 452, p. 186; vol. 895, p. 450). In the transaction of November 15, 1844, Frances A. Minns is specified as Administratrix.

Emerson had known the painter Francis Alexander for many years; he had met him in Rome in 1833 and shared lodgings with him in London (*Letters,* 1:380, 392, and *JMN,* 3:155, 156). Moreover, in 1825 Alexander had painted a portrait of Ruth Haskins Emerson; see *JMN,* 4:272 (the editors of this volume do not recognize that the painter referred to here is the same man Emerson had lodged with in London). It is likely that Alexander knew George Minns, for when Dickens visited Boston in 1842, Minns was one of five signers of the invitation to the dinner given by the "young men of Boston" and Francis Alexander painted Dickens' portrait. Edward F. Payne, *Dickens Days in Boston* (Boston: Houghton Mifflin, 1927), pp. 4–5, 34.

36. Text damaged when the seal was broken; the last three letters of "regard" adhere to the seal.

To Samuel Gray Ward, Concord, March 13? 1845[37]

My dea[r friend,]
going to Boston
here, I learned at Munroes [t]hat you were in town & sought you in Park
Street & State Street in vain. Some special village politics forced me to
return home in the 1 1/2 cars, after leaving your Mss. with Munroe. On
my return I found your letter enclosing the printer's estimate, &c[38] and
⟨shoul⟩ learned your design of a precipitate retreat to the wilds
                                            [s]hould have
                        [f]or Mr Wendell [Phillips] the whole
                                                      splendid
                                        [Lyce]um, wherof
                                            "Curator," in
                                     village discords.
                              not go early to the
post office, I receive a new letter from you dated *Tuesday* and it threatens
your departure tomorrow.[39] I have now but a slender hope that this
sheet can reach you tonight, but on that contingency will say, that if you
have not made the correction in the Ms. I will give them immediate
attention & send you page & line. If the retrospective or the prospective
hours, or those which are both, give you another sonnet, I shall heartily
thank you, if you will send it to me. Have you ever heard W. Phillips? I

37. MS in the Ward papers, Houghton Library, MH; ph. in NNC; p. [4] addressed:
Saml. G. Ward At house of T. W. Ward, Esq | Park Street | Boston |; above the address: Paid.
To be delivered this (Thursday) Evening. Partly printed with an incorrect date by Norton,
p. 60; listed *Letters,* 3:279, with the date corrected to March 12 because of the reference to
hearing Phillips "last night"; Wendell Phillips' Concord Lyceum lecture was delivered March
11. I date the letter the 13th because of the note above the address and the explicit entries
in the MS Account Book for 1845–1849 p. [13]; under the date March 12, Emerson enters
the expenses of his trip to Boston; under the date March 13, he enters: "Letter to S. G. W.
.12." The corner of the letter torn away has slightly damaged the text on the first leaf and
seriously damaged it on the second. The salutation here is suggested by January 31 above.
    38. The printer's estimate is on the verso of a letter to Emerson from James Munroe &
Co (RWEMA); the letter sets forth the terms the publisher offers for Ward's translation of
Goethe's essays on art; to it Ward has added a note of his acceptance of the terms offered.
The letter is dated March 7 and Ward's note is dated March 10. The missing portion of p.
[1] of this letter then must refer to a trip to Boston made on the morning of March 10,
Emerson's early return from the city made necessary by a meeting of the Concord Lyceum
officers, possibly to report a communication from Wendell Phillips, the selection of whom as
a speaker had precipitated the "village politics" and "village discords" referred to in the
letter (see *Letters,* 3:271). I conjecture that the portion of text damaged on p. [2] gives a brief
account of the discord which led to Emerson's and Thoreau's becoming curators of the
Concord Lyceum.
    39. Presumably Ward's "new" letter of March 10 noted corrections (Emerson clearly
writes the singular) in his MS. Ward was leaving to take his wife to New York.

have not learned a better lesson in many weeks than last night in a couple
of hours. The core of the comet did not seem to be much but the whole
air was full of splendours. One orator makes many but I think this the
best generator of eloquence I have met for many a day & of something
better or grander than his own. Fare you well![40] Every friendly power
attend you to your new home, and I cherish the belief that your choice is
an omen of a better day than the present to our old Massachusetts.[41]

Waldo E.

To Caroline Sturgis, Concord March 16 1845 [42]

I was in town yesterday & ⟨brought⟩ carried with me these two letters
of E's, with the expectation of seeing you: but affairs & appointments
took all my time, so I send them now. The principal thing he has been
doing in N. Y. seems to have been cultivating his acquaintance with
W. A. T. of whom it is very entertaining to hear him speak. I send you
one letter to me, because of the account he gives of the new friend. I
make no apology for detaining your vol. of Fourier which I have read
through, and have, at Hawthorne's desire, lent him, for a day or two, but
if you want it, you shall have it immediately. Also when I am next in
town, I mean to look up Mr Sampson Reed, & recall your 1st vol. In
acknowledgment of these good designs I wish you would send me home
W. T.s letters which you retained, & Louise Weston's book & letter.[43]

Sunday Evening

Adams's Express[44] at Doolittle's City Tavern, is a perfectly safe messenger again. I mention this, because I believe I discredited the convey-
ance when the man was sick.

40. Ward's decision to be a farmer rather than a banker, a decision Ward carefully sets
forth in a document of December 2, 1843, addressed to his father (Ward papers, MHi).

41. "Highwood," Ward's Lenox house, about to be built. See April 30 below, letters to
Ward and to his wife, and February 14 above.

42. MS in the Tappan papers, Houghton Library, MH; ph. in NNC; p. [4] addressed:
Miss Caroline Sturgis, | Care of William Sturgis, Esq. | Summer Street | Boston | . The
reference to Fourier and to Ellery Channing's stay in New York make the year 1845. The
Channing letter referred to is that of March 10 (Houghton Library) which describes William
A. Tappan. Channing announces that he will return to Concord "a week from to-day." On
April 5 (*Letters*, 3:281) Emerson tells his brother that "Channing has been here in our house
a week or two." The only possible Sunday on which this letter to Caroline Sturgis could have
been written is March 16.

43. The other Channing letter is probably that of February 9, postmarked February 10
(CSmH). There is only one Tappan letter, dated February 14, but postmarked February 20
(RWEMA).

44. Augustus Adams.

To John Chapman, Concord, March 26, 1845[45]

Concord, 26 March, 1845.

Mr John Chapman.

Dear Sir,

The kind offer of Mr James Brown[46] to take a parcel to you, induces me to send you the copy you were good enough to forward to me of your edition of my Essays, with such errors as I have discovered, marked. The importance of some of the errors leads me to beg that they may be corrected in the plates, if that is practicable, before any new copies are struck off. If that is not practicable, I entreat you to send out no more copies, without a copy of this list of errata inserted after the titlepage, or at the end. I have marked with an asterisk those that I consider important. Two of them, I believe, are errors of my own edition. One of your errours, the misplacing of a motto of "Character" before the Essay on "Manners," may have come from an accidental misarrangement in Munroe's pacquet of proofs.[47] There is a general correction I should like also to make in your edition in regard to the use of quotation marks. My practice is, when I make a bona fide quotation from any person, to make it with double commas, but when the quotation is only rhetorical, or in the form, I use single commas. I have in looking through your copy, marked such errata /as they occurred,/ but do not think them of sufficient importance to print them in the list. These apart, I find your copy very faithful: and if we shall have occasion to print again hereafter, I will try to give you more time.

Yours, with great regard,
R. W. Emerson

45. MS in the Sterling Library, University of London; ph. in NNC; p. [4] addressed: Mr John Chapman | 121 Newgate Street | London | Kindness of Mr Brown | ; postmarked at Liverpool, April 13. Reproduced in facsimile by Mignon, *ESQ* (4th Q., 1973), 19:225–227; printed, p. 228.

46. Of the firm of Little and Brown.

47. Houghton Library has a copy of the English edition with the mottoes reversed. There is no errata slip. A copy in Special Collections, Butler Library (NNC), has the mottoes where they belong. See M. A16.2c note, p. 18.

To Caroline Sturgis, Princeton, Massachusetts, April 1, 1845[48]

Princeton

A strange accident brought me to this nobly placed village not on the side so much as on the shoulder of Wachusett.[49] The wind has blown all day as befits a mountain country; for we must not be cockneys & expect to bring up here the air of walled streets and low villages. So making the best friends I could with this sublime inconveniency, against which I could hardly keep on my feet, and must hold my hat on my head, I climbed up this evening, an hour ago, just before sunset, to the summit of what they call the "Little Wachusett," which is a lower terrace of the hill, and found a view which made my heart beat. Right before me was the strong Monadnoc   to the south a little lay the Hoosac mountains in Berkshire; and I fancied that the hills I saw behind them, were the Catskills. Far around, like great sea monsters, these mountains reared their huge backs in the horizon, and the tamer eastern counties lay spread out at my feet sprinkled with towns, & shining with now & then a river and a pond. The forests that cover all the country at short intervals have quite another look seen from this angle from above, than that which breeds so much reverence as we ordinarily pass below their boughs. They are now a fierce whisker or wild hair-lock of the unkempt Pan. It is good to leave your known melancholy house & grounds, & melancholy neighbor's houses & grounds, and climb these two or three rounds of God's ladder & see counties. At once all is changed, & /all/ assumes a planetary air, & I begin to see the shining of it, when a little further withdrawn, like Mars & Jupiter. If tomorrow is a good day, I shall probably drain this vein of April folly by scrambling to the top of Wachusett.[50]

48. MS in the Tappan papers, Houghton Library, MH; ph. in NNC; p. [4] has a blank space for the address, but no address appears. The final sentence and initials are at the foot of the leaf and appear to have been written with a different pen, possibly added later; see April 8, below, for Emerson's complaint of what appears to be the same pen. I believe Emerson neglected to send this letter until April 6 and that he may have left it at her father's house. Emerson's MS Account Book for 1845–1849, p. [17] under the date April 4, 1845 (3 deleted) has an entry for expenses of this trip to Leominister, Princeton, Sterling, Lancaster, Shirley, and home to Concord. This letter is cited by Rusk with the wrong date, *Life*, p. 541.

49. I have no solid evidence for the "accident"; but I conjecture that Emerson was looking for a place for his brother Bulkeley; see May 10 below for his removal of Bulkeley from McLean Asylum to Richard Hall's in Littleton. In 1848 when Hall could no longer keep Bulkeley, Emerson writes his brother William: "I must go & beat the countryside again, & find him a new home" (*Letters*, 4:116). The itinerary the Account book shows for this 1845 trip is a loop made from Leominister on the railroad back to Shirley, also on the railroad, a trip consistent with beating the countryside.

50. For a trip to Wachusett with Caroline Sturgis, see May 6 below.

It is not strange to you, I hope, that mountains & clouds recall to me the dear friend of these meteors and of me.

I fear I am not to go to Boston until Wednesday of next week when I will hope to see you.

R W E

To Margaret Perkins Forbes, Concord, April 6, 1845?[51]

Concord
6 April

My dear friend,

You have, no doubt, been looking for the little parcel of letters you confided to me, & they ought to have returned to you at once. I read every word, & do not wonder that you find worth & entertainment in them—I mean, of course, Mrs C.'s—for they have both character & talent. And tis honorable to both of you, this later pleasing relation of the school friend,—& charming in the unlikeness of the parties.[52]

Thanks for Caroline's letter. I do not know how you can resist it—tis so earnest an entreaty for what looks so fit & fair. She is a wise child & of happiest nature, always knowing well what she wants, and so secure & perfect in action & manners, action & manners[53] which I find in her writing also. What pity life is not long enough to live hundreds of years with such people, till we are sure we know what they know. Lidian thinks I sent her note a week ago, & here it is still. You must lay the blame where it belongs on your friend,

R. W. E.

51. MS in Special Collections, NNC; ph. in NNC. Of the extant letters to Caroline Sturgis, only one fills the conditions of this letter. See April 1 above which is securely dated 1845 and which did not go through the mails although Emerson left the space for an address on the fourth page. From this letter to Miss Forbes, it is inferrable that Caroline Sturgis had asked to visit Miss Forbes; such a visit would account for his sending, in Miss Forbes' care, the letter referred to.

52. I have no clue to Miss Forbes' friend; it is likely that "Mrs C" was known to Lidian Emerson who had gone to the same school. My conjecture is that Mrs C. is Maria Weston Chapman.

53. Turning his leaf, Emerson repeats this phrase.

To William Henry Furness, Concord, April 8, 1845[54]

Concord, 8 April, 1845.

My dear friend,

I send you a letter to Messieurs Carey & Lea, which I suppose will serve the purpose of an Advertisement, if it be printed to follow the title-page in their edition of Carlyle.[55] As to the request of Mr Carey to retain Carlyles letter, I am not quite ready to grant it, as I do not carry accurately in my memory its contents.[56] If Mr C. only wants a specimen of his writing to lithograph or otherwise copy for publication, he is at liberty to use all that part of the letter which respects this edition. But I should not like ⟨very well⟩ to have ⟨it all⟩ the whole letter published—as well as I can remember its contents, & perhaps can find a letter of mere business. If Mr Carey however only wants an autograph for his private satisfaction, I think I will leave him in quiet possession of this, at least for the present, if he will have it transcribed & send me a copy of it. For I cannot bear to be wanting to so good a friend of Carlyle, as he appears to be.

For the Diadem, I am in good hope to find or make something yet that will not be wholly unworthy, but it cannot be ready today.[57]

Ever yours,
R. W. E.

To Caroline Sturgis, Boston? April 8? 1845[58]

Dear Caroline,

I hoped to have seen you today & not to have left a silent roll without so much as thank you. I dwelt in my cloud of pictures for the last six

---

54. MS in the Furness papers, Van Pelt Library, PU; ph. in NNC; p. [4] addressed: Rev. William H. Furness | Care of Carey & Lea—| Philadelphia | ; printed in *Records*, p. [38]; listed *Letters*, 3:246.

55. The letter intended for the Carey & Hart one-volume edition of Carlyle's *Critical and Miscellaneous Essays* (listed *Letters*, 3:289). See June 2 below for Emerson's second version correcting the name of the firm.

56. Carlyle's letter of February 16 (Slater, pp. 375–378), the original now in the Historical Society of Pennsylvania; see June 2 below. (In this letter Carlyle also misnames the firm, calling it Carey and Lea.)

57. He sent his contributions with his letter of May 6, below; see above February 7.

58. MS in the Tappan papers, Houghton Library, MH; ph. in NNC; I take this note to refer to Miss Sturgis' 1845 stay with the Hawthornes (as a paying guest); see April 30 to Anna Ward below. I incline to the April date because Caroline was not likely to make plans well in advance, and she frequently acted on impulse. Moreover, it is in April that the Hawthornes' plight became virtually public knowledge; Caroline was related to George Bancroft's second wife, and the Bancrofts knew of Hawthorne's financial difficulties. As late as February 24 (a.l.s. to Emerson) Caroline had no intention of coming to stay in Concord; Emerson's March letters show no sign that he expected her there. The earliest possible

weeks in good hope to reflect some skirt of their glory: and as you said I might choose some of the drawings to keep I have counted out six, (one of them a duplicate of one that I return). If I have too many, you shall come & see your children whenever you will, or I can even lend them to you.[59] A book also I have which I like to keep, & do not like to return.[60] You will have to ask for it. I am not to be disappointed of seeing you at Concord. You are to come on the May day. But this wretched sliver of steel with /whitish/ grey ink will not let me write.[61]

Yours ever
Waldo.

Tuesday Night

TO JOHN SULLIVAN DWIGHT, CONCORD, APRIL 20, 1845[62]

Concord, April 20, 1845

My dear Sir,

Your letter was very kind & friendly, and one is always glad that anything is adventured in the midst of so much excusing & impediments; and yet, though I should heartily rejoice to aid in an uncommitted journal, not limited by the name of any man, I will not promise a line to any which has chosen a patron.[63] We shall never do anything, if we begin

---

Tuesday is April 8; but there is nothing to rule out the 15th. I take the letter to have been written in Boston because of the complaint of the pen and ink.

59. In the Tappan papers is a scrap torn from the top of the second leaf of a letter from Caroline to Emerson. The verso of the scrap shows his endorsement "1845" and the single word in Caroline Sturgis' hand "closed"; the recto of scrap reads: "lodgings today—Small country houses, with the thinnest of walls & the Yankeest of inhabitants are not earthly paradises. Poverty consists in a very close neighborhood with the human race. Do not say anything about [me at?] Mrs Hawthorne's I." This scrap could not have been written after Emerson informed her of the Hawthorne's departure from the Old Manse, October 1 below. There is no room for the letter in the correspondence of August and September when the question of where she would live in the winter was agitated. I conjecture that the scrap alludes then to her proposed stay at the Hawthornes' in May. Of Caroline's vacillation, the correspondence of August and September provides ample evidence. I suspect that conversation between the two in the spring followed the same pattern as the correspondence of the summer and fall, and see March 2 above Caroline Sturgis's letter of February 24 (26).

60. Possibly a volume of Fourier; see her letter of September 1 quoted with Emerson's letter of August 23, below.

61. The pen seems to be the same one used for the final sentence of the letter from Princeton, dated April 1, above.

62. MS in the Fruitlands Museums; ph. in NNC; p. [4] addressed: John S. Dwight | Brook Farm | West Roxbury. | Mass. | ; postmarked at Concord, April 21. Printed completely (without date) but incorrectly by George Willis Cooke, *John Sullivan Dwight, Brook-Farmer, Editor and Critic of Music* (Boston: Small, Maynard, 1898), pp. 103–105; listed from Cooke with conjectured date of June 1 in *Letters*, 3:289; printed from the MS by Cameron, *ESQ* (1st Q., 1961), 22:95–96, where the address is erroneously said to be on an envelope.

63. Dwight had hoped to enlist Emerson as a contributor to the new Brook Farm paper *The Harbinger*.

with being somebody else. Then, though I admire the genius of Fourier, since I have looked a little into his books,—yet it is only for his marvellous tactics; he is another French soldier or rather mathematician, such as France is always turning out, and they apply their wonderful ciphering indifferently to astronomy, chemistry, war, or politics.[64] But they are a sub-type, as modern science would say, deficient in the first faculty, and therefore should never be allowed the lead in great enterprises, but may very well serve as subordinate coadjutors, where their power as economists will stand in good stead. It seems sadly true that the scholars & philosophers, & I might say also, the honest & well disposed part of society, have no literary organ or voice which is not desperately sectarian, and we are always impelled toward organization by the fear that our little power will become less. But if things come to a still worse pass, indignation will perhaps summon a deeper voiced & wiser muse than our cool New England has ever listened to. I am sure she will be native, and no immigrant, least of all will she speak French. But she will, I doubt not, have many wreaths of honor to bestow on you & your friends at Brook-Farm; for courage & hope & real performance, God & man & muses love. You see how little & how much faith I have. As far as your journal is sectarian, I shall respect it at a distance: if it should become catholic, I shall be found suing for a place in it.

Respectfully & affectionately yours,
R. W. Emerson

To Caroline Sturgis, Concord? April c. 20 1845[65]

How gladly I would send you my letters from W. T., if I had good ones.[66] That enclosed <u>third sheet</u> which startled your curiosity,—was only a returned letter of Margaret's, which I had sent him to explain her wishes about seeing him, & to describe her residence. What an excellent

---

64. Emerson had been reading Fourier in February and March (see letters to Caroline Sturgis above), and in 1842 and again in 1843 he had been exposed to Albert Brisbane's efforts to convert him (see *Letters*, 3:30 and 146); of numerous journal entries on the subject of Fourierism, one is in substance close to this letter; see *JMN*, 9:100. For a sharp criticism of Brisbane, see *JMN*, 8:208–210.

65. MS in the Tappan papers, Houghton Library, MH; ph. in NNC; p. [4] addressed: Miss Caroline Sturgis, | Care of William Sturgis, Esq. | Boston. | I give this letter an April date because of its similarity in substance and language to his letter to Ward of April 30, below. There is no proof. If the letter were after April 30, it would be addressed to Caroline at the Hawthornes'; it has to be earlier than the 30th, I think, for to write her the day she is expected in Concord seems pointless.

66. There are now no letters from Tappan later than that postmarked February 20; see March 23? above.

book is this "Vestiges of Creation"—something which so many have tried
to write, Mrs Somerville twice, Sir J Herschel, all the Bridgwater treatises,
& so many more, & all failed. This new Vyvyan, if that be his name, has
come as hear to succeeding as a man not a poet could.[67]

To Samuel Gray Ward, Concord, April 30, 1845[68]

Concord, April 30, 1845.

My dear friend,

Yesterday I was in town & saw at Munroe's the last proofsheet of
"Goethe."[69] It seemed a good time to greet you on your mountains, as
you are regaining your freedom again, if with regrets like Gibbon's.[70]
The reluctant spring has yielded us some golden days and I do not know
any idleness so delicious as dilettantism in fruit trees.[71] Grafting & prun-
ing turn a day into pure dream, and seem to promise the happy operator
a dateless longevity, inasmuch as it appears to be a suspension of all
expenditure: Only he must not cut his fingers. Ellery after much balancing & many rejections has suddenly bought twenty acres of land of
various quality, (5 or 6 woodland, the rest pasture, orchard, & tillage)
without any buildings, about 1½ mile from the centre of the village. It
has a noble prospect, lying on the south side of a hill, the top of which is
crowned by his own woods. He pays for it $600. I am to go with him
today to see it.[72] I am sorry it is quite so far off, as I fear he will be the

67. See notes 74 and 77 on the letter of April 30 to Ward. The second book by Mrs.
Somerville is very likely her *On the Connexion of the Physical Sciences*, London, 1834, which
Emerson owned (ELi, p. 253). Emerson has omitted the "e" in Bridgewater.

68. MS in the Ward papers, Houghton Library, MH; ph. in NNC; p. [4] addressed;
S. G. Ward. | Lenox | Mass. | ; postmarked at Concord, April 30. Printed in part by Norton,
pp. 61–62, with the year given incorrectly as 1844; partly printed also from copies by Cabot
in *Letters*, 3:283, under the correct date. Because of Norton's error, the letter is also listed
under 1844, *Letters*, 3:250. And, then, because of a confusion in Cabot's Index, the
letter is listed under 1847, *Letters*, 3:395. Cabot's careless use of ditto marks in his Index
makes it appear that there is a letter to Ward of April 30, 1847, but the Calendar reference
number shows that the letter listed is that to Margaret Fuller.

69. Ward's translation of Goethe's *Zur Farbenlehre* published in May; see March 13 above,
and *Letters*, 3:285–286.

70. Emerson is likening Ward's retreat from Boston and banking to the Berkshire Hills
and farming to Gibbon's release from Parliament and the Board of Trade to return to
Switzerland; see *The Miscellaneous Works* . . . 1837, pp. 249–252. Emerson owned the book,
ELi p. 115.

71. Emerson no doubt has his own pear trees in mind; he had just been setting out new
trees (MS Account Book for 1845–1849, p. 25).

72. Channing had enlisted Emerson's services as early as his letter of December 19,
1844, asking him to "look into the *Cogswell* place, or the place at any rate, next this side of
Bull's," and he sends a list of twenty-eight questions he wants answered. Emerson may have

sooner discontented with it. In other respects it has much to recommend
it. Our little neighborhood prospers in every way. Mr Bradford has just
returned from New York, where he saw Anna,[73] who has sent me the
friendliest letter.—Did you read Vestiges of Creation?[74] I am told the
journals abound with strictures and Dr Jackson[75] told me how shallow it
was, but I find it a good approximation to that book we have wanted so
long, & which so many attempts have been made to write, (by Sir J.
Herschel & Mrs Somerville, & all the Bridgewater Treatis[es] &c. &c.) a
digest, namely, of all the recent results in all the departments of science.
All the competitors have failed, & perhaps it needs ⟨another⟩ a poet for a
task like this, but this new Vyvyan,[76] if it be he, has outdone all the rest
in breadth & boldness, and one only wants to be assured that his facts are
reliable. I have been reading a little in Plato (in translation, unhappily)[77]
with great comfort & refreshment of mind—as always happens to me in
that quarter. The Correspondence of Goethe & Schiller gave me little

---

reported that the Cogswell place was no longer available (see January 13 above), but he
could scarcely have taken the questions seriously. As late as March 10, 1845 (a.l.s. to
Emerson, Houghton Library), Channing had not chosen a place; his purchase could not
have been considered as carefully as his twenty-eight questions of December required. He
tells Emerson that it is only to be near him that he chooses to live in Concord and laments
that Emerson should live "so near the city of Boston, in so flat scenery, in so cold a climate,
with so wretched a soil, where there are bigots in religion and fantasts devoid of rational
opinion. . . ." See McGill, p. 86. McGill suggests but does not explain a relation between
Channing's buying land and building and Thoreau's, but I suspect that Channing is imitating
his friend Ward and indulging a fantasy of wealth. Thoreau did not buy his land; Emerson
lent it to him, willing it to him, probably for his protection, the legacy being revoked when
Thoreau sold the cabin.

When this letter was written, Channing had no property. On May 5 he paid $100 for a
quit claim. For twelve, not twenty acres, he ultimately paid $600 (January 1, 1846) and later
(August 16, 1848) he paid an additional $10 for a quit claim from Caroline Hunt. The first
quit claim was paid to Charlotte Hunt, "Sr." and Charlotte Hunt, "Jr." (Middlesex Registry
of Deeds, MS. vol. 472, pp. 434, 435). He bought the property from David W. Buttrick (idem,
p. 434).

73. George Bradford; see Letters, 3; 282. Anna Barker Ward was spending the early
spring in New York; see letter to her below.

74. Robert Chambers, Vestiges of the Natural History of Creation (New York, 1845), Harding, p. 54. See JMN, 9:211, 233.

75. Dr. Charles Jackson, Emerson's brother-in-law.

76. See JMN, 4:24, for both Sir John Herschel and Mrs. Mary Somerville; and see Letters,
1:342–343. Mrs. Somerville's popularized translation of Laplace was published in 1831 as
The Mechanism of the Heavens; Emerson may have read it at about the same time he read
Herschel; see above, April 30, for the book he owned. See Letters, 2:169, for the fourth and
fifth of the Treatises sponsored by the eighth Earl of Bridgewater; Emerson owned these
two of the eight; for Roget, see Harding, p. 231, and for Bell, p. 25.

Chambers' book was published anonymously; it was attributed to various authors. Emerson's candidate is Richard Rawlinson Vyvyan, author of On the Harmony of the Comprehensible
World (London, 1842).

77. Cousin's translation apparently; see JMN, 9:214–216.

pleasure[78] The Essays on Art will give me much. I shall delight to hear from you. R. W. E.

To Anna Barker Ward, Concord, April 30, 1845[79]

Concord, 30 April, 1845.

My dear friend,

Mr Bradford made so many stops on his way homeward, that I did not receive my letter until Monday noon, as I was stepping into the cars for Boston. I was so glad to have it, that it served me by way of sunbeam in the blue east winds of the city. Now that I am at home again I can more securely give you joy of that happy present & seemingly assured happier future that lie around & before you. Who can so well bear a little absence from a country home in spring, as you so rich in all advantages! Though you do not say it, I have heard too that you gain strength & health in your exile, if an old home can be an exile because there is a new one.[80] Tidings and good tidings come to you by every train from Boston, and tidings by every boat from Berkshire of the planter & builder there, and of the progress of the new house. Favoured child that you are, I think the eminent angel that guards your fortunes has dropped the smallest possible leaf of wormwood in the cup, as if only to temper the sweetness. May a condition so excellent, root itself ever the surer in the only source of strength & increase!

I read a few weeks ago the poems you praise of Miss Barrett. "Lady Geraldine's Courtship" is very charming, full of power, & of fine pictures, and betraying what delicate perceptions![81] To such admirable execution I suppose we must forgive the want of a pure natural melody, which,

78. George H. Calvert's translation of the *Correspondence Between Schiller and Goethe from 1794 to 1805* (New York, 1845); see Harding, p. 241.

79. MS in the Ward papers, Houghton Library, MH; ph. in NNC; p. [4] addressed: Mrs Anna H. B. Ward. | New York. | with a generous space left between the name and the place as if someone else was to add the street address. Below "New York" in John Ward's hand has been added: "with King John's love—& fathers—"; i.e., with John Ward's love and Thomas Wren Ward's; Emerson apparently left the letter at the Park Street home of Thomas Wren Ward to be sent on from there.

80. Before returning to Lenox to superintend the building of his new house (Highwood), Ward had taken his wife to New York where she was to be treated for neuralgia by Margaret Fuller's mesmerist, Theodore Leger (Ward to his father, March 8, 1845, MHi). I think it likely that Emerson heard of the efficacy of the treatment directly or indirectly from Miss Fuller (Margaret Fuller to Caroline Sturgis, March 13 and April 17, 1845, Tappan papers, MH) as well as George Partridge Bradford (see above April 30).

81. Elizabeth Barrett; her *The Drama of Exile and Other Poems* had appeared late in 1844; among others, Poe reviewed it.

the ill natured poets affirm, our brilliant poetess has not. Do you think in heaven the angel Gabriel has perfect nature *and* perfect art? Here we are using the finest hours to train our bushes & graft our apple trees. Ellery has just bought his land. Mr Thoreau is building himself a solitary house by Walden Pond. Caroline Sturgis comes today to board with Mrs Hawthorn during the month of May. Yet the spring is cold & pale.

Certainly, I shall come to Berkshire to see you. But you must try to come here, before you go home. R. W. E.

To Caroline Sturgis, Concord, May 6, 1845 [82]

Dear C.

The weather looks so unsettled this morn.g that I think we must put off our ride another day to be surer of a good prospect.
Tuesday 7 o'c

To William Henry Furness, Concord, May 9, 1845 [83]

Concord, 9 May, 1845.

My dear friend,

I send you two or three little pieces, garnets for your "Diadem,"—if not too late. [84] But I think you gave me *into May,* in your first communication on the subject, for latest day. My wife & my mother have become a little uneasy at the long detention of my miniature effigy which your compatriot Mr Griswold borrowed of the former, and insist that I shall inquire if it is safe, or has at some time been returned in our direction & has miscarried. [85] Will you, if you meet Mr G., say so much to him. I dare say it is quite safe & will come back in a good time.

Yours affectionately,
R. W. E.

82. MS in the Tappan papers, Houghton Library, MH; ph. in NNC; p. [4] addressed: Miss Sturgis—| At Mr Hawthorne's. I date this letter May 6 because the allusion to "a good prospect" suggests the trip to Mt. Wachusett of which there is a record in the MS Account Book for 1845–1849 p. [27], under the date May 9. See also Margaret Fuller's note to Emerson of May 22 quoted in n. 38, *Letters,* 3:289.

83. MS in the Furness papers, Van Pelt Library, ph. in NNC; p. [4] addressed: Care of Carey & Hart. | Rev. William H. Furness. | Philadelphia. Printed in *Records,* p. [39]; listed in *Letters,* 3: 283.

84. He sent three poems; see February 7 above and *BAL,* 5206.

85. The miniature, by Caroline Neagus Hildreth (see April 21 and August 30, 1844 above), was, I conjecture, borrowed by Griswold for his proposed Literature and Art in America (see September 19, 1844); it was used for his *Prose Writers of America,* Philadelphia, 1847 (*BAL,* 6676), an engraving (by John Sartain) from it appearing opposite p. 440. As late as February 1847, it had not been returned; see *Letters,* 3:371.

To Caroline Sturgis, Concord, May 10? 1845[86]

I am sorry to lose an hour of being in your neighborhood, but cannot stave off these objects of my journey &, on consideration, think I shall get the most from your visit by finishing these things now.[87] I wish you were my brother to travel through the world with me. I should go to you, as I do not to Charles K.[88] Now I prize my friend with a foolish extravagance, and you only waste good time for me & I for you, if we come near. Yet you should be my Muse, & give me power. If this fondness of mine should once temper & settle itself, it should be a new & heroic tie better than any we have heard of. Already it is better than most modern things, and looks a little out & over the world. Here is the Spinoza & Cabot's letter. But I have verses to show you on Monday.[89]

To William Wilberforce Lord? Concord, May 16, 1845

[See May 10, above, to Caroline Sturgis where the question of what poet was subjected to critical examination on May 11 is considered. Emerson wrote to a poet clearly, but I merely guess Lord.]

To Augustus Adams, Concord, May 16, 1845

[In the MS Account Book for 1845–1949, p. [29], under the date May 16, 1845, is the entry: "Pd Express for letter to Adams concerning Mrs R. E.'s trunk .12";

86. MS in the Tappan papers, Houghton Library, MH; ph. in NNC; This letter is certainly written during Miss Sturgis' stay in Concord (April 30 through June 7). The conclusion of the first sentence suggests that it was written early in her visit, possibly before Monday, May 11, when judgment was passed upon poems. See May 17 below, and *Letters*, 3:283–284, 285. The allusion to Cabot's essay on Spinoza raises a question. Emerson had received the essay some months before December 17, 1844 (see above letter of that date to Ward) and apparently returned it March 24, 1845 (see *Letters*, 3:279–280). The Cabot letter referred to cannot be the letter that accompanied the manuscript, for that letter, undated, says as little as possible, simply offering it, along with excerpts from Wilkins' translation of the Bhăgvăt-Gēētă for *The Dial* (a.l.s., Cabot papers, Schlesinger Library, Radcliffe). There had surely been at least one exchange of letters between Emerson and Cabot before March 24, 1845, for Emerson had borrowed Cabot's copy of the Bhăgvăt-Gēētă, and this he did not return until he acquired his own (see below October 20). His letter of March 24 had invited Cabot to visit him, and by May 24, Emerson had met him; another exchange of letters is likely. I think it possible that Emerson, reluctant in any case to return the manuscript, had borrowed it back; his letter of March 24 shows he hoped to "have custody of it again."
87. Emerson's MS Account Book for 1845–1849 under the date May 10 shows at pp. [27] and [39] a trip to Boston and to Littleton "for and with R. B. E."; that is, his brother Bulkeley. Letters to William Emerson show that Bulkeley had been in McLean Asylum up to May 11 and that after that he boarded with Richard Hall in Littleton (*Letters*, 3:291–292, 293, 351).
88. Charles King Newcomb.
89. Emerson may mean poems of his own, but see May 17 below where he says he has written to "the poet" to report the judgment made upon them. The poems may be those of Elizabeth Dodge Kinney (see *Letters*, 3:283, and n. 285). Another possibility is the recently

see *Letters*, 3:284, for Ruth Haskins Emerson's lost trunk. Rusk in n. 16 mentions the possibility that Alvin Adams is meant, but it seems clear that it is Augustus Adams who is "our" express man and who is asked to make inquiries all along his routes. The trunk was lost on the way to Boston; Alvin Adams ran an express from Boston to Washington and cities along the way and also north to Portsmouth, New Hampshire. Augustus Adams operated out of Concord.]

To Caroline Sturgis, Concord, May 17? 1845 [90]

Though it rains, I have no book to read to you today: for poor Mamma lost her travelling trunk the other day in getting to Boston & all my messengers having failed to bring me any tidings of it, I must go to town this noon & look myself. I wrote to the poet last night [91] the just judgment of Rhadamanthus & company, yes & of ⟨y⟩Proserpine also. [92] Sat. Morn.

To Messrs. Carey & Hart, Concord, May ? And June 2, 1845 [93]

Messrs. Carey & Hart,

Gentlemen: I have to signify to his American readers, Mr. Carlyle's concurrence in this new edition of his Essays, and his expressed satisfaction in the author's share of pecuniary benefit which your justice and liberality have secured to him in anticipation of the sale. With every hope for the success of your enterprise,

I am your obedient servant,

R. W. Emerson.

Concord, June, 1845.

---

published book by William Wilberforce Lord (see *Letters*, 3:290, and n. 43); Emerson owned the book (Harding, p. 173). I incline to the latter because his letter about Mrs. Kinney's poems is written not to the poet herself but to her husband.

90. MS in the Tappan papers, Houghton Library, MH; ph. in NNC; p. [4] addressed: Miss Sturgis—Care of Nathaniel Hawthorne, Esq; endorsed "1845 May." The date is certain from the reference to the lost trunk; see May 19 to William Emerson, *Letters*, 3:284–285.

91. See notes on May 10 above for conjecture that the poet is William W. Lord, although Emerson may be referring to his letter to William B. Kinney, husband of the poet Elizabeth Dodge Kinney.

92. Rhadamanthus I take to be Emerson; the company would then be George Bradford and possibly Frederic Henry Hodge. Proserpine is Caroline Sturgis. Note that the only letter referred to here that is not securely of 1845 is the letter of May 10 to Hodge, but I think the year of that letter is made secure by this letter to Caroline together with the letter of May 19 to William Emerson; and the three together provide the reasonable date of May 10 for the note to Miss Sturgis that appears above.

93. No MS has been found; text from the printing (p. [3]) of *Critical and Miscellaneous Essays* (Philadelphia: Carey & Hart, 164 Chesnut Street, 1845). See, below, Emerson's letter to Furness about the mistakes in the first version he sent to the firm, April 6, misaddressed to Carey and Lea. The misspelling of "Chestnut" appears on all title pages seen.

To WILLIAM HENRY FURNESS, CONCORD, JUNE 2, 1845[94]

Concord 2 June
Monday Morng

My dear friend,

My note to Mr Carey was shockingly careless, and the insertion of the 'of,' a prank of the imps. I find in my drawer a draft of the note without that superfluity. If the new note, which I enclose, does not end as well as the old one, print from the old one.[95] Also the address was a carelessness: I knew better, & never have confounded the person of the benevolent gentleman who took so much pains that I should see his pictures in good lights, — [96] with any other, though I knew nothing of the history of his partners.

As for the head, which, with your letter, only reached me on Sat. night, (for Munroe kept it, & I have not been in town for /weeks,)/ I like the head very well and though I dare not confide in my memory of a face which I saw for one day twelve years ago, yet this agrees well with my impressions.[97] I go to town today & I think I must take the head with me, & try to find some one who has seen C. recently Dr Russell, or Parker or Mrs Lee. I could heartily wish he had not been drawn with the left arm so placed; or it is ill-drawn, or a little prolonged? I think it a strong likeness: but Carlyle ought not to be as contented with it as he seems to be in his letter, for it certainly does not give the ideal of the grim literary sans culotte. /though this is far better than D'Orsay's/ Somebody will yet draw a more characteristic sketch. As an ⟨head⟩engraving, it seems to me excellent, & the best of Mr Sartain's that I have seen. It is almost painted: and so clear & strong, & without that pomp of darkness. —

94. MS in the Furness papers, Van Pelt Library, PU; ph. in NNC; p. [4] addressed: Rev. William H. Furness | Care of Carey & Hart | Philadelphia. Printed in *Records*, pp. [40]–41; listed in *Letters*, 3:285. The letter is primarily concerned with Carey and Hart's one-volume edition of Carlyle's *Critical and Miscellaneous Essays* (BAL, 5205) and is therefore of 1845, when June 2 fell on Monday.

95. See April 8 above where Emerson refers to the firm as "Carey & Lea"; his prefatory note for the Carlyle volume (p. 3) is dated "June 1845."

96. In 1845 Edward L. Carey was president of the Pennsylvania Academy of Fine Arts; he was a collector of paintings.

97. See Emerson's letter of January 21 to Carlyle for Furness' proposal that Samuel Lawrence's drawing of Carlyle be copied in oil or watercolor, then to be engraved by John Sartain (Slater, pp. 374–375); Carlyle fell in with the proposal (Slater, p. 376). For his change of mind, see Slater, p. 381. Emerson showed the engraving to Charles Sumner, Andrew Russell, and Theodore Parker, who all disapproved; see Slater, p. 379. The frontispiece does not appear in all copies; copies in MH and NNC lack it; copies in NN and CtY have it. The Mrs. Lee referred to is Hannah Farnham Sawyer Lee for whom Emerson had supplied a letter of introduction to Jane Carlyle (Slater, p. 361).

I have not yet recovered my copy of "Dr Francia."[98] If I do, & I have sent for it, I will send it you though I cannot think Mr Carey can find any difficulty in finding it in some library which binds & keeps the ⟨the⟩ ⟨l⟩Quarterly Reviews. It was in the Westminster, was it not?—

I may have an errand for Mr Hering:[99] but if I have not, I shall not write a letter. For I have grown churlish about introductions, & ⟨nev⟩ Englishman-like never introduce until I have been introduced. But it is a great refreshment that you are ever so kind & indulgent to me. Yours affectionately,

R. W. Emerson

Let Mr Carey keep the letter with all my heart but he shall send me a copy.[100] The ladies say th⟨a⟩ey are not content with Mr Griswold's answer. They will ⟨keep⟩have the picture. ⟨What can we⟩ what to say to the ladies?[101]

To Caroline Sturgis, Concord, June 17, 18? 1845[102]

Certainly the way was open for a letter. And with reason enough to write, if there had been any need. If a cloud had risen on the sky as large as my palm, there were reason. but now when the whole firmament glowed with friendly lights when the strong rays of the culminating star

---

98. Carlyle's "Dr. Francia" appeared in the *Foreign Quarterly Review* (July 1843), 31:544–589; see July 28 below for a reprint of the article in *Campbell's Foreign Semi-Monthly Magazine* (September 1, 1843), 4:1–27. I infer that Emerson had lent his copy to someone to whom he may have written to recover it, but I have no clues.

99. Dr. Constantine Hering, Philadelphia homeopathist.

100. Edward Carey had evidently indicated that he wanted the Carlyle letter of February 16, 1845, for himself; see April 8 above and October 15 below.

101. Caroline Neagus Hildreth's miniature; see May 9 above. Emerson's wife and mother were anxious that the miniature be returned.

102. MS in the Tappan papers, Houghton Library, MH; ph. in NNC; p. [8] addressed: Miss Caroline Sturgis. | Care of William Sturgis, Esq. | Boston. | Emerson is replying to an undated (possibly incomplete) letter from Caroline, a letter that is in part a bread-and-butter letter. Emerson has endorsed it "Woburn 1845." As he tells Elizabeth Hoar on June 17 (*Letters*, 3:290), Caroline Sturgis went from Concord to Woburn after her long stay in Concord of May and early June 1845. On Saturday, June 7, she and Emerson went to visit Charles K. Newcomb (*JMN*, 9:222); presumably she left for Woburn after that. The letter cannot be earlier than June 10 and 11. It certainly antedates the letter of July 22 below. The letter to Elizabeth Hoar mentions a visit from Cabot, and so does a letter to Ward (*Letters*, 3:286), of May 28; if the later letter to Elizabeth Hoar refers to the same visit, then this letter to Caroline Sturgis refers to a second visit of Wednesday, June 18. If, on the other hand, the letter to Elizabeth refers to a second visit from Cabot, then this letter to Caroline must be of June 10, 11. (He had seen Parker before June 29 when he wrote Carlyle; Slater, p. 379.) In the absence of any clinching evidence, I give the letter the later date because Caroline Sturgis' letter (see below) reads as if she were well settled in at Woburn, and Emerson's first sentence reads as if some time had elapsed between her departure from Concord and her writing to him.

had absorbed every swart & malign beam and the sky showered good omens, I thought I would wait & see if the bright weather would be eternal. The bright weather hitherto brings no graver penalty than Tasks. Those it begins to open. But it may bring hereafter both graver & dearer freight on its wings severe duties austere counsels, suffering, contest, & conquest; thrice welcome if they shall be common. A life of walks & talks is only less shallow than one of morning calls, and we have a whole armory of unused powers. but what if opportunity should suddenly come in her dreadful forms of pain & violence, public commotion & oppresive demands on time, &c. Can we not so perhaps delight ourselves & the good by demonstrating that beauty is the most robust as she is the most delicate of agents, and is, as the ancient truly pictured her, a god, and the leader & exhilarator of gods. But these fancies of mine you will reckon fables, whether the ancient soothsayer or no. Those wandering lodges will never fix. The Calmuck never takes off his wheels. So you say for I think young people pride themselves on freedom from credulity. But I speak of no circumstances nor shocks, but of the march of things which halteth not. To the eye that never shuts, all well born souls stand united in groups & bands, working & conversing, and the seas that roll & the mountains that separate them are invisible But why stroll so wide? We are wide enough already. Well then the letter of the last winter I had not the smallest disposition to burn.[103] And I had ascended into so calm a turret that if there were still suggestion, though the faintest, of the Néant, in the pencilled note, I had no eyes for it and read only my own in it, the language of home. It is really deep & glad. And every day I am prouder of your powers—no, that is a cold & unworthy way of saying that I heartily enjoy the clear pictures you give me in these writings lately, as in Caronce, In that story a child might suggest all the correction; but the value of the piece is real & rare. How could you keep such things from me so long? Well, you shall enlarge the roads of life, the roads which thoughts and daemons travel, for me.—But to go back & for the last time to the sole criticism which I have to make on these sweet letters and which because I did not say it vexed you at Concord— love is always affirmative, is incapable of apprehending any prohibitions or bounds, the only way in which he excludes or detaches the false, that which does not belong to him from that which does, is by more eager & absolute affirmation & possession of that quality which is his. If my friend must tell me that his shoe-clasp is not mine, I shall tell him that wizards

103. The letter has not been found.

do peep & mutter in the floors of the temples. But if he give me the new music the universe has yielded him, he guides me well; I shall not |think of shoes.|

Wednesday Night

Here is enclosed a sheet which I wrote last night on the receipt of your letter[104] & books & enclosures, all excellent & which came safely. "Fiamma" I have already read to Ellen-of-eager-ears. The book shall follow your direction.[105] Today should have yielded you something better,—but Elliot Cabot came, and Theodore Parker after him, and there was no mount of retreat. And now it is late in the night—Certainly it is in my heart to accept early these friendly invitations to see your new abode. I wish to see you, and I wish also to see how men & women live: and if I can also find when you shall be in town, I shall go. But will the gentle Heart that loveth us all, drive from my door & from my path now until this round moon wanes, every foot led by compliment, curiosity, or affairs,—that I may explore my home, and see if every star is in its place, and hold the sincere truth! The fiery atmosphere in which Love himself dwells, becomes externally a waving formidable sword. In heaven the old diamond law of "Like to like" suffices for all police, but in the bronze sphere with which we are familiar. each individual being heterogeneous in his com-

104. Caroline Sturgis' note (adorned with drawings that were probably made after her letters were returned to her in 1875) reads:
"Dear Waldo,
"There are some kinds of postages [?], rides, gingerbread dinners which can be represented only in gold & if there is any superfluity it must be given to the poor; that is what they do in heaven.
"I cannot write what I wish to say & so will not write at all. I hope I shall see you soon. If I knew when you /were/ ⟨coming⟩ going to Boston I would be there to ⟨meet⟩ see you if you liked to have me—but ⟨I⟩ will you not also come out here some day soon—In my boat I can ⟨I⟩ row away to the woods & tell you how the birds sing there. It is what the country people call 'rather lonesome' here, but I endeavor to think of the Bagvat—do I?
"I send the stories for Ellen to read—will you lend them to Carrie Pratt & Richard Barlow sometime. I carried away your your British Ballads & send you another. I hope I shall soon have some better poems to read, if that may be—You⟨r⟩ forgot to give me the initial poem, did you not?
"Will you also lend the stories to G. Curtis who misguidedly desires to see them."
Caroline Sturgis ultimately published her stories *Rainbows for Children.* Carrie Pratt is possibly the daughter of Minott and Maria Pratt, Brook-Farmers who moved to Concord in 1845; Richard Barlow is possibly a son of Almira Penniman Barlow. George William Curtis, with his brother Burrill, was then living in Concord. See Edward Waldo Emerson's note, *J,* 7:76. Emerson's copy of the Bhăgvăt-Gēētā did not arrive until September 15, but he had been reading a copy borrowed from Cabot.
105. No book with the title British Ballads is listed by Harding or recorded by Cameron. See, however, *Letters,* 2:296, and n. 211, for Alexander Hume's *English Songs and Ballads,* sent on to Emerson by his brother William in May; see also Slater, p. 278 and n. 3. It was probably this book that Caroline carried away with her and apparently never returned.

position, this law cannot secure him good company. Well, shall the rich bronze experiences compensate?—Dear & blessed friend, peace, the peace of eternal morning, that peace which gives transparency to the universe,—abide with you, & disclose holy & happy secret!

To Caroline Sturgis, Concord? June? 22? 1845?[106]

Sunday night

I enclose the letter which came by Saturday's mail;[107] and Cecil, or at least one volume shall go with it.[108] I have been hearing Father Taylor preach today, and, in these poor cow pastures where no Ole Bulls play Niagara, it was very good.[109] But for him, and but for the letter I send, I might obey your command to send you verses—But I will keep them until I come to see your new home,[110] which it is my design to do perhaps one day this week—Thursday or Friday, but I know not.[111] Write by mail, if you prefer another time.[112]

To William Bennett, Concord, June 30, 1845

[Emerson's reply to William Bennett's letter of June 1 (RWEMA) is quoted in catalogue 215 of Dawson's of Pall Mall. The passage quoted reads: "I have no skill & really no title to offer one word of opinion which you seem to invite in relation to the methods which lie before you. The good heart & necessity, these are the two counsellors who order all things well." Bennett's letter written in Quaker plain speech had asked for news of Alcott and Lane, and Emerson apparently obliged, referring to Lane as one who "has rendered a valuable service to the Shakers by his residence among them." Bennett had visited the States in 1843; see *Letters*, 3:174 and n. 250.]

106. MS in Tappan papers, Houghton Library, MH; ph. in NNC; single sheet, without address. Father Taylor of the Seaman's Bethel preached in Concord June 22; see *JMN*, 9:233–235.
107. Possibly a letter from William Tappan.
108. Catherine Gore's *Cecil* (1841); the American edition is of 1845.
109. Ole Bull was then playing in Boston; "Niagara" was one of his own compositions.
110. The "new home" in Woburn, on Horn Pond, is described by Charles G. Loring in his *Memoir of William Sturgis* (Boston: Press of John Wilson & Son, 1864), pp. 51–52, as "commodious" (it was designed as a summer hotel) and "romantic" in its situation. Sturgis maintained the house as a summer residence for his daughters and their children.
111. Emerson's MS Account Book for 1845–1849, p. [33], records the expenses of a trip to Boston and Woburn under the date June 30.
112. Caroline Sturgis' (incomplete) reply to this note is postmarked from Boston June 24; with characteristic vagueness, she accepts Thursday or Friday, suggests also Wednesday, rules out Saturday because "perhaps" she will go "somewhere," says she will "stay at home every morning" until he comes, but advises him not to come at all if work on his oration (for Middlebury) makes him "doubtful."

To Robert Bulkeley Emerson, Concord, June 30, 1845

[In his MS Account Book for 1845–1849, p. [33], under the date June 30, Emerson records the payment for a letter to Bulkeley Emerson; the letter was sent by express. The entry immediately follows one recording the purchase of a railroad ticket from Littleton to Concord for Bulkeley. I infer that the letter was sent by express because the ticket was enclosed.]

To Caroline Sturgis, Concord? July 3? 1845

[See July 6, below, for evidence of a letter sent by Thursday's mail; i.e., mailed July 3. Writing on the 10th, Caroline Sturgis notes that she has received two letters, but that they are long in coming. The two letters must then be this of "Thursday's mail" and that of July 6. It is this lost letter that Miss Sturgis acknowledges in hers of Sunday, July 6th, when she writes: "A boy on a great white horse brought me your letter. . . ." See also Emerson's letter of July 15, below, which shows that he has written three letters to Brattleboro. Miss Sturgis' letter is in the Tappan papers, MH.]

To Caroline Sturgis, Concord, July? 6? 1845 [113]

Sunday

Where is my promised letter as soon as you should arrive at the hills? I am the more impatient because these were not to be common highlands or Spas, but hills of omen which held God knew what magnet or carbuncle in their dark heart whose virtue moved & drew, moved & drew, on one radius as far as Woburn,—on the other radii I have yet to learn how far. Well, you ⟨s⟩will tell me in time, and the music which you hear I shall hear also. You will catch the deepest melodies, for now your ear is so tense,—for a long time familiar with the dialects of the sky. Men can say nothing that pleases. Well, ask the flowing numbers for their inmost oracle,—why we infer gods only from their shadows; why we are plagued with disproportion—we lovers of symmetry; why born & fed on this faith in Unity, we die daily of miscellany;—& all the other eight & thirty articles of the Catechism,—all one. If verily you can come to speech with

113. MS in the Tappan papers, Houghton Library, MH; ph. in NNC; the letter fills all four pages and may be incomplete, but the last sentence is crowded in at the foot of the page. It would have been addressed to Miss Sturgis in care of Dr. Robert Wesselhoeft, Brattleboro, Vermont; see July 15 below. In a note of June 30, postmarked from Boston July 1, Caroline Sturgis says she will leave for Brattleboro "tomorrow" or Saturday, and declares that she will "write directly as soon as I am among those cold waterfalls. . . ." The homeopathist Wesselhoeft favored the "water-cure" and ran a spa in the neighborhood of Brattleboro that attracted a fashionable clientele. In his letter of July 9, Emerson refers to this letter as having been put into the post office in Boston "more than a week ago"; his MS Account Book for 1845–1849, p. [35] shows a trip to Boston on July 8.

some more communicable ⟨G⟩gnome of that reticent race, I am sure he
will confirm the frequent rumour that intimates the existence of Inter-
mediates, a dynasty too of complex & impure genius, next highest over
us, & vehicles to men of the celestial energies. But the co-presence of
archangels I anticipate also. The beloved Sibyl will not lose one accent of
the song, nor fail to make me wise with her wisdom. Tell me also that
which soothes & consoles you, for the breath of these days, I confide
comes to you laden with health. I fancy even that it may bring before
your eyes the graceful woods & waters at Woburn with a shade of regret
at their slighted beauty. Edward Taylor told the people here, most characteristically, that "he had lived half a century of years, & had never
known an unfortunate day;—he did not believe there were any."[114] The
days, I think, have as many coats as an onion; in every new illumination
they put off one, and gain in lustre. These illuminations are retrospective, as we call them, but they seem to belong to an order which does not
respect time. Dear child, nothing ever happens in this star gazing Assyria
where I live, or I would send you something gayer. And yet I believe the
God never fattens his favorites with events, but starves them rather. My
Mother has come home, & Elizabeth Hoar.[115] Margaret writes rather
languidly & rememberingly:[116] and on the whole in the absence of the
rarest luminaries it is a weekday, a plain-clothed working day, & no festa,
in our calendar. Well, poor men love them, & history is kneaded of such
atoms. If dear friends are loving each other, & separated only by a few
hills & woodlands, no day is bad: This is bright. |I wrote you by
Thursday's[117] mail.|

TO CAROLINE STURGIS, CONCORD? JULY 9, 1845[118]

9 July
We are so hard to please that our guardian angels might be excused if
they were occasionally a little snappish   If anybody come to see us we

114. For "Father" Taylor of the Seamen's Bethel, Boston, see *JMN*, 9:208, and for
extended comment, see 9:223 ff.
115. Ruth Haskins Emerson had been visiting her son William; Elizabeth Hoar accompanied her.
116. Margaret Fuller; the brief note quoted in *Letters*, 3:289, n. 38, does not seem to
answer these adverbs.
117. See July 3 above.
118. MS in the Tappan papers, Houghton Library, MH: ph. in NNC; the text fills all
four leaves, but appears to be complete. Mrs. Tappan's customary verses appear upside
down in the right hand corner of the first leaf. Since verses of this kind were written on
other letters when she reread them in 1868, it is safe to assume these were written then too.
Their position makes it clear that if any part of the letter or a cover sheet was lost, the loss

run & hide. If, as now, I sit at my table to write for a few days together, all perception all comparison disappears, and I say—⟨T⟩If only I could talk over this thing five minutes with a reasonable friend!—I looked into "Sybil" of Disraeli: small succour was there: no burning inextinguishable word to set one's thoughts on flame. I wonder a little how that Notoriety supports himself in such position as he must hold. There is a little of literary scampdom in dragging into his fiction Peel & Russell & others, as stock figures, men whom he must face the next day in the House of Commons or in society.[119] It seems a ruinous confession of inferiority, which destroys all power over ⟨our⟩ /the/ imagination of the reader, to say nothing of the outraging improbabilities /a romance made up/ of ⟨a⟩men & things so near us. Nothing but our Anglomania could make such a book readable. How superior is your Cecil,[120] with its earnest unaffected tone, written from a heart which still throbbed at the record of its experiences, and not from class-legislation & class-society. I have also better books but none good enough to diminish the joy your letter brought me, answering, as it did, some eager questions, and being, besides, full of matter, a sufficient, direct & satisfying letter. It does not quite correspond in its informations to the accounts I was prepared to receive of the presentient second sighted child, daughter of the supernal, but flattered also by the obscure powers. Yet health is a gift from Jove himself. That is the amreeta.[121] Health & mountain groves & waters,— what strings & heaps of gifts do not thereon depend! How gladly I would & will come to those walks you offer me if you will only wait for me a little. I infer from your last statement that you will not go with me to the College,[122] but will let me come to B. on my way home, and I will spend

occurred earlier. She has marked the letter upside down at the foot of the fourth leaf with the month and the correct year, Emerson's name, and the note "send JEC." Cabot has added the year below Emerson's dateline. There can be no question of the year. The letter is plainly an answer to Miss Sturgis' letter of Sunday, July 6, written from Brattleboro. A sentence from Emerson's letter is printed from Cabot's copy in *Letters*, 3:292.

119. Emerson can't have known that, in 1845, Disraeli had no difficulty at all in facing Sir Robert Peel or Lord John Russell either.

120. See June 22 above for Emerson's lending Miss Sturgis the American edition of Catherine Gore's novel.

121. In the *Mähäbhärät* the water of immortality; Emerson seems to imply that the "amreeta" is likely to be more efficacious than Dr. Wesselhoeft's hydrotherapy. Emerson's allusion is not to Sir Charles Wilkins' text of the Bhägvät-Gëëtä, but to his n. 78 (p. 145). Wilkins prints his translation of "Episode from the Mähäbhärät," Book I, chap. 15 (pp. 146–151); this is a tale of a great battle between the Söörs and Asöörs for possession of the Ämreetä.

122. Middlebury College, where Emerson was scheduled to give an address on July 22. Since the existing portion of Miss Sturgis' letter of July 6 speaks of "hoping to go to Middlebury with you," I infer that in the missing portion of the letter she makes a different proposal. Their plans subsequently changed.

a day there & then you will be ready to come homeward with me. Meantime if any muse of splendid wing should astonish my ear with the right vibration of the wires /—/ then—you would go with me & hear my report, would you not? But ⟨a⟩what if I never hear such a tone and have never anything to offer you that can please either of us must it not content me that there is surely music, though I am not in the orchestra. God is in mortification & also in triumph, and when the soul is intelligent the substance appears & the surface fades. But the fine orientalism always proves a little too much for poor humanity, and I draw too solid a good from being your friend & from your being mine to care to dissipate it into any universalities. In you solid sense & in your serene mind & in your beating heart I will have you to be & to continue my friend more & more from year to year, as you have done. I know how much certain swift spirits value instant communication, but time has also his indefeasible honours & rewards in this as in all things and this old good will of ours will survive many acquaintances we shall yet form as it has done many already. May the calm strong affectionate wisdom keep & lead you!

To Caroline Sturgis, Concord? July 15, 1845[123]

Tuesday, 15 July

I do not know how you should have failed to receive a letter which I put into the Post Office in Boston & paid for, more than a week ago. Yet you say, you have only two. I can remember nothing that was in it yet I hate to be baulked. It was in reply too, to so good a confession.[124] Now I have with all content this morng your letter of the 10th and only time to say, that I hope you will stay at B. firmly, until I come down the river bank on my way home, which will doubtless be on the 24th or 25th,[125] /or 26th/ The 22nd is my appointment at Middlebury; the 23rd their commencement. It is just possible that I shall go to Lake George on the 24th, as I shall be so near; then I should come to B. & spend the Sunday, and you will be ready to come homeward with me? I have got entangled in a fishing party which is to go down to the sea from Dorchester

---

123. MS in the Tappan papers, Houghton Library, MH; ph. in NNC; p. [4] addressed: Miss Caroline Sturgis—| Care of Dr Wesselhoeft. Brattleboro Vt. For Dr. Wesselhoeft, see July 6, above.

124. It is Emerson's letter of July 9 that replies to "so good a confession"; i.e., to her letter of July 6 which explains her flight from Woburn and too much family (her married sisters and their children). He appears here to be remembering when he mailed his letter, also of July 6; he mailed it on the 8th; she could not by July 10 have received his of the 9th. The third letter he refers to is that of July 3, not found.

125. Brattleboro. He has to mean the Hudson River.

tomorrow,[126] & Ellery goes with me, tonight to Boston. I cannot well take a day now but neither can I not. The "Discourse" is rather grave & cold:[127] no Chakra:[128] The "Calamities of Authors" have never been truly written. Put this first,—that in making a book, that commonly gets dropped out, which the book was written to say. I shall be comforted for your absence from M. that you do not suffer from the dulness of the speech. One thing more I take the pen to say, can you not send me a line to Middlebury, directing me at what house to find you in B. or must I face the learned Paracelsus[129] as your patron & warden? Well you shall have another letter to pay for the lost one & for this O much forgiving friend with much to forgive!

To Caroline Sturgis, Concord, July 17, 1845[130]

17 July Thursday Eve.

The first sentiment so justly expressed at the close ⟨y⟩ of your letter makes me regret the conclusion into which I have settled that I must go alone, and I will not at this late hour make us both uneasy by the hazardous attempt to change it. I jalouse also a little my mountain college⟨,⟩ since they have sent me at my request a printed catalogue of its members, and am tender of showing it to so proud a visiter. May be this brood-hen has clucked but one brave chicken in all the years, and yet Hudson was a bright apprehensive Vermonter.[131] But you are right in your measure of friendship, which is the most solid estate and the most serious concern of a human being, and in its service he may well call many phantoms by their right names. I too could easily have found a

126. Channing, see July 17 below for more of the fishing party.
127. For Middlebury College, reported in the *New-York Daily Tribune* of August 4 (see *Letters*, 3:294–295). The *Tribune* mentions the "local prejudices"; the reporter has evidently seen *The Northern Galaxy* of July 30, 1845 (p. 2), which reads: "Ralph Waldo Emerson of Concord, Ms., discoursed before the Philomathesian Society. . . . The manner and style of Mr. Emerson is highly cultivated and polished. His address was of the high transcendental character, and whatever may be said of its literary merits, we know that many Christian hearts were pained at some expressions which were nothing short of pantheistic atheism."
128. As in the letter of July 9, above, Emerson's allusion is not to Wilkins' text of the Bhāgvāt-Gēētā, but to the "Episode from the Māhābhārāt" he translates for his note 78 and refers back to in his note 96 (p. 152). In the text of the episode the chăkră is described as the "ponderous orb, the speedy messenger, and the glorious ruin of hostile towns" (p. 150). It is deployed as a weapon in the battle between the Sŏŏrs and Asŏŏrs and is the effective agent for the victory of the Soors in their struggle to secure the Ămreetă, the water of immortality. Emerson apparently thought his speech lacked the effective heavenly weapon.
129. Dr. Robert Wesselhoeft.
130. MS in the Tappan papers, Houghton Library, MH; ph. in NNC; p. [4] addressed: Miss Caroline Sturgis Care of Dr Wesselhoeft Brattleboro Vt. Letters destroyed by breaking the seal are supplied.
131. Henry Norman Hudson, lecturer on Shakespeare.

warrant for overstepping my modesty & for urging you to go /with me to
M.[132]/ had I found any sudden & potent infusions of the muse in these
⟨papers⟩sheets that now cover my table. But there is so much dust &
nonsense in these holidays that I thought without a lady you might easily
find the little town a prison of inconveniences, if, as you prophetically
suggested, they quarter me at a private mansion. But when I come back,
I shall indemnify myself at least, by accepting your invitation to B. I am
glad you like your ⟨t⟩encampment so well. Taste after its eye is once
open, never shuts it, is despotic & implacable & though it becomes a
languid pleasure it imperiously requires that the fine statue we know so
well shall have a fit gallery, that is, a fine landscape. After a few visits the
landscape has little to say to us. But persons make us wise, each good one
reflects on all the rest, & reveals what schools of virtues & vices: they
inform & reform & overinform the landscape again, which yields har-
vests of new lights & meanings. But consider—if only they would,—in
how few moments we learn all this from them, and let a ne[w] law of
short & shortest intercou[rse] take place of the tarrying system. You will
understand from all this that I went down below the light house yesterday with fourteen gentlemen, beheld the sea & the fishes, landed on an
island, came back at night under the moon to Dorchester,[133] & have just
now come home hither to read your letter & to write this. Will you not
always continue to make silence & solitude dearer to me, when I am
ordered to silence & solitude?[134]

132. Middlebury.
133. See July 15 above for the fishing trip.
134. Emerson here replies to Miss Sturgis' letter of July 10. Her letter reads: "You are
like Fatima in the tower—always calling out 'Sister Ann, Sister Ann, do you see any one
coming?' I do not go hither & thither hoping for any event, but because I have not courage
enough to stay at home. If I was summoned hither it was only that I might fin⟨g⟩d health in
these springs, & if another radius should reach a⟨f⟩s far as Concord I shall be gladly pleased.
You shall come to be crowned with stars-beams upon the hill-tops, & not with broken
wreaths. You always ask a circumstance & yet ⟨you⟩ say they are no⟨ne⟩thing. To you all have
been given & therefore you may be incredulous if any may be so who receives the circumstance of life.
"These hills breathe the air of the morning & I believe I am the first wanderer among
them; they are so unconscious they ⟨never⟩ can never have echoed their own praises. If it
were not for conscience, if we /were/ Indians who had never heard of manufacturing
districts, the claims of the orphan, & the old man's petition, how happy ⟨are⟩ we might be in
this gay, green world; but one step higher & we shall have passed by the claimer; she ⟨only⟩
beckons to those below but never points upward, & we have only to look steadily into her
eyes & assure her we hear a sweeter song from above & she vanishes from our sight: but
when the song ceases ⟨she⟩ her ⟨is⟩ voice is heard calling, calling, ever from a distance & we
known not whe⟨re⟩nce. But there must be one listener in the woods, one eye to mark the
clouds which no day will ever bring again. It is so good to have all the senses open: to find
delight in the curve of every upblown cloud of dust, in every sparkling drop, in the glance a
transparency of every leaf makes the midsummer a holiday; we wish to be arrayed in festive

To Caroline Sturgis, Concord, July 29? 1845 [135]

Monday Eve

Perhaps you are better without house of your own, when I think, as
now, how hardly I steal the time from a most unlooked for guest—to

garments & gay as in a Carnival, & oare not who throws the sugarplums. Do not ask me what
the gnomes whisper: I have not more thoughts for your little Edie, but am as happy as she is
& can play in a wood-pile all day. I was in a dungeon before I came here, & perhaps shall
return there with a dagger in my heart. I know there is a pain greater than any I have ever
felt. I like to see ⟨all⟩ the possibilities of sorrows: this gives solidity to all the joy that comes,
& with mere fancies I cannot amuse myself.

"It was pleasant at Woburn to see the seven wild children[a] rush out in the morning
merely for enjoyment; & perhaps in the moonlight nights I remember my boar & the
shadowed shores, but here the streams will leap through the valleys & how can I have regrets
—I have never even wished again for the orchards by the river, where I received visits from
the Norwegian prince. Any day is good when it must come, but when there is a choice I am
wayward. I am sorry ⟨when⟩ father is not satisfied who like to have me placed through his
acts but everything must take its own way. Even the demons cannot interfere among men,
but that they are here, close to us, all must believe who see the circles of life. All above, as
below, is organized, & into the innermost being man may not enter. So let us return the
smiles of the angels who look upon our sports, as children return those we so condescend-
ingly bestow. But let the angels know, as we also know for the children, that our place in the
universe holds good with theirs & our games are a part of its music.[b]

"Why did you smile so slyly when I asked if you thought there was melody in you⟨as⟩r
/poems/—because I cannot detect it? Sometimes I think I can.—the words play so easily
along, & they are such as no one else uses—words of great meaning, of thought & not of
images. Now & then a line darts forth like a tongue of flame & the others move harmoniously
around it; but sometimes they hiss & sputter a little as if cold water had been thrown upon
the coals. I wish I had a book of them; they are better to me than they were—perhaps I am
learning to see.

"Do not question the Invisibles but make saw-dust pies with Edith. When you come here
we will hunt rattle-snakes upon the mountains; then we shall know whether we are good or
not; perhaps in this week we shall acquire as much vigor as to kill them with a glance. I am a
hundred times nearer to you here than when I was in Woburn. But we are only neighboring
princes who have sent each other their portraits & now /each/ congratulates ⟨themselves⟩
himself upon having a friend. But can I congratulate you—Yes, for a little while, until the
dearest shall come, & then also, that there may be one to ⟨feel⟩ rejoice in your happiness.
But when shalt thou have that from which thou turnest they face, Kehamah! Kehamah! If
any butterflies come flitting by that will not alight upon the oration, you can send them to
me—Two letters I already have but it takes /them/ a long time to come. You cannot be here
in the moonlight, & I cannot have its full beauty myself, for I do not like to go far away in
the night, alone. I will show you a cathedral here—not an old abbey—At its base is a cascade
for the organ-music, the spire is a pine-tree, rising a hundred feet in a wall of thick /trees/
through whose delicate tracery I can see the sunlit columns & the blue window. There is
nothing more in this glen than the voice of the stream, & perhaps I should not have written
this letter here—but I know not what the hidden things is. "Thursday—July 10th."

[a]The "seven wild children" the oldest 12 and the youngest 2, are Ellen, Edward, and
Marian, children of Ellen Sturgis and Dr. Robert William Hooper; William, Anne, and Alice,
children of Anne Sturgis and the Hon. Samuel Hooper; and Mary Louisa, daughter of Mary
Louisa Sturgis and Robert Gould Shaw, Jr.

[b]Beginning "I am sorry . . .": Emerson quotes this passage in his MS journal CO; see
JMN, 11:428. He unfortunately changes Miss Sturgis' "father" to "he," leaving the passage
open to misreading.

135. MS in the Tappan papers, Houghton Library, MH; ph. in NNC; p. [4] addressed:
Miss Caroline Sturgis. Miss Sturgis' letter of August 5 (see below) acknowledges books and

salute you.[136] Does not every year of the past lifetime yield one guest to the current year? But you reckon me unwary. Well, the glowing days of this summer must be cooled by some grey shades.—I had such calm & pleasant thoughts through all my Monday's ride as I must thank you for, though they came too late to be shared.—All was well under my roof and my little boy[137] crept stoutly towards me at the first glance. E. H. was here this morn, &[138] tonight Ellery has been here with good natured eagerness for my whole story. He to talk of gossips! He will have every thing /that is/ communicable concerning yourself in the first place. He says that he must write to you though he has been waiting for a letter. But plain signs show that there shall be no talk now so I shall hasten to put up what books—all old—I see in token that better may come, if I can recall my estrays, or visit the Atheneum, before I go southward.[139] Here is a letter from Miss Martineau which I found here last night.[140] Send it back again, & I will send it to Margaret, whom it respects. Have you read Carlyle's Dr Francia? It is in this old Campbell's Magazine. The "Mirror Library" you must safely return some day.[141] Farewell   You will never be under the least doubt concerning your brother.

---

continues the subject of a house of her own. Emerson's letter clearly refers to the return trip from Middlebury and Brattleboro, but he must mean either his "Sunday's" ride or he has misdated his letter "Monday night"; since his letter of "Saturday night" (August 2) refers to "the sincere satisfaction of my Sunday" and to his having written her on Tuesday, I think the error is in the dateline, and so I assign this letter to Tuesday, July 29.

136. Miss Sturgis' inability to remain very long with her family is evident from her letters. Burrill Curtis described the relation as one of "affectionate strife," Myerson, *NEQ*, 51:408.

137. Edward Waldo Emerson, not yet a year old.

138. Elizabeth Hoar.

139. He returns a book on the 12th of August; there is no withdrawal until September 4; *ER*, p. 26.

140. Harriet Martineau's letter of July 2, 1845 (RWEMA), says she would like to try mesmerism on Margaret Fuller; Miss Fuller was already under treatment. Miss Martineau, announcing her own good health, enthusiastically credits it to mesmerism. Her book *Life in the Sick-Room* (London, 1844) was well-known in Concord; known too were her articles of the same year in *The Athenaeum* about her successful recourse to mesmerism ("Mrs. Martineau on Mesmerism," *The Athenaeum*, nos. 891–895, Nov. 23–Dec. 21, 1844, pp. 1070–1072, 1093–1094, 1117–1118, 1144–1146, 1173–1174, and gathered by Miss Martineau to be published in 1845 by Moxon as *Letters on Mesmerism*). Her letter also describes the site she has chosen in Ambleside, her intent to build, and her distinguished neighbors (the Wordsworths and the Arnolds).

141. Caroline's undated letter acknowledging the books is postmarked at Brattleboro August 5; addressed to Emerson at Concord, it was forwarded to him in care of his brother at the Wall street address. She writes: "I have received the books very gladly, dear Waldo, & they are all I shall want, so do not search Athenaeums or the shelves of forgetful neighbors for more. Chaucer I had been wishing for, but forgot to mention it; the African Cruise[a] also I meant to ask you to send. Was Miss Martineau's letter sent to awaken an enthusiasm for cottages? Perhaps I shall have one sometimes, a mile from some great man. But there are many things to be considered before one plants his foot upon the ground. It is best for those who are not generous to hold but a small share of the world's property. If I have but one

room(s) no one can claim a part; if I had a house could I permit anyone needing shelter or repose to pass by, yet I have no desire to give ⟨any⟩ /much/ time to vagrants, or even friends, except to the dearest. No—I shall wait until I can live in some kind of a convent or assembly in which many together can make life easier than it is to any one who takes possession of that which others need. See what a tax you have to pay because you have a house with a neat white fence before it. If you were like the wind, everywhere & nowhere, you would always seek & never be sought—Yet in every stage coach ⟨have⟩ comes /to/ you someone to whom the heart or the lips must be opened. In a community, with all its combinations & mechanism, the desire for friendship & recognition would be what it is now—⟨Yet⟩But it would be better⟨e⟩ there, for we should not find a desolate parent in one house, a misunderstood child in another,[b] or both in the same; a poor devoted woman in another, & longing hearts everywhere. I believe I was born to be a sister of Charity for I cannot shut my eyes upon all these wants for a single day, or open them only upon other things; but it is my eyes alone that are active, for with my hands I know not what to grasp. It is good to hear of such persons as Miss M. but one must love far better these little Anna Lorings[c] who look out into the infinite with still eyes. An hour in her presence would do me more good than a broken limb cured or a political romance. We wish for action only ⟨that⟩ ⟨is⟩as ⟨in⟩it may be adapted to the person for a garment floating around him, so do not ask me to build a house of stone or brick & put up ⟨an⟩ a sign, 'Our Home,' as the ⟨lepers⟩ /sailors/ do for I am still but a homeless child. I can have society enough /now/ without sending for Ellen;[d] the Longfellows are here & Tom Appleton is coming—but I flit away from all persons except now & then when the twilights are a little too grey. William Channing[e] is coming,—perhaps while I am here, but I shall only remain a fortnight I think. I wish to be with the children[f] & to leave home with a good grace, if that may be, for wherever my wanderings may be I shall return there again—I would rather go to Sing Sing & take charge of the prisoners. But I shall come near you next winter & can let the future rest in peace. I do not like to go away from here for in moving about one realizes the world altogether too much, especially in returning home. Only those things that whisper of friendship & love are good; arrangements & conveniences are dire accompaniments, & concessions the saddest of all. Tell Ellery I highly approve⟨d⟩ of his proposal to write me a letter—I have ⟨only⟩ been waiting for one to send him an answer. I have only Chaucer for a desk. It is a dear companion for the woods & I wonder I have not read it before. My thanks are all to you for it now.

"This William Aspinwall[g] is a good child he has much honor & delicacy,—but he has no genius or faith, I could not go out into the woods with him but it makes me less solitary to see him sometimes, I did not show you the glen & the pretty stream that runs through the village below a wooded bank. Well! you were here only a little while.

"What did Sophia Hawthorne do with her house?[h] But I cannot go there & it is better not to repeat a happy visit, for some devil or other always follows in the footsteps of angels.

"What a child I was not to ask the good people of Brattleboro to invite you to have lectured here—would you not have done so. It would have been very satisfactory.

"I went to see the Longfellows last eveg—they board in the house opposite. Fanny seems to be in a trance & Mr L. looked like a half civilized German boor but they were both very polite & cordial & talked very prettily. If this were only Fanny Appleton how good it would be to have her here but Fanny Longfellow has lost all her beauty.[i] A little gold-piece should go with this but I shall not forget my privileges. I had a pleasant letter from Susie who talks about my having at least Oct. at Woburn, which gives me a long leave of absence, if I cared for it."[j]

[a] Horatio Bridge, *Journal of an African Cruiser,* ed. Nathaniel Hawthorne, was published in June (*BAL,* 7597).

[b] Caroline Sturgis' mother. The "misunderstood child" could be Caroline Sturgis herself or her sister Susan, whose letters and poems (Tappan papers) reveal distress.

[c] Anna Loring (see August 2 below).

[d] Ellen Sturgis Hooper.

[e] William Henry Channing.

[f] In Woburn to help with her sisters' children; see July 17, above.

[g] A cousin of William A. Tappan whose mother was an Aspinwall.

To Caroline Sturgis, Concord, August 2, 1845[142]

Saturday night

No letter comes, so I suppose you are waiting for mine. It is ungrateful in me to have sat silent all this week, after the sincere satisfaction of my Sunday. But I told you of my guest on Tuesday. The next day brought me two new ones, the writing H. Tuckerman,[143] & the writing Mr Whipple.[144] Yesterday was First of August, and I found at last no outlet of escape and made the best I could of the evil necessity, by reading, the night before, the life of Demosthenes in Plutarch There turned out to be no need of ridiculous heroism, for William Channing unexpectedly came to the Waltham assembly, and made a perfect speech.[145] He increases my respect for the human race. I saw Anna Loring[146] in the grove, & introduced Ellery to her. She was a pleasing sight & presence,—there was a good share of beauty in the company, the grounds were beautiful, on the bank of the river, with a little bay full of water lilies,—but all soon came to look so fantastic & unreal to me, that I began to speak to my companion as lotus eater to lotus eater when he sees the mountains spin & the land begin to flow. I went for my supper to Mrs Ripley's,[147] and found some lively travelled company; but it has taken a bath in Walden, & a tramp over the hills with Thoreau, entirely to restore angularity & grit to the landscape. Ellery asks with great interest concerning you, & at Waltham we conversed long under the pine trees on so singular a subject. I told him you talked of coming here in winter, and that I had asked, why not insist on your own establishment? Ellery

[h] The rent long unpaid, the Hawthornes would soon leave the Old Manse.

[i] Frances Appleton by accepting Longfellow after first refusing him lost some of the admiration contemporary young women had been inclined to give her. The social rule here seems to have been applied in judgment more often than it was obeyed in practice.

[j] If Susan Sturgis goes to Woburn to help with the seven children of their sisters, Caroline is free.

142. MS in Tappan papers, Houghton Library, MH; ph. in NNC; the text fills all four pages and may be incomplete. The date is certain from the reference to the annual celebration in Waltham of Emancipation in the British West Indies. The year is certain from the reference to his engagement to speak at Wesleyan University in Middletown, Connecticut.

143. Henry Theodore Tuckerman; see *Letters*, 3:293, 298.

144. Edwin Percy Whipple.

145. Emerson evidently expected to speak and did so; William Henry Channing's appearance saved him from the need to make an oration. Emerson's remarks are reported in *The New-York Tribune* for August 7.

146. Anna Loring, the pretty and appealing fourteen-year-old daughter of Ellis Gray and Louisa Gilman Loring. She evidently charmed all who knew her; see Lydia Maria Child's *Fact and Fiction* (Boston, 1846) dedicated to her. Caroline Sturgis' letters to Margaret Fuller (Fuller papers, vol. 10, MH) show that Caroline took considerable interest in the girl, particularly this year. Anna Loring would subsequently marry the musician Otto Dresel.

147. Sarah Bradford Ripley.

resisted the last, for it was being old and he requires a connection. He said he had tried to make you acquainted with T.[148] I affirmed that I also had attempted as much. I should gladly have been much more frank, and if you were here, should have asked your leave. But I told him what advantages I thought you should derive from a private housekeeping. We agreed however that you ought to charter the Hawthorns for your householders for the present. They are, as I understand it, still without any resource, & contented enough with Concord.[149] It is still doubtful whether Mr Ripley gets here this winter, and if not, your living with them would enable H. to pay his rent, which, Mr R told me yesterday, had not been paid since the first year,—& which is bad for both: so that you seem the very goddess of a romance descending to solve all the knots. It is very desirable to Ellery & to me that H. should stay in Concord,—which adds another impulse to my counsel: so I hope you will propose to them to find you a house or lodge you in their present one.

I hope you see plainly that it will not be for want of counsel, ⟨that⟩ if you go without a castle, and the very swans sing the indispensableness of it, & to you! Far be such persuasions from me. I only content myself with putting no straw of an impediment in the way of it, if such be your pleasure. Do you like to know that the memory of a day spent with you is more appeasing than the day itself. Restless with you, I am calm & assured in the remembrance, & wish the hours back like noble opportunities. My slow faculties are late in overtaking rare music, which yet comes to them at last out of the voice of my friend.

I go on Monday, as I think, to Boston; thence on Tuesday to Springfield & Middletown: On Thursday to New York; & I shall perhaps stop at Lenox,[150] a few hours or a day, on my return. Then I shall not be in Concord again until perhaps Tuesday—a week. Then I shall return to

148. William A. Tappan. This passage is somewhat cryptic; it hints at there being more to be said on the matter of Tappan and Caroline Sturgis. Although they had never met, Tappan had been writing her, sending his letters to Emerson to be forwarded. See June 9, 1844, above for a likely letter from Caroline to Tappan. He thanks Emerson in his letter of February (postmarked February 20 at Boston) for forwarding letters to a correspondent, a woman, whose address he does not know; and like his letter of December 12, 1844, the letter is marked paid "double." In her letter of February 24 Caroline Sturgis asks Emerson to send on "another white bird," and in her postscript hopes he will send the letter soon. It is plain enough that Channing and Emerson concur in thinking Tappan the right man for her. See Emerson's letters of February 1 above, and August 17 below.

149. The Reverend Samuel Ripley, Emerson's half-uncle, was the owner of the Old Manse and Hawthorne's landlord. See Randall Stewart, *Nathaniel Hawthorne* (New Haven: Yale University Press, 1948), pp. 66–67 and 75–76.

150. To visit the Wards; see *Letters*, 3:294, and August 17 below.

this plotting for the next winter Wm Channing is to spend Sunday after next with me.[151]

To Caroline Sturgis, New York, August 9? 1845

[Emerson's letter of August 17 makes it plain that he wrote Caroline from New York; he would surely have told her all his news of Margaret Fuller; see *Letters*, 3:295–296. Since he opens his letter of August 17 with an account of events of August 10 I infer that he wrote on the same day he wrote his wife. Caroline Sturgis' letter of c. August 20 (see August 17 below) acknowledges three letters, of which two, that of August 2 and that of August 17, are printed here.]

To William Henry Channing, Concord, August 14, 1845

[Cabot's bluebook calendar has an entry reading: "1845. . . . Aug. 14 Just ret'd from Lenox & N. York expecting the Texas convention (to W. H. Channing) The convention will be held 22d Sept. & W. H. C. wanted   They will pay his expenses." See *Letters*, 3:295, for Emerson's plan to go from New York to Lenox, returning on Wednesday, August 14. See p. 296 for his return on the evening of the 13th. See below September 18, for a second letter to Channing, recorded in Cabot's Ledger.]

To Caroline Sturgis, Concord? August 17, 1845 [152]

Sunday, 17 August.

Dear Caroline,

I told you of my visits in New York, but not of all. Sunday morning I went to Brooklyn & found Mr T.'s house, for I mistrusted that the father, whom I had found in his counting room, would not tell the son of ⟨call⟩ my call; and, though he was very civil, 'it seems he had not.[153] William was very glad to be found: I spent an hour with him /there,/ & then carried him to my hotel in the city. He appeared to as great advantage as ever, and surpasses in figure, grace, quiet strength, & charm of manners every-one whom I see: He says good things and provokes you to say good things, but I fear he dreams away his time & leads but an Indian life. I do not like to compromise myself with exquisite spirits, so I asked few questions on matters of fact, but I found he had been travelling with his family all summer, at Trenton Falls, & Niagara, I believe, and at Ticonderoga, & had been close to Middlebury with intent to be there at

151. August 17; see August 23 below.
152. MS in the Tappan papers, Houghton Library, MH; ph. in NNC; the text covers all four pages and may be incomplete.
153. The merchant and abolitionist, Lewis Tappan, father of William A. Tappan.

the Commencement, but was ignorant of the altered day of their festival, & so failed. He has had no companion since Ellery was here, and speaks of him with great justness.[154] In speaking of you, I said—'And you have never seen my friend?' he said, 'No I never see any body—' but presently remarked that he fancied he knew the forms of persons whom he had not seen.—At dinner (at the City Hotel) he asked me if a young girl sitting with others at one end of the table did not resemble you? I looked at the party—there might be a trait—but I would not countenance it— and answered, No. Afterwards in some compassion I told him of George Curtis's remark on the "Roman Girl" in the "Gift," to which he lent earnest heed.[155] In the p.m. I carried him with me up to Margaret's house & introduced him to her, telling him that after he had made his visit, he should leave me with her.[156] Meantime I had acquainted him with my purpose of going up the Hudson River the next day and invited him to go with me, to which he assented. Well we parted at Margarets after I had left them on the rocks together perhaps half an hour with the repeated agreement that we were to meet on board the steamboat next morning at 7, and—I saw him no more. Next morning it rained heavily, the fine new boat that should have sailed was supplied by a night-boat very ill-provided, and in an unusual crowd of passengers I did not find Euryalus,[157] and I went up the river alone. He had said something about "If I wake up so early" but I had foolishly so trusted ⟨him⟩ the sincerity of his intention that I had left my communication with him all incomplete in every part. My vexation was great, and was enhanced of course by a dozen concomitant mischances. I should so gladly too have gone with him to Sam Ward's,[158] whither I told him I was bound, and at Lenox I missed my fine traitor again with new chagrin.—I hope you will forgive me this garrulity about one incident in my journey, in which, of course, you can take no manner of interest. Next time I will write more reasonably.[159]

154. For a brief time after Giles Waldo left for the Sandwich Islands, Ellery Channing had shared Tappan's quarters; *Letters,* 3:381.

155. Daniel Huntington's picture, engraved by John Cheney, is an "embellishment" in *The Gift* for 1845 (Philadelphia: Carey and Hart), p. 212. See *JMN,* 9:196–197, for a record of an observation by Tappan.

156. Margaret Fuller; Emerson had tried to arrange a meeting between Margaret Fuller and Tappan earlier in the year; see above letter dated April 20? See also February 1 above and letters to Henry James of May 6 and July 21, 1843, for Tappan's curious habit of hanging back.

157. Apollo, as a sea god.

158. For the visit to the Wards, see August 23 below.

159. Caroline Sturgis' undated reply (c. August 20)ᵃ is as follows: "Most excellent of brothers,

"I cannot but be a little pleased that the Fates should have sported with you also &

hidden the invisible[b] in a shower on the Hudson, but am sorry the Highlands were dimmer, & ⟨that⟩ the Furies pursued you on your homeward way. I find you a good writer of table-talk & hope you will improve every opportunity of perfecting yourself & but fear the conversations will all be imaginary. I hear however that the mother of the mysterious not the mysterious mother, has just arrived in Brookline, & if filial affection has its wonted sway, you will know where to find an expounder, if you wish for Bible notes.

"Now it is positively true that I have not a single word to write to you in return for three letters of varied & useful information. Whether all thoughts & emotions have flowed away in these streams, I know not, but certainly silence reigns upon the mountain-tops & not even a crow will flap by. I have been reading the Seeress & believe it all, except the Christianity which is as bad as that in Dante, & certain whims & fallacies, into which every mortal falls & every other mortal detects. Her division of 'Spirit, soul & life-spirit,' & so like that which I call soul, character, & the demon, in myself & others that it was quite pleasing, especially the way in which the character forms the next ⟨body⟩form, for which we are all waiting with patience ever-to-be-admired. Tom Appleton came & told Irish⟨ish⟩ [?] stories with the wit of a northern wind among frozen leaves. He looks like an ante-deluvian jumping-jack, & will soon stand at St Peter's gate, demanding admittance without a pass-port in his pocket.[c] Fanny sat in the moon-light like a fading lily, while Mr Longfellow seemed the comfortable personification of all that earth can bestow—

"Finding our evenings but mutilated things, lately Mr Aspinwall, Anna P.[d] & I have hired a small chapel where we study or read aloud & repair all that brambles & bushes bring to despair; Mr A. reads very well[e]—we have Sidney Smith & a store of good books sent from Boston & find our domestic life quite agreeable; but in the moonlight evegs & sunny days the poor little chapel is ⟨quite⟩ deserted again. Rainy days it is pleasant there—we each take possession of a window & watch the apples ripen while we turn over the leaves of our dictionaries.[f] Then we have a family of Jews at Mr Bridge's—⟨Ma⟩ a young man of about twenty, so reverential in his appearance, that he reminds me of Charles[g]—he also has soft, wavy, dark hair & long fringed-eyes—our acquaintance /is confined/ to ⟨low bo⟩ the courtesies of goodmorning &c, which he always proffers with low bows, which seem to say, 'Shall we say nothing more,' but mine are quite negative in character It would be pleasant to know a Jew but I am already involved in such an army of Christians & infidels. He is from South Caroline & has been studying in Phila[del]phia.

"William Channing is coming here next Sunday[h] & we are going to immure ourselves between the walls of pews to hear him preach, Did ⟨p⟩he pass last Sunday with you? You will write to me, although you see that it is quite impossible for me to write to you.

"Always believe Ellery in everything with regard to me; he understands me better than you do when he says I must not have a house of my own.[i] I am a stream that cannot be stayed until it reaches the ocean, so seek not to build ⟨airy⟩any dams, or turn grist-mills with the foaming waters. If the /Hawthornes/ remain in Concord I shall be thankful to stay with them, provided they will let me—if not may heaven take its own; I am not going to make plans for a winter which may be swept away by its own first storm for aught that I care—but to which I shall incline as meekly as the earth is folded in her robe of snow—"

[a] A corner of the second leaf of this letter has been torn away, slightly damaging the text and the complimentary close; the blurred postmark has inverted figures of which the first is clearly "2"; since Emerson's letter of August 23 is a reply, the date cannot be later than August 20 or 21.

[b] In the first paragraph, the "invisible" is a reference to William Tappan; and with the phrase "mother of the mysterious," Caroline Sturgis is referring to Tappan's mother, an Aspinwall of Boston. With the parallel phrase "mysterious mother," she alludes, I think, to her own mother who was sometimes also domiciled in Brookline. The William Aspinwall then staying in Brattleboro was a cousin of Tappan's and was certainly her source of information.

[c] Emerson has evidently lent her his copy of Catherine Stevens Crowe's translation of Justinus Andreas Christian Kerner's *Die Seherin von Prevorst* (see Harding, p. 158). She had probably heard of the book from Margaret Fuller who read it in German (see *Letters*, 3:170, n. 235). Mrs. Emerson had probably read it; in a letter to his wife Emerson identifies Mrs.

To Caroline Sturgis, Concord, August 23 and 24, 1845[160]

Saturday, 23 August
Concord—

Live, my dear friend, where & as you please, only may it please you & Heaven, that your house may be near mine.[161] I showed Lidian the other day your letter which I received in New York, and she very frankly offered to take you as a boarder herself, if the Hawthornes could not. I told her you had no claims such as she is wont to hear of, & this was a case where each of the parties, herself & yourself & myself should deal very unreservedly by yea & nay. For my part, I mustered what possible objections I could lay hold of, and declared that a little experience might prove it unadviseable to so inveterate a clerk as I. I added that if it could be tried, & could succeed, which seemed quite uncertain, it would be a solid satisfaction to me.—So you have one more door open to you in this village of few doors. And I should like to have you bear it in mind, if it were only as an occasion of your treating directly with Lidian some time, by word or pen. Such a benefactress to me as she is in her will in all calm moments,—I wish to acknowledge & to honour as far as I can. For the

---

Crowe by alluding to her translation (*Letters*, 4:19). Kerner is reporting the experiences of a clairvoyante Friederike Hauffe, daughter of a forester of Prevorst.

ᵈ Anna P. is probably Anna Q. T. Parsons, the clairvoyant; see 19 February above.

ᵉ Thomas Gold Appleton, Frances Appleton Longfellow's brother, noted as a raconteur.

ᶠ See Longfellows' poem "Summer Rain," written at Brattleboro in 1845 (Lowell to Longfellow, August 13, 1845; *Letters of James Russell Lowell*, Charles Eliot Norton, ed. (New York, 1894), 1:95–96.

ᵍ Charles K. Newcomb.

ʰ William Henry Channing had been expected to visit Emerson on August 14; see August 2 above.

ⁱ See August 2 above for Emerson's report of his conversation with Ellery Channing about where Miss Sturgis should live; Emerson copied this first clause into his journals in 1851 (MS journal CO, pp. 206–207). The editors of *JMN* (11:428) cite Miss Sturgis' letter, but date it August 23 from the postmark, but the date is impossible.

160. MS in the Tappan papers, Houghton Library, MH; ph. in NNC. The year is in no doubt; the letter answers Miss Sturgis' letter of August 20? printed above with Emerson's letter of August 17. That it was continued on Sunday is implied in "I give your joy of this day"; the 24th was Miss Sturgis' birthday.

The paragraph that opens with the birthday greeting is written on the recto of a single leaf that has no embossed stamp in the left corner and is therefore the second leaf neatly separated from its contiguous leaf. Part of the text is indented to accomodate a seal of which there is no trace. The verso bears no address but has the customary pencilled verses. The letter clearly has its end; the question is whether it is complete. The text reads like a natural continuation, and nothing in Caroline Sturgis' reply of September 1 (below) suggests that there was more than we have. The question then is unanswerable, the evidence allowing a number of conjectures, no one more plausible than another.

161. See August 17 for the vacillating Caroline's latest allusion to winter plans in the final paragraph of her letter of c. August 20.

rest, I can easily entertain or reject such a proposition for the present as your convenience or wishes may incline you, so only that (whilst you keep your independence) you consider me in whatever plans respect permanent residence. For I delight in that Roman word for friendship, necessitudo: I delight that absolute & selfsufficing people should find each other necessary to them, and whilst inhabiting the highest grounds should have the wisdom & the security of yielding to each the stern uncomplimentary human supplies. I will harness our horses, I will buy you wood —You shall show me my blunder, you shall cheer me moping. The stars will stoop to show a well to their favourites. But I have expanded my short errand unconscionably, and have left me no room to tell you of my journey, which gave me many things to note. At Lenox, I found my visit made a little too much to their new house than to my old friends the builders, but this absorption will not last always. The best thing we can find anywhere is now & then a sensible person whose eyes we seem to borrow to look at the road & passengers, by way of test of our own, or rather if I should say it more nearly, because of the stimulus of that new colour & angle we acquire some new power over the old perceptions. Moodily, casually, at long intervals, and then perhaps rapidly in successive flashes comes in the great Guest, & strikes us dumb, for we never can manage to say anything we know about him—and existence seems a most unnecessary & pedantic extent of personages and plots, like the getting up of the tedious tragedy in Hamlet to bring out a single loaded word or sense somewhere,—all the rest superfluous. Luckily, charitably, we have some of us been furnished with the love of trifles as well as with the ambition of heaven, & we crack our nuts very ingloriously but very cheerfully in the long eclipse between the revelations. It was a bright thought to hire a small chapel for the afternoons, and, I doubt not, will be extensively imitated. When you come here, you must build one.

I give you joy of this day & of W H Channing your true priest.[162] He came here & seemed the Abdiel of the state. The dialogue between Mr Hoar & him at the office of the former was quite a Homeric picture[163] Had you been there, it would have furnished you with the sternest drawing; such a contrast of figures, & Mr H was Massachusetts itself. W. C. is finished like a belle, and sufficiently apprehensive to be a stimulating companion, with such address too & so many & such polished

162. On August 24 William Henry Channing was to preach in Brattleboro; see Caroline's letter of August 20.
163. Samuel Hoar.

weapons but he disappointed me when I applied one of my old touch-stones.[164] I am an old fashioned chemist, and always use oil of vitriol for gold.

164. See *JMN*, 9:241, for Emerson's evaluation of Channing ("W.C." in the text) after this visit of August 14, 1845.

Caroline's reply of September 1 bears a faint postmark September 5; Emerson's reply is September 9 below. Her letter reads:

"Dear Waldo,

"I hope you will thank Lidian for her kind offer, & I will thank her myself when I see her, but I am sure it will be best for me not to come. I have such a wild way of living that I am a most unprofitable member of any family, & it is pleasanter for both me & my retainers, that I should live with those who are quite indifferent to me, so that my incomings & outgoings may be unnoticed—Lidian would find me more trouble than she anticipates, for I am always unpunctual & generally invisible at meal-times & so unsocial at all times that I must give pain even to the most generous, for in one small household each individual must be felt more or less. I would rather go where I can be *only a boarder* which I cannot be at your house,—or to Sophia Hawthorne's, where they have already sustained a long siege & would know if they could be willing to receive me—but I doubt very much if they would Let us say no more upon winter plans at present for I ⟨have⟩ never have patience to look forward one we ⟨a⟩ek into the future & it will /be/ three months before I shall have to decide upon a location. If there was a community where I /could/ go for a long sojourn I should be glad, but am not willing to go to Brook Farm, that modernized Tower of Babel, & so I must dance around from bandbox to bandbox, until I can finally determine upon some life of my own. I believe in nothing but association unless one has a necessary home in genius or love, to which everything else must be subordinate—but it is not easy for any one to say for himself that such will never be & join dense masses of garrulous reformers. How radiant William Channing is! He surprised me like an illumination. His words bit hard, but there are secret shades to which we retire beyond their reach, not altogether so, however, for his sunlight streams far & wide, but we need not all come forth to fight with the weapons he uses. It always seems as if I must make a confession to him, but presently I remember how external all that I say is, & ⟨that⟩ he cannot penetrate into that which is really my life, so, I thank him in my heart for his inspiration & am silent.

"We have ⟨very cold⟩ magical mornings here now—the mists roll up like silver fires marking the length of the valleys, the mountain⟨s⟩ looms darkly above them, & every pine-bough stands firmly forth against the floating light. But the the cold winds bring the autumn & even the goldenrods are fading. I am going to remain a fortnight or so, & then return to my bereaved family who call upon me to fish in their ponds—Cannot you send me some wonderful book—Something scientific I should like—philosophical; or poetical, but not sentimental—Is there not a volume of Fourier at your house—& will you not lend me De Quincey's Letters. We have many books here but nothing that dives quite deeply enough—⟨y⟩have you not some poems to send. Our sociable evenings are still very pleasant, but we were all born for symphonies—Nature only sings ⟨them to⟩ one oratorio to herself & among men there are so many discords that one does not know exactly where to go—We must have some little air to ourselves as ⟨as⟩ we wander along, & if an echo is returned the notes ⟨would⟩ shall rise purer & ⟨sweet?⟩ louder until they persuade the air & the ⟨har⟩grand harmony will soon begin.

"Do not say of anyone he leads but an 'Indian life'[a]—his feet may be bound with golden chains, which must become sunbeams before he can walk upon them.

"Ellery wrote me a⟨n⟩ most grandfatherly letter; ask him if he has forgotten the days of his youth. It was as short as good advice should always be, but you will not write good advice.

"I did not bring Margaret's book here.[b] will you not send me one of yours to give to some one I should like to have read the story of Mariana W. A.[c], perhaps he will like it—& it should be restored.

"If you should send me ⟨a pen⟩ some books will you also send 1 doz—Thoreau's pencils —6.H. & 6.S."

To, ———— Concord, September 1, 1845?[165]

Concord, 1 September

Dear Sir,

I am very sorry to have neglected so long to have forwarded the book which you promised to look into. Immediately after seeing you, I went to Vermont and on my return set out on a new journey, almost without an interval to Connecticutt & New York,—which is the only apology I have to offer. I hope the Book may yet find you at leisure; for it requires that.

Yours respectfully,

R. W. Emerson.

To Mary Peabody Kenny, Concord, September 9, 1845[166]

Concord 9 September 1845

Mary P. Kenny, Cor. Secy

Madam,

I am mortified that my delay should have gone so far as to have given you the trouble of a second letter. I think you must ascribe some part of the delay to my reluctance to say no to such a request. It is not in my power to accept your invitation. I have nothing at present in my thought to offer to the society, and my time for some months is so pledged to special studies[167] that I dare not promise you anything. I like however to have the door open, that if in the course of the winter I should have anything to say on this subject, [I] may have where to bring it.[168] And with this hope I am thankfully & respectfully your servant,

R. W. Emerson.

————

[a]Said of Tappan in August 17 letter above.

[b]Margaret Fuller's semi-autobiographical story "Mariana" was included in *Summer on the Lakes,* 1844.

[c]William Aspinwall, mentioned in earlier letters; Miss Sturgis omits "to" in this postscript written along the top of p. [1].

165. MS in Special Collections, Butler Library, NNC; ph. in NNC; The year is established by the journeys alluded to, those to Middlebury in July and Middletown in August. There is no clue to the addressee; Emerson saw a good many people just before leaving for Vermont including the "fourteen gentlemen" of the fishing party referred to in letters to Caroline Sturgis of July 15 and 17 above.

166. MS in the papers of the Salem Female Anti-Slavery Society, MSaE; ph. in NNC. Single sheet, address leaf removed; the remaining sheet was once mounted, damaging one letter here supplied in brackets. The addressee was the daughter of Deacon Jonathan Kenny and his wife Hannah. *Vital Records of Salem, Massachusetts* . . . (Salem: Published by the Essex Institute, 1916), 1:486.

167. Preparing the new lectures "Representative Men."

168. I find no evidence that Emerson obliged the ladies, but I suspect that if he had done so, he would not have charged a fee. The Account Book for 1845–1849, pp. [75], [77],

To Caroline Sturgis, Concord, September 9, 1845[169]

Concord, 9 Sept.

Here is Humboldt's first part,[170] if you have daylight enough in the Chapel to read the bad type. But the book is good, and promises better: it has the breadth of march that always distinguished the encyclopaedic man. I have not been in Boston since I had your letter, or you should have a book: now I confine myself literally to your commands. I have now even time to write you a word of rhyme or reason. Foolish house building and what comes of it has murdered many days.[171] and Webster & what comes of him seek to murder what survive; and this very night, it appears, I must forth in the rain to see the omniarch at Mr Cheney's.[172] I hear already the cry of preparation; so you shall hear from me again quickly. From Thoreau's diminished stock I procured this bundle, which does not exactly conform to your order.[173] Ellery lives with H. T. at the pond, in these days, in the absence of his wife![174] I am to read a course of lectures, six or seven, to the Boston Lyceum in November & December I believe.[175] My "Schelling on Freedom" is a little too good a book to send you to the mountains.[176] I am afraid it would not read well, & up to its real worth. But come here, & I will show you great sagas in it. I have no tidings of evanescing travellers. The world remains full of little people & a grand design. We quarrel with one another, but, I am sure, shall grow very amiable when our power to execute our fancies is increased. A little sleep & a little health & a little success improve our beauty & gentleness largely, and these things come not by striving, & plainly tell us that that

---

shows only one trip to Salem, March 25, 1846, when he lectured for the Lyceum (Charvat, p. 22). See also below August 27, 1851, and August 2, 1852.

169. MS in Tappan papers, Houghton Library, MH; ph. in NNC; p. [4] addressed: Miss Caroline Sturgis. The year cannot be in doubt for Emerson is executing the commissions specified in Miss Sturgis' letter of September 1; see August 23 above.

170. Alexander Humboldt's *Cosmos;* probably A. Prichard's translation.

171. The house for his sister-in-law, Lucy Jackson Brown, for which there are many entries in his account books; see note to Thoreau below of c. October 8.

172. Concord was still one of the county seats of Middlesex County, and the coming of distinguished lawyers like Daniel Webster might be the occasion for a party; this time Webster's host was John M. Cheney, cashier of the Concord bank; see September 15 below. For Emerson' entertainment of Webster in 1843, see letters of August in that year. Omniarch is a Fourierist term.

173. Of pencils; see Miss Sturgis' letter above.

174. According to McGill, p. 86, the Channings moved into their new house on September 3; this information that he is living with Thoreau at Walden is then startling, but possibly the exclamation point is Emerson's comment on Ellen's being away, for it was Ellery who was subject to fugues.

175. The series "Representative Men"; see September 15 below.

176. James Elliot Cabot's MS translation of Friedrich Schelling; see *Letters,* 3:298.

we shall owe the new & better life to our star, & not to taking thought. I am timid & slow of belief, I dare not hold fast a hand for fear that my friend is wishing to withdraw it; but underneath the doubt is a faith which will survive it. So bear with me if you can.[177]

To Caroline Sturgis, Concord, September 15, 1845[178]

Concord, Sept 15, 1845

Did I not say you should have a sheet of paper with or without cause? There is nothing to tell you out of the library, and, shall I say, less than nothing ⟨n⟩in it? No, for I have my copy from London of the Bhagvat Geeta.[179] And E. H. loaned me today "Margaret," which though certainly not of the same strain as the oriental, is honest & original New England. I fancy it to be written by a brother of Louise Weston, from one or two circumstances that I heard of or put together. But I may be wrong.[180] Also, I have become the owner of an English Plato, and do turn over the majestic leaves.[181] Also I read Swedenborgs Animal Kingdom,[182] Humboldt, & Schelling;[183] for you are to know that I am to read in Boston to the Lyceum six or seven discourses, to wit, on Plato, or the Philosopher; on Swedenborg, or the Mystic; on Shakespeare, or the Poet; on Montaigne, or the Skeptic; on Napoleon, or the Man of the World.[184] perhaps more, but these names sometimes loom so much, that I may think it

177. Miss Sturgis answered this letter, but mislaid her reply; see her letter of September 22 below with Emerson's letter of September 15. Finding the missing letter, she mailed it September 27; see October 1 below.

178. MS in the Tappan papers, Houghton Library, MH; ph. in NNC; p. [4] addressed: Miss Caroline Sturgis | Care of Dr Wesselhoeft | Brattleboro | Vt. | ; postmarked at Boston September 17.

179. See *Letters*, 3:303–304, and below October 30.

180. Sylvester Judd's novel. See Lowell's comment, *Letters*, Charles Eliot Norton, ed., 1:106. The source of this misinformation may have been Calvin Farrar, who had known the brothers of Louise Weston at Bowdoin; on May 1, 1845, he wrote from Boston that he was coming to Concord and was bringing a letter to Emerson from Miss Weston.

181. He had hitherto owned only the French translation by Cousin. He now acquires Thomas Taylor's translation in five volumes (1804); see Harding, pp. 215–216. As the Boston Athenaeum records show, he had been borrowing the volumes before September 4 (*ER*, p. 26). He bought the volumes from Charles Lane; MS Account Book, for 1845–1849, p. [47], entry of October 8; he paid $27.50.

182. James John Garth Wilkinson's translation, 1843–1844, Harding, p. 262; also a translation by Augustus Clissold, Harding, p. 263; the MS Account Book for 1845–1849, p. [53] shows the purchase of Swedenborg's *Conjugal Love*, from the publisher Otis Clapp. The book is marked but not by Emerson. Sophia Hawthorne is the likely vandal. The Account Books show the purchase of other books by Swedenborg, but neither Emerson nor anyone else read them; they are unopened.

183. *Cosmos;* see September 9 above, and see the same letter for his refusal to lend James E. Cabot's MS translation of Schelling's "Essay on Freedom."

184. See *Letters*, 3:304, 306.

better to substitute others. Did I not tell you of Webster?[185] Well the cannon missed fire though it was loaded to the lips much to the chagrin of the company. The ca⟨u⟩se was given to the jury by the Judge under an ruling or instruction before Webster was required to speak and the jury bro't in a verdict. It was the more pity because he had got well heated & declared to Mr Cheney that he meant to blow off the roof of the house. He behaved well & looked like the omniarch of your phalanxes.—(which word reminds me that I have no vol. of Fourier One, Sampson Reed has, &, ere this, must have left with J. Munroe & Co; but the vol. which I had last was taken away with your consent & sent I know not whither.)[186] As for Webster, Cranch, who was here, thought he had never seen him more fit to be painted.[187]

I will not now begin to write a letter which is always due to you, was never written, & I suppose never will be, (that is, as we poor humanities construe never), but when I say nothing to you I know very well that I say nothing. Do not fail to send me word of your movements.[188]

To John Minter Morgan, Concord, September 16, 1845

[Emerson's MS Account Book for 1845–1849 has at p. [45] under the date September 16, 1845, the note "Letter to Mr Morgan"; the charge of thirty-three cents is that for a letter to England. I conjecture that Emerson here records a reply to John Minter Morgan's letter of May 20, 1845. Morgan had sent him his *The Christian Commonwealth* (London: 1845).]

To William Henry Channing, Concord, September 18, 1845

[Cabot's Ledger, p. 263, has an excerpt from a letter to William Henry Channing, dated September 18, 1845. It reads: "Concord Sept. 18 '45 the antitexas convention is really to be held on next Monday, 22d inst. in this town & they rely on yr presence & help. The antisl. soc. in the town will account it their privilege to bear yr travel. exp Rockwood Hoar will speak & W Phillips is looked for." See August 14, above, for an earlier letter to Channing on the same subject.]

185. See September 9, above, written just before he went to a party in Daniel Webster's honor at the home of John Milton Cheney.
186. Caroline asked for a volume of Fourier in her letter of September 1; see August 23 above. The books are hers.
187. Christopher Pearse Cranch was visiting in Concord; see *Letters*, 3:302; he had given up preaching for painting.
188. Caroline's reply of September 22 apologizes for a mislaid letter (see October 1 below), says she expects to be in Woburn in a week and to come to Concord to live "in one of those miniature towers of Babel among your sandy roads—"

To James Munroe, Concord, October ? 1845

[In the Emerson papers (RWEMA) is the address sheet of a letter to him endorsed by him: "J Munroe Camb Lyceum Oct." See Emerson's letter of December 29 to Richard Fuller where he says that he has "given the men of old Cambridge their choice of the first two Wednesdays of Feby." (*Letters*, 3:321). I take this scrap to refer to a letter making this offer. "Oct" may be simply Emerson's endorsement and not a note of his reply, but he certainly wrote a letter and probably a second one to confirm the date.]

To Caroline Sturgis, Concord? October 1, 1845 [189]

I do not know whether the fine sentence in your letter concerning the Children of the Mist, points at any sentence of mine it is of no importance, it is certainly elegant & I admired it.[190] But all things with me are of a sad earnest, and I am very negligent of professing love, since whatever really draws me, draws me as daylight & gravitation do, & many years do not release me from my friends. I do not know whether I have ever dared to expect in recent years any concurrence of the circumstance to my affection & scarcely more any concurrence of affection to my affection. The guiding Genius has required a covenant of the heart that it shall adjourn to a quite infinite future its rightful satisfactions. If at any time I rebel, the Genius knows very well how to whip me with my defects & send me to my cell again; so that I had long ago in one plane of life almost ceased to believe that any peer of mine, my quantitative & qualitative peer, if you will forgive the expression, could see through so many & many surfaces, and nobly love me, nor can I now perhaps for any long time together maintain the belief. Against this skepticism I have, dearest friend, our singular friendship, every passage of which I religiously regard. But the Genius is sometimes sinister then when he should be best, and fine as are your influences, & noble as is your appreciation, I am not quite contended. We do not wish to feel the weight of ourselves in the presence of our friend, but only power to unite, to rise & to raise. If we have powers which our friend never saw exerted, we long to

189. MS in the Tappan papers, Houghton Library, MH; ph. in NNC. The text virtually fills the four pages; it is certainly complete.

190. The greater part of this letter was evoked by the opening paragraph of Caroline Sturgis' "lost" letter, undated but written c. September 12 in reply to Emerson's letter of September 9 (see above). The opening paragraph of Caroline's letter reads: "Has it not been written by all the scribes & pharisees, that he who believes the other wishes to withdraw the hand already desires to withdraw his own—but such whispers come from the children of the mist, & we hear not the slightest murmur of their voices."

summon them also from their subtle cells to elevate the hour. With you
therefore it must happen that I should say, well there is a better friendship yet for both of us to dwell in together. How then can you tolerate
this? and I anticipate your discontent, and fortify myself again in my
solitude.—This whiff of sentiment has expanded itself, you see, into a
very long dull smoke—to end in my old saw, that I dearly love my friend,
but never expect a return in the world that now is. Great & generous
wonderfully is my friend's nature, and great demands are made on her
by her brother's infirmities, but, though I have not ended my shrift, I
will break it off.—The lost letter came, & this day came the new letter,
with tidings that you were ill, & do remain. Last night I looked for you
in the down train. May the fever be gone.[191] As for Concord, Sophia
Hawthorne goes out of town on Thursday, they quit us then. The house
is to be vacant all winter, except during the repairs of some rooms by
carpenters. I asked Mr Ripley if he would not have you for a tenant until
spring? "Yes, if she will endure the hammering." So you had better bring
Margaret Curson [192] & a manservant & live there. I think I may escape
out of Concord for a day or two on one of my pen & ink excursions
presently but it will not last longer. If you come & make the promised
visit, call Lidian to council as to houses & places. Margaret has not come
but is I believe daily expected.[193] Come here by all means and to this

191. The "lost" letter is postmarked from Brattleboro September 27: the new letter,
dated September 29, is postmarked September 30 and reports the illness that keeps her
another week in Brattleboro. In both letters the question of where she shall live is agitated.
In the first she writes: "Your next housebuilding must be your share of a great palace—
Seeing William Channing has taught me this—but the palaces are as yet only pasteboard &
'paint' This generation has not where to lay the head—we must live in barns for a while &
see what will come of it. I have thought a little of ⟨coming⟩ going to the Community this
winter but am not ready to throw myself before the Juggernaut—But where else can I go—
If Sophia Hawthorne leaves Concord & I say, 'not to your house,' there can be ⟨n⟩/no/other
place but some small room with six children wailing responses to a fretful /mother/ above,
beneath, on every side. One might as well go to an Association at once for in these the world
has a chance to begin anew. But this Brook Farm seem little more than a great market where
they label themselves heroic martyrs, & sell pigs adorned with ornamental frost work—
William Channing will be their good angel, but he will have to talk until he will desire to
learn Patagonian & forget his native tongue. When you see Sophia H. will tell her I
cannot accept her pleasant invitation to stay a little while in Oct. because I must confine
myself to the delights of Woburn—I cannot answer her letter because I have already eight
to write, & not one of them will ever be written—"
    This "communitarian" fantasy prompted by hearing William Henry Channing preach
gives way to one of a different sort in the letter of the 29th. Here the devotee of the
picturesque and the sublime speaks: "I wish I could have a lodge, for a constancy, in your
garden—but your garden should be a forest & your house beside a stream, & its tall turret
should overlook mountain & valley."
    192. Of the Curson family of Curson's Mill. Curzon is the preferred form.
    193. In her letter of the 29th, Caroline had asked if Margaret Fuller had arrived: "I
shall not wish to see her & she will not wish to see me—Women should all have a hemisphere

house and if I should not be at home stay till I come, and then, only stay long enough to tell me all you have learned in Brattleboro, unless you decide to sit down & board with Lidian; for I am a spacious reader for these six or eight weeks to come[194] Have I answered any of your questions? Ellen Hooper and Anna H. and Susan Sturgis came hither the other day & called at this & other houses—.[195] I was very sorry that I was in Boston all the while.

1 October

To Henry David Thoreau, Concord, October 8? 1845[196]

Dear Henry

Can you not without injurious delay to the shingling give a quarter or a half hour tomorrow morning to the direction of the Carpenter who builds Mrs Brown's fence? Cutler has sent another man, & will not be here to repeat what you told him so that the new man wants new orders.[197] I suppose he will be on the ground at 7, or a little after & Lidian shall keep your breakfast warm. But do not come to the spoiling of your day.

                                                                        R. W. E.

Wednesday
p. m. 5 o'clock
H. D. Thoreau

---

to themselves & send ambassadors to each other like great queens. . . ." See October 15 below for Margaret Fuller's visit.

194. Reading for the new series of lectures, "Representative Man." In the "lost" letter, Miss Sturgis had promised him a new listener, William Aspinwall, "so you shall have a listener for the first time & that is always the best." And then she adds: "Yet it is often good to hear the same music again; the bird whom we first heard singing in the sky, in our childhood, must always be heard with delight."

195. Caroline Sturgis' sisters: Ellen (Mrs. Robert Hooper), Anne (Mrs. Samuel Hooper), and Susan.

196. MS in Houghton Library, MH; ph. in NNC; printed by Cameron, *ESQ* (1st Q., 1961), 22:96. Cameron suggests an August date for this note, but Emerson's MS Account Book for 1845–1849, p. [49], shows under the date October 10 a payment to Thoreau of $5.00 "for building fence." In the same Account Book, p. [44] Emerson's full record of the expenses of the new house for his sister-in-law Lucy Jackson Brown shows two payments to Thoreau (of $5.00 each), one for "building drain and laying cellar floor" and the other for "building fence"; payment for the first is recorded as "sundry labours," p. [43], under the date August 26. Mrs. Brown moved in on September 9, p. [45]. Since the fence need not have been built before she moved in, I have conjectured a date for this note close to the date of payment.

197. Isaac Cutler, carpenter.

To Caroline Sturgis, Concord, October 15, 1845?[198]

Concord, Oct 15.

And when will you come to our browning meadows, dear friend, & consider our endurabilities for a winter?[199] I have little & lessening chances for any excursion, and should be loth to be absent at your coming. If you go to town /Boston/ some days, write me now what day you will surely be there & I will go to see & hear the wonders of the months. Or you shall summon me, if you so choose, to our Abbey,[200] & I will try to come. Margaret has just gone from us to Chelsea & Brook Farm. I am very busy, the lot of all limited people By the side of Jove's ⟨there⟩throne are many crystal vases, each containing virtuous gases, one spherule of which no bigger than a drop weighs down the globe of the

198. MS in the Tappan papers, Houghton Library, MH; ph. in NNC; p. [4] addressed: Miss Caroline Sturgis | Care of William Sturgis, Esq. | Boston. | ; postmarked at Concord, October 15. The reference to Margaret Fuller's visit and Caroline Sturgis' reply of October 20 make the year certain.

199. Miss Sturgis' letter written from Woburn, postmarked at Boston, October 20, reads in part:

"I shall not come to Concord until it is necessary to find a permanent abode for the winter—the last of this month or the first of next—& so will you not come to see me here. I have been waiting for the present chaos to subside, & now that order will resume some sway I hope you will come & pass a day—any day next week—on Tuesday I shall go in to hear Ole Bull, but that is the only engagement I have—Cannot you ⟨come⟩ send ⟨Mond⟩ me word what day & then I certainly shall be at home—You can come /in the cars at/ ¼ before 12, & stay until the last of the P.M. Ellen also is here ⟨in⟩ with a little black silk dress, diamond pin, & diamond eyes. The Abbey is too shady & cold to sit in but we can go into some sunny field among the fading asters.

"I have a fine plan to propose for next winter—that I should live in your barn—but do not say a thing about it, or that I may or must not come, until I have seen it myself & judged of its capacities. I have an equal dread of loneliness & any domestic arrangement which the shingle palaces of Concord would permit, but a barn would be a golden mean such as is rarely found. . . .

"Margaret has just been here & I had a very good time with her, & am glad she came—I am sorry I said even for a moment I did not want to see her, but I seem to have an endless distrust towards my friends—no wonder when I live among people who look upon me with cold & criticizing eyes—the constant drop will wear upon the stone, so every one who loves me must forgive me forever & aye. . . .

"I wish to see you very much but I have not followed the track of any star or measured the height of any mountain peak, & you must be content with lowly things from me—"

Caroline Sturgis came to Concord sometime at the end of October, apparently staying briefly with the Emersons, but leaving when she arranged to stay with "Mrs Ball" (letter from her of November 1); she returned to Concord November 5 to spend the winter. How long she stayed is not certain, but she was still in Concord when in February 1846 Channing took it into his head to go abroad. See *Letters*, 3:327, and in McGill, p. 88, where her letter to Margaret Fuller is quoted.

200. Emerson presumably accepted the invitation above; the MS Account Book for 1845–1849, p. [51], shows under the date October 22, that he went into town and stayed the night in the American House. I think he took poems to show her and that she is the "critical friend" referred to in his letter of October 29 to his brother William, *Letters*, 3:310.

earth, and, better, countervails all the various energies,—salt, acid, alkali, animal life—in the monster ball. Ever yours,

To William Henry Furness, Concord, October 15, 1845 [201]

Concord, Oct. 15, 1845.

My dear friend,

I should have answered your letter so richly accompanied too,[202] immediately but that I saw that the best answer to a part of it would be to send you the last letter which I had from Carlyle, and which I had lent to a friend here who must & will read his letters. I enclose it that you may not only read its good news of himself, but see his answer to my remark ⟨that⟩ (in a letter written before I saw you in Boston) that I had heard nothing from Philadelphia respecting the promised £50, since the death of Mr Carey,[203] and that I hesitated about writing to you on this subject. You will see by his letter that he has not received the money. Pray do not afflict Mr Sartain with C's grim humours, into which he is always relapsing,—about the picture.[204]

Thanks, and very humble thanks too, for the fine book you send me, so rich & stately that my poor little verses look very few & short,—and I wish they had been better. Great is your art & skill. I enclose also a note of thanks, /(which read,)/ to Mr Hart, for his generous gift.[205] I doubt not also that my first thanks are due to you in the matter. And as far as I can remember in life you ever stand in the shape of a benefactor to me. I shall write a hymn to you one day.

You must send me back this letter of T.C.;[206] and also remind some right person, friend of Mr Carey, that the *copy* of t[he] letter I gave him was never s[ent][207] to me.

Your affectionately,
R. Waldo E.

201. MS in the Furness papers, Van Pelt Library, PU; ph. in NNC; p. [4] addressed: Rev. William H. Furness.| Philadelphia. | Pa. | ; postmarked at Concord, October 15. Printed in *Records*, pp. [44]–45; listed *Letters*, 3:309.

202. Of October 8, *Records*, pp. [42]–43. Furness had sent *The Diadem* for 1846 and the watercolor copy of Samuel Lawrence's sketch of Carlyle, the latter the gift of the publisher Abraham Hart.

203. Carlyle's letter of August 29 (Slater, pp. 379–381); Furness had asked whether Carlyle had received any money from Carey and Hart (see Slater, pp. 381–383).

204. The portion of the Carlyle letter that refers to the "frightful picture by Lawrence"; John Sartain, the engraver.

205. In *Letters*, 3:309.

206. The letter of February 16, which Emerson had given to Edward L. Carey; see April 8, above.

207. The breaking of the seal damaged two words.

To John Chapman, Concord, October 30, 1845[208]

Concord, Oct. 30, 1845

John Chapman, Esq.

Dear Sir,

Mr Munroe, ⟨print⟩without authority from me, advertised my Poems as "in press," much to my vexation. I did intend to get them ready for New Years; but unlooked for interruptions made me lay them aside for a couple of months. I may print them by Wiley & Putnam, but, if I do, shall reserve, as I told them, your right of publication in England.[209] I will endeavour to send you a fair Ms. copy of the whole /work/, before I begin printing here. But I cannot say when it will be, as it indispensably requires a few if only three or four of my best days, to end the MSS; and in the two next months, /or longer/, I see no day of leisure.

Yours respectfully,

R. W. E.

I received safely the copy of the Bhagvat Geeta, with much satisfaction: but of two prices marked on it, could not determine which was yours.[210] If you know anything of Dr M'Cormac of Dublin, if he visits your shop please to say to him, that I have heard from him twice, by his books kindly sent, and shall now write to him, I hope, by an early steamer.[211]

To Robert Adams, Concord, November 1, 1845[212]

Concord, 1 Nov. 1845

Robert Adams, Esq

Dear Sir

Forgive me for my delay in replying to your letter which in some confusion of my papers was mislaid & which after much seeking I have just recovered. I think it will not be in my power to comply with the

---

208. MS in Houghton Library, MH; ph. in NNC; p. [4] addressed: Mr John Chapman | Bookseller | 121 Newgate Street | London. | ; postmarked Liverpool? November 18.

209. See *Letters*, 3:297, 301, 308, for abortive negotiations with Wiley and Putnam through Evert Duyckinek.

210. In a letter of May 30, Emerson had asked Chapman to find for him a copy of Wilkins' translation of the Bhagvat Geeta (*Letters*, 3:288); see Harding, pp. 26–27. He had received it by September 15; see letter of that date above.

211. Probably the same "Dr M'Cormac" to whom he had Chapman send a copy of his *Poems*; see *Letters*, 3:359, where Rusk (n. 144) suggests Henry MacCormac, translator of *The Meditations of Marcus Aurelius, with the Manual of Epictetus*, 1844.

212. MS in the Barrett Collection, Alderman Library, ViU; ph. in CUL; p. [4] addressed: Robert Adams, Esq | Fall River, | Mass.|; postmarked at Concord November 1. Emerson's only certain lecture in Fall River (February 11, 1846) was for the lyceum, not for a group of ladies.

request of the ladies, your friends. My time is necessarily devoted to certain studies, which are very jealous, & allow of few & rare departures from their demands. I shall be glad to esteem the invitation you send me, as a door left open for me in case anything good & reasonable should come into my thoughts, on that subject of Slavery; but, at present, sad as it is, I have nothing to say of it.

Yours respectfully,
R. W. Emerson.

To Henry MacCormac, Concord, November 15? 1845

[See October 30 above, where Emerson tells Chapman he hopes to write Dr. Henry MacCormac "by an early steamer." There is no certainty of a letter, but MacCormac had sent Emerson his translation of the *Meditations of Marcus Aurelius* (see Harding, p. 17) and apparently other works as well.]

To William J. Rotch, Concord, November 17, 1845[213]

Concord, Nov. 17th, 1845.

W. J. Rotch, Esq., Secretary

Dear Sir: —If I come to New Bedford, I should be ready to fix, say the first Tuesday of March, and the second. But I have to say, that I have indirectly received a report of some proceedings in your Lyceum, lately, which, by excluding others, I think ought to exclude me. My informant said, that the application of a colored person for membership by purchase of a ticket in the usual manner, had been rejected by a vote of the Lyceum; and this, for the first time. Now, as I think the Lyceum exists for popular education, as I work in it for that, and think that it should bribe and importune the humblest and most ignorant to come in, and exclude nobody, or, if any body, certainly the most cultivated,—this vote quite embarrasses me, and I should not know how to speak to the company. Besides, in its direct counteraction to the obvious duty and sentiment of New England, and of all freemen in regard to the colored people, the vote appears so unkind, and so unlooked for, that I could not come with any pleasure before the Society.

---

213. No MS has been located; text from *The Liberator* (January 16, 1846), 16:10; listed *Letters*, 3:312. Daniel Ricketson appears to have been the agent in securing the letter for publication in *The Liberator;* see *Letters*, 3:322–323, and note 1 where Rotch's willingness to release the letter is reported in a letter from Ricketson to Emerson (December 29, 1845). Ricketson says also that the letter was read aloud to the members of the New Bedford Lyceum and that Charles Sumner had taken a similar action. Emerson's second letter to Rotch has not been found; see *Letters*, 3:312 and 323. The manifest typographical error of "ignorent" for "ignorant" has been corrected.

If I am misinformed, will you—if they are printed—have the goodness to send me the proceedings; or, if not printed, their purport; and
oblige,

Yours respectfully,

R. W. Emerson.

To Jerome Hall Woodman Colby, Concord, November 17, 1845[214]

Concord, 17 Nov. 1845

J. H. W. Colby, Esq

Dear Sir,

I believe I must not promise myself the pleasure of coming to Dover,
this winter.[215] If, however, some of my contingent engagements should
not prove binding, perhaps you will let me ask hereafter for a late day in
your Lyceum.

Yours respectfully,

R. W. Emerson.

To John Andrew Peters, Concord, November 17, 1845

[Goodspeed's *The Flying Quill*, Spring 1984, item 29, describes a letter to John A.
Peters and quotes it: "I do not know but that I was a little inconsiderate in my
conversation with Col. Goss, in leaving him with the impression that I could easily
come to Bangor . . . at least certainly not before March. Will you not then let me
keep the visit before me as a good and pleasing hope. . . ." See *Letters*, 1:415–416,
n. 45, for Colonel Cyrus Goss of Bangor. Emerson did not lecture in Bangor until
October of the following year (see Charvat, p. 22.)]

214. MS in the Feinberg Collection, MiD; ph. in NNC; single leaf, the address leaf torn
away. Printed by William White, "Thirty-Three Unpublished Letters of Ralph Waldo Emerson," *AL* (May 1961), 33:160. J. H. W. Colby is listed in a Dover directory as a student in the
law office of D. M. Christy; he is surely the Jerome Hall Woodman Colby (1821–1853) listed
in the *General Catalogue of Dartmouth College,* class of 1842; he subsequently migrated to
Manitowoc, Wisconsin, where he became a judge in the Probate Court.
215. Emerson had lectured in Dover, N. H., on February 12, 1845 (see December 29?
1844, above for correction of Charvat); he was not to lecture there again until 1851.

To CHRISTOPHER GORE RIPLEY, CONCORD, NOVEMBER 29, 1845[216]

Concord, 29 Nov, 1845.

C. G. Ripley. Esq.

My dear Sir,

I have told Mr Robert Haskins[217] that if he cannot elsewhere succeed in raising the money he wants, I will procure him one hundred dollars [to be loaned him on the note of himself & his son Augustus Parsons[218] of Waterford payable in one year, with interest,] provided that he satisfies you that the security which he offers on his house & land in Waterford is good & sufficient.[219] If you can give so much attention to the affairs as to satisfy yourself on my part, I shall be your debtor.

Yours ever,

R. Waldo Emerson.

To CHRISTOPHER GORE RIPLEY, CONCORD, DECEMBER 1, 1845[220]

Concord, 1 December, 1845

C. G. Ripley, Esq.

My dear Cousin,

I could not hope to understand Mr Haskins's story,[221] & told him I would not attempt it; but as he referred to you, I seized on that good fortune and said he should have the money if he could satisfy you that there was any /landed/ security The letter was further to avail him, in case of your favorable opinion, as an assurance to Mr. Matteson[222] Thanks

216. MS in Houghton Library, MH; ph. in NNC; p. [4] addressed: C. Gore Ripley, Esq. | Court Street. | Boston |. This letter, that of December 1, and the two letters of December 17 below are concerned with the unfortunate consequences of Aunt Mary Moody Emerson's "fancy-practice in real estate"; Emerson explains the matter to his brother William in a letter of February 13, 1847; see *Letters*, 3:371–373. Christopher Gore Ripley, the son of Samuel Ripley, Mary Moody Emerson's half-brother, often acted for her.

217. Emerson's uncle.

218. Augustus Parsons was Robert Haskins' son-in-law. Emerson may be asking for two co-signers of the note, but in that ease one would expect him to have written: "himself, his son, & Augustus Parsons." (The square brackets may have been added by Ripley.) Robert Haskins' son, Samuel Moody Haskins, is mentioned in December 1, below, as lending his father $100 toward the sum needed to get back the property Mary Moody Emerson had virtually given away.

219. As the letter of December 1 shows, the property had never been Robert Haskins'.

220. MS in Houghton Library, MH; ph. in NNC; p [4] addressed: C. G. Ripley, Esq. | Court Street, | Boston |.

221. Robert Haskins, Emerson's uncle. The letter referred to is, I believe, that of November 29 above; its formal salutation suggests that it was meant to be carried by Robert Haskins to Gore Ripley and used also "as assurance to Mr Matteson."

222. In the explanatory letter to his brother William, Emerson spells the name Matthewson and specifies that he is jeweler in Providence. The deed (RWEMA) by which Emerson

for your explicit information. A little daylight is so welcome.[223] There is then no security of land. Still, all that I understood of his story returns, —that he is to lose a valuable farm for the want of 200 dollars, whilst his son S. Moody[224] stands ready to raise $100. I say then that if Mr Ralph Haskins will become responsible for him (by endorsement, if that is sufficient,) I will lend ⟨him⟩ /Mr Robert Haskins/ one hundred dollars for a year. If Mr Ralph Haskins[225] refuses his name, I am willing to lend to Mr Parsons[226] on anything which you shall ascertain to be real security; & ⟨I⟩in that contingency, I will be at the cost of proper inquiries. Yours affectionately,

R. W. Emerson.

To Christopher Gore Ripley, Concord, December 9, 1845[227]

Concord, 9 Dec.

My dear Cousin

Will you not, if you are at leisure on some Thursday Evening, give us your countenance at the Lyceum?[228] Will you not give my love to Elizabeth, & to Mr & Mrs Simmons,[229] & ask them if they will ⟨not⟩help us also? I enclose, for the day, such slips of card, as the Lyceum officer[230] (I do not admire his taste,) sent me. I understood him that each card would admit a party of several persons. I do now know whether for one or for several evenings; I shall learn tomorrow, & will send more if these are not good.

Ever yours,
R. W. Emerson.

---

conveys the property back to Mary Moody Emerson shows that the jeweller is Allen C. Mathewson. According to the Providence directory for 1845, Mathewson was a manufacturing jeweler of the firm of Allen and Mathewson, 9 Broad St.; the firm is also specified in the deed. The deed was registered in Oxford County, Maine, January 22, 1846, 73:107–108.

223. A possible sign of desperation is that p. [4] of the November 29 letter has $300 written on it nine times in addition to other figures and Emerson's name six times.

224. Samuel Moody Haskins.

225. Ralph Haskins, Emerson's uncle and Robert Haskins' brother.

226. Augustus Parsons, Robert Haskins' son-in-law.

227. MS in Houghton Library, MH; ph. in NNC; p. [4] addressed: C. G. Ripley, Esq. | 9 Court Square | Boston|.

228. Emerson was giving for the Boston Lyceum his series on "Representative Men"; the lectures were delivered on Thursday evenings.

229. Elizabeth Ripley and Mary Ripley Simmons (Mrs. Charles Francis Simmons) were Gore Ripley's sisters.

230. Nathaniel W. Coffin; see *Letters*, 3:314.

To Christopher Gore Ripley, Concord, December 17, 1845[231]

Concord, 17 Dec. 1845

My dear Cousin,

I am really not at all master of this business, and too little intelligent of what you have told me to have the grounds of a decision,—what with this weeks study,[232] what with my increasing correspondence with New York.[233] I must even put myself in your hands, and you must do the best you can. If you think Aunt Mary can only be relieved by my paying 400, and if you think me eventually secured to this amount; pay it. I enclose a cheque on the Atlantic Bank, which will be good in Providence. But why Matthewson[234] & Co. are at liberty to fluctuate between 300 & 500, whether they extort or not, & how far it behoves us to submit to them, I know not at all.[235] I am very sorry the time presses us so, for I hate to jump in the dark. I did not receive your letter till night. If you wish a more unlimited discretion than I have described, use it.[236]

Yours affectionately,

R. Waldo Emerson

231. MS in Houghton Library, MH; ph. in NNC; p. [4] addressed: C. G. Ripley, Esq. | 9 Court Square | Adams' Express Boston|.

232. See November 29 and December 1 above; for a lucid account of Mary Moody Emerson's "fancy-practice in real estate" see *Letters*, 3:371–373.

233. The correspondence with New York concerned Carlyle's new book, which so far as Emerson knew at the time, was about to be pirated by Wiley and Putnam; see *Letters*, 3:315–325, *Passim*.

234. The Providence jeweler (see December 1, above), to whom Aunt Mary had sold a portion of her Waterford property.

235. Emerson's MS Account Book, 1845–1849, has three entries on this matter. The first, p. [57], under the date December 8 is, as indicated, partially deleted; it reads: "Cheque on Suffolk Bank to ⟨C. G. Ripley,⟩ Esq for contingent ⟨use at Providence⟩ ⟨300.00⟩." The second, p. [59] under the date December 27 reads: "Pd. Matthewson for a deed of 25 acres of Land in Waterford, Me. $300.00" The third of November 23, 1846, p. [95], records the payment of $23.00 to C. G. Ripley "for professional services & expenses in the business of - M. M. Emerson last winter."

236. Acting for Mathewson, Thomas Davis of Providence wrote Gore Ripley on the same day: "I ought in justice to Mr Matthewson to state that his proposition to Mr Haskins was to receive $220 cash & a note for $200. . . ." (a.l.s., RWEMA). A letter of November 18, 1846, from Davis to Ripley shows that the matter was not clearly settled a year later; Davis is replying to a letter of November 16, 1846 (Emerson's copy, RWEMA), from Ripley inquiring the meaning of a letter to Emerson from a Mr. Johonnot "whom I conclude to be a clerk of Messrs Matthewson & Allen." The question is whether a note (taken by Haskins and guaranteed by Augustus Parson) for $100 payable to Emerson and endorsed by Emerson to Mathewson and Allen was endorsed by him as "without recourse to him" or not. Davis' reply assures Ripley that it is so endorsed. An Andrew Johonnot is listed in Providence directories for 1847–1848 as "clerk" at the same address as Mathewson & Allen, from which fact it can be conjectured that he is the Johonnot who alarmed Emerson and Gore Ripley with what appeared to be a demand for the additional $100 owing to Mathewson & Allen. Ripley's

To Christopher Gore Ripley, Concord? December 17, 1845 [237]

Postscript

Dear Gore,

I think to enclose to you a note to the Cashier of the Atlantic Bank. If you do not draw the cheque, you shall withhold the letter to him. If you draw or forward the cheque, please to present the letter to the Cashier first.

Yours

R W Emerson

To Benjamin Dodd, Concord, December 17, 1845

[See the second note of December 17, 1845, above, to Christopher Gore Ripley, for a note to the cashier of the Atlantic Bank, Benjamin Dodd.]

To Sampson Reed, Concord, December 24, 1845 [238]

Concord, Dec. 24, 1845.

My dear Sir,

I enclose my card which is good at the gates of the Lyceum. I ought to speak of Swedenborg tomorrow evening.[239] I am sure it would give me much more pleasure to hear you speak on the same subject.

Yours respectfully,

R. W. Emerson.

---

letter was written from Concord suggesting that Emerson got hold of him at once for a reply; manifestly Emerson was fearful that Aunt Mary's "fancy practice" might cost him another $100.

237. MS in Houghton Library, MH; ph. in NNC; p. [4] addressed: C. G. Ripley, Esq. | 9 Court Square | paid | Adams's Express Boston. This postscript is separately addressed and separately sealed. It pretty clearly belongs with the letter of December 17 above.

238. MS in the University Libraries, OOxM; ph. in NNC; p. [4] addressed: Sampson Reed, Esq. | of | Reed, Wing, & Cutler—| Boston. | ; postmarked at Boston, December 24. Listed *Letters*, 3:320–321. The paper is unlike any Emerson ever used; I infer that the stationery was borrowed in Boston.

239. Emerson gave the third lecture of the series "Representative Men" at the Odeon on December 25 for the Boston Lyceum (Charvat, p. 21).

1846

To William Davis, Concord, January 12, 1846

[In 1945, Rusk saw this letter to Davis in MHi (Miscellaneous MSS); the letter is now missing from its place in a bound volume, and more than one search has failed to recover it. Rusk's note shows that the letter was dated from Concord January 12, 1846, signed R. W. Emerson, and addressed: William Davis, Esq.| Plymouth,| Mass.|; it was postmarked at Concord January 12. Rusk's précis of the letter reads: ". . . Will accept but wants to arrange time. Has made two contingent promises at Providence and Worcester. Will offer time after ten days. . . ." See January 28 below for his offer of March 5 and 6.]

To William Davis, Boston, January 28, 1846[1]

Boston 28 Jan. 1846

Col. Wm Davis—
Dear Sir,

Will Thursday & Friday 5th & 6th March suit your convenience in the Lyceum, for my Lectures?[2] If so, please address me at Concord.[3]—The same evenings in the following week are equally free for me, if you like them better.

Yours respectfully,
R. W. Emerson

To Rufus Griswold, Concord, January ? 1846

[See below, March 30, to William Furness for evidence that Emerson wrote Griswold probably in January in an effort to recover the miniature that had been sent to him in 1845.]

1. MS in Miscellaneous MSS., MHi; ph. in NNC; p. [4] addressed: William Davis, Esq. | Plymouth. | Mass. | ; postmarked at Boston January 28.
2. Charvat, p. 22, lists only one lecture at Plymouth. Emerson's MS Account Book for 1845–1849 has an entry for expenses, p. [74]; the entry is undated. The entry for the receipt of $30.00 "at Plymouth" is dated March 7, p. [18].
3. See above, January 12, for note of a lost letter to Davis.

To WILLIAM HENRY FURNESS, CONCORD, FEBRUARY 25, 1846[4]

Concord, Feby, 25, 1846

My dear Furness,

To pass over my gross omissions of epistolary duty to you ward, dum tacent clamant,[5]—& come immediately to the errand of today—be it known to you; that Carlyle had been repeatedly charged by me to send his Cromwell book over to us in Ms. which Munroe & Co were ready to print advantageously for him. At the last, he was driven a good deal, & the printers there would not let him wait for a Ms copy; so he apologized to us & did the best he could; sent me a letter, saying, "I have sent you by last steamer an early copy of the whole work, which you will get, at least, a month before any bookseller in America can have it." -&c. sent ⟨to⟩thro Wiley & Putnam.[6] I had not received any such parcel by that last steamer. I sent Horace Greeley Esq to demand such copy of Wiley & P. They "declined giving it up, until their edition, then in press, should be ready; & had their authority from Carlyle's publishers, of whom they had bought a copy."[7] So we were baulked, & angry, without sin.

I sent Carlyle an account of this matter. He went down to his "Chapman & Hall" there, & got an explanation, which was provoking enough truly, but exculpated Wiley & Putnam.[8] It seems, he had gone into their shop, & written my name on a blank leaf, & ordered an early copy bound up & forwarded to me by the going steamer. Chapman said, "If it is to be reprinted by Mr E., why bind it? send it in sheets." Carlyle, they say, made reply, "O I will not bother him with that; bind it."[9]

He did not wish to send it me in a form that seemed to expect us to reprint. But Chapman bethought himself—& went immediately over to W & Putnam, & offered them an early copy, for £10. They said,

"But you must send no other." He said,

"only one for Mr E., who will not print, Mr C. says"

4. MS in the Furness papers, Van Pelt Library, PU; ph. in NNC; p. 4 addressed: William Henry Furness. | Philadelphia | Pa. | ; postmarked at Boston, February 26. Printed in *Records*, pp. [46]–49; listed, *Letters*, 3:328.

5. Emerson apparently liked this phrase; see November 18, 1833, above, and *JMN*, 5:171; 6:139. In all these uses, he has the verbs in the singular. Here he is closer to Cicero's *In Catilinam*, I, viii. In all he uses "dum" for Cicero's "cum" spoiling the original. Here certainly what he gives doesn't make sense. He ought to have used Cicero's adverb, but changed the verbs to the first person singular. Elsewhere he has no qualms about changing a quotation to suit his end.

6. Letter of November 11, 1845; see Slater, pp. 383, 386.

7. See letters of December 1845 in *Letters*, 3:315–320, and Slater, pp. 386–387. Letters to Horace Greeley and to Wiley and Putnam have not been found.

8. December 15, 1845; *Letters*, 3:317–318, and Slater, pp. 386–387.

9. January 3, 1846, Slater, pp. [388]–389. And see also *Letters*, 3:324–326.

"Yes, but he may give it to one who will"—

"Then you need not hasten his copy"—said Chapman —

And thus was our learned & witty friend defrauded by little & little of all advantage here from his most saleable book. He was very much vexed at the whole affair. ⟨Now he⟩

Chapter Second.

Now he has a second edition preparing, and bethinks him that he can make possible, out of that, some reparation to Munroe, who was to have shared with him the advantage of the first edition, and /he/ sends us the letter which I conclude to enclose to you.[10]

I have gone to Munroe, with this letter, & said, What will you give for the new edition? Is it worth anything to you? Munroe & Co do not seem inclined to meddle with it at all, fearing that not only the Appendix, but what new matter shall be inserted in the text of the book, will be instantly reprinted from them. It occurs to me, that the next party—(I have yet mentioned it to no other,) is your friend Mr Hart. Perhaps he may see how the work may be printed once more here with some security from pirates. If he cannot in the existing circumstances attempt anything for the mutual advantage of Carlyle & himself, he is at liberty if he chooses, to receive & print the proofs or such part as he will. And I know Carlyle will be gratified to have this disposition made of them, as he is very sensible of the liberality of Carey & Hart's behaviour in their edition of his Miscellanies.

Will you now add to all your loveliness this new merit of considering & properly communicating this affair, & sending me an early reply as the days are few in which anything can be done. And send me home my Carlyle letters, of which you will have 1,2,3, is it not? & I no copy. Yours affectionately

R. W. Emerson

All is clear in respect to Wiley & Putnam. They explained very circumstantially their part in the affair to me, & I wrote to them acquitting them of all charges, & I printed a paragraph to the same effect in the Boston D. Advertiser.[11] But they were told, at the same time, how vexed we were to be thus honorably plundered by them. Of course, we owe them & their editions no respect.[12]

10. February 3, 1846, Slater, pp. 390–391.

11. January 27, 1846; *Letters*, 3:324. *Boston Daily Advertiser*, January 31, 1846; see n. 10, *Letters*, 3:326.

12. By March 24 (*Letters*, 3:329) Emerson found that the "Charms of wrath" had begun to pall. His long efforts on Carlyle's behalf brought him debt and vexation, but his persistence never flagged.

To E_____ T_____ Rice, Concord, March 9? 1846

[In a letter of March 7, 1846, E. T. Rice invites Emerson to give a lecture for the lyceum of South Berwick, Maine: he proposes March 18, but there is no record of a South Berwick lecture in the 1846–47 season. The addressee may be Edwin T. Rice (later of New York), who married Lidian Emerson's cousin Augusta Jackson; see *Letters*, 4:278 and 436, n. 110.]

To Reed and Cutler, Concord, March 14, 1846? [13]

Will Messrs Reed & Cutler send me 7 lb Supercarbonate of Soda
7 lb. Cream Tartar
4 lb. Saleratus —
& charge the same to their obed.t serv.t

R. W. Emerson

Concord, 14 March.

To Anna Barker Ward, Concord, March 25? 1846 [14]

Concord, Wednesday Morn

Dear Anna,

Lidian depends on seeing you today which is so bright for us all. And she prays you to bring the children with you. It is really very easy to do

13. MS in CSmH; ph. in NNC; single sheet without address. This order cannot be earlier than 1846, the first year in which Sampson Reed's firm is listed in Boston directories as Reed and Cutler, as it continued to be through 1869. I find no entry in the account books which would provide a more nearly secure date.

14. MS in the Ward papers, Houghton Library, MH; ph. in NNC; p. [4] addressed: Mrs Anna Ward. | At house of T. W. Ward. Esq. | Park Street. This letter cannot be earlier than 1845 or later than 1847 when on September 26 the Ward's fourth child (Eliza) was born. The youngest child named in the letter is Thomas Wren Ward (Emerson has plainly written "Sam," but Ward's only son was named for his grandfather). The child was born in October 1844, three months after the birth of Edward Waldo Emerson. When the boy was born, the Wards had already moved to Lenox, not returning to Boston permanently until 1850. They did, however, make annual visits in the early spring, staying with Ward's parents at the Park Street address. The first of these visits was made in 1845, but the manner in which Emerson refers to the children does not suggest so early a date; Tom, four months old, and "little Ned," seven months old, would be scarcely up to even infant sociabilities. In 1846, the Wards came to Boston at the end of the first week in March (Martha Ward, a.l.s., March 3, 1846, to Samuel and Anna, MHi) and stayed through the first week in April (Samuel Ward, a.l.s., April 12, 1846, to his father, MHi). A Wednesday in 1846 is possible, with the exception of March 11 when Emerson went to Fall River to lecture. Emerson was thereafter firmly fixed in Concord on Wednesdays between March 24 and April 8, for he was giving his series on "Representative Men" for the Concord Lyceum. I choose 1846 because it seems unlikely that in 1847 Emerson would misname Ward's son; moreover, the Wards in later years made their visits to Boston in February, for in this year, 1846, Ward discovered that he had stayed too

so and Ellen & Edith & little Ned do present their compliments to their several contemporaries, Anna, & Lily, and Sam Ward,[15] and wish to show them their nursery & swing. The Fitchburg coach will come for you at 1 o'clock and the day is the best.

Ever yours
R. Waldo Emerson.

To WILLIAM HENRY FURNESS, CONCORD, MARCH 30, 1846[16]

Concord, 30 March, 1846

My dear friend,

That essential point, the date, the last day of grace or opportunity for the contributors to the Diadem,—you have not named. You must write again & say it, for in these negative ages it is often the sole inspiration. When I know that, I will honestly respect the /coming/ fact, in my writing or in my revising of that which is written; and will either send you something passable, or give you timely notice that I cannot. I am really intending to print my verses before the next new year though it seems like taking advantage of the times of dearth when we bring what we know to be inferior fruit to market.

You will be glad to know that from unpromising correspondence Wiley & Putnam have offered what I consider pretty good terms for the new Carlyle book of which near 300 pages arrived by the last steamer.[17]

May I trouble you once more about that miniature ⟨sent⟩ /lent/ to Mr Griswold.[18] He took it from my wife, perhaps fourteen months ago. I wrote to him perhaps two months since, requesting him to send it to me by express. I have no reply whatever. Is he in Philadelphia? If he is, will you obtain it from him, & send it to /care of/ J Munroe & Co. who will

late for the good of his farm (letter of April 12 cited). February in New England suggests sleds not swings. I choose March 25 because by the 24th "spring" had "really come" (see *Letters*, 3:330). In 1847 the Wards made the Boston visit in February, returning to Lenox March 4.

15. Lydia Ward, born in late April 1843, and Edith Emerson, born in late November 1843; and Edward Emerson and Thomas Ward (see above) both born in 1844.

16. MS in Special Collections, Mugar Library, MBU; ph. in NNC; p. [4] addressed: William Henry Furness. | Philadelphia. | Pa. |; postmarked at Concord, date blurred. The postscript was evidently written after Emerson had started to fold it for sending. See *Records*, p. [52] for Furness' letter of March 20 to which this letter is a reply. For the poem provided, see June 10, 1846, below.

17. See Slater, pp. 393–394, and n. 2; and pp. 396–398, and nn. 1 and 2.

18. See, above, May 8, 1845, and, below, June 10, 1846, to Furness, and April 5, 1847.

pay the Express. To put it in a book, which I will restore, is the safest way. This absurd fuss would make a good Farce.

Yours affectionately,
Waldo Emerson

I shall take the liberty to pay postage on this letter as I learned that a double or treble letter I sent you about Carlyle went unpaid.

To Wiley and Putnam, Concord, April 9, 1846[19]

Concord April 9, 1846

Messers. Wiley & Putnam
Gentlemen:

Mr. Carlyle's *Sartor Resartus* was reprinted for the first time from *Fraser's Magazine,* by Munroe, at the request of my friend Mr. Russell[20] and myself, but at Munroe's own risk and profit. Mr. Carlyle received no benefit from it, and I know not what claims Munroe makes on the book, or whether any.

The *French Revolution* I published, for the author, through Little & Brown. That edition was long ago sold. Of the new and converted edition in three volumes Mr. Carlyle sent over to Little & Brown 500 copies which were sold for his benefit. He has no interest that I know of in any existing American edition.

I collected the *Miscellanies* and published them by Munroe for the author, two editions of the first series, or volumes one and two; and one edition of the second, volumes three and four. When Munroe's stock of complete sets were nearly exhausted, Carey & Hart made me a proposition that they would give Mr. Carlyle fifty pounds sterling for the right to reprint the *Miscellanies* as a part of their series of Foreign Essays. I accepted the proposition; they paid that sum to Mr. Carlyle about a year ago, they purchasing the odd copies of the first series of which I believe, there remain a hundred or more, in sheets. I gave Carey & Hart a certificate of Mr. Carlyle's consent to and interest in the work which I believe they prefixed to it. He has every wish to protect their copies from any competition.

19. No MS has been found, text from George Haven Putnam, *George Palmer Putnam* (New York: G. P. Putnam's, 1912), pp. 102–103; printed also in the 1903 edition. Both printings have in the first sentence the manifest error of "fifth" for "first," here corrected. A draft of this letter is printed in *Letters,* 3:330. There are substantial differences between the draft and the letter as sent. See Slater, pp. 397–419, for letters about the arrangements with Wiley and Putnam, an arrangement not to Carlyle's advantage; see his complaints of December 2, 1856 (Slater, p. 517).
20. LeBaron Russell.

Chartism and *Past and Present* were both published by Little & Brown, for the author, from early copies (the letter from a copy partly in manuscript) sent out to me. I have not by me any recent account from Little & Brown, but I believe they have never quite closed the sales of their editions, the New York printed edition[21] of *Past and Present* having spoiled our sale.

With the exception of the *Miscellanies*, I should be glad if you will make, by direct proposition to Mr. Carlyle, any arrangement for a correct and uniform publication of his works, from which he shall derive a fair advantage. I shall cheerfully recommend to him such an arrangement.

Respectfully
R. W. Emerson.

To Mary Moody Emerson? Concord, May? 1? 1846

[Entered in his Bluebook Calendar 5 with the key number 1806 is a letter that Cabot described as a "fragment" about the Everett Inaugural Dinner (April 30, 1846) and Webster's speech on that occasion, with comment on Everett revealing Emerson's changed attitude toward him. Cabot enters this as a letter to Lidian Emerson; but I find nothing to show that Mrs. Emerson was away on April 30, or May 1. In the calendar, the letters number 1807–1814 are to Mary Moody Emerson; I therefore conjecture that if this is a letter it may be to her; she was familiar with Emerson's early admiration of Everett. See *JMN*, 9:379–381, for Emerson's journal entry about the occasion.]

To Samuel Longfellow, Concord, May 13, 1846[22]

Concord, 13 May, 1846

Mr Samuel Longfellow,
Dear Sir,

I have recovered the old hymn which you ask for, & send a copy of it.[23] In transcribing it, I have mended it, I hope, a little; yet it is easy to see that a little labour would make it much better. But I am constrained today to let it go as it is, or not at all; and you shall print it or leave it, as you will.

Yours respectfully,
R. W. Emerson.

21. The 1912 reading "copy" is here emended to the 1903 "edition" which makes sense, as "copy" does not.
22. MS in Craigie House; ph. in NNC; p. [4] addressed: Samuel Longfellow. | Cambridge. | Mass. | ; postmarked at Concord May 14. The poem occupies pp. [1–2]; the text of the letter is on p. [3]. Printed by Cameron, *ESQ* (1st, 1958), 10:34.
23. The hymn is the one written for the ordination of the Reverend Chandler Robbins, Emerson's successor as pastor of the Second Church (*Works*, 9:223–224, 448). The text

We love the venerable house
Our fathers built to God;
In heaven are kept their grateful vows,
Their dust endears the sod.

Here holy thoughts a light have shed
From many a radiant face
And prayers of ⟨humble virtue made⟩ /tender hope have spread/
/A/ ⟨The⟩ perfume ⟨of⟩ /through/ the place.

And anxious hearts have pondered here
The mystery of life,
And prayed the eternal Spirit to clear
Their doubts, & aid their strife.

From humble tenements around
Came up the pensive train,
And in the Church a blessing found
Which filled their homes again;

For faith & peace & mighty love
⟨What⟩that from the Godhead flow
Showed them the life of heaven above
Springs from the life below.

They live with God, their homes are dust,
But here the children pray,
And, in our fleeting lifetime, trust
To find the narrow way.

On him who by the altar stands,
On him the Spirit fall;/

Emerson sends Samuel Longfellow differs from other printed versions; I reproduce it below. The hymn is printed in *A Book of Hymns for Public and Private Devotion*, ed. by Samuel Longfellow and Samuel Johnson (Cambridge: Metcalf, 1846) as Hymn 423, with the title "The Home Our Fathers Built to God." The text follows the revisions that Emerson makes here, except that the second line of the last stanza reads: "On him thy blessing fall!" The faulty meter of the third line is corrected by the deletion of "to." In *Selected Poems*, 1876 (*BAL*, 5274), the line is corrected by changing "Spirit" to "Light" and retaining "to." Curiously, the original false rhyme of the third line in the second stanza and, of necessity, the original reading of the fourth line are retained. See *JMN*, 3:370–375 for what appear to be the earliest versions.

Speak through his lips they pure /commands,/
Thou Heart that lovest all!

TO JOHN CHAPMAN, CONCORD, MAY 15, 1846[24]

Concord 15 May 1846

Mr John Chapman,
Dear Sir,

I was sorry to have let slip the occasion of the writing by the last steamer to acknowledge your letter. I am sorry again that I have so little good account to give of my forwardness to take advantage of the good opportunities you continue to offer me. This volume of poems though now pretty certain I hope to be ready for the next Christmas still remains in imperfectness.[25] The Seven Lectures which I read in the winter in Boston, I shall, no doubt, print some day; but they are quite too incomplete for print now.[26] I am, in these very days, revising & enlarging them, but I dare not fix a time when they will be ready to send to you. Munroe & Co have pressed me to /re/print the first /& second/ series of Essays ⟨&⟩ in two uniform volumes.[27] But I do not find even that easy, for I wish, if I can, to keep the first series in one volume; & the second needs a considerable addition to go as its companion. In one or another way we must soon execute this last plan.

Though I have so little satisfaction to give you on these points I believe you must take my word for it that I am not quite idle & after a few months I shall hope to give you something to print.[28]

With great regard,
Yours,
R. W. Emerson.

24. MS in the Berg Collection, NN; ph. in NNC; p. [4] addressed: Chapman, Brothers. 121 Newgate Street, London, sent by Harnden's express; stamped May 29 in England. Listed from auction catalogue, *Letters*, 3:332.

25. See BAL 5210 and 5211 for the English and American editions of *Poems* (M. A18. 1 a and M. A18. 1 b). See also below two letters of December 29 and *Letters*, 3:356.

26. *Representative Men* (BAL, 5219; M. A22. 1 a) was not published until November.

27. *Essays. First Series* was reprinted in October 1847. *BAL* 5231, where the intercalary poems are listed (M. A10. 5 a). The Second Series was not reprinted until 1850 (*BAL*, 5220; M. A16. 4 a).

28. The MS for the English edition of *Poems* was sent to Chapman in mid October (*Letters*, 3:356). The MS of "Concord Hymn" is in the Sterling Library, University of London; the Berg collection has other portions; the rest is scattered.

TO WILLIAM HENRY FURNESS, CONCORD, MAY 22, 1846[29]

Concord, 22 May, 1846.

My dear Friend,

I have nothing to send to the new Diadem.[30] I am sorry for it. But I have promised to do what I can to make a volume of poems, and those which I can suffer to pass for publication are so few, that I dare not diminish the number by a single quatrain or couplet. Then for prose, I am like some bookdealers who will never sell me the thing I want, for it will break a set. With the most vigorous recollections, I cannot remember that I ever wrote anything detached & of reasonable dimensions. You see my desperate imbecility, & will leave me to time & my tub[31] for recovery.

I am trying to put into printable condition my seven Lectures on Representative Men; but the topics were so large, & seem to require such spacious & solid reading, that what might pass to be spoken, does not promise to be fit to print in a hurry.[32]

Your abominable
R. W. Emerson

TO DANIEL MARTINDALE, CONCORD, JUNE 10, 1846[33]

Concord, 10 June, 1846.

My dear Sir,

When I left Middletown I had a great good will to print my Oration, at the request of yourself & your associates; yet, I think you will remember that I reserved a right to refuse it. There were some pages in the discourse concerning the "practical" & the "speculative man" which seemed to me incomplete, and I was willing to wait a little that I might express a little more adequately my sense of this matter. By waiting a little I became busy in new studies—somewhat spacious reading & writing for a course of lectures last winter in Boston The proposed question, too, had its attention & enlargement, but dragged in with it a piece of the Oration

29. MS in the Furness papers, Van Pelt Library, PU; ph. in NNC; p. [4] addressed: William H. Furness. | Philadelphia. | Pa. | ; postmarked at Concord May 22. Printed in *Records*, p. [53]; listed in *Letters*, 3:333.

30. But see below, June 10, for Emerson's contribution of "The World-Soul" to *The Diadem for MDCCCXLVII* (*BAL*, 5209).

31. Emerson is probably alluding to Archimedes here, not Diogenes.

32. See May 15 above to Chapman and notes.

33. MS in NBuHi; the original of this letter cannot now (1985) be found; ph. in NNC; p. [4] addressed: Daniel Martindale | Wesleyan University | Middletown | Conn. | ; postmarked at Concord June 10. Printed by Benjamin F. Gronewald, "Emerson at Middletown in Connecticut," *ESQ* (2d., 1956), 11:56.

into a lecture on Goethe, and, I fear, a piece more into one on Montaigne, so that the original integer has suffered irreparable dismemberment.[34] What arguments the difficulty, ⟨is⟩ I have been much importuned to publish the Seven Lectures, and, as they give me ampler room for treating the topics before me, I am inclined to comply. There remains a part of the Middletown discourse, which was special to the occasion & to the condition of the societies—I will look it over, & if it will serve any good purpose it might do to publish "an Extract" from it in your local newspaper, or in any Literary Journal that circulates in the College. I will see if this can be done with the paper, & if I find something, will communicate with you again. Meantime, you will please communicate the substance of this letter as the best apology I can now make to the Literary Societies.[35] whose kindness and attention to the oration & the orator deserved from me every attention.

Yours respectfully,
R. Waldo Emerson.

I did not receive your letter until yesterday eve. on my return from a journey.[36]

To WILLIAM HENRY FURNESS, CONCORD, JUNE 10, 1846[37]

Concord 10 June 1846

My dear friend,

I enclose a piece, which, for want of a better name, I call "the World Soul." Anima mundi was the name, but we are bound at least in poetry to speak English. I had the poem when ⟨you⟩ ⟨w⟩ I wrote before, but in the smallness of my portfolio of new pieces, dared not send away one of so many lines, until you tell me that I may print it in my new book, if I have one, in spite of you. Yours, however, will, I suppose, appear first. —I have heard that Margaret Fuller printed a verse or two of this piece

---

34. See *Letters*, 3:294–295 and 296 with n. 73. Cabot, *Memoir* 2:752, describes Emerson's use of the materials of this lecture given at Middlebury and Wesleyan in 1845.

35. The societies were the Philorhetorian Society and the Peithologian Society; Martindale belonged to the latter.

36. The MS Account Book for 1845–1849, p. [85], under the date June 9, 1846, shows the expenses of a trip to Jaffrey (New Hampshire) and return to Boston. The entry includes a note of twenty cents spent at Mt. Monadnoc.

37. MS in the Furness papers, Van Pelt Library, PU; ph. in NNC; p. [4] addressed: William Henry Furness. | Philadelphia | Pa. | ; postmarked at Concord, June 10, with four additional pages bearing the MS of Emerson's poem "The World-Soul"; "by R. Waldo Emerson" has been added not in Emerson's hand between the title and the first line of the text. Printed in *Records*, pp. [54]–59; listed in *Letters*, 3:334.

once in the Tribune,[38] but I never saw them. She printed /if she printed,/ from a copy I had lent to Elizabeth Hoar. I am almost tempted to send you another copy of the same piece, that you may select your own reading from the Variorum. But I will not bother you. I will only say, that in the copy from which I now transcribe this, the 8th stanza has only one quatrain, and I have just added four lines to make it complete. And now it strikes me that the poem was a little more intelligible before. If you think so, leave out the quatrain.[39]

My wife insists that you shall hear once more of Mr Griswold. He wrote me in April, I think, that he should be in Phila. in May, & would immediately send home the lady's miniature. If he is at home, jog his elbow for the lady's sake.[40]

Yours gladly,
R. W. Emerson.

The World-Soul.

Thanks to the morning light!
Thanks to the seething sea,
To the uplands of New Hampshire,
To the greenhaired forest free;
Thanks to each man of courage,
To the maids of holy mind,
To the boy with his games undaunted,
Who never looks behind!

Cities of proud hotels,
Houses of rich & great,
Vice nestles in your ⟨chimney⟨chambers⟩ chambers,
Beneath your roofs of slate.
It cannot conquer folly—
Time-&-space-conquering steam,
And the light-outspeeding telegraph
Bears nothing on its beam.

38. See above, May 22, 1846, and *BAL*, 5209. In her "Asylum for Discharged Female Convicts," the second, third, and fourth stanzas, *The New-York Tribune*, June 19, 1845, p. 1. Lines 3 and 4 of the second stanza differ from the text sent to Furness reading: "A stack of smoking chimneys, | A roof of frozen slate." Possibly the subject, if he knew it, of Miss Fuller's article suggested the revision that gives the present text. A manuscript in the Tappan papers (Houghton Library) has the lines as they appear in Margaret Fuller's article.

39. Henry Howard Furness, printing the poem, notes in bracketed inserts the differences between this text and that of the 1884 edition of Emerson's *Poems*.

40. For Rufus Griswold's borrowing from Lidian Emerson, Caroline Hildreth's miniature of Emerson, see above, May 8, 1845, and March 30, 1846; and, below, April 5, 1847.

The politics are base,
The letters do not cheer,
And tis far in the deeps of history
The voice that speaketh clear;
Trade & the streets ensare us,
Our bodies are weak & worn,
We plot, & corrupt each other,
And we despoil the unborn.

Yet there in the parlour sits
Some figure of noble guise,
Our angel in a stranger's form,
Or woman's pleading eyes,
Or only a flashing sunbeam
In at the window-pane,
Or Music pours on mortals
Its beautiful disdain.

The inevitable morning
Finds them who in cellars be,
And be sure the all-loving Nature
Will smile in a factory.
Yon ridge of purple landscape,
Yon sky between the walls
Hold all the hidden wonders
In scanty intervals.

Alas, the Sprite that haunts us
Deceives our rash desire,
It whispers of the glorious gods,
And leaves us in the mire;
We cannot learn the cipher
That's writ upon our cell,
Stars help us by a mystery
Which we could never spell.

If but one hero knew it,
The world would blush in flame,
The sage till he hit the secret,
Would hang his head for shame;

But our brothers have not read it,
Not one has found the key,
And henceforth we are comforted,
We are but such as they.—

Still, still, the secret presses,
The nearing clouds draw down,
The crimson morning flames into
The fopperies of the town;
Within, without the idle earth,
Stars weave eternal rings,
The sun himself shines heartily
And shares the joy he brings.

And what if Trade sow cities,
Like shells along the shore,
And thatch with towns the prairie broad
With railways ironed o'er;—
They are but sailing foambells
Along Thought's causing stream,
And take their shape & sun-colour
From him that sends the dream.

From Destiny does not like
To yield to men the helm,
And shoots his thought by hidden nerves
Throughout the solid realm;
The patient Daemon sits
With roses and shroud,
He had his way, & deals his gifts,—
But ours is not allowed.

He is no churl or trifler,
And his viceroy is none,
Love-without-weakness,
Of Genius sire and son.
And his will is not thwarted;
The seeds of land & sea
Are the atoms of his body bright,
And his behest obey.

He serveth the servant,
The brave he loves amain,
He kills the cripple and the sick,
And straight begins again;
For gods delight in gods,
And thrust the weak aside,
To him who scorns their charities,
Their arms fly open wide.

When the old world is sterile,
And the ages are effete,
He will from wrecks of sediment
The fairer world complete.
He forbids to despair,
His cheeks mantle with mirth,
And the unimagined good of men
Is yearning at the birth.

Spring still makes spring in the mind
When sixty years are told,
Love wakes anew this throbbing heart,
And we are never old.
Over the winter glaciers
I see the summer glow,'
And through the wild-piled snowdrift
The warm rosebuds below.

To Maria Weston Chapman, Concord, June 22, 1846[41]

Concord June 22, 1846

Mrs Chapman
Dear Madam,
I thank you for your kind invitation to Dedham, which honours me.
But you shall not advertise me.[42] I am so easily led away to holidays, that

41. MS in the Mugar Memorial Library, MBU; ph. in NNC; addressed, p. 4, to Mrs.
M. W. Chapman | 53 Federal Street | Boston | ; postmarked at Concord, date blurred, but
letter is endorsed by Mrs. Chapman June 22.
42. Emerson's Fourth of July Oration for the town of Dedham (Charvat, p. 22) was
printed in *The National Anti-Slavery Standard* (July 16, 1846), 7:25–26; it is reprinted by Louis
Ruchames in his "Two Forgotten Addresses by Ralph Waldo Emerson," *AL* (Jan. 1957),
28:427–429. Mrs. Chapman is surely Maria Weston Chapman, a co-editor with Sydney Gay,
of the *Anti-Slavery Standard*.

I should be a sad idler, if I did not check my truant disposition, and I have laid out so much work for this summer, that whenever I see so much as a good hope of a working day, I turn my back on all things else. It is therefore a bad sign for me, if I go to the Festival. But I will, if you please, keep open for me the freedom of the day, and if my private studies do not prosper, I will cheer myself with the generous resources you open of the company of the great & the good at Dedham. It is a real consolation in this darkness & disgrace of our politics, to see the vivacity & the growth of that Church of Liberty which you love & which loves you so well. I also am very grateful to you & to your fellow apostles.

My wife & my mother acknowledge your friendly invitation.

Yours respectfully,
R. W. Emerson

To Sydney Howard Gay, Concord, June 23, 1846[43]

Concord, 23 June 1846

Sidney H. Gay.
Robert F. Wallcut
Dear Sir,

Please to receive the names of George P. Bradford & of Mrs Lucy C. Brown both of this town, as subscribers for one year to the Antislavery Standard. I enclose two dollars from them.[44]

Yours respectfully,
R. W. Emerson.

To Daniel Jefferson, Concord, June 29, 1846[45]

Concord, 29 June, 1846.

Mr Daniel Jefferson.
My dear Sir,

You must think me ungrateful in my long delay, but I was very sensible of the sincere good will which dictated your letter, and I did

43. MS in the Gay papers, Special Collections, Butler Library, NNC; ph. in NNC; single sheet, address leaf torn away.

44. Emerson's MS Account Book for 1845–1849, p. [86] shows that Emerson paid for his sister-in-law's subscription.

45. MS in Special Collections, Butler Library, NNC; ph. in NNC; p. [4] addressed: Mr Daniel Jefferson | 15 Ford Street | Old Ford: Bow: | London | ; sent by Harnden's express; stamped July 14 in England. Printed (inaccurately) in *The Manchester Guardian*, December 3, 1889, p. 12; listed in *Letters*, 3:337. As Rusk notes, Daniel Jefferson's letter of April 3, 1846,

really set myself about fulfilling your request in regard to a miniature.[46] But on repeated trials of the Daguerre process, my friends declared that I was a very bad subject for that style, and that every impression was a painful misrepresentation which they could not consent to let go abroad for the use which you proposed to make of the effigy.[47] So we will, if you please, let your friendly design slumber for a time, the rather that I believe some old companions of mine think of getting a very skilful artist here to try his crayons on me, some day. If that should be done, perhaps I will send you a copy by the machine. But too much of this.

I do not well know what to say to the point of difference you indicate between us in regard to the immortality. I think we are continually casting off shreds of personality & selfishness which have got consecrated in the popular mind; and one who has the habit of requiring self-evidence in every article of his creed, will, I apprehend, be sensible of a slight coldness or deadness in almost every remark that is made in houses concerning future life. It is a very traditional unintelligent form of words, and not a direct poetic emancipating emanation of the thing spoken of. Now I think it by no means our duty to reproduce the whole real nature in propositions; but it is our duty, when we cannot attain to the expression of any fact, ⟨not to⟩ /to abstain from/ degrad⟨e⟩ing it by a verbal flourish. The perfection of the creed is of no importance compared with the perfection of the credence.

Let us have no impatience with the good Heart which beats so tranquilly at the centre of nature. Does it not make the most affecting appeal to our magnanimity on its own? Why should we pin it down to a testamentary certificate with notarial specification of its good meaning to our nominated selves in some dated futurity,—when the universe flows with wild bounty, the inmost fact of our consciousness cannot be discrimi[n]ated from that good agency. But I find I am not now ready to say anything: let me not seem to say. ⟨I⟩Though I did not mean to sit down to write to you, until I was in an open mood. I have to thank you

---

evoked this reply; Jefferson's enthusiasm for Emerson's writings was qualified by his wish to hear more from Emerson on the subject of immortality.

46. Jefferson had asked for a calotype of Emerson and offered to pay for it.

47. The "repeated trials" are described in a letter to Carlyle of May 31 (Slater, p. 400). The MS Account Book for 1845–1849, p. [86], under the date June 15, 1846, has an entry of the payment to Harnden of $1.00 for sending "first miniature" to England; this one was for Carlyle (Slater, pp. 402, 403). Emerson was not so dissatisfied as not to order extras, for also on June 15 he paid the daguerrotypist Albert S. Southworth $4.00 for a "second miniature" and on June 24 laid out $12.50 (no mean price) for a "Daguerrotype miniature in an extra case."

for your too liberal appreciation of my few & most inadequate writings. There are times when I fancy I shall yet succeed in doing some justice to those capital questions which engage all[48] thinking men. But amid these delusions there is always the consolation that the truths that baffle us are quite sure of fit expression first or last, and we need not be officious. I shall gladly hear more of your thought as you find new books & new experiences. With all affectionate hope, yours respectfully,

R. W. Emerson.

To Amasa Barrett, Concord, July 5? 1846[49]

Dear Sir, I will come to Bangor in the course of Sept. or Octr, as the Lyceum shall choose, and read a course of not less than 3 Lectures provided the Lyceum will permit me to read three in a week, at the rate of 25.00 each lecture. I will read 3, 4 5 or 6 Lectures al

To Maria Weston Chapman, Concord, July 6, 1846[50]

Mrs Chapman
Dear Madam,

I send you such an account of what I attempted to say at Dedham as I can now give. I think it is a little plainer on paper than it was in the ear, what I would be at, & I hope not more dull. If it should be too late, or, for any cause, suppressed, it will please me well.

Yours with great respect,
R. W. Emerson

Concord, 6 July, 1846.

48. Emerson washed out two words here. I do not see "all think," but I believe that is what he wrote before realizing that he needed a verb to keep his expression succinct.

49. This rough draft is written at the foot of the second page of Amasa Barrett's letter of July 1, 1846, to Emerson (RWEMA); ph. in NNC; listed *Letters*, 3:337. Barrett's reply of July 22 accepts the proposition for three lectures and will take more if the Lyceum has the funds; he recommends a Monday afternoon steamer from Boston. See below, August 5.

50. The MS has not been located; text from a copy provided (1948) by the Carnegie Book Shop; the copyist's error "then" is here corrected. The letter is twice listed and partially quoted by Cameron in *ESQ* (1st, 1956), 3:6, and (4th, 1958), 13:38, from Carnegie Book Shop Catalogue 142 (1949). See above, June 22, for Emerson's reply to Mrs. Chapman's invitation to take part in the Fourth of July meeting of the Massachusetts Anti-Slavery Society.

To John P. Welch, Concord, July 26, 1846[51]

Concord —
July 26, 1846

John P. Welch
Treasurer
Dear Sir:

I believe you took my name as subscriber to one share of new stock in the Fitchburg Railroad. You will please credit me with twenty-five dollars for the first assessment out of such dividend on seven shares as may be due to me on 1 August.[52]

R. Waldo Emerson

To Mary Moody Emerson, Concord, July 27, 1846

[In the MS Account Book for 1845–1849, p. [90], an entry dated July 27 reads: "Cash sent to Miss Mary M. Emerson to her demand. 20.00" It is likely that a note at least accompanied the money.]

To Caroline Sturgis, Concord, August 3, 1846[53]

Concord, 3 August, 1846.
Monday Eveg

Shall I appoint you to answer the question in your letter, or shall I be so simple as to dot all the answers down? The letter gave me so much pleasure that I will not refuse to be caught in the fine trap you have baited for me. The letter gave me pleasure,—that is very little to say. In the whirling world, which so infects the manners of its children, a little permanence in character is sublime, & at the same time is it not the most pathetic of all things? I am indeed happy, whenever you turn to me, yet

51. The MS has not been located; text from a copy annotated by Rusk as sent "by Angelers Press, Los Angeles, Cal. Dec. 12 1839." It is possible that this is the same letter as that listed in *Letters*, 3:339, under the date July 24.

52. Emerson's MS Account Book for 1845–1849, p. [88], under the date July 25, 1846, has an entry: Fitchburg Rail Road first assessment on my share of new stock 25.00." Later entries record his payments of subsequent assessments.

53. MS in the Tappan papers, Houghton Library, MH; ph in NNC. The text fills all four pages. A cover sheet must have been addressed to Miss Sturgis at Lenox. Emerson is replying to a letter, dated Woburn, Sunday, July 26, of which only the first leaf remains (Tappan papers). She tells him that she is going to Lenox on the 28th, reports that Margaret Fuller will be in Boston on the 30th, and asks for a letter "really about yourself & not statistics."

could I expect from you less? The prayer of one of my old saints, was, "to be changed into that which changeth not." [54] But for what you say of clouds & walls,—once more I think, did you seriously mean I should reply? Well, then, if you wish to see how it looks, I will try for once.— From me certainly you did not expect any caprice, as really my temperament & antiquity made it less likely. But it was of course impossible for me to speak to a commanded spirit. All friends are commanders; all conversation which we use ⟨&⟩or desire, is absolute. When any one looks over my shoulder, I stop writing, nor can I speak to an overlooked party. —Not therefore do I or could I make the smallest impediment in your career of woman. O no, but say, it was always to be looked for,—go, & do as all have done. But in so doing, do not also expect a friendship that is incompatible with that. Least of all expect me to take /a/ modester share in the conversation. You know—none better—how painful my sense of my own ⟨un⟩worth⟨i⟩/less/ness to you & to all—Yet certainly I will have no friend, rather than suffer the smallest abatement ⟨in⟩of my claim on my friend. But more than enough to you, who, as I feel all the time, anticipate what I say. I write also to say that I know nothing more of you than you now or heretofore say to me, for I do not like to ask for any other person what I ought to learn from you.—I wish you had sent your letter & its varied accompaniments, all which I here acknowledge, by Adams's Express, (which goes daily from the City Hotel,) [55] & not sent it to Miss Peabody's Depot of Contingency, where I found it after many days almost by chance. [56] I should have come to town to have seen you on your transit. You would have been confiding and I should have learned much in little time. Now you are at Lenox, and if you are to stay or to go, you will send me some word. I will roll up & send you some /new/ poems, of which I have many for me. But whether to send you all such? Shall I send you Chapman? [57] It is ready for you. Is the money in the letter 6.00 for "Chapman" /and 75 for Davis/? [58] I can think of nothing else, and I know not how you guess at that. I will look into it, but believe the price

54. Emerson's version of St. Paul, I Cor. 15:51.
55. Augustus Adams.
56. Probably on Friday, the 31st when, as he says below he saw Margaret Fuller for an hour. Miss Sturgis may have left her letter at Elizabeth Peabody's book shop on the assumption of his being in town to see Miss Fuller. It is tempting to infer that Caroline Sturgis deliberately avoided both Emerson and Margaret Fuller.
57. George Chapman's translation of Homer.
58. The MS Account Book for 1845–1849, p. [93], under the date October 23 records the payment of .75 to Charles B. Davis, the Concord postmaster (1845–1849) "for Miss Sturgis."

was 5.75.* I shall leave at Dr Hooper's,[59] when I am next in town, your mother's vols. of Swedenborg,[60] which, I hope, she has not despaired of. Ellery came safely home, on 4 July, in the same ship he sailed in, after spending 16 days in Rome, and going nowhere else, except as the Marseilles steamer touched both in going & returning to Civita Vecchia, at Genoa & Leghorn.[61] He is very well, & has had a gratifying visit, & says that his journal is original, at least, & reads well; professes that he will write it off, & be ready to print. Alas, the turret in the woods is not yet built, but still remains probable enough.[62] Margaret I saw for an hour on Friday. P.M.

Waldo

---

*If I rightly read the bill, it is 5.15, but I will inquire.

To Amasa Barrett, Concord, August 5? 1846

[As he had agreed in his letter of July 22 (see July 5 above), Amasa Barrett, for the Bangor Lyceum, names the first Tuesday in October (6th) as the day for the first lecture and hopes for six lectures (a.l.s., August 3, 1846, RWEMA). Emerson gave five lectures; see Charvat, p. 22, and *Letters*, 3:355. In his reply to Barrett, Emerson apparently agreed to six lectures and went to Bangor with that expectation.]

To Charles Lane, Concord, August 17, 1846[63]

Concord, 17 August, 1846

Received of Joseph Palmer one dollar in full of all demands for rent, crops, stock, tools or other claims in respect to the farm of Charles Lane in Harvard, held in trust for Charles Lane.

R. Waldo Emerson.

Charles Lane.

59. Dr. Robert Hooper, husband of Ellen Sturgis.

60. The MS Account Book for 1845–1849, p. [90], under the date August 24, records the purchase from Sampson Reed of Swedenborg's *Animal Kingdom*, 2 vols. for $7.25. Emerson's library now includes two translations of the work, one by James John Garth Wilkinson (1843–1844) and the other by Augustus Glissold (1845–1848), the latter the gift of the London Swedenborg Association (ELi, pp. 262–263). Possibly Emerson bought the Wilkinson translation at this time to replace the volumes borrowed from Caroline's mother, Elizabeth Davis Sturgis.

61. Caroline Sturgis had contributed to the funds collected for Channing's brief and limited trip to Europe (*Letters*, 3:327; McGill, pp. 86–87). The child born in Channing's absence was named Caroline Sturgis.

62. Channing's plan for building a house remained a fantasy.

63. MS in the Fruitlands Museum Library; ph. in NNC. This is the bill of sale which Emerson executes as Trustee for Charles Lane, the owner of the Fruitlands property.

To Rufus Putnam, Concord? September? 22? 1846

[Rufus Putnam's letter of September 21, 1845 (RWMEA), is endorsed by Emerson: "Yes, late." As corresponding secretary for the Salem Lyceum, Putnam asks for a lecture, leaving the date to be set by Emerson. See February 17, 1847, Charvat, p. 23.]

To Samuel Gridley Howe and Others, Concord, September 23, 1846[64]

Concord, September 23, 1846.

Dr. S. G. Howe, and Associates of the Committee of Citizens:

If I could do or say anything useful or equal to the occasion, I would not fail to attend the meeting on Thursday.[65] I feel the irreparable shame to Boston of this abduction. I hope it is not possible that the city will make the act its own, by any color or justification. Our State has suffered many disgraces, of late years, to spoil our pride in it, but never any so flagrant as this, if the people of the Commonwealth can be brought to be accomplices in this crime,—which, I assure myself, will never be. I hope it is not only not to be sustained by the mercantile body, but not even by the smallest portion of that class. If the merchants tolerate this crime,—as nothing will be too bad for their desert,—so it is very certain they will

64. No MS has been located; text from *Address of the Committee Appointed by a Public Meeting*, Held at Faneuil Hall. September 24, 1846, p. 31. There is a typescript copy in the Emerson papers (RWEMA) presented in 1888 to Edward Waldo Emerson by Francis J. Garrison (of Houghton, Mifflin). With the exception of one comma, the text is identical to that of the pamphlet printing from which it clearly derives. A version printed by Vincent Y. Bowditch in his *Life and Correspondence of Henry Ingersoll Bowditch* (Boston, 1902), 1:182–183, differs from the pamphlet and the typescript only slightly. The last sentence reads "stains" instead of "stain"; there are three differences of punctuation, and the passage "If it shall turn out, ... wealth came of an end." is set up as a separate paragraph. Since the typescript is faintly marked to set off the same passage, I infer that it served as "copy" for Bowditch's book, published by Houghton, Mifflin. Bowditch follows his printing with a misleading remark: "In addition to the letters just mentioned, I have found in one of his scrapbooks the records of the famous meeting at Faneuil Hall in the handwriting of John A. Andrew, who acted at secretary. . . ." The slight textual differences between Bowditch's printing and the pamphlet do not give his text the authority of a manuscript source; Garrison's note to Edward Emerson does not imply a manuscript, and the chances are that the "friend" who called his attention to the letter was Vincent Bowditch very likely working on his book at the time. The occasion of the meeting, called by Henry Ingersoll Bowditch and Samuel Gridley Howe, was the connivance of a Boston merchant and the captain of a ship owned by him in the return to New Orleans of a runaway slave who had hoped to escape his bondage by stowing away in a north-bound vessel. The slave having been returned, the object of the meeting was to "pillory" the merchant and his captain as "unmitigated sycophants before the slave power, and the meanest of traitors to Massachusetts liberty and laws" (Bowditch, 1:181).

65. Emerson's letter is a reply to a printed letter bearing a manuscript postscript by Dr. Howe; the postscript asks for an "expression of your views."

have the ignominy very faithfully put to their lips. The question you now propose, is a good test of the honesty and manliness of our commerce. If it shall turn out, as desponding men say, that our people do not really care whether Boston is a slave-port or not, provided our trade thrives, then we may, at least, cease to dread hard times and ruin. It is high time our bad wealth came to an end. I am sure, I shall very cheerfully take my share of suffering in the ruin of such a prosperity, and shall very willingly turn to the mountains to chop wood, and seek to find for myself and my children labors compatible with freedom and honor.

With this feeling, I am proportionably grateful to Mr. Adams[66] and yourselves, for undertaking the office of putting the question to our people, whether they will make this cruelty theirs? and of giving them an opportunity of clearing the population from the stain of this crime, and of securing mankind from the repetition of it, in this quarter, forever.

Respectfully and thankfully,
Your obedient servant,
R. W. Emerson.

To Caroline Sturgis, Concord, September ? 1846

[A letter from Caroline Sturgis to Emerson (Tappan papers, Houghton Library, MH), without dateline, but written in mid-October (15? from the blurred postmark) from Lenox suggests that there may have been an exchange of letters after August 3 (above). From the equivocal final paragraphs of Caroline's letter, I infer that if Emerson sent anything with the poems she refers to, it was only a note. Her letter is as follows:]

[Dear Waldo,

I must tell you the simple truth about the poems; at first I could not read them because they had all the old words in them, but I remembered that every spring brings the same flowers, every night the same stars, & having thus soothed my feelings I found pleasure in them as thoughts—perhaps not as poems. Should not a poem be an old thing transmuted into a new one—into something rich & strange; withering leaves changed into gold as in these October days. Although Jack Frost may be the alchemist the transformation should appear to be ⟨a⟩effected by the sunshine. Philosophy is still philosophy although delivered in rhyme by Alphonso the Nice,—yet one likes to hear him speak—the wisest things. I liked the Bacchus best—ᵃ ⟨the⟩it was the first I read & made the day wider, as your words always do, although they sometimes send the little breezes away to die among the mountain hollows.

Your poems are too good not to have been written, better than they would be in prose, & yet I take a mischievous delight in seeing how ingeniously they are

66. John Quincy Adams presided at the meeting.
ᵃSee *Works*, 9:25, 125, for the poems named here.

contrived, & always ⟨find⟩think ⟨that⟩ you should have heard Beethoven's[b] music, seen a Bayadere, had a frolic with the children, or followed the ⟨m⟩Muse longer in silence through your pine-vistas & not have written down her words before they were fully uttered. Impulse is what we who /sadly/ confess ourselves to be statues, do most of all need. I should like to have red hair & eyes like a comet. But red-haired people are always a little too active; they cannot stand still but have to shift from one foot to the other to keep their balance. It is worth coming to Lenox for, to see ⟨Mr⟩ Charles Se⟨g⟩dgewick; a man loving to all, yet penetrating & full of humor—one whom every one must like.[c] About the fine arts he knows nothing but stands firm on his own ground & respects all that one could wish to know. He makes the atmosphere of the place—even Sam seems to attune himself thereto but cannot put his whole heart into social life. It is good to be where there are no aims & reforms—where it is warmhearted, free, lively & with so much beauty as to prevent it from being wearisome. Why have you not been here this summer—I thought you would go to Taconic & make us a call. We have proposed sending for you to hear music, smoke cigars, drink milk-punch, & hunt wood-cock—But there is only one woodcock in the country & that more invulnerable than Achilles, only one musician & he has departed & cigars & punch may be had nearer home—But now we can offer valleys full of crimson & gold & purple hazy mountains, beside our own personal pretensions. Sam's house is good—à la Wilhelm Meister; Anna's bust is the queen of it & most lovely to see. I dwell in a shingle palace,[d] nearby, among fields & woods contented enough as the world goes; one must never say anything about being happy, but thank God when he is so. I have been alone the last week & may be so yet longer.

I wanted to tell you which lines I liked best, but they are too many to be written,—but one should like the poem throughout & not lines or verses—these are good still with a sharp edge, but must be polished & curved into scimitars— not drawn out into long swords.

---

[b]The pianists Frederick and Ogden Rackemann were friends of the Wards. Ogden Rackemann was in Lenox in late August 1846 (MS copy of Anna Barker Ward's diary, entry of August 20, Ward papers, Houghton Library); it was probably he who played the Beethoven. His brother Frederick would later marry Charles Sedgwick's daughter. The Rackemann brothers are credited by John Sullivan Dwight with bringing classical music to Boston, as "the first" to give Boston the music of Chopin, Liszt, and the sonatas of Beethoven (Justin Winsor, ed., *The Memorial History of Boston*, Boston: James R. Osgood, 1881, 4:428). Their concerts of 1839–1840 were attended by Margaret Fuller and her friends.

[c]Charles Sedgwick, County Clerk, charmed everyone who met him. The Sedgwicks and the Wards had become close friends. The Sedgwick letters (MHi) show considerable admiration of Samuel and Anna Ward.

[d]"Highwood"—the Wards' new house. The "shingle palace" is the red cottage later to be leased to Hawthorne. Hiram Powers' bust of Anna Ward; Powers had begun the work in December 1837 when Anna Barker was in Rome with her cousin Eliza Rotch Farrar (a.l.s., Anna Barker to her brother Thomas, December 31, 1837, Ward papers, Houghton Library). Ward made haste to secure it after their marriage, but to finish it Powers required a partial life mask. Further trouble with the marble and the workmen delayed its completion until 1844 (a.l.s., Ward papers, Houghton). It arrived late in that year and was kept for a time at 3 Park Street where Charles Sedgwick saw it on January 20, 1845 (a.l.s., MHi).

Chapman I enjoy reading on the mountains[e]—Tell Mr Bradford I am grieved
to say that I cannot find St Evremond[f] at Woburn, or any where & think it must
have been spirited away—are you sure the one in your library is not his—I can
perhaps find one at the Antiquarian book-store or ⟨you⟩will you not enquire for
me there ⟨if⟩ if you can purchase one & give it to him before he knows of the loss
I shall be greatly obliged—I am sorry to trouble you about it—still more so about
that foolish Mr Davis[g]—I was rather provoked at his trying to cheat me, & in
such an absurdly obvious manner, but he had best have the money ten times told
& sink into forgetfulness—You say nothing about Concord & its inhabitants—
Lydian, Elizabeth, Mrs Ripley,—Ellery, do you see? Have you heard from Margaret—Nothing humbles human beings so much as seeing their names in too
close proximity—Ellery & Margaret! in one breath when such a wide sea rolls
between them.

I know that I should like the poems better than a letter—& I do,—but I like
all kinds of gossip beside—it reads well by the fire in an autumn evening—I wish
some days you could come in & make me a visit as at Concord last winter or I
could come into your study & make all the essays flutter about, but other days I
am flying over the hills, chasing lights & shadows, into I know not what abysses—
across which you would swing yourself on a rope bridge without once looking
down—Well! they find diamond mines in South America, but one has to travel to
them on mules.

> Farewell—
> With love alway
> Caroline.

To Henry David Thoreau, Concord, September? 30? 1846?[67]

Will Mr Thoreau please to bear in mind that when there is good
mortar in readiness, Mr Dean must be summoned to fit the air-tight stove

---

[e]See August 3 for the Chapman book; possibly Chapman's *Human Nature*, the first to be
written and published (1844) by Chapman. It does not seem likely that John Weiss' translation of Schiller's *Aesthetic Letters* (published by Chapman in 1845) is the book referred to.

[f]There are no volumes by Saint-Évremond in Emerson's library; see *JMN*, 9:189, 193,
for quotations recorded in 1845. Which work George P. Bradford claims is not known, but
it is probably *Ninon de L'Enclos*.

[g]See August 3 above for Mr. Davis.

67. MS in the Berg Collection, NN; ph, in NNC; printed by Sanborn, *AM* (June 1892),
69:742, with the date December 2, 1847; and in Harding and Bode with the same date, p.
195. Listed in *Letters*, 3:445, with doubts of the date assigned by Sanborn.

Mr. Dean and airtight stoves figure in the MS Account Book for 1840–1844, but no
entry can be connected with a schoolroom and Thoreau. A project of 1846 seems to satisfy
the conditions. See *Letters*, 3:347 and 348, where in September letters to his wife, Emerson
describes a project to build living quarters requiring a chimney over the schoolroom in the
barn, indicating in the second letter that Thoreau is to do the work.

The MS Account Book for 1840–44 shows that a stove costs $10. The MS Account Book
for 1845–1849 has an 1846 entry under the date September 30 (p. [91] for a payment to
Thoreau of $15. "in advance." This note authorizes Thoreau to buy a stove and to hire Mr.

to the chimney in the school-room; unless Mr T. can do it with convenience himself.

To Daniel Austin, Concord, October 22, 1846[68]

Concord, 22 October, 1846

Rev. Daniel Austin, Chairman.

Dear Sir,

You shall, if you please leave my name out, this season, from your list of lecturers, & oblige your obedient servant.

R. W. Emerson

To Harrison Gray Otis Blake, Concord, October 23, 1846[69]

Concord, 23 October 1846.

My dear Sir,

Your letter came when I was out of town, [70] or you should have had an earlier reply. I will not judge of the advantages of town or country for your school, but am glad for my part that you are within my reach. I am often in Boston, especially in summer, when I cannot think of any soul in the city whom I would cross the Common to see:—in summer, when many good persons have left the town. The paucity of engaging traits in the population is insofar an unfavorable reply to your inquiry concerning rational inhabitants, who are ever the smallest & most diminishing minority. And yet we are such moody & relative creatures that the true answer to this question is always subjective—Now there is no friendship, no wisdom: and now there is on every side nothing but friendship and wisdom;—according to our positive or negative fit. Tis weather weather all. What a strict symbol of our secret life are these Octobers & Novembers ben/i/gn & detestable, days of swift and contrasting succession. Tis a variegated surface, but the core is immutable; and so with ours. Well, I

Dean when the "mortar" is ready. Under "Masons" in Dickinson's Almanac a James Dean is listed. The formality of the note and the advance payment are accounted for by Emerson's impending trip to Bangor.

68. No final manuscript has been found, text from the draft printed *JMN*, 10:399. It is canceled by a diagonal line. It appears upside down on MS. p. 190. A final letter must have been sent. It is a reply to Daniel Austin's letter of October 12; Austin asks Emerson to state the Wednesday prior to the middle of January and name the subject of his lecture; he offers a fee of $10. He writes from Cambridge.

69. MS in the Houghton Library, MH; ph. in NNC; p. 4 addressed: H. G. O. Blake, Esq. | 1⟨4⟩7 ⟨Montgomery Place⟩ /Harrison Avenue/ | Boston | ; the corrections in the address do not appear to be Emerson's; postmarked at Concord, October 23. Listed *Letters*, 3:357.

70. Emerson was in Bangor, Maine, between October 6 and 13.

own again the grand old Law[71] in your feeling & action in regard to your pupils.[72] These are the penalties & deep rewards of truth. Everlasting honour & love to him who dares to be just & perseveres to the end. He fancies he is alone & nobody; nay that is some constitutional defect in him not incident to other men who are better mated & averaged, and really he is fighting the battle of us all with all things for spectators: & every increment of spiritual strength so private, so indispensable, lifts him another & another degree in the eternal hierarchy. Meantime we must be men too I know how necessary it is to have somebody to eat one's bread with whose eyes & tongue do not contradict God & themselves. And I confide that you will quickly find such

> queis arte benigna
> Et melior luto finxit praecordia Titan[73]

I think I can even help you to the neighborhood & faces of such. But I rely at last, as ever, on that central efflux which proceeding from every good man convicts & converts malignants & dunces, for that they, under this magnetism, exhibit extraordinary symptoms, & pay the most unlooked for homage. But if I have not begun to answer your letter, it is because I mean to come soon to see you.

Yours, R W Emerson.

To John Boynton Hill, Concord, November 24, 1846[74]

Concord, 24 Nov. 1846.

J.B. Hill, Esq.
My dear Sir,
    Lest you should think I have forgotten my instructions from you touching the Buddhists, I hasten to send you this though imperfect apparatus. Here is the principal book, Upham, that is to be found on the subject. Colebrooke at this moment is not to be had. Perhaps I shall soon be able to procure it: then, it shall go. Meantime, I send a cingalese

71. Compensation.
72. Blake's letter evidently concerned his decision to become a schoolmaster although he was trained for the ministry. He is listed in Worcester directories in 1846 and thereafter as a teacher. He does not appear in directories of 1844 and 1845. Emerson's letter suggests that Blake was considering Boston instead of his native Worcester. Blake's doubts of his calling may well have begun with Emerson's Divinity School Address; see above, August 1, 1839.
73. Juvenal, *Satires*, XIV, 34–35; see *JMN*, 6:21; and *JMN*, 4:367, and textual note, p. 446; Emerson here also writes incorrectly "melior."
74. MS privately owned; ph. in NNC; p. [4] addressed: John B. Hill, Esq. | Bangor. | Me.; see November 25 for Emerson's sending this note (unpostmarked) by express with the books referred to. The MS has been carelessly repaired, but the text can be made out. Printed from an inaccurate copy in *Letters*, 3:360–361.

poem.[75] In the absence too of the Bhagavad Geeta, I have torn from a Common-place Book this fine French sketch of Cousin, which you must put together and read.[76]

> With great regard & respect,
> Yours,
> R.W. Emerson

To John Boynton Hill, Concord, November 25, 1846[77]

Concord 25 Nov. 1846

J. B. Hill, Esq.
My dear Sir,

It occurs to me that it may ensure the safer arrival of my parcel to your hands, if I advertise you that I sent this morning by one of your Expresses a package containing a couple of books from the Cambridge Library to your address, with a letter[78]

> Yours ever,
> R. W. Emerson.

To Amory Dwight Mayo, Concord, November 27, 1846

[Emerson has endorsed a letter of November 26, 1846, from Amory Dwight Mayo (RWEMA): "Yes, 30 Dec.," the date Mayo asks for. See *Letters*, 3:357, for note of Mayo's letter of October 14 asking for a lecture in Gloucester. Replying, Emerson named no date. See Charvat, p. 22, where the undated December entry for Gloucester can be corrected.]

75. See *ER*, p. 48, for Emerson's borrowing from the Harvard Library on November 18 Edward Upham's *The History and Doctrine of Budhism* and John Callaway's translation of the Cingalese poem *Yakkun Nattannawà*. Which of Henry Thomas Colebrooke's works he could not find is not clear. See *ELi*, p. 63, for the two Emerson subsequently owned.

76. Possibly from Blotting Book III which has pages missing and is of the right date for Emerson's reading of Cousin. See *Letters*, 6:246, for Emerson's long-remembered debt to Cousin's "sketch" of Hindu literature.

77. MS privately owned; ph. in NNC; p. [4] addressed: John B. Hill, Esq. | Bangor - Maine | ; postmarked at Concord, date blurred.

78. Of the two Expresses going to Bangor, only Jerome & Co. had a service on Wednesdays; in 1846, the 25th of November fell on Wednesday.

To John Weiss, Concord, December 19, 1846[79]

Concord, Dec. 19, 1846.

Dear Sir,

Yes, that will be a most amiable arrangement. You shall come hither 27 January, & spend the night with me I will go down the next day & read my lecture to you, on the 28th. So be it.[80]

Yours,

R. W. Emerson.

To George A. Blanchard, Charles A. Evans, and
Moses T. Willard, Concord, December 20, 1846

[B. Altman advertised this letter in *The New York Times*, November 27, 1977. The same letter is listed *Letters*, 3:363. Emerson is answering a letter of December 16 (RWEMA) from the Committee representing the Lyceum of the New Hampshire town of Concord, which had affecting associations for him. He offers to lecture for expenses only. George A. Blanchard replied on the 29th (RWEMA) to ask if Emerson may be considered engaged for February 3. There had to be additional correspondence to settle the date and arrange for the second lecture. Until December 31 Emerson had supposed himself engaged to the Boston Mercantile Library Association for February 3. He may have received Thomas J. Allen's letter of the 31st (RWEMA) in time to agree to Blanchard's proposal of the 3rd of February. In any case, Charvat (p. 23) requires correction, for in Emerson's MS Account Book for 1845–1849, p. [10], under the date February 1 is the record of expenses ($4.70) for a trip to Concord N. H., and return. There is no entry for the second trip. The lectures had to have been given before February 10, for on that date Emerson enters in his Account Book (p. [28]) the receipt of $10.00 for travel "twice" to Concord, N.H. One trip may have been on February 3 and the other on or before February 1.]

To Frederic Henry hedge, Concord, December 22? 1846

[In a letter of April 24, 1847, to Emerson (privately owned), Hedge says he has heard from Emerson "several times" since they saw each other in Bangor in October and "once to the tune of two & half hundred pages." Hedge is referring to *Poems* (*BAL,* 5211); I conjecture that a letter was written Hedge on or about December 25, the date of some presentation copies of the book. Hedge apologizes for his "long delayed thanks" for the book. See *Letters,* 3:360, for another letter written after the Bangor lectures.]

79. MS and ph in NNC; the address leaf is missing. The MS records of the Concord Lyceum (CFPL) show that the Reverend John Weiss lectured in Concord on January 27, 1847.

80. This letter fixes the date of Emerson's Watertown lecture as January 28 (see Charvat, p. 22); Weiss was then serving the First Unitarian Church in Watertown. Emerson enters in his MS Account Book for 1845–1849, p. [100], his payment of Weiss' railroad fare.

To Alexander Ireland, Concord, December 28, 1846[81]

Concord, 28 December, 1846.

A. Ireland, Esq.

Dear Sir,

I was very glad to be reminded by your concise note; written on shipboard & conveyed to me by Mr Garrison,[82] of our brief intercourse thirteen years ago, & which, it seems, has not yet quite ended.[83] Your affectionate expressions towards me & my friends are very grateful to me: and, indeed, what better thing do men or angels know of than an enduring kindness?

In regard to your inquiry, Whether I shall visit England now or soon? —the suggestion is new & unlooked for, yet opens to me at once so many flattering possibilities, that I shall cheerfully entertain it, & perhaps we may both see it ripen, one day, to a fact. Certainly, it would be much more practicable & pleasant to me to answer an invitation, than to come into your cities & challenge an audience.

You have been slower to visit Mr Wordsworth than I was, but, according to all testimonies, he retains his vigour & his social accomplishments. He could not now remember me in my short & unconnected visit, or I might easily send him (s)assurances, from me & many others also unknown to him, of a regard that could not fail to gratify him.

Yours, with the best wishes of these days,

R. W. Emerson.

To Herbert P. New, Concord, December? 29?1846?

[In his MS Journal O, p. 368, *JMN*, 9:468, Emerson altered the following list: "Letter to A Ireland C Lane L. Withington Herbert P New J. A. Heraud." Since all the other letters are known to have been written either because they exist or were acknowledged by their recipients, it is reasonable to suppose that Emerson at about the same time acknowledged New's communication of November 15, 1846 (RWEMA), from Evesham, Worcestershire; New had sent a poem "Expec-

---

81. MS in the Barrett Collection, Alderman Library, ViU; ph. in NNC; p. [4] addressed: Alexander Ireland, Esq. | At the ⟨Manchester Athenaeum⟩/"Examiner" Office/ | Manchester. | England. | ; sent by Harnden's express; stamped January 13, 1847, at Liverpool and January 14 at Manchester. Printed in part by Ireland, *In Memoriam Ralph Waldo Emerson* (London: Simpkin, Marshall, 1882), p. 57 and pp. 77–78; listed in *Letters*, 3:365.

82. William Lloyd Garrison; see *In Memoriam*, pp. 56–57.

83. See *Letters*, 3:393–396, for Emerson's 1833 acquaintance with Ireland as well as for his visit of that year to Wordsworth.

tations" written on hearing that Emerson was to publish a volume of poems (see *BAL*, 5210, for Chapman's announcement of October 14, 1846).]

To James Munroe and Company, Concord, December 29, 1846[84]

Concord, 29 Dec.

Gentlemen

Please to send to J. P. Cushing[85] Esq Watertown and to James Lawrence at the house of Mr Abbot Lawrence[86] these two copies of Channings Poems.

Also I send a copy of my book for Rev W. H. Channing which please send to house of Dr Walter Channing.[87]

Please send me by bearer ten copies of "Emerson's Poems."

I wish Mr Dennett[88] would see that copies of my book are sent to the following New York Editors

J. L. O'Sullivan, *Demo Review*

W C Bryant, Esq

Home Journal, of Willis[89]

I am not sure that I specified these for mine on Friday, as I did for

84. MS in the Feinberg Collection, MiD; ph. in NNC; p. [4] addressed: J. Munroe & Co. Printed by White, *AL* (May 1961), 33:160–164. The MS of the letter proper is on a single sheet of quarto blue paper folded to make four pages. The text fills pp. 1–2. Affixed by sealing wax to the lower half of p. 3 is a scrap of paper containing the order to correct p. 167 in the plate.

The enclosed list of persons, titles, and addresses is largely in Emerson's hand; exceptions are noted below. This list is on a strip cut from a single sheet of the blue quarto paper; the strip is about half the normal width. A line drawn through the entire list appears to signify that copies of the book have been sent to those listed. (A name and address on the verso is not in Emerson's hand and appears to have nothing to do with the subject.)

BAL, 3061. Emerson has again secured William Ellery Channing's publication by attaching it to his own; the contract (October 21, 1846, RWEMA) with Munroe for the publication of his *Poems* carried with it a parallel agreement to publish Channing's *Poems, Second Series* (see Emerson's correspondence with Furness of 1844 above and in *Records*, p. [25] Furness' comment). Emerson signing both parts of the contract made himself legally responsible for the cost of printing both books. Finding no record of Emerson's making payments on Channing's behalf, I conjecture that the underwriter was Samuel Gray Ward, though I have no kind of evidence. By the terms of the contract Emerson would be responsible for all the presentation copies here listed, including Channing's.

85. John Perkins Cushing.

86. James Lawrence was Abbott Lawrence's son.

87. William Henry Channing, Dr. Walter Channing's nephew.

88. Boston directories list William Dennet as an employee of J. Munroe & Co.

89. John L. O'Sullivan's *Democratic Review* has a notice of both books (with others) in "New Poetry in New-England" (May 1847, 2:382–398). William Cullen Bryant's *New York Evening Post*, January 4, 1847, p. 2, notices only Emerson's volume. Emerson's *Poems* are reviewed in Nathaniel Parker Willis' *The New-York Evening Mirror* (February 1, 1847), 5:2. His *Home Journal* of March 13, 1847 (p. 4) quotes a notice from *The Christian Register*.

Channing's book. I did myself inscribe copies for Mr Greeley,[90] Mrs Child,[91] & Dr Parsons[92] for the Knickerbocker.

I wish also a copy sent to the "Harbinger," at Brook Farm[93]

———

I enclose an important correction that can easily be made on the plate for p 167, & that must be attended to before any more printing is done. ———Please send it to the printer or to Mr Phelps or where is fit. Yours respectfully

R. W. Emerson

Nathl ⟨J⟩I Bowditch
R. F. Fuller 6 Court Street[94]
2 copies A Adams 2 Winthrop Place[95]
Dr Frothingham Summer St[96]
Richard Hildreth Esq[97]

———

N. Hawthorne. Salem/E. P. Peabody
T. Lee, Esq. Temple Place[98]
Prof. J. Lovering. Cambridge[99]

H. Greeley, Esq. (Tribune) N.Y.
Wm Emerson Esq N.Y.
10 Wall St
Mrs L. M. Child. N.Y.
H. G. O. B.[100]
Rev. W. H. Furness, Philadelphia[101]
Southern Quarterly Charlestown[102]

90. Horace Greeley for *The New-York Tribune*. Channing's *Poems* were reviewed in the issue for January 1, 1847, p. 2; Emerson's in the issue for January 9, p. 1.
91. Lydia Maria Child.
92. Thomas William Parsons. Emerson's *Poems* are mentioned in "The Editor's Table" in *The Knickerbocker Magazine* for March and April 1847 and Channing's in the issue for May (29:272–275, 370–372, 473).
93. John Sullivan Dwight reviewed both in *The Harbinger* (January 16, 23, 1847), 4:91–94, 107–108.
94. Richard Fuller, Margaret Fuller's brother.
95. Abel Adams.
96. Nathaniel Langdon Frothingham.
97. See above, April 26, 1844.
98. Thomas Lee.
99. Joseph Lovering, Hollis Professor of Mathematics.
100. Harrison Gray Otis Blake.
101. William Henry Furness.
102. This entry is not in Emerson's hand. Emerson's *Poems* and Channing's are reviewed in *The Southern Quarterly Review* (April 1847), 11:493–499.

H. G. O. Blake Montgomery Place.
Dr LeBaron Russell Otis Place
C. G. Ripley, Esq. Office, <u>Court Square</u>[103]

N Y[104]

____

Willis ____	Courier.[105]
W. C. Bryant	Atlas—sent
Knickerbocker	Chronotype Dana[106]
Dr Parsons	Advertiser
____	Transcript[107]

To John Chapman, Concord and Boston,
December 29 and 31, 1846[108]

Concord, 29 December, 1846.

Mr John Chapman.
Dear Sir,

I send you a copy of each of Mr Channing's two series of Poems,[109] &
will suggest to you the question of publishing them in England. Mr
Channing is an immense favorite with a small company of readers here,
but, as far as the sale of his first series shows, of a very small company; as
no more than 250 copies have been sold how in several years. He has just
published the second series, which meets with much more favour now at
its first appearance; but it is too early to say what its success may be. He

103. Christopher Gore Ripley.

104. Entries under this general heading "NY" duplicate matter annotated above. The
names of Parsons (Thomas William) and Dana (Charles Anderson) are not in Emerson's
hand.

105. *The Boston Daily Courier,* December 29, 1846, p. 2, under New Books gives a brief
notice of Emerson's *Poems.*

106. Channing's *Poems* had been reviewed at length in *The Daily Chronotype,* December
23, 1846, p. 1; Emerson's *Poems* received a short notice in the issue of January 2, 1847, p. 2.

107. Only Channing's *Poems* are noticed in *BET,* December 24, 1846, p. 2. *BDA* has no
notice of either book. Emerson does not list *The Christian Examiner,* but in an article "Poetry
and Imagination," Cyrus Bartol includes a notice of Emerson's *Poems* and Channing's (March
1847, 40:255–262, 254–255). Other notices appear in *The North American Review,* and *Brownson's Quarterly Review.*

108. MS in the Chapman papers, Sterling Library, University of London; ph. in NNC;
p. [4] addressed: Chapman, Brothers. / 121 Newgate Street | London. | ; postmarked: FEB |
Jan 13 | 1847, and stamped Forwarded By | Harnden & Co. | Boston. | Printed by Mignon,
ESQ (4th G., 1973), 19:228–229.

109. *BAL,* 3057 and 3061. *BAL* does not list an English edition of Channing's poems.

has, in my judgment, more poetic talent than any American. I wish, if you incline to the experiment of republication, you would show the books to any lovers of poetry among your friends, & collect their judgments. I should be especially glad if it should turn out that Mr Channing might gain in England some money one day, for his verses.—Mr C. is living on his little farm in this town, & is a nephew of the late Dr Channing.

I have to thank you for the very handsome volumes you have sent me, ⟨Con⟩ "Characteristics of men of Genius," wherein, certainly, our old arid North Americans & Dials have come to unlooked for honour.

I send you a copy of the Boston edition of my "Poems."[110] The printing of it has convinced me that I was guilty of a great rashness in sending you the work in manuscript: for I see how impossible it is in printing from a manuscript so far from the author to avoid a hundred blunders. So I assure myself that with all your superior intelligence /&/ best heed, I shall yet find a multitude of errata in your edition,[111] for which I shall be obliged to thank my own bad writing: to say nothing of corrections more or less material which I have made on my own text, in the course of ⟨re⟩printing. May I then request of you, before a single copy more is printed from your office, that an exact comparison should be made, page for page, & letter for letter, betwee[n] your book & ours, and your edition correc[ted] from ours.—Three or four poems especially [occur] to me which I wish to be thus corrected "Xenophanes (in the last line.) "Musketaquid," "Threnody," and the "Daemonic Love."—[112]

I will beg you to send a copy of the volume to Mr Charles Lane at Ham with my regards. And to send Miss Margaret Fuller whenever she is in London one copy & any more copies she may wish in my name.[113] If it is quite convenient also to send Miss Harriet Martineau a copy,

110. *BAL,* 5208; M, D14.

111. *BAL,* 5211; M, A18.2a

112. *BAL,* 5210; M, A 18.1a The tipped-in errata slip, present in some copies of the English edition lists corrections for "Threnody" but not for the other poems named here. Possibly Chapman got out the slip when he received this letter but before he received the corrected American edition. A list of the errors is laid in MS Journal GH; see *JMN,* 10:127. The mutilation noted in *JMN* may be deliberate, for the text of "Threnody" reads "locks" in all printings. The errata slip has five errors not in the *JMN* list in which there are eight errors not in the errata slip.

For Emerson's distress over the errors, see his letter of January 31, 1847, to Carlyle (Slater, p. 413). In England in 1848, he sent home for copies of the American "Fourth" edition to give his English friends.

The text was damaged with the breaking of the seal; the fragment torn away is still affixed to the wax.

113. Margaret Fuller left for England August 1, 1846, bearing letters of introduction from Emerson.

inscribing it, "sent to Miss Martineau at the special direction of Mrs. Lidian Emerson, I should like it so.

Yours respectfully,

R. W. Emerson.

P.S. 31 Dec. /Boston./ I am sorry on arriving in town today, to find that all freight was put on the steamer yesterday, & that my ⟨b⟩three books (2 Channings Poems & my own) cannot go. Perhaps I shall not have to wait quite a month. I suppose I need not remind you that I requested that copies of my Poems might be sent to Mr Carlyle, J A Heraud Esq Rev D Thom J. J. G. Wilkinson & Dr M'Cormac[114]

Can you further oblige me by communicating to Mr Heraud my respects & saying to him that I fully intended to reply to his letter by this steamer, but have no intelligence at present that will be valuable to him; & shall write to him by the next steamer.[115]

114. In his letter of October 30, *Letters*, 3:258–259; see also Slater, p. 413. John A. Heraud, David Thom, James John Garth Wilkinson, and Henry MacCormac.

115. See below, January 31, 1847, and *Letters*, 3:369–370, for Emerson's letter (draft and final version) to Heraud.

1 8 4 7

Concord 2 Jan. 1847

Gentlemen,

I have before me a list of all the names of persons to whom I have sent my Poems, to this date. This list (which includes the names of H. Greeley & T. M. Brewer) makes sixty eight 68 copies.

[add copies sent to	Daily Advertizer	
	Chronotype	1
	Transcript	1
	Courier—Mr Whipple	1
	Harbinger	1
	?/Atlas—Mr Field	1
	—	
	W. C. Bryant	1
	Home Journal	1
	Dr Parsons for Knickerbocher	1
	Southern Review	1
		10
add copies remaining in my possession		⟨7⟩8

8<5>6 copies

This /as far as I know,/ is the whole number of copies received by me up to this date & includes all which were charged to me on 31 December.

Will you have the goodness to charge me with these, cancel other

---

1. MS in the New England Collection, MnM; ph. in NNC; p. [4] addressed: James Munroe, & Co. | Boston.; without postmark or sign that the cost was charged to the post office account. The letter may have been delivered by hand. Listed *Letters*, 3:368.

charges contained in this & <an> for any copies I may hereafter distrib-
ute, record in your Account the names to which they are sent.[2]

Yours respectfully,

R. W. Emerson

To Mary Moody Emerson, Concord, January 28? or 29? 1847

[To a letter of "Sab" January 24, and February 4, to Elizabeth Hoar (RWEMA),
Mary Moody Emerson adds a note (February 4) to Emerson: "I received your
kind letter of 29 & send a deed. What does it mean to cancel my note of 15? As
you have not an eventual but a stronger & better memory I will ask that the note
be taken care of as your excellent mother lost one wh I gave for you /on interest/
thinking you might lose by my Executor if you did not preserve it. Yours & L in
love & hasty." A letter to William Emerson (see *Letters*, 3:372), and an Account
Book entry explain in part this cryptic utterance. In the MS Account Book for
1845–1849, p. [100], under the date January 28, 1847, is an entry reading: "by
letter to Miss M. M. Emerson to discharge a debt due from her to A. Parsons
which debt is secured by a deed of an acre of land to A. P. 11 July 1844 which
deed is now to be transferred to me 29.00." In the Emerson papers is a sheet of
receipts signed by Robert Haskins: the first of these is for "Twenty-nine Dolls $\frac{21}{150}$
the same being paid by her to A. Parsons to cancel his claim on an acre of land
conveyed to him as security for taxes paid by him July 11. 1844." As for the note
Miss Emerson refers to, it is not clear whether the figure 15 is for the date of the
note or the sum borrowed. A. Parsons is Augustus Parsons of Waterford, Maine.]

To John Abraham Heraud, Concord, January 31? 1847[3]

Mr John Heraud
Dear Sir,

I received your letter & the accompanying file of programmes, of the
Semi annual Review[4] with much interest. I have spread them abroad
among such persons here as I thought would like to know the design.
There is no reason to expect in Boston any other pecuniary aid to such a
work than simply a number of subscribers for single copies of the work.

---

2. The list here repeats four names listed in the letter to Munroe of December 29, 1846,
above: *The Harbinger*, W. C. Bryant, *Home Journal*, and Dr Parsons for *The Knickerbocker
Magazine*. The names of newspapers and periodicals are duplicated as well.

3. MS in the Emerson papers (RWEMA), Houghton Library, MH; ph. in NNC. This
draft at one point differs substantially from the letter as actually sent (*Letters*, 3:369–370). A
reply to Heraud's letter of November 28, 1846, the draft could have been written anytime
after mid-December. In his December 31 postscript to John Chapman (see December 29,
1846, above) Emerson had sent Heraud a message promising to write by the "next steamer."

4. That is, *The Half-yearly Review*.

[And] With regard to [literary] aid, /in the composition of the work itself/ we have no new writers who have shown much force combined with a /due/ catholicity, unless it be Elizur Wright editor of a daily paper in Boston called the Chronotype and a Mr Charles A. Dana [no] a Socialist, now connected with the New York Tribune (newspaper.)[5] The abolition movement which has taken a strong hold on the conscience & mind of our people is educating both the one & the other & already seems to have ripened a few minds to that degree that the abolition of /negro/ slavery no longer seems to them the only duty /end/ for which /the while/ man was created. The very sensible influence of this agitation on the politics of this country, long denounced as futile or mischievous, is lately sensible & salutary, and it brings with it a whole connexion of related subjects all tending to novelty & expansion

I feel the justice of your[6]

I confide that the whole expression of thought in America will presently share a juster & wider view

Mr Thoreau of this town is a person of profound mind who if he lives will certainly be heard from in your country as well as in ours. Mr Alcott may never succeed as he has not hitherto succeeded in giving a written expression to his bold & original & religious thinking but he may be reckoned on as a sure ally of everything great & good You must not fail to talk with Margaret Fuller on the subject who is well acquainted with the best people in Boston & New York & a very ingenious /the most eloquent/ & independent of women. For myself I shall not promise any very efficient aid, though I may easily contribute a paper or two as the work goes on but my papers when good for anything have no timeliness but are as fit for one book or year as another I have no great special skill as a periodical writer

To Sarah Margaret Fuller, Concord, January 31? 1847

[In the MS Account Book for 1844–1849, p. 100, under the date February 1, 1847, Emerson enters the cost of "postage to Liverpool" for his letter to John A. Heraud and a letter to Margaret Fuller, the cost .66 for the two letters. See *Letters*, 3:576, n. 29, for Emerson's addressing letters to Margaret Fuller in Paris in care of Brown, Shipley, & Co., Liverpool. She had written from Paris on November 16, 1846; see *Memoirs*, 2:184–187.]

5. The final version does not name Dana and the *Tribune*.
6. Nothing of these reflections on the abolition movement appears in the final version.

To Charles Lane, Concord, January 31? 1847

[In his MS Account Book for 1844–1849, p. [100], under the date February 1, Emerson enters the cost of postage "to the ship on letters to Carlyle, Chapman & Lane .6 .72." See Slater, p. 413, for the January 31 letter to Carlyle. Emerson is probably answering Lane's letter of January 3 (RWEMA).]

To John Chapman, Concord, January 31? 1847

[In his MS Account Book for 1844–1849, p. 100, under the date February 1, Emerson enters the cost of postage "to the ship on letters to Carlyle, Chapman, and Lane .6 .72." This letter to Chapman may have included a request to send a copy of the English edition of *Poems* to William Thom, as Charles Lane in his letter of January 3 (RWEMA) had asked, having suggested that Thom send Emerson his poems; *Rhymes and Recollections* published in 1844 and reprinted in 1845. Lane writes "Wm. Thom of Inverness," but Thom of Inverary seems to be the only possibility. See Slater, pp. 412–414, for Emerson's letter of January 31 to Carlyle.]

To Martin P. Kennard, Concord, February 7, 1847

[Advertised and quoted in part by B. Altman (*The New York Times*, December 3, 1972), this letter is written to the jeweler M. P. Kennard and is addressed to him at his office; the object is framed to show both the text and the address. Kennard was a jeweler in the firm of Bigelow Brothers and Kennard, Boston. Kennard was manifestly a member of the committee on lectures for the Boston Mercantile Library Association, for the letter says that the subject of the lecture for Wednesday is "Eloquence" (see Charvat, p. 23). Emerson says further that he will be spending that night at Dr. C. T. Jackson's (his brother-in-law's) and asks that he not be addressed by a title to which he has no claim; i.e., "Reverend."]

To William Lock Brown, John Sedgwick, Charles Carroll Moore, Concord, February 8, 1847

[In the Emerson papers, RWEMA, is the address leaf of the letter of January 26 written by the committee for the literary societies of New York University; Emerson has endorsed it: "answered 8 Feb that I wd come unless I write within 15 days to the contrary." See *Letters*, 3:369, for Emerson's inquiries about the "University of the City of New York," of which he seems never to have heard although it was then sixteen years old and proving a rival to Columbia. His correspondents were all members of the Class of '47 in the college of Arts and Pure Sciences.]

To Sarah Ann Clarke, Concord, February 9, 1847[7]

Concord
Tuesday 9 Feb

My dear Sarah,

I shall be quite unable to keep my people at home if you persist in disturbing discipline. Edith accepts your invitation in the most determined manner, & hopes to find Lilla[8] at your house.

And my wife & Ellen mean to come to tea with me. So we shall have the best opportunity to confer on what is past & what is to come. Yours ever,

R. W. Emerson

Miss Clarke.

To Thomas Treadwell Stone, Concord, February 13, 1847

[In a letter of February 12, 1847 (RWEMA), Thomas Treadwell Stone invites Emerson to be his guest when he comes to lecture in Salem; there is no proof of a letter, but an answer is surely required. Emerson lectured in Salem on February 17 (Charvat, p. 23).]

To Caroline Sturgis, Concord, February 14, 1847[9]

Concord Sunday 14 Feb

My dear friend, I have had many regrets & much more than regrets, since I saw you, in recalling what I said of my poems,—that they were not historic, &c: for, on remembering certain poems, to which I make no doubt you alluded, it is quite plain what their meaning was when they were written. I have only to say in explanation of my positiveness, that such pieces are consciously fabulous to any actual life & purposes of mine, when I write them, & so manifestly. that, after a short time, they take rank in my memory with other people's poetry, as intellectual exer-

7. MS in the Clarke papers, Houghton Library, MH; ph. in NNC; Of the three possible years when the 9th of February fell on a Tuesday after Edith Emerson's birth and before her marriage, the year 1847 is the only possible one; in 1858 Emerson was not at home on February 9, and in 1864, Edith was in New York. The tenor of the letter implies that the girls are still children.

8. Lilian Clarke, daughter of James Freeman Clarke and niece of Sarah Clarke.

9. MS in the Tappan papers, Houghton Library, MH; ph. in NNC; There is no address of any kind on p. [4]. Of the years when February 14 fell on a Sunday; 1847 is the most likely. In September 1846 Emerson had sent her some poems in MS, a selection from his forthcoming volume, eliciting from her some praise and some objections. See her letter of October 1846 printed above. The subject was evidently taken up again, possibly on February 10, when he saw her and others after his lecture on "Eloquence" (see Letters, 3:377), as well as on the 11th (Thursday) when according to this letter he saw her again.

cises, &, after a little while, are as readily exposed to other eyes as odes on Napoleon or Apollo. But the seeing you—suggested that these poems, which the day before were poems,—were personalities, & they instantly became unspeakably odious to me.[10] I seem to have surprised myself in an offence which I never forgive in another. And that offence too against you.

To you the verses are & will be nothing. That firmness of yours which nature made so admirable to me, would ward off all the poems in America like snowflakes.—And, I suppose, I might know in all private conversation how to testify to the clearness & perfectness of your position. But these considerations did not much avail me in my regrets of Thursday evening.—

Yet there is for us a ground of absolute truth & confidence careless of occasions & interviews, & remaining unaltered through all the connections & histories into which we severally enter. And this is shaken by untruth, & by nothing else. The calling in by trumpeting poetry, of millions of witnesses, though it may be very idle, would be indifferent, so long as I am what I say & do not equivocate to myself. This friendship has been the solidest social good I have known, & it is my meaning to be true to it. Once more your entire friend,

W.

To William Lock Brown et al., Concord, February 23? 1847

[See above February 8 for note of Emerson's letter of February 8 in which he promised to write again within fifteen days if he changed his mind about addressing the literary societies of New York University, and see *Letters*, 3:369, n. 2, for the fact that he did not make the address. William Emerson replied on January 31 to his brother's letter of January 28 (*Letters*, 3:368) asking for information about the "University of the city of New York." He reports it to be "a college, & not a high school; as those things go in the U.S." and adds in a postscript: "I do not believe that said University is on a footing with Harvard & Yale, but it probably is with Columbia College & the 2d class colleges" (a.l.s. privately owned).]

10. The nicety of Emerson's conscience is such that it is rash to conjecture which poems were turned into "personalities" and so became "odious" to him. That Emerson should use in poems, letters, and journals the same or similar phrases is not to the purpose; parallels of this sort are so much to be expected that they have no evidential value. Miss Sturgis might recognize herself in "Hermione" and her complaints of the Concord landscape in the opening of "Musketaquid," and she would know that "Monadnoc" grew out of Emerson's April trip to the nearer mountain Wachusett and the May excursion they had made together (see April 1, 1845, and May 6, 1845, above). A draft of a portion of "Monadnoc" is dated by Emerson May 3, 1845, when the May trip to Wachusett was in prospect and the April trip in memory, yet I think any reader of the poem finds it "fabulous to any actual life & purpose" of Emerson's. Both Caroline Sturgis and Emerson could easily tolerate the many obvious "personalities" in Ellery Channing's poems, if not in each other's poems.

To Alexander Ireland, Concord, February 28, 1847[11]

I owe you new thanks for your friendly and earnest attention to the affair of Lectures which you have put me on, but I had not anticipated so prompt an execution of the project as you suggest. Certainly I cannot think of it for April (1847).[12] For September I will think of it, but I cannot at present fix anything. I really have not the means of forming an opinion of the expediency of such an attempt. I feel no call to make a visit of literary propagandism in England. All my impulses to work of that kind would rather employ me at home. It would be still more unpleasing to me to put upon a few friends the office of collecting, an audience for me, by much advertisement and coaxing.[13] At the same time, it would be very agreeable to me to accept any good invitation to read lectures from institutions, or from a number of friendly individuals who sympathised with my studies. But though I possess a good many decisive tokens of interest in my pursuits and way of thinking from sundry British men and women, they are widely sundered persons, and my belief is that in no one city, except perhaps in London, could I find any numerous company to whom my name was favourably[14] known. If I were younger, it would give me great pleasure to come to England and collect my own audience, as I have done at home here; and I have that confidence in my favourite topics and in my own habits, that I should undertake the affair without the least distrust. But perhaps my ambition does not give to a success of this kind that importance it has had for me. At all events, in England I incline rather to take than to give the challenge. So that you see my project requires great frankness on your part. You must not suffer your own friendly feelings to give the smallest encouragement to the design. . . . You inquire what are the rates of remuneration of lecturers here. . . .[15] I am glad to hear what you tell me of your employments and position. I doubt not life has taught and is teaching us both one lesson. It would be strange, but most agreeable to

11. The MS has not been located; text from Ireland, *In Memoriam,* pp. 57–58. See *Letters,* 3:379–381, for text from a MS draft (RWEMA), and note 39, for the text of Ireland's letter of February 3 to which this letter is a reply. The elision marks are Ireland's.

12. The year is Ireland's insert.

13. Since Ireland in other instances took liberties with Emerson's text; he may have done so here. Emerson's draft has "painful" here, not "unpleasing" and has "puffing" not "advertisement."

14. Emerson's draft has "favorably" here and "favourite" below; Ireland puts the "u" in the first and takes it out of the second.

15. Ireland omits the financial details here, possibly because they were out of date when he printed the letter. See *Letters,* 3:381.

me, to renew again our brief yet never-forgotten acquaintance of thirteen or fourteen years ago in Edinburgh.—[16] With ever kindest regards.

To WILLIAM EMERSON, CONCORD, MARCH 1, 1847[17]

Concord 1 March 1847

William Emerson, Esq.

My dear Sir,

I have pleased myself all winter with the expectation that in the last week of February or the first week of March I might find myself in a situation to claim your kind promise to afford me an opportunity of going into the woods with you above Bangor, to see the timber cut, & the lumberers in their camp. &c. I have taken some care to avoid cumbering myself with engagements that should find me at this season. But now that the time has come & is passing, I find that it is still not quite practicable to me.[18] It were long to tell you my hindrances, which, I fear, too, would be hardly intelligible out of a scholar's study; but I have reluctantly given up the thought of making you a visit at present. I do not however relinquish the claims you were so good as to give me, but I retain my strong desire to see the forest & mean one day to climb Mount Katahdin.[19] On many accounts, in site of the difficulties of travelling, it is Maine in summer that I wish to see.[20] Please to accept my renewed thanks

16. This paragraph is not in the draft. Emerson is replying to Ireland's opening account of what has happened since they first met in 1833. It is evident that in 1833, Emerson had told him of Ellen Tucker Emerson's death.

17. MS in the Bangor Public Library; ph. in NNC; p. [4] addressed: William Emerson, Esq. Bangor Maine.; postmarked at Concord, March 1. Printed by Vernon R. Lindquist in his "Unpublished Letter Reveals a Bangor Friendship," *University of Maine Bulletin* (1968), 2d ser., no. 88, 155–156. The William Emerson here is not a relative.

18. Lindquist makes rather too much of what is simply a polite explanation. He is mistaken in listing as one of the "hindrances" the editing of *Poems*, for by March 1847 the book was already in print (late December 1846). There were no "tenants" (Lindquist, p. 157, n. 5) in Emerson's house; see *Letters*, 3:331, and 4:117, for the arrangement by which the Emerson family became "boarders" in their own house; i.e., Emerson hired a housekeeper. (Emerson's specification of sixteen or eighteen people in his letter of recommendation for Mrs. Goodwin includes his family and friends and hers, six at the least; he gives the maximum numbers because he is recommending her for a job in a large institution.) Among the hindrances were the illness of the Emerson children, the vexing affair of the intractable Harro Harring, the planting to be done in the Warren lot, and the necessity of straightening out his finances if he were to go to England; see *Letters*, 3:371–383.

19. Emerson mentions this desire to Margaret Fuller, letter of February 28, when he had not altogether given up hope of making the trip to Maine (*Letters*, 3:377).

20. Emerson's early (1834) admiration of his Bangor acquaintance was not cooled by the "destruction of the forests," as noticeable in 1834 as in 1846, but by William Emerson's offensive remarks on Judge Joseph Story; see *Letters*, 3:335, and *JMN*, 9:458.

for your kind offers, and my best hopes for your continued health. With remembrances to Mr & Mrs Goss,[21]

Yours respectfully,
R. Waldo Emerson.

To Caroline Sturgis, Concord? March? 1847[22]

Dear Caroline,

Thanks for the letters which are all excellent, and Mr Sedgwick's in a new style. Have you read "Hazlitt's Conversation of James Northcote," which is far superior to anything else with Hazlitt's name, and as full of the high common sense as the talk of Johnson or Burke. I also admire the "Suspira" of De Quincey which I discovered the other day, & return —Happiest days to you!

W.

To Samuel Gray Ward, Concord, March 25, 1847[23]

Concord, 25 March, 1847.

My dear friend,

I have had two letters from you which were both most welcome. You shall surely keep the books as long as you read them.[24] We can like any book so little while! Though its pages were cut out of the sky, & its letters were stars in a short time we cannot find there with any turning of leaves

21. Mr and Mrs Cyrus Goss, *Letters*, 1:415, and for the recent meeting, *Letters*, 3:353, 354; see also Lindquist, p. 157, for the relationship between the Gosses and William Emerson.

22. MS in the Tappan papers, Houghton Library, MH; ph. in NNC; a single leaf, the verso addressed: Miss Caroline Sturgis. The stationery and the fine pen are those in use in 1847, in, for example the letter of February 14 to Miss Sturgis. It is certainly written after Caroline Sturgis' long stay in the Berkshires in 1846 where she succumbed to Charles Sedgwick's charms. The letters referred to here are, I think, from him. The letter is possibly of this interlude, and it so happens that both the books referred to are mentioned by Emerson in March 1847 (*JMN*, 10:17, 49–50). The allusion to De Quincey's book reads: ". . . If people are grieved we go over the sorrow in words & the more cunning the repetition of it in words the better consoled they are; or we lend them a book:—cure with music still. Administer literature, as 'Suspira de Profundis.'" The letter here certainly implies that Caroline has lent him the De Quincey. (By March Caroline was back in Boston; the letter and the books were perhaps left at her father's house.)

23. MS in the Ward papers, Houghton Library, MH; ph. in NNC; p. [4] addressed: Saml. G. Ward. | Lenox Mass. | ; postmarked at Concord, March 25. Printed by Norton, pp. 63–65; a draft differing from this text is in *Letters*, 3:386–388.

24. Ward had visited Emerson in February (*Letters*, 3:377); Emerson evidently lent him some books at that time. In Lenox, the Wards and the Sedgwicks frequently met to read aloud (letters in the Ward papers and Sedgwick papers, MHi).

the celestial sentences or the celestial scents we certainly found there once; and I am of opinion that relatively to individual readers the fiery scriptures in each book either disappear once for all from the context after a short time, or else, have a certain intermittency & periodical obscuration, like "revolving lights." Perhaps too there are cycles of epiphany & eclipse in bookshops. Certainly I have seen nothing that craved to go to Lenox since you gave me leave to look for you. But I shall not yet quite resign my commission.

Theodore Parker & others are considering just now once more the practicability of a new Quarterly Journal, & they seek for an editor.[25] They came to me & then to C. Sumner. I promised my best help, but no editorship. Sumner declined also. Then I am invited on some terms— not yet quite distinct & attractive enough—to England, to lecture: in Manchester & Birmingham, & Carlyle promises audiences in London.[26] But though I often ask where shall I get the whip for my top, I do not yet take either of these. The top believes it can fly like the wheel of the Sisters, with a poise like a planet and a hum like the spheral music, yet it refuses to spin. I have read in the Cosmogonists that every atom has a spiral tendency, an effort to spin. I think over all the shops of power where we might borrow that desiderated push, but none entirely suits me. The excursion to England & farther, draws me sometimes, but the kind of travel I should prize, the most liberal, that made it a liberty & a duty to go, /is/ not to be found in hospitable invitations. And if I could really do as I liked, I should probably turn towards Canada, into loneliest retreats, far from cities & friends who do not yield me what they would yield to any other companion. And I believe that literary power would be consulted by that course & not by the public road. When my meditations draw to any head, I shall hasten to apprise you; and perhaps I shall, if they do not. Yours affectionately,

R. W. E.

25. This is Emerson's first reference to the proposal for a new periodical, to be called *The Massachusetts Quarterly Review;* for its history see Clarence Gohdes, *The Periodicals of American Transcendentalism* (Durham, N. C.: Duke University Press, 1931), pp. 157–193. Parker had written Emerson on March 14 (a.l.s., RWEMA) proposing the journal and declaring Emerson the ideal editor. See *Letters,* 3:391–392, and notes for the first formal meeting to discuss the plan. For Emerson's uncomfortably equivocal relation to the venture, see *Letters,* 3:397 and 409. To the first number Emerson contributed an unsigned address "To the Public" (December 1847, 1:1–7; *Works,* 11:(383–393, with the title "Editor's Address").

26. For the slowly developing plan to lecture in England, see December 28, 1846, above, *Letters,* 3:379–381, and Salter, pp. 417–418.

To Benjamin Marston Watson, Concord, March 26, 1847[27]

Concord, 26 March, 1847

My dear Sir,

I am endeavouring to lay out a good plan for the disposition of my trees in my new orchard and I do not find all the notes I took in Plymouth[28] I have mislaid the rude list I made in your nursery which was to be a transcript of the *order* we agreed on.—if indeed I made such a list & did not merely add the principal new names you gave me to an old list of yours which I carried with me in a pocket book.[29]

Will you have the goodness to send me a copy of the order, as you have it, with the prices annexed.[30] Perhaps I shall not venture to put quite so many pears into my ground at once, but shall let my neighbors have a few of them here: And John Moore in proposing exchanges, wishes to see my accurate list.[31] Perhaps you will send me, at the same time, that table of directions, which I need so much, for their treatment. I have Downing's[32] "Fruit Frees of America," but like to have line upon line.

Perhaps for this cold spring the 7 or 8 April will be better than the 1st for the transit of the trees. You has better pay for the freight *to* the Fitchburg Rail Road & charge me with the same.

The snow still lies in our woods and a few patches along the walls, but today it is rapidly disappearing.

27. MS in the Watson papers, Hillside Collection, MPlPS; ph. in NNC; p. [4] addressed: Marston Watson, Esq. Plymouth Mass; postmarked at Concord March 26.

28. Benjamin Marston Watson was the husband of Lidian Emerson's childhood friend Mary Russell, who had been for a time Waldo's and Ellen's teacher. Emerson was to buy many trees from Watson. This purchase was for the "Warren lot" (2 acres, 66 rods), east of the house lot, bought January 6 from Cyrus Warren and paid for April 1 (see *Letters*, 4:362, 371, and n. 9 of the corrected printing of 1969). On the last page of the smaller of Emerson's MS notebooks "Trees" (*JMN*, 8:454), is a detailed description of the property. The purchase and planting of this lot delayed Emerson's decision to go to England (see below July 31). The MS Account Book for 1845–1849, p. [105] under the date March 31, records the payment of $500.00 to Warren for the lot and under the date April 2, p. [105], the payment of $1.00 to Thoreau for surveying it.

29. Emerson lectured in Plymouth on March 5 and 6; see my article "Emerson's Lecture Schedule . . . Revised" (*HLB*, Autumn 1973, 21:399). He is referring here to conversation with Watson then, but also to his original selection of the trees some time before November 27, 1846; see letter to his brother of that date (*Letters*, 4:362), and Watson's letter cited below.

30. Watson replied on March 28 (letter laid in the larger of the MS notebooks "Trees," Houghton 125), listing the trees selected "last autumn" and presenting a bill of $76.75.

31. John Moore, son of Abel Moore, Concord sheriff, Emerson's admired neighbor; see *JMN*, 8:536; 10:20.

32. Andrew Jackson Downing, *The Fruits and Fruit Trees of America* (Harding, p. 83). In his reply, Watson observes: "Mr Downing's remarks are excellent and cover the whole ground," and then he gives Emerson detailed instruction for preparing the ground and for planting the trees. He proposes to send the trees on April 5.

I am heartily grieved that the winter has been such a heavy one to Mrs. Watson and that we do not hear much better tidings of her health yet.[33] Tell her that every one of our household holds her in anxious & affectionate remembrance.

And when you write please to give me the best news of her you can.

Yours respectfully,
R. W. Emerson.

To Mary Rotch, Concord, March 28, 1847[34]

Concord, 28 March,
1847.

My dear friend,

It was a great pleasure to hear from you, if only by a question in philosophy. And the terrors of treading that difficult & quaking ground shall not hinder me from writing to you.[35] I am quite sure however that I never said any of those fine things which you seem to have learned about me from Mr Griswold, and I think it would be but fair, as he deduces them, that he should explain them, &, if he can, show that they hold. No, I never say any of these scholastic things, and when I hear them, I can never tell on which side I belong. I never willingly say anything concerning "God" in cold blood, though I think we all have very just insights when we are "in the mount,"[36] as our fathers used to say. In conversation sometimes, or to humility & temperance the cloud will break away to show at least the direction of the rays of absolute Being, and we see the truth that lies in every affirmation men have made concerning it, & at the same time the cramping partiality of their speech.

---

33. Watson reports his wife's improvement and conveys her gratitude for "your volume of poems which has been our pleasantest visiter this year."

34. MS in the Emerson papers (RWEMA), Houghton Library, MH; ph. in NNC; the text fills all four pages. Printed by Cabot, 2:498–500; listed in *Letters*, 3:388–389.

35. Emerson is answering the Quaker Mary Rotch's letter of March 22 (RWEMA); she has just bought Rufus Griswold's *The Prose Writers of America* (Philadelphia, 1847; *BAL*, 6676). Griswold had written of Emerson (p. 440): "His prominent doctrine, is that the deity is impersonal,—a mere being, and comes to *self-consciousness* only in individuals. The distinction of this from pantheism is this, that while pantheism 'sinks man and nature in God,' Mr. Emerson 'sinks God and nature in man.'" Quoting this passage, Miss Rotch asks: "Is this also just to you?" She is particularly anxious to know whether the phrase "comes to self-consciousness only in individuals" is "correct." See Emerson to Griswold, April 5, below. See also my article, *HLB* (October 1973), 21:390–391, for Ellis Gray Loring's account of a conversation in 1838 with Emerson on this subject, and, above, correspondence with Henry Ware, Jr., July 28 and October 8, 1838.

36. This expression may be derived from Deu. 5.4 "The Lord talked with you in the mount out of the midst of the fire."

For the science of God our language is unexpressive, & merely prattle: we need simpler & universal signs, as algebra compared /with/ arithmetic. Thus I should affirm easily <u>both</u> those propositions, which our Mr Griswold balances against one another, that, I mean,—of "Pantheism" & the other <u>ism</u>. Personality, too, & impersonality, might each be affirmed of Absolute Being; and what may not be affirmed of it, in our own mind,? And we when we have heaped a mountain of speeches, we have still to begin again, having nowise expressed the simple unalterable fact. So I will not turn schoolman today, but prefer to wait a thousand years before I undertake that definition which literature has waited for so long already. Do not imagine that the old venerable thought has lost any of its awful attraction for me. I should very heartily,—shall I say, <u>tremulously</u> think & speak with you on our experiences or gleams of what is so grand & absorbing: and I never forget the statements so interesting to me you gave me many years ago of your faith & that of your friends. Are we not wonderful creatures to whom such entertainments & passions & hopes are afforded?

Yours with respect & affection,
R W Emerson

To Frederic Henry Hedge, Concord, Spring? 1847

[In a letter of April 24, 1847, privately owned, Hedge says that he has heard "several times" from Emerson "since we parted last October." See *Letters*, 3:360, for one such letter to Hedge and December 22 above for a conjectured second letter. There is no sharp evidence for a third letter, but twice is scarcely "several times."]

To Alexander Ireland, Concord, April 1, 1847[37]

My townsman, E. Rockwood Hoar, Esq., is ordered by his physicians to quit his professional duties for a time, and to travel for his health. Mr. Hoar is an eminent practitioner at the Massachusetts Bar, and was lately a member of our State Senate. As he proposes to visit Manchester in his route, I use the opportunity to beg you to introduce him to the Athenaeum, and to give him any local information that you may think may be useful to him.—Yours with great regard.

37. No MS has been located; text from Ireland, *In Memoriam*, p. 78; listed *Letters*, 3:390. Ireland gives place and date; for all the letters he prints he gives this information in a consistent form throughout; it is unlikely that Emerson did so.

To Benjamin Marston Watson, Concord, April 3, 1847[38]

B. M. Watson.

Concord, ⟨2⟩3 April 1847

My dear Sir,

Above written you have an order on the Atlantic Bank for $76.75 for the amount of your bill for trees, &c.[39] I have dated it 6 April to allow for the possible tardiness of my kind agent in town. I notice in your list that one item "3 Louise bonne de Jersey"[40] is set down twice. Now I will not have six of Louise be she never so good; but you shall, if not too late, supply the place of one triad with good apples. Thanks for your kind attention to the wants of my land here. I shall not, I fear, do all you advise, but shall keep it in mind & do what I can.[41] I made it a part of my bargain in buying the land that the seller should subsoil-plough it for me. — But the whole land is covered now with solid snow

We are all very much relieved by your report of Mrs Watson's health.

Yours, R. W. Emerson.

38. MS in the Hillside Collection, MPlP; ph. in NNC. The first leaf has become separated from the second and is separately filed in the collection. The paper is of the same color and the edges fit perfectly. The two pieces are not of the same size because the upper portion of p. [1] bearing the order on the Atlantic Bank has been cut away. It was to allow for this that Emerson turned his sheet half way around and wrote the the balance of his letter across the recto of the second leaf, leaving the verso of the first leaf blank.

39. See March 26 and notes for Watson's letter of March 28. Emerson enters the payment of Watson's bill under the date April 7 in his MS Account Book for 1845–1849, p. 107.

40. A variety of pear described by Emerson in the larger notebook "Trees" as "A large beautiful Pear; pale green with a dark blush, juicy and rich. . . ." The small notebook "Trees" [A], *JMN*, 8:534–536, lists the trees received from Watson April 10; the list corresponds to that provided by Watson in his letter of March 28 (see March 26, above) but is not identical. There are seventeen fewer pear trees; I infer that some of these were given to John Moore as proposed in his letter of March 26, above. Five were apparently given to "Mr Munroe." Watson's list had only one apple tree, but after his own list Emerson enters the one "June eating apple" of Watson's list, followed by eight apple trees. Apple trees being a good deal cheaper than pear trees (thirty-seven cents each as against a dollar), I infer that these were substituted for the unwanted Louise Bonne de Jerseys.

41. Watson had provided detailed instructions for ploughing, harrowing, and fertilizing the land.

To Rufus Griswold, Concord, April 5, 1847[42]

Concord, April 5, 1847.

Dear Sir,

I received the entire paquet you were so good as to forward me by Ticknor & Co, containing a copy of the "Prose Writers,"[43] and Mrs Hildreth's miniature with the engraved copies of the same.[44] I beg you to receive my thanks for these gifts. If the popularity of the book is to be judged from my own experience, it is quite certain; for I have not been able to keep it on my table long enough for any real examination, one friend after another borrowing it in swift succession. A friend at New Bedford[45] has written to me to know whether Mr Griswold rightly represents my opinions in respect to Pantheism, &c.. I replied, that as far as I understood the two statements which Mr G balances against each other, I should affirm them <u>both</u>. And I do not think that we are at all bound to be masters, in this science, even of our own opinions, but only to be very obedient pupils and exact reporters of that which appears to us.

Respectfully Yours
R. W. Emerson.

42. No original has been found; text from a copy made by Horace Binney Wallace in Phi; ph. in NNC. Wallace heads his copy with the note: "Copy of Letter, addressed to 'Rufus W. Griswold, Esq. Philadelphia, Pa." and in the lower left corner enters over his signature the note: "(true copy made by H. B. W.: April 10, 1847)." Listed in *Letters*, 3:390.

43. Griswold's *The Prose Writers of America* was published early in March by Carey and Hart (*BAL*, 6676).

44. Griswold had borrowed from Mrs. Emerson the miniature of Emerson by Caroline Neagus Hildreth; he had had the original since 1844 causing Mrs. Emerson some anxiety as Emerson's letters to W. H. Furness show; see, for example, May 9, 1845, above. Griswold evidently included in the pacquet copies of Sartain's engraving from Mrs. Hildreth's miniature (see *Prose Writers*, facing p. 440).

45. Mary Rotch, March 22; see March 28 above.

To Eliza Cabot Follen, Concord, April 8, 1847[46]

Concord, 8 April, 1847.

Mrs Follen

Dear Madam,

I send you the papers respecting Harro Harring you were so good as to send me, & the volume "Dolores."[47] I wrote to Mr Stallknecht,[48] with thom I had formerly a slight acquaintance, & received a reply expressing the kindest consideration for Harro, but representing the difficulties which Mr S. found in attempting to serve him. He promised, however, new efforts. My brother William in New York has called on Harro, & will serve him, if he can. I have attempted to put the novel into the hands of our Munroe & Co., but thus far Harro makes terms not quite acceptable. We shall not despair quite yet. Yours respectfully,

R. W. Emerson.

To James Elliot Cabot, Concord, April 9? 1847

[In his letter of April 11, 1847, to Convers Francis, Emerson lists the men who have already promised him or Alcott to visit Emerson on the 14th; of those listed, it seems to me likely that Emerson wrote to Cabot and Sumner as well as to Stetson and Stone whom he names and Weiss whose reply to Emerson exists. See *Letters*, 3:391–392.]

To Charles Sumner, Concord, April 9, 1847

[See, above, note of letter to Elliot Cabot for the likelihood of a letter also to Sumner.]

46. MS in the Barrett Collection, Alderman Library, ViU; ph. in NNC; p. [4] addressed: Mrs Follen. | Cambridge.

47. Eliza Follen had sent Emerson a manuscript by Harro Paul Harring, a copy of his novel *Dolores* (New York: Marrener, Lockwood, 1846), and a letter she had written Harring. Her covering letter of March 2 (RWEMA) makes it clear that she has no very high opinion of the man or his work and thinks he should be told the truth. She leaves it to Emerson to send on her letter if he thinks best. She had enclosed also a letter from Margaret Fuller to Emerson, a letter of introduction for Harring; see *Letters*, 3:381, n. 42.

48. Frederick S. Stallknecht was Harring's attorney; Emerson's letter of March 7 (listed *Letters*, 3:281), has not been found. For Harring's affairs, see Emerson to his brother William, *Letters*, 3:381–383. The letter from Stallknecht to Emerson (March 10, RWEMA) shows that Harring had the unlovely habit of abusing those who befriended and served him. From Stallknecht's account of Harring's behavior, I think it can be conjectured that Mrs. Follen had also suffered on Harring's behalf and had turned to Emerson only when she could no longer cope. Emerson gives his brother William a less guarded account of Stallknecht's letter; see *Letters*, 3:386. See finally Emerson to Margaret Fuller, June 4, *Letters*, 3:401.

To James Munroe, Concord, May 31, 1847[49]

Concord, 31 May

Mr Munroe,

Dear Sir,

Please to look at this proof of the title page, &c. of the Essays: and instruct Mr Metcalf how to *date the copyright,* as you will observe he balances between 1841 and 1847. If you think it advantageous to take out a new one for me, please to do so.

Yours respectfully,

R. W. Emerson.

to John Chapman, Concord, May 31, 1847[50]

Concord, 31 May, 1847

Mr John Chapman,

Dear Sir,

I am very much concerned to learn that my book of Poems is to be the occasion of loss to you, which I had ventured to hope might be a benefit. I find too that we cannot help you in the way you suggest, for our ⟨book⟩ /second edition/ was already printed when your letter arrived. I should have replied to you by the following steamer, but your letter found me on the island of Nantucket from which for many days, was no egress for many days for man or letter by reason of an easterly gale.[51] I thank you heartily for your kind invitations to England & London. It is by no means certain that I shall go thither ⟨at⟩ /in the/ present year: Mr Ireland & Mr

49. MS in Miscellaneous MSS, Houghton Library, MH; ph. in NNC; p. [4] addressed: James Munroe & Co | Boston |. The date is clear from the text; the reference is to the second edition of *Essays, First Series* (*BAL,* 5213). A new copyright was taken out August 27, 1847, M. A10.5.d, p. 51.

50. MS in the Sterling Library, University of London; ph. in NNC; addressed p. [4]: Chapman, Brothers. | Booksellers. | 121 Newgate Street | London. The blurred Liverpool stamp seems to be of June 15. Printed by Mignon, *ESQ* (4th q., 1973), 19:229–230.

51. Emerson was on Nantucket Island the first two weeks in May to give his series of lectures on "Representative Men." Charvat, p. 23, correctly notes that Emerson has entered the payment of $70 for these lectures under the date April 19 (MS Account Book for 1845–1849, p. [30]), but the date is surely Emerson's error for May 19; the immediately preceeding entry on the page is also dated the 19th of April; the entry immediately following is dated June 14. That the lectures were given in May is clear from this letter; it is the mid-month mail boat he has missed. See also *Letters,* 3:395–398, and journal entry of May 24, *JMN,* 9:62–64. His entry for the expenses of the Nantucket trip (MS Account Book, pp.[105–109]) is dated May 3. His payment for this letter appears under the date June 2, p.[112].

Carlyle hold out very pleasing inducements, and I gladly entertain the project,[52] but have not yet decided, as indeed there is no need of decision for some months yet.

I must cherish the hope in some manner to relieve you of any burden that has fallen on you ⟨by⟩through printing my book.

Yours respectfully,
R. W. Emerson

To Frederic Henry Hedge, Concord, June 2? 1847

[Emerson's letter of introduction to Carlyle must have been sent to Hedge with a covering letter. See *Letters*, 3:399 and Slater, pp. 424, 425.]

To Thomas Carlyle, Concord, July 1, 1847[53]

Concord, 1 July, 1847

Dear Carlyle,

My cousin, Mr George S. Emerson,[54] of Boston, desires an introduction to you, which I also wish to secure for him. It may be a long time before he brings you this line, as he sails for Havre & visits the Continent of Europe, before he goes to England. I am quite sure that on his way homeward his wish to see you will not be less.

Yours affectionately,

T. Carlyle, Esq. R. W. Emerson.
London.

To Thomas Cogswell Upham, Concord? July ? 1847

[In a letter to Mrs. Emerson, October 26, 1847 (RWEMA), Thomas C. Upham mentions a letter from Emerson. The letter had acknowledged the receipt of Upham's *Life and Religious Opinions . . . of Madame de La Motte Guyon* (New York, 1847); see Harding, p. 285. Upham's letter to Emerson of July 25 (RWEMA) says he is sending the book for Mrs. Emerson; I conjecture that Emerson's acknowledgment was written in late July. As his letter of October 26 shows, Upham had

52. See Slater, pp. 417, 419, and Emerson may have just received Carlyle's letter of May 18 (Slater, p. 423).

53. MS in the George Barrell Emerson papers, MHi ph. in NNC; with envelope addressed: Thomas Carlyle, Esq. | 5 Cheyne Row: | Chelsea: London | G. S. Emerson, Esq. | Inadvertently omitted by Slater, who returned it to me for publication here.

54. Only son of Emerson's second cousin George Barrell Emerson. See *JMN*, 11:125. This letter of introduction was apparently never used.

borrowed from Mrs. Emerson a work by Mme. Guyon when he was writing his book. See also February 8, 1835, above.]

To Alexander Ireland, Concord, July 31, 1847[55]

Concord 31 July 1847

A. Ireland, Esq.

My dear Sir,

I owe you hearty thanks for your effective attention to my affair, which was attractive enough to me in the first proposition, and certainly assumes in your hands a feasible shape. I have a good deal of domestic immoveableness—being fastened down by wife & children by books & studies by pear-trees & apple-trees[56]—but after much hesitation can find no sufficient resistance to this animating invitation and I decide to go to England in the autumn. I think to leave home about the 1 October, perhaps in the steamer, but more probably in the sailing packet[57] which leaves Boston for Liverpool on the 5th of each month;—and, at any rate, shall expect to be in England before the 1 November. From the 1 November, I will take your advice as to the best order of fulfilling these engagements you offer me at Manchester, Sheffield, & Leeds. In regard to the subjects of my lectures, I hope to send you by the next steamer some programme or sketch of programme that may serve a general purpose. I could more easily furnish myself for so "numerous" a course as seems to offer itself if there were any means of preventing your newspaper reporters from publishing such ample transcripts as I notice (in the "Examiners" you were so good as to send me—) of Mr Marston's Lectures.[58] But I will see what I have to say.—Meantime, I beg you not to give yourself any farther pains in this matter which I fear has already cost you much. It will give me pleasure to speak to bodies of your English people. but I am sure it will give me much more to meet with yourself &

55. MS in the Barrett Collection, Alderman Library, ViU; ph. in NNC; p. [4] addressed: Alexander Ireland, Esq | "Examiner" Office | Manchester. | England. | ; stamped at Liverpool and at Manchester August 14. The signature has been cut away. Printed by Ireland, pp. 78–79; printed in *The American Writer in England* (Charlottesville: University Press of Virginia, [1969]), pp. 42, 44; listed *Letters*, 3:406.

56. The recently purchased Warren lot and its planting are referred to her; see *Letters*, 3:371, 388, 402, and 412, and, above, March 26 and April 3.

57. He chose a sailing packet, the *Washington Irving*, leaving as scheduled October 5 (*Letters*, 3:419).

58. Probably John Westland Marston, Alcott's friend; see *Letters*, 2:231. Emerson was to find the full reporting of some English newspapers an annoyance, the more so that he did not have many lectures on hand. The newspapers giving the full reports were those friendly to nonconformists and to the Mechanics Institutes for which Emerson gave the lectures; the Tory press carefully ignored them.

other honoured individuals in private: and I see well, that, if there were no lecturing, I should not fail to find a solid benefit in the visit. I write a note of reply to Mr Hudson, to go with this.[59]

With great regard, Your friend & servant,

To WILLIAM HENRY FURNESS, CONCORD, AUGUST 6, 1847[60]

Concord, 6 August, 1847.

Dear Furness,

It was very wrong in you not to come & see me in any of these your northern flights. The last of your Boston visits, for example, I set down as a clear case of contumacy, that you would neither come to me nor be at home where I went to see you. I hope you had my card, which I left at Dr Gannett's.[61] But now I write because Henry D. Thoreau has a book to print.[62] Henry D. Thoreau is a great man in Concord, a man of original genius & character who knows Greek & knows Indian also,— not the language quite as well as John Eliot—but but the history monuments & genius of the Sachems, being a pretty good Sachem himself, master of all woodcraft, & an intimate associate of the birds, beasts, & fishes, of this region. I could tell you many a good story of his forest life. —He has written what he calls, "A Week on the Concord & Merrimack Rivers," which is an account of an excursion made by himself & his brother (in a boat which he built) some time ago, from Concord, Mass., down the Concord river & up the Merrimack, to Concord N.H.—I think it a book of wonderful merit, which is to go far & last long. It will remind you of Isaak Walton, and, if it have not all his sweetness, it is rich, as he is not, in profound thought.—Thoreau sent the manuscript lately to Duyckinck,—Wiley & Putnam's[63] literary Editor, who examined it, &

59. See *Letters*, 3:407, for the letter to James William Hudson and note 137 for Hudson's letter to Emerson. At the time Hudson was Secretary and Librarian of the Leeds Mechanics Institution and Library Society and also Secretary of the Yorkshire Union of Mechanics' Institutes. Ireland had written Hudson in June; his letter was read at the meeting of the Leeds Institution on June 29, whereupon it was resolved that the members "would be happy to engage Ralph Waldo Emerson to deliver three or four lectures through the Yorkshire Union Committee not to exceed twenty Guineas for the course." Liverpool (Lancs.) had acted even earlier (see notes September 30, 1847, for the resolution of April 13, 1847). The effort to persuade Emerson to visit England had begun in 1846 when Carlyle and Chapman both urged him to consider such an undertaking.

60. MS in the Furness papers, Van Pelt Library, PU; ph. in NNC; p. [4] addressed: Rev. William H. Furness | Philadelphia. | Pa. | ; postmarked at Concord, August 7. Printed in *Records,* pp. [60]–62.

61. Ezra Stiles Gannett.

62. See Emerson's postscript here.

63. See *Letters*, 3:384, for Emerson's letter to Evert Duyckinck on Thoreau's behalf.

"gave a favorable opinion of it to W. & P." They have however declined publishing it. And I have promised Thoreau that I would inquire ⟨it⟩ publishing it. And I have before we begin to set our own types. Would Mr Hart,[64] or Mr Kay[65] like to see such a manuscript? It will make a book as big as my First Series of Essays. They shall have it on half profits, or on any reasonable terms. Thoreau is mainly bent on having it printed in a cheap form for a large circulation.

You wrote me once & asked about Hedge.[66] I esteem & respect him always more & more. He is best seen at Bangor. I saw him there last October & heard him preach all day. He is a solid person who cannot be spared in a whole population of levities. I think he is like one of those slow growing pear trees whose fruit is finer every year & at last becomes a Beurré Incomparable.[67] I bade him goodbye seven or eight weeks ago, on board the "Washington Irving,"[68] & expect to see him in England next spring. Do you know that I am going thither in October? Will not Henry Thoreau serve as well as another apology for writing to you. Yours ever,

R. W. Emerson.

It may easily happen that you have too many affairs even to ask the question of the booksellers. Then simply say that you do not; for my party is Anacharsis the Scythian, and as imperturbable as Osceola.[69]

To Joseph Palmer, Concord, August 7, 1847[70]

on $400. Interest $18.86 to 14 June
on 300 Interest 4.50 to 14 Sept. 3 months

23 36

64. Abraham Hart.
65. The Philadelphia directories for 1847, list Kay & Brother, booksellers, and, separately, James Kay, Jr., and John L. Kay.
66. Frederic Henry Hedge whom Emerson heard "all day" October 11, 1846; see *Letters*, 3:355, and for Hedge's sailing, see *Letters*, 3:399. For Carlyle on Hedge, see Slater, p. 428–429. Furness' letter inquiring about Hedge is not among those found.
67. Emerson is preoccupied with pear trees as he lays out the Warren lot.
68. The sailing ship Emerson would travel on.
69. Of the Seminole leader's imperturbability Emerson may have heard directly from William Batehelder Greene, who fought in the Seminole wars before becoming a preacher; see *JMN*, 7:207, and n. 31. There is no way of knowing which of the attributes Emerson has in mind. For Furness' efforts, see his letters of August 16 and September 10, *Records*, pp. [63] and 66.
70. MS in the Fruitlands Museums; ph. in NNC; p. [4] addressed: Mr Joseph Palmer | Still-river | Harvard | Mass.
The property in Harvard, Massachusetts, bought by Charles Lane for the experimental community known as Fruitlands was sold by Lane to Joseph Palmer. A copy of the deed

Concord, 7 August, 1847

Mr. Joseph Palmer,

Dear Sir,

I received lately a letter from Charles Lane who remains at Ham near London. He wishes me to demand payment of the balance of your note for $400.00; namely $300. of principal, and 23.36 on interest at the beginning of next month. That I may give you the less inconvenience, I will name the latest day that will give me time to complete his affairs, namely, the 1⟨5⟩4th September.

About the 1 October, I shall probably sail for England, & in the course of the month expect to meet Mr Lane at London. I shall depend on your promptly keeping this day, the 1⟨5⟩4 September, in your payment.

It will give me great pleasure to carry any good news of yourself or of your good hopes for mankind to Mr Lane. I shall probably remain in England a few months. In the meantime, I will leave at home a power of attorney with Mr Hoar or some other gentleman to act for me & for Mr Lane, if anything should require it in my absence.

Yours respectfully,

R. Waldo Emerson

To Eliza Cabot Follen, Concord, August 9, 1947[71]

Concord, 9 August, 1847.

Mrs Follen.

Dear Madam,

I enclose Dr Nichol's letter again. I am very glad he means to come to us; and the Lowell Institute could not have a better organ, if he speaks as well as he writes. He little knows what a hermit I am, when he fancies that I can aid his design with the gentlemen who control these things,

---

(RWEMA) is dated August 18, 1846. In the collections at Fruitlands is a bill of sale, dated at Concord, August 17, 1846, and signed by Emerson. It reads: "Received of Joseph Palmer one dollar in full of all demands for rent, crops, stock, tools, or other claims in respect to farm of Charles Lane in Harvard, held in trust by me for Charles Lane." Emerson acting as Lane's trustee is collecting the mortgage, not fully paid off until April 6, 1852; see below letters of September 7, 1849, and October 1, 1850, and *Letters*, 3:340, 402, 462; 4:158, 287. The payments, made by Palmer's son Thomas, are recorded in Emerson's account books along with the remittances to Lane. The payment asked for here was made as requested and is recorded in the MS Account Book for 1845–1849, p. [32] under the date September 16.

71. MS in Special Collections, Butler Library; NNC; ph. in NNC; p. [4] addressed: Mrs E. L. Follen. | Brattleboro. | Vt.| ; postmarked at Concord August 9. Listed in *Letters*, 3:408, from dealer's catalogue, with the conjectured date August 6. Mrs. Follen, on August 4 (RWEMA), had sent Emerson a letter to her from John Pringle Nichol, the English astronomer; she solicits Emerson's help in getting lecture engagements for Nichol.

and whom I suppose I do not know; but I will certainly give him the
compliment of making known to Mr Lowell[72] my love of his book & how
desirable I think his public instructions would be.—I am sorry that he
thinks any reserve necessary. It would be very easy, if the programme of
the Lowell Institute be full, to procure him good offers from ⟨the⟩ two of
the Boston Societies, as, the "Mercantile Library Assoc.", and the "Boston
Lyceum", or the "Diffusion Soc.y."—[73] I could represent his claims to
their respective Directors,—and, if he has a talent for lecturing, it will be
easy for him, /besides/ to collect a large audience as a private class.—One
thing I regret—and the more for the kind confidence he so unexpectedly expresses in me,—that I am not likely to see /or hear/ him. I shall
sail for England about the 1 October, where I have promised to read
some lectures to certain "Institutes" in the Northern Counties. I shall
probably remain in England for six months. It will give me great pleasure
to aid you in Dr Nichol's affair as far as I can.

Yours respectfully,
R. W. Emerson.

To John Lowell, Concord, August ? 1847

[See above, letter to Eliza Follen, August 9, where Emerson certainly promises to
write the founder of the Lowell Institute on behalf of John Pringle Nichol.]

To Samuel Gray Ward, Concord, August 23, 1847[74]

Concord, 23 August, 1847.

My dear friend,

I am glad to have a token from you though it be only the back of a
circular which I certainly did not send you.[75] This country is practical
and as I promised aid oh surely aid to the new journal provided only I

72. Possibly Emerson wrote letters to these institutions, as well as to John Lowell, though
no such letters have been found. See *Letters*, 3:433, 434, and 436, for Emerson's meeting
with Nichol in Liverpool. See *Letters*, 2:399, and *JMN*, 7:427–429, for Emerson's familiarity
with Nichol's *Views of the Architecture of the Heavens* (New York, 1840).
73. Society for the Diffusion of Useful Knowledge.
74. MS in the Ward papers, Houghton Library, MH; ph. in NNC; p. [4] addressed:
Saml. G. Ward. | Lenox. | Mass. | ; postmarked at Concord, March 23. To his ink endorse-
ment Ward has a pencil note "going to England."
75. See *Letters*, 3:409, for the offending circular (advertizing the new magazine *The
Massachusetts Quarterly Review*) got out by Theodore Parker, whose draft for the circular gives
no indication of the use to be made of Emerson's name. Emerson from the first had rejected
an editor's role; see above, March 25 to Ward.

was no editor & had no responsibility whatever, I am suddenly greeted a week or two after like yourself with a circular on which my name stands printed, and foremost too, conductor of this blessed hope of time; now too, when in five weeks I go to England to stay all winter & probably all the spring. Sometimes I could wish it was the Adirondack mountains[76] —whose summits I have repeatedly & wishfully gazed at from Vermont —a wholesomer place, no doubt, than England, and a great deal easier to live in. Wife & children, house & farm will keep you safe prisoner in Berkshire, till, in another September, I can accept your challenge. Perhaps too, I shall find you some books in London,[77] though I have found none here. Ever Yours,

R. W. E.

To Nicholas Marie Alexandre Vattemare,
Concord, August 27, 1847[78]

Concord, 27 Aug. 1847

Alexander Vattemare, Esq.

Dear Sir,

I return your two books with my thanks. The design is a good one, and for books printed by corporations, civil or academical, seems the most natural disposition of them. The scheme will attract me more the more it promises to bring to a library here, the works of private authors in France, and vice versa:[79] Yet it seems less practicable in that point; since, though the author might gladly send his book to one city or a few cities,—any large number he could not supply; and the project, of course, contemplates the largest number of cities & states, in its league. But I look with the best hope to the future developments of this pleasing design.

The two little books of mine which I was to send you, are not quite

76. Ward had been climbing in the Adirondacks; see *Letters*, 3:414.

77. For Emerson's "commission" to secure books for Ward, see March 25 above.

78. MS in Special Collections, Butler Library, NNC; ph. in NNC; p. [4] addressed: Alexander Vattemare, Esq. Boston. Listed by Cameron, *ESQ* (4th q., 1958), 13:38.

79. A journal entry of August 24 (*JMN*, 10:156), explains part of this letter; Vattemare had conveyed to Emerson a request from the French ministry of public instruction for two books by Emerson. The note does not mention the books Emerson says he returns. In a journal of 1850 (*JMN*, 11:205), Emerson describes Vattemare as a "high historical ambassador of the learning of all nations, by day. By night, he puts off his citizen's cloak, & puts on a conjurer's harlequin cap, & as M. Alexandre, juggles & ventriloquises for his bread."

ready—new editions of both being just about ⟨ready to⟩to appear,—but they shall go to the Mayor in a few days.[80]

Yours respectfully,
R. W. Emerson.

To Calvin Farrar, Concord, September 9, 1847[81]

Concord, ⟨Aug⟩ September 9, 1847

Calvin Farrar, Esq.
Dear Sir,

My wife besets me this evening with an errand which I must not choose but perform, and bribes me with the interest the matter possesses for the family of my friend Mr Alcott.

Mrs. Emerson knows or fancies that yourself and Dr Kittredge are in search of a lady to discharge the duties of Matron to your interesting Establishment,[82] and she thinks that our neighbor & friend Mrs Alcott possesses the energy experience & economy which the office demands. On ⟨her⟩ /Mrs E's/ return home, she was gratified by Mrs Alcott's volunteering the remark ⟨a⟩in conversation, before she had spoken to her on the subject, that what she wished for herself was to be at the head of a Watercure. Mrs E described to her the institution at Waterford, & asked her if she would like to go there   Mrs Alcott said nothing would please her better   And Mrs E. who fears the intercepting of her messages if they should go in messages to our honored relative (whose authority with us is despotic)[83] and not presuming herself to address Dr K. or yourself, lays her commands upon me.—I understand, shortly, that if there is a place of this kind to be filled, Mrs Alcott is ready & willing to undertake it; and, if you desire it, will come to Waterford at any time, & spend a

---

80. *Essays, First Series* (*BAL*, 5213) and, I believe, a second printing of *Poems;* see letter to Chapman of May 31, above.
81. MS and ph. in NNC; p. [4] addressed: Calvin Farrar, Esq. | South Waterford Maine. | ; postmarked at Boston September 10.
82. Calvin Farrar of Waterford, Maine, and Edward A. Kittredge, M.D., acquired in May 1847 land adjacent to Farrar's property and set up a "Water Cure Establishment," which Mrs. Emerson had seen on her visit to Waterford August 23–30.
83. Farrar, a Bowdoin graduate, had known the brothers of Louise Weston, the disturbed poet in whom Emerson had taken an interest in 1844–1845. Farrar had thought of marriage; but Miss Weston's mental state markedly worsened in 1846 (a.l.s. Farrar to Emerson, September 1846) and he could not "think of her with a view to wed." He appears later to have presented himself to Elizabeth Hoar as a serious suitor. He was a close friend of Emerson's aunt Mary Moody Emerson, who for a time boarded in his house, and for whom he carried books and messages back and forth between Waterford and Concord.

week at the House, for conference with you.—I hope, after all this writing in obedience to the ladies, ⟨I⟩they themselves have not been betrayed into mistaking their own wishes for yours?[84]

Yours Respectfully,
R. W. Emerson

To Bryan Waller Procter, Concord, September 30, 1847[85]

Concord, Mass.
30 September, 1847.

B. W. Procter, Esq.

My dear Sir,

I am not a little gratified by the very kind expressions of your note & by the little book which I received a few days ago from the hands of Mr Fields.[86] In the expectation of being in London a little while in the course of the coming winter, the timidities of a home keeping countryman are in no small degree allayed by the assurance that he has more & better friends in England than he dared to believe.

The valued book you send me is not quite a stranger, though I had not possessed it before. I find in it some new & some very old acquaintances.[87] One piece of yours which I knew by heart,—I believe five & twenty years ago—the Pauper's Funeral, I do not find here.—As I read these, and lately some other English poems, I esteemed it the felicity of England & of every one of her writers the quiet pride with which she accepts from so many accomplished men the costly gifts of poetic power & culture as only their reasonable service. In my judgment, it is far happier to be one in a chorus of poets, than to wear the bays alone.

Your obedient servant,
R. W. Emerson.

84. Since nothing came of this scheme to provide a living for the Alcotts, it seems likely that Emerson's diagnosis here is correct.

85. Text from Emerson's MS copy or draft, Emerson papers (RWEMA), Houghton Library, MH; ph. in NNC; printed by Procter in his *Bryan Waller Procter, An Autobiography* (Boston: Roberts Brothers, 1877), pp. 294–295; listed *Letters*, 3:418.

86. Emerson is answering Procter's note of August 17 where the name of the bearer is written Field with an *s* added later.

87. In Procter's printing, this sentence reads: "I have been enlarging my knowledge of some of your living poets lately; and now again in these pages it occurred as the felicity of England and . . ."

To ALEXANDER IRELAND, CONCORD, SEPTEMBER 30, 1847[88]

Concord, 30 September, 1847

Alexander Ireland, Esq.

My dear Sir,

I have decided after a little hesitation & advising with better sailors than myself, to follow my inclination in taking passage in a ship, & not in the steamer. I have engaged a berth in the "Washington Irving," which leaves Boston for Liverpool next Tuesday, 5 October. The owners are confident, that with ordinary fortune we shall arrive in Liverpool in twenty days. But I shall not complain if the voyage should be a little longer. On my arrival in Liverpool, I will endeavour to see Mr Hogg[89] of the Institute there, and shall probably think it best to go directly to Manchester to meet yourself, & to settle with you the plan of my little campaign.—I suppose that I shall be ready to read lectures at once as soon as the proper notices can be given: or, if more time is required by the Institutes, I can go to London & make a short visit before I begin.— I know that I ought to have sent you some synopsis, long ago; but it has never been quite certain to me what I could promise as I have been endeavouring to complete some lectures not even yet quite finished.—I think I will now reserve my table of contents until I see you.—

Yours with great regard,

R. W. Emerson.

To SAMUEL GRAY WARD, CONCORD? SEPTEMBER 1847

[Since Emerson's August 23 letter, above, does not ask Ward for a contribution to *The Massachusetts Quarterly Review* and his October 3 letter implies such a request,

88. MS in the Feinberg Collection, MiD; ph. in NNC; p. [4] addressed: Alexander Ireland, Esq. | Office of *The Examiner* | Manchester | England. | Printed by Ireland, p. 79; and by Joseph B. Ames, "Some Literary Autographs," *The Critic* (Sept. 1906), 49:235; listed *Letters*, 3:418.

89. Thomas Hogg, Secretary of the Liverpool Mechanics' Institution, MS records, now in the Liverpool Record Office, Brown, Picton, and Hornby Libraries, Liverpool. The records of this institute are more nearly complete than those of other institutes, possibly because until recently the records had remained in the same building (built in 1844), the building in which Emerson gave his lectures and where I first saw the records. The MS Minute Book, 1847–1848, of Lectures, Library, etc. shows that the resolution to invite Emerson to lecture "as soon as he arrives" was passed as early as April 13, 1847. Arriving October 22, Emerson began his Liverpool lectures on November 3. On November 16, after four of his six lectures, the Institute voted to ask him to deliver another course before his departure from England. Possibly it could then be foreseen what the record of December 28 shows: that Emerson's course would pay for itself and even yield a small profit because of the number of non-members attending. According to this record the average attendance was 770. Since none of the Institute's other lecturers (in that year or any other) provided a

I infer that a letter asking for a contribution was sent to Ward in September, possibly after the meeting with Parker on September 3 (see *Letters*, 3:416 and n. 165).]

To Mary Botham Howitt, Concord, September 30, 1847

[The MS of Emerson's letter of September 30, 1847, to Mary B. Howitt is listed in James Lowe's catalogue 20, item 42. It is quoted in part and one of the two pages is reproduced in facsimile. The text is virtually the same as the revisions leave it in the draft printed by Rusk, *Letters*, 3:419–420. In the letter as sent Emerson substitutes "Miss" for "Margaret" in his allusion to Margaret Fuller. The MS confirms Rusk's n. 174 of the placement of the sentence about the obscurity of his friends.]

To Henry Hall, Concord, October 1, 1847

[Under the date October 1, 1847, Emerson's MS Account Book for 1845–1849, p. [125] has the following entry: "Mem This day sent /to/ Henry Hall Esq Rutland, Vt. by mail the original of Benajah Root's letter to the Concord Church in 1776 and agreed to leave for him with G. B. Emerson Esq the Ticonderoga letters of /Rev./ W. Emerson;—all to be safely restored to me.]" The Reverend Benajah Roots's letter of October 21, 1776, "to the Church and People of God at Concord" gives an account of the illness, death, and burial "with honors of war" of Emerson's grandfather (MS owned by RWEMA). The name is Roots; Emerson has misplaced the apostrophe. In a letter of May 27, Henry Hall of Rutland, Vermont, says that he is trying to gather "historical incidents . . . relating to this vicinity" and asks for the loan of Roots' letter. See Amelia Forbes Emerson, *Diaries and Letters of William Emerson* (Boston: Privately printed, 1972).]

To Samuel Gray Ward, Concord, October 3, 1847[90]

Concord, 3 October, 1847

My dear friend,

You gave me the best answer that could be concerning assistance to the Mass. Quarterly Review,[91] and Cabot,[92] who is editor, & Parker, who is 'The Ten', rejoice in a good hope. I suppose what is prepared for the

---

profit, the eagerness to secure another American is perhaps explained; an entry of July 24, 1848, records the rumor that Longfellow may be coming to England, and it is proposed that he be invited to lecture.

90. MS in the Ward papers, Houghton Library, MH; ph. in NNC; p. [4] addressed: Saml. G. Ward, Esq. | Lenox | Mass. | ; postmarked at Boston October 5; i.e., the date of Emerson's embarkation on the pacquet ship *Washington Irving*.

91. Ward had promised a contribution to *The Massachusetts Quarterly Review;* for the first number (December), he supplied an article on the sculptor Hiram Powers' famous "Greek Slave" (1:54–62); see *Letters*, 4:60, for Emerson's comment.

92. Elliot Cabot had taken the job Emerson, Sumner, and Parker had refused.

first Number[93] should come to Cabot by the 15 October. If you are not ready then,—as soon thereafter as can be, for the next Number. Parker & others have exerted themselves to good purpose, & the journal looks very well.

By the good help of Mr T. W. Ward,[94] Mr Abel Adams,[95] & other sufficient friends, my canoe will get launched for England, I doubt not, next Tuesday. On the whole, it is as easy as the falling of an apple from the tree. If the canoe will only float back again staunch & dry to its wharf! Meantime, I shall hope to send you some good news & to hear from you.

Yours affectionately,
R. Waldo Emerson

To James Martineau, Liverpool, October 24, 1847[96]

Waterloo Hotel
Sunday Evening

My dear Sir,

I decide to go to Manchester tomorrow morning, and I hope to find myself at London by night. I must pay for this pleasure by losing your company on Wednesday, but I mean to make myself amends in that particular on my return to Liverpool[97] at the end of the week or the beginning of the next.

With kindest remembrances to Mrs Martineau

Your friend & servant,
R. W. Emerson.

93. Emerson wrote "number" and then used the printer's mark for capitalizing the initial letter.

94. Ward's father, Thomas Wren Ward, had supplied a letter of credit, part of which was to cover the money Emerson had been collecting for Charles Lane from the sale of the Fruitlands property to Joseph Palmer (see above, August 7), and *Letters*, 3:425. Emerson's MS Account Book for 1845–1849 records under the date October 2 (pp. [124]) the payment of $450.00 to T. W. Ward "to be credited to me in a/c with Baring & Brothers, London." See also *Letters*, 3:419.

95. Abel Adams held Emerson's power of attorney and was prepared to be called upon should Mrs. Emerson get into any difficulties; see *Letters*, 3:427, 431–432.

96. MS in the Martineau papers, Manchester College, Oxford (the town not the university), ph. in NNC; the date is established by Emerson's letters to his wife of October 27, 30, and November 1 (*Letters*, 3:423 and 426). See Slater, pp. 430–431, for the Carlyle letter that lured Emerson to London on October 25. Below the signature in a shaky hand is an erased pencil note: "Mr. Emerson's writing." The note shows up clearly in the photocopy, if not in the original.

97. Emerson has written [over] in the left margin below the phrase "on my return to Liverpool" which ends his first page.

To William Henry Furness? Liverpool, November 4, 1847[98]

Liverpool, 4 Nov. 1847.

My dear friend,

I find Dr Nichol here among excellent friends who highly love and honour him—now just embarking for Boston, and as he means to be at Philadelphia I wish that you & all good men who have long since learned to value him by his Architecture of the Heavens, should not fail to see & know him. Dr. Nichol has the design of reading lectures at Boston, & you will think of what is necessary to give your "Mercantile Library" an opportunity of hearing him. Did I or did I not write the letter that was in my heart at parting, of thanks & love for your kind farewell?

Yours affectionately,
R. Waldo Emerson.

To James William Hudson, Manchester, November 5, 1847[99]

Manchester
5 November, 1847.

J. W. Hudson, Esq.
Dear Sir,

I received yesterday just before leaving Liverpool your letter of 3d instant, and I suppose I shall not receive the further details you promise me until tomorrow P.m. when I shall find news from you at the Waterloo Hotel.[100] I only write now to say, that I will talk over the whole series of engagements you now offer me with Mr Ireland, and, I doubt not, that with his eyes I shall quickly be able to see ⟨which⟩ what is the most judicious order in which to arrange so many opportunities of speech as your friendly care has provided for me. I shall, of course, respect the prior claims of the Institutes you name in Sheffield & elsewhere.

In Liverpool, I shall now have lodgings at 56 Stafford Street, Isling-

---

98. Ms in the Southern Historical Collection, NcU; ph. in NNC. Of the two Philadelphians Emerson might address as "friend," William Henry Furness is more likely than Samuel Bradford. Furness' letter of September 19, 1847 (*Records.* pp. [65]–66), is clearly a bon voyage note. Furness tells Emerson of a wish "to write a line" to him before he goes "across the water" and to offer him "the hearty good wishes of a friend"; it concludes with the hope of hearing of Emerson's "doings in the old country" and sends a message for Carlyle. The body of the letter expresses warm admiration for Emerson's writing and recalls affectionately their school days.

99. MS in Alderman Library, ViU; ph. in NNC.

100. Hudson's letter of the 3rd does not survive; see *JMN*, 10:437–441, for Emerson's final schedule. Hudson did not arrange for the London lectures.

ton. and in Manchester, at ⟨2⟩Mrs Massey's, 2 Fenny Place, /P/ /Peru St,/ Higher Broughton: [101] yet here, <u>Mr Ireland</u> will certainly be a surer address.

Respectfully, your

obedient servant,

R. W. Emerson

To RICHARD DAVIS WEBB, MANCHESTER, NOVEMBER 5, 1847 [102]

Manchester

Nov. 5 1847

Richard D. Webb, Esq.

Dear Sir,

I have just received in a letter from my wife in Massachusetts your very kind note to me dated 16 September. I thank you heartily for the frank & generous welcome you send me from so far, Your name was indeed well known to me, [103] but I could not have anticipated this personal kindness. I dare not say, at present, whether it is even probable that I shall visit Dublin; it would be a great privilege; but I find it not easy to combine all the objects I have first proposed to myself. But if I shall succeed in going into Ireland, I shall not fail to pay my respects to you personally for that large benevolence, which, in embracing so many, has reached also to your sincerely obliged servant,

R. W. Emerson

To HARRIET MARTINEAU, MANCHESTER, NOVEMBER 11? 1847

[On November 10 Thomas Hogg of Liverpool enclosed to Emerson the calling card of Harriet Martineau's brother-in-law with the message that the gentleman lives near the Institute and would like to have Emerson call on him any afternoon for tea at six. In a letter of November 13 Harriet Martineau writes that she is glad that her poor mother has met Emerson and that he knows something of her "beloved sister Ellen Higginson." She understands that Emerson is very busy and

101. Emerson started to insert "Peru St." in the margin, but a blot obliged him to add it above the line. See *Letters*, 4:435, where Emerson has "Post Office Street."

102. MS in Trinity College Library, University of Dublin; ph. in NNC.

103. Emerson is answering Webb's letter of September 16, 1847 (RWEMA), which offers the hospitality of his house (176 Great Brunswick St., Dublin). He hopes that Emerson will be "calling in to see poor Ireland by the way." And he adds: "I am not aware that you have been invited to Ireland nor do I think it likely in our distracted condition." (He refers to the potatoe famine.) He assures Emerson that he will not be "bored with abolitionism or any other ism . . ." The Quaker printer Webb was well-known to American abolitionists. See Walter Merrill's biography of Garrison, *Against Wind and Tide* (Cambridge: Harvard University Press, 1963), p. 173 and passim. Webb was active also in other reform movements.

cannot now tell her when he can come to visit her in Ambleside. She had written him on the 5th inviting him to visit. Emerson has apparently availed himself of the invitation to tea. Emerson had been in Liverpool on the 10th, returning to Manchester the morning of the 11th.]

To Abel Adams, Manchester, November 17, 1847

[In a letter of January 14, 1848 (RWEMA), Abel Adams acknowledges three letters from Emerson and gives the dates. The first is of November 3, 1847; see *Letters*, 3:430–431. The second is perhaps the apparently incomplete letter printed by Rusk, *Letters*, 3:431–432, with the conjectured date of November 3 and conjectured to be an enclosure with the first letter. It is clear from Emerson's letter to his wife begun on November 13 and completed on the 18th that the expected S.S. *Cambria* was to make its return trip on the 18th; see *Letters*, 3:439.]

To John Nayler, Manchester? November 18? 1847

[In a letter of November 17, 1847 (Emerson papers, RWEMA) John Nayler, newly elected secretary of the Leeds Mechanics' Institution, asked Emerson if he would be in the neighborhood of Leeds on December 1 when the Institution planned to hold their annual soirée. At their meeting on the 16th, the members had voted to invite Emerson and to pay his expenses. The vote instructed Nayler to write (MS Minutes of the Institution for 1847, p. 349). There is no evidence that Emerson attended; on December 1, he was to lecture in Preston. The letter, however, calls for a reply.]

To Joseph Boult, Manchester? November 23? 1847

[Emerson must have written to Joseph Boult, Honorary Secretary of the Roscoe Club, Liverpool, on or near November 23, 1847. In a letter of November 24, Roscoe accepts the arrangement Emerson has proposed. On November 30, Emerson gave a "Reading" for the Essay and Discussion Society of the Club for which he received £5,5s (*JMN*, 10:438, 411).]

To Thomas Elford Poynting, Manchester, November 23, 1847

[In the Sotheby Parke-Bernet Catalogue of Autograph Letters . . . February 20 and 21, 1978, four letters by Emerson to the Reverend T. E. Poynting of Eccles are listed. The first (item 401) is of November 23, n. y., dated from Higher Broughton, Manchester, 2 Fenny "Place." It is certainly of 1847 and is a reply to Poynting's letter of November 21, 1847 (RWEMA); Poynting gives his address as Monton Parsonage, near Eccles. In his letter, Poynting describes himself as an unknown admirer; he invites Emerson to "honour our homestead" by coming to visit. Thomas Elford Poynting is listed in Frederick Boase' *Modern English Biography* (vol. 6, supplement to vol. 3) as the pastor of Monton Chapel, Eccles. He is the author of two sermons with titles that suggest that he might well have been an admirer of Emerson; they are *God in Nature* and *Glimpses of the Heaven that Lies*

About Us. Emerson's letter says that he hopes to accept the invitation but is now trying to settle lecture engagements in Ireland through a friend. William Allingham of Donegal could not arrange the lectures.]

To Harriet Martineau, Manchester, November 24, 1847[104]

Manchester, 24 November

My dear friend,[105]

You are bent, as ever since I knew you, on being a benefactor to me: and now I have two notes from you unanswered on my table, one reaffirming your hospitable commands from your own roof, & now the one accompanying Mrs Turner's invitation to Nottingham. I believe I shall only have need of your name as a spell to open all doors & all hearts with. I have used it already at two houses at Liverpool, & it is likely to have equal potency elsewhere. I have written just now to this kindest Mrs Turner, to say that I am promised at least to two friends at Nottingham;[106] but I shall certainly call upon her; though that seems a great risk, after she has created for me such a grand reputation in her house. I do not yet know when I am to go thither; much less, when I am to have the day of seeing & thanking you.

R. W. Emerson.

To Henry U. Ward, Manchester, November 24, 1847[107]

Manchester
24 November

Dear Sir,

I have to acknowledge the receipt of your note of the 17th instant.

Respectfully
R. W. Emerson.

Henry U. Ward, Esq.

104. MS in the Barrett Collection, Alderman Library, ViU; ph. in NNC. The date and the addresses are established by Emerson's letter of the same day to Catharine Turner and by Miss Martineau's letter to Emerson of November 20, 1847 (RWEMA). An annotation on p. [4] of the MS erroneously suggests William Allingham as the addressee. See *Letters,* 3:440–441 and n. 237.

105. Emerson met Harriet Martineau on his first visit to England in 1833 (*Letters,* 1:393); the acquaintance was renewed during her 1835–1836 visit to America (*Letters,* 2:24 and n. 70; *JMN,* 5:86). For Miss Martineau as the agent of Emerson's acquaintance with Margaret Fuller, see *Letters,* 2:32, n. 90. Now in 1847 Emerson says of her she "pursues me with kind letters & introductions of friends" (*Letters,* 3:444).

106. M. Attenburrow and Joseph Neuberg; *Letters,* 3:445, 446 and n. 259.

107. MS in Special Collections, Butler Library, NNC; ph. in NNC; unaddressed single sheet. Ward's note of November 17, 1847 (RWEMA), asks for an autograph.

To WILLIAM BELL SCOTT, MANCHESTER, NOVEMBER 29, 1847 [108]

2 Fenny Street, Higher Broughton
Manchester, Nov. 29, 1847.

William B. Scott, Esq. [109]

Dear Sir,

I received on Saturday your book with the kind note accompanying it. I certainly did not "read the poem through at one sitting" but I found that it concerned me very much, & there is good prospect of its continuing to do so. I have read in it a good deal yesterday with high pleasure, but I have not finished it; and yet have no tidings to send you beyond this acknowledgment. I must add however that it was a great satisfaction to find the Bhagavat Geeta, which I unwilling left in my library at Concord, here fairly & wonderfully understood in England.

But I will give you at another hour some account of my speed with the poem.

Respectfully & thankfully yours,
R. W. Emerson.

To HENRY DAVID THOREAU, MANCHESTER, DECEMBER 2, 1847 [110]

Manchester, 2 Dec. 1847.

Dear Henry,

Very welcome in the parcel was your letter, very precious your thoughts & tidings. [111] It is one of the best things connected with my coming hither that you could & would keep the homestead, that fireplace shines all the brighter,—and has a certain permanent glimmer therefor. Thanks, evermore thanks for the kindness which I well discern to the youth of the

108. MS in the Brotherton Collection, University of Leeds; ph. in NNC; printed in *Autobiographical Notices of the Life of William Bell Scott*, ed. W. Minto, New York: Harper, 1892, 1:240.

109. The addressee was the master of the government school of design at Newcastle-upon-Tyne and the brother of the painter David Scott who did a portrait of Emerson. On November 23, William Bell Scott wrote that he was presenting to Emerson his book *The Year of the World: A Philosophical Poem* (London, 1846); see Eli, p. 244, where the date is incorrectly given as 1864. A portion of the half-title has been cut away; there may have been a presentation inscription, but Emerson was not in the habit of vandalizing his books as Alcott was.

110. Ms in the Berg Collection, NN; ph. in NNC; p. [4] addressed: Henry D. Thoreau | Concord | Mass. | ; postmarked at Liverpool December 14 and at Boston December 25; above the address on the left is "P Hibernia S." Printed by Sanborn, *AM* (June 1892), 69:741–742; Harding and Bode, pp. 194–195; listed *Letters*, 3:445.

111. Thoreau's letter of November 14; Harding and Bode, pp. 188–192.

house, to my darling little horseman of pewter, leather, wooden, rocking & what other breeds, destined,[112] I hope, to ride Pegasus yet, and I hope not destined to be thrown, to Edith who long ago drew from you verses which I carefully preserve,[113] & to Ellen who by speech & now by letter I find old enough to be companionable, & to choose & reward her own friends in her own fashions. She sends me a poem today,[114] which I have read three times!—I believe, I must keep back all my communication on English topics until I get to London which is England. Everything centralizes, in this magnificent machine which England is. Manufacturer for the world she is become or becoming one complete tool or engine in herself—Yesterday the time all over the kingdom was reduced to Greenwich time. At Liverpool, where I was, the clocks were put forward 12 minutes. This had become quite necessary on account of the railroads which bind the whole country into swiftest connexion, and require so much accurate interlocking, intersection, & simultaneous arrival, that the difference of time produced confusion. Every man in England carries a little book in his pocket called "Bradshaws Guide",[115] which contains time tables of every ⟨d⟩arrival & departure at every station on all the railroads of the kingdom. It is published anew on the first day of every month & costs sixpence. The proceeding effects of Electric telegraph will give a new importance to such arrangements.—But lest I should not say what is needful, I will postpone England once for all,—and say that I am not of opinion that your book shoul[d] be delayed a month.[116] I should print it at [on]ce, nor do I think that you would incur any risk in doing so that you cannot well afford. It is very certain to have readers & debtors here as well as there. The Dial is absurdly well known here. We at home, I think, are always a little ashamed of it,—I am,—and yet here it is spoken of with the utmost gravity, & I do not laugh. Carlyle writes me that he is reading Domesday Book.—[117] You tell me in your letter one odious circumstance, which we will dismiss from remembrance henceforward.[118]

112. Edward Waldo Emerson; Thoreau had suggested that the boy would like "wooden or pewter horses."

113. *Collected Poems*, ed. Bode, p. 397, from Emerson's copy (RWEMA).

114. See *Letters*, 3:444, and 4:7.

115. In November, commuting between Manchester and Liverpool, Emerson must have become well acquainted with Bradshaw.

116. *Week on the Concord and Merrimack Rivers*, for which both Emerson and Thoreau had vainly attempted to find a publisher.

117. See Slater, p. 435; Emerson's MS clearly reads "Domesday" here not "Doomsday," as Harding and Bode have it.

118. Thoreau's account of Miss Ford's (Foord) unwelcome proposal of marriage and his rejection of it; Harding and Bode, pp. 190–191.

Charles Lane entreated me, in London, to ask you to forward his Dials to him, which must be done, i⟨n⟩f you consent, thus. Three bound vols are among his books in my library The 4th Vol is in unbound numbers at J Munroe & Co's shop received there in a parcel to my address a day or two before I sailed & which I forgot to carry to Concord It must be claimed without delay It is certainly there, was opened by me, & left. And they can enclose all 4 vols. to Chapman for me.— [119] Well I am glad the Pleasaunce at Walden suffered no more but it is a great loss as it is which years will not repair.— [120] I see that I have baulked you by the promise of a letter which ends in as good as none   But I write with counted minutes & a miscellany of things before me. Yours affectionately,

R. W. E.

To Arthur Hugh Clough, Manchester, December 3, 1847 [121]

2 Fenny Street
Higher Broughton.
Manchester, 3 Decr

Dear Sir,

Your kind note, after some delay, reached me, through Mr Bulley, when I was in Liverpool. I am very heartily obliged by your courtesy. There are few objects in England so attractive to me as Oxford, which you so frankly open to me. I shall esteem it a high privilege to claim the opportunity of seeing the Colleges, which you offer me, as soon as I find myself in your neighbourhood. I fear, it will not be until after the vacation.

Mr Bulley prepared for me a new interest in your name, by reading

119. John Chapman.
120. Thoreau had reported the burning of woods to the southeast of Emerson's Walden property where Thoreau's cabin was built; the fire was one of many ignited by sparks from the railroad.
121. MS in the Clough papers, Bodleian Library, Oxford; ph. in NNC. Printed in the *Emerson-Clough Letters,* ed. Ralph L. Rusk and Howard Lowry (Cleveland: Rowfant Club, 1934), No. 2; reprinted by Frederick L. Mulhauser, *The Correspondence of Arthur Hugh Clough* (Oxford: Clarendon Press, 1957), 1:186; listed *Letters,* 3:446. Samuel Bulley had sent Clough's letter of November 26 to Emerson with a covering letter dated November 30, 1843 (RWEMA). Emerson had met Clough's sister at Bulley's. Clough makes the meeting serve as an introduction to Emerson whom he invites to visit him at Oxford (*Emerson-Clough Letters,* no. 1, Mulhauser, 1:186–187), where there are young men who would welcome him.

to me extracts from a pamphlet published in Oxford, to which I paid honour.[122]

With thanks,

Yours respectfully,

R. W. Emerson.

To Abel Adams, Manchester, December 3, 1847

[In his letter of January 14, 1848, Abel Adams lists a letter of December 3, 1847, as the third of three letters he has received. Rusk, *Letters*, 3:441, lists a conjectured letter of November 25, citing a notebook entry of that date reading: "To Baring & Brothers for A Adams 70..0.0" (*JMN*, 10:413). Since there had been a mailboat on the 18th of November, there would not be another until December 3.]

To William Ellery Channing, Manchester, December 9? 1847

[In a letter dated only January 1848, but postmarked at Manchester January 31, 1848 (RWEMA), Elizabeth Hoar tells Emerson that Ellery Channing has brought her Emerson's letter to him. In his letter of December 5, Emerson tells Margaret Fuller (*Letters*, 3:447), that he has heard from Channing "this week." Emerson's reply had to have been written in December, but for which steamer there is no way of knowing. He wrote his daughter Edith on the 9th, his wife on the 16th (for a steamer of the 18th), and his wife, Sarah Bradford Ripley, and his brother, on the 26th (*Letters*, 3:448–458). The last of these dates is the least likely. I choose the earliest date for no better reason than that Miss Hoar's letter is about events of December (e.g., the marriage of Caroline Sturgis and William Tappan, December 12).

There were other letters to Channing, in 1848, of which I find no trace; Mrs. Emerson in an undated letter of early May 1848 (RWEMA) describes Channing as being "quite jocose" about Emerson's "apologetic letters to him." In a letter of February 1848 (Houghton Library) Channing tells Mrs. Emerson that he is writing Emerson a letter to go by the steamer of the 26th.]

---

122. Clough's *A Consideration of Objections against the Retrenchment Association* (Oxford: Francis Macpherson, 1847). Bulley had read from the pamphlet on November 20 after Emerson's last Liverpool lecture. The Retrenchment Association at Oxford had proposed cutting their expenditures for food and drink in sympathy with the victims of the potatoe famine in Ireland.

To EDWARD TRUELOVE? MANCHESTER, DECEMBER 15, 1847[123]

> 2 Fenny Street Higher Broughton
> Manchester, 15 December.

Sir,

I am sorry that I cannot give you any precise answer to your inquiry concerning my lectures, in which you express an interest so complimentary. It is certainly my meaning to go to London after a few weeks,— perhaps six or eight weeks,—and, when there, I may venture to accept propositions to read a short Course. Hitherto, I have declined, or rather postponed, the friendly overtures from that quarter.

> Respectfully,
> R. W. Emerson.

To JOHN HARLAND, MANCHESTER, DECEMBER 15, 1847[124]

> 2 Fenny Street, Higher
> Broughton, 15 Decr

Dear Sir,

I return the Heimskringla with special thanks for so excellent a book. I shall procure it in London, &[125] send it home to some good friends,[126] who, I know, will value it as I do. I fear, I have trespassed on your bounty in detaining the volumes so long. I had the best will to return it, a week ago; but it chanced that I left town in great haste, being belated, & was forced to leave the books on my table.

> With renewed thanks,
> Yours respectfully,
> R. W. Emerson.

123. MS in the Feinberg Collection, MiD; ph. in NNC; printed by White, *AL* (May 1961), 33:161–162. Emerson received several invitations from London to lecture there; it is impossible to determine with certainty to which request this is a reply; however, a letter of December 10 from Edward Truelove is closest in date (RWEMA). He is the secretary of the Literary and Scientific Institution with its address John Street, Fitzroy Square. There is no record of Emerson's lecturing there.

124. MS in the John Harland Autograph Collection, Manchester Central Reference Library. Copy in NNC. The date is secured by the Manchester address and Harland's letter, from the office of the *Manchester Guardian*, to Emerson of November 23, 1847 (RWEMA). Harland sent Emerson, Samuel Laing's translation of Snorri Sturluson's *Heimskringla* with the hope that "Carlyle or yourself might make it the subject of one or more suggestive lectures or essays."

125. Emerson bought the book in London in March 1848 (*JMN*, 10:207); listed by Harding, pp. 252–253. The receipt for the purchase of the book is laid in MS Ledger for 1849–1872 (pp. 82–83); it is dated March 21, 1848; the charge was £1.6.0. He read from it in his 1869 series of "Readings" (*Letters*, 6:52, n. 2; 61–62, and nn. 40 and 41).

126. One friend was Caroline Sturgis Tappan; see below May 4, 1855, and *JMN*, 11:224.

To WILLIAM MATHEWS, MANCHESTER, DECEMBER 15? 1847

[In *ABPC*, 1985, a letter of 1847 to Mathews is described as thanking him for an invitation. See *Letters*, 3:451 and 455 for Emerson's visit to Birmingham and for Mathews "hospitably entertaining him and promising a letter of introduction to Brunel." Apparently Sir Marc Isambard Brunel, Emerson identifying him as the builder of the Thames Tunnel. See below, March 25, 1848, for William Mathews and index for later correspondence.]

To MARY CARPENTER? MANCHESTER, ENGLAND, DECEMBER 15, 1847

[A letter of December 15, 1847, is listed in Parke-Bernet's catalogue of December 1, 1948; listed also by Cameron in *ESQ* (3d Q., 1956), 3:6, and again by Harding in (4th q., 1958), 13:39, quoting from *The Collector*, April 1948, p. 87, item M696; dated from Higher Broughton, Manchester, December 15, n.y.: ". . . I dare not yet say when I am likely to have the many privileges you so freely offer me at Bristol, perhaps not until I go to London, where I mean to be after a few weeks." See below July 3, 1848, for Mary Carpenter who is the likely addressee.]

To THOMAS ELFORD POYNTING, LEICESTER, DECEMBER 21, 1847

[Item 402 in the Sotheby Parke-Bernet catalogue cited above (November 23) is a letter to T. E. Poynting, December 21, in which Emerson asks if he may visit on Christmas Day. Listed also (item 328) in Robert T. Batchelder's Catalogue 24, where it is described as dated from Leicester and expressing regrets that he has been prevented from accepting Poynting's invitation "which gave me so much pleasure"; he proposes to "come out and spend an hour or two." List A of Priscilla Juvelis quotes another sentence from this letter: "I believe I have had no day in Manchester when even so short a visit could be securely announced & made." Poynting's reply of December 24 (RWEMA) says "Nothing would be more delightful to us" and provides train schedules.]

To GEORGE CRAWSHAY, MANCHESTER DECEMBER 24, 1847[127]

> 2, Fenny Street, Higher Broughton,
> Manchester, December 24, 1847.

Dear Sir,

Your kind note was received last night, and awakens the warmest interest. It is not yet quite certain that I am to lecture at Newcastle, but on such a showing as yours I see not how I can avoid going thither. I believe I must frankly accept your invitation, and make you a short visit,

---

127. No MS has been found; text from the *Newcastle Monthly Chronicle*, November 1889, p. 495; Emerson's Manchester address is misprinted as "Ferry" Street, here corrected; he probably used ampersands where the text has "ands."

whether I go to the Institute or not.[128] Will you let me keep this good hope before me? and when I see the opportunity of realizing it, I will write to you.

Yours respectfully,

R. W. Emerson

TO THOMAS ELFORD POYNTING, MANCHESTER, DECEMBER? 24? 1847?

[Item 404 in the Sotheby Parke-Bernet catalogue cited above (November 23) is a letter dated from Manchester "Friday" to the Reverend T. E. Poynting putting off his "promised visit owing to the arrival of two friends whom he cannot reject." The same letter described as accompanied by addressed envelope is listed in the J. F. F. Autographs, Inc., catalogue 1582, item 126. It is quoted in part: "Accept my regrets . . . two friends whom I cannot reject have volunteered to come and dine with me in my lovely lodgings and at such an hour I fear will preclude any hope of a visit. . . . As you have given me to[o] long a grace you must still extend it a little and as how [soon?] as I can fix a new hour . . . do not expect me tomorrow and do not cease to expect me. . . ." I believe this letter to have been written on Friday, December 24, 1847; see *Letters*, 3:454, where Emerson, in a letter of December 25, tells his wife that Alexander Ireland and John Cameron are coming to dine with him. See January 2, 1848, below, where Emerson expresses his regret at not having been able to visit Poynting on Christmas Day.]

128. Crawshay provided for the *Chronicle* a note of Emerson's stay with him at his home on Westgate St. describing Emerson as a "delightful inmate" and indicating that they found common ground in their interest in Fourierism: "He induced me to get the 'Bhagavad-Gita,' . . . and predicted to me a great infusion of Oriental thought into English thought. The grounds of his prediction, which has come true, were that in this respect there was a vacuum in England that would necessarily be filled up." See also *Letters*, 4:16, and n. 53; above, November 29. A manuscript copy (not in Crawshay's hand) of Crawshay's introductory remarks here is in the Ireland papers, Manchester Central Reference Library.

1848

To Thomas Elford Poynting, Manchester, January 2, 1848

[Lot 403 in the Sotheby Parke-Bernet catalogue cited above (November 23, 1847) is a letter to Thomas Elford Poynting of January 2, 1848, regretting that he could not visit Poynting on Christmas Day (see December 21 and 24, 1847, above). This letter is quoted: "Since . . . I have been down to Worcester, seeing and hearing many things. Now that I am home again here it is but for a day as I have to go into Yorkshire tomorrow morning to spin again among the Lecture rooms. I would willingly escape from this tedious task, but am holden by supposed engagements . . ." Listed also as item 5 in Robert T. Batchelder's Catalogue 29 with the same quotation.]

To Charles Bray? Rawdon, January 4, 1848

[In *The Flying Quill*, Winter 1982, p. 4, Goodspeed's lists a letter dated "at Mr Forster's, Rawdon near Leeds, 4 January." The letter acknowledges an invitation to visit Coventry. Emerson says he will come if he can, but "I dare not say that I will bring any lectures." The year has to be 1848; on his Yorkshire lecture tour, he visited Carlyle's young friend William Edward Forster at Rawdon on January 4. The addressee is, I believe, Charles Bray who entertained Emerson in Coventry July 11, where he met George Eliot (see *Letters*, 4:98 and n. 352).]

To William? Fisher, Jr., Leeds, January 7, 1848[1]

Leeds, 7 January.

Dear Sir

I am much obliged to you for the renewed invitations you kindly send me and promise myself the pleasure of seeing you on Monday p.m.

1. MS in the Barrett Collection, Alderman Library, ViU; ph. in NNC. The Leeds address makes the year 1848 certain. In a letter from Sheffield of January 3 (RWEMA), W. Fisher, Jr., asks Emerson to let him know the day of his arrival and his train. If he should not be recognized by whoever comes to meet him, he is to take a cab to Fisher's house. See *Letters*, 4:3, 4, for evidence that Emerson stayed with Fisher on his visit to Sheffield. This letter is certainly a reply to Fisher's note of the 3rd. Fisher is possibly the son of the William Fisher elected in 1843 as a Councillor for the Borough. See Alfred Gatty, *Hallamshire. The History . . . of the Parish of Sheffield . . .* (London: 1869), p. 203.

about 4 o'clock as I notice that the train which leaves Manchester at 1.30 arrives at Sheffield at 3.39. In the good hope of seeing you so soon, I am

Yours respectfully,

R. W. Emerson

To ———, MANCHESTER, JANUARY ? 1848

[See entry, below, for January 15, where an earlier note to the same correspondent is mentioned.]

To ELIZABETH DAVIS BANCROFT, MANCHESTER? JANUARY 15? 1848

[In her letter of January 10, 1848 (RWEMA), Mrs. George Bancroft asks Emerson a number of questions and reports that Monckton Milnes wants to know where he is. She asks Emerson to write her in reply. He would certainly have answered this letter from his wife's old friend. His itinerary was such that I think the 15th would be his first opportunity to write. Milnes meanwhile had got his Manchester address from Carlyle and had written Emerson on the 15th (a.l.s., RWEMA).

George Bancroft, in Paris, has met Victor Cousin who is eager to know something about the American named Henry who had translated his work and about the Tappan who had written a "masterly" reply to Jonathan Edwards on Freedom of the Will. Caleb Sprague Henry is the translator. Henry Philip Tappan published, in 1839, *A Review of Edwards's "Inquiry into the Freedom of the Will."*

Emerson apparently knew Henry; See *Letters,* 1:341; *JMN,* 3:205, 316, and I think that the "Mr Henry" in *JMN,* 13:81, is the same "Mr. Henry" in Emerson's letter to his brother. Rusk does not risk an identification; the editors of *JMN,* vol. 3, do. There is no evidence that Emerson knew Tappan, the more distinguished of the two, until 1850 when Tappan's New York address appears in his journal (*JMN,* 11:243). He may have met him earlier if Mrs. Bancroft is right in thinking that she had met him at George Ripley's "in the good old days in Boston." There is no solid evidence that Emerson ever read Edwards' *Inquiry,* though his father owned it and his Aunt Mary read it more than once.

[Tappan, but not Henry, was elected "correspondant de l'Académie des Sciences morales et politiques (section de Philosophies)" February 2, 1856 (Le Comte de Franquerille, *Le Premier Siècle de l'Institut de France* . . . Paris, 1895, 2:249). Cousin had inquired about the two men with the intent to propose them as *correspondants.*]

To ———, MANCHESTER, JANUARY 15, 1848

[A letter of January 15, n.y. (Altman's, 1977), written from the Fenny Street address in Manchester says that an engagement for the 19th is now fixed so that he will be away from Manchester for a week. Emerson refers to an earlier note and says he still intends to visit his correspondent. The note reads as if the addressee lived in Manchester. The addresses of both William Staley and Francis

Espinasse are recorded in his notebooks (*JMN*, 10:126, 129, 284). The engagement for the 19th was in Beverley (*JMN*, 10:440).]

To Richard Monckton Milnes, Manchester, January ? 1848

[I think it likely that there was at least one letter to Milnes in January 1848. On the fifteenth (RWEMA) Milnes wrote of his hope that Emerson could visit him in Bawtry before February 13 when he would have to be in London for the meeting of Parliament. Milnes wrote again on the 20th (RWEMA), telling Emerson exactly how to get to Bawtry, writing "If you are able to come." That Milnes underlines "are" suggests that Emerson had written in doubtful hope of accepting the invitation.]

To James William Hudson, Manchester, January 26? 1848

[James W. Hudson's letter of January 24, 1848 (RWEMA), invites Emerson to dine with him *en famille* on February 14; his letter of January 31 thanks Emerson for accepting the invitation (a. 11. s., RWEMA). Hudson was now living in Glasgow.]

To Henry David Thoreau, Manchester, January 28, 1848[2]

2 Fenny Street; Higher Broughton;
Manchester; 28 January 1848

Dear Henry,

One roll of letters has gone today to Concord & to New York,[3] and perhaps I shall still have time to get this into the leathern bag, before it is carted to the wharf. I have to thank you for your letter which was a true refreshment. Let who or what pass, there stands the dear Henry,—if indeed any body had a right to call him so,—erect, serene, & undeceivable. So let it ever be! I should quite subside into idolatry of some of my friends, if I were not every now & then apprised that the world is wiser than any one of its boys, & penetrates us with its sense, to the disparagement of the subtleties of private gentlemen. Last night, as I believe I have already told Lidian, I heard the best man in England make perhaps his best speech. Cobden, who is the cor cordis, the object of honor &

2. MS in the Berg Collection, NN; ph. in NNC; p. [4] addressed: Henry D. Thoreau | Concord. | Massachusetts. | ; to the left of the last line: By steamer | from Liverpool | ; postmarked at Manchester January 28. The Huntington Library has a copy in Sophia Thoreau's hand of the first four sentences of this letter. Printed by Sanborn, *AM* (June 1892), 69:745–746, and in Harding and Bode, pp. 205–206; listed *Letters*, 4:13. Substantive errors are noted below.
3. Emerson refers to letters to his wife, mother, and brother; see *Letters*, 4:5–13.

belief to risen & rising England.[4] a man of great discretion, who never overstates, nor states prematurely, nor has a particle of unnecessary genius or hope to mislead him, no wasted strength, but calm, sure of his fact, simple, & nervous in stating it, as a boy in laying down the rules of the game of football which have been violated—above all educated by his dogma of Free Trade, led on by it to new lights & correlative liberalities, as our abolitionists have been by their principle to so many Reforms. Then this man has made no mistake he has dedicated himself to his work of convincing this kingdom of the impolicy of Corn Laws, lectured in every town where they would hear him, & at last carried his point against immense odds, & yet has never accepted any compromise or stipulation from the government. He might have been in the ministry. He will never go there, except with absolute empire for his principle, which cannot yet be conceded. He had neglected & abandoned his prosperous calico-printing to his partners. And the triumphant League have subscribed between 60 & 80 000 pounds, as the Cobden Fund; whereby he is made independent.—It was quite beautiful, even sublime, last night, to notice the moral radiations which this Free Trade dogma seemed to throw out, all unlooked-for, to the great audience, who instantly & delightedly adopted them. Such contrasts of sentiment to the vulgar hatred & fear of France & jealousy of America, that pervades the newspapers.[5] Cobden himself looked thoughtful & surprised, as if he saw a new Future. Old Col. Peyronnet[6] Thompson, the Father of Free Trade, whose catechism on the Corn Laws set all these Brights[7] & Cobdens first on cracking this nut, was present, & spoke in a very vigorous rasp-like tone. Gibson,[8] a member of the /Brit./ government, a great Suffolk Squire, & a convert to these opinions, made a very satisfactory speech and our old Abolition Friend, George Thompson,[9] brought up the rear; though he, whom I now heard for the first time, is merely a piece of rhetoric & not a man of

4. Emerson attended the Free Trade Banquet on January 27; the fragment so dated and conjectured by Rusk to be part of a letter to Lidian (*Letters*, 4:10) must have contained his account of Richard Cobden's speech. The League Emerson refers to is the Anti-Corn-Law League. Lord John Russell had asked Cobden to join his cabinet. The sum raised for Cobden was £80,000. In the MS *cor cordis* is underlined, but in a different ink, possibly by Sanborn.

5. Emerson clearly writes "pervades" not "pervaded" (Harding and Bode, p. 206).

6. Harding and Bode, p. 206, print "Perronnet," but the MS plainly reads "Peyronnet" for the name of Thomas Perronet Thompson, author of *Catechism on the Corn Laws* (1827).

7. John Bright was also a speaker on this occasion; see *Letters*, 4:12.

8. Thomas Milner Gibson, vice-president of the Board of Trade under Lord Russell.

9. Thoreau had met Thompson in 1842 (*JMN*, 8:265). See Rusk, *Life*, pp. 227–228, for Thompson's visit to Emerson in 1835 under the aegis of Mary Moody Emerson. See *JMN*, 8:90, 91, for Emerson's estimate of Thompson, an estimate he sees no reason now to change. This letter confirms the fact that Emerson did not hear Thompson when he was in America

facts & figures & English solidity, like the rest. The audience play no
inactive part, but the most acute & sympathizing; and the agreeable
result was the demonstration of the arithmetical as well as the moral
optimism of peace & generosity. Forgive, forgive this most impertinent
scribble.[10] Your friend,

R. W. E.

I surely did not mean to put you off with a Report when I begun.[11]
But———

To Henry Sutton, Manchester, January 31, 1848[12]

2 Fenny-street, Higher Broughton
Manchester, 31 January.

My dear Sir,

I hear with pleasure that through some—I hardly know whose—
agency, you are to come hither next Saturday.[13] Dr Hodgson[13] is to
administer to our friend Mr Neuberg;[14] I pray you to esteem yourself
my guest, and come directly to the above-written address. I hoped that
Mrs Massey,[15] my landlady, would be able to give you a bedroom: she

in 1834–1835. Thompson lectured on slavery in Concord on January 27, 1835; his speeches
receiving comment in both the *Yeoman's Gazette* and the more sympathetic *Concord Freeman*.
His speeches were given for the newly founded Middlesex Anti-Slavery Association on the
day of its first annual meeting. Thompson would subsequently address the Concord Lyceum,
January 15, 1851, on "British Politics." And see below, November 14, 1850, for the possibility
that in that month and year he spoke to the Middlesex Anti-Slavery Association again.

10. Emerson clearly writes "impertinent," not "impertient," Harding and Bode, p. 206.

11. The postscript reads "surely" not "really" and "begun" not "began," Harding and
Bode, p. 206. Printing Thoreau's reply of February 23, Harding and Bode are undisturbed
by the discrepancy between Thoreau's reference to his Concord Lyceum lecture "last week"
and the date they supply from Alcott (pp. 208, 209). The date of the lecture has to be
February 16, not January 26. Unfortunately, for this season the MS records of the Concord
Lyceum (MCo) were carelessly kept; the secretary lists only the names of the lecturers,
Thoreau's name appearing last. In the cash books of the Lyceum, Thoreau's name does not
appear at all, but the payments recorded and dated for the other lectures given in that
season leave February 16 as the only possible date for Thoreau's lecture. Elizabeth Hoar,
writing Emerson on February 23 (?25) (RWEMA), reports that she has heard that it was a
good lecture. There is no evidence that it was given twice or that Thoreau gave two different
lectures; see Harding, "A Checklist of Thoreau's Lectures," *Bulletin of the New York Public
Library* (1948), 52:81. The lecture was "Resistance to Civil Government."

12. No MS has been located; text from Henry Sutton, "Emerson. Reminiscences of His
Visits to Manchester. I," *Manchester City News*, May 20, 1899; part 2 appears in the issue for
May 27. Printed by Kenneth W. Cameron, "Emerson, Thoreau, and the Poet Henry Sutton,"
ESQ (4th q., 1955), 1:12. Cameron's source is a clipping from the *Manchester City News*.
Sutton's acknowledgment and acceptance of this invitation is dated from Nottingham, February 2, 1848 (RWEMA).

13. William Ballantyne Hodgson; see *Letters*, 3:379, n. 39.

14. Joseph Neuberg, whom Emerson would later introduce to Carlyle; see Slater, p. 446,
n. 3.

15. For Emerson's arrangements with Mrs. Anne Massey, see *Letters*, 3:437.

has only undertaken to find us one close by, and you are to have your bread and water with me.[16] In this assurance.—Yours.

R. W. Emerson

To George Searle Phillips, Manchester, January? 31? 1848

[On February 3, 1848, George Searle Phillips (pseud. "January Searle") writes Emerson (a.l.s., RWEMA) that he cannot be in Manchester on Saturday, but will walk over the mountains (from Huddersfield) to see Emerson on Sunday. Phillips is, I believe, replying to an invitation like that addressed to Henry Sutton. He was at the dinner party on Sunday and gives an account of it in his book about Emerson (1855); see Scudder, pp. 88–95, 212.]

To James William Hudson, Manchester? February 1? 1848

[J. W. Hudson's letter of February 4, 1848 (RWEMA), implies that he has had a letter from Emerson asking him not to offer the lectures on "Napoleon" and "Domestic Life" to the towns in Scotland where he is arranging Emerson's lecture engagements. It is inferrible from Hudson's letter that Emerson has remarked on the long reports of these lectures that have appeared in the English newspapers. Hudson offers the improbable assurance that the English newspapers "are scarcely known" in Scotland. See *Letters*, 3:452, for Emerson's early dismay in finding his lectures so fully reported in the English papers, and see also 4:4. See Appendix C, 2.]

To George Crawshay, Manchester, England, February 7, 1848[17]

2, Fenny Street, Higher Broughton,
Manchester, February 7, 1848.

Dear Sir,

I find that I am promised to your Mechanics' Institution at Newcastle[18] on Wednesday evening next, so that I am setting forth on my journey

---

16. Townsend Scudder provides an account of the dinner party given by Emerson on February 6: Sutton and Neuberg from Nottingham were among the guests; see Scudder, *The Lonely Wayfaring Man* (New York: Oxford University Press, 1936), pp. 86–95; for his sources, p. 212. The accounts he uses are all retrospective, written many years after the occasion and, one suspects, highly colored. Emerson could not have felt himself too far from home in this mixed company of ecstatic mystics and cool Unitarians, of eccentric poets and entrepreneurs of Mechanics' Institutes, nonconformists all in their several ways, even the very successful lecturer, George Dawson, Baptist preacher of whom George Searle Phillips ("January Searle") had rude things to say—to Alexander Ireland's indignation (Scudder, p. 94). Phillips had walked over the moors from Huddersfield (c. 25 miles); the highest point, Stanedge, was 1,271 ft.

17. No MS has been found; text from the *Newcastle Monthly Chronicle*, November 1889, p. 495; "Fenny Street" incorrectly printed as "Ferry."

18. Emerson gave two lectures for the Mechanics' Institution of Newcastle-on-Tyne. The MS Minute Book of the institution (Central Reference Library, Newcastle-on-Tyne), entries of December 6 and 15, 1847, show that originally the "celebrated lecturer from America"

northward to-day, and promise myself the privilege of visiting you on Wednesday p.m. I hope it will be my good fortune to find you at home. If affairs have chanced to call you thence, I shall blame my imprudence in not giving you earlier notice of my designs on you.[19]

Yours respectfully.

R. W. Emerson

To Lydia Jackson Emerson, Barnard Castle, February 9, 1848[20]

2/Barnard Castle Feb. 9th/ On 1st March I go to London, & perhaps I shall have lectures there,[21] & money; & perhaps not. I have received no proposition, such as was mentioned before I came, from Carlyle. There are many objections to opening my mouth again, & in London I cannot now tell how it will be. I have abundance of invitations from institutions of all kinds in London, but hitherto have accepted none.

---

was asked for three lectures: "Shakespeare," "Napoleon," and "Domestic Life" at seven guineas a lecture. He appeared for his first engagement on February 9 with two lectures in hand: "The Natural Characteristics of the Six Northern States of America" and "Shakspeare." Offered a choice, the audience asked for "Shakspeare"; a show of hands was called for and Emerson obliged by reading the "Shakspeare." On the following evening he was allowed to give the new lecture. *The Newcastle Guardian* (February 12) recounts the story of the people's choice and chooses to report only the new lecture given on the 10th, the Shakespeare lecture having been already and often fully reported.

The new lecture, given first at Barnard Castle February 8, is, I think, a revision of the last lecture in the 1843 series given in Philadelphia (Charvat, p. 19). In the folder of MSS for this series (MH), there are only scraps remaining for the last in the series.

The Newcastle institution had bought Emerson's *Essays*, "1st and 2nd series" on January 3 (MS minutes) and on March 12 they list his *Poems* as the first of several new books ordered.

19. See *Letters*, 4:16 for Emerson's comment on Crawshay; and see also Rusk's, note 53, and here February nine below.

20. MS copy by Elizabeth Hoar for Ruth Haskins Emerson, Emerson papers (RWEMA), Houghton Library, MH; ph. in NNC. For the beginning of this letter, see *Letters*, 4:14. In copying this letter of the 9th and the letter of the 10th (*Letters*, 4:15–16), Miss Hoar mixed up the sheets of the letters, as she explains in a note to Mrs. Emerson. She has therefore, numbered this passage "2" and inserted the dateline. Originally—again as her note explains—there was an additional half sheet bearing the first part of this letter of the 9th; the half sheet has disappeared, leaving still a hiatus in this letter; see *Letters*, 4:14, where the text ends abruptly in the middle of a sentence. Miss Hoar's note reads in part: "The half sheet I enclose, is first in order, then what is marked 2 on the second page—then, the letter beginning on my first page follows these, as the date will testify—you will not care to know how I made the blunder—" See *Letters*, 4:68, for Emerson's comment on Miss Hoar's service as a copyist.

21. In the Emerson papers now there are six invitations to lecture in London; missing is the letter from the Metropolitan Early Closing Association received January 27 (see *Letters*, 4:12). The invitation of the Marylebone Literary and Scientific Institution of November 13, 1837, is one of the extant six. There may have been others. Not until early May did he yield; see *Letters*, 4:65, 80, and n. 288 for the Marylebone lectures, and 4:84 and nn. 296, and 103 for the lectures given for the Metropolitan Early Closing Association. Emerson had no illusions about the use being made of him; see *Letters*, 4:80, 83, 87, and 94.

Also, I wish to go to Paris for a few weeks.[22] That is a great point. Here you have the whole dull fact of my economics. I may set out for London 1st March, if I prosper in the next fortnight, with 80 pounds in my pocket—If then, I do not spend, but continue to receive, I can easily send money home to you, & the Concord Bk. It was a great disappointment to me that Munroe had no money for me in January. I am truly sorry for your anxieties in the matter.—But all this check and vexation is very little or nothing while you send me on the same sheet such good stories of the children & of friends.[23] Perhaps I shall not be able to win another moment to write, as I am now in flight for Newcastle to-night, & there am to spend the day with private friends yet unseen, Mr Crawshay's[24] family, & then for Edinburgh. But I will try to put another sheet into the envelope—Love to all, Yours Waldo E.

There is a great deal of destiny as in other trifles, so in the writing of such a letter as this, this odd scroll from an epicurean author on his travels to his saintly wife.

To Sir Archibald Alison, Edinburgh, February 14? 1848

[Sir Archibald Alison, Sheriff of Lanarkshire, invited Emerson to dine on February 22 (a.l.s., RWEMA). Emerson would have replied. Engaged to lecture in Dundee on the 21st and Perth on the 22nd, he would have to refuse. Since he thought Alison a "coxcomb," he was probably not displeased (see Letters, 3:447.]

To George Crawshay, Edinburgh, February 14, 1848[25]

Edinburgh, Monday Evening, Feb. 14, 1848.

My dear Sir,

Forgive me the strange slowness in keeping my promise; but I have been in a whirl ever since I left your door, and could ill command a minute or a pen.[26] But the train kept its word and arrived at or near 8:15. A porter came at once to the carriage window to see if Mr E. was

22. The decision to lecture in London cut short his visit to Paris.

23. Mrs. Emerson, who could be sardonic, once wrote her husband who had complained of not hearing from her: "You practice Stoicism for us both you know" (February 10, 1838, RWEMA).

24. George Crawshay, from whose firm "Gateshead Iron Works" in newcastle, Emerson would write his next letter of February 10 (Letters, 4:15); see above December 24, 1847, and February 2, 1848, and below February 14 and March 2.

25. No MS has been found; text from the Newcastle Monthly Chronicle, November 1889, p. 495.

26. See Letters, 4:18ff., for Emerson's account of his visit to Edinburgh. See, above, February 1, for the Edinburgh lectures.

within. Dr Brown was waiting for me.[27] Your message had been faithfully forwarded, and happily the lecture had been appointed for 8 1/2 o'clock. I was driven to the Phil. Society's rooms, where I found kind secretaries with hot coffee, and the audience were kept waiting by apologizing directors only fifteen minutes, so that all prospered well. There was a great company, so the forewarning was important. I have seen Professor Wilson and Lord Jeffrey, and to-day dined with De Quincey. I trust that Mrs Crawshay is in firmer health, though the weather is so wild. I am still revolving many good things I learned at your house, and shall not have done with them for a long time. But in the present haste must postpone all to a future note.

Yours with great regard,
R. W. Emerson.

To Alexander Ireland, Edinburgh, February 17, 1848[28]

Some friends here wish me to read my lecture on Plato to the Phil. Society, on Saturday night, at half-past eight o'clock. It lies in one of my bureau drawers at Mrs. Massey's. Now will you proceed with beneficent action at once to Fenny-street, demand a candle, and open the various newspaper envelopes in my drawers until you eliminate and extort 'Plato,'[29] and send it by post immediately to me, care of Dr. Brown,[30] 1, Cuthbert's Glebe Edinbro'? The good Misses Massey will assist your search,[31] and yourself will reward your pains. I have seen your father and mother, and Mr. Chambers, and others your friends,[32] and all your despatches and benefits have safely arrived.—Ever yours.

27. Dr. Samuel Brown, John Wilson ("Christopher North"), Francis Jeffrey. For his meeting with De Quincey, see *Letters*, 4:19, and *JMN*, 10:220–221.

28. No MS has been located; text from Ireland, *In Memoriam*, pp. 79–80; listed *Letters*, 4:17. The manifest typographical error of "with" for "wish" (fourth word) is here corrected.

29. The MS minutes of the Edinburgh Philosophical Institution (Central Library, Edinburgh), record a decision, February 17, to ask for a fourth lecture to be advertised in the newspapers, posted in the rooms of the institution, and announced by Emerson at the close of his third lecture, February 18. In the *Scotsman* for February 19, p. 1, the subject announced is "Plato," but see *Letters*, 4:18, n. 57, for the fact that the lecture actually given was "Eloquence," from which it may be inferred that Ireland could not get the MS of "Plato" to him in time.

30. Dr. Samuel Brown; see February 25 below.

31. Emerson's Manchester landlady and, I infer, her daughters.

32. See *Letters*, 4:19; Ireland's parents at whose house Emerson met Robert Chambers, author of the admired *Vestiges of Creation*.

To ———, EDINBURGH, FEBRUARY 17, 1848[33]

Edinburgh, 17 Feby, 1848

Sir,

I am much obliged to you & to your friends for the kind invitation you send me; but I find it to be quite out of my power to make at present any new engagements to lecture; so that you shall, if you please, not think of it again.

Yours respectfully
R. W. Emerson.

To DR. SAMUEL BROWN, PAISLEY, FEBRUARY 25, 1848[34]

Paisley
Friday Evening, 25 Feby

I have got the shirts & the book,[35] O Man of many virtues, and, in the point of hospitality, sorely tried, & not found wanting! ⟨you⟩ and now you will make me proud by bringing all th⟨is⟩e cluster of accomplishments I have so admired, to me, and suffer me to boast of them as those of my friend! ah! you will quite spoil the poor dumb honourer of science & of honour, who came to you only to receive incessant & costly benefits.[36] Well, I shall carry it with me this romantic experience, and affirm to doubting souls that goodness & greatness & genius are still allied with common sense and all household merits & charities. And now may the sure months ripen the thought and the practice which the best of mankind, I am sure, will most confidently await at your hands! Did not Coleridge say of the Immortality, that there was nothing against it but its own sublimity?[36a] that is, we have very weak eyes. But I am resolved that grandeur is evidence, and I rely on you because your thought has nothing vulgar. But it is too late at night to write, so I shall wait till I have seen Wordsworth, which I hope I may on Sunday, to send you some fit

<hr>

33. MS in the Barrett Collection, Alderman Library, ViU; ph. in NNC. There is no clue to the addressee. John Grey of Hexham asked for a lecture in a letter of February 11, and G. W. Yapp, secretary of the Whittington Club, London, asked for a lecture on February 3 (RWEMA).

34. MS in the Barrett Collection, Alderman Library, ViU; ph. in NNC; listed *Letters*, 4:24, from Brown's letter of April 3. Three words in the MS have been glossed, probably by Brown.

35. In his letter of February 23 (RWEMA) Brown had told Emerson to expect a package to be delivered to him in Glasgow by John Sanderson; the package contained the shirts and handkerchiefs and a copy of Catherine Stevens Crowe's book *Aristodemus*.

For Emerson's admiration of Brown and Brown's hospitality, see *Letters*, 4:18, 23.

36. Emerson is apparently recalling a passage at the close of Essay 14 in *The Friend*.

token.[37] With friendly regards to Mr Craig,[38] I pray you also to tell Mrs Crowe,[39] that I am very sensible of her great kindness. Yes, I will do as you say in regard to Marston,[40] with a good will too. I shall take rooms, when I first go to London, in Chapman's house 142 Strand.

Very heartily, your friend,
R. W. Emerson

Samuel Brown.

To ROBERT STEWART, AMBLESIDE, ENGLAND, FEBRUARY 28? 1848[41]

Ambleside
29 Feb.y 1848

Dear Sir,

I promised to send you word of my safe arrival in these poetic regions. I met with no accident on the Caledonian Railway though I saw the

37. Brown's letter of April 3 shows that Emerson did not write him from Ambleside.
38. H. Craig, Brown's faithful associate.
39. Catherine Stevens Crowe; see *Letters*, 4:18–19, and, below, July 10.
40. John Westland Marston (*Letters*, 4:86), but in a note (RWEMA) dated only "Monday Evening" (February 28 certainly) in reply to this letter of Emerson's, Brown corrects his letter of February 23 where he had introduced Marston, the dramatist, to Emerson in mistake for Theodore Martyn, musician, poet, and translator who contributed to *Tait's Edinburgh Magazine* under the pen name of "Ben Gaultier."
41. MS in the National Library of Scotland; ph. in NNC; printed by Fish, *AL* (March 1955), 27:27. This letter, though dated 29, must have been written on the 28th; for the evidence see appendix C, 3. The addressee is not the poet born in Elderslie in 1806 as Fish, with reservations, conjectures. The poet was a hand-loom weaver unlikely to be the Robert Stewart listed as a member of the Paisley Athenaeum (MS list of members, Paisley Central Reference Library).
The prospective history of Paisley alluded to here is by John Parkhill; the imprint reads: "Paisley Robert Stewart, 4 Cross. 1857." In Paisley directories (1848/1849; 1851/1852) Robert Stewart, "bookseller, stationer, and bookbinder," is listed, his address given as 4 High Street. Number 4 High Street is also "4 Cross." At that time, Paisley streets were numbered up one side and down the other with "103 High Street," for example, falling also at "Cross" as the directories cited indicate in parentheses. High Street began at "Old Bridge," the low numbers 1–4 falling on the south side of the street between the "Cart Water" crossed by the Bridge at St. Mirren Street. Conversion tables for renumbering the streets (1923) show that no. 4 High Street fell at the corner of St. Mirren Street and High. On a map of 1839, St. Mirren Street runs diagonally into High Street to a square labelled "Cross," having "coffee rooms" on the east side and Moss Street on the west, with noticeable open space on the south. ("Cross" may signify that a roadside cross was or had been there.) This letter is surely addressed to the bookseller. Other Robert Stewarts, e.g., the tailor at "103 High (Cross)," are unlikely. K. W. Kinshalwood kindly supplied the map and information from conversion tables.
Emerson's MS Notebook "England and Paris" p. [7], *JMN*, 10:441, has Stewart's name against the date February 25 and the place Paisley. Since the entry appears in his lecture schedule, and on March 7 Emerson is still hoping for money from Paisley, it is certain that Emerson was in Paisley to lecture (see *Letters*, 4:30). Scudder is in error in listing a lecture as given on February 16 (*PMLA*, March 1936, 51:246). Not only the letter here but also Emerson's accounts (*JMN*, 10:420) show that the 16th is impossible. There are no expenses

frightful wreck of the carriages at Ecclefechan;[42] & on the whole, had the most agreeable ride through the finest scenery.[43] Yesterday, I had a ⟨very⟩valuable hour with Mr Wordsworth, who is in vigorous health, though 77 years old; and, tomorrow, I shall set forth once more for Manchester & London.

With many pleasing recollections of Paisley, which I hope yet by the aid of your fine book to deepen & inform, I remain your obliged servant,

R. W. Emerson.

Robert Stewart, Esq

To Elizabeth Hoar, Ambleside, February 28 and 29? 1848[44]

Dear E—

I have been here with Miss Martineau a couple of days, & ere I pack my bags again for Manchester, & London, you shall have a token of the fine pleasures of this country & its tenants. Miss Martineau lives here in great advantage & comfort, in a good stone house which she has built in a beautiful position, where, to be sure, all possible sites are excellent, and with Windermere before her windows, the rude hill Loughrigg on one side, Wansfell a higher hill on the other & Fairfield which rises 2900 feet & more, not far off, behind her. Her two maids make all her family; & her days, as you will believe, are spent with perfect method. She is in perfect health, as I can bear witness, after this day's riding & running. I came here yesterday morning, from the North, &, about 3. oclk. we set forth for Mr Wordsworth's house which is a mile & a half from her

for travel to Paisley on the 16th; the only expense entered is for a cab in Edinburgh. Expenses for the trip to Paisley are entered under February 25. Moreover, *The Renfrewshire Advertiser* of February 26 briefly reports the lecture, and it was advertised in the *Glasgow Saturday Post* of February 19.

42. The first sentence here makes it clear that news of the wreck of February 25 on the Caledonian railroad reached Paisley before Emerson's departure and accounts for Stewart's concern for Emerson's safe arrival; Emerson's train would take him over part of the same route. The disaster was occasioned by heavy rains that washed away the embankment between Kirtlebridge and Ecclefechan (*The Scotsman*, February 26).

43. Emerson is here, I think, alluding to the view of Lune Gorge and the Westmorland Fells. The Carlisle-Preston line Emerson traveled on was built by Joseph Locke; his choosing to take the line over Shap Fell was admired as a feat of engineering by engineers if not by Wordsworth who wrote an indignant sonnet.

44. No MS has been found; text from a copy (probably incomplete) made by Elizabeth Hoar for Ruth Haskins Emerson; ph. in NNC; listed Letters, vol. 4, with conjectured date of March 2. The copy is headed: "To E.H.—Ambleside—with vignette of Ullswater." The matter of the letter covers three days—the 27th, 28th, and 29th, the last an extra day, Emerson staying over to see Lake Ullswater.

gate.[45] Wordsworth waked up a little heavily from his after dinner nap on the sofa, but soon began to talk on the great French news. He had, of course, all the strongest English prejudice against the French. He had lived in France a year & a half, & they were an idle people; the women did the work in the manufactories, in the shops, even in the counting houses; the men carried out a fowling piece, or only liked to play at billiards, or faire le cour aux dames. Even the disasters of poor old Louis Philippe,[46] a vagabond at this day, did not seem much to touch the Tory poet. His opinions, however, about many important things are capricious, & rest on anecdotes & narrow experiences. We talked of Jeffrey[47] —No Scotchman could write English. Robertson[48] has only two or three set forms of sentences. (Gibbon, no Scot, could not because he first learned French. Carlyle could not, he was a high offender. Tennyson we came upon, & he expressed great regard & respect for him, whom he personally knew, thinks him to have most genius of all the poets, but some affectation; in short Wordsworth had just such opinions good & bad, as you in your chamber could write out for him. Why should I tediously remember them? And yet it is good to see his great rough weather-beaten face, the dome of his brow, & sometimes a fine smile. His nose is so large & corrugated as no picture would dare to represent it. But he is very temperate, and is all his life long, of a very frugal habit. Mrs Wordsworth was present, & took part in the conversation, Miss Martineau leaving me there, after a little while, to finish my visit. I stayed an hour & a half, & we ran over many topics, & he set out to walk towards Miss M's with me, but it rained, & I would not suffer it. He is 77 years old, but assured me he does not feel his age in walking or journeying. That night, in a tempest of rain, the Arnolds came & spent the

45. Leaving Emerson alone to enjoy his visit with Wordsworth, Miss Martineau was being tactful; Wordsworth was to her as she was to him (and Mrs. Wordsworth) an irritant and certainly no novelty (Scudder here, pp. 134–135, needs correction). As Scudder notes (p. 135), Wordsworth was still suffering over the death of his daughter, but according to a letter by his wife he could "with almost indifferent persons . . . rally a little and appear quite himself." Very likely Emerson qualified as an "indifferent" person. Mary Wordsworth's letter is written on Wednesday, February 2, 1848, though she has dated it "Tuesday 2nd Feb." *Letters of Mary Wordsworth*, Mary E. Burton, ed. (Oxford: Clarendon Press, 1958), p. 293. See *Works*, 5:294–296, for Emerson's published account of his visit with Wordsworth.

46. Louis Philippe had abdicated February 24 and would take refuge with the daughter of the American banker Joshua Bates (see notes, March 9, below). Without *The Prelude* to tell him, Emerson could not understand Wordsworth's complicated feelings about the French.

47. Francis Jeffrey.

48. The historian William Robertson.

evening—very beloved people here, & very well deserving.—The next day Mr Greg[49] provided three ponies, & with him & Miss M. I rode seven or eight miles, & saw, I think, the best of their mountains & lakes;[50] then walked to Fox How, (of the Arnolds); then to Stock Gill Force, a waterfall; then dined with the Arnolds again at Mr Greg's. And so ended the day—Can my letter choose but end? Your brother Waldo.

To George Crawshay, Manchester, March 1, 1848[51]

2, Fenny Street, Higher Broughton
Manchester, March 2, 1848

My dear Sir,

Your kind note found me still in Scotland, where I had a pleasant visit, and satisfied on many points and persons my Western curiosity. Thence I came to Ambleside, where I spent a couple of days most agreeably; saw Wordsworth for an hour and a half;[52] had much talk with Miss Martineau of her coming book;[53] saw the excellent family of the Arnolds, and particularly Mr Greg,[54] under whose guidance I had a good ride on horseback among the mountains and waters; and yesterday returned home hither. I think to set forth toward London to-morrow, perhaps may stop at Birmingham one night, and I mean to remain in or near London until 1st May. If you shall be there in the interim and will send your address for me to Mr Chapman, 142 Strand, I shall not fail to see you. These wondrous French news must occupy you fully in these

49. William Rathbone Greg; in her letter of July 2, 1845, Harriet Martineau declared the Gregs her "nearest & dearest friends hereabouts."

50. Emerson's MS notebook "England Paris 1847–1848," p. [19], *JMN*, 10:421, shows that on February 29 he bought Wordsworth's *Guide Through the District of the Lakes,* and he lists it among the books he is bringing home from England (*JMN*, 10:336); it is not now in his library.

51. No MS has been found; text from the Newcastle *Monthly Chronicle*, November 1889, pp. 495–496, with "Ferry" incorrectly for "Fenny" in the address. Here and in his letter to Margaret Fuller with the same dateline (*Letters*, 4:25, and n. 86), Emerson says he leaves for London "tomorrow," but he tells Carlyle (Slater, p. 40), and Shuttleworth below under the same dateline that he leaves that day. I believe the letter to Margaret Fuller and this letter are of March 1 and that the letter to Allingham below may also be of March 1. See Appendix C, 2.

52. See Letters, 4:25 ff, and 33, and, above, February 28, to Elizabeth Hoar.

53. *Eastern Life,* published in April.

54. William Rathbone Greg; Emerson normally spells the name with two g's and probably did so here.

days and hours.[55] I desire to be kindly remembered by[56] Mrs Crawshay, and am yours, with best regards,

R. W. Emerson.

To John Shuttleworth, Manchester, March 2, 1848[57]

2 Fenny Street
Higher Broughton.
2 March

Dear Sir,

I leave Manchester for London this afternoon, & after making an unsuccessful attempt to pay my respects to you & Mrs Shuttleworth at your house, yesterday afternoon, have only left this opportunity of bidding you farewell. I had the pleasure of seeing friends of yours, Mr Kenrick[58] at York, & Mr /& Mrs/ Gaskill[59] of Wakefield, at Leeds. In the good hope of seeing you again,

Yours with great regard,
R. W. Emerson.

To ———, Manchester, March 2, 1848

[A letter of this date was offered for sale in Henry Southeran's catalogue No. 513, p. 36, where it is described as giving an account of his movements.]

To William Allingham, Manchester, March 2? 1848[60]

2 Fenny Street; Higher
Broughton; Manchester,
2 March;

My dear Sir,

I was vexed indeed by learning from your note received on my way through Westmoreland, day before yesterday, that I had seemed to you

55. The revolution in France; since Emerson last wrote Crawshay, February 14 (see above), Guizot had resigned (February 23) and Louis-Phillipe had abdicated (February 24). See above February 28 to Elizabeth Hoar.

56. The text reads "remembered by"; "to" is the more likely preposition here.

57. MS in the John Rylands Library, Manchester, England; copy in NNC. There is no doubt of the year.

58. The Reverend John Kenrick, whom Shuttleworth had earlier invited to Manchester to meet Emerson; unable to accept, Kenrick, on January 7 (RWEMA), invited Emerson to stay with the Kenricks when he lectured in York, January 13.

59. James Milnes Gaskell, cousin of Monckton Milnes, and his wife Mary, whom Emerson met at the home of the Reverend Charles Wickstead of Leeds. See Letters, 4:58.

60. MS in the Beinecke Library, CtY; ph. in NNC; printed by Cameron, ESQ (1st q., 1958), 10:34; listed Letters, 4:28. Emerson's reference to going to London is inconclusive; I

negligent of your last kind communication. I even fancied that I had already written to you long since, as I should have done. But I have lived such a wandering desultory life since I have been in this country, and with so violent a change of all my habits, that you must forgive me this omission. I recei⟨ie⟩ved & read with great interest your note & lines which I had at Birmingham, and certainly thought of nothing less than dropping my new correspondence. I esteemed it, rather, something quite secure, & which could well bear the silence of many days. Perhaps I shall soon find a little leisure for an adequate return for the same. Meantime, I pray you to appreciate the compliment of my replying to a note which came to me open through another correspondent; which pleases me never.[61] I am on my way to London, where my address is (Care of John Chapman, 142 Strand.)

R. W. Emerson

To Elizabeth Davis Bancroft, London, March 5, 1848[62]

142 Strand
5 March 1848

My dear Mrs Bancroft,

Certainly I shall accept with great pleasure the invitation which Mr Bancroft sends, & you endorse, for Tuesday 14th instant.[63] But for the fine card of Lady Morgan,[64] I shall come & take advice of you, confiding that you will not mislead a quiet villager, who only wishes to see wise & truly informed people, into fine company.

Yours with best regards,
R. W. Emerson

---

question the date because the letter is less hurried than those of his day of departure. I think it may have been written on the 1st; see note to letter to Crawshay above.

61. Writing from Donegal on March 4, Allingham acknowledges this letter and explains that he had sent his last letter open to George Gilfillan, minister of the Free Church of Dundee, with whom Emerson had stayed on February 20 and again on the 23rd (*Letters,* 4:23, 24) because he thought "it would have found you in this house." Gilfillan in a letter to Allingham of February 25 reports Emerson's departure on the 24th and says he will forward Allingham's letter to Ambleside (*Letters to William Allingham,* p. 119). See also Cameron's article "William Allingham and Emerson—Some New Evidence," *ESQ* (1st q., 1957), 6:23–26.

62. MS in Special Collections, the University Library, DGU; ph. in NNC. Printed by John D. Hirsh, "Ralph Waldo Emerson, Mrs. Bancroft, and Lady Morgan in 1848," *Notes & Queries* (June 1978), n.s. 25:228–229. Emerson took more pains than usual in the writing of this letter; it is very neat and carefully spaced.

63. See *Letters,* 4:37 and 41, for the Bancrofts' dinner party on the 14th.

64. Emerson refers to this card to Lady Morgan's soirée in a letter of March 23 and 24, 1848 (*Letters,* 4:41); the card was procured for him by Mrs. Bancroft. Emerson apparently

To Alexander Ireland, London, March 9, 1848[65]

142 Strand, London.
9 March, 1848.

My dear friend,

As usual, with surest punctuality, the morning brought your note & its order for £35.. which was duly deposited with the Barings.[66] Mrs Paulet's note also came, & must be at once acknowledged[67] In reply to your query about the Examiner,—Carlyle did certainly write the article, as indeed it was easy to divine,[68] and has another paper, I suppose, ready for the next. I find him full of strong discourse. He is in the best humour at the events in France. For the first time in his life, he takes in a daily paper,—the Times. And yet I think he has not much confidence in the ability of the French to carry such great points as they have to carry. He interests himself a good deal in the Chartists & in politics generally, though with abundant contempt for what is called political. He talks away on a variety of matters, on London, on the Universities, on Church & State, on all notable persons, on the delusion that is called Art, on the Sand novels, &c &c. I think him a most valuable companion, & speaking the best opinions one is likely to hear in this nation. It is by no means easy to talk with him, but there is little need of that, as he enjoys his pictures & his indignations highly. The guiding genius of the man & what constitutes his superiority over other men of letters is his commanding sense of justice and incessant demand for sincerity. And I can not

knew enough of Sydney Owenson Morgan to doubt that she would have charms for a "quiet villager." When he met her, he found "a sort of fashionable or London edition of Aunt Mary . . . the high moral genius left out" (*Letters*, 4:48).

65. MS in the Olin Library, NIC; the MS is tipped in John Forster's *The Life of Charles Dickens*, vol. 1, pt. 2, between pp. 340–341; ph. in NNC. Printed in part by Ireland in his *In Memoriam*, pp. 80–81. A bracket before "I find him . . ." and light question marks before and after the next to the last sentence are evidently Ireland's markings. Listed, *Letters*, 4:38.

66. This sum is entered as received on account from Ireland in Emerson's MS Notebook "England and Paris," p. 14 (*JMN*, 10:417).

67. Mrs. Elizabeth Paulet's letter, n.d., endorsed by Emerson "March 1848" (RWEMA), was evidently forwarded by Ireland from Manchester. She hopes to see him again in Liverpool.

68. "Louis-Phillipe," *The Examiner*, No. 2092, March 4, 1848, pp. 145–146. Louis Phillipe had fled first to Belgium. See *Letters*, 4:34, 38, where Emerson tells Lidian and Abel Adams that Louis-Phillipe is now in England, the guest of the daughter of Joshua Bates, American banker, close friend of Thomas Wren Ward. Bates' London home was in Portland Place. His daughter, his only child, had married Sylvain Van de Weyer, Belgian Minister to the Court of St. James's.

help thinking that he has more books, or at least one more book to write of more efficiency than any he has written.

I expect your visit ⟨patiently⟩ as[69] soon as the hard work is over.

Yours
R W Emerson

To Elizabeth Paulet, London, March 9? 1848

[See above, March 9, to Alexander Ireland for evidence that Emerson intended to answer a letter from Mrs. Paulet; her undated letter is there referred to.]

To George Bancroft, London, March 9, 1848[70]

142 Strand
9 March.

My dear Sir,

I send you my special thanks for the kind care with which you have remembered my wants & have sent me this ample supply of tickets. I shall not fail to observe your direction.

Your obliged servant,
R. W. Emerson.

To William Arthur Case, London, March 12, 1848[71]

142 Strand
12 March

Dear Sir,

Mr Chapman is very desirous of seeing yourself & Professor Newman here with a few other gentlemen on Thursday evening. Perhaps then you will indulge him & me in this change, and let me meet yourself &

69. Emerson may have thought "patiently" infra dig.
70. MS in the Bancroft papers, MHi; ph. in NNC. Of the year there can be no doubt. The prompt kindness of Bancroft is recorded in several letters; see *Letters*, 4:30 and 33–34. I believe this note acknowledges the receipt of tickets for the houses of Parliament (*ibid.*, p. 34).
71. MS Add. 50956, fl. 90, BL; copy in NNC; the year is established by the address. Case, with an address at 20 Upper Gower Street, is listed in the "England and Paris" notebook (*JMN*, 10:442), and Mrs. Case at the same address is listed in the London notebook (*JMN*, 10:287). Case (1818–1872), a Fellow of University College, London, became an assistant master in 1849; in 1866 he opened a private coeducational school in Hampstead. His house at 20 Upper Gower St. was for University College students who were then known as Caseites. Francis William Newman was one of the founders of University College. The "few other gentlemen" were very likely also connected with the college.

your friend here, instead of at your house.—I do not kn⟨?⟩[72]ow but an option of Thursday or Friday was left to Mr Newman, but with a preference for Thursday

Yours with great regard,
R. W. Emerson.

W. A. Case, Esq.

TO DAVID SCOTT, LONDON, MARCH 13, 1848[73]

142 Strand ⎤ 13 March
London ⎦ 1848

My dear Sir,

When I reached Manchester, on my return from Scotland, I was sorry to find that I had exhausted my little stock of the American Edition of my "Poems," of which I expected to find several copies, whereof one was to have gone to you. So I left with Mr Ireland a copy of the old "Essays" in their revised form, with your address; & now in a week Mr Chapman will send you copy of the "Poems" in which I will try to mark the errata.[74] If they do not arrive at your door within ten days, you must write to me to show cause.—I carry with me a bright image of your house & studio,[75] & all your immortal companions therein, and I wish to keep the ways open between us, natural & supernatural. If the good Power had allowed me the opportunity of seeing you at more leisure, & of comparing notes of past years a little!—and it may yet be allowed in some where & when. —But was I not to send you some autograph for your friend? I must try to add it in the same envelope. I am here to remain I know not how long, but fully occupied this far in exploring my part in London.

Your friend,
R. W. Emerson.

72. The word "know" is written over a partially washed out word.

73. MS in the Pattee Library, PSt. A brief passage is quoted in William B. Scott's biography of his brother; Rusk lists it, quoting the passage in *Letters,* 4:100; he follows Scott's erroneous dating. And from David Scott's reply to this letter, Rusk lists, 4:40, a conjectured letter from Emerson of c. March 18. Scott's letter is dated March 29.

74. Emerson, shocked by the numerous errors in the English edition of his *Poems,* had brought with him copies of the American edition. In his letter of the 29th Scott says he has not received the books.

75. Scott's portrait of Emerson was later purchased by three citizens of Concord and now hangs in the Concord Free Public Library.

To Charles Lane, London, March 15? 1848

[Charles Lane's letter of March 17, 1848 (RWEMA), expresses his pleasure in Emerson's proposed visit to Alcott House, Ham, and suggests that the railroad is the best way to come. This letter seems to imply a letter from Emerson, but the visit is to be made with John Chapman who may have made the proposal Lane refers to.]

To Anna Brownell Jameson, London, March 20, 1848

[Listed *Letters,* 4:40, and by Harding, *ESQ* (4th q., 1958), 13:35, from Ben Bloomfield's List D 1-8, 1953, without year, but 1848 from the London address, the addressee given only as Mrs Jameson. Emerson says that his plans have changed and that he will call "at a quite early hour, soon after 8." There are two undated letters (RWEMA) from Anna Jameson to Emerson, one endorsed by him "March" asks him to come tomorrow, Monday, between 8 and 12 p.m. March 20 fell on a Monday in 1848. Apparently there was an earlier note from Emerson.]

To Samuel Gray Ward, London, March 20, 1848[76]

London, 20 March 1848

My dear Ward,

It was a great pleasure to see your handwriting, the other day, for the first time for long. A day or two afterwards I saw Mrs Butler who had also news from you, which she promised to share, if I would come & see her. But I fear she has already left town, & I have not used my privilege. She will quickly come back, they said. I made a point first of seeing her as Cordelia,[77] with Macready for Lear, and I found them both excellent. What shall I say to you of Babylon? I see & hear with the utmost diligence, and the lesson lengthens as I go; ⟨t⟩so that, at some hours, I incline to take some drops ⟨of⟩ or grains of lotus, forget my home & selfish solitude, & step by step establish my acquaintance with English society.[78] There is nowhere so much wealth of talent & character & social accomplishment, every star outshone by one more dazzling, and you cannot move without coming into the light & fame of new ones. I have

76. MS in the Ward papers, Houghton Library, HU; ph. in CUL; printed in part by Cabot, 2:554–555, and more fully but not completely by Norton, pp. 66–70; listed *Letters,* 4:40. Emerson rarely crosses a letter, but here he has written his postscript across p. [1].

77. Emerson probably saw this performance on March 17 (*Letters,* 4:44, n. 157). Ward knew Frances Kemble Butler well; she consulted him and corresponded with him (Ward papers, MHi). Emerson's MS Pocket Diary for 1848, *JMN,* 10:448, shows a dinner engagement at George Bancroft's on March 14; it was on that occasion that he talked with Mrs. Butler (*Letters,* 4:41). William Macready's Lear was famous.

78. Emerson had written Abel Adams on March 10 of his resolve to do the London season (*Letters,* 4:39).

seen I suppose some good specimens chiefly of the literary-fashionable &
not of the fashionable sort. Macaulay is quite the king of every circle
where he goes, by the splendor & the speed of his talking. he has the
strength of ten men, I may well say, and any table talk of his is an exploit
to found a reputation on. Mr Hallam is affable, but comparatively quiet.
Bunsen is reputed a man of learning & wide information & is much a
man of society, but he talked little where I saw him. Milnes is the most
gentle friendly all knowing little-caring omnipresent person that can be;
you see him so often that you think it must be Boston not London. lord
M⟨r⟩orpeth's virtues give him the highest consideration both in public &
in private circles. Mr Charles Austin is a lawyer of great reputation & of
a social talent that makes him the only fit match for Macaulay. Milman is
a very polished man and Mrs Milman a superior woman, and they are
the centre of a distinguished circle. Carlyle does not very often dine out
or go to breakfasts, so that I do not well know how he, who is a wonderful
talker, manages his tomahawk among these Romans. I have seen also
Lady Harriet Baring, esteemed the wittiest woman in London, and am to
dine with her this week,—a lady in great respect. Kinglake, I have seen,
a sensible man enough, but he does not look the Eothen; And Barry
Cornwall, at whose house I found him & Thackeray, you should never
mistake for a poet. They have all carried the art of agreeable sensations
to a wonderful pitch, they know everything, have everything, they are
rich, plain, polite, proud & admirable: But though good for them, it ends
in the using. I shall or should soon have enough of this play for my
occasion. The seed-corn is oftener found in quite other districts.[79] But I
am very much struck with the profusion of talent which allows every
body to be ignorant of the authors of paragraphs, articles, & books,
which all read with admiration, but have not any guess of the writer.

79. To his wife, Emerson makes a less guarded comment on Macauley (*Letters*, 4:43);
this letter to Lidian of March 23, 24 covers the same ground in more detail than Emerson
here gives Ward. Emerson met Macauley, Henry Milman, Chevalier Bunsen, and Lord
Morpeth at the Bancrofts' (March 14); at Henry Milman's for breakfast March 18, he met,
in addition, Charles Austin, barrister, brother of the jurist John Austin, and the historian
Henry Hallam. The MS Pocket Diary, *JMN*, 10:449, shows that he dined on March 23 with
Carlyle's friend William Bingham Baring and his wife Lady Harriet (the daughter of a peer
and therefore holding the courtesy title in her own right). On the following day he dined
with Baring's father, Lord Ashburton. Lady Ashburton, née Bingham, was an American.
The Barings were well-known to Ward, for his father was, and he himself would become,
the American representative of their banking firm. Emerson had dined at Bryan Waller
Procter's on March 15, and there met Alexander Kinglake and Thackeray. Writing Margaret
Fuller a month later, he would catalogue the "great men" and conclude: "theirs is bread that
ends in the using, & no seed" (*Letters*, 4:62).

Tennyson whom I wished to see more than any other, is in Ireland, and I fear I shall miss him.[80] I saw Wordsworth to very good purpose in Westmoreland, and all the Scottish gods at Edinburgh. Perhaps it is no fault of Britain,—no doubt tis because I grow old & cold, but no persons here appeal in any manner to the imagination. I think even that there is no person in England from[81] I expect more than talent & information But I am wont to ask very much more of my benefactors,—expansions that amount to new horizons. But this is very idle gossip, & when I come home, I will mend it by giving you all my impressions of these fine people —if I can remember them. Meantime do not fail to write me immediately. With kind remembrance to Anna. Your friend,

R. W. Emerson.

Thanks thanks for your duty to the M. Q.y.[82]—Mrs Bancroft is a great favorite here. To her, & to the Carlyles, & to Milnes,[83] I owe |the| most ⟨of⟩& best of my opportunities. I am very sorry to hear that we are very ill represented in other courts and that American diplomatists cannot speak French or Spanish or German. If you cannot send better, come yourself!

To Arthur Hugh Clough, London, March 20? 1848

[Clough's letter of March 12 required a reply and his letter of March 22 implies that he has received one, *Emerson-Clough Letters*, nos. 3, 4; Mulhauser, 1:201, 202.]

To Lidian Emerson, London, March 23 and 24, 1848

[A copy of this letter (made by Elizabeth Hoar for Emerson's mother, Ruth Haskins Emerson, RWEMA), adds a note explaining the blank (*Letters*, 4:44): "Lidian says that blank after 'reads' stands for my book,' I mean that Lady Byron reads &c."]

---

80. He met Tennyson finally in May; for Wordsworth, see February 28 above. His letter of c. February 22 to his wife gives an account of the "Scottish Gods" (*Letters*, 4:17–23).

81. Emerson omits the necessary relative pronoun here.

82. Emerson had solicited from Ward an article for *The Massachusetts Quarterly Review*; see above October 3, 1847.

83. The ubiquitous Richard Monckton Milnes, later the first Baron Houghton, was notoriously friendly to Americans.

To Henry David Thoreau, London, March 25, 1848[84]

London, 25 March, 1848.

Dear Henry,

Your letter was very welcome and its introduction heartily accepted.[85] In this city & nation of pomps, where pomps too are solid, I fall back on my friends with wonderful refreshment. It is pity, however, that you should not see this England, with its indiscribable material superiorities of every kind; the just confidence which immense successes of all sorts have generated in the Englishman[86] that he can do everything, and which his manners, though he is bashful & reserved, betray; the abridgment of all expression, which dense population & the roar of nations enforces; the solidity of science & merit which in any high place you are sure to find (the Church, & some effects of primogeniture excepted) but I cannot tell my story now. I admire the English I think never more than when I meet Americans—as, for example, at Mr Bancroft's American soiree, which he holds every Sunday night.—Great is the self respect of Mr Bull. He is very short sighted[87] & without his eye-glass cannot see as far as your eyes, to know how you like him, so that he quite neglects that point. The Americans see very well, too well, and the travelling portion are very light troops. But I must not vent my ill humour on my poor compatriots—they are welcome to their revenge & I am quite sure have not reason to spare me[88] if they too are at this hour writing letters to their gossips. I have not ⟨been⟩gone to Oxford yet, though I still correspond with my friend there, Mr Clough. I meet many young men here, who come to me simply as one of their school of thought, but not often in this class any giants. A Mr Morrell[89] who has written a History of Philosophy, and Wilkinson[90] who is a socialist now & gone to France, I

84. MS in the Berg Collection, NN; ph. in NNC; single sheet, without address. Printed by Sanborn, *AM* (June 1892), 59:749, and in Harding and Bode, p. 212; listed *Letters,* 4:45. Emerson is acknowledging a letter dated February 23 by Sanborn; Harding and Bode (p. 207) accept the date but do not reconcile the inconsistency of a lecture given January 26 (p. 209) with Thoreau's reference to the lecture's being given "last week'; see above January 28 for argument that the lecture was given February 16. Emerson had received Thoreau's letter by March 8 (see *Letters,* 4:35) in the same mail with one from Lidian.

85. Thoreau apparently enclosed a letter of introduction, but I have no clues.

86. The text clearly reads "all sorts" not "all pasts" and "the Englishman" not "this Englishman."

87. "Self respect" and "short sighted" (the latter hyphenated in Webster, 1849), are run together, but so are other words taken as two by Harding and Bode.

88. The text clearly reads "reason to spare" not "weapon to shave."

89. John Daniel Morell, *An Historical and Critical View of the Speculative Philosophies of Europe in the 19th Century* (London: John Johnstone, 1847).

90. James John Garth Wilkinson, Swedenborgian friend of Henry James, Sr.

have seen with respect. ⟨But⟩ I went last Sunday for the first time to see
Lane[91] at Ham & dined with him. He was full of friendliness & hospitality has a school of 16 children, one lady as matron, then Oldham,[92]—
that is all the household. They looked just comfortable. Mr Galpin,[93] tell
the Shakers, has <u>married</u>. I spent the most of that day in visiting Hampton Court & Richmond & went also into Popes Grotto at Twickenham &
saw Horace Walpoles Villa of Strawberry Hill. Ever your friend,

Waldo E.

To Arthur Hugh Clough, London, March 25? 1848

[Clough's letter of March 22 expects and needs a reply which Emerson surely
wrote; *Emerson-Clough Letters*, no. 4, (Mulhauser, 1:202); see March 20 above.]

To J——— Thomas? London, March 26, 1848[94]

142 Strand.
26 March

Dear Sir,

I am very much obliged by your friendly interest, and am well aware
that I have been long since a debtor to your good will. I have not quite
yet made up my mind to give any public or private lecture in London;
but the kind suggestion of many friends is making such an attempt more
probable to me. When I decide to do that, I will not forget your friendly
notice.

Yours respectfully,
R. W. Emerson.

91. The visit to Charles Lane's school at Alcott House, Ham, was made on Sunday,
March 19.
92. William Oldham, spiritualist, whom Alcott had met in 1842.
93. Probably William Galpin, associated with Alcott House and with Robert Owen,
serving as vice president of Owen's Rational Society. See *The New Age, Concordium Gazette and
Temperance Advocate*, (May 20, 1843), 1:21 et passim.
94. MS in the Beinecke Library, CtY; ph. in NNC. The year is obviously 1848 although
someone has marked it "1860." There is no clue to the addressee, but very likely the letter is
written to one of the institutions which had already invited him to lecture; "long since"
implies one of those whose agent had written him on his arrival in England. I suggest the
Marylebone Literary and Scientific Institution, because the letter seems to be keeping a door
open. J. Thomas, the secretary, had written Emerson November 13, 1847; and it is for this
institution Emerson would give a series of six lectures on "The Mind and Manners of the
Nineteenth Century" beginning on June 6. For this organization he would give a seventh
lecture on June 26.

To William Mathews, London, March 29, 1848 [95]

142 Strand London
29 March

My dear Sir,

I have been so variously occupied,—with my little skill as traveller, too,—that I have not seen Mr Carlyle,—since I saw you, until last night; and then I arranged with him, that, if it would suit your convenience, you & I should call on him this evening. I am sorry to learn at your Hotel that you have left town. I am going tomorrow to Oxford, for a ⟨fo⟩ couple of days; and when you are in town again, if you will be good enough to call on me, as you pass, we will fix an evening for Chelsea.

Yours respectfully,
R. W. Emerson.

W. Mathews, Esq.

To Katherine Barland, London, April 2, 1848 [96]

142 Strand London
2 April 1848

My dear Miss Barland,

I should have sent an earlier reply to your note received the other day, but that it found me just leaving town for two or three days, nor was I, in the mean time, in circumstances to write. I hasten now to say, that I

95. MS in the Beinecke Library, CtY; ph. in NNC; Cameron prints the letter in *ESQ* (1st Q., 1958), 10:34. The year is in no doubt. William Mathews had entertained Emerson at his Birmingham home, December 24, 1847 (*JMN*, 9:190; *Letters*, 3:455). There may have been an earlier letter to Mathews, for on February 27, Mathews acknowledges Emerson's gift of his *Poems* (RWEMA). See also, above, entry for December 15, 1847.

Emerson may have met Mathews through James John Garth Wilkinson, whose daughter Florence would subsequently marry Mathews' son Benjamin. That the Mathews moved in Swedenborgian circles is clear from Mrs. Mathews' letter of April 12, cited below in a note to letter of July 14; they were known also to Wilkinson's American friend Henry James, Sr. (see *Henry James Letters*, 1;104, 2:169–170). The Mathews were certainly prominent in Birmingham, for Mrs. Mathews, née Rachel Attwood, was the sister of Thomas Attwood, first M.P. for Birmingham, who would inherit the poet Shenstone's estate, The Leasowes. And Mathews was acquainted with the railroad engineer Marc Isambard Brunel (*Letters*, 3:455). His brother Jeremiah Mathews was a highly regarded land agent in the Midlands; and the nephew named for him would be a founder of the Alpine Club.

96. MS in the library of the University of Edinburgh; copy in NNC; printed by Fish, *AL* (March 1955), 27:29; listed *Letters*, 4:53, with conjectured date of April 15. The text fills six pages, the last two appearing on a sheet now attached by a strip of paper. Fish quotes Miss Barland's extravagant poem in praise of Emerson. Rusk cites her letters to him: one of March 25, to which this letter is a reply, and the other of April 20, her acknowledgment of this letter which she finds "kind."

was touched & gratified by the kind confidence with which you honour me. But I ought perhaps to advertise you, that, in all questions touching life & affection, I am reckoned a little stoical,—not a good sympathizer.[97] I could heartily wish you more peace than you seem yet to have found; but that is never far off from a strong mind. Health is more <u>natural</u>, & far more common than sickness, and, at some rate, we must have it. And I cannot but observe that the feeling is spreading through all society, that we are somehow acountable for our distempers, & must blush for our rheumatism & typhus. Why not then for moral infirmity of every shade? But I have to say—that I found in my readings in your little book of Poems, such indisputable evidence of good sense, & of all those fine gifts that go to make a good ear, & metrical talent, that I should be forced, if I were within reach of your conversation, to speak to you as to one who need suffer no longer than she liked, since the finest works & pleasures are open to you; & the same power that enables you to succeed in them, qualifies you to exert yourself with security in many other directions. Perhaps now I am less disposed than ever to concede any point to our domestic foes—that I have lately been making some sketches towards a chapter on the Culture of the Intellect. That is a chapter in our mysterious Book of Life, which draws on all our means physical & metaphysical, —on our science & on our tears—and the attraction of the subject for me is the lofty invitation which it at all times sends into our low & squalid indolence, summoning us to a kingdom of inspiration & miracle without end. I wish you would yourself look that way. The very topics that will first arrange themselves in your mind will nerve you, & lead you on; and, strange to say, it is still new & unexplored ground. But I am outrunning all limits of a note, & yet could not say less.[98] Thanks for the verses, too; though you have written many better. With my best wishes & assurances ⟨to⟩of your restored & augmented health & happiness, I remain Yours,

R. W. Emerson

97. Miss Barland had written on March 25: "I remember well your . . . admonitions. I have thought much on that remark of yours that lowliness is better than Stoicism. I fear that heretofore I have been too prone to seek refuge in Stoicism."

98. Letters of February 19 and March 1, 1848 (RWEMA) to Emerson from John Sanderson of Glasgow show Sanderson to be involved with Miss Barland and drawn into her quarrels with her sister. By Dr. Samuel Brown, who judges "her insanity . . . the product of disappointed sentimentalism rather than deep feeling," Sanderson has been advised "to break off the acquaintance"; he will do so if Emerson gives the same advice. Emerson could not have found being drawn into such an affair either welcome or pleasant.

Writing Emerson on April 22, 1849, Dr. Samuel Brown would report: "Kate Barland come to see me one day in Oct. almost as mad as ever . . . returned at Xmas—well, sane, happy, herself again. She continues so, Sanderson & folly are forgotten."

To Alexander Ireland, London, April 3, 1848[99]

I had hoped to have seen you here ere this. My London adventures already make too long a story to write. I spend my time not quite unprofitably, but in a way that must soon have an end, or it would make an end of my comfort. Yet I cannot decline these valued opportunities of seeing men and things which are offered me here. Excepting Tennyson, I believe, I have seen all the literary and many of the political notabilities who interested me. On Thursday last, I went to Oxford, and spent two days and more, very agreeably there, and made the acquaintance of many good men.[100] I have not quite yet decided how long to stay, or whither next to go, but soon must. I carried our good friend Neuberg,[101] the other night, to Carlyle, who was in better mood than usual. I have a good chamber for you here, waiting your advent, and am ever yours. I doubt about Paris a little, being very impatient to be at home and at work.

To William Mathews, London, April 8, 1848[102]

142 Strand
8 April. Evening

My dear Sir,

I saw Carlyle today & he promised to be at home to early tea on Tuesday Evening if we would come & see him. Will you not go—say, from this house at 7 o'clock—on that evening with me?[103]

Yours faithfully,
R. W. Emerson.

To _____, London, April 10, 1848

[Listed by K. W. Cameron, "Emerson's Manuscripts Ungathered and Migrant, Pt. 2," *ESQ* (1st q., 1957), 6:27 from Emily Driscoll's catalogue 16 (December

99. No MS has been located; text from Ireland, *In Memoriam*, p. 81; listed *Letters*, 4:52.
100. See *Letters*, 4:47–48, for visits to Oxford.
101. Joseph Neuberg of Nottingham, later became one of Carlyle's friends.
102. MS is the Beinecke Library, CtY: ph. in NNC; printed by Cameron in *ESQ* (1st q., 1958), 10:34. See March 29 above. Mathews had returned to London by April 12 (a.l.s., Mrs. Mathews to Emerson, April 15, 1848, RWEMA). This letter with others to Mathews were acquired together by Professor Cameron. The letter is endorsed: "To Wm Mathews Esqr | of the Leasowes | Father of B. St John Mathews Esq." The handwriting looks like Mathews'. It is his wife's family that inherited the poet Shenstone's famous property.
103. Emerson enters the visit of April 11 to Carlyle in his Pocket Diary for 1848 (*JMN*, 10:450).

1956); in both it is incorrectly dated 1847; the error is repeated by Cameron, in his Part 4, *ESQ* (2d q., 1966), 43:144 from the Sixth Cooperative Catalogue (February 1959) of the Antiquarian Booksellers Association of America (Middle Atlantic States), item 197. The letter (of one page) postpones an engagement because Emerson has "promised on Friday to dine with Dr Forbes & to hear Professor Faraday's lecture." I find no clue to the addressee; the MS Pocket Diary for 1848 lists the dinner engagement with Edward Forbes, *JMN*, 10:450.]

To William Ellery Channing, London, April 20? 1848

[In her letter of c. May 21, 1848 (RWEMA), Lidian Emerson says that Channing mentions Emerson's "apologetic letters" to him. And in a letter to Elizabeth Hoar dated "⟨March⟩ April 1848" (Houghton Library) Channing complains that she does not show him her letters from Emerson though he shows his to her. There are no other clues to these letters; I let this entry stand for them. Mrs. Emerson is acknowledging the letter to her of April 20 and 21 (*Letters*, 4:54–58); he seems to have taken time for letter writing that week.]

To Robert Hutton? London, April 23, 1848 [104]

142 Strand
2⟨2⟩3 April

My Dear Sir,
  It will give me great pleasure to visit you on 6 May, & to meet Miss Martineau.

Your greatly obliged servant,
R. W. Emerson.

To Charlotte Augusta Bailey, London, April? ? 1848

[In an undated letter of 1848 (RWEMA), Charlotte Augusta Bailey acknowledges a "kind note" and invites Emerson to breakfast. A second letter from Mrs. Bailey (endorsed by Emerson May 1848) gives her full name and the address 271 Holborn. See *JMN*, 10:451, for the Pocket Diary entry of April 27, 1848, showing that Emerson dined at this address on that day, and p. 184, for "Mrs. Bailey" at this address. London directories give 271 and 272 High Holborn as the address of Daniel and Edward Bailey, smiths and ironmongers.]

---

104. MS in the Humanities Research Library, TxU; ph. in NNC; added to the dateline is "48," the figures do not look like Emerson's and appear slightly below the line. Listed in *Letters*, 4:61. The MS Pocket Diary for 1848 shows an engagement with Mr. Hutton for May 6 (*JMN*, 10:451); on May 3 Emerson breaks the engagement (*Letters*, 4:65). See *Letters*, 4:41, n. 148, for evidence that Robert Hutton, former M.P. for Dublin, was Harriet Martineau's acquaintance.

To Alexander Ireland, London, May 3, 1848 [105]

I have stayed in London a great while, yet have not quite finished my visit. I am going to Paris, I think, on Saturday, and mean to stay there but a short time, as it is decided, almost against me, that I shall read lectures here three weeks hence. Ah, if I knew what to call those lectures! they have grown from day to day and have not yet a name. But the indecision whilst I have been writing here, whether to read or not, and which I had once decided so, has left me quite unable to send you any word to Manchester. . . . It will also be too late at Manchester for any of those private classes which hovered in your friendly imagination. Besides it is late in the year, and it will be high time for me to set my slow sail for the Capes of Massachusetts. In my short and crowded days here I have given you no account of myself, yet I have found London rich and great, quite equal to its old fame. I have seen a large number of interesting persons, and I suppose the best things—the Parliament, Oxford, the British Museum, Kew Gardens, the Scientific Societies, the Clubhouses, the Theatres, and so forth. I attend Mr. Owen's lectures at the Royal College of Surgeons; Faraday, at the Royal Institution; Lyell, Sedgwick, Buckland, Forbes,[106] I hear at the Geologic Society; and two nights ago I dined with the Antiquaries, and discussed Shakespeare with Mr. Collier.[107] Dr. Carpenter has shown me his microscopes,[108] Sir Henry Delabeche his geologic museum,[109] and I have really owed many valuable hours to the scientific bodies. Now the Picture Galleries are open, and I have begun to see pictures and artists. It is very easy to see that London would last an inquisitive man a good while, and find him in new studies, but the miscellany is distracting, and quiet countrymen will soon have enough of dining out and of shilling-shows. Yet I value all my new experience, and doubtless shall not wish it less when I am safe in my woods again. In Paris I shall remain three weeks to see the revolution, and to air my nouns and verbs. Mr. Bancroft,[110] who has just returned,

105. No MS has been located; text from Ireland, *In Memoriam*, pp. 82–83; listed *Letters*, 4:82–83.

106. See *JMN*, 10:525–528, for Sir Richard Owen, his lectures and his friendship with the painter J. M. W. Turner. Emerson has less to say of Michael Faraday and the distinguished geologists Sir Charles Lyell, Adam Sedgwick, William Buckland, and Edward Forbes.

107. The Society of Antiquaries where Emerson on May 2 met John Payne Collier; see *Letters*, 4:61.

108. See *JMN*, 10:257, for William Benjamin Carpenter's microscopes.

109. Sir Henry Thomas De la Beche, president of the Geological Society.

110. Goerge Bancroft.

takes the most favourable views of their politics, and says the workmen have quite got through all scheme [*sic*] of asking Government to find them labour, repudiate the whole plan, &c. By the last steamer I had no letters from home;[111] if the letters of the due ship come to you, speed them to your ever obliged and grateful.

TO JAMES ANTHONY FROUDE, LONDON, MAY 6, 1848[112]

142 Strand London
6 May, 1848

My dear Sir,

Two friends of mine from Lowell, near Boston,—one for his health & both for pleasure,—are making a tour in England, & wish to see Oxford. In the absence of Clough, I have ventured to give them a note to you, that they may have, what is a great satisfaction to an American, the seeing of an Oxford Fellow in loco. Mr Ames[113] is a lawyer of some eminence, and a son of Fisher Ames, a statesman of great note with us, in his time. Mr Warren[114] is or was a banker, a man of worth too, but I am sorry to see him so much an invalid.

I got to Paris today,[115] for three weeks. On my return, it is decided, almost against my will, that I shall read six lectures in London.[116] I have directed Mr Chapman to send you my card to them, and if you are in London, on any of their days, you must come. Yesterday, I saw Tennyson[117] & am to see him again today. He has the most favorable

111. He found his letters two days later at Baring's; see *Letters*, 4:68.
112. MS in the Alderman Library, ViU; ph. in NNC. Of the young men other than Clough whom he met at Oxford, Emerson speaks most often of Froude (see *Letters*, 4:56, 60, 62). That the letter is addressed to Froude is clear from Froude's letter of June 6 (RWEMA) to Emerson; Froude writes: "I am sorry indeed that I was absent from Oxford taking holyday when your friends came. I need not tell you how much pleasure it would have given me to be of service to them."
113. Seth Ames, son of Fisher Ames, was married to Margaret Bradford; see above, note for letter of February 1841.
114. Pelham W. Warren, president of the Railroad Bank, Lowell. He is listed in Lowell directories of the 1840s as boarding at the Merrimack House, where Emerson stayed when he lectured in Lowell in 1837–1838 at Warren's invitation. Warren was an officer in the bank for sixteen years from its founding in 1831. See *Letters*, 4:67. In n. 240, Rusk, from the shipping list in *The New-York Tribune*, gives Warren's middle initial incorrectly as "M." and his residence as Boston.
115. Clough had gone to Paris where Emerson met him later; see *Letters*, 4:74.
116. At the Marylebone Literary and Scientific Institution; see *Letters*, 4:80, n. 288.
117. May 5, 1848, at Coventry Patmore's; for Emerson's comment on Tennyson, see *Letters*, 4:74, and *JMN*, 10:537–539, 565.

aspect, simple, solid with an unmistakeable sign of general strength & superiority. In the assurance of seeing you again,

Yours,
R. W. Emerson.

To Mary Carpenter, London, May 6, 1848[118]

142 Strand London
6 ⟨April⟩ /May/ 1848

My dear Miss Carpenter,

The hope of seeing you & Bristol, I grieve to say, grows less & less. I go to Paris today for two or three weeks. On my return, it is at last decided that I am to read six lectures in London.[119] But it will then be so late in the season & in my season of vagabond living, that I shall be hastening to Liverpool & Boston. But even at this time, I do not wish quite to shut the door you have so hospitably kept open for me, so that I will not pledge myself not to come to Bristol.

Yours gratefully,
R. W. Emerson.

To Richard Chenevix Trench? London, May 6, 1848[120]

142 Strand, 6 May

My dear Sir,

You were kind enough to promise me the opportunity of seeing your friend Mr Maurice when I should name an evening.[121] I have been quite

118. MS in the Pattee Library, PSt; ph in NNC. Stains from mounting and a tear in the second leaf do not affect the text. See July 3 below for Emerson's second failure to visit Miss Carpenter in Bristol.

119. He refers to the six lectures he would give for the Marylebone Literary and Scientific Institution, beginning on June 6.

120. MS owned by the Jenkins Company (Austin, Texas); quoted in Catalogue 167; ph. in NNC; the address gives the year 1848.

121. The only usable clue to the addressee is the name of John Frederick Denison Maurice. The appearance of Maurice's name in *JMN*, 10:282, is of no help; it appears in MS Journal "London" in a list of books bought or considered as purchases. Maurice, however, had been a close friend of John Sterling. They had met at Trinity College, Cambridge. Maurice's first wife was the sister of Sterling's wife. Maurice also knew Carlyle. It seems reasonable to look for the addressee among Maurice's friends. There are two possibilities.

The first I select is Richard Chenevix Trench (b. 1807). He too had been at Trinity College and closely associated with Sterling (b. 1806) and Maurice (b. 1805). The three together had founded the Apostle's Club. In *the Letters and Memorials*, gathered by Trench's son (London, 1883), the letters are chiefly to Maurice and Sterling. In 1848 Trench was the Dean of Westminster and so living in London as Maurice was also. Carlyle could well have told Emerson of the connection, and Emerson would surely wish to meet friends of Sterling. Emerson later shows some interest in Trench. In 1855 he borrows from the Athenaeum

MAY 1848

occupied all this week & now rather suddenly have decided to go to Paris |today| for a fortnight. It appears, that I am to read lectures when I return. In that case, I shall be sure to have the opportunity of asking you some more questions, & you must continue to be as thoroughly kind & communicative as you have been, to yours gratefully,

R. W. Emerson

In the contingency of the lectures, I shall beg Mr Chapman to send you a card.

To THOMAS GOLD APPLETON, PARIS, MAY 25? 1848

[Two letters by Thomas G. Appleton in the Howe Collection, CFU, make it plain that there was a letter by Emerson, possibly on the 25th or 26th. The first of Appleton's letters is a single leaf: it has at the top "Paris—1848" in a hand that is not Appleton's. The letter invites Emerson to dine with him "tomorrow" and then to call on the Countess Baudrand (see notes May 27 below). The second, fully

---

Trench's *The Lessons in Proverbs*, keeping it for more than two months; in the following year he withdrew Trench's *Calderon;* see *JMN*, 14:24–43, for comment. See Cameron, *ER*, pp. 30 and 110, for these borrowings. In *JMN*, 15:436, are notes of two of Trench's works on language. (His role in initiating *OED* is well known.)

The second possible addressee is Archdeacon Julius Charles Hare (b. 1795). At Trinity College, Cambridge, Hare had been the tutor of Maurice, Sterling, and Trench. In 1844 he had married Maurice's sister; Maurice's second wife was Hare's half-sister. Hare's edition of Sterling's *Essays and Tales . . .* with a memoir of his life was published in 1848. See Harding, p. 258; the book was the gift to Emerson from the publisher; see *Letters*, 4:53. Thanking the publisher, Emerson said the book had "the highest interest" for him. Carlyle no doubt spoke to Emerson of his intense disapproval of the memoir, disapproval that provoked him to supply his own. Emerson's hope of meeting Hare was not likely to be chilled by Carlyle's strictures. Sterling had been Hare's curate when he was rector at Herstmonceux. By 1848, Hare was Archdeacon of Lewes (Sussex). Though not living in London, he could easily have visited often, especially in the "Season." There is, however, Dr. Samuel Brown's flat statement in a letter to Emerson: "By the bye you were mistaken in thinking you had seen Archdeacon Hare." Brown is replying to Emerson's letter begun at sea and finished at Concord (see below, entry for July 26 and 28). Without the text of Emerson's letter, just what Brown means by "seen" is not clear, but leaves the supposition that Emerson did not meet Hare without ruling out altogether the possibility that he did. He certainly must have named him in his letter to Brown. (The Hare Emerson met in Italy in 1833 was the older brother, Augustus William Hare; see *Letters*, 1:383; he died in Rome the following year.)

In the absence of any evidence that Emerson met either Julius Hare or Richard Trench, I should suggest also William Jacobson, the Regis Professor of Divinity at Oxford, on the supposition that he might know the Professor of Divinity at King's College, University of London, one of the chairs held by Maurice.

Apparently Emerson never did meet Maurice, perhaps it is just as well. Maurice regarded Emerson's Neo-platonism as one of two dangerous extremes, the other being Romanism. In a letter to Charles Kingsley, he gives an account of a ferocious battle between himself and Carlyle on the subject of Emerson. The "growler" Carlyle vigorously defending Emerson and Maurice, no mean growler himself, attacking him. Each contender had a backer of mild disposition; Carlyle's was John Sterling. (*The Life of Frederick Denison Maurice*, Chiefly told in his own letters, edited by his son Frederick Maurice; London, Macmillan, 1884, 1:346–347.) No doubt, if Emerson had met Maurice, he'd have been advised to go back to Plato and his teacher Socrates and leave Proclus et al. alone (*Life* of Maurice, 2:134).

dated, letter, May 27, 1848, makes it clear that some confusion of date arose for which Appleton takes the blame, as well he might; for his first letter is an open invitation; he specifies the "next day" but then adds on "any day your engagements permit." Emerson apparently proposed either the 27th or the 28th, but Appleton's letter of the 27th regretfully says he is busy both days and is the more sorry because he had been free on the 26th.]

To Thomas Gold Appleton, Paris, May 27, 1848 [122]

Sat. noon.

I am glad to hear of the arrival of your friends.[123] I believe I cannot spare Monday for any countess [124] but Rachel, who plays for the last time, &, I am told, her Lucrece is specially good.[125] But I have pestered you enough on the subject of that visit. We will adjourn it for the present, with many thanks.

R. W. E.

To Frederick J. Foxton, London, June 10? 1848

[Frederick J. Foxton with his complete address: Gwlch, Cwyn, Rhayder, Radnorshire, is listed twice in *JMN*, 10:130 and 282. The first list is of 1847 and is headed: "Memoranda for the Voyage." In this journal (GH), entries made in England do not begin until MS p. 112, *JMN*, 10:178. Emerson may then have heard from Foxton before he sailed for England. All three surviving letters from Foxton are of 1848. The first, dated March 25, is noted by Rusk, *Letters*, 4:45, where a reply of March 30 is conjectured; this conjecture is warranted by Foxton's

122. MS in the Parkman D. Howe Collection, FU; ph. in NNC. The place and date, May 27, 1848, not in Emerson's hand, appears in pencil crowded around his dateline; on the verso of the first leaf is a note in the same hand: "Letter written by | Ralph Waldo Emerson | Thomas Gold Appleton." | ; on the verso of the damaged second leaf, also in the same hand, appears: "In Paris—/⟨no date, time of Rachel⟩" | This note with its deletion indicates that the supplied date was added late. It was perhaps this annotator who inserted a superfluous comma between "for" and "the last time." It is not in the same ink Emerson used.

The damaged second leaf, its upper portion roughly torn away and the two leaves partly separated, was crudely repaired with a strip of paper containing writing in what appears to be the hand of the annotator.

That the date is correct is clear from Appleton's dated letter of May 27, 1848, also now in the Howe collection, FU, in which Appleton proposes a Monday visit to the countess. See, above, May 25, for Appleton's original invitation and the confusion that followed.

123. The sentence is crowded in as if it were added after the rest of the letter was written. In his letter, Appleton had named the Bartletts and Mr. Ames of Lowell, probably the Sidney Bartletts of Boston, and Seth Ames, who appear in Emerson's letters from England and Paris.

124. The countess was the wife of General Baudrand (Marie Etienne François Henri, Comte de); she would subsequently marry the the painter Ary Scheffer.

125. Emerson saw Rachel three times, the third being in her performance of François Ponsard's *Lucrèce*, which, as this letter shows, had to have been on Monday, the 29th, *JMN*, 10:269; see also *Letters*, 4:73, 75, 77, 79, and notes.

letter of June 8 apologizing for not replying because of illness and Emerson's
being in Paris.

[The third letter is July 5, endorsed 1848. This letter makes it clear that
Foxton has met Emerson; since there is no record of Emerson's visiting Wales,
though Foxton had invited him, I conjecture that Emerson had written to invite
him to come to London. Foxton's third letter shows too that Emerson had suggested books. Foxton had not been able to find the "Bhagavad Gita" in any
language but French; he apparently found Thomas Taylor's Proclus. The meeting was evidently satisfactory to Foxton who writes "whether we meet again or
not I shall never cease to feel a deep & affectionate interest in all you do or say or
write." He promises to write only when his heart is full.]

To George William Frederick Howard, Lord Morpeth, London, June ? 1848

[In a letter of June 17, n.y. (RWEMA) Lord Morpeth invites Emerson to dine on
June 28. A second note without date regrets that he has just missed Emerson but
is glad to secure him for the 28th; he suggests, however, a preference for July 8
and asks for a reply to be sent to him at Whitehall Place. From the note and from
Emerson's letter to his wife of June 21 and 23 (*Letters*, 4:86), I infer that Lord
Morpeth had called at Chapman's for his answer to the invitation of the 17th.
That he did call at Chapman's after hearing Emerson's lecture of June 17 is a
matter of record; see Rusk's n. 303, 4:86.]

To Jane Webb Loudon? London, June 20, 1848 [126]

20 June

142 Strand

My dear Madam,

I am truly sorry that I can not accept your attractive invitations certainly not for Thursday & I fear not for Saturday because of one certain
& one contingent engagement, both probably inevitable. I shall yet keep
before me [127] privilege you offer me for Saturday & if I am released shall
come to you with great pleasure.

Yours respectfully,

R. W. Emerson.

126. MS in OC; ph. in NNC. The London address makes the year secure. This is a single
sheet, the second leaf apparently removed. The letter shows signs of having been at one time
mounted. At the foot of the second page in a hand that is not Emerson's appears: "(To Mrs.
Loudon | Bayswater);" Jane Webb Loudon, widow of Claudius Loudon, lived in Bayswater.
Mrs. Loudon's name does not appear in Emerson's journals or notebooks; nor does her
letter to him survive.

127. Emerson omits the definite article here.

TO WILLIAM ALLINGHAM, LONDON, JUNE 24, 1848[128]

London, 24 June 1848.

My dear Sir,

I was very glad of your letter & verses though they came at a moment so busy for me that they could only cheer me but draw no reply. Henry Sutton too of Nottingham,[129] an excellent youth, wrote to me almost on the same day ⟨t⟩concerning something of yours which he had read in Howitt. And I showed "the Pilot's daughter" to Coventry Patmore & to Clough[130] a good Oxonian who came to see me, & they both liked it well. The more lonely & barricaded round with walls of Fate you find yourself, the better omen for the future days so that only the⟨se⟩ /passing days/ are made divine by obeying the oracle.[131] Our enemies are our /best/ friends, is an experience of all observant men. I should gladly have seen you with eyes, & in these days of travel & revolution, that may yet happen. But your way is onward & upward, & I confide that we shall meet if that be best, as the old saints believed. At present, I am preparing to leave England on Saturday fortnight, or at most three weeks, from Liverpool. And in today's distractions can only acknowledge your kindness by these hurried lines. In constant hope & regard,

R. W. Emerson

TO JOHN ROLT, LONDON, JUNE 27? 1848

[In a letter of June 26, 1848 (RWEMA), John Rolt invites Emerson to dinner, offering several dates; an undated letter from him makes it clear that Emerson

128. MS in the Beinecke Library, CtY; ph. in NNC; printed in *Letters to William Allingham*, H. Allingham and E. Baumer Williams, eds. (London: Longmans, Green, and Co., 1911), p. 44; listed in *Letters*, 4:92; printed by Cameron, *ESQ* (1st q., 1958), 10:36–37. With his letter of June 11, Allingham had sent a copy of his poem "The Pilot's Daughter," *Letters to William Allingham*, p. 43, and pp. 295–299.

129. In his letter to Emerson of June 8, Sutton says that on reading a poem by Allingham in the last issue of *Howitt's Journal*, he recalled Emerson's comment on Allingham's verse. The poem by Allingham is "Cant" in the issue of June 3, p. 362. A tuneless social satire, the poem is derivative, but I find no comment by Emerson that is pertinent. In his notebook "PY Ledger" (a collection of observations on poetry largely culled from earlier journals), there is this judgment (p. 117): "I like much in Allingham's poetry, but you must not remember the masters. Chaucer, Milton, Shakspeare, have seen mountains, if they speak of them. The young writers seem to have seen pictures of mountains."

130. In a letter to Allingham of February 20, [1849], Clough recalls Emerson's having shown him the poem (*Letters to . . . Allingham*, p. 152).

131. In his letter of June 11 (RWEMA) Allingham describes himself as living "so solitary" that he "cannot remember in the last eleven months to have spoken or listened with direct pleasure to any 'articulate' man" (*Letters to . . . Allingham*, p. 43). Emerson offers him the doctrine of compensation.

has been somewhat bemused by so many choices and wished to be sure that July 3 is convenient. See *JMN*, 10:286, 442, for the engagement.]

To Arthur Hugh Clough, London, June 28, 1848[132]

London 28 June 1848

My dear Clough,

I have discovered that the steamer of July 8, from Liverpool, goes to New York; & I must wait one week longer for the Europa, which sails for Boston, on the 15th. You shall not therefore expect me in Liverpool quite so soon as I said. But I gain another point, for Appleton[133] promises to go with me to sea. In the good hope of seeing you again, yours,[134]

R. W. Emerson.

To Mary Carpenter, London, July 3 1848[135]

⟨the⟩London, 3d July.

My dear Miss Carpenter,[136]

As usual I am slow to say what yet I may say gladly, that I will carry with great pleasure to America any letters or parcels which you will honour me with. And I shall receive & read with interest the record of your own thoughts which you promise me in a book. Did you not tell me that perhaps I should find you at Liverpool? I leave Liverpool in the Europa on the 15th, & shall be on the 14th, probably, at Lynn's Waterloo Hotel. Perhaps, however, on second thought the following address is surest—R W Emerson, on board the /steamer/ Europa, sailing 15 July. Care of Messrs D. & C. MacIvor Water Street Liverpool./

And with best wishes & thanks, Yours,

R. W. Emerson.

132. MS in the Clough papers, Bodleian Library, Oxford; ph. in CUL; printed in *Emerson-Clough Letters*, no. 6 (Mulhauser, 1;214); listed *Letters*, 4:92.

133. Thomas Gold Appleton.

134. Clough saw him off.

135. MS in Letter Book "D," Manchester College in Oxford; ph. in NNC. The dateline is not sharply written. Emerson has run the figure "3" into a skimpy "d." The 3d of July is a likely date; Emerson wrote several notes of this sort that day.

136. Mary Carpenter, philanthropist and reformer, concerned with education for the poor and the delinquent, and with prison reform. In 1848, she lived in Bristol, from which presumably she had written Emerson. She was the author of a *Memoir of Joseph Tuckerman* (London: Christian Tract Society, 1849). For the Reverend Joseph Tuckerman, see, above, notes to letter dated July 25, 1830.

To ———, LONDON, JULY 3, 1848 [137]

142 Strand

Monday 3 July

Dear Sir,

I am sorry to find that I shall not be able to join your pleasant party at dinner tomorrow in obedience to your kind invitation. I find my whole week disposed of by a few excursions to Cambridge to Salisbury, Winchester, & other points, which I must not leave England without seeing. With grateful acknowledgments of your courtesy, & best wishes, I am

Yours respectfully,

R. W. Emerson.

To JOSEPH NEUBERG, LONDON, JULY 6? 1848

[In a letter of July 5, 1848 (RWEMA), Joseph Neuberg reminds Emerson that he has promised to show him "Chitsworth." He offers Emerson two arrangements, depending on what day he comes. Emerson would have to answer the letter specifying his choice. See July 11 below for Emerson's visit to Chatsworth.]

To JOHN KENYON, LONDON, JULY 10, 1848 [138]

Monday 10 July

My dear Mr Kenyon,

I found the other day your friendliest note just as I was departing for Cambridge,[139] & now, on my return from Stonehenge & Salisbury & Winchester, last night, I received your note & gifts. If I did not know as all men know your great heart, I should almost suspect you of the design of some poetic angels who load some sinner with costly benefits to melt a

137. MS in the Beinecke Library, CtY; ph. in NNC; printed by Cameron, *ESQ* (1st q., 1958), 10:36. Cameron (who once owned the letter) identifies the addressee as William Mathews, but there is no evidence in Emerson's MS Notebook "England Paris 1847–1848" that Emerson had any engagement with Mathews in July. On the 11th Mathews writes Emerson from Birmingham, and see below Emerson's letter of July 14 regretting that he could not visit Mathews on his way to Liverpool. (Mrs. Mathews had long since invited him to do so.) The addressee is likely to be a Londoner, but there is no clue.

138. MS in Houghton Library, MH; ph. in NNC. The year is in no doubt.

139. In his note of July 4 (RWEMA), evidently written after the trip to Windsor and Eton that day, Kenyon writes of his pleasure in having come to know Emerson in person. The letter accompanied Emerson's great coat, which Kenyon has not asked him "to come and fetch" because he "may need it at Cambridge." Kenyon's second letter of July 7 accompanies the gift of his *Poems*, 1838, and evidently also *A Rhymed Plea for Tolerance*, 1833. See Harding, p. 158, where the 1838 volume inscribed by Kenyon is listed. Kenyon, a poet and philanthropist with many literary friends, is perhaps best known for his intimacy with the Brownings during their courtship and after their marriage.

bad heart; and all the more, that I had a somewhat heavy return from
Windsor, having discovered very quickly that I had blundered out of my
true place[140] which kind Heaven, and a courtesy that held also of the
kind Heaven, had given me. But now what does it mean that I read on
the envelope of these melodious books, Mr K. leaves town on Saturday I
hope he is in town again on Monday & Tuesday,[141] as it is my purpose to
come & make my farewells personally at York Terrace. I shall carry these
good books to the sea, & try their quality there, though I know already
something of their virtue long since; & they shall keep your name in all
honour for me & for many more on the skirt of Concord woods in
Massachusetts. Nor can I doubt that you will yet come yourself into the
great company of the friends you have so effectually served & cherished,
let us show you your New England.[142] I shall venture to add to my note
a⟨n⟩ /new/ American edition of my book.[143]

Respectfully & gratefully yours,
R. W. Emerson.

To Catherine Stevens Crowe, London, July 10, 1848[144]

Monday, 10 July

My dear Mrs Crowe,

I am very sorry that I cannot use the fine privilege you & Mr Rogers
offer me.[145] I must leave London in a few hours, I think, perhaps not till
tomorrow p.m. to begin my tour to Liverpool, which is to combine many
points. I have been out of town ever since I saw you, except sometimes at
night to sleep in London; have seen Windsor, Cambridge, & now Stonehenge, Salisbury, & Winchester, with Carlyle: excellent sights, excellent

---

140. Apparently Emerson got separated from the rest of the party (and his top coat) on
the return from Windsor.

141. Emerson means today and tomorrow, the 10th and the 11th.

142. Kenyon's kindness to Americans is well attested from George Ticknor on.

143. Emerson was giving his English friends the fourth printing of the American edition
of his *Poems* (for the errors in the English edition, see above, December 29, 31, 1846, to
Chapman). Samuel Brown, in a letter of May 13, says David Scott has received a copy
promised him and hopes to have his copy soon; he refers to it as a "fourth" American
edition. A copy presented by Emerson to Mrs. Ellen Fisher, the inscription dated at Manchester, "3 Feby 1848," has "Fourth Edition" on the title page (Special Collections, NNC);
Emerson had made corrections for this printing (M. A 18.2d).

144. MS in the Barrett Collection, Alderman Library, ViU; ph. in NNC. There is no
doubt of the year. Quoted (inaccurately) more than once in catalogues, most fully in Paul C.
Richards' Catalogue 39, 1969, item 2286. See *ESQ* (4th q., 1958), 13:34–35 for others.

145. I have no clue to the "privilege" referred to here, unless Samuel Rogers has invited
Emerson to another of his famous breakfasts.

company.[146] And now, as Burke has said, "I must shut the book, I have had my day."[147]

So do you thank Mr Rogers for me, whose hospitalities on one bright morning, months ago,[148] I shall always remember. And farewell you too, who made me so rich & proud in Edinburgh. I shall never be quite contented until you come to see me in my own house at Concord; keep you that well in your generous mind.

Ever gratefully yours,

R. W. Emerson

To Alexander Ireland, London, July 11, 1848[149]

It now appears certain that I cannot reach Manchester, do what I can, before 9-4 p.m. on Thursday. So you must give me tea and toast and a bed that night, and despatch me early next morning to Liverpool, where Mrs. Paulet[150] has always been promised the homage of a day. I am very sorry that I am so late and crowded and speedy; 'tis the inevitable fate of my nation. But I could not go without a call at Chatsworth,[151] which I must report to some friends at home, and I stop at Coventry[152] one night first. I have just got home from Stonehenge, whither I went with Carlyle, and Chapman has made out the plan of my new journey to you the best he could.—Yours ever.

146. See *Letters,* 4:97, for this tour.

147. See *Letters,* 4:93, for earlier use of this quotation from Burke.

148. See *Letters,* 3:425–426, for breakfast at Rogers' in October 1847, and *Letters,* 4:19, for dinner given Emerson in Edinburgh by Mrs. Crowe for Dr. Samuel Brown. In London, June 22, Emerson took her to call on the Carlyles (Slater, pp. 149–150).

149. No MS has been located; text from Ireland, *In Memoriam,* pp. 83–84; listed *Letters,* 4:99, and see n. 357, where Rusk gives the substance of the letter.

150. Elizabeth paulet, whose letter (undated, but of July 11) inviting him to Seaforth House reminds him of his promise.

151. The engineer George Stephenson, by July very ill, had invited Emerson to visit him and see Chatsworth; see *Letters,* 4:455. Here, however, Emerson is referring to Joseph Neuberg's invitation of July 5 (RWEMA). In *English Traits,* Emerson has nothing to say of Chatsworth. Cameron prints Neuberg's letter, *ESQ* (4th q., 1955), 1:11.

152. To visit Charles Bray in Coventry where Emerson met George Eliot and from which he made a visit to Stratford-on-Avon under the guidance of Edward F. Flower, *Letters,* 4:98, and n. 352.

To William Mathews, Manchester, July 14, 1848[153]

Manchester

⟨13⟩ 14 July

My dear Sir,

I hoped until the last days of my stay in London that I should make Birmingham one stage, & stay over one train with you in my journey northward. But a sort of necessity of seeing Chatsworth,[154] & one or two other points, and with a party, prevented me; and I came here last night, & go this morning to Liverpool, with the expectation of sailing in the steamer tomorrow, and now shall not see you until you come to make your American visit, which, I hope, is really no improbable contingency. Meantime, it is a serious regret to me not to see you & Mrs Mathews, once more; I had much to say to you. I am sorry too not to see Gill,[155] & one or two other friends at Birmingham I made a little journey with Carlyle to Stonehenge, Salisbury, & Winchester,[156] which took three days instead of two, & so deranged my final plans, that I have missed you. With kindest regards to Mrs Mathews, I am Your affectionate servant,

R. W. Emerson.

To William Henry Furness, Liverpool, July 14, 1848

[See below letter of July 15, 1848, where Emerson tells John Nicholson that he encloses a letter to Furness on behalf of William Nicholson.]

153. MS in the Beinecke Library, CtY; ph. in NNC; printed by Cameron, *ESQ* (1st q., 1958), 10:37. William Mathews' home was in Birmingham; a letter of April 12 from Mrs. Mathews (RWEMA) expressed the hope that Emerson would be their guest when he again visited Birmingham. Chapman, with the help of Bradshaw, had shown him the impossibility of getting a stay in Birmingham into his crowded journey from London to Liverpool (*Letters*, 4:98). The correct year 1848 has been added to the dateline in a hand other than Emerson's. Mathews has again endorsed the letter as to "William Mathews Esqre of the Leasowes."

154. See July 11, above, for a note of the visit to Chatsworth.

155. Thomas Hornblower Gill (*Letters*, 3:455 and n. 284); see Scudder, pp. 90–92. From Birmingham also came the Reverend George Dawson, who with Gill had been a guest at Emerson's Manchester dinner party.

156. July 7–9; Emerson in *English Traits* gives a chapter to this trip (*Works*, 5:263–290).

To John? Nicholson, Liverpool, July 15, 1848 [157]

Liverpool 15 July 1848

⟨dea⟩Sir,

Mr Newman desired me to send you a letter or two to friends in the United States.[158] I have been so much pressed with hasty visits, letter writing, & other duties of a departing traveller, that I was not able to do this at all in London, & have not now done it well. But I send you a note to my brother W. Emerson Esq.,[159] New York City, who ⟨m⟩knows all men whom I know there, & many more, and one to Rev. Mr Furness, in Philadelphia, my best acquaintance, & really an excellent one, in that city.

But my hope of serving your brother,[160] lies in his coming to me, at Concord, Massachusetts, which is only one hour's distance from Boston, on the Fitchburg rail road; (Give him, if you please, that direction that he may not be misled into Concord, New Hampshire.)[161]

It will give me great pleasure to obtain for him such information as Boston people can give him.

Yours respectfully,

R. W. Emerson.

157. MS in the Feinberg Collection; MiD; ph. in NNC. The letter is folded and addressed: Dr. Nicholson | Penrith. Printed by Cameron, *ESQ* (1st q., 1958), 10:37, where it is described as written to William Nicholson. I believe it to be addressed to one of Dr. Nicholson's brothers. The letters enclosed are for William Nicholson, the "brother" to be helped, and this letter then cannot be to him. The letter shows signs of being written in haste.

158. Francis W. Newman's letter (n.d., but of 1848, RWEMA) answers Emerson's request for information about William Nicholson.

159. For the letter to William Emerson, see *Letters*, 4:100; as this letter shows, the place is certainly wrong; if the letter to Wm. Emerson was written on the 13th then the place should be Manchester. The letter to Furness has not been found.

160. Emerson did write additional letters for William Nicholson in November 1848; see *Letters*, 4:123–124, and November 3 below. Nicholson finally settled in Cleveland (*Letters*, 4:365).

161. This warning is owing to the error of John Pringle Nichol, who visiting the States in November 1847 went looking three times for the Emerson household in Concord, New Hampshire, while Mrs. Emerson, Elizabeth Hoar, William Ellery Channing, and Thoreau, expecting him for dinner, waited for him in Concord, Massachusetts. See *Letters*, 3:455, for Emerson's fear that Nicholson might have made such an error. In a letter to Emerson of November 29, 1847 (RWEMA), Elizabeth Hoar describes the first of these fiascos, and Ellen Emerson, inaccurately, tells the story in her Life of Lidian (MS, pp. 208–209).

In the manuscript, the word "rail road" is divided at the line without a hyphen. The spelling moved from being two words, then hyphenated, and then one word. The changes occurred within a relatively short period of time. Emerson's inconsistent use of end-line hyphenation leaves his intent in doubt.

To Samuel Gray Ward, S.S. *Europa*, July 22, 1848[162]

> At sea
> Steamship Europa
> 22 July 1848.

My dear friend,

The daily presence & cheerful smiles of your brother[163] make it almost imperative, if I had not besides a just debt, to write you a page, and it will be some sunshine in these headwinds & long disgust of the sea, to remember all the gallery of agreeable images that are wont to appear with your name. What games we men so dumb & lunatic play with one another! What is it or can it be to you that through the long mottled trivial years a dreaming brother cherishes in a corner some picture of you as a type or nucleus of happier visions & a freer life. I am so safe in my iron limits from intrusion or extravagance, that I can well afford to indulge my humour with the figures that pass my dungeon window, without incurring any risk of a ridiculous shock from coming hand to hand with my Ariels & Gabriels. Besides, If you & other deceivers should really not have the attributes of which you hang out the sign, you were meant to have them, they are in the world and it's is with good reason that I rejoice in the tokens. Strange that what is most real & cordial in existence should lie under what is most fantastic & vanishing. I have long ago found that we belong to our life not that it belongs to us, & that we must be content to play a sort of admiring & secondary part to our genius. But here to relieve you of these fine cobwebs, comes an odd challenge from a fellow passenger to play chess with him; me too, who have not played chess, I suppose, for 20 years. Tis of a piece with the oddity of my letter, & I shall accept that, as I write this. Shadows & Shadows. Never say, I did it. Your loving fellow film.

Sea weeds. Two very good men with whom I spent a Sunday in the

162. MS in the Ward papers, Houghton Library, MH; ph. in NNC; quoted by Cabot 1:367; printed in part by Norton, pp. 71–75, as two letters; quoted by Edward W. Emerson in a note, *Works*, 5:397–398; listed (as two letters) in *Letters*, 4;100. Norton breaks this eight-page letter with the word "Seaweeds," but there is no very good reason for dividing this MS into two; there is only one dateline, one salutation, one complimentary close, and one signature. Perhaps it was not all written in one day (it was interrupted obviously), but there is virtually no space at the foot of p. [4] so that "Seaweeds" has to begin on a new sheet. All of it was written at sea, unlike the clearly two letters written to Samuel Brown (See August 8 below); there was certainly no reason for not mailing the whole at once, under a single cover, once Emerson got home. The letters to Brown, on the other hand, had to go by the same pacquet but not necessarily under the same cover.

163. Ward's brother Thomas William Ward (see *Letters*, 4:101).

country near Winchester[164] lately, asked me if there were any Americans, if there were any who had an American idea? or what is it that thoughtful & superior men with us would have? Certainly I did not retort, after our country fashion, by defying them to show me one mortal Englishman who did not live from hand to mouth but who saw his way. No, I assured them there were such monsters hard by the setting sun, who believed in a future such as was never a past,[165] but if I should show it to them, they would think French Communism solid & practicable in the the comparison. So I sketched the Boston fanaticism of right & might without bayonets or bishops, every man his own king, & all cooperation necessary & extemporaneous. Of course, my men went wild at the denying to society the beautiful right to kill & imprison. But we stood fast for milk & acorns, told them that musket-worship was perfectly well known to us, ⟨but⟩that it was an old bankrupt, but that we had never seen a man of sufficient valour & substance quite to carry out the other, which was nevertheless as sure as copernican astronomy, and all heroism & invention must of course lie on this side. Tis wonderful how odiously thin & pale this republic dances before blue bloodshot English eyes, but I had some anecdotes to bring some of its traits within their vision, & at last obtained a kind of allowance; but I doubt my tender converts are backsliders before this.—But their question which began the conversation was so dangerous, that I thought of no escape but to this extreme & sacred asylum, & having got off for once through the precinct of the temple, I shall not venture into such company again, without consulting those same thoughtful Americans, whom their inquiry concerned. And you first, you who never wanted for a reason of your faith, choose now your colours & styles, & draw in verse, or prose, or painted outline, the portrait of your American. Yours, at least, will have verisimilitude marrow & mountain life.[166] Forgive these ricketty faltering lines of mine; they do not come of infirm faith or love, but of the quivering ship. Ever your friend,

R. W. E.

164. July 9. Arthur Helps and Carlyle. See *Works,* 5:286–288, for another report of this conversation.

165. One is certainly Alcott and another Thoreau.

166. Emerson is alluding to Ward's decision to give up banking and commerce for farming and painting; within a year Ward would have to return to business to help his father.

To Samuel Brown, S.S. *Europa*, July 26? and Concord, July 28? 1848

[This letter to Dr. Brown and the letter of August 8 below are treated by Rusk as if they were one letter; see *Letters*, 4:102. Rusk had only Brown's reply of November 9 to go by. Having the letter of August 8 in hand makes it clear that there were two letters; both went out on the *Europa*'s return voyage and would reach Brown at the same time, hence Brown's allusion to the second as a "postscript." In his letter, Brown refers to the content of the letter written partly at sea and partly at Concord. Emerson evidently mentioned Brown's friend Edward Forbes (see *Letters*, 4:63) and tells him that the author of an article on his Essays that appeared in Blackwood over the initials W.S. is the author of a play Emerson never heard of, a tragedy entitled "Aethelwold." The author of the play was William Henry Smith. Emerson had wanted to know. Emerson apparently inquired also about the painter David Scott; Brown reports him as ill. He has apparently also remarked upon his travels in England and on his pleasure in being at home. The remainder of Brown's letter answers Emerson's of August 8.]

To Samuel Brown, Concord, August 8, 1848 [167]

Concord, 8 August, 1848

My dear friend,

I had hardly got safely & happily home, before Theodore Parker came to me with his "Mass. Quarterly Review." He & Cabot have almost alone written the three Numbers that have yet appeared. He wants aid, & your aid, and was proposing to write to you, as he said, "to ask a paper on "*Mesmerism.*" " I said, who shall write to Dr Brown but I? [168] He is my friend, and I am too glad of any need to communicate with him.— For the Journal, it is not as good, not nearly as good as I wish it. I wish it to be rather a Magazine than a Review & am frightened lest it should die of dulness. [169] Honestly, I should like it best if it looked least like other journals, & only heartily contented its authors. I should like it if it should prove at last a record of friendship & of their studies for some sincere

167. MS in the Barrett Collection, Alderman Library, ViU; ph. in NNC. This letter is listed in *Letters*, 4:102, as part of a letter written at sea, c. July 26 and continued at home c. August 6. Brown, replying on November 9, 1848 (RWEMA), is answering two letters; of which this is the second, written just in time to go by the *Europa* on her return voyage (see *Letters*, 4:104, and n. 369).

168. Emerson's MS journal LM lists two names under the heading "Mass Quarterly Review/ Write to"; the first is that of Brown; the second, Horace Bushnell (*JMN*, 10:338). Samuel Brown's "The Methodology of Mesmerism" appears in *The Massachusetts Quarterly Review* (September 1849), 2:401–444. (Emerson repeated the pronoun when he turned his leaf.)

169. See letters to Parker, *Letters*, 4:103–104; 106–110, and September 15 below, also letters to Cabot, *Letters*, 4:111–113. Emerson wants another *Dial*.

persons who quite forgot politics & popularity, but carried the Law of the World in their hearts. Do you not think you can send us something that you you care for? If you do not fancy to give us a supreme view of Mesmerism, why, then, choose your own topic. Send me word what the North British, or other journal in which you write, pay for matter, & I will see that our publishers are as good.—If this can be, I shall write myself with far more courage & good will, & shall enlist new friends. I am not expected to help them, until the Number which appears 1 December.—I talked in London with Chapman, & then with Patmore, Froude, Clough & others of an "Atlantic Journal" which shd. be written from London & Boston—It was Chapman's project.—I only hear these things; never lead them. I only mention it, because Patmore said,—"You shall have Samuel Brown's New Chemistry, & my theory of Architecture in one Number!" [170] ⟨m⟩So might it be! I would be editor, writer, & printer almost, if anything half so good as what I hope from your ⟨s⟩laboratory might come through our Record.—It is unfortunate for all friendly designs of this kind the foolish load of postage our governments have now saddled us with. But by sending letters unsealed to Chapman, he can I doubt not forward them to me without postage. I will write him tonight. Tell me of the laboratory what you may.

With love, R. W. E.

To John Chapman, Concord, August 8, 1848

[See above, August 8, to Dr. Samuel Brown for evidence that Emerson wrote Chapman the same day.]

To Horace Bushnell, Concord, August ? 1848

[See August 8, 1848, above for note of a journal entry that is a reminder to write Horace Bushnell as well as Samuel Brown on behalf of the *Massachusetts Quarterly Review*. There is no contribution by Bushnell to the *Review*, and therefore no certainty that Emerson wrote him, but since he did write Brown, a letter to Bushnell is a possibility.]

To Elizabeth Davis Bancroft, Concord, August ? 1848

[In a letter (on stationery with a mourning border) of October 15, 1848, to Lidian Emerson, Elizabeth Bancroft acknowledges "Kind and welcome notes" from both

170. Coventry Patmore had not yet published anything on his theories or architecture unless he is the author of a review of the Earl of Lindsay's *Sketches of the History of Christian Art* (London: 1847) in *The Critic* (March 6, 1847), no. 114, pp. 177–180. The Earl of Lindsay's book is in any case the probable source of Patmore's theory of the symbolic relationship of Egyptian, Greek, and Gothic architecture.

Emersons. She writes: "Since I received them I have been made very sad by the death of both my brothers. . . ." She goes on to speak particularly of her brother Thomas and his "blighted life." According to *The Plymouth Church Records* (Part 2), Thomas Davis died in September 1848; no specific date is given, but the entry follows one of September 18. The same records record the death of Nathaniel Morton Davis on July 29 (*Publications of the Colonial Society of Massachusetts*, 23:688, 687). I conjecture that the notes from Emerson and his wife were written on the occasion of the death of Nathaniel Davis occurring just as Emerson returned from England. Mrs. Bancroft's letter reads as if their notes had been received before Thomas Davis' death.]

To Frederic Henry Hedge? August 21, 1848[171]

Concord, 21 August, 1848.

My dear friend,

I was heartily glad to see your kind summons, & have to say, with Elizabeth Hoar, that nothing Cambridge has to offer us on its holiday, is so attractive as the invitation to your house. Yet I dare not say that in the huge pile of trifles that I busy myself in these days to dispose, I see no end or vacation so soon as Thursday. Therefore you must not expect me.

Yours affectionately,
R. W. Emerson.

To Theodore Parker, Concord, September 15, 1848[172]

Concord, 15 September, 1848.

My dear Sir,

Your letter announcing your resolution respecting the Journal reached me duly, but I waited to see Cabot who delayed his coming until yesterday.[173] As Cabot has been so prompt in throwing down his arms, I who was plotting to throw down mine, must persist in my mutiny, even though I should repent it one of these days with tears. I could heartily

171. MS in the archives of the American Unitarian Association; ph. in NNC; a single sheet, the second leaf having been torn away. There were not many people whom Emerson addressed as "dear friend" and for whom he signed himself "affectionately." He did address Hedge in that fashion, and on other occasions. Hedge offered hospitality for the commencement weekend. A letter to Hedge might reasonably wind up in the papers of the Unitarian Association. There is, however, no proof. The invitation was for Phi Beta Kappa day. See *JMN*, 10:340, for a list of the trifles, the more demanding for his having been so long away.

172. MS in the Barrett Collection, Alderman Library, ViU; ph. in NNC; p. [4] addressed: Rev Theodore Parker | West Roxbury | Mass. | ; postmarked at Concord September 15. Quoted by Walter Harding from catalogue, *ESQ* (4th q., 1958), 13:35.

173. See *Letters*, 4:111–112, 114–115, for Emerson's letters to James Elliot Cabot.

wish that communication with you were a little easier, as I should like well to exculpate myself from what may easily seem to you very little performance, after much implied promise. But I wanted what perhaps is here & now an impossibility, a journal of pure literature & ethics, which must be very jealous of its philanthropic & political contributors, every man writing on oath, and the journal much preferring to go without its complement of pages than to have less than the best. But I understand very well—though I did not until I saw you last week[174]—your own interest in the enterprise, and you have every right to make it good, & I shall gladly aid you, if I can, by some contribution; though it becomes me henceforward to be very discreet in promising aid, after this experience. And now I shall promise myself great public results from your courage & energy in dealing with the great questions of the day; which, if I, warned by vision or by no vision, do not touch, I do not the less but the more honour & thank those who can & do.

Yours ever gratefully,
R. W. Emerson.

To James Dinsmoor, Concord? October 5? 1848

[James Dinsmoor, corresponding secretary of the Lowell Institute, Lowell, Massachusetts, wrote Emerson October 3 (RWEMA) asking for four lectures and offering any Wednesday dates after November 15. Emerson has endorsed the letter "Answered yes." Rusk notes this only in his index, *Letters*, 6:415. See Charvat, p. 23, for the dates; no subjects are specified; Dinsmoor leaves the subjects to Emerson's choosing.]

To Daniel Austin, Concord? October 7? 1848

[In a letter of October 5, 1848 (RWEMA), Daniel Austin asks Emerson to give two lectures for the Old-Cambridge Lyceum. In his tentative list of 1849 lectures, Emerson lists Cambridge for March 7 and 15. The MS Account Book for 1845–1849, p. 66, lists under the date March 8 the receipt of $15.00 from James Munroe for the Cambridge Lyceum. His only Cambridge lecture in the 1848–1849 season is that of March 7 (Charvat, p. 24; *JMN*, 10:456).]

174. Emerson saw Parker on September 5, going to West Roxbury for the purpose (*Letters*, 4;111); he gives his brother an account of the meeting (*Letters*, 4:113–114) and makes his differences more explicit than he does in this firm but tactful letter. The immaculate text and careful script suggest that Emerson worked it out in drafts first. Emerson clearly wanted another *Dial*; see journal entry (December 8 or 9, 1848), *JMN*, 11:59–60. John Edward Dirks, in his *The Critical Theology of Theodore Parker* (New York: Columbia University Press, 1948), defines the differences between Parker and Emerson (pp. 23–32 et passim). And see *JMN*, 14:352–358.

To Chandler Starr, Concord? October? ? 1848

[See below, October 19, to William Emerson; Emerson must have written a refusal of the invitation to address the New England Society of Brooklyn.]

To William Emerson, Concord, October 19, 1848[175]

Concord, 19 October, 1848.

Dear William,

I had an invitation lately from a New England Society of the City of Brooklyn to deliver a discourse before them on 22 December It came from a Mr Chandler Starr, & was endorsed by Horace Greeley. Of course, I could not think of it though the subject was attractive & I should have liked well a visit to New York. But it would have cost me a month, & my year has not months enough now. Bulkeley remained here until last Friday.[176] I went to Littleton a week before that &, with the help of /Rev./ Mr White[177] found a Mr Hoar, who, on leaving the matter with Mr White, did, some days after, consent to take B. to board. On Friday I went with Bulkeley, and though Mr Hoar was out of town, I saw his wife & family & left him. Mr Reuben Hoar is a large farmer, has sons & daughters, has a variety of plain work, lives at a distance from the village,—it is I fear 3 miles from the railway-station,—and they appear to be very sufficient and amiable people. But the principal thing was, they were willing to take him in. After he has been with me a little while, I should dispute no price less than the. Asylum's that should be demanded for his board. He is an intolerable talker, and will not let you be, —with his innumerable trifling wants. Mr Hoar is to take him now on trial & on such terms as shall be agreed on hereafter. That was our first arrangement with Mr Hall, & formerly with Putnam. I paid Mr Hall for Bulkeley's board for 17 weeks from ⟨26⟩29 May to 26 Sept at 1.13 the old rate—

175. MS in the Emerson papers (RWEMA), Houghton Library, MH; ph. in NNC; p. [4] addressed: William Emerson, Esq. | 10 Wall Street | New York. | ; postmarked at Concord October 20, endorsed by William Emerson as received on the 21st and answered on the 27th. Listed in *Letters*, 4;119.

176. See *Letters*, 4:114, 116. See *Letters*, 3:292 and 417, for Richard Hall of Littleton, who sold his farm in September 1847 and could no longer board Bulkeley Emerson. See *Letters*, 1:252, for Bulkeley's boarding with Israel Putnam of Chelmsford, an arrangement that held until 1845 (see above April 1, 1845, n. 49), Bulkeley being periodically confined to McLean's Asylum.

177. William Hunt White, a nephew of Samuel Hoar, and see Hurd, *The History of Middlesex County*, 2:875.

$$19.21$$

to cash　　.30

to horse & carriage　　.75　　20.26

Paid besides for my two visits to Littleton by cars and for Bulkeleys return

$$30 \times 5 = 1.50$$

Kendall twice for R.B.E.　　.25

sundries for do　　. 6

cash for do　　.10　　1.91

$$22.17^{178}$$

I fear every days mail may bring me a letter from Mr Hoar, for the late chan[ge] had left Bulkeley much more excitable than usual.

Did I tell you that Eddy's rocking horse[179] & my casts of Isis were lost in the Ocean Monarch?[180] The bill of lading was bro't me by Joseph Lyman.[181] Lidian & the boy received the news at Plymouth, & Nathaniel Russell,[182] to whom Lidian had once sold an old family rocking horse, only junior to the Trojan Horse, magnificently explored his garret, & made it a present to Eddie. The horse arrived in Concord amidst uproarious acclamations of our youngest people. We are all expecting to hear Susan shall come.[183] Has she gone to Portsmouth? With love from us all to you all.

Yours ever

Waldo.

178. These expenses are recorded in the MS Account Book for 1845–1849, p. [134], under the dates October 6 and 13, 1848. The first payment to Reuben Hoar is of February 2, 1849, p. [150].

179. See *Letters*, 4:7 and 82–84, for Edward's desire for a rocking horse.

180. The *Ocean Monarch* caught fire eight hours out of Liverpool, August 24, 1848. Richard C. McKay, *Some Famous Sailing Ships* . . . (New York: G. P. Putnam's, 1928), p. 65. The bill of lading is in Miscellaneous Business papers (RWEMA). In the same box is the receipt, July 5, 1848, for the purchase of "2 busts & figure" for £1.14.0.

181. Joseph Lyman had been a close friend of Charles Chauncy Emerson (see *Letters*, 1:281).

182. For "Captain" Nathaniel Russell, see *Letters*, 2:85, and above, November 6, 1835, July 27, 1841.

183. William Emerson's wife, Susan Haven Emerson, whose family lived in Portsmouth, New Hampshire.

To William Buell Sprague, Concord, October 25, 1848[184]

Concord, October 25, 1848.

My dear Sir: It will be easy, as it is grateful, to me to answer your inquiries in regard to Dr. Ripley, as I still have by me some sketches which I attempted of his character very soon after his decease. Indeed, he is still freshly remembered in all this neighbourhood. He was a man so kind and sympathetic, his character was so transparent, and his merits so intelligible to all observers, that he was very justly appreciated in this community. He was a natural gentleman; no dandy, but courtly, hospitable, manly, and public spirited; his nature social, his house open to all men. I remember the remark made by an old farmer, who used to travel hither from Maine, that "no horse from the Eastern country would go by the Doctor's gate." Travellers from the West and North and South could bear the like testimony. His brow was serene and open to his visitor, for he loved men, and he had no studies, no occupation, which company could interrupt. His friends were his study, and to see them loosened his talents and his tongue. In his house dwelt order, and prudence, and plenty; there was no waste and no stint; he was open-handed and just and generous. Ingratitude and meanness in his beneficiaries did not wear out his compassion; he bore the insult, and the next day his basket for the beggar, his horse and chaise for the cripple, were at their door. Though he knew the value of a dollar as well as another man, yet he loved to buy dearer and sell cheaper than others. He subscribed to all charities, and it is no reflection on others to say that he was the most public spirited man in the town. The late Dr. Gardiner, in a Funeral Sermon on some parishioner, whose virtues did not readily come to mind, honestly said,—"He was good at fires."[185] Dr. Ripley had many virtues, and yet all will remember that, even in his old age, if the fire bell was rung, he was instantly on horseback with his buckets and bag.

He was never distinguished in the pulpit as a writer of sermons, but in his house his speech was form and pertinence itself. You felt, in his

184. No MS has been found, text from Sprague's *Annals of the American Pulpit,* 8:117–118; printed also by Alexander Ireland in *Ralph Waldo Emerson* (the second edition of *In Memoriam*) (London, 1886), pp. 191–196. Listed *Letters,* 4:120. Reprinted from Sprague by Cameron, "Emerson on His Father and Step-Grandfather," *ESQ,* (1st q., 1957), 6:18–19.

In this fine portrait, Emerson is concerned, I think, to make up for any injustice he may have done his step-grandfather. For his thought that his aunt Mary Moody Emerson may have prejudiced him against Ezra Ripley, see MS journal NY (1869), p. 217 (*JMN,* 16:175). Cf. the account of Ezra Ripley prepared for the Concord Social Circle, *Works,* 10:379–395.

185. John S. J. Gardiner, rector of Trinity Church, Boston, died in England September 11, 1831 (see *Letters,* 1:308, n. 74). Said of Bishop Samuel Parker; see *JMN,* 8:90, and n. 42.

presence, that he belonged by nature to the clerical class. He had a foresight, when he opened his mouth, of all that he would say, and he marched straight to the conclusion. In private discourse or in debate, in the vestry or the lyceum, the structure of his sentences was admirable,— so neat, so natural, so terse, his words fell like stones, and often, though quite unconscious of it, his speech was a satire on the loose, voluminous, patch-work periods of other speakers. He sat down when he had done. A man of anecdote, his talk in the parlour was chiefly narrative. I remember the remark of a gentleman, who listened with much delight to his conversation, at the time when the Doctor was preparing to go to Baltimore and Washington, that "a man who could tell a story so well was company for kings and John Quincy Adams."[186] With a very limited acquaintance with books, his knowledge was an external experience, an Indian wisdom, the observation of such facts as country life, for nearly a century, could supply. He watched with interest the garden, the field, the orchard, the house and the barn, horse, cow, sheep and dog, and all the common objects that engage the thought of the farmer. He kept his eye on the horizon, and knew the weather like a sea-captain. The usual experiences of men,—birth, marriage, sickness, death, burial, the common temptations, the common ambitions, he studied them all, and sympathized so well in these that he was excellent company and counsel to all, even the most humble and ignorant. With extraordinary states of mind, with states of enthusiasm, or enlarged speculation, he had no sympathy and pretended to none. He was very sincere, and kept to his point, and his mark was never remote. His conversation was strictly personal, and apt to the person and the occasion. An eminent skill he had in saying difficult and unspeakable things; in delivering to a man or a woman that which all their other friends had abstained from saying; in uncovering the bandage from a sore place, and applying the surgeon's knife with a truly surgical spirit. Was a man a sot, or a spendthrift, or too long time a batchelor, or suspected of some hidden crime, or had he quarrelled with his wife, or collared his father, or was there any cloud or suspicious circumstance in his behaviour, the good pastor knew his way straight to that point, believing himself entitled to a full explanation; and whatever relief to the conscience of both parties plain speech could effect, was sure to be procured. In all such passages he justified himself to the conscience, and commonly to the love, of the persons concerned.

186. Edward W. Emerson credits this remark to his uncle Edward Bliss Emerson (*Works*, 10:591).

Many instances, in which he played a right manly part, and acquitted himself as a brave and wise man, will be long remembered. He was the more competent to those searching discourses, from his knowledge of family history. He knew everybody's grandfather, and seemed to talk with each person, rather as the representative of his house and name than as an individual. In him has perished more local and personal anecdote of this village and vicinity than is possessed by any survivor. This intimate knowledge of families, and this skill of speech, and still more his sympathy, made him incomparable in his parochial visits, and in his exhortations and prayers with sick and suffering persons. He gave himself up to his feeling, and said on the instant the best things in the world. Many and many a felicity he had in his prayer, now forever lost, which defied all the rules of all the rhetoricians. He did not know when he was good in prayer or sermon, for he had no literature and no art; but he believed, and therefore spoke.

He was eminently loyal in his nature, and not fond of adventure or innovation. By education, and still more by temperament, he was engaged to the old forms of the New England Church. Not speculative, but affectionate; devout, but with an extreme love of order, he adopted heartily, though in its mildest forms, the creed and catechism of the fathers, and appeared a modern Israelite in his attachment to the Hebrew history and faith. Thus he seemed, in his constitutional leaning to their religion, one of the rearguard of the great camp and army of the Puritans; and now, when all the old platforms and customs of the Church were losing their hold in the affections of men, it was fit that he should depart, fit that, in the fall of laws, a loyal man should die.

Yours, with great respect,

R. W. Emerson.

TO JAMES FREEMAN CLARKE, CONCORD? OCTOBER 28, 1848

[In the letter calendar in his MS journal for 1848–1849 (MHS) James Freeman Clarke lists under the date October 28, 1848, a letter from Emerson. This letter may have concerned Clarke's effort to secure a lecture from Emerson for his Freeman Place Chapel; see *Letters*, 4:118–121, and nn. 416, 417, 427.]

TO HENRY A. JONES, CONCORD, OCTOBER 30? 1848

[In a letter of October 29, 1848 (RWEMA), Henry A. Jones, corresponding secretary of the Portland Lyceum, invites Emerson to lecture, offering the first, third, or fourth Wednesday in December. He wants a reply by return mail so that he may advertise Emerson as one of his lecturers "by Wednesday next." Emerson

lectured in Portland on January 31, 1849 (Charvat, p. 23; *JMN*, 10:454). In a
letter of February 12, 1849, Jones describes the Lyceum as pleased with "the
beautiful simplicity of your 'Voyage to Europe' &c." There is no other record of
this title.]

To Samuel Hill, Concord? November 1, 1848

[Emerson has endorsed Samuel Hill's letter of October 30, 1848, asking for a
lecture in Woburn "Yes (in Feby probably)." Rusk notes this evidence of a letter
in his Index, *Letters*, 6:969. The Pocket Diary for 1848–1849 (*JMN*, 10:454) lists
the Woburn lecture under the date January 11; the receipt of $10.00 for the
lecture is listed in the MS Account Book for 1845–1849, p. [42], under the date
January 12. There is no evidence that he gave more than one lecture.]

To Joseph Longworth, Concord, November 3, 1848 [187]

Concord, November 3, 1848

Joseph Longworth, Esq.
Sir,

   My friend W. E. Channing to whom I applied to introduce my friend
Dr Nicholson to a few good men in Cincinnati, whilst he thinks it important that Dr N. should see you, flatters me by saying that you will forgive
me if I address you directly without the privilege of a personal acquaintance.[188] I decide to run the risk, & throw myself on your indulgence to
the extent of this letter, whose object is to pray for the bearer, Dr
Nicholson, such advice & information as you may supply to an accomplished English gentleman proposing to emigrate with his friends to
⟨c⟩this country. Dr Nicholson is a physician who has taken his degrees at
the University of Berlin; and his brother, Dr John N., at the University
of Oxford. They, with their families, are planning a removal into the
United States, & Dr William Nicholson now comes to see where. They
are most favorably known at home for their learning & their personal
worth; & all good men here have an intere⟨n⟩st in confirming them in
their purpose. Will you furnish him with any hints which your local
knowledge[189] may suggest in regard to land & living in Ohio, toward

187. MS in the collections of OCHP; ph. in NNC. Instead of using the blank fourth page
for the address, Emerson used the first leaf of another piece of stationery and, after folding
his letter, used the extra leaf to form an evelope addressing it lengthwise. It is addressed:
Joseph Longworth, Esq. | Cincinnati | Ohio | Dr W. A. Nicholson | . See *Letters*, 4:123–124.
The letter is very neatly written.

188. Emerson would later become acquainted with the addressee, son of the well-known
wine-grower Nicholas Longworth. See below May 17, 1858, and *Letters*, 4:308, 330. For other
letters on behalf of William Nicholson, see, above, July 15.

189. Emerson breaking "knowledge" at the end of the line uses a double hyphen.

which his eyes seem now to be directed. And when you or any friend of yours /shall/ come to Boston, I shall be particularly gratified if you will make me useful to you.

Yours respectfully,
R. Waldo Emerson.

To James Handasyd Perkins, Concord, November 3, 1848

[See *Letters*, 4:123–124, where Rusk cites a letter from William A. Nicholson belatedly acknowledging letters of introduction Emerson had sent for him. In his letter Nicholson names Joseph Longworth (see above) and "Mr. Perkins" whom he has visited. With the letter to Longworth above, a letter to Perkins seems the more likely. Rusk provides the probable identification of Perkins.]

To William A. Nicholson, Concord, November 3, 1948

[Since Emerson's letter introducing Nicholson to Joseph Longworth did not go through the mails, I infer that Emerson sent the letter, along with the likely letter to James H. Perkins, directly to Nicholson with a covering note.]

To George Lyman Emerson, Concord, November 17, 1848

[Under the date November 17, 1848, in the MS Account Book for 1845–1849, p. [139], is a note: "Cash sent in letter to G. L. Emerson 10.00."]

To _____, Concord, November 18, 1848

[In Catalogue 14 of Charles Yale, Pasadena, item 493, is a letter of November 18, 1848, described as of eighty-two words about lectures. It is possibly the letter of this date to Charles Timothy Brooks listed *Letters*, 4:123. In a letter of November 16, 1848, Charles Timothy Brooks had asked Emerson to lecture for the Mechanics' & Manufacturers' Association in Newport, Rhode Island; Emerson accepted the date proposed, December 7 (see Charvat, p. 23).]

To George Walden, Concord, December 2, 1848 [190]

Concord, 2 December, 1848.
George Walden, Esq. Secretary.
Dear Sir,

I find myself engaged for the evenings you name, 4 & 5 January, and it would not be practicable, I think, for me to accept your invitation for

190. MS in the Barrett Collection, Alderman Library, ViU; ph. in NNC; without address leaf. Emerson lectured in Northampton and Cabotville (now part of Chicopee) on the February 22 and 23, 1849 (Charvat, p. 24); these engagements are entered in the MS Pocket Diary for 1848–1849 (*JMN*, 10:456). Under the same dates in MS Account Book for 1845–

any earlier day than in o⟨f⟩ne of the last weeks of February. For so distant a day, I do not like to promise; but if the 22 & 23d February suit your Lyceums, you shall hold me for them, unless /I hear from you, or unless/ I give you a seasonable notice with cause why I should not come.

Yours respectfully,
R. W. Emerson.

To Sarah Ann Clarke, Concord, December 11, 1848[191]

Concord, 11 December, 1848.
Great is your courage, my dear friend, to perplex yourself with these rough rambling manuscripts;[192] but if you ask, I suppose I must dare to bring them. I am much bound by the kind invitation to your house, and, when the Lecture evening is fixed, I hope to accept it,—certainly in part; & Elizabeth[193] shall be duly informed. I saw Mrs Newcomb, at Providence,[194] & found her entirely favorable to Elizabeth's design, & yours.

Affectionately yours,
R. W. Emerson.

To William Henry Furness, Concord, December 16, 1848[195]

Concord, 16 December, 1848.
My dear Furness,
I am very glad to see your faithful hand again, always of the best omen to me & to whomsoever it concerns itself for. But I hardly dare accept the opportunity you offer me of printing a chapter on Montaigne. All that I know, or, all that I know how to say, about him, is written in one of Seven Lectures, which, together, I call "Representative Men," & Montaigne there stands for the class *Skeptic*. I mean some day to print these together, whenever I shall have more adequately finished the resisting figures of Plato & of Swedenborg.

1849, p. [64], he records the receipt of $15.00 from each; and in the calendar of lecture engagements at page [166] he records the two engagements.

191. MS in the Clarke papers, Houghton Library, MH; ph. in NNC; this is a single sheet; the address leaf is missing.

192. Miss Clarke has evidently asked to borrow the MSS of the lectures. I infer that she has invited him for the first evening of his Freeman Place Chapel lectures (arranged by her brother, james Freeman Clarke) or for the day after.

193. Elizabeth Hoar probably.

194. Charles K. Newcomb's mother whom Emerson saw on the 5th.

195. MS in the Furness papers, Van Pelt Library, PU; ph. in NNC; p. [4] addressed: Rev. W. H. Furness. | Philadelphia Pa. | ; postmarked at Concord December 16. Printed in *Records*, p. [67]; listed *Letters*, 4:126.

I am much obliged to you for the pleasing & most readable tract on the Art-Union, which you sent me, the other day. It gave me exact & agreeable information. It would give me the greatest pleasure to see the Author of that tract.[196] Do you think I ever shall?

Yours affectionately,
Waldo E.

To Edward Everett Hale, Concord, December 28, 1848 [197]

Concord, 28 December, 1848.

My dear Sir,

I am much gratified by your friendly proposition, and am not without hope of holding you to it one of these weeks. Just now I am balancing & must perhaps today decide what has been suggested from Boston, whether to read there as a private course the London Lectures you speak of. If I should do so, I could not come to Worcester for five or six weeks, as these lectures are a study for me, & will require that I stay much at home whilst they are on foot. If I do not go to Boston, I should like very well to come to Worcester,[198] /at once,/ if you will warn the class that three of the six lectures are intended to be the "Natural History of the Intellect," and do eagerly ask a thoughtful ear. The other three were not objectionable, that I know, on the score of taxing too much the attention of the class. I call the series, "Mind & Manners in the XIX Century," and would read them at Worcester, for twenty dollars for each lecture.[199] It would give me much pleasure on many accounts to go thither, & if you think it worthwhile I will endeavour to arrange it.

Yours respectfully,
R. W. Emerson

196. *An Address Delivered Before the Art-Union of Philadelphia in the Academy of Fine Arts.* . . . (Philadelphia, 1848). Furness gave this address on October 12. The work is not now in Emerson's library.

197. MS in Houghton Library, MH; ph. in NNC; p. [4] addressed: Rev. Edward E. Hale. | Worcester. | Mass. | ; postmarked at Concord, December 30. Reproduced in facsimile by Julian Hawthorne in "Personal Glimpses of Emerson," *The Booklovers Magazine* (February 1903), 1:159, 163, 166. This article is reproduced by Cameron, *ESQ* (4th q., pt. 3, 1967), 49:159. The Library of UCLA had reproductions of this letter and the others in the same article; I saw these before the *ESQ* article appeared, but do not know whether the reproductions indicate some other printing, there being nothing with them to show the source.

198. See Charvat, pp. 23–24, for the final schedule of lectures as given in Worcester. See *Letters*, 4:133, 134–135, for Emerson's difficulties in meeting the schedule as arranged.

199. Worcester was able to pay him a little more than the $120 as agreed upon here (see *Letters*, 4:135, n. 29, and Charvat); the extra $18.00 did not cover Emerson's expenses, not to mention the loss of his wallet with $15 or $20 in it (MS Account Book for 1845–1849, p. [151]).

1849

To Epes Sargent, Concord? January 1? 1849.

[Emerson's letter of January 13 below shows that he had written Epes Sargent to ask that the *Boston Evening Transcript* print no verbatim report of his lecture before the Mercantile Library Association. Emerson gave two lectures for the association: the first on December 27, the second on January 3 (Charvat, p. 23).]

To Charles H. Brigham, Concord, January 5? 1849

[Charles H. Brigham had first proposed a lecture in Taunton, Massachusetts, in a letter of January 4, 1849 (RWEMA), asking for an early reply; his second letter of January 10 is dated 1848, but is clearly of 1849 and is an answer to a letter from Emerson. See note below under January 12 for further correspondence.]

To Henry Wadsworth Longfellow, Concord, January 5, 1849[1]

Concord 5 January 184⟨8⟩9

My dear Longfellow,

I send you a poem which you must find time to read, and which I know you will like. The author is /or was lately/ a Fellow of Oriel College, Oxford, and was Dr Arnold's favorite pupil at Rugby.[2] I knew him at Oxford, & spent a month in Paris with him, valued him dearly, but, I confess, never suspected all this poetical fury and wealth of expression. Will you not, after trying his verses, leave it for me at James Munroe's in Boston, say on Wednesday or Thursday?—Ellery Channing has kept Jasmin from me,[3] until lately; so it must stay yet a little longer with me.

Yours ever,
R. W. Emerson.

1. MS in the Longfellow papers, Houghton Library, MH; ph. in NNC; p. [4] addressed: Professor Longfellow. Printed by Samuel Longfellow in *Final Memorials of Henry Wadsworth Longfellow* (Boston: Ticknor, 1887), pp. 29–30; listed, *Letters*, 4:128.

2. Arthur Hugh Clough, *Bothie of Toper-na-Fuosich* (Oxford: F. MacPherson, 1848); the book is no longer in Emerson's library. Longfellow's *Evangeline*, published in 1847 (*BAL*, 12089), suggested to Clough the use of hexameters (Clough to Emerson, February 10, 1849. *Emerson-Clough Letters*, no. 8; Mulhauser, 1:240–241). See below January 11.

3. Longfellow had evidently loaned Emerson a book by the Gascon dialect poet Jacques Boé called Jasmin ("le Perruquier Poète"). Longfellow's MS diary (on deposit, Houghton

To James Freeman Clarke, Concord, January 8, 1849

[In the letter calendar in his MS journal for 1848–1849 (MHi), James Freeman Clarke lists under the date January 8, 1849, a letter from Emerson. A letter from Clarke to Emerson dated January 11, "1848," but endorsed by Emerson 1849, acknowledges tickets and recommends "our Sexton" as doorkeeper for Emerson's lecture series to begin January 15, 1849. Clarke says the doorkeeper will attend to fires and lights. In his letter of January 8, Emerson had apparently inquired about the lighting and had enclosed the tickets with it. See Charvat, p. 22, for this series given in Clarke's Freeman Place Chapel.]

To William Henry Furness, Concord, January 10, 1849[4]

Concord, 10 January, 1849.

My dear Furness,

Here is a curious coil in Carlyle's last letter, which I know not how to begin to unwind except by letting him tell his own story, and to you, poor you, who were born for a benefactor to him & to me. You must even go through patiently with your destiny.—Thus runs the letter, under date 'Chelsea, 6 December, 1848.'

"You are to be burdened with a foolish ⟨piece⟩bit of business for me again; do not grudge it, but do it since it has come on course! Here is the matter. About three years ago, (I think in the end of 1845) Mr Hart, of the firm Carey & Hart in Philadelphia, sent me, as you may remember, a draft for £ 50, payable by some house in Liverpool; it was in return for liberty to print (without grumble from me) the Book of Essays; and, though an old silent[5] friend in Philadelphia negociated the immediate details, you, too, I believe, had a hand in the affair, & were privy to it all along. Well, this draft arrived; come to me while I was at Alverstoke in Hampshire with Mr Baring (Hon. W. Bingham Baring, now Lord Ash-

---

Library), shows that the book was Jasmin's *L'abuglo de castèl-Cuillé* and that his brother-in-law Thomas Gold Appleton had brought it to him from Paris in 1847 (Longfellow's MS diary, entry of June 12, 1847) Longfellow declares Jasmin "a true poet," refers to the book as "The Blind Girl of Castell-Cuillé," and lists it in his MS 1847 book list as "L'Abugle de Calèt-Cuilés." Appleton, who must have returned to Europe in the winter, may have told Emerson of it in July 1848 when he came home again on the same ship with Emerson. In an article of May 1, 1837, collected in his *Portraits Contemporains* (2:1846), Sainte-Beuve had named the poem as Jasmin's most remarkable work.

4. MS in the Furness papers, Van Pelt Library, PU; ph. in NNC; p. [4] addressed: Rev. William H. Furness. Philadelphia, Pa.; postmarked at Concord January 10. Printed in *Records*, pp. [68]–69; listed in *Letters*, 4:128. The portion quoted from Carlyle is in Slater, pp. 443–444.

5. See Slater, pp. 381, 383; and, above, October 15, 1845, for more about Carlyle's £50. The "silent friend" is Furness.

burton,)[6] probably about this very season of the year: whether the Liverpool House had accepted, I cannot now say; but their acceptance not being doubtful the paper (payable probably in 60 days or so,) was of course perfectly equivalent to the sum marked on it; and accordingly Mr Baring, when I spoke of negociating it, & inquired his advice, How? volunteered, as my only Banker is a Scotch one at Dumfries, to give me at once in return for it a draft of his bankers (the Drummonds, of Charing Cross here,) by whom the paper would be duly managed without trouble to anybody, and the £ 50 at once paid me. And so undoubtedly the £ 50 was at once paid me, & I got it, & spent it, & returned some acknowledgment to Mr Hart for it; & had entirely forgotten it, when, about a year a year ago, Mr Baring surveying his Banker's Account Book, told me he could not find that item in it; was by me invited to search farther; has searched farther, set his Bankers to search,—& now, the other day, ascertains finally that there is no such payment or transaction recorded in his favour,—& that, in brief, he must have lost the Carey & Hart Draft for £ 50, payable by some Liverpool House, and that it was never presented for payment, & consequently never paid! This he told me, the other night; and I, of course, heartily vexed at this act of carelessness, engaged to inquire. The things now to be done, therefore, are two, first to ascertain from Mr Hart, what the exact particulars of the draft were, (this will be tolerably easy, I suppose,) & then, secondly, whether, supposing the money were never demanded, it is now in the hands of the Philadelphia, or of the Liverpool House, or in whose hands, —in short, what is possible for limited but honest human nature, pursuing correctness under impediments, still to do in the matter. Ascertain me these two things, this one last thing, like a good fellow; and I will let you lie quiet for a very long time to come!"—

So far the Homeric Carlyle. I think you must carry the matter to Mr Hart, for him; though certainly Mr Baring's carelessness is inexcusable.[7] But he is a good man, I saw him two or three times, & found him very friendly, & hospitable, and he has been for many years a valuable friend to Carlyle.

6. Emerson had met William Bingham Baring and his wife Lady Harriet through Carlyle; Baring had become the second Baron Ashburton on the death of his father, Alexander Baring, in May 1848.

7. Furness investigated the matter and reported to Emerson, January 15 (*Records*, p. 70); Emerson was able to write Carlyle on January 23; see Slater, p. 449, and his note for Emerson's error in copying Furness.

And so I leave my burden with you, for this present; and am as ever Yours affectionately,

R. Waldo Emerson.

To ARTHUR HUGH CLOUGH, CONCORD, JANUARY 11, 17? 1849[8]

Concord, 1⟨1⟩⟨6⟩7, January 1849

My dear Clough,

I cannot tell you how great a joy to me is your poem. It came to me on the very day when a frightful calamity had come into the house of a dear friend here, whom I was on the way to visit,[9]—and I had that night a strange balance to adjust, of grief & joy. For this poem is a high gift from angels that are very rare in our mortal state. It delights & surprises me from beginning to end. I can hardly forgive you for keeping your secret from me so well. I knew you was good & wise, stout of heart & truly kind, learned in Greek, & of excellent sense,—but how could I know or guess that you had all this wealth of expression, this wealth of imagery, this joyful heart of youth, this temperate continuity, that belongs only to high masters. It is a noble poem. Tennyson must look to his laurels. It

8. MS in the Clough papers, Bodleian Library, Oxford, with envelope addressed: Arthur H. Clough. | Care of Mr John Chapman | 142 Strand, | London. |; verso stamped in England February 5; ph. in NNC. Printed in *Emerson-Clough Letters*, no. 7; and by Mulhauser, 1:232–233. The date Emerson gives his letter and the date Rusk and Lowry assign to it (23rd) are both puzzling, for on neither the 16th nor the 23rd was Emerson in Concord. The letter had to have been written by the 23rd to catch the Cunarder leaving on the 24th. It could not have been written earlier than the 10th or 11th when Longfellow returned the book with his letter of the 9th quoted by Emerson. The date looks as if it had been written over; what I see is "11" altered to "16" and immediately to "17"; the second digit does not look like Emerson's normal writing of either "6" or "7," but the descending stroke is heavy as the first digit is and both the curl to the right and the horizontal stroke to the left at the top are light as if done at the same time with the same pen. It seems to me that the greater part of the letter could have been written in Concord on the 11th and the rest written on the 17th. This supposition would square with the Concord dateline and with Emerson's letters of the 23rd to Longfellow and Carlyle. Both these hurriedly written letters are dated from Boston. To Longfellow Emerson writes: "I have written to Clough, to thank him for his poem, & have not forgotten to inform you of your friendly verdict" (*Letters*, 4:130). In his note to Carlyle, he complains of Carlyle's silence about the poem and of finding no notices of it in the English periodicals (Slater, p. 250). Evidently the January issue of *Fraser's Magazine* (39:103–110) with Charles Kingsley's review was not available in the States when Emerson made his search (see *Wellesley Index* for citation of a Kingsley letter of January 15 and Mulhauser, 1:240, for Clough's letter to Kingsley of February 10). Emerson's letter to Clough does not read as if it were written in a hurry, though it does read as if it were written piecemeal.

9. The death of George Samuel Emerson, son of George Barrell Emerson, December 22, 1848. On that day Emerson entered in his journal his initial response to Clough's poem (*JMN*, 11:63); for a second reading and comment, see *JMN*, 11:92.

makes me & all of us richer, and I am recalling every passage of speech & action of my staid & reticent friend, to find the hints & parallels of what I read. I have no time now to write at all, much less to tell you what I think. But I sent the poem to many friends, each for one night, & have the best report from all. Three of them have ordered copies immediately, & you shall have a sale here quickly. Longfellow I sent it to, & he writes moderately enough, yet I will transcribe his note,[10] as Longfellow is prized on your side the water. "Altogether fascinating, & in part very admirable is the poem of Mr. Clough. Tom Appleton read it aloud to us the other evening, the audience consisting of my wife; my brother, an engineer; Lowell, the poet; a German friend, a man of letters, well versed in our vernacular; & myself. All were much delighted with the genial wit, the truth to nature, & the extreme beauty of various passages & figures; all agreed that it was a poem of a very high order of merit; no one criticized.—In the morning, I found Appleton reading it again to himself; in the afternoon, my wife doing the same thing, &c"—then he praises "the /fine/ delineation of the passion of love," & congratulates himself on the hexameters, &c &c

Well, Carlyle has written me, & never mentioned this. I looked into your journals, & find no notice yet. It is named somewhere, but they have not found out that they have got a new book! Well, keep your secret if you can, & as long as you can. Alas for you! Your silent days, I believe, are now nearly ended. Thanks & joy & love to you!

R. W. Emerson.

To Nathaniel Hawthorne, Boston, January 12, 1849[11]

Boston, 1⟨1⟩2 January, 1849.

My dear Sir,

I did not mean to come Salem[12] until my Boston Course was ended; but to avoid troubling you with my hesitations, I will accept at once your day, &, come next Wednesday.[13] Kindest thanks for your friendly invita-

10. See *Letters*, 4:130, for Longfellow's letter of January 9 given in full in n. 9; the letter is substantially the same as Longfellow's MS journal entry of January 7 (on deposit, Houghton Library).

11. MS in the Phillips Library, MSaE; ph. in NNC; p. [4] addressed: Nathaniel Hawthorne, Esq. | Salem | Mass.| ; postmarked at Boston; the postmark is blurred but the second digit is clearly not 1. Printed by Rusk, "Emerson in Salem," *Essex Institute Historical Collections* (July 1958), 94:194–195. Emerson omits "to" in the first sentence.

12. January 17 (Charvat, p. 23).

13. The town of Salem was known among lecturers for being inhospitable; Hawthorne, acting as secretary for the lyceum, was breaking with tradition in offering a bed and a

tion to your house. I am a bad guest, but if you will let me run away suddenly next morning, I will come. Yours with great regard,

R. W. Emerson.

To Charles H. Brigham, Concord, January 12? 1849

[Rusk lists this letter under the conjectured date January 10 (*Letters*, 4:128), but it has to have been written after that date, for on January 10, Brigham of Taunton wrote a letter clearly of 1849 but misdated 1848 (RWEMA); this letter Emerson endorses "Yes 13 February." And to Emerson's offer of February 13, Brigham replies with his letter of January 29, 1849, apologizing for the delay, accepting the date February 13, but saying that the directors had agreed that they could not pay more. Emerson must have written a third letter to Brigham of which there is no record.]

To Orson S. Murray, Concord, January 12? 1849

[In the MS Account Book for 1845–1849, p. [146], under the date January 12, is the entry: "Paid (enclosed in a letter) to O. S. Murray, Fruit Hills, Twenty Mile Stand, Warren County, Ohio; for C. Lane, 6.00." Emerson is probably renewing Charles Lane's subscription to *The Regenerator*, "a free paper for the promotion of universal and progressive improvement"; see *Letters*, 3:406. According to the Union List, however, the paper ceased publication on April 8, 1848.]

To Epes Sargent, Concord, January 13, 1849 [14]

Concord 13 Jany 1849

Epés Sargeant, Esq.
Dear Sir,

I have to beg once more for the new Private Course of lectures [15] I am attempting, next Monday, & the following Mondays, the same forbearance I begged lately for one before the Mercantile Library,—that you will not make any <u>verbatim</u> reports in your paper. [16] I do not think, to be sure, that the subjects, [17] which will be in part metaphysical, will be very likely to tempt your Reporter But, at all events, I beg, he will not try. These new [18] lectures are rather studies than finished discourses, and I

---

welcome to a lecturer who preferred hotels but who could scarcely refuse a former fellow townsman.

14. MS in the Barrett Collection, Alderman Library, ViU; ph. in NNC; single sheet, address leaf torn away.

15. "Mind and Manners in the Nineteenth Century," five lectures at Freeman Place Chapel, not entirely new, for they had been given in London; see *Letters*, 4:80, n. 288.

16. *Boston Evening Transcript.*

17. See above December 28, 1848.

18. Either Emerson smudged his letter here or he wished to wash out the word "new"; it is blurred but legible.

hope, one day, to complete, revise, & print them, or the substance of them.

Of course, they are entirely open to your strictures & criticism

I enclose my card, and am, in advance,

Yours thankfully,
R. W. Emerson.

To Horatio Woodman, Concord, January 13, 1849?[19]

Concord
Saturday 13 Jany.

My dear Sir,

I was detained in town all yesterday, & find at home, this morning, some neglected suitors with unexpectedly long arms, who will not suffer me to go to town, as I meant.

Regretfully,
R. W. Emerson

Mr Woodman.

To Benjamin Rodman? Concord, January 13? 1849

[Benjamin Rodman, in a letter of January 11, 1849 (RWEMA), invites Emerson to lecture for a second time in New Bedford, offering a Tuesday evening in March. Emerson presumably wrote a refusal. Rodman mentions the subject of the first lecture as "England," not noted in Charvat, p. 23, and asks for "London." His letter also alludes to the ruckus of 1845 when Emerson refused to come to New Bedford because of the exclusion of blacks; Rodman writes: "You can have as many colours in the audience as the variety in our good city affords" (see above, November 17, 1845). Rodman's letter of February 2 (RWEMA) shows that Emerson replied. The invitation is repeated by Joseph Ricketson, in a letter of January 12, who offers January 29 or February 5 or February 12, all impossible dates for Emerson who may have written Ricketson as well as Rodman.]

19. MS in the Woodman papers, MHi; ph. in NNC; Of the years when January 13 fell on a Saturday, only 1849 is possible. This letter cannot have been written in 1866, for Emerson was en route to La Porte, Indiana, on the 13th of January in that year; nor can it have been written in 1872, for he was then en route from New York to West Point. The handwriting and the alertness of the letter make 1877 impossible; of the remaining dates, the year 1855 is ruled out by Emerson's letter of that date to his wife from the American House in Boston. Woodman had written Emerson on January 2, 1849 (RWEMA), evidently having had need of Emerson's testimony as to the marriage of a client.

To Sarah Ann Clarke, Boston, January? 16? 1849?[20]

American House
Tuesday p.m.

My dear Sarah,

I find myself so light-bodied & so light-headed in my further movings about today that I think it will hardly be prudent for me to promise for any more visits this week, and I regret very much not to be counted in your party.

Yours ever,
R. W. Emerson.

Miss Clarke.

To William S. Whitwell, Boston? January 16, 1849?[21]

Tuesday, 16th Jan

Dear Sir

In fear lest our little plan for tonight was not exactly settled, I called to say that it is my design to go out tonight from Boston to /W/ Newton in the evening train (5 P M. I believe) and I am to depend on your charity for a bed & for carriage to the Waltham station tomorrow morning.[22]

Yours respectfully,
R. W. Emerson

To Rebecca Duncan, Concord, January 19, 1849[23]

Concord, 19 January, 1849.

I have never forgotten I think for one day the friendliest note which I received many weeks ago & which I have not yet answered only because

20. MS in the Clarke papers, Houghton, MH; ph. in NNC. The date given this letter is not solid, but see above the letter of December 11, 1848, from which it is clear that Miss Clarke has planned a gathering of some kind to coincide with the opening of Emerson's lectures in the Freeman Place Chapel, the series arranged for by her brother (see Charvat, p. 23). The first lecture was given on Monday, January 15, 1849. That Emerson was in Boston the next day is evident from a letter to his brother of January 16, dated from Boston; see *Letters*, 4:128–129. See also the note below to Whitwell.

21. MS in the Whitwell papers, MHi; ph. in NNC; a single sheet folded, with the addressee's name on the resulting page [4] as well as at the foot of the letter proper. Emerson lectured in West Newton in January only in 1849 when the 16th fell on a Tuesday. The note was evidently left at Whitwell's Boston office, 119 Washington St. (see *Letters*, 4:132 and n. 15).

22. The Salem lecture, see above January 12, is crowding Emerson.

23. MS in the Barrett Collection, Alderman Library, ViU; ph. in NNC; p. [4] addressed: Miss Rebecca Duncan.| Charlestown| Mass.|; postmarked at Concord on the 19th. Printed in

these weeks are the busiest in my year and I adjourn all letters but those of necessity. But since you think me worth challenging twice[24] I must write, if only to thank you for your good will, and to express my hearty content if there is a new lover & seeker of truth. I was very sensible of the intelligence that dictated the first note, & very proud of my reader. I am still better pleased, if the world grows too fair & serious to permit you to be calm. It is the turning hour of our fate, the suspicious hour, when the old brute walls of the world become at last transparent and we discover eyes peering through them filled with light fairer than the sun.

I write as I say only for good will & for congratulation. I dare not offer, certainly not at present, the counsel you ask for,—perhaps never. Perhaps you will never find it at the hands of man. You say, you have heard lectures of mine, & ⟨t⟩one in Boston. I am then particularly desir⟨e⟩ous [t]hat you will hear the third one of my present course in town.[25] It comes nearer, in some points, to the truth of the day & hour, than any thing I have written lately. Meantime, though I am often a bad correspondent, I shall be very glad to hear from you again: & am, with best wishes, yours respectfully,

R. W. Emerson.

To Amos Adams, Concord, January 24, 1849

[In a letter of January 23, 1849 (RWEMA), Amos Adams, president of the East Lexington Lyceum, asks Emerson to give his lecture on England on any Wednesday evening in February; Emerson had to write Adams his choice of the date, February 28; see Charvat, p. 24, and *JMN*, 10:456. Charvat does not give the subject.]

To Reuben Hoar, Concord? February 2, 1849

[In the MS Account Book for 1845–1849 under the date February 2 (p. 150) is a detailed account of expenses for the care of Bulkeley Emerson followed by the

---

part in "Theodore Parker's Bettine," *Boston Evening Transcript*, July 12, 1897, p. 6; quoted in catalogue of Goodspeed's Book Shop, January–March 1922; listed in *Letters*, 4:129. Text on third leaf slightly damaged when the seal was broken.

24. Emerson is referring to Miss Duncan's letter of November 19, 1848, and her letter of January 15, 1849 (RWEMA). In the latter, she says: "I did not expect you to write me before—now I *do* expect this—if you choose, I mean. . . ." She already has Theodore Parker to give "help & counsel," but wishes Emerson's direction as well.

25. The third lecture (January 29) was "Tendencies and Duties of Men of Thought" (*Letters*, 4:80, n. 288); Emerson considered the first three in this series the more important and gave them the general title of "The Natural History of the Intellect" (see letter to H. G. O. Blake of December 28, 1848, above). See Edward Emerson's notes to the essay entitled "Instinct and Inspiration" (*Works*, 12:65–89, 442–444).

note: "Sent Mr Hoar in a letter. 23.00." To date is made secure by a letter of February 3 to William Emerson, where Emerson reports paying the bill "yesterday" (*Letters*, 4:132).]

To James Dana, Concord, February 2, 1849

[In a letter of February 1, 1849 (RWEMA), James Dana of Charlestown invites Emerson to tea and to stay the night when he lectures in Charlestown (February 6 and 19). The letter requires an answer.]

To Susan Inches Lyman, February 11, 1849

[Susan I. Lyman writes Emerson on February 10, 1849 (RWEMA), saying that her mother wanted Emerson to stay with her when he came to lecture in Northampton, February 22 (Charvat, p. 24, *JMN*, 10:456). Emerson could scarcely ignore an invitation from Anne Robbins Lyman whose hospitality he had enjoyed in 1827 (*Letters*, 1:215). He may have written directly to Mrs. Lyman.]

To David W. Horton, Concord, February 15, 1849

[In a letter of February 14, 1849 (RWEMA), David W. Horton asked for a lecture for West Cambridge (now Arlington) on Tuesday evening next; i.e., the 20th. He asks for an early reply to his Boston office. Emerson apparently refused.]

To Samuel Gray Ward, Concord, February 27, 1849[26]

Concord, 27 February, 1849—

My dear friend,

I have two letters from you, each well entitled to a considerate answer. For the first, & the expansion you give to Mr Alcott's project, expansion & restriction too, I listen gladly this time, as always, to any scheme for uniting good men.[27] Was it Burke who said, "When bad men conspire, good men must combine."[28] And I am so credulous about association,

26. MS in the Ward papers, Houghton Library, MH; ph. in NNC; p. [4] addressed: S. G. Ward.| Care of T. W. Ward, Esq| Boston.|; postmarked at Concord February 27.
27. The Town and Country Club is meant; I conjecture that Ward had received the circular sent out in February inviting him to attend a meeting on March 20 to "discuss the advantages of organizing a Club or College, for the Study and Diffusion of the Ideas and Tendencies of the Nineteenth Century . . ." from the MS Minutes published by Cameron, "Emerson, Thoreau, and the Town and Country Club," *ESQ* (3d q., 1957), 8:2.
28. Emerson is quoting inaccurately from memory a passage from Burke's "Thoughts on the Cause of the Present Discontents." He had long since used the passage in his lecture on Burke (*EL*, 1:196). In the edition of Burke's *Works* that he owned (Harding, p. 45), the passage appears in 1:423.

that if such a covenant were offered me as you sketch, I doubt not, I should sign it. But I am the worst of leaders, and mean never to be editor or principal or instigator again, to any party of more than one.[29] I shall work with joy in any enterprise of pure literature, work as friend & contributor, and should like to have you, or Cabot, or both, for my commanders.—But here comes the interruptor of my letters,—& I have only room to say that I must & will come & see you before you go. I am so engaged this week as to see no night when I shall be at home until Saturday.[30] Will you not come & dine with me Saturday? You shall have all the Behmens I can muster. I am sorry to find you have not my Swedenborgs.[31] In my English absence, they have all disappeared & I tried to persuade myself that I had promised them to you, & hoped that Miss Peabody or other attendant spirit had conveyed them so. Now I must look elsewhere for you.

Ever yours,
R. W. E.

TO CHARLES F. HILLS? CONCORD, FEBRUARY 28, 1849[32]

Concord
28 February 1849.

Dear Sir,
    I have much pleasure in complying with your request.

Yours respectfully,
R. W. Emerson.

29. Emerson is alluding to his unhappy experience with the *Massachusetts Quarterly Review*, and perhaps also to *The Dial*.

30. Emerson evidently saw Ward in town on Saturday; see *JMN*, 11:73; the entry is undated, but it has to be for March 3, for the Wards had returned to Lenox by March 10 (MS copy of diary of Anna Barker Ward, Ward papers, Houghton Library). The MS Account Book for 1845–1849 shows the expenses of fares to Boston between entries dated March 2 and March 7 (p. 152), with the exception of this one entry, all the travel expenses on this page can be tied to lecture engagements.

31. See Eli, p. 34, for works of Jakob Boehme in Emerson's Library; for Swedenborg, see pp. 262–264.

32. MS owned by Joel Myerson; ph. in NNC. In the Emerson papers is a letter of January 18, 1849, from Charles F. Hills of Lowell asking for an autograph. There is nothing to prove that this letter obliges Mr. Hills, but the dates are compatible. In the catalogue advertising this letter, two signed poems are listed with it. Apparently both are written on sheets of paper of the same size as the letter and are dated "Concord Feb 1849." The first is the couplet beginning "Of all wit's uses" (*Works*, 9:351) and the second is a slight variation of 12–15 from "Nature I" (*Works*, 9:225).

To David? H. Merriam, Concord, March 2? 1849

[In a letter of February 28, 1849 (RWEMA), D. H. Merriam of Fitchburg, Massachusetts, asks for a lecture before April 15, and he asks for a note of Emerson's fee. Emerson apparently replied offering March 31 and asking for $15.00; see Charvat, p. 24, and *JMN*, 10:457. I conjecture the addressee to be David H. Merriam; see William A. Emerson, *Fitchburg Massachusetts Past and Present* (Fitchburg: Press of Blanchard & Brown, 1887), pp. 35–36.]

To Samuel Barstow, Concord, March 2? 1849

[In a letter of March 1, 1849 (RWEMA), Samuel Barstow of Woonsocket, Rhode Island, asks for a lecture on the 6th, 7th, or 8th of March and asks for a reply. The MS Pocket Diary shows Woonsocket deleted after March 20 where Alcott's name appears (*JMN*, 10:456). In the list of lecture engagements at the end of the MS Account Book for 1845–1849 p. [167],—a list for February 1 through April 6, 1849—Alcott's name was entered for March 20 and Woonsocket entered first for April 2, deleted, and then entered for April 3. Normally the MS Account Book lecture lists are earlier and less accurate than the Pocket Diary lists; in this instance I suspect that Emerson began to use the pocket diary for 1849 before he transferred to it long-standing engagements. He may have had to write Barstow more than once to settle the Woonsocket engagement. See *JMN*, 11:77, for the Town and Country Club meeting at Alcott's.]

To George Foster, Concord, March 2? 1849

[George Foster of Andover, Massachusetts, writes on March 1 (RWEMA) to ask Emerson to give the last lecture of the Andover course on March 16. Emerson endorses the letter "yes on Thursday 15 if desired, if not Thurs 22nd." Emerson enters Andover under March 15 in the lecture list at the end of the MS Account Book for 1844–1849, p. [167], but in the MS Pocket diary for 1849, he has Chelmsford for that date, *JMN*, 10:456. His travel expenses, however, bear out the Account Book listing, though the date for his Andover expenses is March 13 (p. 153). Tuesday the 13th is the date for the Concord Social Circle, whose meetings he was reluctant to forgo. I conjecture that he may have gone to Andover on Monday.]

To Ida Russell, Concord, March 9, 1849

[In a letter of March 10, 1849 (RWEMA), Miss Ida Russell of Milton acknowledges a letter accepting an invitation to lecture; she expects Mrs. Emerson and the children too and proposes the 22d as the date. Her letter of March 8 implies earlier correspondence, and there must have been a later exchange, for the date of the Milton lecture is March 26 in both the MS Account Book, 1845–1849, p. [167] list and the Pocket Diary for 1849 (*JMN*, 10:456). No payment is recorded and there is no record of expenses.]

To James Russell Lowell, Boston? April 13, 1849[33]

Meeting for choice of officers, determination of place; &c holden next Tuesday Apr 17 at 10 o'c AM 12 West Street.

R. W. E.

To Daniel Webster? Telegram, Concord, April 14? 1849

[Emerson's MS Account Book for 1845–1849, p. 157, has under the date April 14 this entry: "Telegraphing a letter to Washington for Dr C. T. J. 1.56." For a second telegram certainly to Daniel Webster, see April 16 below. Emerson's letter of April 13 to his brother-in-law Charles T. Jackson shows that a letter from Jackson's wife to Mrs. Emerson initiated Emerson's participation in Dr. Jackson's troubles with the Department of the Interior. Letters to Emerson of April 18, 24, 25 and May 9 (RWEMA), particularly that of April 24, show Jackson convinced of a "plot" to remove him from his post as geological surveyor of mineral lands in Michigan. See *JMN*, 11:112 and n. 113, for Jackson's putative enemies John W. Foster and Josiah D. Whitney. For further action by Emerson on behalf of his brother-in-law, see *Letters*, 4:140, 141–142, and nn. 45, 53. The Bartlett Emerson refers to in his letter of April 24 is Sidney Bartlett, a member of Webster's firm, not Homer Bartlett, as Rusk conjectured. In the letter of April 13 Emerson's comment on Dr. Gould alludes to Augustus Gould's having assisted Morton in preparing the apparatus for administering ether; see here Appendix C. Jackson's letter of April 18 summoned Emerson to Boston to secure the influence of Abbott Lawrence.]

To Daniel Webster, Telegram, Boston? April 16, 1849

[In his MS Account Book for 1845–1849, p. 157, Emerson records under the date April 16: "Telegraphing a letter to D. Webster; Washington; for Dr C. T. J. 3.88." Under the same date he records the payment of $100.00 to Sidney Bartlett "for a retainer for Daniel Webster in cause of Dr C. T. Jackson at Washington." See April 14 above for the trouble occasioning Emerson's action on his brother-in-law's behalf. As he wrote his brother William, May 23: "My time was sadly occupied for a fortnight in Dr Jackson's affair" (*Letters*, 4:146).]

To Officers of the Fitchburg Railroad, Concord, April? 1849[34]

their reduced value in our eyes on account of the change of the near-lying lots into public grounds. On consideration I have decided that I

---

33. MS in the Rare Book Department, Perkins Library, NcD; ph. in NNC. The note is written on the verso of the first page of the Town and Country Club printed prospectus. Emerson has written "[Over" below the printed matter. Page [4] is addressed: J. R. Lowell, Esq.| Cambridge.| Mass.|; it is postmarked from Boston; the month is clear; the blurred date appears to be "13." Lowell did not attend; see Cameron, *ESQ* (3d q., 1957), 8:3.

34. MS draft in Emerson papers (RWEMA), Houghton Library, MH; ph. in NNC. This fragment cannot be later than May 1, 1849, or earlier than December 2, 1845. The parcel

will consent to sell the land you ask for on these terms, that the Railroad
Company shall buy all the land which I own or represent on ⟨the⟩ both
sides of the pond at one hundred dollars per acre. The land on the
Concord side of the pond will probably measure ⟨thirteen⟩/⟨fourteen⟩/
/say 27./————/twenty seven/ acres; that on the opposite shore, say thirty
four or thirty five acres

Respectfully
R. Waldo Emerson

To William Batchelder Greene, Concord? May 2? 1849

[In *Letters*, 3:171, Rusk lists a letter to Greene of the conjectural date May 2,
1843; he inferred the letter from Greene's letter (RWEMA) dated, as he read it
"May 2.d '43—evening." The last digit is not clear; it could be read as "8" instead
of "3"; furthermore Emerson's endorsement reads: "W B Greene/ May 184⟨8⟩9."
In Rusk's notes is the record of a letter to him (December 7, 1950) from Earl E.
Coleman calling his attention to a pamphlet by W. B. Greene, *Transcendentalism*
(West Brookfield, Mass., Power Press of Oliver S. Cooke & Co., 1849). Greene's
letter is written from South Brookfield; it speaks of "reading proof" of his "tract"
and does so in the way of recollection. It is clear from his letter that both Emerson
and Mrs. Emerson have read the pamphlet and talked to Greene about it. Greene's
letter refers both to a meeting with Emerson "today" and to his "note," which
clearly he has just received. The year "1849" would appear to be correct for this
unlocated note to Greene. (There is an 1843 publication by Greene, but it is not
about Transcendentalism.)]

To Waldo E. Haskins, Concord: May 5? 1849

[In the MS Account Book for 1845–1849, Emerson enters under the date May 5,
1849 (p. [162]), this note: "Cash sent in letter as gift to Waldo E. Haskins, care of

------

south of Walden Pond was not purchased until November 29, 1845, the deed dated December 2; the grantors were Abel Moore and John Hosmer. (MS Ledger for 1836–1848, loose
sheet laid in at p. 162; and Middlesex County Registry of Deeds, MS vol. 473, p. 351.) What
was in fact sold to the Fitchburg Railroad by May 2 for $31 (MS Account Book for 1845–
1849, p. 66) was a small portion from the parcel purchased in 1845; the portion sold was
"according to the deed" dated May 1, 1849, signed by Emerson July 18 (Middlesex Registry
of Deeds, MS vol. 568, pp. 31–32) and the "surveying notes of Mr Thoreau 1 A., 122 rods"
(MS Ledger for 1849–1872, p. 63). In the ledger entry cited, the figures for the whole
property are given according to Thoreau's notes. On the south side of the pond before the
sale to the railroad were 41 acres and 51 square rods and no the opposite shore lying partly
in the town of Lincoln were 39 acres and 89 square rods, before the court decision that later
awarded 10 acres and 7 square rods to Charles Bartlett. See *Letters*, 5:112, n. 70, for this
action of tort, and, below, March 11, 1850. Underestimating the acreage and overestimating
its value, Emerson certainly composed this draft before Thoreau surveyed the property and
before the actual sale of the small portion known as the "Island." Thoreau's survey of this
property must have been made before May 1, 1849; it is the second item listed under
Emerson in Marcia Moss *A Catalogue of Thoreau's Surveys* (Geneseo, New York: Thoreau
Society, 1976), p. 7, where it is assigned to the winter of 1849–1850.

E. B. Clayton & Sons, John St. N.Y. 10.00." Haskins had written Emerson on April 30 (RWEMA) asking for the loan of 2 or 3 dollars on easy terms. See *Letters*, 4:172 and 174, for Waldo Haskins' later borrowing from Emerson and then returning $100.00.]

To HARRISON GRAY OTIS BLAKE, CONCORD, MAY 11, 1849[35]

Concord, 11 May, 1849

Thanks, my dear friend, for your persistent kindness & care of ungrateful me. Your note found me on the way to some dismal affairs,[36] which have kept me in Boston for many days—irrecoverable days—but I was glad to have a ray of sunnier light in this very thicket. I hoped to use the occasion to write the letter long due but can only write new promises. Perhaps you will send me in a day or two some hint of your experiences in Bhagavat Geeta, that will be a text, & will find me in better leisure As it is I have only space to thank you & greet you affectionately.

Yours,

R. W. Emerson

To THOMAS WENTWORTH HIGGINSON, CONCORD, MAY 16, 1849[37]

Concord, 16 May
1849

My dear Sir,

I was in town yesterday & Mr Alcott showed me the list of subscribers to the Town & Country Club and I read at or near the end of the list the names of two ladies, written down, as he told me, by your own hand. On the instant, I took a pen & scratched or blotted out the names. Such is the naked fact. Whether the suggestion I obeyed was supernal or infernal, I say not But I have to say that I looked upon the ⟨only⟩circumstance of the names of two ladies standing there upon our roll as quite fatal to

35. MS in Beinecke Library, Cty; CtY; ph. in NNC; p. [4] addressed: H. G. O. Blake.| Worcester.| Mass.| and is postmarked at Concord, May 11. Printed by Stanley Williams in *JEGP* (October 1927), 26:481; listed *Letters*, 4:142. I have no clue to Blake's service to Emerson; I conjecture that Emerson had proposed Thoreau as a lecturer in Worcester; Thoreau did lecture in Worcester in April 1849.

36. The dismal affairs are probably those of his brother-in-law Charles T. Jackson. See *Letters*, 4:140, 141–142, and April 14 and 16 above.

37. MS in CSmH; ph. in NNC; without address leaf. Printed by Higginson in "Glimpses of Authors . . . IV" in *Brains*, (December 10, 1891), 1:104, and again in *The Outlook*, 74:222; printed by Sanborn and Harris, 2:462–463, and by Sanborn in *Recollections*, vol. 2, tipped in opposite p. 306. Listed *Letters*, 4:144.

the existence of our cherished Club.[38] I had stated to the Club the other day that "men" was used designedly & distinct⟨ly⟩ively in the first draft, & the Club by vote decided that it should stand so.[39] I had moreover /yesterday/ just come from a conference with some gentlemen representing the views of an important section of the members, who, alarmed by the pugnacious attitudes into which the Club was betrayed the other day, were preparing to withdraw, & whom I had assured that all those who had long been projecting their literary Club, would not be deprived of their object, & something else thrust on them,—when to my surprise I found this inscription of names of ladies. I erased them at once, that no man might mistake our design. I really wish that you would join with us in securing what we really want,—a legitimate Club Room; & very many of us will, I doubt not, heartily join with you in obtaining what is also legitimate, but not what we now seek, a social union of literature, science, &c for the sexes. But we claim a priority /of time/ in our project, & do not wish to be hindered of it, when it is now ripened & being realized. I am quite sure it is the wish of the great majority of persons who have acted in it hitherto, to establish a club house; & you must let us do it, & you must heartily join & help us do it.

Yours with great regard,
R. W. Emerson.

To John Chapman, Concord, May 23, 1849[40]

Concord, 23 May, 1849.

My dear Sir,

I am just printing "Nature" again, & the Orations, &c. which have never been collected in this country. As soon as I get through with this

---

38. The Town and Country Club was probably foredoomed by its size, its eccentrics, and its reformers.

39. Emerson is referring to the club meeting of May 2 at which Higginson had proposed that the by-laws concerning membership be amended to read "men and women" instead of "men." There ensued a lively debate and a succession of amendments to amendments and of votes that left the sense of the meeting more open than Emerson's letter suggests. See *ESQ* (3d q., 1957), 8:4–6, where the minutes of the meeting are printed by Cameron. Higginson, replying on May 19, rightly reminds Emerson that, in a final vote, the club having defeated all amendments consented to understand "men" as meaning all human beings, the vote being 22 to 16.

40. MS in Special Collections, University Research Library, CLU; ph. in NNC. The cutting away of the complimentary close and signature has damaged the text on p. [3]. The letter is surely addressed to John Chapman who would publish the English edition of *Representative Men* (*BAL*, 5219; M. 22. 2a, p. 216). It was in 1849 that Emerson sent Carlyle

long delayed reprint I am to print (probably by Phillips & Sampson, who have long proposed it,) my lectures on Representative Men;[41] & that book I shall be contented to send you in the way you propose, say on a scheme of half profits. These publishers proposed to have it ready in September. I dare not affirm it.

I have received the "Aurora" in good order, and it is the print I wished. No bill has come with it. If you will advise Munroe & Co. of the price, I will pay it to them. My thanks to Mr Delf for his kind attention.[42]

I learn from Carlyle that he duly rec/e/ived his barrel of corn which went through your hands. I send in the same way, by the steamer of tomorrow another barrel, containing some varieties of corn & meal; as he professes great interest in the subject. Again my agents here agree to send it /to London,/ without expense to any of you. If that agreement is not executed, if you have paid anything on this[43]

I noticed in some London advertisement of yours, that I was named as an editor of the Mass. Q. Review. Never say it again. I have never been a conductor even, since the first Number, and, at the end of the first Volume, formally renounced it; as Parker knew & should have said.[44] I have received Froude's book,[45] & the Dublin Review; both, I suppose from you. Who wrote of me in Dublin[46] He does me great honour.[47]

------

the barrels of Indian corn here referred to (see Slater, pp. 451–452, 454); both shipments are entered in the MS Account Book for 1845–1849: the first under the date March 20, p. [154], and the second under the date May 17, p. [163].

41. BAL, 5218; M. 22. 1.d.

42. A letter of May 2, 1849, from William Emerson shows that the print of Guido Reni's "Aurora" was ordered as a gift for William Emerson from his mother. Thomas Delf secured it.

43. Probably no more is missing here than a request that Chapman report if the barrel of corn let him in for any expense.

44. For Emerson's difficulty with Theodore Parker, see above, September 15, 1848, and Letters, 4:111–114.

45. See Eli, p. 111, for James A. Froude's The Nemesis of Faith, published by Chapman in 1849.

46. The article in The Dublin Review (April 1849, 26:152–179), is attributed to MacCarthy in a list of articles appearing in vol. 118; probably Dennis Florence MacCarthy. It is not altogether complimentary; MacCarthy finds Emerson "original to a fault," praises his style, and acknowledges his sincerity, but doubts that his work will survive.

47. Probably no more is missing here than the complimentary close, signature, and perhaps the addressee's name.

To Henry Wadsworth Longfellow, Concord, May 24, 1849[48]

Concord ⎱
24 May ⎰ 1849

My dear Longfellow,

I am heartily obliged to you for Kavangh,[49] which I read on Sunday[50] afternoon with great contentment,—though hindered by "the Steamer"[51] & other accidents, from acknowledging it. It had, with all its gifts & graces, the property of persuasion, & of inducing the serene mood it required. I was deceived by the fine name into a belief that there was some family legend, & must own (like palates spoiled by spices) to some disappointment at the temperate conclusion. But it is good painting, & I think it the best sketch we have seen in the direction of the American Novel: for here is our native speech & manners treated with sympathy, taste, & judgment. ⟨But⟩One thing struck me as I read,—that you win our gratitude too easily; for, after our much experience of the squalor of New Hampshire[52] & the pallor of Unitarianism, we are so charmed with elegance in an American book, that we could forgive more vices than are possible to you. Is it not almost June, & did you not agree to trust yourself for one day to my guidance?

Yours,

R. W. Emerson

To Elizabeth Palmer Peabody, Concord, June 1, 1849

[In *Letters,* 4:149, this letter is listed from Cabot's Bluebook Index. Cabot's Blue-book Calendar 5, number 1954, gives the date and has a note that the letter was written "on rec't of Aesth. Pap." Cabot quotes a fragment as follows: "My old gem, S. Reed's 'Genius' I confess caught my eye first. I think that as beautiful as I found it the day when I was Bachelor of Arts & hear[d] it spoken." Miss Peabody's short-lived periodical, *Aesthetic Papers,* was published in May with Sampson Reed's essay at pages 58–64. Sampson Reed received his M.A. from Harvard in 1821 and was a speaker, as Emerson was, on Commencement Day. Emerson quotes

48. MS in the Barrett Collection, Alderman Library, ViU; ph. in NNC; printed by Samuel Longfellow, *Life of Henry Wadsworth Longfellow* (Boston: Ticknor, 1886), 2:140; listed *Letters,* 4:147.

49. Emerson's misspelling of the title. Longfellow's "tale" *Kavanagh* was published May 12 (*BAL,* 12096). The presentation inscription of Emerson's copy is dated May 19; Emerson subsequently gave the book to the Concord Free Public Library (Harding, p. 172).

50. The text in *Life* reads incorrectly "Saturday."

51. Emerson is referring to the mail boat; see *Letters,* 4:144, where two unlocated letters to England are listed, and one letter is printed; and see above, May 23 to Chapman.

52. Possibly an allusion to Isaac Hill, New Hampshire editor and politician, of whom Emerson had a low opinion. See *JMN,* 5:47; 11:277.

from Reed's oration in a journal entry of 1821 (*JMN*, 1:293–294). There are two MS copies of Reed's oration in the Emerson papers. One of them is inscribed (verso of front cover): "The property of William Emerson, presented by his respected brother, R. W. E."; the other is also inscribed (verso of cover): "Chas. C. Emerson from his friend Joseph Lyman Oct, 1830." Both Rusk (*Life*, p. 87), and the editors of *JMN* credit William Emerson (Reed's classmate) with acquiring a copy for Emerson, but the inscription in the first copy suggests the opposite, and in July 1830 (RWEMA) it is to William that Charles Emerson writes to borrow his copy. Emerson does not become enthusiastic about Reed until the publication of *The Growth of the Mind*; see *JMN*, 3:45, and, above, letter of early October 1826 to Mary Moody Emerson in reply to her criticism of Reed.]

To Elizabeth Palmer Peabody, Concord, June 11, 1849

[The entry under this date in *Letters*, 4:152, is a ghost created by an error in Cabot's first Bluebook Index where he crowds it in after his correct entry for a letter of June 1 (see above) and gives both the same key number 1954; he enters both June 1 and June 11 again in Index II, giving only June 1 the key number. In the more nearly accurate listing in Bluebook Calendar 5 only the June 1 letter appears against the key number 1954: The ghost letter is, I think, an offspring of June 11, 1849, to Theodore Parker (*Letters*, 4:151), which does not appear in the first Bluebook Index, but does appear in Index II with its own number 1513 and in Calendar 4 under that number.]

To Gilbert Lewis Streeter, Concord, June 11, 1849[53]

Concord, 11 June, 1849.

G. L. Streeter, Secretary.

Dear Sir,

Forgive me for not making an earlier reply to your kind note. I am not quite ready today to promise compliance with the request of the Lyceum: but you shall put my name on your contingent list, & I may probably come when you want me.[54]

Yours respectfully,
R. W. Emerson.

53. MS in the Gilbert Lewis Streeter papers, Phillips Library, MSaE; ph. in NNC; p. [4] is addressed to G. L. Streeter, Esq.| Salem.| Mass.|; postmarked at Concord June 12.
54. There is no record of a lecture in Salem in the 1849–1850 season.

To Marianne L. Welford, June 28, 1849[55]

Concord, 28 June, 1849

My dear Mrs Welford,

I thank you heartily for your kind remembrance. Your friendliest thoughts only make me regret the more my few & short hours in New York, which did not allow any visits, not even my return to Mr Welford's store, which I had promised myself. I should very gladly have renewed our brief London acquaintance, & have learned your American experience, which I am curious to know,—& how the English home looks in the distance? I am rarely in your city, but shall not fail to see you—I hope—when I am there again. With kind regards to Mr Welford,

Your obliged servant,
R. W. Emerson.

To Alexander Ireland, Concord, July 5, 1849[56]

You will think I died and was buried soon after I left Manchester. No, I escaped the sea and survive until this day, but with no studies or fortunes worth transmitting news of so far; yet not despairing, one of these days, to send you something. But here is my friend, Rev. James Freeman Clarke, an excellent and accomplished man, who can tell you of every good thing in Boston and America, and whom you must furnish with good tidings to me of all your circle.—Your affectionately.

55. MS owned by Kenneth Cameron in 1952; ph. in NNC; printed by him in *ESQ* (1st q, 1958), 10:37. Charles and John G. Welford are listed in New York City directories of 1848–1849 as owners of a bookstore at 424 Grand Street. Mrs. Welford's note (RWEMA) of June 19 (7 Astor House) provides no clue to her identity; she expresses her regret at missing his call at the bookstore, but does not mention her meeting with Emerson in England. Possibly this is the same "Mrs Welford" described (1869) by Henry James, Jr., as "father's old friend"; see *Henry James Letters*, 1:92. James' letter leads to the inference that she was a Swedenborgian, for his news of her comes from William White, well-known Swedenborgian. My guess is that Emerson had met her in 1848 through William Mathews or J. J. Garth Wilkinson, both Swedenborgian friends of Henry James, Sr.

56. The MS has not been located, but see *Letters*, 4:155, for its listing in auction catalogue of 1926; text from Ireland, *In Memoriam*, p. 84.

To Samuel Gray Ward, Concord, July 12, 1849[57]

Concord, 12 July, 1849—

My dear Ward,

The Club is not so out at elbows as your friend fancied, for besides other good men whom I do not remember, Cabot was there, who is always bright, erect, military, courteous & knowing, a man to make a club: Then Edward Bangs, Edward Tuckerman, Hawthorne, a good Atkinson whom Cabot brings, Hillard, Lowell, Longfellow, & other men of this world,[58] have all shown themselves once,—&, with a little tenderness & reminding, will all learn to come. There is a whole Lili's Park[59] also with tusks & snakes of the finest descriptions. Belief is the principal thing with clubs as well as in trade & politics. And really we have already such good elements nominally in this, that the good luck of a spirited conversation or one or two happy rencontres would now save it. Henry James of N. Y. is a member, & I had the happiest half hour with that man lately at his house, so fresh & expansive he is.[60] My view now is to accept the broadest democratic basis, & we can elect twenty people every month, for years to come, & yet show black balls & proper spirit at each meeting. So, I pray you to shine with all your beams on our young sprout. For the rest, I shall be heartily glad to draw the advantage from your return, and you must, when you get wonted, show me how. The best way for me will be an afternoon hour 4 to 5, or 5 to six; for our fixture is not sun or moon, but "the special" at 7 P. M.[61] I have serious thoughts of beginning a correspondence with you.

Yours affectionately,

R W E

57. MS in the Ward papers, Houghton Library, MH; ph. in NNC; printed in part by Norton, pp. 76–77, and by Edward W. Emerson in *EYSC*, pp. 6–7; listed *Letters*, 4:155.

58. Edward Bangs, Boston lawyer, and Edward Tuckerman, Amherst professor of botany, are named by Emerson in what appears to be a preliminary or prospective list of members of the Town and Country Club, MS journal RS, *JMN*, 11:78–79; the list is apparently of December 1848; there is a later list (1850) in MS journal AZ, *JMN*, 11:237–238. Atkinson does not appear in either list, but does appear in a third list in Journal BO (*JMN*, 11:329) as W. P. Atkinson, the name deleted. Probably William Parsons Atkinson is meant. He was a Harvard graduate, B.A. '38, subsequently professor of English and history, M.I.T. Cabot, of the class of '40, may well have know him. This list appears under a heading: "Say for a Boston Club."

59. The allusion is to Goethe's "Lili's Park," 2:90–95 of *Werke*, the 1828–1833 edition owned by Emerson; Eli, p. 118.

60. See August 28 below.

61. The last train to Concord.

To Harper and Brothers, Concord, July 13? 1849

[See July 14 below for evidence of a letter to Harpers. The letter (and that of c. July 2, listed *Letters*, 4:154), certainly concerned copies of the American edition of John Carlyle's translation of Dante, copies Emerson was to present on John Carlyle's behalf. For Emerson's letter to John Carlyle, see Slater, p. 457, and n. 3. The date of this note to Harpers has to be after July 6, for Emerson tells Carlyle that the books were ready after James Freeman Clarke sailed. Since Emerson did not send S. G. Ward his copy on July 12 (see above), but on the 19th, I conjecture the note to be of the 13th. See also *Letters*, 4:128, 132.]

To Ellen Tucker Emerson, Concord, July 14, 1849[62]

Dear Ellen,

Tell your Uncle William that I have received & acknowledged the books sent lately by the Harpers.[63] The children have told you their news but they have not told you that Edith brought home an Approbation, today & another last week. I believe she has eight. You must be sure to secure Approbations from Aunt Susan & from Ellen E.[64]

Papa

14 July.

To Samuel Gray Ward, Concord, July 19, 1849[65]

Concord 19 July

The Horticultural paper never came, & I am left to guess your opinions on Downing.[66] Do not fail to inquire on your side, for my postmaster

62. MS in the Emerson papers (RWEMA), Houghton Library, MH; ph. in NNC. This note is a postscript to a letter of July 13 by Mrs. Emerson to her daughter Ellen, then visiting the William Emersons in New York (*Letters*, 4:150).

63. See above July 13.

64. See *Letters*, 4:156 and 157, for further information about "approbations" for, I take it, good work and good conduct. Ellen is being asked to be a judge of her own conduct.

65. MS in the Ward papers, Houghton Library, MH; ph. in NNC; p. [4] addressed: S. G. Ward.| Boston.|; printed by Norton, p. 76; listed *Letters*, 4:155. The year is secured by the allusion to the American edition of John Aitken Carlyle's translation of Dante, copies of which were received by Emerson c. July 13 (see above July 14). In early June 1849 Ward had been summoned to Boston, his father's health making it likely that he would have to return to banking; on the 13th of June, he had decided to do so. He had been in Boston for a month and was about to return to Lenox for a ten-day visit (MS copy of part of the diary of Anna Barker Ward, Ward papers, Houghton Library).

66. Andrew Jackson Downing. Ward as the builder of a country estate ("Highwood," Lenox, Massachusetts) would necessarily be interested in Downing's works. No signed article by Ward about Downing has been found, but in Downing's own periodical, *The Horticulturalist and Journal of Rural Art* (June 1849, 3:555–557), is an article signed "W., Lenox, Massachusetts" and titled "The Effects in Landscape of Various Common Trees." The article is followed by a comment in brackets: "We recognize, in the above excellent paper, one of the most cultivated and artistic minds in the country; and we are glad to find the rich store

is positive here. I send you, I am ashamed it is so late, with Dr Carlyle's compliments, a copy of his Dante. The Doctor's presentations are slow, fault of the Harpers, who forgot their author for a time. But the book is worth waiting for, the most conscientious of translations. Confirm me if you can in my estimate of it. I read it lately by night with wonder & joy at all his parts, & at none more than at the nerve & courage which is as essential to poet as to soldier. Dante locked the door & put the key in his pocket. I believe, we value only those who do so.⁶⁷

R. W. E.

To Ellen Tucker Emerson, Concord, July 21, 1849⁶⁸

Saturday, always pleasant to Eddy & Edie, because a holiday itself, & to be followed by another, is pleasanter than ever today, with its welcome rain to to the burned land, & I hope it shines with happy light, clear or cloudy, to Ellen.

To William Lloyd Garrison, Concord, July 24, 1849⁶⁹

Concord, 24th July, 1849.
Dear Sir;

I hardly know how to resist your kind invitation to the anti-slavery meeting at Worcester, though, except for the generosity of the business, which makes a commanding claim on us all, I can scarcely find a reason for my going, as all my attention is devoted to quite different and engrossing matters.⁷⁰ But I think I will try the benefit of the good day

of observations, which we know the writer has accumulated, are beginning to rise to the surface, and overflow a little for the good of others. We shall always welcome with pleasure any contribution of 'W.' in this journal. Ed." That "W." is Ward seems likely, though I have no confirming evidence.

67. See letter to John Carlyle, Slater, p. 757, and n. 3. As the letter to John Carlyle shows, Emerson selected the American recipients of this American edition; Slater lists them.

68. MS in the Emerson papers (RWEMA), Houghton Library, MH; ph. in NNC. These lines were added by Emerson to his wife's letter to their daughter. Mrs. Emerson's postscript to her letter is dated July 21 and the letter is postmarked with that date; July 21 fell on a Saturday in 1849 when Ellen spent the summer on Staten Island with William Emerson and his family. Another letter to Ellen (Letters, 4:156–157), remarks upon the hot, dry weather.

69. No MS has been located; text from The Liberator (July 27), 19:119; Emerson is answering Garrison's letter of July 20 (RWEMA).

70. Emerson had been revising the essays to appear in Nature, Addresses, and Lectures and preparing Representative Men; the first to be published in September, the second in November (BAL, 5218, 5219; M A21.1.a, A22.1.a).

you offer me, as far as hearing goes, and, if I think of any thing to the purpose, I will say it.[71]

Yours with great respect,
R. W. Emerson.

William Lloyd Garrison.

To Rebecca L. Duncan, Concord, August 16, 1849[72]

Concord, 16 August, 1849.

I am heartily obliged to you for all your kind thoughts, which you must continue by all means to cherish. And I shall hold you to your good intent of coming to see me.[73] But you shall not come now. I am the most morose & nervous of all men, not to be helped even by your compassion, having covenanted with myself & certain booksellers to furnish them some papers ⟨in⟩ /near/ the ⟨l⟩end of October; which papers, as the days go by, do not draw near to completion.[74] I am daily threatening to quit my home & try the stimulus of new air & country, for a short time. Neither is my poor sick wife in condition to give you any welcome. So you must pity me, out of all the energy & charity Monadnoc lends you.[75] And I will yet hope to keep my slow word with you concerning some books.

With joy in all your happiness,

Yours,
R. W. Emerson.

To Henry James, Sr., Concord, August 28, 1849[76]

Concord, 28 August, 1849.

My dear James,

It is a great many days ago but not a month since I being at the Town & Country Club heard a conversation concerning the inviting some

71. Emerson did attend the Massachusetts Anti-Slavery Society's celebration of the abolition of slavery in the West Indies, held in Worcester August 3. He found something to say; his remarks are reported in *The Liberator* (August 17, 1849), 19:131; reprinted by Louis Ruchames, *AL* (January 1957), 28:431–433.

72. MS in the Barrett Collection, Alderman Library, ViU; ph. in NNC; quoted in catalogue of Goodspeed's 1922; listed *Letters,* 4:161.

73. The aggressive Miss Duncan had written on August 12 (RWEMA) of her "wish to meet you again at your own home"; see October 24 below.

74. *Representative Men,* published in November 1849, *BAL,* 5219; see October 10, below, to Chapman and *Letters,* 4:149, 157, 159.

75. Miss Duncan had written from Stoddard, New Hampshire.

76. MS in the James papers, Houghton Library, MH; ph. in NNC; printed by Perry (1:56–57) with some errors and additional punctuation; listed *Letters,* 4:160. James' reply of August 31 is printed by Perry (1:57–59).

gentleman to read a paper to the Club, in November. I hastened to say, that we had been foolishly wearing homespun & eating Indian corn, now for two or three of our holidays, like farmers shut up in a snow drift, when we might have dressed in Cashmeres & dieted on grapes & pomegranates, for, did we not number distinguished colleagues far from Frog Pond & unconchituated? So I proposed you as the ⟨per⟩proper person to read us the Memoir on the vacant day.[77] Immediately I was told, that you were not a member. I affirmed that you ⟨was⟩were, for Alcott had long ago assured me that he had taken all the proper steps to make you one, & you had signified to me at N.Y. your good will to it, as I remember. Besides, I think it was Dwight who told me, you had a paper that would suit us.—The Treasurer replied, that you had not complied with a vote necessary to membership, & paid his subscription.[78] I declared you intended membership, & I would be surety for his five dollars. Then you were unanimously elected orator—I meaning instantly to sit down & apprize you first of the facts, entreat your assent, nay, preclude all possibility of doubt or denial, on your part. But a heap of things has hindered me from hour to hour & /from/ day to day; &, I suppose, you got some formal secretary's notification, & who knows but you had forgotten there was a club, & refused to come. I have seen nobody since, & do not know what correspondence has been. But if you have hesitated, or if you have refused, I beseech you to reconsider it all, & accept, as the loveliest thing you can do. Then you will come & see me here in my fen, & we will finish that score of conversations we begun some two or more months ago.[79]

Yours,

R. W. Emerson.

77. In Emerson's journal AZ (1850), *JMN*, 11:237–238, is a clearly incomplete list of members; James' name does not appear; nor is his name in the list of 1848 in Journal RS, *JMN*, 11:78–79. And from the longest list I have seen his name is missing, but so is Alcott's. See Cameron, *ESQ* (3d q., 1957), 8:17. See M. A20, 1 and 2.

That is, not residents of Boston, the Frog Pond in the Boston Common being as well-known a symbol as the codfish. Lake Cochituate (Emerson misspells it) had been merely Long Pond until in 1846 construction began on an aqueduct to bring drinking water to the city of Boston; the Indian name was then restored, the occasion celebrated with a poem by Lowell. The delays in completing the construction were the occasion of local jokes. See *JMN*, 11:130, for a similar use of the Frog Pond and Cochituate under the heading "Brag."

78. John W. Browne and James W. Stone had been elected respectively as treasurer and recording secretary at the meeting of May 2; Cameron, *ESQ* (3d q., 1957), 8:4.

79. He saw James in New York when he took Ellen to his brother's on June 5 (*Letters*, 4:150); see above July 12, 1849, for allusion to a visit to James, and see also *JMN*, 11:128.

To JOHN AITKEN CARLYLE, CONCORD, AUGUST 28, 1849

[Printed by Slater, pp. 457–458, with misleading note; the MS is a copy in Charles Eliot Norton's hand, in the Norton papers, Houghton Library; no original has been found. This is, I believe, the letter listed under the conjectural date September 5, *Letters*, 4:161, the last of the three letters referred to by John Carlyle in his letter to Emerson of September 28, 1849 (RWEMA); see *Letters*, 4:153.]

To THOMAS PALMER, CONCORD, SEPTEMBER 7, 1849[80]

Concord, 7 September, 1849.

Dr Thomas Palmer,

Dear Sir,

I find on my return from New York,[81] where I have been for a few days, your letter, and its enclosed sum of fifty four dollars, being one year's interest to the 18th August last, of Joseph Palmer's note of $900.00 payable to me in trust for Charles Lane. I requested you to take up the note, as I find on the note itself that it should be paid now. You say, that Mr Lane promised your father "that he should not be distressed," and it is not now convenient to him. In that case, I shall not at present proceed any farther, but will send the interest to Mr Lane, & will inform him of ⟨w⟩your wish. Perhaps it will be equally convenient to him to let it lie as it does. I have had no letter from him for nine or ten months, & did not know at all of this understanding between your father & him.[82]

I enclose your father's deed.[83] He brought it to me, or sent it to me, & asked me to have it recorded for him at Worcester, & he would some time take it of me. I accordingly sent it with Mr Lane's to Worcester by express. The Registers fee ⟨re⟩for recording your deed was 45 cents: half

80. MS in the Berg Collection, NNC; ph. in NNC; p. [4] addressed to Dr Thomas Palmer.| Fitchburg.| Mass.|; postmarked at Concord, September 8; listed in *Letters*, 4:161, from bookseller's catalogue.

81. Emerson had gone to New York to bring his daughter Ellen home from her visit with the William Emersons.

82. Palmer's letter of September 4 (RWEMA) acknowledges Emerson's letter of August 18 (*Letters*, 4:158); Emerson enters a record of both letters in his MS Account Book for 1849–1853, p. 25, under the date August 22. In the same Account Book, he enters, p. 6, the receipt of $54.00 from Thomas Palmer for Joseph Palmer's interest on the note referred to here. The MS Ledger for 1849–1872 under the date September 11, 1849, p. 14, has an entry reading: "By cash paid S. G. Ward for a Bill of Exchange for £137 3d drawn on Baring & Co. in favor of Charles Lane, & sent to him by Steamer Caledonia 12th Sept. 58.37½" See below September 12.

83. The deeds are to the property in Harvard, Massachusetts, where Lane and Alcott had tried to maintain their community, Fruitlands. Thomas Palmer had asked for the deed of his father's "Harvard lands" in his letter of September 4. See *Letters*, 4:117–118, for Emerson's earlier effort to collect this debt for Charles Lane.

the fee of the Express was 12½ cts: so you will have the goodness to charge yourself with 57 cents, which you can pay when your interest falls due again.

Yours respectfully,

R. W. Emerson.

To Henry James, Sr., Concord, September 7, 1849[84]

Concord, 7 September, 1849.

My dear James,

I was heartily glad to find you had decided aright, in spite of my negligence to hold up candles. Socialism is as good a topic as a brave man who likes it can choose.[85] We all have a leaning towards it from the 'anxious benches,' an expectation of being convicted & converted, on account of a certain geometry that is in it, notwithstanding that we are born hermits. I hear with some terror that you are going to Europe, I who never see you, & perhaps shall not, if you stay on this side. But New York looked amiable & intelligent whilst I knew you were in it. And now that we are to have a club, we might hope to see the members once a year. But you will not go till I have seen you, & learned to share in the project. So, with kind remembrances to Mrs James,

Yours

R. W. Emerson—

84. MS in the James papers, Houghton Library, MH; ph. in NNC; p. [4] addressed: Henry James, Esq.| 58 West Fourteenth Street| New York.|; postmarked at Concord September 7. Printed by Perry, 1:59–60; listed in *Letters,* 4:161. An extract from this letter in the hand of Cabot is misdated 1847 by Cabot and is catalogued by Houghton Library under the date 1843; the extract begins with the second sentence here.

85. Emerson is answering James' letter of August 31 in which James says he has accepted the invitation to give a speech for the Town and Country Club (see August 28 above). He asks Emerson's advice, for he "would greatly like to consider socialism from the highest point of view, but the name is a stench in the nostrils of the devout and honourable . . ." (Perry, 1:58). He will wait for Emerson's verdict; if it is unfavorable, he would like to lecture on sin. It is not surprising that offered this choice Emerson should prefer the topic of socialism and that he should think of the evangelicals' anxious seat.

In the MS records of the Club, James' topic is given as "The Antagonism between Socialism and Civilization," Cameron, *ESQ* 3d q., 1957), 8:9, the subject differently conceived by his son in the novel *The Princess Casamassima* to be written thirty-five years later.

To Samuel Gray Ward, Concord, September 12, 1849[86]

Concord, 12 September, 1849

My dear Ward,

I enclose $1.37 due on Charles Lane's Bill.[87]

You will be in town in the winter,[88] it is a great happiness,—& will know how to extract the Club of the Club. Cabot, Channing, Alcott, Hillard, Longfellow, Edward Bangs,[89] there are many bright men whom the slightest arrangement would assemble—perhaps to the comfort of all—can they not bring their cigars to the Club Room or to the next room on a given evening. In these days when Natural History is so easily paramount, I should put most trust, as I myself should prefer, that the nucleus of the company should be ⟨naturalist⟩savans.[90] But Tuckerman, I believe, is in Europe, & Desor is gone exploring.[91] These people are a very clean disinfecting basis. But I wish to see you & Cabot.

Ever yours,

R. W. Emerson

To William Buell Sprague, Concord, October 5, 1849[92]

Concord, 5 October, 1849.

My dear Sir: I fear you have the worst thoughts of me as far as the virtues of a good correspondent go. I ought to have warned you at first that I am a reprobate in that matter. Yet, I did, on the receipt of your

86. MS in the Ward papers, Houghton Library, MH; ph. in NNC; p. [4] addressed: Saml. G. Ward. | Office of T. W. Ward & Co. | State Street | Boston |. Printed, with first sentence omitted in EYSC, p. 7–8, and by Norton, pp. 76–77; listed *Letters*, 4:155.

87. Since Charles Lane's return to England, Emerson had been acting as trustee of his affairs in America, chiefly the collection of the mortgage payments of Joseph Palmer who had purchased the Fruitlands property in Harvard, Massachusetts. Emerson had usually transmitted the payments to Lane through the Wards. See September 7 above for Emerson's acknowledgment to Palmer's son for interest received. Possibly the small sun mentioned here is for fees for bills of exchange.

88. See July 19 above for note of Ward's decision to return to banking and Boston.

89. This move to extract a small club from the Town and Country Club gives Edward Waldo Emerson slight ground for deriving the Saturday Club from it. Of the men named here only Longfellow (1857) and Cabot (1861) became members of the Saturday Club founded in 1856. William Henry Channing, see October 5 below where Emerson specifies William Channing, whose cousin William Ellery Channing is usually designated Ellery.

90. Edward Emerson read the word "savants." Emerson in his MS journals spells the word as he does here; e.g., see LM, p. 49 (*JMN*, 10:311).

91. Edward Tuckerman, Amherst, professor of botany, lichenologist. Edward Desor, Swiss-born geologist, assistant to Agassiz. Desor had contributed to Parker's *Massachusetts Quarterly Review* (see Gohdes, pp. 167, 168, 169).

92. No MS has been found, text from William Buell Sprague's *Annals*, 8:244–245. Listed *Letters*, 4:166. Reprinted from Sprague by Cameron, *ESQ* (1st q, 1957), 6:17.

letter, in the summer, make, with my mother, some investigation into the history of my father's preaching, that he might make his own answer, as you suggested, to your inquiry concerning his opinions. But I did not find, in any manuscript or printed sermons that I looked at, any very explicit statement of opinion on the question between Calvinists and Socinians. He inclines obviously to what is ethical and universal in Christianity; very little to the personal and historical. Indeed what I found nearest approaching what would be called his creed, is in a printed Sermon "at the Ordination of Mr. Bedee, of Wilton, N. H."[93] I think I observe in his writings, as in the writings of Unitarians down to a recent date, a studied reserve on the subject of the nature and offices of Jesus. They had not made up their own minds on it. It was a mystery to them, and they let it remain so.

Yours respectfully,
R. W. Emerson.

To Samuel Gray Ward, Concord, October 5, 1849[94]

Concord, 5 October, 1849.

My dear friend,

I tried yesterday at Park Street & at State Street, and missed you.[95] I should be delighted with your plan of a circle, if it can be brought about: but, I fear, I am the worst person that could be named, except Hawthorne, to attempt it. If Tom Appleton were here, & had not lost all his appetites, he is the king of clubs. But I suppose he is full. Cabot, Bangs, & William Channing are the men I should seek, & Henry James of N. Y. if he were here, as he used to talk of coming. You must remember,—by the way,—that he is to read a lecture on Socialism to the T. & C. Club, on the first Thursday of November at 11½ o clock.[96] You must hear ten minutes of it. He is an expansive expanding companion, & would remove to Boston to attend a good club a single night. As it is he is going, I think, to Europe with his family. He seems to wish to be forbidden. Whom do you think it desireable to secure?

Ever yours,
R. W. Emerson.

93. Sprague quotes from the sermon Emerson cites, *Annals*, 8:245–246.

94. MS in the Ward papers, Houghton Library, MH; ph. in NNC; p. [4] addressed: S. G. Ward, Esq., | Merchants' Bank Building | State Street. | Boston |; postmarked at Concord October 5. Printed in part in *EYSC*, p. 8.

95. The home of Ward's father was 3 Park Street, his office was at 63 State Street.

96. See, above, August 28.

To John Chapman, Concord, October 10, 1849[97]

Concord, Oct. 10 1849.

Mr John Chapman,

Dear Sir,

I am sorry to hear that Mr Delf[98] should have given you any ground to distrust his honesty. I earnestly hope he will explain himself to your satisfaction. I have not yet written to him since receiving his letter: and, as you choose to make my book more important than I did, I am content to send you the Ms. copy, if I can, in advance of our printing. It now seems pretty certain that I shall not get any copy delivered to the printers here before 1 November,[99] & I will try to send you the whole or a part ⟨of⟩at the same time. But I am so bad a workman against time, that you cannot quite rely on me.

If I get to the light in England, as soon as here,[100] I shall wish to scatter perhaps a good many presentation copies there, which you must let me have at cost; & I will send you my list of names to be inscribed.[101]

Yours ever;

R. W. Emerson.

To Rebecca Duncan, Concord, October 24, 1849

[Rusk lists this letter from a dealer's catalogue and notes Miss Duncan's reply of October 26. Her reply shows that she has finally got the invitation to visit him at Concord that she has been asking for for some time, see August 16 above. Her letter concludes "On Wednesday then, at 12."]

To Samuel Gray Ward, Concord, November 15, 1849[102]

Concord, 15 Nov. 1849.

I should have acknowledged your note yesterday, or the day before, but that I have still believed each day I was going to town & to see you.

97. MS in the Berg Collection, NN; ph. in NNC; listed in *Letters*, 4:167, from auction catalogue.

98. Thomas Delf, formerly of the American publishing house of Wiley and Putnam, had been with Chapman in London but had severed his connection with Chapman in June; see *Letters*, 4:159, and n. 119. The book is *Representative Men;* see *BAL*, 5219, for "London Editions:" and MA 22. 1a, 2a, 3a, pp. 190–191. Emerson had met Delf in New York in 1842; see *JMN*, 8:202, 203.

99. An entry in the MS Account Book for 1849–1853, p. 55, under the date January 1, 1850, reads: "paid Elizabeth Weir for copying 'Representative Men.' 8.00."

100. In 1849, the mail boats normally left on the 1st and the 16th of the month.

101. See below under the conjectured dates November 21 and December 21.

102. MS in the Ward papers, Houghton Library, MH; ph. in NNC.

But the weary blotting book holds me fast.[103] I shall have ended it the sooner. O yes, I shall gladly cooperate in the bright design that promises pure pleasure.[104] The first day I come, I will see you if at home.

Yours,

R. W. E.

To Mary Moody Emerson, Concord, November 18? 1849

[In a letter to Mary Moody Emerson, Elizabeth Hoar writes: "Waldo tells me he has written you about the farm & that he saw Gore & wrote you about the $5.00." It is not clear whether Miss Hoar is referring to one letter or two.

[Christopher Gore Ripley managed, or tried to, Mary Moody Emerson's affairs, but she characteristically embroiled others in her difficulties (see, above, letters of November 29 and December 1, 9, 19, 1845).

[Miss Emerson's letter of December 23 to Lidian Emerson refers to property in Gorham (Maine); she wants Lidian to tell Emerson that she "must give an obligation for a deed before he moves all from Gorham" and she wants her to ask him if Gore Ripley should "come down"; i.e., "down east," to Waterford, Maine. Possibly there is another letter to Miss Emerson in December.]

To John Chapman, Concord? November 21? 1849

[Emerson's Journal AZ, *JMN*, 11:188, has the following note: "I sent Chapman orders to send copies of "Representative Men" to T. Carlyle J. A. Carlyle Earl of Lovelace Arthur Helps Mrs Paulet W. E. Forster John Forster Arthur H. Clough Miss Ellen Rendall Dr Samuel Brown Edinburgh Edwin Field J J G Wilkinson." The closest dated pages of this journal are p. 5, November 17, and p. 24, December 14, *JMN*, 11:185, 193. See above October 10 for his forewarning to Chapman of such a list and below for a supplementary list. See *BAL*, 5219, for Chapman's announcement of the English edition which was apparently not ready until January 5, 1850. Carlyle received his copy on January 8, Slater, p. 460, n. 2. William King became the the first Earl of Lovelace when he married Byron's daughter.]

To James Russell Lowell, Concord, December? 1? 1849?

[A letter to Emerson from James Russell Lowell is listed by Cameron, *ESQ* (2d q., 1966), 43:142 from Carnegie Book Shop Catalogue 256, October 1961. The letter is described as dated "Boston, Saturday," and is quoted as follows: "Miss Bremer has promised to stay a day longer, & she & Mrs. Kemble are to dine with us . . ." It was in December 1849 that Frederika Bremer made her visit to Elmwood

---

103. Emerson is referring to the manuscript of *Representative Men*. To his friend George P. Bradford, he writes on the same day: "I being to see daylight through all the blottings of my book, which ought to be done" (*Letters*, 4:170), and see Rusk's note of a letter of December 8 from the publisher (*Letters*, 4:171). Emerson had hoped to finish the book by the first of the month.

104. The "bright design" is for the "Club of the Club"; see above September 12.

where Lowell and his first wife were living with his father. Her own account of her visit is dated December 15 and Lowell announced his expectation of her visit "next week" in a letter to his friend Briggs of November 25 (*Letters*, Norton, ed. 1:169). His letter to Emerson is then of either December 1 or 8, and I infer it to be an invitation to dinner requiring an answer, though it could be an explanation of Lowell's being unable to meet Emerson. The quotation is, to say the least, tantalizing. I prefer the first inference if only because it permits both gentlemen to be courteous. For Miss Bremer's visit to the Lowells, see her *Homes of the New World*, Mary Howitt, tr. (London: A. Hall, Virtue, 1853) 1:130–131.]

To George Stillman Hillard, December 3? 1849

[In a letter of December 3, 1849 (RWEMA), George S. Hillard tells Emerson that Edward Twisleton, English visitor, wishes to meet him and asks if Emerson expects to be in town "in the next few days" or could Twisleton find Emerson at Concord. Edward Turner Twisleton hoped to persuade his countrymen to adopt the New England free school system and on his second visit to the States in 1851 sent Emerson a questionnaire on the subject. His letter of October 3, 1851 (RWEMA), reads as if he had met Emerson on this first visit. Presumably Emerson answered Hillard's letter. See *Letters*, 4:261, for the exchange of letters in 1851. Since the questionnaire Emerson had filled out and Twisleton returned for modification to suit his purposes is still in the Emerson papers, it is inferable that Emerson had no inclination to oblige. This inference is confirmed by Twisleton's book: *Evidence as to the Religious Working of the Common Schools in the State of Massachusetts* (London: James Ridgway, 1854). Here his American respondents are quoted (Longfellow among them), but Emerson is not cited.]

To Edward Everett Hale, Concord, December 13, 1849[105]

Concord, Dec 13 1849

My dear Sir,

I have been out of town a couple of days, or you should have had an earlier answer.[106] It is true, I am a little alarmed at your proposition, not knowing what matter I can find in my portfolio that will fit the audience, and quite incapable as I am, at this moment, indeed at all times, of writing to a given assembly;—but I cannot find any flaw in the claim, & must say, yes, a little in the dark. I am truly glad you have attempted to

105. MS in the Hale papers, Houghton Library MH; ph. in NNC; p. [4] addressed: Rev. E. E. Hale.| Worcester| Mass.|; postmarked at Concord December 14. Printed by Hale in facsimile, *The Outlook*, "James Russell and his Friends," (May 7, 1898), 59:40; listed in *Letters*, 4:172.
106. Emerson is replying to Hale's letter of December 8 (RWEMA) inviting him to lecture in a series for the support of a church for black people; he says: "most of the lectures are on subjects having some bearing on the present position of the blacks in the world." The topic is not required however.

aid our hapless countrymen in a way that suits them so well, & to which there can be no objection. Send me word what are the vacant nights in the Course—& I will choose mine. You shall pay my expenses, but no fee.[107]

Yours ever,
R. W. Emerson.

To Francis? A. Howe, Concord, December 16? 1849

[Writing Emerson on December 17, 1849 (RWEMA), F. A. Howe of Harvard, Massachusetts, is pleased to consider Emerson engaged to lecture on December 25 (see Charvat, p. 24); the tenor of the letter makes it clearly a reply to one from Emerson. F. A. Howe is possibly the Francis A. Howe whose name appears in a list of members of the Harvard school committee (Henry S. Nourse, *History of the Town of Harvard Massachusetts . . .* , Harvard, 1894, p. 378).]

To John Chapman, Concord? December? 21? 1849

[In his MS Journal AZ, *JMN,* 11:188–189, Emerson follows his note of having sent Chapman a list for presentation copies of *Representative Men* with the reminder: "I must add to the list by the next steamer Miss Martineau Dr Jacobson C. E. Rawlins, Jr John Kenyon Esq." See above October 10 and November 21. Dr. Jacobson is surely William Jacobson (see *JMN,* 10:247 and n. 173); Rawlins is Charles E. Rawlins, Jr; see below May 21, 1863.]

To Reuben Hoar, Concord, December 21? 1849

[In the MS Account Book for 1849–1853, under the date December 21, 1849, p. 49, is an entry reading: "Pd by cash enclosed in a letter to Reuben Hoar, Esq his bill of board &c for R. B. Emerson, but no sum is entered.]

107. Acknowledging this letter on December 27 (RWEMA) Hale offers Emerson a list of dates (all six) from which to choose. Of the dates offered by Hale, only two—February 5 or 12—can be fitted into Emerson's 1850 lecture schedule; the MS Account Book for 1849–1853 (p. 26) shows under receipts the sum of $4.00 from E. E. Hale for expenses to Worcester; his costs appear at p. 67 under the date February 5. This lecture of February 5 is not listed in Charvat.

To Samuel Gray Ward, Concord, December 26, 1849[108]

Concord, 26 Decr

I was in town an hour or two yesterday, thoughtless of Christmas, when I left home, & was punished for my paganism[109] by not finding you, & not finding any one with whom I had to do, at their posts. But, for your club news, it is the best that can be. I saw Bangs two or three days ago, & Bradford on Sunday.[110] Both heard gladly, but both made the same doubt—they had nothing to bring. Yet they will doubtless both be counted in. Bradford "did not know but he was *borné* on some points; thought the Club had better give the supper, & not the member.[111] Then there is always the same supper, and tender persons will not offer you wine, but the guilty broad shouldered Club only. Certainly it is better to have the Club the perpetual host, and not each bashful member. The persons named by Longfellow ar⟨l⟩e doubtless desireable,—Appleton in the superlative degree, but I suppose him all preoccupied.[112] Yet Longfellow should know. Billings I do not know; nor Perkins: yet have no objection. Agassiz, again,[113] I suppose quite too full already of society. What night is best? Monday is freest. For me I think Tuesday & Wednes-

108. MS in the Ward papers, Houghton Library, MH; ph. in NNC; printed in full in *EYSC*, pp. 8–9; listed in *Letters*, 4:173. Endorsed 1849 by Ward and clearly on the topic of the Club; see above letters of September 12 and October 5 and below that of December 29. Emerson's MS Account Book for 1849–1853 under the date December 27 (p. 53) shows that Emerson went to Groton via Boston, though he could have gone directly from Concord via the Fitchburg line. Charvat (p. 24) has no date for the Groton lecture, but he does have the date of December 25 for Harvard, Mass., which is a few miles from Groton. The Harvard date is secure from a letter of December 17 from F. A. Howe (RWEMA).

109. As for the paganism that brought him in town on Christmas day, few New Englanders celebrated Christmas unless they were of German extraction or had adopted German customs. The family holidays were Thanksgiving and Fast Day (falling in March or April). An anthropological note is provided by Arthur Hugh Clough in a letter of December 3, 1852, to Carlyle (Mulhauser, 2:343): "Yesterday week, Thursday, Novr 25th, was the great New England festival, puritanically substituted for Xmas, which has only begun to be observed again of late years, chiefly by the aid of German 'Trees.' This feast, which is a sort of puritan-Hebrew ingathering, is fixed by the Governor, after harvest is over, towards the end of Novr, and is a very great and universal holiday. Church-going, and good dinners and games at family-meetings, etc., etc."

110. Edward Bangs. George P. Bradford.

111. Emerson does not close the quotation which I conjecture closes here.

112. Because Appleton was Longfellow's brother-in-law. Perkins is Charles Callahan Perkins, art and music critic, who with Appleton, was active later in establishing the Boston Museum of Fine Arts. Billings was very likely the artist. Hammatt Billings who visited Longfellow in 1847 hoping to illustrate *Evangeline*. Both Perkins and Billings appear in Longfellow's diaries.

113. Of the men named here, aside from Longfellow himself, only Appleton and Agassiz became members of the Saturday Club: Agassiz a charter member of 1856, Longfellow elected in 1857 and Appleton in 1859.

day are inconvenient for the Club Tuesday chiefly because our village Club of 25 farmers[114] &c meets on that night & I do not wish to resign.

But we must ballot for every night in the week, & for which has the most marks.

Ever yours,

R. W. E.

To CHARLES NORTHEND, CONCORD, DECEMBER 26, 1849

[Rusk prints a letter of December 26, 1849, to an unnamed addressee, 4:173; Emerson agrees to lecture in South Danvers (now Peabody). That the addressee was Charles Northend is evident from Emerson's letter to Thoreau, below, February 6, 1850.]

To SAMUEL GRAY WARD, CONCORD, DECEMBER 29, 1849[115]

Saturday, 29 Dec.

My dear S.

I shall be in town, Monday, & will go to your office at 3 o'clock. Bradford named /Geo./ Russell,[116] & thought he would like to join us. Rockwood Hoar, the new judge, is a very able man, & social: do you know him? Eustis the new Professor at Cambridge is said to be valuable;[117] & I have always hoped to know Tuckerman,[118] the botanist; who I believe is just now in Europe. I am not sure that I feel the /need/ of pressing none but householders.[119] Minors & cadets make better clubs, & I am willing to run the risk of being the oldest of the party. But I will see you on Monday if you are in town.

Yours,

R. W. E.

114. The Concord Social Circle.

115. MS in the Ward papers, Houghton Library, MH; ph. in NNC; printed in part in *EYSC*, p. 9, listed in *Letters*, 4:173. Endorsed by Ward 1849 and clearly related to earlier letters above about the club. The 29th of December fell on Saturday in 1849. Ebenezer Rockwood Hoar had been appointed a judge of the Court of Common Pleas in July 1849, taking office in September (Winfield Storey and Edward W. Emerson, *Ebenezer Rockwood Hoar*, Boston: Houghton Mifflin, 1911, p. 79.) Of those named, only Rockwood Hoar was a member of the Saturday Club when it finally came into existence.

116. I have no clue to the George Russell referred to; a George Russell is listed in 1849 directories as a physician. George Robert Russell is a possibility.

117. Henry Lawrence Eustis, professor of engineering, Lawrence Scientific School.

118. Edward Tuckerman, see above July 12.

119. These letters suggest the varying conceptions of the club; Longfellow wants members interested in art; so does Ward; Emerson wants young men and scientists.

To HENRY WADSWORTH LONGFELLOW, CONCORD, DECEMBER 30, 1849[120]

Concord 30 Dec 1849

My dear Longfellow,

Mr Scherb brought me the welcome gift of your Poems,[121] which, I observe, like their predecessors, receive the best compliment of being at once read through by all experimenters. I hope much in these days from Ward's cherished project of a club that shall be a club.[122] It It seems to offer me the only chance I dare trust of coming near enough to you to talk one of these days of poetry, of which, when I read your verses, I think I have something to say to you. So you must befriend his good plan. And here is a token—I send you my new book,[123] & will not have any sign that you have received it until the first club meeting.

Ever yours,
R. W. Emerson

120. MS in Longfellow papers, on deposit, Houghton Library, MH; ph. in NNC; p. [4] addressed: H. W. Longfellow Esq. Printed by Samuel Longfellow in *Life,* 2:154; listed in *Letters,* 4:54.

121. *The Seaside and the Fireside,* presentation inscription dated December 25, 1849 (Harding, p. 172; *BAL,* 12099). Emmanuel Vitalis Scherb, Longfellow's friend, v. *Life,* 2:120, *et passim.*

122. In the Longfellow papers is a copy of a printed flyer for the Town and Country Club addressed to Longfellow and bearing on the first page: "P.S. Your name is requested." The handwriting is not Emerson's or Alcott's. These flyers were circulated in April 1849.

123. *Representative Men, BAL,* 5219.

1850

<hr/>

To Elias? Nason, Concord, January 1, 1850[1]

Concord 1 Jany 1850

Dear Sir,

I will venture to offer you Friday, ⟨e⟩8 February, evening, for my lecture to your Lyceum.[2] It is just possible that I may yet wish to change it, with sufficient reason & notice, however.

Yours respectfully,
R. W. Emerson.

In advertising me, you shall please omit the title of *Reverend,* to which I have no claim.[3]

To William Henry Furness, Concord, January 3, 1850[4]

Concord 3 January 1850

My dear friend,

I was heartily glad to see your dear handwriting once more, glad of all it signified & ⟨& t⟩ of the fine little book that came with it. I am today (as too often, & all but always) the hack of petty engagements, & am besides forced to some caution in the use of my eyes, but must write, though so tardily, a few lines. Schiller's Song of the Bell,[5] I may as well avow, I have

<hr/>

1. MS in the Barrett Collection, Alderman Library, ViU; ph. in NNC; p. [4] addressed: Mr Nason| Manager of Newburyport Lyceum.| Newburyport| Mass. Above the dateline is written, apparently in the hand of the addressee: "R. W. Emerson's Autograph—| E. Nason." The addressee is possibly Elias Nason who founded a school for young ladies in 1840 and in 1844 became principal of the Brown High School (John J. Currier,) *History of Newburyport . . .* Newburyport, Mass.: Published by the Author, 1906, 1:324, 326).

2. In the MS Account Book for 1849–1853, p. [67], Newburyport is listed as of February 8 in a detailed record of expenses incurred between February 4 and 9; on p. 26, under the date February 8, is recorded the receipt of $20. from the Newburyport Lyceum.

3. See the similar postscript to a letter of December 26, 1849 (*Letters,* 4:173); the correspondent, not named by Rusk, is probably Charles Northend; see February 10, 1850, below.

4. MS in the Furness papers, Van Pelt Library, PU; ph. in NNC; p. [4] addressed to Rev. William H. Furness.| Philadelphia| Pa.|; postmarked at Concord January 3. Printed in *Records,* pp.[73]–74; listed in *Letters,* 4:175.

5. Emerson is replying to Furness' letter of December 27, 1849 (*Records,* p. [72]). Furness has sent him two copies of his translation of Schiller's *Song of the Bell . . .,* one copy being for Carlyle. Emerson's copy was evidently lost and replaced by Furness in April; see *Letters,*

always been content to take on trust; I have never read it in German; I do not like it very well: have even fancied that it owed something of its wide currency to its illustrations by Retsch,[6] & to the music which has been added.[7] More of my stupidity I will not now parade: but since you have been drawn to praise it with such faithful work, I shall give it one more chance to captivate me and have already read your gay translation once through,—which to me is only learning my way. All joy & peace & honour dwell with you, whatever you attempt & do!

I learn with great interest that your son is in Boston.[8] I had never heard of it:—only last summer, that he was in N. Y. Why did you not send him to me at once: I beg you to do so now; or send me his address, & I will ⟨at⟩immediately be at one with him

I am going however, next week to Albany, & the whole of the following week am to be in the city of New York. Immediately thereafter, I shall be permanently here, and will not be deprived of my share of beauty & art, do you tell him. I sent you my new book to the care of Mr Hart.[9]

Ever affectionately yours,
Waldo Emerson

To James John Garth Wilkinson, Concord, January 18? 1850

[Under the date January 5, 1850, Rusk lists this letter (4:175) from J. G. G. Wilkinson's reply of February 8. Wilkinson says he read *Representative Men* "a month ago" and Emerson's letter "a few weeks since." It is likely that Wilkinson received his copy of the English edition of the book from Chapman on the 8th of January as Carlyle did; see December 21, 1849, for note of Emerson's order to Chapman for the book to be sent to Carlyle and Wilkinson among others. Since Emerson's letter apparently reached Wilkinson after he had the book in hand, I think the letter has to be later than the 5th.]

4:190, and n. 82. The third copy is described by Harding (p. 241) as dated April 5, 1850, and "inscribed from the translator"; the volume includes translations from Goethe by Frederic Henry Hedge; it is inscribed by Furness.

6. Emerson may have seen an 1834 London edition of Schiller's poem (Black, Young & Young) with illustrations by Moritz Retzsch (the misspelling above is Emerson's). The Retzsch illustrations were to be used (1851?) in *Gems of German Verse* (Philadelphia: W. P. Hazard, n.d.), edited by Furness and including the Schiller and additional translations by Furness, Hedge, and others.

7. Schiller's poem was set to music by both Justin Heinrich Knecht and Andreas Jakob Romberg; the latter setting was evidently the better known, being issued by Novello with a text in English.

8. William Henry Furness, Jr. (see below November 1, 1852, to Greenough), who later would paint portraits of Emerson (see below December 17, 1871) and of his daughter Edith.

9. *Representative Men*.

To Henry David Thoreau, Saco, Maine, February 6, 1850[10]

Saco, Maine,
Wednesday 6 Feb

Dear Henry

I was at <u>South Danvers</u> on Monday Evening,[11] & promised Mr C. Northend, Secretary of the Lyceum, to invite you for Monday 18th Feb. to read ⟨as⟩ a lecture to his institution. I told him there were two lectures to describe Cape Cod,[12] which interested him & his friends, & they hoped that the two might somehow be rolled into one to give them some sort of complete story of the journey. I hope it will not quite discredit my negotiation if I confess that they heard with joy that Concord people laughed till they cried, when it was read to them. I understand Mr N., that there is a possibility but no probability that his absent colleague of the Lyceum has filled up that evening by an appointment But Mr N will be glad to hear from you that you will come, & if any cause exist why not, he will immediately reply to you.[13] They will pay your expenses, & $10.00. You will go from the Salem depot in an omnibus to /Mr/ N.'s house. Do go if you can. Address <u>Charles Northend, Esq. South Danvers.</u>

Yours ever
R. W. Emerson.

To James Russell Lowell? Concord? February 21, 1850?

[Listed *Letters,* 5:179, from *Catalogue of a Large Collection of Autographs . . . Donated to the Great Western Sanitary Fair, to be Sold . . . March 15th, 1864.* See Appendix A, 1850.]

10. MS in the Berg Collection, NN; ph. in NNC; addressed: Henry D. Thoreau.| Concord| Mass.|; postmarked at Saco, Me., February 7. Printed by Harding and Bode, p. 255; listed in *Letters,* 4:178, from auction catalogue. Emerson was in Saco on February 6, 1850 (*Letters,* 4:179; Charvat, p. 24), and in that year the 6th of February was a Wednesday.

11. South Danvers, Massachusetts, now Peabody, where Emerson lectured.

12. Thoreau had made a trip to Cape Cod in October 1849; his lectures on his trip had been given for the Concord Lyceum on January 23 and 30 (MS records of the Concord Lyceum, CFPL).

13. On a 1984 postcard, Goodspeed's listed a letter of Thoreau dated February 8 which refers to Emerson and arranges to read the lecture on "Cape Cod."

To Samuel Gray Ward, Concord, February 24, 1850[14]

Concord, 24 February, 1850

My dear friend,

Elizabeth Hoar wishes to prepay this letter to Margarita Marchesa;[15] but has done so before ⟨and⟩on letters which, she thinks, Margarita had to pay for again. Caroline T. told her that you could pay it & it would be paid. Do so, and I will bring you the money from Elizabeth H.

I saw Longfellow at Lowell's two days ago, & he declared that his faith in clubs was firm. "I will very gladly," he said, "meet with Ward & you & Lowell & three or four others, & dine together." Lowell remarked— Well, if he agrees to the dinner, though he refuses the supper, we will continue the dinner till next morning!—Meantime, as measles the influenza & the magazine appear to be periodic distempers, so, just now, Lowell has been seized with aggravated symptoms of the magazine,—as badly as Parker or Cabot heretofore, or as the chronic case of Alcott & me. He wishes to see something else & better than the Knickerbocker.[16] He came up to see me. He has now been with Parker, who professed even joy at the prospect offered him of taking off his heavy saddle, & Longfellow fosters his project. Then Parker urges the forming of a kind of Anthology Club:[17]—so out of all these resembling incongruities I do not know but we shall yet get a dinner or a "Noctes."[18]

Ever yours,
R. W. E.

14. MS in the Ward papers, Houghton Library, MH; ph. in NNC; p. [4] addressed: Sam.l G. Ward, Esq.| Merchants' Bank Building.| State Street.| Boston|; by Edward W. Emerson in *J*, 8:105, and in *EYSC*, p. 10; no printing is complete.

15. Margaret Fuller Ossoli. Caroline Sturgis Tappan.

16. Although published in New York, *The Knickerbocker Magazine* counted on its Boston contributors, among them Lowell. To the earnest, the magazine would appear frivolous.

17. The club to which Emerson's father and Lowell's had belonged, founders of the *Monthly Anthology* which later became *The North American Review*.

18. John Wilson ("Christopher North") et al., *Noctes Ambrosianae*, part factual, part fictional record of the conversations of an Edinburgh dining club, originally printed in *Blackwood's Edinburgh Magazine*.

TO HENRY JAMES, SR., CONCORD, FEBRUARY 25, 1850[19]

Concord, 25 February, 1850

My dear James,

Your letter & your book[20] arrived safely at my door many days ago, but I have not done with either of them. I came away from New York hugely contented that the good City had at least one expansive person within its expansive arms,[21] & meaning to make much of my opportunities & write you many letters But I began soon to accuse myself of improvidence in not really possessing myself of your points of view when you were stating them. It is surely best that conversation should be a luxury, & not a lesson.—But when one sees a doctrinaire, and only once in many years,—taking notes would be pardonable. The next time I find you, I ought to make you repeat point by point all the salient angles and towering pinnacles, & re-draw all the boundary walls of your citadel; for I am so unused to good company that each new stroke on my memory obliterates the last & I bring home little but this regret for great losses. It is sadly true. I had the feeling many times that we both had much to exchange, and I certainly saw that here was knowledge both critical & affirmative, which I wished to see to the end of. I shall not rest, then, until I have made another experiment.—The book, I said, will contain these things. But it does not. Your writing is not as good a statement as your speech.[22] At least, I think not. I do not pretend yet to have mastered the book. I read many fine things in it, and admirable special statements.

But I am awed & distanced a little by this argumentative style: every technical For & Suppose and Therefore alarms & extrudes me. and moreover I find or fancy (just as Wilkinson finds me guilty of unitarianism)[23] that you have not shed your last coat of presbyterianism, but that a certain catachetical[24] & legendary Jove glares at me sometimes, in your

19. MS in the James papers, Houghton Library, MH; ph. in NNC; p. [8] addressed: Henry James, Esq.| 58 West Fourteenth St.|New York.|; postmarked at Concord February 25. Printed by Perry, 1:61–62; listed in *Letters*, 4:180.

20. James, *Moralism and Christianity* (New York: J. S. Redfield, 1850).

21. Emerson was in New York for eight days, lecturing for the Mercantile Library Association on January 22 and 29 (Charvat, p. 24). James had invited Emerson to be his guest, and apparently Emerson did spend part of his visit there (Perry, 1:60, 66–67), but clearly not all of it, for a letter from William Emerson (February 2, RWEMA) shows that Emerson left brushes behind in the Staten Island house.

22. In his reply (March 1, Perry, 1:67), James takes this criticism in good part and begs for more.

23. James John Garth Wilkinson whose "notes" James says he is forwarding to Emerson with his letter of February 26 (Perry, 1:65); James appears to mean Wilkinson's letter of February 8.

24. Perry corrects Emerson's misspelling here.

page, which astonishes me in so sincere & successful a realist. Then lastly
& mainly—a curious cavil you will think for me to make,—your statement is not made with that completeness which seems imperative on one
broaching matters so vital & dear. Mr. Scroggins has gathered from you
some valuable revolutionary hints, some fine gunpowder to explode the
Capitol, but is not quite sure that he has the whole plan for building
Atlantis. But grain for grain: for every atom of gunpowder you must
send him a garden seed.—I see well that the book is full of nobleness, &
bright with health & reason, and as I become better acquainted with it,
perhaps it will defend & acquit itself. At all events you my friend, ⟨wi⟩must
& will. I beg you to make kindest remembrances from me to your wife,
⟨Miss Ja⟩ & to your Sister;[25] & give my love to the boys.—Your "Mercantile Library" has many echoes, & I have not yet done receiving applications from its Jersey neighbors, for lectures; and am seriously thinking
of going to them, &, possibly, much farther to Pittsburg & to Cincinnati,
from whence I have summonses.[26]

Yours affectionately,
R. W. Emerson.

To William Davis, Concord, February 27, 1850[27]

Concord, 27 February, 1850.

Dear Sir,

I believe I must not think of accepting your friendly invitation to read
lectures in Plymouth this season.

Yours respectfully,
R. W. Emerson.

William Davis, Esq.

To Henry James, Sr., Boston? February 27, 1850?

[With the letters to James (MH) is an envelope postmarked Boston, and dated
February 27. It is addressed to James at the 58 West 14th Street address, and has

25. Emerson probably remembered that "Aunt Kate" was not "Miss James," but not
knowing her name played safe; Miss Catherine Walsh was Mrs. James' sister.

26. Emerson did accept New Jersey invitations (Charvat, pp. 24–25), and in May made
his first trip to the Middle West, lecturing in Cincinnati by intent and Cleveland by accident
(Charvat, pp. 25–26). There was no lecture in Pittsburgh. Emerson improved the occasion
of his trip by coming home the long way to see St. Louis and the Mississippi, arriving home
on June 28 (see *Letters*, 4:209–215). See below May 7, 1850.

27. MS in bound volume of Miscellaneous MSS, MHi; ph. in NNC; single sheet without
address.

to have covered a letter written in 1850 or 1851 (it has no stamp). There is no known letter to James of February 27.]

To George Bancroft, Concord, March 5, 1850[28]

Concord, 5 March, 1850.

My dear Mr Bancroft,

Mr Emanuel Vitalis Scherb (of Basle, in Switzerland,) means to stop a day or two in New York, on his route to Georgia, & very naturally, as he is a good scholar, desires to see your face.[29] Mr Scherb has been reading lectures on European poetry to classes of ladies in Boston, and, as I understand, with unusual success. He has been our townsman here in Concord for some months; and an amiable man who knows books, is every where valuable.

My wife charges me to convey to Mrs Bancroft, with her kindest remembrances, the request, that, if Mr Scherb should, one of these days, read lectures in New York, she will go & hear them.[30] Excellent man, will you not come to Concord, on the nineteenth of April?

Yours faithfully,
R. W. Emerson.

To George Barrell Emerson, Concord, March 5, 1850[31]

Concord, 5 March 1850.

Dear George,

I am promising myself the pleasure of dining with you this P.m. but find it necessary to be at home this morning & shall take the noon train, which though it promises to leave Concord at 1.08., /p.m./, sometimes makes us wait 30 minutes; so you must give me a little latitude ⟨a⟩in your hour of dining,—though I count myself sure of being at your house very near to 2:30.

Yours affectionately,
R. Waldo E.

28. MS in the Bancroft papers, MHi; ph. in NNC.
29. Emmanuel Scherb was a friend of Longfellow's; see Samuel Longfellow, *Life*, passim.
30. See *Letters*, 4:186, March 23, 1850.
31. MS in the Ralph Lowell papers, MHi; ph. in NNC; single quarto leaf folded and addressed: George B. Emerson, Esq | 2 Pemberton Square| Boston.| The occasion appears to be without any special significance; just a visit with his cousin.

To Henry James, Sr., Concord, March 6, 1850[32]

Concord, ⟨5⟩6 March, 1850

My dear James,

You must check & abolish some of that superlative good nature of yours or it will lead the possessor into bogs & desarts. I am balancing whether to carry my popgun & thimbleful of paper bullets to Brooklyn, to New Jersey, & to the adjacent hamlet of New York,—forced to make a new answer too by a letter from Marcus Spring, and forthwith comes your welcome, wider than the arms of Massachusetts Bay, and I rashly wrote to Mr Spring[33] yesterday that I would come ⟨the⟩next week. This morning I woke up wiser, & wished my letter unwritten. But my venture in it is so small, that I will persist now that I am in. I shall write today to two Jersey people, in Paterson, I believe, & in Newark, who have written to me; and for New York,—you, you, O unhappy man! must ⟨first⟩be my first counsellor. /Mr/ Greeley & Mr Ripley[34] ⟨ha⟩assured me that I might find an audience. I think you must go to them, & ask them what kind of audience & what place & what manner of advertisement they contemplated, and they & you, or you alone, if you know him, must fix on some bookseller or factor that will do all but read the lectures, for me. For the matter of lectures, I have besides the two which I read to the Mercantile Library,[35] one on "Books" one on "Eloquence" one on "Natural Aristocracy" one on the "Superlative in manners & in literature",—a sort of sketch of the Eastern & Western races—; and three Lectures which I call "Natural History of the Intellect." Even at the bottom of my portfolio I find a lecture on "London", which, w|h|ere there is no Intellect at all, might be thought of. Out of this medley you see I might boldly promise /a Course of/ three or four chapters with some courage. and under some such programme as "Lectures on the XIX Century", which has served me before. With that name, however, my story on the "Spirit of the Times," would need to come in. Here you have all my story. If the omiscient "Tribune," or if a good bookseller thinks that such readings in

32. MS in the James papers, Houghton Library, MH; ph. in NNC; p. [4] addressed: Henry James, Esq.| 58 West Fourteenth Street| New York.| ; postmarked at Concord March 6. Printed by Perry, 1:67–69; listed *Letters*, 4:182.

33. Marcus Spring, Quaker reformer; see Thoreau's description of Spring's estate, Eagleswood, and the community there (Harding and Bode, pp. 439–440). It is with Spring and his wife that Margaret Fuller traveled in 1846.

34. George Ripley had become a reviewer for Horace Greeley's *Tribune*.

35. In England first and then in Boston. See Charvat (pp. 24–25) for lectures in Brooklyn and New York and in Newark and Paterson.

New York will pay my tax bills & bad gardening in Concord, I shall try the experiment. Do then, unfortunate man, whom heaven in its anger has afflicted with a good heart, go ask the question. I mean to come to N.Y. say on the 13th. I shall go to the Astor House. Reproach me not with my ingratitude. It never was heard of in credible history that a man went twice in the same season to the house of his friend. I shall go to the Astor,[36] that I may the more unblushingly spend the whole day at your house. Meantime I shall ripen all the nettleseed I can find on the subject of a late Book.[37] With kindest remembrance to your tutelar gods,

Yours,   R. W. Emerson.

To Henry David Thoreau, Concord, March 11, 1850[38]

Concord, 11 March 1850

Mr Henry D. Thoreau,
My dear Sir,

   I leave town tomorrow & must beg you, if any question arises between Mr Bartlett & me,[39] in regard to boundary lines, to act as my attorney, & I will be bound by any agreement you shall make.

Will you also, if you have opportunity, warn Mr Bartlett, on my part, against burning his wood lot, without having there present a sufficient number of hands to prevent the fire from spreading into my wood,— which, I think, will be greatly endangered, unless much care i⟨t⟩s used.

   Show him too, if you can, where his cutting & his post-holes trench on our line, by <u>plan</u>. and, so doing, oblige as ever,

Yours faithfully,
R. W. Emerson.

36. In his letter of March 1, James had invited Emerson to be his guest again (Perry, 1:66–67).

37. James' book, see February 25 above.

38. MS in NNPM; ph. in NNC; p. [4] addressed: Henry D. Thoreau. Concord.| Printed by Sanborn in *AM* (June 1892), 69:750, and in Harding and Bode, p. 256. The purpose of the letter accounts for its formality; Thoreau could show the letter as authorizing him to act for Emerson.

39. See *Letters*, 5:24 and 112, with n. 70, for an account of later difficulties with this neighbor, Charles Bartlett. For a more detailed account, see Kenneth W. Cameron's "Emerson's Fight for his Walden Woodlots," *ESQ* (1st q., 1961) 22:90–95; Cameron prints this letter, p. 90. See *JMN*, 12:210–213, for entry of June 17, 1857, written the day after a Jury heard the case.

To Henry Wadsworth Longfellow?, Boston, March 12, 1850[40]

Boston March 12. 1850

Sir.

You are invited to meet, for the purpose of advising a Committee ap⟨oin⟩pointed to present a plan for reorganizing the Town & Country Club at their room No. 15 Tremont Row, on Thursday, 14th inst. at 3 o'clock P.M.

Respectfully
R. W. Emerson
James T. Fisher
Geo. B. Loring   Com.
S. G. Ward
Wm. O. Johnson

To Frederick William Ricord, New York, March 14, 1850

[Listed by Cameron, *ESQ* (2d q., 1956), 3:5, and again (4th q., 1958), 13:39 from George A. Van Nosdall List 1,026, August 1946, item 56, described as addressed to Mr Ricord and as inserted in the Hogan copy of *Essays*, 1841 and 1844 *sic*, and as dated from the Astor House, March 14, n. y. The lecture schedule and titles determine the year (see Charvat, p. 24). The letter, apparently quoted in full, reads: "I think you may depend on me at Newark, next Friday Evening, since you say that is the best for you, and I will bring you the lecture on 'England,' if you choose it. Mr. Marcus Spring, however, who heard my lecture tonight on 'Natural Aristocracy,' chooses that for me to read at Brooklyn. Please to say to Mr. Kinney, with my respects, that I shall certainly accept his hospitable summons. With great regard, your obedient servant, R. W. Emerson." Kinney is William Burnet Kinney, see *Letters*, 4:196–197. Emerson's correspondent is surely Frederick William Ricord, librarian of the Newark Library Association and later State Superintendent of Schools.]

To William M. Gillespie, Concord, March? ? 1850

[As corresponding secretary of Phi Beta Kappa, Union College, Schenectady, New York, William M. Gillespie, in a letter of March 14, 1850 (RWEMA), notified Emerson of his election as poet for the next anniversary, July 23. One letter certainly was necessary.]

40. MS in the Longfellow papers; Houghton Library, MH; ph. in NNC. The letter including all the signatures is in the hand of James T. Fisher and may be his composition, although Emerson was chairman of the committee (a.l.s., Fisher to Emerson, March 7, 1850, RWEMA). This document was originally in Craigie House, and was probably addressed to Longfellow; his brother Samuel, also a member of the club, lived in Fall River in 1850.

To Henry James, Sr., New York, March 18, 1850[41]

Astor House
Monday night

My dear James,

I have been looking through my "London" & on the whole I think it will not do to venture it on such short notice. It has been drained of its best things to cram the "England," and and I could not, so soon as Wednesday night, make good those defects. If we must take Wednesday Night,[42] I think we must take "Books."

Another vexation for you. Mr Spring sent up to C. S. Francis bookstore this P.m. for a supply of tickets for Brooklyn, to eke out an imperfect supply already provided.[43] I believe he got 50 tickets of Francis, and as I thought I heard,—"all he had."[44] Therefore Francis[45] must immediately be provided with more or you are a ruined benefactor.

R. W. E.

Alas! I have no postage stamps! they must come by & by to you. meantime you shall pay!

To William Henry Furness, New York, March 20, 1850[46]

Astor House. New York
20 April, 1850

My dear Furness,

William Emerson sent me yesterday your kind note, an autograph within & without, very refreshing to behold. I should like extremely to come to Philadelphia, and have at this moment but one objection, and that the gravest; namely, that you, you & your friends, but chiefly you,

41. MS in the James papers, Houghton Library, MH; ph. in NNC; with envelope addressed: Henry James, Esq. | 58 West Fourteenth Street. | New York.| ; stamped by Boyd's Express, March 19. Printed by Perry, 1:69; listed in *Letters*, 4:185.

42. I find no evidence of a Wednesday engagement during this second visit to New York; the fourth lecture for Hope Chapel was given on Thursday, the subject "Books" (Charvat, p. 24).

43. On the 15th, Marcus Spring had written Emerson to send to Brooklyn "one or two hundred tickets"; the Brooklyn series opened on the 18th (Charvat, p. 24).

44. James evidently underwrote the expenses of ticket printing, advertising, and the rent of the hall (see *Letters*, 4:196). See below, April 9, for Emerson's return to New York for the settlement of accounts.

45. Charles S. Francis with whom Emerson had had dealings earlier on behalf of Carlyle (see *Letters*, 2:104, 186–187).

46. MS in the Furness papers, Van Pelt Library, PU; ph. in NNC; printed in *Records*, pp. [77] −78. The letter of March 24 below shows that Emerson misdated this letter; the two together settle his going to Philadelphia where his lectures began on April 3. It was certainly written in March. See *Letters*, 4:184.

will feel a certain conscience to shoulder my affair,—a thing painful, nay intolerable, to think of, and which shall not be done. But if you can think of a Bookseller who would undertake the charge, and would do all but read the lectures, I should like very well to read four or five, and should come with the more courage that they have been unexpectedly successful here. I am quite clear that there should be a functionary in each of our cities who would be General Undertaker & Factor for Lectures, and who should transact for Agassiz, Dana, Mitchell, & me.[47] But it is now too late in the season, or will be before I can leave N.Y.; where, I must still read three lectures, it seems, (tomorrow /Thursday/[48] Tuesday, & probably Thursday or certainly two. We will talk of it for next winter, and, meantime, our aesthetic broker can be ripening. The blessings of all the days fall on that roof which invites me so hospitably!—but I am inveterate churl, & never carry my tediousness to the houses of my friends. If however, you can send me some disengaged worldly opinion that the experiment is still worth trying, I shall be heartily glad of an apology for coming to a faithful gossip with you.

Yours affectionately,
R. Waldo Emerson.

To Henry Whitney Bellows, New York, March 21, 1850

[In the Barrett Collection, Alderman Library, ViU, is an envelope addressed to Rev. Henry W. Bellows. 32 East Twentieth St New York. The envelope is stamped Paid and surcharged at New York March 21. The only possible year before postage stamps were required is 1850. The envelope cannot belong with the letter dated by Rusk March 23, 1860 (Letters, 5:207–208), which it now accompanies (as it did when letter and envelope were in the Colson estate).]

To William Henry Furness, New York, March 24, 1850[49]

Astor House, New York
24 March, 1850

My dear Furness,

Since you are pleased to be peremptory & foolhardy in your good nature, I think I must even try your project. I must hold you to your

---

47. Richard Henry Dana, Jr., is meant. "Mitchell" is the Cincinnati astronomer J. Ormsby Mitchel, whose name Emerson habitually misspelled.

48. "Thursday" written above "tomorrow" is a gloss not an insert. See Charvat, pp. 24–25, for the New York lectures.

49. MS in the Furness papers, Van Pelt Library, PU; ph. in NNC; printed in Records, p. [75]; listed Letters, 4:188. Henry Howard Furness prints with this letter (p. 76) a long

own terms, & it is the bookseller & not you who shall shoulder the affair, even though the audience should so be reduced one half. I do not think I can come to Philadelphia until Tuesday or Wednesday,—for safety, Wednesday,—of next week. It would be safe to advertise for Wednesday Evening, 3d April. We can promise two or three lectures per week, as you think best; two probably. Here, I am in the hands of a good friend of mine, Henry James, & /of/ Parke Godwin,[50] and they settled that it should be a two shilling audience. I incline to this cheaper ticket; though it is a moot point, & many advisers said, Fifty cents.[51] The booksellers must decide that, too. Here, we have had no Course announced, but only a series of unconnected ⟨1⟩Lectures, from night to night. Did I give you the titles of such as I have here that are pronounced producible?

England   } read here at my last visit.
Spirit of the Times }
Natural Aristocracy.
Eloquence.
Books.
The superlative in manners, character, & races.[52]

Of all these I think the fourth seemed to be best received here, though perhaps each has had its friends. I am promising to read one lecture here, as I believe I told you, to please myself, called "Instinct & Inspiration." And so, awaiting your commands with confidence & love, I am yours,

R. Waldo Emerson.

---

postscript that cannot belong to this letter; see below, December 18, 1853, for the postscript and the argument that it belongs with that letter.

50. Of *The New York Evening Post,* Bryant's future son-in-law.

51. See May 7, below, for Emerson's preference for cheaper tickets and yet his willingness to abide by local practice.

52. See Charvat, p. 25, for the final schedule with one lecture repeated. Emerson separates the titles with a short rule between each pair and by means of a brace indicates that the first two titles are not new.

To John Jay, New York, April 1, 1850[53]

Astor House
Monday morng, 1 April.

John Jay, Esq.
My dear Sir,
    I learn from Philadelphia this morning that my friends have promised me there on Wednesday Evening: So I regret that I shall not have[54] promised pleasure of seeing you & Mrs Jay on Wednesday Evening. I mean to indemnify myself at another hour as early as I can.

With great regard
Your obliged servant,
R. W. Emerson.

To Henry James, Sr., Philadelphia, April 9, 1850[55]

United States Hotel
Phila, 9 April, 1850.

My dear James,
    I suppose you think I went to ruin as soon as I left your protection, and I confess I had had my share of sunshine, & was not entitled to any more good fortune for the present. Still the winds of heaven ⟨never⟩have not blown out all their odours & benefits and I have found some old & some new friends here. The weather was bad with rain & snow but what a day was Sunday! I heard[56] sermon from William Furness, then dined with an old playmate of my infancy, Saml Bradford,[57] Treasurer here of the Reading Rail Road, and walked with him & an excellent Walter Langdon,[58] the whole delicious afternoon on the Schuylkill ⟨Ri⟩Banks.

53. MS in the Jay papers, Special Collections, Butler Library, NNC; ph. in NNC. Emerson lectured in Philadelphia in April only in 1850, in which year the 1st fell on a Monday. See above letters to Furness, March 20 and 24. In England, Emerson had traveled to Windsor and Eton with the Jays, George Hillard, and the Englishman John Kenyon; see above July 10, 1848; *Letters*, 4:95; *JMN*, 10:272–274. Rusk and Sealts, following Rusk, identify Jay as William Jay, but in the Columbia collection of Jay papers there are letters by John Jay showing that he was abroad with his wife (Eleanor Kingsland Field) in the spring of 1848 and in England. And this letter suggests an earlier social relation.

54. Turning his leaf, Emerson omitted a definite article here.

55. MS in the James papers, Houghton Library, MH; ph. in NNC; with envelope addressed: Henry James Esq.re | 58 West Fourteenth Street | New York. |; postmark blurred; printed by Perry, 1:70; listed *Letters*, 4:198.

56. Emerson omits the article here.

57. Bradford, Furness, and Emerson were schoolboys together.

58. Walter Langdon was a friend of William Emerson (*Letters*, 2:149; 4:195). Langdon's gift to Emerson of a French edition of Montaigne is acknowledged by Emerson on April 18 (*Letters*, 4:200); the edition was bequeathed to Cabot (Harding, p. 193); and see *Letters*, 4:202.

Yesterday I spent with some Quakers of Germantown, Wistars[59] & Fishers[60] well worth the seeing, in a park & old house worthy of England, and Lucretia Mott too is a benignity which is nature's ultimate in that kind. But I did not sit down to tell you my history but only to make an effort to secure a meeting with you, on my way home. I have been indiscreetly persuaded this morning to stay one night more, namely, Thursday (beyond my plan) hitherto & repeat one of my grindings.[61] It follows that I shall have no time to stay in N. Y. if I mean, as I must, to get home on Saturday night.[62] I am to carry with me Mrs William Emerson, and it will take a little longer time for her to go, than if I went alone. I shall reach N. Y, I am told, about 11.30 A.M. on Friday, and will go then to the Astor House. I have written my brother that I will come thence immediately to his Office & learn what route & hours he & his wife have decided to take—probably to New Haven, Friday p.m.[63] Then I shall go, say 12.30 to the Astor. Will you not see me there? If I do not find you, I shall go up to your house, & to Bancrofts also, & to one or two more, that I wish to visit. And it is plain you must leave me at the Astor House some note of your whereabout. So with all love & joy in you & in yours, I am

Waldo Emerson

To Lucretia Coffin Mott, Concord, April 18, 1850[64]

Concord, 18 April,
1850.

My dear Mrs Mott,[65]

It was very negligent in me to leave Philadelphia without complying with the easy task you laid on me to write my name on a paper. Yet, in my last day, & evening, I had scarcely a moment alone. I send you for your friend a verse from the Persian poet Hafiz, of which the English

---

59. Descendants of Dr. Caspar Wistar.

60. William Logan Fisher (*Letters*, 4:196; *JMN*, 11:292–293.)

61. See Charvat (p. 25) for the repeated lecture in Philadelphia.

62. Emerson returned to New York to settle his accounts left in James' charge. His MS Account Book for 1849–1853, in an undated entry of March, records (p. 28) the receipt of $116 from Marcus Spring for his Brooklyn lectures and of "about $390," "after all expenses were paid," from Henry James for his New York lectures. On the same page are listed his receipts from Newark, Paterson, and Philadelphia. In an undated entry of April (p. 72) he calculates his expenses for the whole circuit at $117.75 and his net receipts as "about" $630.

63. Susan Haven Emerson did not after all travel to Concord with Emerson (*Letters*, 4:202).

64. MS in the Barrett Collection, Alderman Library, ViU; ph. in NNC.

65. See April 9, 1850, and *JMN*, 11:249, for Emerson's admiration of Lucretia Mott.

translation is is mine.[66] My wife & I are very much obliged to you for your truthful & loving defence of Woman. We also entertain a good hope of seeing you & your husband,[67] one day, in our house which is on the Fitchburg Rail Road, one hour from Boston.

With grateful remembrances,
Your affectionate servant,
R. Waldo Emerson

To ———, Concord, May 3, 1850

[Listed by C. F. Libbie in the catalogue of the Leffingwell Collection, sale of January 6–8, 1871.]

To Ainsworth Rand Spofford, Concord, May 7, 1850[68]

Concord, Mass.
7 May, 1850

A. R. Spofford, Esq.
Dear Sir,

The kind invitation you convey to me from so many friends in Cincinnati[69] awakens again the wishes & hopes of many years to see the

---

66. Emerson encloses the following quatrain signed and dated R Waldo Emerson. | Concord, April, 1850.|:

> Go, leap into the waves,
> And have no doubt, nor care,—
> And the flowing of the seven broad seas
> Shall never wet thy hair.

Revised and with an additional quatrain and the title "Faith," the verses appeared in *The Liberty Bell* for 1851 (p. 79); for the final version, see "Persian Poetry" (*Works*, 8:261), first published in the *Atlantic Monthly* in April 1858 (1:732). See below October 24; November 17, 18, 1850, and December 27, 1851, for other translations from Joseph von Hammer-Purgstall's German texts.

Emerson bought Von Hammer's edition of Hafiz (Harding, p. 124) from Elizabeth Peabody in April 1846 (MS Account Book for 1845–1849, entry of April 9, p. [81]); he acquired Von Hammer's *Geschichte der schönen redekünste Persiens* (Harding, p. 125) in October 1850, buying it from Theodore Parker (MS Account Book for 1849–1853, entry of October 30, p. 110). In Emerson's MS poetry notebooks, particularly in notebook 10, there are a good many translations from Hafiz and other Persian poets.

67. James Mott.

68. MS in the Manuscript Division DLC; ph. in NNC; printed by C. Carroll Hollis in his "A New England Outpost . . ." *NEQ* (March 1965), 38:67. The letter is separated at the fold; the postscript is on the second leaf. The letter is gauzed.

69. The invitation signed by a hundred citizens of Cincinnati is referred to in Emerson's letter to Carlyle of August 5; *Letters*, 4:224 (Slater, p. 462). Spofford, then a bookseller, subsequently Librarian of Congress, was evidently entrusted with making the arrangements for Emerson's first Western lecture engagements. The five lectures became eight (listed, Charvat, pp. 24–25). For the unplanned Cleveland lecture, see David Mead, *Yankee Eloquence in the Middle West* (East Lansing: Michigan State University Press, 1951), pp. 26–27.

Ohio River & all that lies between it & my home. I do not well know how to go, as I had just settled myself here to some summer work, both in my house & on my land, which must wait.[70] But after thinking it twice over, the project of the journey is very attractive to me, & I decide to come, & shall leave home next Saturday or Monday.[71]

In regard to Lectures, you are at liberty to make such arrangements for me as you think best. And you may announce a Course of Five, as you suggest. Perhaps tomorrow I will write you again in regard to subjects.[72]

Yours respectfully,
R. W. Emerson.

I observe that you set your course tickets at one dollar. You must do what is best in your city, consulting your usage. But at New York my friends, I believe, convinced themselves that Mr Horace Greeley, with whom it had been left, should have made the single ticket 50 cents, instead of 25. The lecturers complained of me as an injurer of the profession[73]

To Sewall and Munroe, Concord, May 9, 1850[74]

Concord, 9 May, 1850.

Will Mr Sewall have the goodness to send me by the Bearer, (the Concord Express)

70. The MS Account Book for 1849–1853 shows a number of expenses connected with his house and land including the purchase from Cyrus and Nathan Stowe of two acres of woodlot in Lincoln (April 22, p. 79; and Middlesex County Registry of Deeds, MS Vol. 589, p. 186); and a payment (among several for various chores) to Thoreau for "trenching the line of blackthorn hedge from Watts's line west along the edge of the upland" (April 30, p. 83), and see below, May 9, for an order for hardware.

71. Emerson gives details of the Western trip in a letter to Lidian (*Letters*, 4:209–214); a lost earlier letter of May 17 may have described the fire in the lake steamer *America* that brought him ashore in Cleveland. The MS Account Book for 1849–1853, p. 91, records the expenses entailed by his additional travel. Under June 7 he enters the expenses of the journey "from Concord to Cincinnati including visit to Niagara" as $38.65. Under the date June 18, he gives as $191.80 the total expense of the journey to Cincinnati, Mammoth Cave, to Cairo, St. Louis, Galena, and home by way of Lake Ontario, Oswego, Albany, and Worcester. He took in a good deal on this journey through territory of which he had only read or heard of from such friends as Ward, Channing, Clarke, and Margaret Fuller. (For this trip, see also *JMN*, 11:533–538.)

72. See note under May 10 below.

73. For himself, Emerson would have preferred the lowest charge, but he was first and last an accommodating man.

74. MS in the Feinberg Collection, MiD; ph. in NNC; p. [4] addressed: Sewall & Munroe | Liberty Square. | Printed by William White, *AL* (May 1961), 33:162. Emerson clearly spells the name Sewall; White has Sewell. The hardware dealer James S. Munroe is listed in Boston directories with his address after 1850 as 7 Liberty Square. The MS Account Book for 1849–

1. a strong spring to shut a front /wooden/ gate.

———

2. a strong spring to shut an inner house-door. price about 1 dollar

———

3. 1 pair strong hinges, say 4 inches by 2

———

4. a couple of strong hasps [a drawing appears here] for a barn door & a gate.

———

and charge the same to the account of

R. W. Emerson

To William Buell Sprague, Concord, May 10, 1850[75]

Concord, 10 May, 1850.

Rev Dr Sprague.

My dear Sir,

I have been so much a truant from home, that all my correspondence has fallen into most discreditable disorder, But if you have not forgotten it, I was to send you a manuscript of Dr Ripley; one of William Emerson, my grandfather; & an autograph of Miss Bremer. These I send.[76] An autograph of Rev Daniel Bliss, Mr Emerson's predecessor, I doubted not to find also; but a Col. Bliss of Buffalo, has been last summer, in Concord, & carried off all such papers /as/ he could find.[77]

With kind remembrance,
Yours respectfully,
R. W. Emerson.

———

1853 (p. 104) records a payment of 2.81 to Sewall & Munroe on September 30. For his Christmas card in 1938, Carroll A. Wilson reproduced an undated note to James S. Munroe. The note is written in pencil on a glazed calling card; it reads: "Will Mr Munroe/ send Mr E. an effect-/ tive Rat Trap/ 2 inch chisel/ 2 auger/." On the obverse of the card appears in ink: Mr R. W. Emerson. I conjecture that the card was left at Munroe's shop. I have no clue to the date.

75. MS in the Dawes Memorial Library, OMC; ph. in NNC. The letter is inlaid, the second leaf trimmed slightly damaging the final letter and punctuation of the first line of the complimentary close. At some later time, an attempt was made to eradicate the addressee's name by washing it out and, when that didn't work, scratching was tried; the letter "R" in "Rev" is palpably rough to the touch. Whoever sought concealment did work carefully.

76. William Buell Sprague, from Albany, acknowledges Emerson's package in a letter of May 15 (RWEMA).

77. There are still papers of the Reverend Daniel Bliss, his sons, and his wife in the Emerson papers (RWEMA). The borrower (?) was Colonel John Bliss; see entry 900 in John H. Bliss, *The Genealogy of the Bliss Family* (Boston, Mass.: Printed by the author, 1881), p. 152.

To Ainsworth Rand Spofford, Boston? May 10, 1850

[In his letter to Spofford of May 7 above Emerson says he may write again "in regard to subjects" for his lectures in Cincinnati. The Library of Congress had an envelope addressed to Spofford; it is postmarked at Boston May 10 and possibly covered a second letter, but there is no certainty, for the envelope could have covered the letter of the 7th. (1984) The above entry was entered when the Library of Congress still had the envelopes accompanying the papers of Spofford, formerly head of the library which has apparently discarded them.]

To Alexander Ireland, Concord, May 12, 1850[78]

Concord, 12 May, 1850

My dear Ireland,

I received many weeks ago a note from you for which I found no answer,—I am sorry for it,—& so sent none. I am so disconnected from all the common systems of lucrative work, that when I hear of an applicant, I inquire of other people if there is room. Mr Greeley (of N.Y.)[79] said "none for literary work; we refuse such applications in great numbers." Rev Dr Furness of Philadelphia, said, "I always advise the Englishman to come; I know of so many instances of success."—My belief is that there is, for all men of energy, much more room, & opportunity here, than with you: but almost no more promise here, than with you, for any infirmity. In the case of your friend, I should think it not wise,—from my impressions of his tendencies & turn of mind,—to make the adventure. I saw him but little, & learned something of him from his friends, the Fishers,[80]—I saw no writing, heard no public speaking, and have no knowledge of what public talent he possesses; but he did not inspire me with any confidence in his good sense, or in his reasonable expectations from society. So I only praise the more your & Mr Fisher's generous fidelity to him. I was very glad to see your hand & name, & you must not fail to write me ⟨a similar⟩ again when you have the like application to make for another person. Tis likely, I may give you a much better answer. But mainly I look & shall not cease to look for your own arrival, though late, yet sure, it must be, on your tour of observation. Mr Law-

78. MS in the Berg Collection, NYPL; ph. in NNC; printed with many minor omissions by Ireland, pp. 84–85; listed in Letters, 4:202.

79. Horace Greeley.

80. I have no clue to the identity of this prospective emigrant from England, if Fisher is W. Fisher, Jr., then possibly he came from Sheffield; see above January 7, 1848.

rence, I see, tells you once a month, in London, that "we are a great nation,"[81] and my dear Carlyle tells you that we are a very dull one; but nature never disappoints, and our square miles and the amounts of human labour here are incontestable & will interest all your taste, intelligence, & humanity. Forgive me that I never write. My eyes are not good, & I write no letter that is not imperative. I remember you at all times with kindest thankfulness & high esteem. I heard with joy that Espinasse was well placed, to command his time & studies. Of Mr Ballantyne too his paper brought me good news.[82] And Mr Kehl of Huddersfield gave me good tidings of others of your friends.[83] Yours affectionately,

R. W. Emerson

To Norton S. Townshend and H. D. Clark, Cincinnati,
MAY? 30? 1850

[In a letter of May 24, 1850 (RWEMA), Norton S. Townshend and H. D. Clark ask Emerson to repeat, in Columbus, Ohio, the lectures he is giving in Cincinnati; members of the constitutional convention now meeting and residents of Columbus would like to hear them. See *Letters*, 4:208, for record of a reply to a similar invitation from Pittsburgh. It is likely that Emerson replied to this invitation too, but there is no proof. Both Townshend and Clark are listed as delegates in J. V. Smith, *Report of the . . . Proceedings of the Convention for the Revision of the Constitution of the State of Ohio* (Columbus: S. Medway, Printer to the Convention, 1850), 1:3, 5.]

To Gilbert Lewis Streeter, Concord, June 29, 1850[84]

G. L. Streeter, Esq.
Dear Sir,

On my return home I find your note, but I do not like to promise a lecture for so distant a day. You shall if you please make up your list

---

81. Abbott Lawrence, minister to England, 1849–1852.
82. Francis Espinasse of the *Manchester Examiner* when Emerson met him; see *Letters*, 3:447. Espinasse was one of Emerson's guests at the dinner he gave in Manchester; see *Letters*, 4:15, and Espinasse, *Literary Recollections and Sketches* (London, 1893), pp. 156–166; Scudder, pp. 48, 93, 149, passim. Thomas Ballantyne, editor of the *Manchester Examiner;* see *Letters*, 4:11 and 15, and Scudder, pp. 42, 93.
83. See *JMN*, 10:216, for Kehl of Huddersfield.
84. MS in the Gilbert Lewis Streeter papers, Essex Institute; Emerson returned from his first Western trip on the 28th.

without regard to me; &, next winter, if you find any vacancies, perhaps
I shall be ready to come.[85]

Yours respectfully,
R. W. Emerson

To Thaddeus William Harris, Concord, July 1, 1850

[Laid in the MS Account Book for 1849–1853 between pp. 18–19 and used as
scratch paper is the beginning of a letter to the librarian of Harvard; in spite of
the date, it appears to be a false start of the letter dated June 30 (*Letters*, 4:214–
215).]

To Marcus Spring, Concord, July 23, 1850[86]

Concord, 23d July, 1850.

My dear Sir

The morning papers add no syllable to the fatal paragraphs of last
night concerning Margaret Fuller; no contradiction and no explanation.
At first I thought I would go myself and see if I could help in the
inquiries at the wrecking ground, and act for the friends. But I have
prevailed on my friend, Mr Henry D. Thoreau, to go for me and all the
friends. Mr Thoreau is the most competent person that could be selected; and in the dispersion of the Fuller family, and our uncertainty
how to communicate with them, he is authorized by Mr Ellery Channing
to act for them all.[87]

I fear the chances of recovering manuscript and other property, after
five or six days, are small, and diminishing every hour. Yet Margaret
would have every record of her history for the last three or four years;
and whatever is found by anyone would easily be yielded up to a diligent
seeker. Mr Thoreau is prepared to spend a number of days in this object,
if necessary, and you must give him any guidance or help you can. If his

85. He would lecture for the Salem Lyceum on January 21, 1851; since no date is set
here, there would have to be a later exchange of letters between Emerson and Streeter, the
Corresponding Secretary of the Salem Lyceum. See Charvat, p. 25, for the 1850–1851
season.

86. No MS has been located, text from Sanborn, *Recollections*, 2:415; an earlier printing
by Sanborn is in *The Critic* (March 1906), 48:254–255; Cameron reproduces the printing in
Recollections, *ESQ* (4th q., 1958), 13:39; listed *Letters* 4:220. See *Letters*, 4:219, for a similar
letter to Horace Greeley. Rusk's n. 17 quotes the *Tribune* account of the wreck of the
Elizabeth.

87. Channing was married to Margaret Fuller's sister. Arthur Fuller, Margaret's brother,
joined Thoreau on the 24th.

money does not hold out, I shall gladly pay any drafts he may make on you in my name.[88] And I shall cordially unite with you in any expense that this painful calamity shall make necessary.[89]

Yours faithfully,
R. W. Emerson.

Marcus Spring, Esq.

To George Barrell Emerson, Concord, August 2, 1850[90]

Concord, 2 August, 1850

Dear George,

Can you recommend to us a good ⟨private⟩teacher for our private school? Miss Whiting has[91] taught some twenty children, girls & boys, for two years, with great success; but refuses to begin a new year. We want a lady who can fill her place: she ought to be able to fit a boy for college; yet the majority of her scholars will not read latin. We want, of course, character & complete command of the school. We can easily guarantee $550.00 a year, and, if the teacher makes the school famous, she can make the income from $600. to $650. I suppose.

We have already applied to Elizabeth Ripley,[92] but she peremptorily refuses. Can you not think of a lady who can serve us? Do you know whether Miss Adam could come? And is she competent? Do you know

---

88. The MS Account Book for 1849–1853 under the date February 23 has this entry (p. 96): "Cash to Henry D. Thoreau for expenses of journey to N. Y. and Fire Island 70.00." Under the date July 30 is the entry (p. 40): "Received of H. D. Thoreau unexpended balance of 70.00 paid him for expenses in journey &c to Fire Island Beach. Cash paid him 70. Expended by him 29.00 advanced to Channing 10.00 . . . Balance repaid me 31.00." (William Henry Channing accompanied Thoreau to Fire Island.)

89. Plans for the *Memoirs* were underway by August 2 (*Letters*, 4:222).

90. MS in the G. B. Emerson papers, MHi; ph. in NNC. Emerson's second cousin was the head of a distinguished and successful school for girls in Boston.

91. Ellen Emerson, in her life of her mother, gives Miss Whiting's name as Jane (MS, p. 207c, 2d set of these numbers). The MS Account Books show payments to Miss Whiting from November 1848 through July 1850, some entries giving the initials "L. J." Louisa Jane Whiting was a native of Concord; she and her sister and brother (William Whiting, Jr.) all had attended the Concord Academy when its principal was Phineas Allen. The Emerson children had earlier been taught by Mary Russell, Ellen Fuller Channing, and Anna Alcott.

It is in a conversation with Bronson Alcott that Ellen Emerson in 1858 recalled Miss Whiting. She writes her sister (a.l.s., November 8, 1858): "Mr Alcott made me a speech which I couldn't understand about myself and Idealism and I told him so, and he asked me whether I was a school madam or a scholar and whether I had dreams of teaching. I said I shouldn't make a good teacher and he doubted whether there were any, as I went out I told him that Miss Whiting's scholars thought she was a perfect teacher, and I thought that such a thing was possible. And he called after me 'That is Idealism.' "

92. Elizabeth Ripley, daughter of Emerson's half-uncle Samuel Ripley.

Anna Ware? & her sister Elizabeth?[93] Now, if you will please to give me your best thought on these premises in a note,—not answering all my questions, but the right one only,—You will greatly benefit the cause of education in Concord, & add another to a multitude of kindnesses to your affectionate cousin

Waldo E.

To Caroline Sturgis Tappan, Concord, August 3, 1850[94]

Concord, 3 August,
1850.

Dear Caroline,

William Henry Channing writes me an urgent letter wishing me to write some sort of ⟨w⟩life, which he calls "Margaret and her Friends."[95] On his invitation, I ⟨have⟩went to see him, & we talked an hour of it. Many questions rose. Can one do it? Perhaps not, but three might, namely, S G W, W H C, & I. But are the materials to be had? Nothing could be done without the full concurrence of the above named three, & then your own; &, of course, that of the family. But will you, & Sam W., & William Channing, consent to surrender all these old letters, to me, or to the three? I have written to Ward, whom I failed to see after talking with W. C. If ⟨we⟩all shall agree in heroic consent & surrender, will the compiled history be publishable?—I think it must be written in the

93. I have been unable to find the Misses Ware or Miss Adam in *The Boston Almanac* for 1849 (S. N. Dickinson) which not only has a list of teachers but has also an account of every Boston public school. And neither of them attended the Teacher's College in West Newton (originally in Lexington and now in Framingham).

94. MS in the Tappan papers, Houghton Library, MH; ph. in NNC; the MS ends abruptly at the foot of the fourth page; the rest of the letter is apparently lost.

95. On August 1, as Emerson tells Ward in his letter of August 2 (see *Letters*, 4:222). From Lenox Caroline Tappan replied on August 7 (MNS). She thinks the three Emerson mentions could certainly select "what is most valuable" until the time she went to New York. "That was an new era. The persons she knew best there were more vehement, adventurous, & various than her friends here; less moral, less poetical, less beautiful than some she had known, but she enjoyed their freedom from the puritanism that had annoyed her here." She names those who would have knowledge of her life in Italy and says she will try to see Mr. & Mrs. Cranch who are nearby in Sheffield. With Ossoli, "she was happy . . . having the affection & sympathy of daily life without being impeded or overwrought." Mrs. Tappan would not want the Fullers to read her own letters unless "it were Eugene. . . . I think no one else is to be trusted." She reminds him of Charles Newcomb and of Jane King and Sarah Clarke.

Horace Greeley's name is not mentioned by Emerson or by Caroline Tappan, but he had a book on his mind too, as his letter to Emerson of July 27 shows; Rusk prints Greeley's letter in full in his note to Emerson's reply of August 5 (*Letters*, 4:224–226, and n. 198).

bravest mood of Spiridion, or of Bettine, better yet, of Dante,—mystically in Novalis's sense,[96] that is, "as if the world were one pair of lovers." When it is written, it will be the rarest book, but it will /then/ be unanimously decided by

TO GEORGE BARRELL EMERSON, CONCORD, AUGUST 5, 1850[97]

Concord, 5 Aug. 1850.

Dear George,

Thanks, thanks for your explicit & guiding letter. But you shall not speak with Miss Maynard,[98] until our "parents" have had a meeting, this evening. Before writing to you, I had suggested to them that instead of a lady we might perhaps obtain young Ephraim Ball,[99] who graduated the other day at Cambridge, and I found,—on carrying the tidings of your note to the minister & others who had begged me to write to you,—that they were a little perplexed in their minds between the lady & Mr Ball. So tonight we hold a meeting, & tomorrow I will tell you the issue.

Did I tell you, that I have had no news lately from Mrs. Wilson at Cincinnati? I sent her word, a few days ago, that Mrs /H. I./ Bowditch will take her daughter to board,[100] and I asked for a ratification of my doings in her behalf.

Yours affectionately,
R. Waldo E.

96. *Spiridion* is George Sand's novel. Bettina von Arnim, "Novalis" is Friedrich von Hardenberg's pseudonym; Emerson probably has *"Heinrich" von Ofterdingen.* in mind.

97. MS in the G.B. Emerson papers, MHi; ph. in NNC.

98. Miss Helen M. Maynard.

99. Ephraim Ball is certainly Ephraim Merriam Ball, born in Concord November 10, 1829, son of Nehemiah Ball and his wife Mary.

100. See *Letters,* 4:221, for a letter to Mrs. Caroline Wilson of Cincinnati, who wrote Emerson on August 9 to confirm Emerson's arrangement for her daughter to live with Henry Ingersoll Bowditch's family and attend George Barrell Emerson's school. A letter from Mrs. Wilson of December 3 to Emerson (RWEMA) shows that her daughter finally lived with a Mrs. Lathrop; her letter is a letter of thanks, so possibly Emerson made this arrangement too, entailing further correspondence of which there is no trace. It is in this letter that she proposes to make a bust of Emerson; see *Letters,* 4:330.

To George Barrell Emerson, Concord, August 7, 1850[101]

Concord, 7 August-
1850

Dear George,

We have decided, after a longer demurring than I anticipated,[102] to invite Miss Maynard to teach our school. I shall write to her today, if I have time, if not, tomorrow to describe our condition.

With thanks, yours,

R. W. E.

P.S. I have written to her.

To Helen M. Maynard, Concord, August 7? 1850

[Emerson's letter of August 7, above, shows that he wrote Miss Maynard the same day. His Account Books for 1849–1853, 1853–1859, show that Miss Maynard held the job until 1855 when she was succeeded by Frank B. Sanborn. Emerson's Account Books give only initials, but Helen M. Maynard of Waltham is listed as a member of the class of 1848 in the *Catalogue of Teachers and Alumnae, 1839–1900* of what is now Framingham State College. The first teacher's college in the United States, founded in Lexington in 1839, moved to West Newton in 1844, and to Framingham in 1853. Miss Maynard is listed in the catalogue as having married Joseph Keyes and as living in Concord. See, below, letter to Mrs Joseph Keyes, then living in Watertown, October 25, 1857.]

To Nathaniel Prentiss Banks, Concord, September 1? 1850

[In a letter of August 31, 1850 (RWEMA), Nathaniel P. Banks asks Emerson to lecture for the Rumford Institute of Waltham. Emerson apparently wrote a tentative acceptance, settling the date later, see below January 25? 1851.]

To Caroline Sturgis Tappan, Concord, September 1, 1850[103]

Concord
1 September, 1850.

Dear Caroline,

I waited to learn what our friends should find at Canton,[104] before replying to you. Ellery,[105] yesterday, brought me all my letters to Mar-

101. MS in G. B. Emerson papers, MHi; ph. in NNC.
102. See, above, letters of August 2 and 5.
103. MS in the Tappan papers, Houghton Library, MH; ph. in NNC; Rusk quotes from a copy by Cabot a fragment of this letter under the date September 5 (*Letters*, 4:227).
104. Margaret Fuller's mother, Margaret Crane Fuller, lived in Canton, Massachusetts.
105. Ellery Channing.

garet; and said, that he had sent Sam. G. Ward his; & will tomorrow send to you the package of letters & Journals which Margaret had rolled up & marked with your name—in the inscription leaving you some option to ⟨to s⟩save or to burn. I hope you will let the burning be as figurative as, the commentators say, the sacrificing was by Jephthah of his daughter. At least, I thought the permission "to save the poetry," ought to cover a large part of Margaret's MSS.

Of course, our project of a memoir depends entirely on what shall be found & furnished, mainly on Journals & letters. Elizabeth H.[106] has translated /for the family/ the entire correspondence between Margaret & Ossoli whilst she was at Rieti; I have seen nothing, but am told it is the finest document of character, & has no word of America in it.—Richard Fuller[107] sends me word he has sixty letters. If Charles K. N.[108]—to whom I have not written, were amenable to any power of mine, I should have as good as sixty thousand. Indeed no heaven could be better than that of which each of my friends is a hint, & unhappily is content with hinting. The Allston Gallery[109] is complete still & will remain so, I doubt not, through September: but I doubt you will find it has lost some of its old glories. If you mean that you are to be here to see it,—I beg you will send me word where I can see you.

R. W. E.

To J. Peter Lesley, Concord, September? 12? 1850

[The Reverend J. Peter Lesley in a letter of September 14, 1850 (RWEMA), is replying to a question put him by Emerson. Lesley, a geologist, outlines possible popular lectures on Caves. Since later correspondence (*Letters*, 4:235–236) shows that Emerson, as a curator, invited Lesley to give a lecture on Caves for the Concord Lyceum (on January 8, 1852), I conjecture that Emerson had sounded him out on the subject in a letter of early September. There is no proof.]

To Robert Bulkeley Emerson, Concord, September 16, 1850

[Emerson's letter of this date to his wife, see below, says he is going to write his brother Bulkeley.]

106. Elizabeth Hoar.
107. Margaret's brother.
108. Charles King Newcomb.
109. Exhibition of paintings by Washington Allston in the studio of Chester Harding, School Street. Caroline had inquired if the Allston Gallery was still open. Emerson should also have told her where to send the letters she is willing to contribute.

To Edmund Quincy, Concord, September 16, 1850[110]

Concord 16 September
1850

My dear Sir,

I see that the fifteenth day has past & I who have kept my eyes on the watch for any verse or prose old or new that I could think would serve your turn must report the muse absent, perhaps dead. I am very sorry, but I am never more at a loss than when asked to send a scrap for an annual; & even the high connections of the Liberty Bell will not animate my imagination.[111] But the day, though descending, is not yet closed, & I shall not remit my vigilance whilst this month lasts, if anything that commends itself to my fancy ⟨for⟩or judgment, for your purpose, should turn up. So think of me with what forgiveness you can

R. W. Emerson.

To Lydia Jackson Emerson, Concord, September 16, 1850[112]

Concord, 16 Sept. 1850

Dear Lidian,

Up to this date the children & the seniors are as well as usual. I am glad you find such comfortable rooms,[113] & especially such good company as the Warrens. I could heartily wish, not only that the Bancrofts, but the Bartletts had stayed, so that you might have had all the warmth of a friendly crowd, which is the best cure for a cold & other bad habit of

110. MS in the Jay papers, Special Collections, Butler Library, NNC; ph. in NNC; listed *Letters*, 4:229, with the conjectured date, September 15, from Quincy's reply; quoted by Rusk, *Life*, p. 366.

111. For the 1851 *Liberty Bell*, edited by Quincy, for sale at the annual National Anti-Slavery Bazaar, held at the end of December 1850. See below, October 24, for note of a second letter to Quincy, submitting contributions. For a list see *BAL*, 5221.

Quincy's acknowledgment (September 29, RWEMA) of this letter is worth quoting: "I rec'd your note some fortnight ago in which you report the health of your muse in a failing state, if not entirely past praying for . . . I think a little wholesome rage is a good thing to set one agoing . . . I should advise you to read the infernal fugitive slave bill & then the case of the first victim under it as told in last night's (Sat.) Traveller." Quincy refers to the case of James Hamlet, arrested in New York City September 27, to be returned to Mary Brown of Baltimore. The money to buy Hamlet back and restore him to freedom was raised by New Yorkers. Stanley W. Campbell, *The Slave-Catchers 1850–1860* (Chapel Hill: University of North Carolina Press, 1968), p. 115, citing Samuel May, *The Fugitive Slave Law and Its Victims* (New York: American Anti-Slavery Society, 1861), p. 11.

112. MS owned by the Raymond Emerson estate; ph. in NNC; listed *Letters*, 4:229.

113. In the Samoset House, Plymouth.

body.[114] You must use up the occasion of your neighborhood to Mr Abraham Jackson, to talk with him concerning the subjects of Dr C. T. J. s letter.[115] We have no company here, but I shall write this morning to Bulkeley, to invite him to come to the Cattleshow, & spend two or three days. If you decide to stay longer than a week, you will want money, which I will send. Mother & I ⟨w⟩attended, on Saturday, the funeral of Major James Barrett,[116] who died at 89 years The benignant dignified old man was the best representative of a Massachusetts farmer. He & his had been on their land, I suppose, ever since the planting of the town. Mr Frost recited to the mourners Bryant's verses at "an old man's Funeral" very happily.[117] The company was large, & the afternoon tranquil.

Affectionately,

W.

To Amos Bronson Alcott? Concord, September, 18, 1850

[The MS Account Book for 1849–1853, under the date September 18, has the note (p. 103): "Paid in a letter for tickets to A. B. A. 1.00." Alcott was living in Boston, 88 Athenaeum Street, in September 1850. Emerson is writing for tickets to one of Alcott's "Conversations." The letter need not have been written to Alcott himself; an entry of 1851 (January 17, p. 123), shows the purchase of tickets for Alcott's lectures from Miss Peabody.]

To Thomas Palmer, Concord, October 1, 1850[118]

Concord, Oct. 1, 1850.

Dr Thomas Palmer.

Dear Sir,

I hear nothing from you concerning Charles Lane's interest due on the 18 August last, /from your father,/ & concerning the payment of the

114. Probably Mr. and Mrs. George Bancroft. Mrs. Bancroft was a native of Plymouth. In a letter to her sister of September 15 (RWEMA), Lidian names a number of her friends, Abby Hedge Warren (Mrs. Charles Warren) and Margaret Bartlett Warren (Mrs. Winslow Warren) among them. See, above, April 21, 1836, for a Rebecca Bartlett.

115. Dr. Charles T. Jackson, Lidian's brother; Abraham Jackson, their relative, managed their common property. I do not find the letter referred to here.

116. Major Barrett was a descendant of Humphrey Barrett, whose name appears in the earliest records of Concord.

117. The Reverend Barzillai Frost; Bryant's poem "The Old Man's Funeral," written on the death of a patriarch, makes the dead man the speaker.

118. MS in Houghton Library, MH; in extra-illustrated copy of Edmund Clarence Stedman's *Poets of America* (Cambridge, 1885), vol. 1, opp. p. 134. ph. in NNC.

balance still due him of the principal; concerning which I wrote you particularly in August.[119] Be so kind as to let me hear from you on this matter, by return of mail.

Yours respectfully,
R. W. Emerson.

To Caroline Sturgis Tappan, Concord, October 9, 1850[120]

Concord, 9 Oct.
1850

Dear Caroline,

What have you for me from Margaret's manuscripts,[121] and when will they come? Ellery has brought me several weeks since all or nearly all that the family have of her journals: and I have received nothing else from any quarter, except a few old letters from Mrs Barlow;[122]—W H C sending nothing,[123] & S G W demurring,[124] & now too going to London. Meantime her journals have been so seriously mutilated by the knife[125] & by erasure, that the valuable material I possess is very small. The autobiography which she once seriously begun, &, I remember, gave me some notes from time to time of its progress,—. I find no trace of. It was probably lost with her. Perhaps you will be able to send me soon,—if not MSS., at least, ⟨a⟩some report of what material you shall at last send

119. See, above, letter of September 7, 1849, to Thomas Palmer, son of Joseph Palmer. On October 15 Palmer paid all the interest and the fees for filing the deed to the Harvard property but said in his covering letter that his father could not pay the principal (RWEMA). See below October 22.

120. MS in the Tappan papers, Houghton Library, MH; ph. in NNC.

121. See, above, September 1.

122. Almira Penniman Barlow, estranged wife of David Hatch Barlow. See *JMN*, 11:257–259, for Emerson's record of her remarks on Margaret Fuller's death.

123. Channing would procrastinate throughout the enterprise, and Ward would withdraw altogether.

124. Ward evidently destroyed a number of Margaret Fuller's letters to him; as her copies of two letters to him (Fuller papers, Houghton Library) show, she had fancied herself in love with him (1836–1838).

125. The mutilation of the Margaret Fuller MSS is shocking, some of it attributable to William Henry Channing, but some of it her own doing. Like Alcott she tinkered with her journals and papers, making new and misleading combinations and copies. Her papers (those at Houghton and MB) are still (1974) in a chaotic state. Two volumes of copies carelessly put together without regard to date and sequence do not help matters. And the *Memoirs*, also, is not a helpful guide, though Emerson's portion of it is a credit to his intelligence and honesty. See November 17, 18 below for his reflections on reading the manuscripts Caroline finally sent him.

me,[126] so that I may judge whether the enterprise of a Memoir is to be persisted in.[127]

Yours,

R. W. Emerson.

To Franklin Forbes, Concord, October 16? 1850

[In a letter of October 15, 1850 (RWEMA), Franklin Forbes invites Emerson to give a lecture for the Bigelow Mechanic Institute of Clinton, Massachusetts. He offers any Wednesday in the season and asks for a reply. Emerson lectured for the institute on February 20 (Charvat, p. 26) and had surely to write Forbes at least one letter to accept and a second to settle a date; see below January 25? 1851.]

To Amory Dwight Mayo, Concord, October 18? 1850

[In a letter of October 17, 1850 (RWEMA), Amory Dwight Mayo invites Emerson to lecture for the Gloucester Lyceum in the coming season. Since Emerson did lecture in Gloucester January 22, 1851 (Charvat, p. 25), there had to be at least one letter to Mayo to settle the date.]

To Charles Lane, Boston? October 22? 1850

[Emerson's MS Account Book for 1849–1853, under the date October 22, has this entry (p. 109): "Bought a bill of exchange on London of Harnden & Co for £ 10, 18, 2d in favor of Charles Lane 54.54 Sent the same in letter by mail pre-paid .24." This is the interest on the note of Joseph Palmer, Emerson acting as Lane's trustee. The date is probably right; the mail steamer usually left Boston on the 23rd or 24th of the month. See Letters, 4:234, where this letter is listed from the evidence of Lane's acknowledgment of November 21. See above September 7, 1849.]

126. Caroline Tappan replied vaguely in a letter of October otherwise undated (MNS). She apologizes for not answering at once, but notes that Emerson has not supplied her with an address to which she should send the manuscripts selected. Her father's house in Boston is closed. Emerson's letter supplying an address is dated November 6, presumably her letter is late in October.

She tells Emerson that she does not want Anna Barker Ward to read them or any woman but Elizabeth Hoar who "has a finer sense of personal relations & is at the same time more impersonal in them than any other. . . . And to me she has always been a good angel."

127. With the lecture season upon him, Emerson has reason to be annoyed by delays.

To Edmund Quincy, Concord, October 24, 1850[128]

Concord, 24 Oct. 1850

My dear Sir,

In fulfilment of my half promise, & I hope not quite too late, I send you some translations from the Persian. They are my translations, rather free, from Von Hammer's German literal versions of Hafiz; and one of Nisami.[129] If they are not fit for your purpose, please return them, & forgive

Your unpardonable servant
R. W. Emerson.

Edmund Quincy, Esq.

To Caroline Sturgis Tappan, Concord, November 6, 1850[130]

Concord, 6 November, 1850.

Dear Caroline,

Your parcel[131] for me should be addressed to the Care of Augustus Adams, Concord Mass. Express, City Tavern, Boston. I believe every afternoon has brought me either a guest or an importunate trifling affair, and I who write letters in afternoons, am thrown into disgraceful arrears. William H. Channing, of whom you ask, has been a traveller for some weeks, and is now in Boston, where a letter addressed to No 83 (is it not?) Mount Vernon Street, will reach him. He was to have come here, on Saturday last, but failed. The Storys have come home, but I have not yet seen them.[132] They explained satisfactorily, I was told, everything which Boston & South Boston & East Boston wished to know, even to the marriage certificate. Charles K. N. is to come tomorrow or next day, & spend a few days with me.[133] I have had his "Edith" or "Cleone" or

128. MS in the Barrett Collection, Alderman Library, ViU; ph. in NNC.
129. See above, September 16, to Quincy for the half-promise of a contribution to the anti-slavery annual *The Liberty Bell* for 1851. See *BAL,* 5221, where Emerson's contributions are listed. Quincy systematically dunned his prospective contributors. See *New Letters of James Russell Lowell,* M. A. DeWolfe Howe, ed. (New York: Harper, 1932), pp. 38–40. The Anti-Slavery Bazaar was held in December 1850, at which time the annual, dated 1851, was for sale. For Emerson's other translations from Von Hammer's German versions of Persian poetry, see above, April 18, and below, November 17, 18.
130. MS in the Tappan papers; ph. in NNC.
131. Of Margaret Fuller papers.
132. William Wetmore Story and his wife (Emelyn) had been in Rome and Florence and had seen a good deal of Margaret Fuller, Ossoli, and the child. Boston suspected the worst. Letters of 1839 show that Margaret Fuller had no high opinion of Story (Hudspeth, 2:41–42, 45), but in Italy she had need of American friends.
133. Charles K. Newcomb.

"Caroline" now for a year, & have deciphered a great deal of it, & think it always better. Tennyson was good, but Wordsworth was better.[134] I shall faithfully await your parcel.[135]

Yours,

R. W. E.

To George Thompson, Concord, November 14, 1850 [136]

Concord, 14 Nov. 1850.

Dear Sir,

I had the pleasure many years ago of detaining you on your journey for a short time at my house.[137] I shall presume on that half hour's acquaintance to bring a request with which I am charged by an admirable woman, Mrs Nathan Brooks of this town,—a request which she & other ladies have warmly at heart,—that you will give us an evening, the earliest you please to name, when you will address the friends of liberty in this town.[138]—I think, it goes far to make a thing right & important to be done,—that Mrs Brooks requests it. The Evening is the best time. If

---

134. Both *In Memoriam* and *The Prelude* were published in 1850.

135. In her long covering letter (MNS) for the packet she sends him, Caroline Tappan writes of what she has heard from New York. She has apparently heard from Nathan who "says you cannot write a biography of Margaret without his letters to her; he wishes to have them himself. . . ." Mrs. Greely reports on messages from the spirit world received by a Mr. Harris. "From Mr. Nathan and Mr. Harris you might gather materials that would make the old Boston State House reel to its foundations." She offers too an acute observation of her own that "Margaret's great want was of a sense of art"; she sees that "now in her writings, her relations with persons, her whole life." One page of her letter describes life in the Berkshires: "No one comes to this Western land, & there are so many cows, horses, & baaing lambs about us I begin to think we have retired to the Ark, & the world is hidden by a flood. Miss Peabody flew hither as a messenger dove & I have seized upon her with great vivacity—it is so pleasant to hear anyone talk the human language. My little girl lives in pantomime; if she should ever speak linguists would have an opportunity to study the original language. The words she uses at present are 'More' and 'Don't' and they have not been taught, but the spirit of the age has fallen upon her—Mrs Hawthorne & her children gather flowers and draw white chalk figures on the black board—Mr. H. writes in red chalk on his own private black board. I'm afraid the de'il will carry him off if he walks so much in solitary places;—but the only choice here is between the village post-office & the solitudes of the mountains. One may go for three days for a poem & three weeks for a novel—but he has been three months writing his & I know the hero will prove chicken-hearted for he has seen nothing living except chickens during that time."

136. MS in Special Collections, Butler Library, NNC; ph. in NNC.

137. Emerson refers here to George Thompson's visit to the States in 1835. In 1848 he heard Thompson speak in England; see January 28, 1848, below. Emerson had no very high opinion of this English abolitionist, but characteristically he is ready to serve the anti-slavery cause as he can.

138. On this visit of 1850–1851 Thompson also spoke for the Concord Lyceum. Mary Merrick Brooks was an active member of the Middlesex Anti-Slavery Society.

you can & will come, as we hope,—in advance of all other petitioners, I shall depend on the pleasure of receiving you at my house.

In which good hope, I remain

Yours respectfully,

George Thompson, Esq. M.P.   R. W. Emerson

To Caroline Sturgis Tappan, Concord,
November 17 and 18, 1850 [139]

Concord

Sunday noon 17 Nov.r

Dear Caroline,

The parcel came safely & on Friday morning. I read much & I believe the largest part of it.[140] I ⟨w⟩find it perfectly like all I had read before of Margaret's, & thoroughly creditable to her. So much wit, ready & rapid learning, appreciation, so much probity constancy & aspiration, when shall we see again? Then what capacity for friendship! Her discriminating & proud election of her friends from afar, her brave & flowing intercourse with them, her quarrels, patience, pardons with & of them, are all good. But if I could have had any doubt earlier, I can have none now that those elevations & new experiences of which she sometimes wrote & spoke, & which she well knew how to adorn with a whole literature of mystical symbols, were quite constitutional, & had no universal sense whatever—The best effect of these fervid pages is the fine praise they give to every thing liberal, and the admonition to self reliance & courage. I grieve to find in them so much grief, belief in a bitter destiny, &c., which her clear mind & great heart should not have admitted, though the head ached & the knees shook. But she used her gifts so well, & against so much resistance, that almost none has a right to blame her.—Yes, it is too obvious that all her estimates of men, books, pictures, were distorted a little or much by her highly-refracting atmosphere, &

139. MS in the Tappan papers, Houghton Library, MH; ph. in NNC. For the portion of the letter dated November 17, the year 1850 is secure; Emerson had received the Margaret Fuller papers he had asked for in his letters, above, of September 1 and October 9. November 17 was a Sunday in 1850. The note of the 18th is written on a single sheet of the same stationery and is now catalogued in the Tappan papers as a separate letter. It is certainly a postscript for the letter of the 17th. Sending Emerson Margaret Fuller's letters with a letter Emerson has endorsed "Nov. 1850," Caroline inquires if he has heard Jenny Lind (a.l.s., MNS). Emerson had heard the singer in England; he heard her also in Boston in October 1850. His MS Account Book for 1849–1853 under the date October 13, 1850 (p. 107), records the purchase of three tickets "to Jenny Linds Concert," fares for himself, "E." (Elizabeth Hoar or Ellen Emerson), and his wife, and the cost of the programs.

140. See November 6 above.

therefore her statement is never catholic & true. But as an impulse & ⟨a⟩inspiration to whole files & companies of young men & women, & these the best, the memory of her decisive choices & of the marvellous eloquence in which she conveyed them will remain one of the best things our time has afforded us.—I had large & vague expectation of what amount of manuscript you would send, & perhaps had some disappointment in the actual reading.—I had hoped from what Ellery said, there were two or three Journals, & that you would not burn them; and I hoped there would be more recent letters, from New York, & from Europe. But a seal seems to be set when she leaves Boston. Nothing of any importance comes to me, after that time. I saw William Story & his wife, last week; they give the friendliest pictures of Margaret; that was pleasant,—⟨but⟩ and describe her agreeable relations with her Italian ladies & with the Brownings.[141] /and repeated the story I had heard from the Springs of the first acquaintance with Ossoli./ But no mots & no action. William Channing[142] will use his own materials so that I have nothing more to look for. Charles K.[143] N. has written again to say that he has been ill & is not quite yet able to come.—The whole reading has been an Egyptian chamber to me, filling me with strange regrets that my first dealing with the facts themselves was hardly more substantial than with these shadows of them. But I shall have more to say. Ever Yours,

R. W. E.[144]

18 Nov

You ask of Jenny Lind. I heard her but once in Boston, and, as it chanced for me it was much more satisfactory than my seeing her in the Opera in London; I know no more than to be entirely contented, though, as you know, my musical suffrage is worth nothing. Your allusion to Eastern Sages almost tempts me to send you the Megha Duta,[145] which I believe you have not seen. But it is not, at least in metrical translation, up to its frame, so I will let you off with some transcripts from my own

141. Robert and Elizabeth Barrett Browning.
142. William Henry Channing.
143. Charles King Newcomb.
144. The last page of this portion of the letter ends here; Emerson then uses the space above the dateline on p. [1] for the rest of the letter and its close.
145. See Harding, p. 156. Emerson acquired Wilson's translation of Kalidasa's poem *Méga Dúta* in England; in his MS journal LM (*JMN*, 10:336), he lists it among the books he brought home. See *JMN*, 5:392, for what appears to be Emerson's first encounter with Horace Wilson's translation of this Sanskrit poem. See *JMN*, 10:91, for Goethe's comment on this translation. John Chapman's invoice for the purchase of the book is dated May 3, 1848 (Miscellaneous business papers).

versions from Von Hammer, which are always attractive to me till they in plain English.

<u>Body & Soul</u>   <u>Enweri</u>

In China, once painted a painter a hall,
O hearken! no better did ever befall!
One half from his brush with rich colors did run,
The other he touched with a beam of the sun,
So that all which attracted the eye in one side,
The same, point for point, in the other replied.
In thee, friend, the well-painted chamber is found,
Thine the high vaulted roof, & the base on the ground;
Is one half depicted with colors less bright?
Beware that the counterpart blazes with light.[146]

To George Lyman Emerson, Concord, November 21? 1850

[In the MS Account Book for 1849–1853, p. 112, under the date November 21 1850, is the entry: "Sent G. L. Emerson, Ogunquit, Me. from Mrs R Emerson— gift 5.00."]

To Benjamin Rodman, Concord, November 22? 1850

[In a letter of November 21, 1850 (RWEMA), Benjamin Rodman extends his customary invitation to be his guest when Emerson lectures in New Bedford January 7, 1851. There is no record of payment for the lecture, but the expenses of the journey are recorded under the date January 7, 1851, in the MS Account Book for 1849–1853, p. 120.]

To C. H. Morse, Concord, November 25, 1850[147]

Concord, 25 Nov. 1850.

Dear Sir,

I acknowledge the receipt of your note of the 21st instant.

Yours respectfully,
R. W. Emerson.

146. Emerson published an improved version of his translation of these verses in *The Atlantic* for April 1858 (1:732; see *Works*, 8:262). Emerson's use of the plural "versions" implies that he sends here more than "Body & Soul"; her letter of January 19, 1851, mentions the "Phoenix" and other "translations." Apparently she separated a contiguous leaf here; it may have had additional poems as well as the address. She had so much enjoyed the verses that she had sent for a copy of the *Divan* but does not "find the originals" in it and so believes "they were written by a modern Hafiz" (a.l.s., MNS, see January 22 below).
147. MS owned by the late Henry Wadsworth Longfellow Dana, who in 1948 sent a photostat (NNC) to Rusk. I have not been able to locate the original. The note appears to be merely a reply to a request for an autograph. See *Letters*, 4:513, for a note to a Charles E.

To John Chapman, Concord? November 25? 1850

[In the MS Account Book for 1849–1853 under the date November 25 is the bracketed entry (p. 113): "Wrote to John Chapman." This entry in the record of payments is a long way from the 1850 record of receipts; p. 46, under the date November 20 is entered the receipt of £10 with the value in dollars 50. The entry shows that John Chapman sent an order on Phillips, Sampson, & Co. "for cash for Ms copy of Representative Men." Emerson's letter must be an acknowledgment of the money.]

To Joseph Breck, Concord, December 1? 1850

[In a letter of December 3, 1850 (RWEMA), Joseph Breck confirms December 17 as the date for Emerson's lecture for the Brighton Lyceum (see Charvat, p. 25); he is clearly replying to a letter from Emerson. There may well have been earlier correspondence.]

To Alexander W. Harvey, Concord, December 22, 1850[148]

Concord, 22 December, 1850.

Dear Sir,

I have received your courteous invitation,[149] &, a little earlier, a similar one from Rochester promising that yours should come.[150] I have read the Lecture[151] you speak of many times & thought the public pretty well acquainted with it through the newspapers. But I can I doubt not with a little revision make it better worth your hearing. For the time, I shall not be able to come in January, & should prefer the last of February, or the beginning of March. For the terms, which you ask me to fix, it seems rather a costly plan to invite me to go so far to read one lecture.[152] But I am content to come to Rochester & Buffalo, & read a lecture in each place for a hundred dollars & my expenses: that is to say, Each Lyceum shall pay me $50. and half the cost of my going & returning. But if it is desired, I will without additional charge read another lecture in each

---

Morse of New York, possibly the same correspondent. At the foot of the leaf is a note: "Bought by H. W. L. Dana, May, 1940, for $3.00 from Heise." The handwriting is Dana's.

148. MS in the Beinecke Library, CtY; ph. in NNC; endorsed by Harvey on p. [4] as answered. There must have been a second letter to Harvey settling the matter of dates, but I do not find it.

149. Harvey was the manager of the Young Men's Association (*Letters*, 4:243).

150. Emerson lectured in Buffalo, February 10 and 11, and in Rochester, February 6 and 7, 1851 (Charvat, p. 25).

151. "England"; the second lecture was the new one, "Power."

152. Buffalo paid him $65, and Rochester, $75, and Buffalo paid his hotel bill. His travel expenses came to $44.50 (MS Account Book, 1849–1853, pp. 54, 52, and 126). The unexpected addition of a lecture at Syracuse (*Letters*, 4:242–243) delayed his return home, but gave him an additional $25 and paid his hotel bill (MS Account Book 1849–1852, p. 54).

place, provided you will permit me to read it on the following evening, so that I may not be absent from home more than eight days.

Yours respectfully,

R. W. Emerson.

A. W. Harvey, Chairman.

To Nathaniel Hawthorne, Concord, December 22, 1850[153]

Concord, 22 December,

1850

My dear Hawthorne,

Mr George Bradburn, better known, I think, in the sectarian & agitation, ⟨w⟩than in the literary world, desires to try his luck in solving that impossible problem of a New England magazine. As I was known to be vulnerable, that is, credulous, on that side, I was attacked lately by Hildreth (of U.S. History,)[154] and urged to engage in it. I told him to go to Lowell,[155] who had been for a year meditating the like project; that I wished a magazine, but would not think of an experiment & a failure, that if he would assure himself, before he begun, of the cooperation of Hawthorne, Cabot, Thoreau, Lowell, Parker, Holmes, & whatever is as good, if there be as good,—he should be sure of me. So I promised nothing. A few days ago, (having heard nothing further for three weeks,) I had a letter from Theodores Parker, desiring me to write to you, & ask your interest & cooperation in Mr Bradburn's magazine, & to assure you that all articles are to be paid for. So I hope, since they proceed so gently, you will not be taught to deny them, but will let them lay siege to your heart with these soft approaches. A good magazine we have not in America, and we are all its friends beforehand. If they win you, I shall think a great point is gained.[156]

Yours affectionately,

R W Emerson.

153. MS in the Berg Collection, NN; ph. in NNC; printed by Julian Hawthorne, *Nathaniel Hawthorne and His Wife* (Cambridge: University Press, 1884), 1:381–382; listed *Letters*, 4:238.

154. George Bradburn in 1850 was on the staff of Elizur Wright's *Boston Chronotype;* in 1851 he would move to Cleveland. He was one of five Lowell factory workers who would subsequently become Unitarian preachers. See *JMN*, 11:317, and Frances Bradburn, *A Memorial of George Bradburn* (Boston: Cupples, Upham, 1883) passim. Theodore Parker had written Emerson December 10 about Bradburn's project and had asked Emerson to solicit Hawthorne's aid. I find no letter from Richard Hildreth, nor any letter from Bradburn.

155. See February 24 above for a comment by Emerson on Lowell's "distemper."

156. Hawthorne's reply of December 30 is chilling and acute; he knows no solely literary magazine, American or English, that is successful or that could be (Nathaniel Hawthorne, *The Letters, 1843–1853*, Centenary Edition, 16:379).

1 8 5 1

To T——, WELLINGTON, CONCORD, JANUARY 11, 1851 [1]

Concord, 11 January, 1851

Dear Sir,

I believe I must not venture to promise a lecture to your lyceum at present,—as I am to be absent from home during, perhaps, the largest part of the month of February.

Yours respectfully,
R. W. Emerson.

T. Wellington, Sec.y—

To CAROLINE STURGIS TAPPAN, CONCORD, JANUARY 22? 1851

[With a letter of January 19, 1851 (Sophia Smith Collection, MNS), Caroline Tappan sent Emerson three letters of Margaret Fuller that she had omitted from the packet already sent. She tells him also that Mrs. Fuller has asked to see her daughter's European letters and says that two of the three may be lent to Mrs. Fuller; she has marked one of them "Not." She has sent the journals to Elizabeth Hoar so that she may copy the poems; the "books" are then to be given to William Henry Channing who can then give them to Emerson, "& afterwards cut out some leaves & let Ellen [Fuller Channing] & Mrs. Fuller see them." She is clearly nervous about letting the Fullers see everything; that "their hearts are full of her" does not "answer for perception—and besides other persons are constantly mentioned in her letters and journals." She asks if Charles [K. Newcomb] has come and whether Hedge has anything for him; she names also George Davis "who has much acuteness & great goodnature."

This letter seems to require an answer if only to acknowledge the safe arrival of the manuscripts sent. Emerson had time to reply; he does not leave for his New York State lectures until the first week in February.]

To FRANKLIN FORBES, CONCORD, JANUARY 25? 1851

[Franklin Forbes' letter of January 27, 1851 (RWEMA), appears to be a reply to a letter from Emerson settling the date (February 19) of his lecture for the Bigelow

---

1. MS owned by Joel Myerson; ph. in NNC; single sheet roughly torn from its contiguous leaf. The year might be read as 1857, but Emerson was not in Concord on January 11 of that year. In 1851, his Western engagements kept him away from home for more than two weeks into February. He was home a week earlier in 1857. The addressee may be T. W.

Mechanics Institute of Clinton, Massachusetts. See Charvat, p. 26, where the date
February 20 is entered for the Clinton engagement, with Concord down for the
19th.]

To Nathaniel Pembroke Banks, Concord, January 25? 1851

[Nathaniel P. Banks' letter of January 31, 1851 (RWEMA), appears to reply to a
letter from Emerson settling the date (February 22) for his lecture for the Rumford Institute of Waltham. Charvat, (p. 26) following Emerson's MS Account
Book for 1849–1853, p. [54], lists the lecture as for the Waltham Lyceum, but
Banks' original letter of invitation specifies the Rumford Institute (a.l.s., August
31, 1850, RWEMA).]

To J. B. Allen, Concord? February ? 1851

[In the Emerson papers (RWEMA), Houghton, there is a leaf torn from a letter
by Allen to Emerson, endorsed by Emerson: "J. B. Allen. Feb. 1851 Yes Tuesday
4 March if you like it." Emerson lectured in Stoughton, Massachusetts, on March
4 (Charvat, p. 26).]

To Charles Sumner? Concord, March 15, 1851[2]

Concord, 15 March, 1851.

My dear Sir,

I return at last your two valuable volumes of Fremont,[3] & of Emory &
Johnston's Journals[4] with many thanks. The only reason why they have
been kept so long, is that they were found so good. I use the occasion to
make a special ack⟨w⟩nowledgment of the two volumes you have sent me
of agricultural matter, from the Patent Office. My eyes have not suffered

Wellington, coal dealer, with yards in Worcester and in Southbridge according to a Worcester County Business Directory of the time, but there can be no certainty here.

2. MS in the Fales Collection, NYU; ph. in NNC; printed by White, *AL* (May 1961),
33:162. I conjecture that the addressee is Charles Sumner who sent Emerson books of this
sort; see *Letters*, 4:447–448. The last digit of the year could be read as "7," but see March 21,
below, for the eye trouble referred to here.

3. In May 1846 Emerson had bought a copy of John Charles Fremont's Report of the
Exploring Expedition to the Rocky Mountains ... (MS Account Book for 1845–1849, entry of
May 16, p. 84); the book is not now in Emerson's library. What he is referring to here is
probably the edition of 1851 (Buffalo) which had additions descriptive of California and the
gold regions.

4. The second book referred to is William Hensley Emory (White misreads the name as
Emery), *Notes of a Military Reconaissance from Fort Leavenworth ... to San Diego,* Washington,
Senate Executive doc. no. 7, 1848; pt. 3 of this work contains the journal of Captain
Abraham Robinson Johnston. An abridged edition of the same year has a New York imprint;
this New York edition has been reprinted by the University of New Mexico, 1951; it does
not include Johnston's journal. Emory, lieutenant colonel in the Army Corps of Topographical Engineers, became a general during the Civil War; Emerson's nephew William Emerson
served under him.

me to make much examination of their contents; but if I cannot find use
from them, I mean to find some other owner who can.

With great regard,
Your obliged servant,
R. W. Emerson

To Mary Merrick Brooks? New York, March 18, 1851[5]

New York, 18th March, 1851.

Dear Friend:

I had more reasons than one to regret leaving home at this time, and,
if my present engagements were not of two seasons' standing,[6] I should
have made every effort to relieve myself. For your Liberty meeting,[7] I
think it has a certain importance just now; and, really, at this moment, it
seems imperative that every lover of human rights should, in every
manner, singly or socially, in private and in public, by voice and by pen,
—and, first of all, by substantial help and hospitality to the slave, and
defending him against his hunters,—enter his protest for humanity
against the detestable statute of the last Congress. I find it a subject of
conversation in all cars and steamboats, and everywhere distributing
society into two classes, according to the moral feasibility of individuals
on one part, and their habitual docility to party leading on the other. I
do not know how the majority of to-day will be found to decide.

Sometimes people of natural probity and affection are so warped by
the habit of party, and show themselves so unexpectedly callous and
inhuman, that it seems we must wait for the Almighty to create a new
generation, a little more keenly alive to moral impressions, before any
improvement in institutions can be looked for. But, as far as I have
observed, there is, on all great questions, a tide or undulation in the
public mind—a series of actions and reactions. The momentary interest

<hr />

5. No MS has been located; text from *The Liberator* (April 18, 1851), 21:4; listed *Letters*,
4:245, where Rusk conjectures that the addressee is Mary Merrick Brooks who answers to
the *Liberator*'s specification "one of our young ladies." Mrs. Brooks, born in 1801, was not
exactly "young" in 1851; Sophia Thoreau, born 1819, more nearly answers the adjective,
though it may be used in mere gallantry. Like Mrs. Brooks, Sophia Thoreau was a member
of the executive committee of the Middlesex County Anti-Slavery Society (MS Records,
MCo).

6. Emerson's series of lectures in Pittsburgh (Charvat, p. 26), did not end until April 1;
and he had to return via New York to pick up Mrs. Emerson and his son Edward. He
arrived home on April 5 (see *Letters*, 4:247).

7. The Liberty Meeting, held April 3 in the orthodox church, to protest the Fugitive
Slave Law had the compelling event of the arrest of Thomas Sims to make the meeting of
more than usual importance.

carries it to day; but, presently, the advocates of the liberal principle are victorious,—and the more entirely, because they had persisted unshaken under evil report. And, as justice alone satisfies every body, they are sure to prevail at last.

If the World has any reason in it, it is forever safe and successful to urge the cause of love and right. I know it is very needless to say this to you, and others like you, who cannot, if they would, help serving the truth, though all the world be gone to worship Mammon. But it is the only answer I know how to make to our mathematical compatriots. So, wishing you a day of happy thoughts and sympathies on Thursday, I remain,

Yours respectfully and gratefully,

R. W. Emerson.

To Lidian Emerson, Pittsburgh, March 21, 1851

[A sentence that Emerson added after he folded this letter for the envelope is omitted from *Letters*, 4:245–247, because it is barely visible. The letter was evidently kept for some time folded; the exposed flaps are evenly foxed (not, I think, scorched), concealing the writing. A negative photograph (NNC) reveals it; the sentence reads: "Love to William and Susan with whom you must stay as long as the children will let you, and send this to mother."

An incomplete copy of this letter in the hand of Edith Emerson Forbes (RWEMA) inserts this sentence after "I ought to leave this place" as if it were part of the main body of the letter, but it is not. The letter is still incomplete as Mrs. Emerson's endorsement notes. Written across one of the two flaps, the message appears perpendicular to the text of the final page when the letter is fully opened.]

To Ainsworth Rand Spofford, Pittsburgh, March 21, 1851[8]

Pittsburgh, 21 March, 1851.

My dear Sir,

I thank you & your & my friends for whom you speak, in the kind invitation you send me,—but, I believe, I must not think of coming to Cincinnati, at present,—though now upon your river. Indeed I come to

8. MS in the Manuscript Division, DLC; ph. in NNC; originally with envelope addressed to A. R. Spofford, Esq. | Cincinnati | Ohio. | Kindness of Mr Mitchell./ Listed *Letters*, 4:247; printed by C. C. Hollis, NEQ, 38:72. The envelope and all the others that accompanied the letters to Spofford have evidently been thrown out; they are not now with the letters, but will be described. Spofford, who was to become head of the Library of Congress, had carefully saved them. The bearer named (but misspelled by Emerson) here is the astronomer C. Ormsby Mitchel.

Pittsburgh,[9] with great difficulty, & against strong reasons, only because the correspondence was more than a year old, & had been renewed two or three times, and, /the/ time being at last fixed, I thought it best to keep it, in spite of new circumstances which made me wish to be at home. So I have come with only half a heart, & shall not,—and that is a main thing, —be able to complete the Course I had sketched in my programme. Only four of the six lectures I have been preparing are sufficiently complete to read, and the first & the last must be supplied by proxies. Besides this Course which was designed for Boston is pretty likely to be as heartily & considerately written as anything I can do, & may be read in Boston, say in October, or November, and will be much better worth your hearing afterwards, than now, if it were yet presentable.[10] So we will adjourn all talking of it until another Spring. My eyes have been & are very weak,[11] which is one of my "reasons", or I should already have been in correspondence with some of your people to whom I have long been in debt. But now Mr. Mitchell is just departing for Cincinnati so I must stop my letter in the midst.

Your affectionate servant,

A. R. Spofford.   R. W. Emerson.

To Henry James, Sr., Pittsburgh, March 29, 1851 [12]

Pittsburgh, Pa.
29 March 1851

My dear James,

Here is Dr Robert Jackson of Blairsville, a good man, whose society has been a great comfort to me in the Iron City and we have talked

---

9. See February 25, 1850, for an earlier invitation to Pittsburgh and *Letters*, 4:241–242, for a draft of Emerson's reply to the invitation from the Young Men's Mercantile Library Association for this season. For the first lecture Emerson gave them "England"; see *Letters*, 4:246, for Emerson's comment on the willingness of audiences to hear a "poor old" lecture and their thinking him "an erratic old gentleman, only safe with safe subject."

Emerson's account of the state of the lectures in the series "The Conduct of Life" is not clear. The lecture "Power" was not given in Pittsburgh, but it was ready and had already been given elsewhere (Charvat, p. 25). The lecture "Fate" (first in the Boston series) was not ready. "Worship," the last in the series, was ready enough for Emerson to offer it in Pittsburgh.

10. Cincinnati got the series in 1852.

11. Emerson's eyes had been troubling him for some months; he would the next year get his first pair of spectacles (MS Account Book for 1849–1853, entry of September 27, p. 223).

12. MS in the Pattee Library, PSt; ph. in NNC; printed by Emil A. Freniere, "Emerson and Parker Letters in the Jackson Papers," *ESQ* (1st q., 1961), 22:46, as from the estate of

much of you, & I have bid him go & find you when he goes to New
York.

Yours affectionately,

Henry James, Esq.   R W Emerson

To Emily Mervine Drury, Concord, April 14, 1851 [13]

Concord, 14 April 1851

My Dear Mrs. Drury,

I received your kind note just as I was leaving home for Pittsburgh,
Pa., quite a month ago.[14] The Bhagavad Geeta had only a day or two
earlier set forth on its travels, because my bookseller told me, that it
could not well find a safe carrier until their "Trade-sales" began.[15] I hope
it has reached you ere now: and when it comes, I confide that you will
remember my rules not to read it except in the best hours, and to read it
as one of the bibles of the world. I am gratified, of course, that you find
my books readable & veracious—to a degree. But you have not done
what you was charged to do do, I mean, to make the exceptions, & show
the vices of these writings. But, at this moment, in the cruelty & ignominy
of the laws, & the shocking degradation of Massachusetts, I have had no
heart to look at books, or to think of anything else than how to retrieve
this crime.[16] All sane persons are startled by the treachery not only of the
officials, but of the controlling public of the moment, in Boston. It is one
sad lesson more to destroy all national pride, all reliance on others. "In
ourselves our freedom must be sought."[17] But against & over all this, we
must hope, & firmly assure ourselves.

Your affectionate servant,
R W Emerson

Dr. Robert Montgomery Smith Jackson of Blairsville, Pennsylvania. The edges of the letter
are browned, curled, and torn from exposure; the text is unaffected except for the signature; there may have been a period. With the letter is an address cut from blue paper and
mounted; it probably belongs to a different letter though it is to James. With it too are a
number of letters of introduction written by others for Dr. Jackson. Jackson is listed by
Emerson as an honorary member of the Town and Country Club (*JMN*, 11:237). He would
later be one of Charles Sumner's physicians.

13. MS in the Beinecke Library, CtY; ph. in NNC; printed by B. D. Simison, *MLN* (June
1940), 55:427; listed *Letters*, 4:248, under the conjectured date of April 17.

14. The Emersons left for New York on March 15th (*JMN*, 11:522).

15. On May 8 Mrs. Drury acknowledges the book and this letter with apologies for
causing him anxiety (RWEMA). The spring auction sales of the New York Book-Publishers'
Association of New York were normally held during the last week in March.

16. The arrest of Thomas Sims under the Fugitive Slave Law. See below, notes for May 14.

17. Emerson seems to be adapting Wordsworth's "in ourselves our safety must be sought"
(Poems Dedicated to Independence and Liberty, Part I, 27, l. 6).

To Theodore Parker, Concord, May 9, 1851 [18]

Concord, ⟨8⟩9 May, 1851

Dear Parker,

Your note which seems to have been mis-sent to Canton,[19] came last evening. I am not sure that is worth while to read my lecture in Boston I am to read it in Lexington, in Fitchburg, & it is asked for in Cambridge, & in Waltham also.—which, if I do, you see, is stumping Palfrey's district.[20] Then I think to print it, and send it to my Boston class in that form. I have no strong choice, but is it not better to omit Boston, & serve the Country!

Yours faithfully,
R. W. Emerson

To William Pembroke Mulchinock, Concord, May 9? 1851

[In the MS Account Book for 1849–1853, under the date May 9, p. [137], is the entry: "Cash loaned to W. P. Mulchinock, & sent by letter 10.00." See also *Letters*, 4:248 and n. 29.]

To Emily Mervine Drury, Concord, May 14, 1851 [21]

Concord, 14 May, 1851

My dear Mrs. Drury,

I am glad you are coming so near us, & I hope you will keep your day. I shall be in town tomorrow, & will seek for you at the Tremont House, and arrange when you shall come & see me.[22] I am now, for a few days, repeating in many places in my county of Middlesex, a speech on the Slave-Bill, which was made by me, last week, to some of my townsmen, at their request. Now, I go about the county with it, in the hope that Dr Palfrey, my friend, will be elected at the next canvass.[23]

18. MS in the Phillips papers, Houghton Library, MH; ph. in NNC; with envelope addressed: Rev. Theodore Parker.| Boston|. Emerson is answering Parker's letter of May 7 (RWEMA) asking that he give his address on slavery in Boston so that "we in this benighted City may hear it."

19. Parker's handwriting would account for the letter's going to Canton instead of Concord.

20. See Appendix C, 4.

21. MS in the Barrett Collection, Alderman Library, ViU; ph. in NNC; listed in *Letters*, 4:250, p. 38, from a copy in Marietta College Library. Faint pencil quotation marks enclose the passage beginning: "I am now" and ending "next canvass." They are manifestly not Emerson's.

22. In a letter of May 8 (RWEMA), Mrs. Drury asks him to write to her in Boston to tell her when she may see him and how to return to him his copy of the Bhăgvăt-Gēētā.

23. See Appendix C, 4, for Emerson's efforts on behalf of Palfrey.

For the Bhagavat,—if I should fail to find you—if you leave it for me at James Munroe & Co s bookstore, 134 Washington Street, it will be safe.[24]

With my regards to Mr Drury,

Yours respectfully,
R. W. Emerson.

To Ainsworth Rand Spofford, Concord, May 23, 1851[25]

Concord, 23 May, 1851

My dear Sir,

I received day before yesterday your letter & its enclosure of $5.00 for Mr Thoreau. He begs me to thank you for your care of his interests, and said, that it was the first money he had received from his book.[26]

I am, for my part, more deeply indebted to you. I received, I believe before I went to Pittsburgh, your pamphlet of the "Higher Law," & ran through it with interest enough, but without a suspicion as to the authorship.[27] On my return ⟨m⟩home, I had another copy, with your name, to my surprise & pleasure. I not only sat down, & read it over again with care, but, my townsmen coming to me for an expression of opinion on the Fugitive Slave Law, I sat down, &, in trying to write a discourse, only succeeded I believe in reproducing yours; carried it down to the village, & read it to the citizens, with good acceptance.[28] I have since been called to read it over in several towns; which I have done, & though I have tried again & again to scratch out your part of it, I have only succeeded in a degree, and fear I shall /not/ hide the most unblushing plagiarisms, if I print it, as they say I must. But the law is so bad, & the servility of the

24. Mrs. Drury was only one of many friends to whom Emerson lent the *Bhāgvăt-Gēētā*, whose lesson he seems to have forgotten temporarily. See below, January 9, 1852, for his revulsion from his "sallies into politics."

25. MS in the Manuscript Division, DLC; ph. in NNC; printed by C. C. Hollis, *NEQ*, 38:73.

26. Spofford's letter of May 13 explains that the $5.00 is from the sale of six copies of *The Week on the Concord and Merrimack Rivers* which had been obtained from the publisher, Munroe, on Emerson's order. One copy was deducted for donation.

27. *The Higher Law Tried by Reason and Authority: An Argument Pro and Con.* Spofford's pamphlet appeared in two forms: a 54-page pamphlet with a New York imprint (S. W. Benedict) and a 48-page pamphlet with a Cincinnati imprint (Truman & Spofford). Emerson presumably saw the New York printing first; as he tells Spofford in a letter of March 15, 1852, Horace Mann and others had attributed it to the New York anti-slavery lawyer John Jay. The pamphlet is not now in Emerson's library.

28. Emerson did not print the address, but see Slater, p. 470, for his letter of July 28 where he regrets not printing and admits it was undertaken to clear his own skirts. See also below, January 9, 1852.

people such, that it is better to say the right thing over & over in twenty places, than to be silent in nineteen. So with my hearty thanks to you for your excellent & timely pamphlet; as well as for your large love & good will,

Yours,

A. R. Spofford   R. W. Emerson.

To Caroline Sturgis Tappan, Concord, June 13, 1851 [29]

Concord, 13 June 1851

Dear Caroline,

Margaret's papers so long postponed now occupy all my days. They suggest many questions touching persons & facts, which, as I read, I wish to ask you. If I can come to Lenox, will you give me half a day? [30] But really it is not so much for facts, as for a conversation with you about Margaret. Any time within a few /or many/ weeks, will serve this purpose, if you chance to have company, or fatigues, at present. William Channing has set his heart on bringing this doubtful enterprise to an early completion.

Yours,
Waldo E.

To James Munroe, & Co., Concord, June 13, 1851 [31]

Concord 13 June 1851

Gentlemen,

No, I will not write a preface to this book, for several reasons; one is, that, in the book, I find rather marked praise of my books. [32] But I think the book a very good one for our market. [33] I have run through it rapidly & find it even more readable than "Friends in Council", with the same

29. MS in the Tappan papers, Houghton Library, MH; ph. in NNC. See June 20 below for Emerson's conjectured hope to get to Lenox to hear what Caroline Tappan could tell him for the *Memoirs* of Margaret Fuller.

30. Caroline replied on the 17th to tell him that she had only just received his letter and that company is expected this week, but that there will be no visitors next week or the week after. (a.l.s., MNS).

31. MS in Special Collection, Butler Library, NNC; ph. in NNC; listed in *Letters*, 4:251, from bookseller's catalogue, without name of addressee.

32. The book is Arthur Helps' *Companions of My Solitude* published by Munroe in 1852. Correspondence in Houghton Library shows that Charles Eliot Norton sponsored the American edition. It has no prefatory note of any kind. The praise of Emerson along with a quotation from *Nature* appears on pp. 207–208.

33. In Emerson's library is a copy of the English edition (London: William Pickering, 1851); see Harding, p. 131.

elegance & quiet domestic conversational tone. It has a taking title too. ⟨If⟩ I hope you will print it. I would, if you wish, write a few prefatory lines, without my name. If you can spare this copy, I will buy it.[34]

Yours respectfully,
R. W. Emerson

James Munroe, & Co.

To Caroline Sturgis Tappan, Concord, June 20, 1851 [35]

Concord
20 June 1851

Dear Caroline,

I am glad you are at home, but I cannot yet fix the day when I can go to Lenox. William Channing is to come here next Wednesday, & I have invited him to stay a fortnight, which time I thought our affair would require. I am told he will not stay; but I think he may. If not, I shall like to come to Lenox, as soon as he leaves me. But if I do not come within the term of free days you have named, I shall write again to assure myself that I do not find you in a crowded house. I must bring you Madame Arconate's letters,[36] and ⟨Mrs⟩Mr Cass's sketch of his acquaintance with Margaret.[37]

Waldo E.

34. See *Works*, 5:286–289, for an account of Emerson's visit to Helps at Bishops Waltham in 1848; for another version, see above, July 22, 1848.

35. MS in the Tappan papers, Houghton Library, MH; ph. in NNC. Mrs. Tappan did not receive his letter of June 13 until the 17th when she replied to tell him that visitors are expected "the last of this week" but next week is free (MNS).

36. Constanza Arconati, Marchesa Visconti. Margaret Fuller's letters to her friend were conveyed to Emerson by William B. Kinney who sent them from Turin on May 2, 1851. Emerson is referring to these letters, I believe, but he may be referring to the letter from Madame Arconati to him from which he selected the motto for his chapter "Visits to Concord" (*Memoirs*, 2:201). See *Letters*, 4:296–297, for an apology to Madame Arconati.

37. Lewis Cass, Jr., Chargé d'affaires at Rome, 1848–1849. The account referred to here is, I believe, the one written by Cass to Margaret Fuller's sister, Ellen Channing; this letter is printed by T. W. Higginson in his *Margaret Fuller Ossoli* (Boston: Houghton Mifflin, 1884), pp. 234–238.

To George R. Robinson, Concord, June 24, 1851 [38]

Concord, Mass.
24 June 1851

George R. Robinson, Secy M. L. Association
Dear Sir,

I am very much flattered by the kind invitation which you send me from your association: but I am at present only able to return my thanks & my good wishes. I find myself so engaged, for months to come, in unavoidable tasks,[39] that I dare not at present promise myself liberty for so long an excursion as to Saint Louis. But you shall, if you please, let this summons lie on the table, for a time; and, one of these days, it may be more practicable to us, on both parts, to give it effect.[40]

Respectfully,
Your obedient servant,
R. W. Emerson

To Caroline Sturgis Tappan, Concord, June 24, 1851 [41]

Concord
24 June, 1851

Dear Caroline,

William Channing writes that he is ill, & will not come here till the second week in July: so I think of taking the Western Road on Saturday.[42] But as you know I have my garden & my grass to remember, you will not expect so large a farmer with any certainty. With salutations to William Tappan, Yours,

R. W. E.

38. MS in the papers of the St. Louis Mercantile Library Association; ph. in NNC. With an envelope addressed: George R. Robinson, Esq | Sec.y Mercantile Lib.y Assoc.n | St Louis | Mo; | postmarked at Concord June 24. Printed by John Francis McDermott, "Emerson at St. Louis 1852: Unpublished Letters and Telegrams," *ESQ* (1st q., 1957), 6:7; listed *Letters*, 4:252.

39. *The Memoirs of Margaret Fuller Ossoli.*

40. Emerson lectured in St. Louis in December and January (see Charvat, pp. 27–28).

41. MS in Tappan papers, Houghton Library, MH; ph. in NNC.

42. June 28; see *Letters*, 4:253. The expenses of the trip to Lenox are recorded in the MS Account Book for 1849–1853 under the date June 27, p. 144.

To William Allingham, Concord, July 14, 1851[43]

Concord Massachusetts

14 July 1851

My dear Sir,

I have not had such a cordial holiday for a long time as the receipt of your book of Poems made for me, now more than a month ago. I had been stung, every now & then, with compunctions for my letting drop the little correspondence /with you,/ which made a joyful and affectionate episode as I well remember, in my six months' residence in England, three years ago. But I had submitted to my bad habit, which had lost me, with yours, the correspondence of a little phalanx of benefactors, & I clung to my Silence, & wondered what indemnity it would ever bring to compensate for such losses.—But I am deeply gratified by the return of your friendly star on my horizon, and I, and all my friends here, have heartily enjoyed this new light. I have read all the poems with much interest. I found in them the old joy which makes us more debtors to poetry than to anything else in life. "The Pilot's Daughter,"[44] which was my first acquaintance, is still a superior poem in any eyes. "The Music Master" has merits which cannot belong to a short poem; and "our Mountain Range," & the Burial Place,"[45] and the "Touch Stone",[46] are, for different reasons, prized. My friend W. E. Channing, a man who has more poetic genius than anyone I know, though with some defects which have hitherto prevented him from writing a single good poem,—is charmed with the sea landscape that runs through them all, & he finds a volume of verses in one line,

"When, like a mighty fire, the bar roars loud"—and Mr. Thoreau also, a stoic among the Muses, whose prose poem of "Concord & Merrimack Rivers," I fear has never reached Ireland,—rejoices in many of these pieces. The book has already passed from house to house, I read some of your pieces in our newspapers, & my copy departs this day to a

43. MS in the Beinecke Library, CtY; ph. in NNC; printed in *Letters to William Allingham*, pp. 44–46, and by Cameron, *ESQ* (1st q., 1958), 10:38; listed *Letters*, 4:253. Allingham had sent Emerson his *Poems* (London: Chapman and Hall, 1850); *ELi*, p. 9. The book is inscribed by Allingham to Emerson. The notes (on rear end paper) referred to by Harding are my three page references, none for the poems mentioned in the letter.

44. Allingham, in his letter of October 12, 1851 (*Letters*, p. 47), tells Emerson that he put "The Pilot's Daughter" first in his volume because of Emerson's kindness (see above June 24, 1848).

45. Emerson omits the quotation mark before "The Burial Place."

46. See *JMN*, 11:372, for a comment on Allingham and *J*, 8:207, for Edward Emerson's note of Emerson's liking "Touchstone."

valued friend at the feet of the Hoosac Mountains in this State.[47] I am sorry I cannot manifest any gratitude beyond good reception. I am a tardy writer, & am now engaged in preparing with W. H. Channing (not W. E. C.) a volume of memorials of the life of Margaret Fuller, a remarkable woman, & dearly valued friend of ours. With thanks & with hopes,[48]

Your affectionate servant,

William Allingham.   R. W. Emerson.

To Caroline Sturgis Tappan, Concord, July 14, 1851 [49]

Concord, 14 July, 1851

Dear Caroline,

I am sorry, I could not command Allingham's Poems sooner; but they were lent.[50] I confide to you, with some reluctance, so talismanic is it, Charles's Edith.[51] You shall have it—for three months, and on the 14 October you must send it back to me.[52] If he /C./ should come to see you in the interim,[53] that will make no difference,—you must not give it to him, though he should kneel for it. I have written a note to Allingham this day. William Channing left me this morning: he has been here only a week. Sam Ward renews his assurances that he will have nothing to do with our affair.[54] But there are people on whom words make no impression.

R. W. E.

47. This is, the Berkshires; Caroline Sturgis Tappan; see letter to her here of the same date. The Tappans had leased from Samuel Gray Ward his house, Highwood, in Lenox. Later, the Tappans would purchase the property from Ward.

48. Allingham's letter of October 12 shows that he owned *The Week*, wanted *Walden*, and owned Margaret Fuller's *Woman in the Nineteenth Century;* but he complains of the difficulty of getting American books.

49. MS in the Tappan papers, Houghton Library, MH; ph. in NNC.

50. See above, of the same date, letter to William Allingham.

51. Charles King Newcomb's novel.

52. On October 9 Caroline wrote that she could not return the MS because she could not read it "in these golden shadowy Indian summer days. . . ." She will return it on December 15. "You will have it in time to take to Mass on Christmas morning," an allusion to Newcomb's lifelong inclination to join the Roman church. There was very likely a reply to this letter. In October Emerson sent her George Sand's *Le Compagnon du Tour de France,* which she acknowledged in her letter of October 9; he probably wrote at the time.

53. C. is, I believe, Newcomb himself; Emerson would refer to William Ellery Channing as Ellery (see August 12 below) and to his cousin as William Channing as he does in this letter.

54. Samuel Gray Ward is showing characteristic reticence; it was originally supposed that he should take part in the enterprise; see correspondence of 1850, *Letters*, 4:228–231, 237. By July 23, Emerson's words evidently had made an impression; and by August 8 Ward had at least selected passages from Margaret Fuller, but had not written any comment (*Letters*, 4:254, 255). The passages quoted in the *Memoirs*, 2:244–250, were probably supplied by Ward. He ought to have had a hand in the passages on art, but these are by Emerson.

To WENDELL PHILIPS, CONCORD, JULY 25, 1851 [55]

Concord, 25 July, 1851.

Thank you, my dear Sir, for your friendly invitation to Worcester, which honors me.[56] But I know my poverty on the like occasions too well to go oftener than is necessary. Besides I have an extending task which will not get done, nor suffer me to leave home until it is.[57] Yours, with entire respect,

R. W. Emerson.

To JOSEPH MAZZINI, CONCORD, JULY 29, 1851 [58]

Concord. 29 July, 1851.
Massachusetts

Dear Sir,

I think it is nearly a twelvemonth since I addressed a note to you, which my friend Carlyle kindly undertook to forward.[59] I have received no answer, & fancy it may have miscarried. The purport of the note was to request in behalf of the family & friends of Margaret Fuller, Marchesa Ossoli, the communication of any information you my possess respecting her life & labours, during her residence in Italy. Every trace of her Manuscript Journal & the materials of her projected "History of the Revolution" has disappeared; and, in preparing a Memoir, we have to rely only on her letters, & notes furnished by a few friends who met her, more or less often. These make a meagre outline of three years, which, we have heard, were active & eventful. If your public duties will permit you /to/ send me any brief notes of facts or conversations in which she

55. MS in the Phillips papers, Houghton Library, MH; ph. in NNC; with unstamped envelope addressed: Wendell Phillips, Esq. | Lynn. | Mass.|; postmarked at Concord July 25. The year in the dateline could be read as 1857, but the envelope would then have had to bear a stamp.

56. Emerson is possibly answering an invitation to attend the Anti-Slavery Society's commemoration of the abolition of slavery in the West Indies.

57. Work on the Memoirs of Margaret Fuller.

58. MS in the Manuscript collections of NjMoHP; ph. in NNC; listed *Letters*, 4:255. (In England Mazzini anglicized his name; searching for Emerson's letters in England, I came upon a good many by Mazzini all signed "Joe."

59. See *Letters*, 4:262–263, for Emerson's October 9, 1850, printed from a draft, and see Slater, p. 463, and for Carlyle's assurance that Mazzini did write a reply, see p. 478. For this second letter, see Slater, pp. 469–470, and 474. Emerson was apparently encouraged to try again by Carlyle's report of seeing Mazzini frequently. Why Emerson never got replies is a mystery. It does not seem altogether likely that the Home Office was still confiscating Mazzini's foreign mail. That they had done so was exposed in 1849; among others Carlyle had indignantly protested.

bore a part, any indication of her character or of the impression made by her,—it will add very much to the value of our picture, & where it is most deficient. Mr William H. Channing & Mr Sam. G. Ward[60] are joined with me in this attempt to draw a portrait of our friend.

With entire respect
Your obedient servant,
R. W. Emerson

Joseph Mazzini, Esq.

TO CAROLINE STURGIS TAPPAN, CONCORD, AUGUST 12, 1851[61]

Concord, 12 August,
1851

Dear Caroline,

I promised Miss Bremer, who was here the other day, & said, she was going to Lenox,[62]—with Mrs Kirkland—, I believe, that I would commend her to your good offices. She is indeed a very worthy ladylike person, with a quiet perseverance that is as strong as a fanaticism & which leads her safely from sea to sea, & from island to island. She has been to the Falls of Saint Anthony, & to Cuba—where she stayed ⟨3⟩three months. In our region, Elizabeth Hoar & Mr Alcott interested her. And she really wished to sound the religious belief of her companion.[63] Ask her to show you her sketchbook,—full of drawings.

Another thing. Ellery, I learn today, has written you a letter, to ask if you would like to have him come to Lenox, in these very days, & could insure him a quiet room?—this in sequence to some invitation brought from you by me.[64] He has been looking for an answer for some days, but

60. Ward had been charged with the delivery of the 1850 letter.
61. MS in the Tappan papers, Houghton Library, MH; ph. in NNC.
62. Frederika Bremer, whose novels in English had been read aloud by Lucy Jackson Brown to the pleasure of her sister Lidian Emerson and of Elizabeth Hoar who owned them all. It was by Mrs. Emerson's agency that Frederika Bremer visited Concord twice (Ellen Emerson, MS life of Lidian, pp. 207, 207b); see *Letters*, 4:176, and notes for the visit of December 3, 1849, and that of January 17, 1850. There was apparently a third visit. Miss Bremer gives an account of her first two visits in her *Homes of the New World* 1:116–117, 153. Emerson's MS Account Book for 1849–1853 has, at p. 61, a record of the expenses for carriages and railroad fares for bringing Miss Bremer to Concord on January 17.
63. Her companion was Caroline Stansbury Kirkland.
64. That Ellery Channing visited Lenox is confirmed by a letter to Emerson of December 18, 1851, when Caroline returns Newcomb's "Edith." She reports of Ellery that "he has grown quite gossiping & agreeable." Of Newcomb's story, she notes "good things in it about "Margaret" citing p. 59 and identifying her as " 'the antedated one' & the one of intellect & will."

none comes. Did you have his note? A wonderful new book is Wilkinson's "Human Body,"[65] One volume.

Ever yours,
R. W. E.

To Elizabeth Palmer Peabody, Concord? August 16, 1851?

[Cabot lists this letter with his number 1983 in his Bluebook Calendar 5 where no year is given. In the Bluebook Index from which Rusk takes it, Letters, 4:255, the letter is given the date 1851. In neither list, does Cabot give a hint of the content, but if it turns up, it should have Cabot's number on it in green crayon. If this letter is of 1851, then it very likely concerns Margaret Fuller. A journal entry falling just before a dated entry of August 11 reads: "Miss Peabody ransacks her memory for anecdotes of Margaret's youth . . ."; JMN, 9:431. In a letter to Emerson of September 8 (RWEMA), James Freeman Clarke asks for Miss Peabody's letters about Margaret, but his letter of September 17 reports that Channing has "taken charge of the Groton & Providence chapters" (Memoirs, 1:143–198).]

To Adeline Roberts, Concord, August 27, 1851[66]

Concord, 27 August, 1851

Mrs Adeline Roberts. Cor. Secretary
Dear Madam,

I am so unwilling to refuse your kind & honouring invitation,[67] that I have postponed my answer for two mails; but the matter will ⟨me⟩not mend, & I beg you to say to the Ladies of the society, that the Discourse they have indicated is not fit to read to them, at present; nor will the tasks, to which I am already engaged, permit me either to ⟨fit⟩make this fit, or prepare another.[68] With the highest respect, & I must add, gratitude to them for their exertions in a good cause, I beg them to take my name from the programme.

R. W. Emerson

To Joseph Williamson, Jr., Concord? September? 1851

[A single sheet torn from a letter from J. Williamson, Jr., of Belfast, Maine (RWEMA), is endorsed by Emerson: "I will answer & fix a day if I can by and by."

65. James John Garth Wilkinson's The Human Body and Its Connection with Man (Harding, p. 301), dedicated to Henry James, Sr. See Letters, 4:255.
66. MS in the papers of the Salem Female Anti-Slavery Society, Phillips Library, MSaE; ph. in NNC; the address leaf is missing; the remaining sheet was once mounted. See above, September 9, 1845, to Mary P. Kenney, and below, August 2, 1852; in the latter Emerson gives the addressee as "Miss" Roberts.
67. I conjecture that the ladies have asked for Emerson's address on the Fugitive Slave Law given as a stump speech to support the candidacy of J. G. Palfrey; see, above, May 14.
68. Probably work on the lecture series "The Conduct of Life."

That he did answer is clear from October 24 below. Joseph Williamson, Jr., an attorney, was Secretary of the Belfast Lyceum in 1850–1851 according to his own *History of the City of Belfast in the State of Maine.* . . . (Portland: Loring, Short, & Harmon, 1877), 1:325.]

TO ELIZABETH PALMER PEABODY, CONCORD? SEPTEMBER 24, 1851

[Cabot's Bluebook Calendar 5 lists this letter with the number 1982 and a note that it is about Emerson's wanting "a French governess to teach his children Fr *speaking*." (Listed in *Letters*, 4:260, from Cabot's index which has no note of the content.) Elizabeth Peabody was interested in current theories of language and had attended Charles D. Kraitsir's lectures on language.

[The letter may also have made some comment on Margaret Fuller, for in his MS journal CO (*JMN*, 11:440), in an entry following shortly after a page dated September 15 (*ibid.*, p. 439) Emerson refers to a letter received "lately" from Elizabeth Peabody and he quotes it (omitting the closing quotation mark): " 'Hawthorne always said, that Lloyd F. explained the faults of Margaret, I do not know if you ever knew that creature. He seems to be the Fuller organization, Fullerism unbalanced, unmixed with the oversoul, which sweetens & balances the original demon, & yet he is unquestionably what the Scotch people call an 'innocent'; for he is so self-sufficient, & exacting, & insolent, unawares, unconsciously, & in the purest good faith. He acts & feels according to his constitution, & God is responsible for his ugliness. He was put, perhaps, as a sign what original ugliness could be overcome by a glorious spirit, which had a vision of the good & true & beautiful, with a will & determination to conquer. Margaret's life was the result of this strange association." Lloyd Fuller was Margaret's youngest brother; Hawthorne may have known him when he was a troublesome student at the Brook Farm school.]

TO JOHN CHAPMAN, BOSTON, OCTOBER 1, 1851[69]

⟨Concord⟩
Boston 1 October 1851

Mr John Chapman,
Dear Sir,
Mr William Henry Channing, Mr J. F. Clarke, Mr F H Hedge,[70] & I, are preparing a Life of Sarah Margaret Fuller, Marchesa Ossoli, which is already partly printed & which Phillips Sampson & Co mean to ⟨?⟩publish about 1 December This work is, on the part of its authors or editors, a labor of love; and, besides being a monument & a justification of our valued friend, we should be glad to give it the greatest pecuniary value to her family that is possible; the rather that there is an amount of debt

69. MS in the Manuscript Collections of NjMoHP; ph. in NNC.
70. James Freeman Clarke and Frederic Henry Hedge; this is the first indication that Hedge had a hand in the book.

against her, which we may reasonably hope to pay, by the profits of the book.

Mr Channing has the chief charge of the book. I had promised only my ⟨c⟩Chapter, estimated at about 180 pages, perhaps not so much. I begged him secure it an English copyright, by arranging with you to ⟨print⟩ publish it one day earlier in London. I grieved to learn, a few days ago, that he had neglected this precaution—and he is now, & will be at New York. In these circumstances I propose to you to publish the work in London from sheets which will be sent to you with each successive steamer, until the whole is printed. Messrs Phillips & Sampson will hold back, at last, 15 or 20 days, in order that you may, using all despatch,[71] obtain copyright, by publishing first, in England. I have asked Messrs P. S. & Co., what ⟨a⟩ terms Mr Richard F. Fuller (who represents Madame Ossoli's family,) might reasonably expect from you? Mr Phillips said, "*12½ percent /*on the retail price."/ in case our plan succeeded. If that rate suits you, let these be the terms; If not, send me by the next steamer the best terms you can give to the family. I have great confidence that the book will have an interest for a considerable public, on your side. The second volume is in large part European. By the next steamer, you shall have a quantity of ⟨proofs⟩ revises.[72]

With great regard,

R. W. Emerson.

over

The book is to be 2 volumes /12 mo/ substantially of the size & form of Mr Carlyles Life of Sterling.

To Lucy Stone, Concord, October 7, 1851[73]

Miss Lucy Stone, <u>Secretary</u>—
Dear Madam:

I had mislaid your note of invitation to the Convention at Worcester,[74] and have only just found it, after many days. I see plainly that I shall not have any opportunity to come to it, for I am tied fast at home by a task which will not end until after a fortnight. I am by no means sure that I should find any message worth bringing to you if I were free. I hope I

---

71. Emerson has either failed to dot an i or write "despatch" by intent.

72. Chapman evidently refused. The book was published in England by Richard Bentley, *BAL*, 6501.

73. No MS has been found; text from *The New-York Daily Tribune*, October 17, 1851, p. 7, where it is described as dated from Concord, October 7, 1851; listed in *Letters*, 4:260.

74. "The Woman's Convention" at Worcester, October 14, from which Emerson was not unhappy to be excused; see *JMN*, 11:443–445.

shall have your forgiveness, when I tell you that my task is the inditing the "Life of Margaret Fuller."

Respectfully,
R. W. Emerson

To MIRON J. HAZELTINE, CONCORD, OCTOBER 20, 1851 [75]

Concord, 20 Oct. 1851

Dear Sir,

You shall if you please hold me engaged for Wednesday Evening, 3 December. As, however, my winter arrangements are quite imperfect at present, I hope you will permit me, if that Evening shall hereafter appear particularly inconvenient for me, to change it for another, within your Course, ample notice being given.

Yours respectfully,
Miron J. Hazeltine, Sec.y   R. W. Emerson

To JOSEPH WILLIAMSON, JR., CONCORD, OCTOBER 24, 1851 [76]

Concord Oct 24 1851

J Williamson, Jr. Secretary.
Dear Sir,

I wrote you some time since to say that I would come to Belfast on 6 Nov.r, if that day were still unengaged. I have waited many days for your answer, which I have not yet received. It has now become necessary to answer some other correspondents, who have received contingent promises; and I think it safest to give you notice that I shall not, in the circumstances, attempt to come to Belfast, but shall wait to arrange with you another day,[77] in your Course,—believing you to be probably supplied for the above-named day.

Yours respectfully,
R. W. Emerson.

75. MS in the Schmucker Library, PGC; ph. in NNC; single leaf. The date Emerson proposes here is the one he enters for Lowell, Massachusetts, in his tentative list of lecture engagements, MS Account Book for 1849–1853, p. 291; but the Account Book shows no receipt of payment from Lowell giving Charvat (p. 26) grounds for listing the engagement with a question mark. Miron J. Hazeltine is listed as a law student in the Lowell directory for 1851.

76. MS in the Feinberg Collection, MiD; ph. in NNC. Printed by White in *AL* (May 1961), 33:163. Listed in *Letters*, 4:262, from a letter to Emerson of January 1, 1852. For Williamson, see above, September letter.

77. Williamson went ahead to advertise Emerson as one of the Belfast Lyceum lecturers,

To George B. Warren, Jr., Concord, November? 1? 1851

[See, below, November 19, for evidence of this earlier letter to the Secretary of the Troy, New York, Lyceum.]

To Samuel Gray Ward, Concord, November 3, 1851 [78]

Concord 3 November
1851

My dear friend.

Henry James is to lecture at the Masonic Temple, on Wednesday night.[79] If that is really the first night I am sorry, I shall be engaged.[80] But I am very uneasy lest his name, little known here, should not secure him an audience. His lectures are really brilliant, and I was told that he swallowed up all the doctrinaires & neologists of New York, and is left sole Aesthetic Doctor, & Ductor Dubitantium, in that city. He is the best man & companion in the world, and, (for I believe you do not personally know him,) I entreat you to let your faith conduct you to his Theatre. He is to stay at the Revere House.

Ever yours

S. G. Ward.   R. W. E.

---

although he had shown this letter to William P. M. Means of Augusta who inferred correctly from the tone of it that Emerson had "no idea of visiting Belfast" (a.l.s., Means to Emerson, January 1, 1852, RWEMA). See below November 3, n. 80.

78. MS in the Ward papers, Houghton Library, MH; ph. in NNC. Quoted by Edward W. Emerson, *EYSC*, p. 325, and by Perry, 1:72, from *EYSC*.

79. James had written Emerson on October 30 (Perry, 1:71–72) giving the schedule of three proposed lectures in Boston. Perry picks up Edward Emerson's quotation from this letter to Ward and mistakenly infers that Emerson has heard James' lectures and is commenting on them. See *Letters*, 4:263, for Emerson's similar letter to Edward Bangs urging him to hear James.

80. Emerson's MS Account Book for 1849–1853 shows under the date November 5 (p. 165) the purchase of "two tickets to H. James's lectures"; and a letter from James T. Fisher, November 5 (RWEMA), reports that James' lecture is postponed to "next Friday." There was nothing, then, to prevent Emerson from hearing James' first lecture after all, for he certainly did not lecture in Augusta, Maine, in November; Charvat conjectures a lecture there November 6 (p. 26). That Emerson did not lecture in Maine until March is clear from letters of October 24, above, and November 28 (*Letters*, 4:266). Moreover, a letter of January 1, 1852 (*Letters*, 4:273), from William P. M. Means of Augusta shows that Means has seen Emerson's letter of October 24 and that Emerson has not been in Maine, though Means has hopes that he will be.

The engagement Emerson refers to here is pretty certainly in New Hampshire. A letter dated "Tuesday 4 November," without year is assigned to 1851 by Rusk for sound reasons. This letter puts Emerson in New Hampshire on the 5th but back in town on the 6th. According to the lecture schedule on the last pages of the MS Account Book in 1849–1853, p. [290], Emerson had an engagement in Manchester, New Hampshire, on November 5. The list gives North Danvers not North Adams (Charvat, p. 26) as his engagement for November 25.

To John Greenleaf Whittier, Concord, November 5? 1851

[In a letter of November 3, 1851 (RWEMA), John Greenleaf Whittier, writing for the Amesbury Lyceum, asks for a lecture on February 1 or else on the Thursday before Emerson lectures in Newburyport. A later letter from Whittier (see *Letters*, 4:270) shows that Emerson must have answered that he was engaged for January 1 (see Charvat, p. 26), and offered a date late in January. In the MS Account Book for 1849–1853, p. [291], Emerson's working list for 1852 has a deletion against the date January 29, the only Thursday in January he had free. The deleted name clearly ends "bury" and appears to begin with "A." Whittier, in his letter of January 8, cited by Rusk, says the "last of Jan.y" has been assigned to a lecturer from a distance, and they hope to "hear from thee on the 26th of Feb.y." The wording suggests that Emerson had offered the 26th of February as an alternative date. It is entered in the Account Book list. I think there need not have been a letter from Emerson on January 6 as Rusk conjectures. For later difficulties see, below, February 20 and 21, 1852.]

To George W. Otis, Jr., Concord, November 10, 1851[81]

Concord, 10 Novr
1851

Dear Sir,

It is a little uncertain whether I may not wish to change the day you offer me, when it is close at hand, as I am pressed by some invitations in the city & state of New York, whose days are not yet quite determined. I wish, then, you would allow me to accept your day, with some understood privilege of changing it hereafter, with mutual consent, to another day mutually convenient, timely notice being given. As it stands, I ⟨w⟩shall aim to be at the Ferry, at 7 p.m. on 22 Jan.y[82]

Yours respectfully,
R. W. Emerson.

Geo. W. Otis, Jr

81. MS in the Bancroft Library, CU; ph. in NNC; single sheet without address.

82. This letter concerns the lecture engagement for Chelsea, Massachusetts (see Charvat, p. 26). Emerson enters the engagement in his MS Account Book for 1849–1853, p. [291], in his list for January 1852 under the date 22 adding "7 P.M. Ferry." There may have been a second letter confirming the date.

To Moncure Daniel Conway, Concord, November 13, 1851[83]

Concord ⎱ 13 November 1851
Mass ⎰

Dear Sir,

I fear you will not be able except at some chance auction to obtain any set of the Dial.[84] In fact, smaller editions were printed of the later & latest numbers; which increases the difficulty.

I am interested by your kind interest in my writings, but you have not let me sufficiently into your own habit of thought, to enable me to speak to it with much precision. But, I believe, what interests both you & me, most of all things, & whether we know it or not,—is, the morals of intellect: in other words, that no man is worth his room in the world, who is not commanded by a legitimate object of thought. The earth is full of frivolous people who are bending their whole force and the force of nations on trifles; & these are baptized with every grand & holy name, remaining of course totally inadequate to occupy any mind; & so skeptics are made. A true soul will disdain to be moved except by what natively commands it, though it should go sad & solitary in search of its Master a thousand years. The few superior persons in each community are so by their steadiness to reality, & their neglect of appearances. This is the euphrasy & rue that purge the intellect & ensure⟨s⟩ insight. Its full rewards are slow but sure; & yet I think it has its reward on the instant, inasmuch as simplicity & grandeur are always better than dapperness. But I will not spin out these saws farther, but hasten to thank you for your frank & friendly letter, & to wish you the best deliverance in that contest, to which every soul must go alone.

Yours, in all good hope,

M. Conway.   R. W. Emerson

To Samuel Gray Ward, Concord, November 19, 1851[85]

Concord, 19 Nov.r 1851.

My dear friend,

If I had not been sent off to town untimely yesterday, you should have had a letter, if only to thank you for honouring me with these free

---

83. MS in the Berg Collection, NN; ph. in NNC; printed by Conway in *Emerson at Home and Abroad* (Boston: Osgood, 1882), pp. 6–7; listed in *Letters*, 4:265; frequently reprinted as the first letter of this friendship. Conway's reply of December 12 is in the Conway papers, Special Collections, Butler Library, NNC.

84. Conway would name his Cincinnati magazine (1860) for *The Dial* of 1840–1844.

85. MS in Ward papers, Houghton Library, MH; ph. in NNC; printed in part, *Letters*, 4:266, from a copy.

thoughts; and now I have only time to say, I weigh them well. Swedenborg is one of the eternal men, & with Dante & Shakespeare has strangely
loomed up in the last age, yet differs from these two in being manifestly,
as yet, an unsettled reputation. You are right in taxing me with ignorance
of his mind. I would read him if I could, but it is one of his demerits, it is
part of his fate, that I cannot.[86] But, from year to year, I watch his great
form striding through the shades, and, when a favorable moment arrives, I dare to accost him. In one of these moments, he will, perhaps,
deign to open his mind.—But I will come to this point, again, with you.
Yours.

R. W. E.

S. G. W.

To George B. Warren, Jr., Concord, November 19, 1851[87]

Concord, 19 November, 1851.

Dear Sir,

The proposition I made you in my last letter has such manifest order
& convenience for me, that I venture to renew it, and, since you say that
the meeting of the Debating Club is the only obstacle, I will beg you to
communicate with the President or Directors of the Club, and make my
compliments to them, & ask the favour that they will adjourn their
meeting on Monday 2 February so as to allow me to address the Lyceum
on that day.[88] I wish to come to Troy, & I wish that I may find the
Debating Club among my audience. And my tasks at home so press on
me that I wish to economize my time as much as I can.[89]

Yours respectfully,
R. W. Emerson.

G. B. Warren, Jr. Sec.y

86. In the MS notebook 51, p. 100, Emerson writes: "Swedenborg that joyless genius:
never was insight so tedious."

87. MS owned by Joel Myerson; ph. in NNC. The addressee is possibly George B.
Warren, Jr., listed in the Troy directory as a druggist.

88. Charvat, p. 26, lists a lecture at Troy under the questioned date of February 9, 1852.
That Emerson did not lecture at all in Troy in this 1851–1852 season is certain, for in a
letter of June 12, 1852 (RWEMA, see *Letters*, 4:298), Derick Lane of Troy writes: "The
disappointment last year of not hearing you . . . was great." Lane's letter also identifies the
group as the Young Men's Association.

89. In his tentative schedule listed in the MS Account Book for 1849–1853, p. 291,
Emerson has Rochester down for February 2, with Troy entered for February 3 and Buffalo
for February 4. The manifestly more convenient order he seeks here is Troy, Rochester,
Buffalo. Correspondence with Rochester is likely, and with Auburn substituted for Troy on
February 2, changed at the last minute to February 9 because of bad weather (see *Letters*,
4:275). The MS Account Book (pp. 180–181) gives the expenses of this trip through upstate

To William Henry Channing, Concord? November ? 1851[90]

. . . Only I hate to hear of swelling the book, and I think not Mazzini himself,[91] not Cranch, not Browning hardly, would induce me to add a line of Appendix. Amputate, amputate. And why a preface? If eight pages are there, let them be gloriously blank: No, no preface. . . . I do not mean to write a needless syllable.

New York; no stopover at Troy is recorded, but Auburn is entered. The lecture fees listed (p. 182) also include Auburn but not Troy.

90. No original MS has been found. The text of the first passage with November date is from Edward Waldo Emerson's *Emerson in Concord*, pp. 220–221 (also printed in *Memoirs of Members of the Social Circle*, 2d series, 2d part, same pp.) The text of the second passage is from *Works*, 9:510; Edward W. Emerson's note to the poem "Grace." The first is listed in *Letters*, 4:267, where it is conjectured that the second passage may be from the same letter.

Both passages are about *The Memoirs of Margaret Fuller Ossoli* (Boston, 1852), *BAL*, 6500, M Fy. By October 20, 1851, volume 1 certainly and volume 2 possibly were in page proof (see Emerson to Richard Fuller, *Letters*, 4:261–262). The two passages here clearly refer to page proofs. The unusual pagination of the first printing of volume 1 is, as *BAL* describes it, ⟨v⟩–⟨x⟩, ⟨11⟩–351. *BAL*'s pp. ⟨ix⟩–⟨x⟩ contain the title page and mottoes for chapter 1, the text beginning on p. ⟨11⟩. Channing had evidently informed Emerson that there was room for an 8-page preface; Emerson's veto here accounts for the odd pagination of the book as issued, the table of contents and title page requiring only two leaves, BAL's ⟨v⟩–⟨viii⟩. That volume 2 was in page proof when Emerson wrote the second passage is evident from the printed book, for on p. ⟨115⟩ his poem "Grace," here referred to by its opening phrase, appears in full, but without an author's name; the misattribution to Herbert was deleted leaving between this motto (the first) and the quotation from Alfieri additional leading equivalent to one line of type. Deleting Emerson's poem would have required resetting the page.

It is still possible that we have here two letters, for Channing was tinkering with the text as late as the first week in January 1852. On January 9 (a.l.s., RWEMA), P. A. Ramsay wrote Emerson that Channing had made several changes (verbal and substantive) in the proofs of Emerson's part of the European chapter (2:169–269), leaving it to the publisher to accept them or not according to the difficulty of making the changes, but "we do not desire this responsibility." Ramsay therefore asks Emerson to call to look at the proofs; the publisher is in no hurry now that a set of proofs has been sent to England. (Perley A. Ramsay, printer, is listed in Boston directories for 1851).

The publisher, as early as September 23, 1851 (a.l.s., RWEMA), had asked Emerson to assume responsibility for all decisions himself, because it was too hard to get hold of Channing; and he had reported that part of the copy had already gone to the stereotypers. On September 25 (a.l.s., RWEMA), the third contributor, James Freeman Clarke, already in Meadville, Pennsylvania, says he has learned from the publisher that Emerson has "consented to look over the proofs of the whole work," and he leaves it to Emerson to make such changes as he sees fit. See August 16 above for evidence that Channing had taken over the writing of the Groton-Providence chapter (1:143–198). The second passage here, I think, could not have been written earlier than the first but may have been later.

91. Emerson had been unsuccessful in extracting information from Mazzini though he had solicited the help of Ward, Carlyle, and Lowell; see *Letters*, 3:233, 255, 257, 258, 310; and Slater, pp. 463, 474.

Christopher Pearse Cranch, who was certainly asked for information.

The Brownings, according to Carlyle (Slater, p. 474), were to write to the Storys, but on October 4 (a.l.s., RWEMA), William Wetmore Story wrote Emerson to say that he had not

For your mottoes to your chapter, I saw that the first had the infinite honor done it of being quoted to Herbert! The verses are mine,— 'Preventing God,' etc.,—so I strike them out.

To Julia A. Dalton, Concord, December 2, 1851[92]

Concord, 2 Dec, 1851.

My dear Julia,

For I am sure you will let me call you so, with the privilege of my sort of avuncular acquaintance, which runs back beyond your memory,[93]— and to-day, too, when I come to crave your forgiveness for my intolerable delays. Here is the book you sent me.[94] I read every line of it, long ago, and lent it to the lovers of poetry near me. You will see that Elizabeth Hoar has left her mark in it. I think the writer successful where our American poets are prone to fail, in the sweetness & finish of his melodies. He has a true ear, & the language is very flexible in his hands. Then the book has a great charm for scholars, in the genuine love it betrays of the Greek & Latin muses. Indeed the vigor with which the old talismanic names are articulated again, indicates not only correct taste, but high original powers. My recollections of one very pleasant walk with the author, many years ago, revived on the reading; and I heartily wish he may yet concentrate his genius to resist the anti-poetic influences of Massachusetts. I wish you wd convey to him, if you know him, my thanks

---

heard form them. (Evidently their letter was lost; see Slater, pp. 476, 478–479.) The Storys shortly returned to Europe, but not before Mrs. Story had set the erratic Channing on a new course with a contradictory version of Margaret's preventing her maid from committing murder (2:322–324). The source of the story, William Hurlbert, assured Emerson of the accuracy of his account in a letter of October 17 (a.l.s., RWEMA). That Emerson should betray some exasperation is not surprising. And see letters above to Caroline Sturgis Tappen.

92. No MS has been found; text from a MS copy in the Feinberg Collection, MiD; ph. in NNC; partly printed with the wrong date, 1856, in "Editorial Notes," *The Index*, June 14, 1883, 14:594, from which printing it is listed in *Letters*, 5:50. The handwriting of this copy is not that of Miss Dalton or of Ball. In the same hand on p. [4] is a note, dated 1851, identifying the letter and in the center of the leaf are the initials J. C. R.

93. Miss Dalton's father, Dr. John Carl Dalton, had been a trustee and examiner of the Chelmsford Classical School when Emerson taught there in 1825 (*Letters*, 1:163); the friendship formed there continued; see *Letters*, 3:304–305; and Slater, p. 486.

94. Benjamin West Ball, whose *Elfin Land and Other Poems* (1851) is still in Emerson's library (Harding, p. 20) with a note in Emerson's hand that the book was the author's gift. Apparently Ball sent this copy after he had seen this letter to Miss Dalton, as he had, for this letter of December 29 speaks gratefully of Emerson's "approval." He refers also to their earlier meeting of 1843; see *JMN*, 8:399. Ball was born in Concord, January 27, 1823, the son of Benjamin and Mary Rogers Ball, and was a cousin of young Ephraim Merriam Ball, whose death he mentions in his letter.

and congratulations for his book. I am on my way to Lowell, tomorrow, and promise myself the pleasure of seeing you.[95]

With kindest regards to your father,

> Your affectionate
>
> R. W. Emerson

Miss Julia D——

To Rufus Wilmot Griswold, Concord, December 13, 1851 [96]

> Concord, Mass.

Dear Sir:-

I am very unwilling to lose the occasion you offer me, both of hearing the celebration of Mr. Cooper's genius, and of meeting with so many excellent persons who wish to honour his memory. But my engagements, though not important, are not easily set aside. . . .

I never had the good fortune to see Mr. Cooper; but I have, in common with almost all who speak English, an old debt to him of happy days, on the first appearance of the Pioneers. And, when I remember the unanimity with which that national novel was greeted, I perceive that the whole population is interested in your design, and that the difficulty of the committee will be, not how to draw, but how to exclude.

I am glad the suggestion of erecting a statue has prevailed, and I shall be obliged to you to give me an opportunity of adding my contribution, when it is time. Respectfully, your obedient servant,

> R. W. Emerson.

R. W. Griswold, & C.

95. This letter confirms the date of Emerson's lecture in Lowell, listed by Charvat, p. 26, with a question mark.

96. No MS has been located, text from *Memorial of James Fenimore Cooper* (New York: G. P. Putnam, 1852) pp. 32–33; printed also (with the same omissions) in the *New York Tribune*, February 26, 1852, p. 6; and in the *New York Evening Post*, p. 1. Both papers are reporting Griswold's reading of the letter (and others) at the memorial meeting of February 25, 1852. Listed *Letters*, 4:267, from dealer's catalogue from which the date is derived.

To Elizur Wright, Concord? December 21? 1851[97]

Elizur Wright, Esq.
Dear Sir,
    I shall take it as a favour ⟨a⟩that you will print no report of any of the Lectures of this Course.[98] All of them are as yet quite incomplete, &, after I have had the benefit of one or two rehearsals, I wish to report them myself. I do not wish however to defend them from any criticism.

> Yours respectfully
> R.W. E[merson]

To Samuel Robert Wells, Concord, December 24, 1851[99]

> Concord, 24 Dec., 1851

Dear Sir:
    I like your plan of popular lectures, and shall be content to stand on your programme on the terms you propose. But I fear I shall not be able to take my part in it sooner than 12th or 19th February.[100] I am to read a lecture before the Mercantile Lib'y in N. Y. on Monday, 16th Feby.[101] and should a little prefer to give that association the compliment of my first appearance. I am engaged in and near Boston, until Feby. In regard to subject, what I have to say of Margaret Fuller will be printed in a few days, but, I think, I can offer you a suitable topic.[102]

> Respectfully,
> R. W. Emerson.

J. R. Wells, Esq.

---

97. MS in the Berg Collection, NN; ph. in NNC. The letter is on a single sheet of much stained paper, torn roughly along the left margin. Stains obscure the signature. Listed in *Letters*, 4:268, the date is conjectured from Emerson's letter of January 7, 1852 (*ibid.*, pp. 272–273). Emerson's name (not in his hand) is written in full at the foot of the sheet. See January 13, 1849, to Epes Sargent, above.

98. To Emerson's vexation, Wright ignored this request; *The Commonwealth* reported the first lecture, the only paper to do so (*Letters*, 4:273).

99. No MS has been found; text from *The Chronicle*, no. 229 (June 1939), pp. 42–43. This privately printed periodical was the work of William Inglis Morse, who in 1939 was the owner of this and two other letters printed in the same number. The first initial should be S. Emerson's initial S can look like a J. These lectures were arranged for by the phrenologist Samuel Robert Wells.

100. Emerson gave the lecture "Power" at the Tabernacle on February 10, 1852. (See letter and n. 16, *Letters*, 4:275).

101. See Charvat, p. 26.

102. *The Memoirs of Margaret Fuller Ossoli* appeared in early February, 1852 (*BAL*, 6500).

To Margaret Perkins Forbes, Concord, December 27, 1851 [103]

Concord, 27 Dec.r
1851

My dear friend,

My wife declares that she has committed me in the enclosed note, (which I have not been allowed to read,) to the sending my dried Persian leaves, in return for the Acanthus you keep for me;—my leaves, which, perhaps, you will think ⟨c⟩are stalactites, rather, by the secular slowness with which they form & drop.

But I was greatly taken with ⟨a⟩Hafiz, when I first read him in German translation, /—/ so well, that I sent for the same Von Hammer's translations of the whole Persian Parnassus &, once in a while, have rhymed /some of/ them.[104]

I am very happy that you are so loyal to your old friends, & do hold so nobly by me, though I do not see you. What has life finer or better?

Yours faithfully,
R. W. Emerson

Miss Forbes.

103. MS Autogr. d.33, fol. 320, in Bodleian Library, Oxford; ph. in NNC. The letter is surely to Margaret Forbes and not to her sister. Margaret Forbes' letters to Lidian Emerson show her to have been intensely interested in anything Emerson wrote.

104. See notes, April 18, 1850, above for Emerson's purchase of Von Hammer's German translations of Hafiz and of other Persian poets from which Emerson made his translations.

1 8 5 2

To William Davis, Concord, January 1, 1852[1]

Concord.

1 Jany. 1852.

Dear Sir,

I hate to refuse to come to Plymouth. Indeed, I particularly wish to come. But it is not very prudent to come, whilst I am reading lectures /in town,/ some of which are new, or are meant to be new. Then, 1 February, I go to New York for two or three weeks. I should like, then, to offer to come on or near 1 March; if your appetite for lectures is not saturated before that time.[2]

With great regard,

Your obedient servant,

Wm. Davis, Esq.   R. W. Emerson.

To William Henry Furness, Boston, January 9, 1852[3]

American House, Boston.

9 January 1852

My dear Furness,

I received, some days ago, a letter, of which you are one of the signers, & which, I thought, I had inserted in the folds of my portfolio, as I was to be absent for a few days /from home/ , & would answer it at my first leisure.[4] I am mortified to find I have brought away the wrong letter.

1. MS in bound volume of Miscellaneous MSS, MHi; ph. in NNC. Emerson is answering Davis' letter of December 30, 1851 (RWEMA).

2. Emerson lectured for the Plymouth Lyceum on March 1; Charvat, p. 27, is so far correct; but the fee was $15.00. See January 15 below and notes for Charvat's conflating two Account Book entries.

3. MS in the collection of the Fruitlands Museums; ph. in NNC.

4. In the right-hand margin of the first page, Furness has written the names of the signers: Mr [James Miller] McKim, W. H. Furness, L. [Lucretia] Mott, M [Mary] Grew; E. [Edward] M. Davis, Oliver Johnson, Mr [James] Mott. The same names (with the exception of James Mott) appear on a letter to Emerson of December 31, 1851, from representatives of the Philadelphia Anti-Slavery Society which plans a series of lectures on slavery; they appear to constitute the executive committee of the Pennsylvania Anti-Slavery Society. In addition to Emerson, the committee proposed to invite Henry Ward Beecher, Horace Mann,

But, rather than wait longer, I will make ⟨in⟩now the best answer I can. I own, I received the letter with some terror. Here am I, just escaped from a task that has absorbed near six months, a labor of love, but of very questionable judgment,—Margaret Fullers Memoir,—a great deal of labor bestowed to very small effect, I fear; and postponing to it all my proper tasks already too long postponed,—and now I am to shoot again from my orbit,—& waste another month in Philistia, because an unhappy committee of friends of liberty are mistaken enough to put my name on a list intended for effective orators. And you, only you, in the Committee ⟨of the waste.I sh⟩ will have any appreciation of the waste I shall be guilty of, if I accept. And all why? simply because of the foolish weakness one has, when that word liberty is named. Since it is every where resisted & blasphemed, there seems a sort of imperativeness to stand for it, however badly, and by whomsoever challenged. This then is my answer: I hate to come;—but I will come, if you say I must: if, on second thought, & consideration of my preoccupation of mind & purposes these excellent people do not relent & discharge me. But I can promise no more than this, at best, merely to come. New matter I have none, nor am likely to have. I shall /have/ to copy & reedify the poor statement I got up for my townsmen some time last spring,—and which, like all my sallies into politics, I hate to think of.[5] Show this to your friends & mine, & defend me from them. Yours affectionately,

R. Waldo Emerson.

William H. Furness.

I shall return home tomorrow & find exactly what the letter asks. Also, Explain, I pray, that Philistia is philisterey, and that I dreamed of no allusive jingle.

To Benjamin Marston Watson, Concord, January 15, 1852[6]

Concord, 15 January, 1852

My dear Sir,

I doubt not, you will have thought your letter had miscarried, or that my answer had. But I have really been either so busy, or so much a traveller, that I have hardly had time to write a note, for some days. For

---

Wendell Phillips, Theodore Parker, and William Lloyd Garrison. On January 14, Furness wrote: "It has been decided to put off our famous world-moving course of Liberty-Lectures till next season" (*Records*, p. 79).

5. Address on the Fugitive Slave Law of May 1851; see above May 14, 1851.

6. MS in the Hillside Collection, MP&PS; ph. in NNC; the signature and complimentary close have been cut away; the text appears to be complete.

your plan,[7] it will be very agreeable to me to take a part in it, and, I fancy, I shall presently have precisely the fitting materials, when my two lectures of "Culture" & "Worship" are ready,[8]—which must be for the next two Mondays. But I dare not say that I can come to Plymouth on a Sunday, before the 29 February, or the 7 March; & I think, I should prefer to say 14th March[9] I showed your letter to Mr Thoreau, who likes it well, & replied, that, he will come to you, on that errand, at any time you please,[10] if you will give him sufficient notice beforehand. At all events, I am edified by the sense & courage of your project.

To WILLIAM EMERSON, CONCORD, JANUARY 17, 1852

[In Cabot's Bluebook "III Extracts from letters of R.W. Emerson to Mr Wm Emerson," p. 18, is this passage: "Jan 17 1852 . . I have advanced my date for com'g to N.Y. to 10 Feb. by an agreet. with the 'Peoples's Lect.' folk. . . . I am finishing. this day a lect. on 'Culture' for Mon. Ev'g next week if we have good luck & finish or fashion, for it is not begun, one on 'Worship,' & then our winter's work will be for the rest easy. The 'Economy' to my surprise turned out attractive to a great house, so that I am not so sure of my gravities now that my levities prosper so well." See Charvat, pp. 26–27, for the dates of the "Conduct of Life" lectures in Boston and the "People's Lectures" in New York.]

To HENRY JAMES, SR., CONCORD, JANUARY 24? 1852[11]

Concord Jan 1852

My dear James,

Do not believe your letter lost, nor judge me by the diplomatic deliberation of my rejoinder. Your letter came in due time to gladden me

---

7. Watson had proposed a course of Sunday lectures.

8. In the series on the "Conduct of Life," see Charvat, p. 26.

9. Charvat, p. 27, has only one Plymouth engagement and that for March 1, with a payment of $10. Although in the schedule at p. 291 of Emerson's MS Account Book for 1849–1853, only the March 1 engagement is listed, the same Account Book together with this letter shows that Emerson lectured twice in Plymouth. Payments for both lectures are in the Account Book (p. 182) in an undated entry preceding one for March 8. From the Plymouth Lyceum, Emerson received $15.00; from B. M. Watson, he received $10.00. It is reasonable to suppose that the Sunday lecture for Watson was given on Sunday, February 29.

10. Thoreau gave his Sunday lecture for Watson on February 22 (Harding and Bode, p. 276).

11. MS in the James papers, Houghton Library, MH; ph. in NNC; printed by Perry, 1:73; listed in *Letters*, 4:274. Perry, and Rusk after him, gives the day as the 27th, but the last sentence shows that the letter must have been written the week before the final Boston lecture January 26 (see above January 17) and yet long enough after James' letter of January 15 (Perry, 1:72–73) to account for the first sentence. An envelope in the James papers addressed: Henry James, Esq. West Fourteenth Street | New York. | is postmarked at Boston January 28 with "1852" added in ink. Either Emerson wrote a second January note to James

with its welcome,—much needed, too; for I, as, I suppose, all solitary men, shudder as ⟨this⟩we approach New York, & cannot too palpably realize the existence of sociable angels in the great dreary squares![12] I shall bring my bag of paper, and you shall not perform a martyr's duty again. Twice to be sawed in two was not required that I remember of any saint in Fox's Chronicle. ⟨Is⟩If there is need, we will really dig up that often-delineated, somewhere-really-existing bookseller of the gods & of lecturers.[13] I wish so much to see you, that I cannot think of coming to your house; for I have noticed, that a man ringing a doorbell, feels exorbitant rights over the master of the house; but the man with a passkey has no rights of an assailant, indeed, is as defenceless as the poor master himself. Let not this however be interpreted to deprive me of any of the fine privileges you offer me. But you are a grievous sinner,[14] & I hope your great sin has, ere this, cut you to the heart. It is only a half expiation—your printing & publishing.[15] And the book will not be as good as if you /had/ exposed it fully to our northern air. I have never been able to reach a more than Thomasian faith in the acute disease which drove you from Boston. I crave your wife's pardon for my infirm credulities, & do seriously send her my kindest respects, as I am always the debtor of her bounties. Remember me to your sister;[16] & do not forget me to the boys.

Pity me this day also, for I am in the torments of extorting the lesson that is for next Monday night. Ever yours,

R. W. Emerson.

Henry James.

To David W. Horton, Concord? January 28? 1852

[In a letter of January 27, 1852 (RWEMA), David. W. Horton asks Emerson to lecture in West Cambridge (now Arlington) during February. He asks for a reply addressed to his Milk Street office in Boston. Emerson presumably refused, having New York State engagements for February.]

---

or this letter did not get mailed until the 28th. The envelope is the likely ground for assigning the January 27 dating.

12. James have invited Emerson to be his guest.

13. The jesting allusion is probably to John Foxe's *Book of Martyrs*.

14. James had not completed the course of lectures he began in Boston November 6; see above November 3, 1851, and notes.

15. *Lectures and Miscellanies* (New York: Redfield, 1852).

16. Catherine Walsh, Mrs. James' sister.

To _____, Concord, January 28, 1852

[A clipping (CSmH) from an unidentified bookseller's catalogue lists a two-page letter dated January 28, 1852.]

To William L. Haskins, Boston? January 29? 1852

[In a letter dated January 24, 1852, but postmarked January 28 (RWEMA), Emerson's cousin William L. Haskins asks him if he can lecture in Williamsburg, New York, on Thursday the week before or after February 26. Emerson did lecture in Williamsburg on Thursday, February 19, (Charvat, p. 26), but when he replied to his cousin is uncertain, for he was on his way to New York State on the morning of January 30 and had spent the night of January 29 in the American House (MS Account Book for 1849–1853, p. 180). A similar letter of October 16, 1852, shows that Haskins is "not authorized" to extend this kind of invitation.]

To _____, Telegram, Buffalo, February 4? 1852

[A telegram to Auburn, N. Y., is likely. See *Letters*, 4:275, where Emerson tells his brother of missing the Auburn date of Monday, February 2, and being obliged to substitute Monday, February 9.]

To William Emerson, New York, February 14, 1852 [17]

Dear William,
    The passage in Manilius which expresses so remarkable a coincidence with the Newtonian theory, is, in the Book I, lines 167–171 [18]
                                            Yours affectionately,
                                                    R. W. E.
Astor House
14 Feb.y 1852

To Edward Waldo Emerson, New York, February 17, 1852 [19]

                                            Astor House
                                            17 February 1852
My dear Son,
    I have your two letters & was very glad that you wrote them yourself. You must study hard until the vacation comes, & show Miss Maynard,[20]

17. MS in the Berg Collection, NN; ph. in NNC.
18. From Manilius' *Astronomica;* Emerson quotes the passage he refers to in his MS Journal BO (1851), p. 284; see *JMN*, 11:364.
19. MS owned by the Raymond Emerson estate; ph. in NNC; listed *Letters*, 4:176.
20. See August 5 and 7, 1850, above for the schoolteacher Helen M. Maynard.

& show yourself, that you can get a lesson perfect, alone. I have a friend here, Colonel McKay,[21] who yesterday morning rolled up fifty dollars in bills, & put them in his waistcoat pocket. He went into a bookshop, & bought a book for $3.oo, & put back the rest of his money, as he thought, /in/ ⟨in⟩his pocket. When he went into another store, to buy something else, he had no money. He went back to the bookshop, & asked the bookseller, if he had found any money on his floor. The bookseller inquired how much he had lost. He answered, "Between 40 & 50 dollars." The man told him, that, soon after he left the shop, his dog brought him the roll of money in his mouth, which he had found on the floor: And returned him the lost bills. Colonel McKay offered to buy the dog, but the bookseller would not sell him. I like the dog & his master. I am afraid I shall not see you until the vacation begins.

Papa.

To JOHN GREENLEAF WHITTIER, NEW YORK, FEBRUARY 20, 1852 [22]

Astor House
20th Feb.y 1852

Dear Sir

Thank you for your ready generosity in releasing me. The ⟨2⟩4 March I am engaged, and all the following Thursdays until after 1 April even I

21. Col. James Morrison Mckay changed the spelling of his name to McKaye in 1855 or 1856 and then in 1885 he changed it to MacKaye, the spelling adopted by his son in 1869; Percy MacKaye, *Epoch, the Life of Steele MacKaye* (New York: Boni & Liveright, 1927), 1:53 and note.

22. MS in the Whittier Collection, Clarke Historical Library, MiMtpT; ph. in NNC. Emerson is here answering a letter of February 18 (RWEMA) in which Whittier hopes not to lose Emerson's lecture (see *Letters*, 5:271 and 276). In his letter of January 20 (RWEMA), Whittier had suggested February 26. In his letter of the 18th, he proposes March 4 in answer to Emerson's request for a change of date. In a third letter of February 23 (two letters, in fact, one sent to Concord). Whittier says that February 26 is now taken, and that it would be difficult to "obtain the Hall on the evenings named by thee," but the 27th of February is possible, and he asks for an immediate answer, apologizing for obliging Emerson to write so often. Whittier's letters together with this letter make it plain that the date February 26 in Charvat (p. 27) is wrong. It is also clear from the MS Account Book for 1849–1853, p. 182, that Emerson did lecture in Amesbury before March 8. Under a February heading Emerson enters the receipts for all his lectures between February 3 (Rochester) and March 5 (Augusta); his next entry is of March 16 and is for the two lectures at Salem (March 8 and 9) and the one lecture at New Bedford (March 16). In the first list, the order is the order in which the lectures were given with the entry for Amesbury falling between that for the Williamsburg Lyceum (February 19) and that for Plymouth (March 1). My guess is that Emerson went to Amesbury on February 27 as Whittier proposes in his letters of the twenty-third.

What happened here is that Emerson had asked to be released from the original date of February 26 because he expected to continue his lectures in New York; postponing these lectures (see *Letters*, 5:278, and nn. 22 and 24), he apparently wrote again to Whittier saying

believe till 16th April. But what hinders that you should let me come on another day of the week, say, Friday 12th, 19th or 27th March or Tuesday 23d or 30th March or Wednesday 24th.

If either of these days will serve you, you shall hold me to it, by writing to me here your election. Thanks, too, & homage for the lines of Freedom & for many & many a service to that cause! [23]

Gratefully yours,
R. W. Emerson

J. G. Whittier.

To Luther Rawson Marsh, New York, February 21, 1852 [24]

Astor House
Saturday

Dear Sir,

Mrs Drury was so kind as to intend to ask your attentions for a card to the Webster oration—But I find I must leave town this day. So do not give yourself trouble on that point.

Respectfully
Your obedt. servt.
R W Emerson

---

that he could after all keep the engagement on the 26th, calling forth Whittier's duplicate letters of the 23rd.

23. Whittier's most recently published poem was "The Peace of Europe" in the *National Era*, February 12. It is possible that he sent Emerson a copy of "The Cross" which did not appear in print until February 26, but which had been written on the eighteenth. See T. Franklin Currier, *A Bibliography of John Greenleaf Whittier* (Cambridge: Harvard University Press, 1937), pp. 228, 322.

24. MS in the Baker Library, NhD; ph. in NNC. This letter is clearly one of the two letters written to Mr. Marsh, referred to by Emily Mervine Drury in her letter of March 13, 1852 (RWEMA), and mentioned by Emerson in a letter of February 25, 1852, to his brother (*Letters*, 4:279). The 21st fell on a Saturday in 1852. Emerson was staying at the Astor House (see *Letters*, 4:277) on this visit to New York and was unexpectedly called home. According to Mrs. Drury, it was Mrs. Marsh who had gone to the trouble of getting Emerson a ticket for Daniel Webster's Address for the New-York Historical Society, February 23. The ticket had been "obtained with difficulty" through a committee member; "many names" had been "proposed at the same time, & all rejected but yours."

Rusk, citing Mrs. Drury's letter, gives Marsh's nickname as "Ransie," but it can be read as "Rawsie." Mrs. Drury habitually fails to complete the final stroke of "w"; in her hand, the letter can be read as "n" or "u" and is identifiable only from other letters in the word (there are eighteen letters from her in the Emerson papers). I read the name as "Rawsie" and identify the addressee as the New York lawyer Luther Rawson Marsh whose middle name allows the diminutive "Rawsie." Marsh was a member of The New-York Historical Society (MS Records, vol. 3, 1850–1852, NHi); Emerson might reasonably suppose the ticket to have been supplied by a member of the society, not by a wife. Both Marsh and his wife were brought up in central New York State, and Marsh's mother, Emma Rawson, was the daughter of Dr. Thomas Hooper Rawson of Canandaigua where the Drurys had a home. Marsh's

To John Greenleaf Whittier, New York, February 21? 1852

[See above, February 20, for the possibility that Emerson wrote again to Whittier to say that because of the postponement of the New York lectures, he could now come to Amesbury on the 26th of February.]

To Benjamin Rodman, Concord, February 24? 1852

[In a letter of February 2, 1852 (RWEMA), Benjamin Rodman invites Emerson to be his guest when he lectures in New Bedford March 16. See March 12 below for confirmation of this letter and a second letter withdrawing the acceptance of the invitation.]

To Edward Jarvis, Concord, February 24? 1852

[In a letter of February 23, 1852 (RWEMA), Dr. Edward Jarvis wants to know by Tuesday evening mail (February 24) whether Emerson can lecture in Dorchester on March 4 and 11. Emerson had already committed himself to Medford for the 11th (see *Letters*, 4:276); the MS Account Book schedule (1849–1853, p. 291) gives March 2 and 10 to Dorchester (Charvat, p. 27).]

To Benjamin Marston Watson, Concord, February 24, 1852[25]

Concord, Mass.
24 February, 1852.

My dear Sir,

I am very well pleased to be expected in Plymouth next Sunday, & Monday, and do not mean to fail you.[26]

Yours faithfully,
R. W. Emerson.

B. M. Watson, Esq.

To Sarah Clark Vaughan? Concord, February 26, 1852

[In a letter (incomplete) of February 15, 1852 (RWEMA), Emerson's former student Sarah Clark, now Mrs. John C. Vaughan, tells Emerson she has read in

---

wife, Elizabeth Stewart, was the daughter of the well-known New York abolitionist Alvan Stewart. Apparently both Marsh and his wife were drawn to Swedenborgianism, and Emily Drury shows signs of a similar inclination. Swedenborgians were likely to be attracted to Emerson as well as to each other.

Mrs. Marsh, I conjecture, made her appeal for the ticket to either Augustus Schell, chairman of the executive committee, or to Maunsell B. Field, Recording Secretary, who together constituted the committee chosen to invite Webster to make the address (MS Records, vol. 3, meeting of November 18, 1851).

25. MS in the Hillside Collection, MPlP; ph. in NNC; single sheet; address leaf cut away.

26. See above notes for January 15, 1852, for Emerson's providing both a Sunday lecture (for $10.00) and a lecture for the Plymouth Lyceum on Monday (for $15.00).

the newspapers of his lecturing in Buffalo; she regrets that the railroad is not finished, for she would like to hear him in Cleveland. I believe that it is Emerson's reply to this letter which is quoted in the *Cleveland Herald* of March 2, 1852, where the date is given as February 26. The passage quoted reads: "Your letter I found on my road, but it offered me fruit I could not eat however fair. All my days were promised, for the Lyceums along the Albany and Buffalo road now act in concert, and when they send to us, eastern demagogues, arrange a series of engagements for us. Yet I was glad to be asked glad to be remembered.'" See N. C. Davis, "Emerson and Ohio," *Ohio Archaeological and Historical Quarterly*, (January 1949), 58:101–102, where the newspaper article is reprinted (p. 101); Mr. Davis' article is reproduced by Cameron, *ESQ* (2d q., 1966), 43:142. In his first note Davis says that the letter (evidently meaning the newspaper quotation) was used by Carl D. Mead in his unpublished dissertation 1 "Eastern Lecturers in Ohio" (Ohio State University, 1947), p. 62. Mead, Davis, and Cameron do not attempt to identify the addressee. It is only to someone already known to him that Emerson could say he was "glad to be remembered." See *Letters*, 4:204, 207, and 365, and, below, March 15; the peripatetic Vaughans lived in Cincinnati, then Cleveland, and finally in Chicago (4:540).]

To Samuel E. Sewall, Concord, February 28? 1852

[In a letter of February 27, 1852 (RWEMA), Samuel E. Sewalll, acting as trustee for Abba May Alcott, reports to Emerson Nathaniel Hawthorne's offer to buy the house to which he holds title and the eight acres to which Emerson holds the title, both intending that any proceeds be used for Mrs. Alcott's benefit. Emerson may not have replied by letter, but the sale was agreed to and the deed executed on March 8; see *Letters*, 4:234, with n. 227, and 291–292 with n. 77, and, above, January 13, 1845. Emerson enters his payment to G. M. Brooks (George Merrick Brooks) for drawing the deed under the date March 8 in the MS Account Book for 1849–1853, p. 185. The deed is recorded in MS vol. 625, p. 219, Middlesex County Registry of Deeds; Emerson named as the grantor and Hawthorne as the grantee.]

To Henry A. Page, Concord, March 8? 1852

[In a letter of March 8, 1852 (RWEMA), Henry A. Page of Medford asks Emerson to let him know by return mail the subject of the lecture to be given on March 11. See Charvat, p. 27. Probably the first lecture was "Fate."]

To Samuel B. Bulkeley, Concord, March 9, 1852

[Of the three letters to Samuel Bulkeley printed in *Letters*, 4:282, 283–284, and 287–288, the first is now in PSt, It has with it the envelope that belongs with the second letter, March 22. Bulkeley has noted the proposed dates, 7th or 14th of April, in pencil on the envelope, the dates Emerson offered Bulkeley contingent on railroad connections. Charvat, p. 27, lists the lecture at Norwich under "Apr. 5?" and he has Concord entered for the 7th. Charvat's source is the MS Account

Book for 1849–1853, p. 188, where under the one date, April 5, Emerson lists receipts beginning with Norwich and including Montreal, Dorchester, and Medford in this order, which is not the order of performance. The Concord lecture was given on the 15th; it is so listed in the tentative schedule in the same Account Book (p. 291); the Norwich lecture has to have been given on the 7th.]

To Sarah Rotch Arnold, Concord, March 12, 1852[27]

Concord ⎱ 12 March 1852
Massachusetts ⎰

My dear Mrs Arnold,

My wife begs me to reply to your kind note, as it found her, I am sorry to say, a little more invalid than usual. But I fancy the note was better than her drugs, & will set her upon her feet before sunset. At any rate, she charges me to thank you for your kind invitation, which she is bent on getting well enough to accept; and, meantime, charges me to write to Mr Rodman, that I am to be released from all claims, in order to go with her to visit you.[28] I shall immediately execute this command, & put myself on your hospitality, confiding that Mrs E. will accompany me. Our day is Tuesday the 16th instant, & I think we shall not reach New Bedford. until /by/ the evening train.[29]

With respectful remembrances to Mr Arnold & to Miss Arnold,

Your affectionate servant,
R. W. Emerson.

To Benjamin Rodman, Concord, March 12, 1852

[See above, letter to Mrs. Arnold of March 12.]

27. MS in the Feinberg collection, MiD; ph. in NNC. I identify the addressee as Sarah Rotch Arnold because of a similar letter of February 27, 1856, to a Mrs. Arnold of New Bedrord; see *Letters,* 4:12 and Rusk's note 48. See also in *JMN,* 13:15, a report of a conversation with James Arnold.

28. Benjamin Rodman was ordinarily Emerson's host when he lectured in New Bedford.

29. The MS Account Book for 1849–1853, p. 187, under the date March 19, shows the expenses of the trip to New Bedford including $1.00 "to servant." Since the cost of the trip is the same as it is in an entry for January 7, 1851 (p. 120), I infer that Mrs. Emerson did not go with him.

To Thomas Palmer, Concord, March 13, 1852[30]

Concord ⎱ 13 March 1852
Mass ⎰

Dr Thomas Palmer,
Dear Sir,

I will leave Mr Lane's note & mortgage at Mr Hoar's[31] office in this town, where you shall find it at your earliest convenience. I am gratified to learn this business is in a way to be closed as well.

Yours respectfully,
R. W. Emerson.

To Ainsworth Rand Spofford, Concord, March 15, 1852[32]

Concord ⎱ 15 March 1852
Mass.   ⎰

My dear Sir,

Your letter seems to have lain in the N.Y. Post Office, or in Mr Greeley's desk until three days ago when he sent it me. But I find myself not quite free enough to use the inviting opportunity you hold out to me.[33] If I had received it in New York, I think I should have tried my fortunes with you once more. Now, it is already getting late, & I cannot easily leave home. Mr Vaughan[34] who has been spending a day with me, tells me, too, that, next Spring, all your system of roads will be complete, & that I can go to Cleveland & Cincinnati, & I know not whither else, without a stop. I am very glad Stallo was aroused to defend the good cause.[35] I am always glad that you are. I surprised Horace Mann with your name for the Pamphlet,[36] which he had attributed confidently to

30. MS in the Fruitlands Museum Library, ph. in NNC. For Emerson's long service as Charles Lane's trustee, consult the index and see also *Letters*.
31. Samuel Hoar.
32. MS in the Manuscript Division, DLC; ph. in NNC. The envelope is postmarked, Concord, Marsh 15. Printed by C. C. Hollis, *NEQ*, 38:74–75. The envelope is no longer with the letter.
33. See below, September 30, 1852, to Spofford for completion of plans to lecture in Cincinnati in the winter.
34. John C. Vaughan of Cleveland and Cincinnati, husband of Sarah Clark, a former student of Emerson's (*Letters*, 4:203, 204, 207) and see, above, February 26.
35. John B. Stallo, Cincinnati jurist. Stallo had apparently spoken out against the Fugitive Slave Law.
36. *The Higher Law*, see above May 23, 1851, and notes.

Mr Jay.[37] It seems to me there needs some rally or concentration & strict alliance of friends of freedom & honor through the land. If I were younger, I should go on such a mission, & put all the good men in knowledge & relations with each other. We must have a new & better Loyola[38] to found a better fraternity.

Yours faithfully,
R. W. Emerson.

A. R. Spofford.

To Anna Barker Ward, Concord, March 15, 1852

[Under the date March 15, 1852, Anna Ward records a letter from Emerson accepting an invitation for Sunday, March 21 (MS copy of diary, Ward papers, Houghton Library). See March 24 below for Emerson's having spent Sunday night at a "friend's house." In a diary entry for March 20, 1852, Anna Ward reports that Emerson has come to stay until Monday. The entry for the following day shows that Emerson and Mr. Ward took all the children to church and that the evening was given to a party to "meet Mr Emerson." There were eighteen guests. (MS copy of a portion of Anna Ward's diary, not in her hand, MH).]

To Joseph Williamson, Jr., Concord, March 16? 1852

[In a letter of March 15 (RWEMA), J. Williamson, Jr., of Belfast, Maine, invites Emerson to lecture in Belfast and Rockland on March 24 and 25. He asks for an early reply. Presumably Emerson sent his refusal, but he had apparently never considered lecturing in Belfast which had nevertheless announced him as one of the lecturers (a.l.s., January 1, 1852, William P. M. Means to Emerson, RWEMA). See October 24, 1851, for Williamson's identity.]

To James T. Fisher, Concord, March 24, 1852[39]

Concord
Mass } 24 March 1852

My dear Sir,

I enclose to you 10.00 with my hearty thanks for the friendly privilege enjoyed in your rooms.[40]

---

37. John Jay (1817–1894). Horace Mann had probably seen Spofford's pamphlet with the New York imprint and inferred Jay's authorship from the fact of his having acted in 1847 as counsel for the fugitive slave George Kirk and from his other anti-slavery activities.

38. Ignatius Loyola; see *The Poetry Notebooks . . .* , pp. 148, 150.

39. MS in the Fisher papers, MHi; ph. in NNC; listed in *Letters*, 4:286, from Fisher's reply of March 25.

40. A letter to Cabot of December 22, 1851 (*Letters*, 4:269), shows that Emerson used Fisher's rooms (36 School Street) to meet with friends after his lectures; Fisher's rooms had been used for meetings of the Town and Country Club while it flourished.

How happened it that you failed me on Monday,—you and your friend? I hastened home on Monday morning, from a friend's house,[41] in the city, where I spent the Sunday, to receive you, & your dinner was ready, but where were the guests?[42]

Respectfully your
obliged servant,

James T. Fisher, Esq.   R. W. Emerson

To Elizabeth Davis Bancroft, New York, March 28, 1852[43]

Astor House
Sunday Night
28 March

My dear Mrs. Bancroft

I am grieved to find that I have been nominally three days in the city, & have not been able to reach Twenty-First Street. Tonight I was to have gone thither, but the inevitable dinner would not break up till 10 o'c. And now I have no choice, but must take the morning train to New-Haven & home. So pity me the more, unskilful traveller that I am, —& tell the Historian, with my regrets, that I am reading diligently the new book, and am almost ready for examination in it.[44] Perhaps I shall have something to write him presently of it. I was bringing to him the London Leader[45] with its critique, but he will have seen it already, I was also to

41. At the Wards'; see March 15 above.

42. That Fisher was to bring with him a Mr. Chapin is indicated in his letter of March 25; he proposes "Wednesday next" for the visit. See, below, letter of March 30, which I believe to be written to Fisher. Chapin is possibly Nathaniel G. Chapin, a partner in the firm of Fishers and Chapin (there were three Fishers altogether).

43. MS in the Bancroft-Bliss papers, Manuscript Division, DLC; ph. in NNC. The letter is endorsed (p. [4]) 1852; Emerson was in New York for three days (March 25–28) in that year and dined at Delmonico's on Sunday, the 28th, returning to Concord on the 29th; see letter of the 30th to his brother, Letters, 4:286–287. Charvat (p. 27) has Emerson giving the third of a series of lectures in Medford on the 28th; the 29th is the likely date. The Medford lectures fell on Thursday ordinarily, but when Emerson accepted the 27th as the date for the second of his postponed New York lectures (see letter to Henry James, Sr., March 15, Letters, 4:284), he must have had to put off Medford. It is probably to keep that date that he had to take a morning train and forgo calling on the Bancrofts.

44. Volume 4 of Bancroft's History of the United States, published in February 1852 (BAL, 587).

45. The favorable review in the Leader (March 13, 1852, 3:254–255) praises Bancroft's scholarship, judgment, and style —the latter at Macaulay's expense. The review may have been written by George Henry Lewes, one of the founders of the magazine. It is clearly Lewes who wrote the review of Memoirs of Margaret Fuller Ossoli, for he alludes to Margaret Fuller's unflattering account of him (Memoirs, 2:185), he being no more favorably impressed by her than she by him on the occasion of their one meeting at Carlyle's. The review appears in the issue of February 14 (3:158–160).

bring you these lines enclosed,[46] which I copied fairly, at home, weeks ago, but tho't not fit to send so far. They were attempted to be copied at your house at your bidding when I was last there but I failed

Yours faithfully,
R. W. Emerson

To James T. Fisher? Concord, March 30, 1852[47]

Concord, 30 March.
Tuesday Morng.

My dear Sir,

I find my family on my return more than usually sick & ailing with measles & ⟨their⟩its sequela. If your friend is to remain in town so long, let me see you on Saturday, to dine. But if that day is not to be had, then do you both come out tomorrow at 12, ⟨bef⟩you proposed, & we will manage to get a bachelor's lunch & show you the North Bridge.

Yours with great regard,
R. W. Emerson.

To W. W. Follett Synge, Concord, April 2, 1852[48]

Concord ⎫
Mass.   ⎬ 2 April, 1852.
              ⎭

My dear Sir,

I am sorry it should be April, before your friendly note is answered. I received it with much pleasure for itself, & with hope for what it promised, on the eve of a little visit to New York, and awaited the arrival of the promised book from Mr Lothrop, —[49] which, however, did not come, & has not yet. I think it not right to ⟨wait⟩delay longer to acknowl-

46. No verses accompany the letter now, and there are no stray Emerson lines in the Bancroft-Bliss papers in the Library of Congress or in the Bancroft papers, Massachusetts Historical Society, or those in Cornell.

47. MS in the Barrett Collection, Alderman Library, ViU; ph. in NNC. The 30th of March fell on a Tuesday in 1852, the earliest likely year for this letter, and for measles in the family, see *Letters*, 4:283 and 286; the second letter cited was written also on March 30, the day after Emerson's return from New York. I identify the addressee as James T. Fisher because of Emerson's letter of March 24, above, and Fisher's reply of March 25 (RWEMA) which proposes Wednesday, March 31, as the day he and his friend Mr. Chapin will call. For Chapin, see notes, March 24 above.

48. MS in the Alderman Library, ViU; ph. in NNC; listed *Letters*, 4:287, with conjectured date of April 1 from Synge's letters of March 15 and April 7.

49. Synge had written that he was sending Emerson Charles Howard's anonymous *Persons and Philosophies* (see Harding, p. 141) through the Reverend Samuel K. Lothrop of Boston. In his acknowledgement (April 7) of this letter, Synge says he has written Lothrop.

edge the pleasure which your account of your friend gives me, & to assure you of my determination to take in good part his own account of himself in the book. It is the best proof of worth when a man attaches good friends to him; and I have already a very high esteem for your friend, & for his friend, from the strong regard he inspires. So do not let me fail of receiving my pacquet; —as indeed I will not; —for if Mr Lothrop does not send to me, I shall sent to him, and I will report to you what I find.

Yours with great regard,

W. Follett Synge, Esq.   R. W. Emerson

To Horace Greeley, Concord, April 2? 1852

[J. Peter Lesley, in a letter of March 29 (RWEMA), asks Emerson for a letter of introduction to Horace Greeley. I think Emerson would have obliged Lesley whose wife Susan Lyman he had known since her childhood.]

To William Henry Furness, Concord, April 6, 1852 [50]

Concord, 6 April
1852

My dear friend

My affections always silently flowing toward you are sure to receive a shock of acceleration every month or two—by some good office of yours. It was always so, and these active virtues accuse my sloth & silence. The last of these sunstrokes was a letter or a pair of letters which Miss Osgood showed me in whole or in part, and, on the instant, I promised explicit thanks.[51] Yet I was puzzled by being quoted as having said to Scherb something quite impossible for me to say. Scherb has forgotten, or mis-, conceived. I found Philadelphia unexpectedly kind & open. Yet I may have said that my Philadelphia audiences always have a look as of your gathering, & not mine,—which I fancy to be the fact. As for Goethe, you

---

Emerson wrote Synge again on April 15 with his comment on the book (see *Letters*, 4:290), but this letter has not been found.

Synge visited Concord sometime in 1852; Hawthorne recalls the visit in *The English Notebooks*, Randall Stewart, ed. (New York: MLA, 1941), p. 39. Emerson leaves no record of the visit; Synge was a spiritualist and as such would be more interesting to Mrs. Emerson than to Emerson himself.

50. MS in the Furness papers, Van Pelt Library, PU; ph. in NNC; printed in *Records*, pp. 81–82; listed *Letters*, 4:289.

51. Miss Lucy Osgood or her sister Mary, Medford friends of Furness; see Furness' reply of April 8, *Records*, p. 86. Furness had evidently repeated to Miss Osgood Emmanuel Scherb's version of Emerson's comment on lecturing in Philadelphia.

are clean wrong altogether,—as you will at once feel, if you will sit down
to Eckermann's Conversations for half an hour.[52] Wise, mellow, adequate
talk, on all topics indifferently, always up to the mark. He is among the
Germans what Webster was among the lawyers, as easily superior to the
great as to the small.[53] Medford is a suburb of yours, and I find myself
gladly your parishioner there, & brag that I am your friend,[54]

Waldo Emerson

To George Palmer Putnam, Concord, April 13, 1852 [55]

Concord Massachusetts
13 April 1852

Dear Sir,

I do not remember that any sketch has been taken of my house except
one by an English lady, which she carried away with her.[56] One circum-

52. Very likely Furness had expressed the romantic preference for Schiller over Goethe,
a preference Emerson had once acceded to (see his essay "Thoughts on Modern Literature"
in *The Dial*, October 1840, 1:156), as Furness reminds him (*Records*, p. 85).

53. Daniel Webster did not die until October 24, but for many New Englanders, he had
died with his speech of March 7, 1850.

54. Emerson was repeating his series "The Conduct of Life" in Medford, beginning the
series of six lectures on Thursday, March 11. At least one of the dates given by Charvat
(p. 27) is impossible, that of March 28, for he did not leave New York until the morning of
the 29th (see above March 28). The original schedule as arranged with Henry Page (Page to
Emerson, January 31, RWEMA) was for a lecture every Thursday, the course to end on
April 15. Emerson's trip to New York to complete the unfinished course at Hope Chapel on
March 25 and 27 made it necessary to postpone the third Medford lecture or to make it up
on some day other than a Thursday. Page paid Emerson on May 1 (Page to Emerson,
RWEMA), from which it is to be inferred that Emerson finished the course by April 29. The
question is whether he could have given a lecture in Medford on April 15 and still have
reached Montreal on the night of the 17th (*Letters*, 4:290). A letter of April 13 to Abel
Adams shows that he expected to be in Boston on the afternoon of Thursday the 15th. And
on that day he wrote a letter to Synge (*Letters*, 4:290). The lecture schedule in his MS
Account Book for 1849–1853, p. 291, lists for April the following: 1 Medford, 8 Medford,
15 Concord, 16 ⟨Medford⟩, 20 Montreal, 29 Medford. The Concord lecture was in fact given
on the 7th of April, freeing the 15th. The Account Book list shows that the trip to Montreal,
if not the trip to New York, was prepared for. It is then possible that he made up the
Medford lecture missed on the 25th by giving his fifth lecture there on April 15. There is
nothing against this date. By the first of January 1851, rail travel from Boston to Rouse's
Point, New York, was possible and by August 6, 1851, the Canadian line form Laprairie to
Rouse's Point was complete. Emerson tells his wife that on Saturday, April 17, 1852, he
walked across the St Lawrence River to Montreal, two days before the ice " 'shoved' " (*Letters*,
4:290–291).

55. MS in the Feinberg Collection, MiD; ph. in NNC.

56. Putnam "per F. Saunders" had written Emerson on April 7 that he proposed to
publish an illustrated volume on the "Homes of American Genius," and for it he wants a
sketch of Emerson's house. The "English lady" is possibly Caroline Stansbury Kirkland (see
above August 12, 1851, and n. 59).

The work was published as *Homes of American Authors,* the article on Emerson written by

stance would recommend to me any project you may entertain of procuring a drawing or a daguerre, namely, that my friend Mr Alcott has built on my land a picturesque summerhouse, which would figure advantageously in a sketch.[57] If therefore you think fit to send us a draughtsman, we will treat him as hospitably as we can.

Yours respectfully,
R. W. Emerson

G. P. Putnam, Esq.

To Charles Herrick? Montreal? April 23, 1852

[A letter of April 23, 1852, was advertised by B. Altman & Co. in the *New York Times* of December 5, 1971; Emerson is quoted as saying he will "cheerfully acquiesce in any arrangement for lectures." The only letter to Emerson sufficiently early to elicit this reply is that of Charles Herrick who, on April 10, wrote on behalf of the Young Men's Mercantile Library Association of Cleveland. A second letter from Herrick, May 25, acknowledges Emerson's acceptance of his invitation. Rusk reasonably conjectures for this acceptance a date later than April 23 (*Letters*, 4:293). Emerson lectured in Cleveland on January 20 and 22, 1853.]

To Rodney Smith and Charles Jonathan Alger, Concord, April 25? 1852

[In a letter of April 23, 1852 (RWEMA), R. Smith and C. J. Alger, representing the literary societies of the University of Vermont, notify Emerson that the societies have elected him Orator for their commencement celebration August 3. There is no record of Emerson's having accepted; presumably he wrote a refusal. Smith and Alger were both of the class of '54.]

George William Curtis; see *BAL*, 1345 and 4406; for the 1896 separate printing, see *BAL*, 4264. See below July 12 and *Letters*, 4:301–302, for Emerson's correspondence with Curtis.

Putnam (per Saunders) three times in August dunned Emerson for a page of manuscript to be reproduced in facsimile; see August 30 below. He later sent Emerson proofs of the engraving of his house, Alcott's creation displayed. The painter sent to sketch the house was William Rickarby Miller; his sketch engraved by "I. B. Forest" appears at p. 254. Ion B. Forrest (or Forest) 1814(?)–1870, an emigrant from Scotland, worked for Putnam after 1842. D. McN. Stauffer, *American Engravers* (New York: The Grolier Club of the city of New York, 1907) 1:87, where the surname is spelled with one "r" as well as with two.

57. In a letter of November 6, 1954, Ellen Emerson identifies herself as "posted at the door, convulsively grasping a branch of Boursalt Rose in my hands while the fair Edith sits in a window drawing." (This passage, which describes also Miller's picture of the house, is omitted from Gregg, 1:80–81. The picture of the hosue is reproduced at 1:39. Ellen's letter identifies the girl under the tree as Edith "reading Parents' Assistant.")

To John Albee, Concord? ? 1852?[58]

To a brave soul it really seems indifferent whether its tuition is in or out of college. And yet I confess to a strong bias in favor of college. I think we cannot give ourselves too many advantages; and he who goes to Cambridge has free the best of that kind. When he has seen their little all he will rate it very moderately beside that which he brought thither. There are many things much better than a college; an exploring expedition if one could join it; or the living with any great master in one's proper art; but in the common run of opportunities and with no more than the common proportion of energy in ourselves, a college is safest, from its literary tone and from the access to books it gives — mainly that it introduces you to the best of your contemporaries. But if you can easily come to Concord and spend an afternoon with me we could talk over the whole case by the river bank.

To Reubin Hoar, Concord, May 1, 1852

[The MS Account Book for 1849–1853 under May 1 (p. 201) has this entry. "Paid Reuben Hoar, in a letter sent this day, for RBE's bill of board &c 27.00." Bulkeley Emerson had been living on Reuben Hoar's farm in Littleton, Massachusetts.]

To W. W. Follett Synge, Concord, May 10, 1852

[Listed in *Letters*, 4:293, from Synge's letter of June 28, but that letter is an acknowledgement of June 6, see below. As the letter of June 6 shows, Emerson's letter of May 10 enclosed the text of the petition on copyright laws that he sent to Longfellow on May 10. See *Letters*, 4:292–293 and, for Longfellow's reply, see n. 81.]

58. No MS has been found; text from John Albee, *Remembrances of Emerson* (New York: The Grafton Press, 1901), p. 14; printed earlier in the *New-York Tribune*, July 23, 1882, p. 4; and in *Concord Lectures on Philosophy*, Raymond L. Bridgman, ed. (n.p., n.d., c. 1883), pp. 66–67; listed *Letters*, 4:270, at close of 1851. (In the Emerson papers is a typescript of Albee's lecture for the Concord School of Philosophy; it has no more authority as a text than the printed versions cited above.) Except that the letter was written before Albee visited Emerson in May 1852 (*Remembrances*, p. 14), there is no clue to the date. See below, May 20, 1853, for note of letters by Albee to Emerson.

To Benjamin Marston Watson, Concord, May 12, 1852 [59]

Concord, 12 May, 1852.

My dear Sir,

Mr Channing [60] to whom I applied, this morning, agrees to come to Plymouth, on Sunday, 16th. I had first applied to Mr Thoreau, who could not go for the 16th, but promises to go on the 23d instant. Put him down ⟨i⟩on your list for that day. I shall have to sit firm a little while in my seat, here at home, before I go abroad again; and examine my materials before I undertake a Sunday lecture.

Yours faithfully,

B. M. Watson.   R. W. Emerson

To Charles List, Concord, May 12, 1852 [61]

(Not to be printed.)

Concord

12 May

Mr List

Dear Sir,

In the Commonwealth's report of my speech yesterday, [62] I notice two errors of some importance to the sense. 1: I am made to say "the greatest future" [63] instead of "the greatest fortune;" 2. I am made to say "very

59. MS in the Barrett Collection, Alderman Library, ViU; ph. in NNC.

60. See above, January 15 and February 4, for other correspondence with Watson about his Sunday evening lecture program. Thoreau had already contributed one lecture (see Harding and Bode, p. 276). There is no evidence that Emerson went to Plymouth a second time (see notes to January 15) in the 1851–1852 season. Emerson refers here to Ellery Channing, who may already have contributed to Watson's Sunday evening lectures. In a letter of February 10 from Providence (Houghton Library), Channing reports that Alcott, who had lectured for Watson on February 8, has told him he is "to be speedily summoned." Characteristically, Channing adds: "So the good Watson has secured the latest imitator of the celebrated lecturer Mr Emerson. . . . Alcott was in vast & magnificent spirits about the success of this new description of Church, from whence we may surely predict its total & speedy ruin." Channing, too, counted himself an imitator, for he had been told by Sarah Whitman that he was "exactly" like Emerson, "even to gait, air, voice, turning of the eyebrow &c."

61. MS in Special Collections, University Libraries, OKentU; ph. in NNC. The injunction not to print is Emerson's. After the dateline, a comma and the year 1852 have been added in pencil; the figures are not Emerson's. The year is in no doubt; the subject, Emerson's "Address to Kossuth," establishes it. List was assistant editor of The Commonwealth.

62. This letter makes the date of the address securely May 11; see Charvat, p. 401, where the day is questioned.

63. The MS (Abernethy Library, VtMiM) reads: "the greatest fortune." See June 4 below for the vicissitudes of this phrase. The MS is endorsed at the top of the first page: "Manuscript of Ralph Waldo Emerson's Speech of Welcome to Kossuth at Concord Mass. handed to me by him at its conclusion W. T. Coggeshall." William Turner Coggeshall is the Ohio

generous American" instead of "every generous American."[64] I do not know but these are worth noting in an <u>Erratum</u> tomorrow.

Yours respectfully,
R. W. Emerson.

Also there is a misplacing of the Concord & the West Cambridge speeches of Kossuth[65] Send me if you please four copies of today's paper, which the bearer will pay for.

To Robert Carter, Concord, June 4, 1852[66]

Concord, 4 June, 1852.

Dear Sir,

One or two errors occurred in the Daily Commonwealth's[67] Report of my Address to Kossuth, which were corrected in the Weekly Commonwealth. One or two errata however remain to be marked.

1. In the eleventh line, erase the words[68]
"[As Concord is one of the monuments of freedom;]"
2. One paragraph is improperly broken into two, at the words
"[You have won your own]&c" Here should be no new paragraph, but these words should be printed without a break, as part of the foregoing.—

The third correction I must perhaps leave unmade. I wrote or spoke in the second paragraph; "a man so truly in love with a glorious fortune, that he cannot be diverted to any less." It has got changed in the newspapers to "the greatest future," &, in the weekly Commonwealth, to "the greatest fortune." Perhaps it is safe to leave it so, as the original expression is not precise. If the right word occurs to me, & not too late, I will

---

journalist who accompanied Kossuth on his tour and reported his speeches. On page three a note initialed "HGS" reads: "Corrections have been ordered for the weekly."

64. *Works*, 11:400, has the correct "every."

65. According to the account in *Kossuth in New England*, Kossuth, on May 11, spoke first in West Cambridge (now Arlington) and then later, on the same day, in Concord.

66. MS in the Feinberg Collection, MiD; ph. in NNC; printed by White, *AL* (May 1961), 33:164. This is probably the same letter that Risk lists under the date June 8 in *Letters*, 4:295, from a sale catalogue of 1904. It is certainly the same letter dated June 2 listed by Cameron, *ESQ* (2d q., 1966), 43:143, from Parke-Bernet Sale Catalogue 1956, sale of March 1–2, 1961. The addressee is the editor of *The Commonwealth*.

67. See above May 12, for corrections sent to the *Commonwealth*.

68. Emerson is correcting the text for printing in *Kossuth in New England* ... (see *BAL*, 5223). The corrections Emerson asks for here were made, pp. 222, 223; the text has the reading "a glorious fortune" (p. 223). The text in *Works*, vol. 11, still has the line about Concord (p. 397) and reads "a greatest future" (p. 398). What Emerson wrote is "the greatest fortune"; see May 12 above. The paragraphing is correct (p. 400).

yet send it to you. I presume that you have a copy of the "Weekly Commonwealth," containing this "Address."

Yours respectfully,
R. W. Emerson.

Robert Carter, Esq.

To W. W. Follett Synge, Concord, June 6, 1852[69]

Concord, 6 June, 1852

My dear Sir,

I enclose to you the paper, of which, I believe, I forwarded you a copy, at the same time that I sent this to Mr Longfellow.[70] He has returned it with some good signatures from Boston. I have kept it, a few days, again, for the sake of obtaining Hawthorne's name, which he has just now appended.[71] The paper will, at least, show you what opinion these names may be had for; & you can give it what form you please, & obtain the signatures again.[72]

Yours, with great regard,
R. W. Emerson

W. W. F. Synge, Esq.

To Delia Salter Bacon, Concord, June 12, 1852[73]

Concord, 12 June, 1852.

My dear Miss Bacon,

Your letter was duly received, & its contents deserved better leisure & apprehension, than I have at once been able to command. The only

69. MS in Autograph Collection, Houghton Library, MH; ph. in NNC; listed by Cameron, *ESQ* (2d q., 1956), 3:5, from dealer's catalogue.

70. See *Letters*, 4:292–293, for the letter to Longfellow and n. 81 for Longfellow's reply. The enclosure is in Emerson's hand and reads: "The undersigned, believing, that both equity & national Comity require, that British authors should be protected in the property of their works, in this country, in a degree equivalent to that in which American authors are now protected in the property of their works in Great Britain; and believing, that the interests of American literature dictate the same policy; pray, that such measures may be taken, either by treaty, or by an Act, as shall secure that end."

71. The signers are William Hickling Prescott, Henry Wadsworth Longfellow, Louis Agassiz, Cornelius Felton, George Ticknor, Olvier Wendell Holmes, Edward Everett, Edwin Percy Whipple, Charles Sprague, George Stillman Hillard, Andrews Norton, Nathaniel Hawthorne, and Emerson.

72. Synge's reply of June 28 (RWEMA) is discouraging; he has been advised that the time is not ripe for such a petition.

73. MS in DFo; ph. in NNC; printed by Theodore Bacon, *Delia Bacon* (Boston: Houghton, Mifflin, 1888), pp. 48–50; listed *Letters*, 4:295; quoted by Vivian Hopkins, *Prodigal Puritan* (Cambridge, Mass.: Belknap Press, 1959), pp. 150–151.

alternative was to let it wait a little, for a good hour. And now I write, only that I may assure you it has been received & is appreciated. In the office to which you have in the contingency appointed me, of critic, I am deeply gratified to observe the power of statement & the adequateness to the problem, which this sketch of your argument evince. Indeed I value these fine weapons far above any special use they·may be put to. And you will have need of enchanged instruments, nay, alchemy itself, to ⟨establish⟩melt into one identity these two reputations (shall I call them?) of the poet and the statesman, both hitherto solid historical figures. If the cipher approve itself so real & consonant to you, it will to all, & is not only material but indispensable to your piece. And it would seem best that so radical a revolution should be proclaimed with great compression in the Declaration, & the real grounds pretty rapidly set forth, a good ground in each chapter, and preliminary generalities quite omitted. For there is immense presumption against us which is to be annihilated by battery as fast as possible. And now for the execution of the design. —If you will send me your first ⟨manuscript⟩chapter, I will at once make my endeavour to put it into the best channel I can find, Blackwood or Fraser[74] I think the best. But this, taking it for granted that you decide on trying your fortune in a magazine, first, —which; I suppose, is fame, rather than fortune. On most accounts, the eligible way is, as I think, the book or brochure, published simultaneously in England & here. I am not without good hope of accepting your kind invitation to visit you in Cambridge though I very very rarely get so far from home where I am detained by a truly ridiculous complication of cobwebs.[75]

With great respect,
Yours faithfully,
R. W. Emerson

Miss Bacon.

P.S. What is the allusion in the Literary World of last week, to criticism on Shakespeare?[76] Does it touch us, or some other?

---

74. Although Emerson went as far as asking Clough for the names of the editors of *Blackwood's* and *Fraser's* (see July 14 below), it is not certain that he did write them, for he consistently advised Miss Bacon to offer her theory of the authorship of Shakespeare's plays in a book, not in magazine articles. Although a little late to be conclusive, Emerson's letter of June 13, 1855, to Miss Peabody implies that he abandoned the proposal to write the English editors (see below).

75. Emerson had already met Miss Bacon (*JMN*, 13:25–26).

76. *The Literary World* (June 5, 1852), 10:391, where there is an allusion to those who doubt Shakespeare's existence.

To Theodore Parker, Concord, June 18, 1852 [77]

18 June
1852

My dear Parker,

I am heartily vexed to be so slow in obeying so easy a duty.[78] I am still more vexed at heart for the badness of the inscription. I did my best at the time of it to make a good one. But the Committee, Col Shattuck & Dr Jarvis, I believe, cooked up this, from all that were offered!

Ever yours,
R. W. Emerson

Theodore Parker.

To Elijah P. Clark, Concord, July 5, 1852 [79]

Concord, 5 July, 1852

My dear Sir,

Mr Carlyle's address is, as usual, 5 Great Cheyne Row, Chelsea, London. and I have letters from him as late as 15 May, from that place. He is very punctual in his habit of answering letters, so that I think he ought to be questioned at once on the receipt of the money.[80] I hate to think there should be any loss: and it is not probable there will be.

Yours faithfully,
R. W. Emerson

E. P. Clark, Esq.

77. MS in the Eliot and Emmons Papers, Milwaukee Area Research Center, WMUW; ph. in NNC.

78. Emerson is answering Theodore Parker's letter of June 14, in which Parker, provocative as always, asks Emerson to copy "word for word" the "false inscription" on the Concord Monument. The grandson of Captain John Parker of Lexington was not going to let Concord claim to have offered "the first forcible resistance to British aggression." Emerson obediently copied the whole inscription word for word and line by line, including "AD. 1836" and enclosed it with his letter.

79. MS in the Clark papers, OCHP.

80. The letter apparently refers to money from the American publication of *The Life of John Sterling*. See Slater, p. 472, for Carlyle's sending to Clark a copy of the English printing and having authorized Clark to negotiate an American printing. Carlyle's brother had already sent the book in sheets to Crosby & Nichols.

To George William Curtis, Concord, July 12, 1852[81]

Concord, 12 July, 1852

My dear Sir,

I postponed an answer to your note, until I could consult my trusty neighbor George Minott, through the fence, who knows much more of the old inhabitants than I. I had fancied, that, where my house stands, another had stood before; but I learn, that mine is the first that has been built here, within the memory of man. Neither is the land memorable: no diligence could find the smallest scrap of legend to dignify the homestead, or to connect the bit of upland with Tahattawan & his sagamores.[82] Not even an arrowhead has been picked up on it, by my friend Thoreau. The house was built about the year 1828, by Charles Coolidge (brother of I. Templeman Coolidge, a well-known /Boston/ merchant,) grandson of old Joseph Coolidge of Bowdoin Square.[83] This ⟨(then) young⟩ gentleman had a lively remembrance of the spacious cellars & old horse chestnut trees of Bowdoin Square, and he built the only good cellar that then been built in Concord, & lined his lot with a comely row of horse chestnuts, which are now ripening their twentyfifth harvest The house, when I bought it, in 1835, was ⟨a⟩ plain, convenient, thoroughly built, for the country. The barn, which I found in good repair, had been an old tumble-down, which had been removed from a distance & set cat- ⟨a⟩ cornered on[84] on the edge of Coolidge's lot by an amiable neighbor, who wished to force him to buy the field. Coolidge had no choice but to pay this blackmail, & ⟨bought⟩ /he/ made a good barn of the building. I have enlarged both the house & the barn; & the two acres, which I found attached to it, have grown to nine. I am too small & slovenly a cultivator to be worthy to be called a farmer, yet I have protected my once uncovered place with ⟨q⟩ shade trees, & my orchard counts near a hundred apple & pear trees My house cannot pretend to any special beauty of site. Indeed I have often had to defend it from the reproaches of strangers, on this score. The land slopes down behind the house to the brook, at the bottom of the garden which runs into the Concord River, which runs

---

81. MS in the Curtis papers, Houghton Library, MH; ph. in NNC. Emerson is supplying this information for Curtis' contribution to *Homes of American Authors;* see above, April 13, for the publisher's (G. P. Putnam) letter to Emerson and for *BAL* references. A second letter to Curtis for the same article is in the *Letters,* 4:301–302.

82. Tahattawan was one of the Indians present when the first Concord settlers purchased the land.

83. The Joseph Coolidge house in Bowdoin Square, Boston, was built by Charles Bulfinch: see Whitehill, pp. 51 (fig. 27)-52.

84. Emerson is apparently spelling "cater-cornered" by ear.

into the Merrimack, & the sea. But the spot has eminent convenience, the land is well watered, and we have the advantage of a horizon like the prairie or the sea. But without venturing on the dangerous prolixity of the advantages of my neighborhood, I hasten to end this too long note.

Yours faithfully,

R. W. Emerson

G. W. Curtis, Esq.

I ought not to have omitted to recall to your memory the only decoration of my lawn, namely, Mr Alcotts summer house,[85] built by his proper hands, designed by his own fancy, & which, could it have been a little more technically based & jointed, would have promised a longer duration, which its pleasing form & details well deserve.

TO ARTHUR HUGH CLOUGH, CONCORD, JULY 14, 1852[86]

Concord ⎫
Massachusetts ⎬ 14 July 1852

My dear Clough,

I cannot tell you whether your letter gave me more joy or sorrow. For I am delighted to hear from you, & cheered by so much as the suggestion of your American Hegira. But I hate to believe that your powers & your performings, too, should have found no more decided acknowledgment, at home, than your letter intimates, or than the present project implies. I dare not advise in a matter which balances such a splendid contingency as an English first-rate literary reputation in the scales. I can only speak to the American details you bring into the question. There is always teaching to be done here, to an extent, & at all prices. The best-paid is that, which, in the event of your coming you would naturally be directed to, namely, of young men who wish to enter College at an advanced standing (who mean, that is, to overstep the first, or the two or three first of the four years at Cambridge) and of those who are <u>suspended</u>, or

85. This is a private joke; Curtis would know very well that among the critics of Emerson's dwelling place were Caroline Sturgis Tappan, William Ellery Channing, and Margaret Fuller, scarcely strangers to either Emerson or Curtis. The site, being neither sublime nor picturesque, did not answer to contemporary taste. I suspect that Emerson was amused to find that his property could not evoke any associations with legend or history, and he appears in this letter to be deliberately divesting it of any suggestion of romance. A drawing of the one "picturesque" object, Alcott's summer house, serves as a vignette at the end of the article. See April 13 above, n. 56.

86. MS in the Clough papers, Bodleian Library, Oxford; ph. in CUL; printed in *Emerson-Clough Letters*, no. 11, Mulhauser, 1:315–317; listed *Letters*, 4:300. Emerson is answering Clough's letter of June 17 (*Emerson-Clough Letters*, no. 10, Mulhauser, 2:314–315), but his reply is not exactly to the point of Clough's inquiry about what a young couple needed to marry on.

temporarily dismissed from College, on account of idleness, or other fault.[87] The College authorities (at Cambridge, Mass) are always looking round them for instructers in safe country-towns, on a radius of 10 to 20 miles from Cambridge, to whose supervision they may assign these mau-vais sujets. This is the surer reliance With enlarged acquaintance come the private tutorships of now & then a rich man's son:—not to mention the always impending contingences of well paid literary labor. I cannot, at this moment, speak from any communication with such persons at Cambridge or Boston, who have experience & oversee the ground, but I think your card,—with your names & titles, real powers & excellent prestige,—a very safe one, if you choose to play it, safe for a permanence tho' one may easily meet some trying delays at the outset. For the com-parative expense of which you inquire, Bristed (who lived 5 years at your Cambridge) says, that all necessaries cost there twice as much as at New-Haven (Yale College).[88] Many & many a decent family lives in Boston on a thousand dollars a year, & sends one or two boys to College. Country ministers live & marry, generally, on salaries of 5, 6, 7, /8,/ or /$/ 900. And country doctors & lawyers do not often make more. Yet the minister of our first parish here in Concord has a thousand dollars. Four dollars a week in the country, & six in the city, will buy good private board (which includes /furnished/ lodging, but excludes washing) Economy is making it the rule in this region for everybody to live out of town; for country-rents & season-tickets on the railroads are cheap. But, perhaps, after a little consideration & inquiry, I may send you new details, an American Boeckh.[89] Meantime, I will make you a proposition, a serious bargain. Do you take the first ship or steamer for Boston, come out & spend two or three months here in my house. I will defend you from all outsiders, initiate you step by step into all the atrocities of republicanism You shall look about you, know all the inlets & capabilities of country & town; have good milk, eggs, coffee, & not-so-good-as-English mutton And you shall, on your part, answer a catechism of details touching England, revise my notes on that country, & sponge out my blunders. For I have lately undertaken to set my journal of 1848, & commentaries, in order. Doubt not our industry to employ yours. Hawthorne, Thoreau, & Channing are all within a mile of me.

87. Students who had been "rusticated."

88. Charles Astor Bristed, *Five Years in an English University* (New York: 1852), 2:153; see *ER*, p. 27; Emerson apparently borrowed Bristed in order to answer Clough's questions; he used it also for his *English Traits*.

89. August Böckh; Emerson alludes to Böckh's *The Public Economy of Athens* (London, 1828); see *ER*, p. 48.

I shall not fail to seek more exact information & perhaps a working-plan, as the architects say.

Meantime, let me ask a question or two. A really brilliant Essay was lately read to me in MS., by its author,[90] on the subject of Shakespeare. The author had wrought in a new fashion on the biography,—working in real conviction had made out a most ingenious, if courageous, paradox,—possessed all the requisite learning, & power of statement.—The author, a new person, never before heard of. It was question how to put this new criticism effectively before the right public. The author believed this must be in England, &, I think, proposed to put it into four or five articles in successive numbers of "Blackwood" or "Fraser." I promised to do what I could to put them there. Now I wish you to tell me who is the official editor, or who the approachable literary man of "Blackwood?" Is it Ferrier or Aytoun?[91] or who? to whom I may write a private letter, disclosing & offering my new start? And who of "Fraser's"? So shall Carlyle be relieved of this negociation,—Carlyle, who has just brought to a successful termination, a cumbersom coil concerning Margaret Fuller's MSS, in which, with too much good nature he had several letters to write.[92]

I ought to have congratulated you on the bright tidings you tell me of yourself & your fair intentions. May all to the fairest issue bend! But, first, you must come out & climb Pisgah alone.

Yours affectionately,

R. W. Emerson.

A. H. Clough, Esq.

TO FREDERIC? W. HOLLAND, CONCORD, JULY 20, 1852

[In a letter of July 19, n. y., but endorsed 1852 (RWEMA), F. W. Holland writes that on his own responsibility he is trying to get up a series of lectures for East Cambridge; he hopes Emerson can help him out with six lectures on easy terms. Emerson has endorsed the letter "F. W. Holland Oct 1852"; my conjecture is that Emerson answered the letter with either a request that Holland write again in October or a promise to write again himself. It is clear from Holland's letter that he has no institution behind him, and his proposed fee of $10. is below the going

90. Delia Bacon; see above June 12. Here Emerson is being circumspect; he knew of Miss Bacon's fear that her idea about the authorship of the plays would be stolen.

91. James Frederick Ferrier and William Edmonstoune Aytoun. Clugh's reply of August 6 says J. W. Parker, Jr., is the editor of *Fraser's* and Aytoun of *Blackwood's*. John William Parker is meant. *Emerson-Clough Letters*, no. 12; Mulhauser, 1:319.

92. See Slater, pp. 475–484, for correspondence concerning the recovery of Margaret Fuller's MSS in the possession of Margaret Gillies. Clough had mentioned the *Memoirs* and his having known Margaret Fuller in Rome.

rate. In an 1852 Cambridge directory, a Frederic W. Holland is listed as pastor of the Third Evangelical Congregational Society.]

To Samuel Joseph May, Concord, July 23? 1852

[In a letter of July 23, 1852 (RWEMA), the Reverend Samuel May invites Emerson to the annual commemoration of Emancipation in the West Indies to be held in the Grove, South Framingham, on August 3. He hopes Emerson will speak. Emerson did not attend this meeting, for on August 3 he and his daughter Ellen went to Lynn (MS Account Book for 1849–1853, p. 216), probably to visit Abel Adams and his family; see *Letters*, 4:299. May's letter would not necessarily require an answer, but the invitation to speak does.]

To Abeline Roberts, Concord, August 2, 1852 [93]

Concord, 2 August, 1852.

Dear Madam,

I am again compelled to decline the part you offer me in your proposed Course of Lectures. With sentiments of grateful respect to all the members of your society,

Your servant,
R. W. Emerson.

Miss A. Roberts. 1852

To Arthur Hugh Clough, Concord, August 26, 1852 [94]

Concord   ⎱ 26 Aug.
Massachusetts ⎰ 1852

My dear Clough,

I read with great pleasure that you will come & see us. For the time, I do not know that there are any commanding circumstances here which

93. MS in the papers of the Salem Female Anti-Slavery Society, James Duncan Phillips Library, MSaE; ph. in NNC. See above Emerson's letter of August 27, 1851, addressed to "Mrs. Adeline Roberts, Cor. Secretary," in the same collection. Emerson is here answering Adeline Roberts' letter of July 19, 1852 (RWEMA), asking him to open the series on October 3.

In the *Vital Records of Salem*, the birth of Mary Adaline Roberts is recorded (2:241), the daughter of Mary Wilson and Timothy Roberts, whose marriage (in Danvers) November 24, 1842, is also recorded (4:261). There is no "Adeline" Roberts in the records, but it seems possible that the child, born in 1845, may have been named for her mother or a grandmother. The *Vital Records of Danvers* record the marriage, giving Salem as the home of both parents. Mrs. or Miss Roberts remains of uncertain identity.

94. MS in the Clough papers, Bodleian Library, Oxford; ph. in CUL; printed in *Emerson-Clough Letters*, no. 13; Mulhauser, 2:321–322; listed *Letters*, 4:307. On August 6 Clough had accepted Emerson's invitation of July 14 (*Emerson-Clough Letters*, no. 12; Mulhauser, 1:319–320).

must be considered. Our College & School years begin about 1 September; but, as I doubt not the existence of unlimited opportunities of employment for you here, in teaching,[95] I think you may choose your own time. I spoke with Felton,[96] Greek Professor at Cambridge, since you wrote me before, & he answered very favorably for our plans. I told him, that, if there were not room in Cambridge, I should make the acquaintance of Bristed[97] in New York, to apprize him of your coming. But I hesitate not to urge your coming, as soon as you are ready, in the belief that in coming to America, you cannot come wrong; for, even if you should decide not to love but to hate us, (and I own I think it costs a long enuring or wonting to make a genuine Englishman tolerate our modes,) yet to your perceptions the whole transit & the spectacle will be pleasant & fruitful. My wife & my children & some good neighbors are made happy by the expectation of quickly seeing you; & your chamber is all ready.

Yours affectionately
R. W. Emerson.

To Caroline Sturgis Tappan, Concord, August 26, 1852[98]

Concord, 26 August, 1852

Dear Caroline,

I am not quite contented with Ellen's school, at this moment. All her schoolmates persist in not being of the right age, or the right turn of mind, for her. If I were a little nearer to town, I should send her to Mr G. B. Emerson,[99] or to Mrs Lowell,[100] but the daily transit is too much tax on her strength. I have heard, lately, something of Mrs Sedgwick's s[c]hool.[101] I can easily believe the school is good. The teaching is of something less importance in Ellen's case, that she is a good scholar & will learn easily & well anywhere. But I wish she should have a good, reasonable, & well behaved set of schoolmates. Will you not tell me if you

95. See above, July 14, for Emerson's information about the prospects for teaching.
96. Cornelius C. Felton became a close friend of Clough.
97. See notes to July 14 for Bristed.
98. MS in the Tappan papers, Houghton Library, MH; ph. in NNC.
99. His cousin's school was in Boston.
100. Anna Jackson Lowell (Mrs. Charles Russell Lowell), whose school was in Cambridge (see *JMN*, 13:108); she was James Russell Lowell's sister-in-law.
101. Elizabeth Dwight Sedgwick (Mrs. Charles Sedgwick), whose school was in Lenox where the Tappans had leased Samuel Gray Ward's house Highwood. The Sedgwicks so dominated Berkshire County that it was once said that the very grasshoppers sang "Sedgwick, Sedgwick." Longfellow credits Anna Barker Ward's brother with this bon mot (August 8, 1848, MS diary, on deposit, Houghton Library).

know or can learn that Mrs. S. has a good set of pupils? or, does her celebrity only draw to her, like a great Doctor's, the "difficult cases?" Of course, I wish the best position in every way for her; wish her to board with Mrs S. & have every convenience that any one has. Ellen is thirteen, knows all the elements, reads Virgil, is affable & conscientious. What more can she ask than companions? Write me your knowledge & opinion; and, (if you think it would be well to try a year at Lenox) please learn for me M[r]s S's possibilities. Can she receive her into her house? and when? and what are the terms. But, first, I wish your opinion.

I have long had your bundle of Margarets letters since their return from Mr Channing refolded,[102] tied, superscribed, & ready to send you. But I shall not even let them go with this note, which can travel faster alone. Clough /from Oxford/ is coming to see me in October. Horatio Greenough spent a day with me lately. ⟨C⟩He is a rare companion, deep & wise.

Yours,
R. W. E.

To Harrison Gray Otis Blake, Concord, August 26, 1852

[Listed 1986 in Catalogue 73 of the Alta California Bookstore. See *Letters*, 4:307, where Cabot's copy of parts of the letter is printed. Cabot, making three cuts, signified his omissions by X. Cabot's copy is of 129 words which in Emerson's handwriting would fill about three pages of 8vo notepaper. The catalogue describes the copy as less than half the original.]

To John Chapman, Concord, August 27? 1852

[See *Letters*, 4:304–305, and Slater, pp. 467–482, for the bundle of Margaret Fuller papers that at Emerson's request Carlyle had entrusted to John Chapman on June 25 to be sent to Emerson. Emerson, on August 16, reported to Chapman that he had not received the promised documents. The MS Account Book for 1849–1853, p. [219], under the date August 27, records the payment of 1.50 to the express man Augustus Adams "for a bundle from England." I think Emerson would have written to Chapman and perhaps also to Carlyle to report the safe arrival of the package.]

102. William Henry Channing.

To George Palmer Putnam, Concord, August 30, 1852[103]

Concord ⎱ 30 Augt 1852
Mass.   ⎰

Dear Sir

I am sorry to be so backward to comply with what seemed so slight a request.[104] But I destroy old papers so fast,[105] that I have not without difficulty found, this morning, the enclosed leaves of old copy. You may take which you will,—if indeed either of them should suit you;—only not the page or pages I have crossed out with ink.

Respectfully yours,
R. W. Emerson—

G. P. Putnam, Esq.

To Horatio Greenough, Concord, September 6, 1852[106]

Concord ⎱ 6 September
Mass.   ⎰ 1852

My dear Sir,

I have read your little book twice through, to say the least.[107] I have gone back, & up & down, & criss cross, & now am in a course of reading

103. MS in the Feinberg collection, MiD; ph. in NNC.

104. Putnam had sent three requests for a manuscript page to be reproduced in *Homes of American Authors;* see above, April 13, for the initiation of this project and July 12 for Emerson's cooperation with George William Curtis who wrote the text for the section on Emerson. Emerson finally sent Putnam a leaf from "The Method of Nature," reproduced in facsimile at p. 254.

105. Emerson does not mean that he threw away or burned manuscripts; he plundered them for essays and for lectures.

106. MS owned by Mr. David Richardson; ph. in NNC; p. [4] addressed: Horatio Greenough Esq/ Newport/ R.I./; quoted in part by William J. Griffin in "Thoreau's Reaction to Horatio Greenough", *NEQ* (December 1957), 30:510–511; printed by Nathalia Wright in "Ralph Waldo Emerson and Horatio Greenough," *HLB* (Winter, 1958), 12:103–105. For Emerson's first letter to Greenough, see *Letters,* 4:271–272 (reprinted by N. Wright, pp. 100–101). Miss Wright gives an account of Emerson's meetings with Greenough in Florence, 1833.

107. Under the pseudonym of Horace Bender, Greenough had gathered his periodical articles with additional chapters into a book with the title *The Travels, Observations, and Experience of a Yankee Stonecutter;* before publication he sent it (in sheets, evidently) to Emerson on September 2 (Wright, p. 103), describing the book as "slovenly," and asking for a reading of two chapters. He got a good deal more than he asked for. He had already visited Emerson in August and, a ready talker, made a strong enough impression to evoke from Emerson extravagant admiration. A journal entry of August 18 is a redaction of Greenough's views of religion (monistic) and aesthetics (functionalism), *JMN,* 13:85–86. Greenough was no abolitionist but, as Emerson recognizes, he is no Hunker either. In his reply (September 11) to this letter, Greenough explains his views; he objects to the rise of hypocritical moral arguments against the South and proposes, virtually, a boycott of slave-produced goods. Emerson's criticism of Thoreau's second act of civil disobedience (1846)

passages to my neighbors: and I assure you, it is, a very dangerous book, full of all manner of reality & mischievous application, fatal pertinence, & hip- & thigh-smiting personality, and instructing us against our will. I am not sure of its success as a popular book. The air of haste & of the newspaper, the negligence of ⟨one⟩ some indispensable trifles in literary etiquette will hide its value from some readers, —and its own kindred & lovers whom it goes out to seek will imperatively ask a more elaborate redaction, —a sinking of the ephemeral, & some bridging to the eminent parts: but it contains more useful truth than any thing in America I can readily remember; & I should think the entire population well employed if they would suspend ⟨all⟩other work for one day & read it. As long as they do not, you may be very sure a few of us will profit by the secret & deal it out to them little by little. Meantime, you have been unpardonably careless in your proofreading, and the book now needs a long table of Errata;

The book does not take me by surprise, as it would if I had not ⟨had⟩ seen the man three weeks before; but it was all the more interesting & luminous. So right & high minded as it is, I am only the more sorry that it should confound things on the negro question, & put reason, from a most unexpected quarter into the hands of the base & greedy partisan. That the negro was a pre Adamite, I early discovered, but now that he too reads books, the courtesy to present company seems to require that it be a little parliamentarily stated. Then, though some fond Las Casas[108] or two might fetch negroes to save Indians, tis very certain that the first planter who turned them or their work into doubloons, if he used Las Casas's words lied & knew he lied. Early Grey "would stand by his order."[109] I hold it to be a paramount law of every aristocracy, that its

---

made a similar point in a context arguing that the moral gesture is inappropriate for Thoreau (*JMN*, 9:446–447), and see below September 25. The gist of the rest of Greenough's argument is that since no one is free so long as "relative success" is his objective, then the Negro cannot be free either (Wright, pp. 105–106); Emerson rightly recognizes the uses to which these arguments can be put by the defenders of the status quo. He asks the deletion of this matter from Greenough's book, on the grounds of his principle that no man is obliged to engage in reforming activity, but that he must not stand in the reformer's way.

108. Emerson could have read a defense of Bartolomeo de Las Casas in William H. Prescott's *History of the Conquest of Mexico, Works* (Montezuma Edition, Philadelphia, 1904), 2:73–74, first published in 1843; or he may have heard a defense directly from Sir Arthur Helps, whose *The Conquerors of the New World and Their Bondsmen* was published anonymously in London in 1848, see 1:269–271. The story of Las Casas' original proposal to import Negroes to save the Indians of the West Indies from a kind of labor to which they were unaccustomed and of his later regrets and remorse had been told also by E. L. Taylor in *The Restrospective Review* (1822), 6(2):261–271; Emerson was familiar with this English periodical.

109. Emerson uses Lord Grey's phrase in more than one context; see *Letters*, 4:372, where it is a "rule of common sense" and *J*, 10:217, where Emerson recognizes a "higher"

members do so. I require of every reasonable Saxon man not to hold slaves or praise the holding, —because he belongs by blood & bond to the other party, & nature has not a Saxon ounce to spare. There is plenty of Celtic or Roman blood that can hold slaves as innocently as sharks bite, & the grand harmonies of nature round them all admirably in: yet we are all pained when either quits his order, when a Turk unturks himself to be a democrat, or a Saxon unsaxonises himself for some accidental sympathy When I begun this leaf I did not mean to be betrayed into preaching.

But man & book are a great possession to me. I wish to get the power of them. I am driven once more to revolve the old question, why not a Journal in this country that will combine the sanity & talent of really liberal men? There is plenty of power in New England wasted for want of concentration —& of which the population has need. I am tempted to go out into the highways & drum the rappel⟨le⟩, now that I see this new strength, ⟨that⟩But lest I should make no end of this letter, I subscribe myself

Yours faithfully,
R. W. Emerson

Horatio Greenough.

My brother William, a lawyer in New York, has lately sold his house on Staten Island & is proceeding to build another on his adjacent land. I have written to him to say that if I were about to build, I should apply to you for professional counsel, though I suppose a working plan for a house is not a thing to go to Phidias for.[110] Yet I should not the less wish to know what Phidias would say on the subject. I mean to inclose to my brother a note to you, & if you chance to have any leisure, I bespeak your attention It is an easy trip to the Island & the site of his dwelling is noble. William E is no artist but is docile and is an honest & worthy man.

I find I have omitted to say what struck me not less than the broad good sense of the book, that is the splendor of statement, which is better than Canning.[111]

---

order. See also *Works*, 10:251–252. Emerson had in the making a lecture on "The Anglo-Saxon"; he may have used the quotation there.

110. See *Letters*, 4:312.

111. This paragraph was written after the letter was folded for enclosure in the envelope and appears upside down at the foot of page [12]. See November 1 below for comment on this analogy between Greenough and George Canning.

To NATHANIEL SHIPMAN, CONCORD, SEPTEMBER 17, 1852 [112]

Concord ⎱ 17 Sept.
Massachusetts ⎰ 1852

Dear Sir,

Your letter did not reach me till this morning, being misdirected to Concord <u>New Hampshire</u>. It will give me much pleasure to visit your city in the course of your season, if I can. If I come to Hartford to read a single lecture, the Institute shall pay me forty dollars.

Respectfully,
R. W. Emerson.

Nath. 1 Shipman, Sec.y.

To H. D. HUNTINGTON, CONCORD, SEPTEMBER 18? 1852

[H. D. Huntington, Corresponding Secretary of the Young Men's Mercantile Library Association of Cincinnati wrote Emerson on September 11 (RWEMA). That Emerson replied is clear from his letter of September 30, below, where he says he has set the date as December 7. Huntington is listed in the Cincinnati directory as a member of the firm of Huntington and Brooks, importers of china and glass; his full name is not given.]

To GEORGE B. GOODWIN, CONCORD, SEPTEMBER 22? 1852

[In a letter of September 20, 1852 (RWEMA), George B. Goodwin, corresponding secretary of the Geneseum Society of Genesee College (Lima, New York), invites Emerson to give a lecture. The society proposes to act conjointly with the Athenaeum Society of Rochester. Goodwin asks for a time and terms. In the draft of a letter to Charles H. Peirce of Rochester, Emerson asks that room for a lecture at Lima be allowed in any schedule Peirce can work out for him (*Letters*, 4:316). I conjecture that Emerson let Goodwin know of this intent, without setting a date. The lecture at Lima could not be arranged and should be deleted from Charvat, p. 27, where the question marks against the dates for the lectures at Penn Yan and Elmira can be deleted; see below, December 2, where these dates are secured.]

112. MS in Butler Autographs, CtHi; ph. in NNC. See *Letters*, 4:314, for Shipman's letters of the September 15 and 27. Emerson did not lecture in Hartford in the 1852–1853 season.

To Horatio Greenough, Concord, September 25, 1852 [113]

Concord, 25 September, 1852

My dear Greenough,

I should have replied at once on hearing from you, for I have no more to say now than I had then, but that my hour for writing letters has each day been interrupted. Print, I say, by all means print what you write. The chances are dreadfully against waiting after you have you have got anything to this ripeness. The usefulness of this little book is a commanding reason for printing it; and this to such a theoretic ultilitarian should be much. But I think your name is material to the book.[114] All these opinions & lessons upon houses & furniture & decorating are interesting & authoritative from a sculptor, which the reader would not hold long enough to estimate, if he took up the book as Essays of an amateur. I do not know but I complained of a want of perspective in the book. ⟨It⟩ /The book/ should not, whatever its accidental history be, appear ⟨in the book⟩ as a mere brochure of newspaper articles; for the unity of the thought is apparent enough, & therefore a very little care would give the immensely additional value only varied applications of one thesis. I should say, then, strike out /all/ names & personalities which can be spared, as giving an ephemeral air. Perhaps this applies only to that piece about the critic on Bryant & Durand (Is it Curtis? & certainly the personalities between you & him: [115] superficially, still more important is the suppression of some colloquialisms, some less low, but some intolerable, like nincompoop which is repeated. I have put a few errata on a slip of paper; but the whole pamphlet should have a careful proof-reading.

For the tendency of the whole writing, do not fancy me quite heedless of that, whilst rather we old fellows are only occupied with your central affinities, & delight in the antiquity & eternity of your notes whilst you, (as of course must happen to a doing man,) are more intent on the

113. Ms owned by Mr. David Richardson; ph. in NNC; p. [4] addressed: Horatio Greenough Esq/ Newport R.I./; quoted by Griffin, *NEQ,* 30:511; printed by Wright, pp. 106–107.

114. See Wright, pp. 105–106, for Greenough's letter of September 11; Greenough thinks "the better way will be to let this edition be and only issue a few copies" to solicit criticism.

115. The article appeared in the *New-York Daily Tribune,* May 20, 1852, under the heading "Fine Arts" and is a criticism of Asher Durand's painting of the destruction of Gog and his host. There appears to be no solid evidence that the article is by George William Curtis. For Greenough's reply; see the *Home Journal* of June 19, 1852, and *The Travels . . .* Nathalia Wright, ed. (Gainsville, Fla.: Scholar's Facsimiles & Reprints, 1958), pp. viii–ix and 90–94.

present applications. I see, too, that I must leave you to burn up your own spots like other suns. Yet tis droll to my village eyes, that such a man of the world should share some party crotchets which I have never before found in such dignified heads, such for instance as deep plots of policy ascribed to England, which we commonly think, is only a kind of stupid merchant helping himself by tours de force. For the black question, I see you are incorrigible—for a time.[116] Why offset prostitution against slavery legislation? I do not find the parallelism. We do not ordain prostitution. We ordain kidnapping. Had we tried to force you to prostitution under penalty of a thousand dollars' fine, & jail, you might allege strict parallelism. Besides, the prostitution is not the act of the well-meaning & thoughtful classes who are aggrieved by slavery; —no; but precisely of the overfed & animal class, who at the north, like Slavery, &, at the south are the drivers & breeders. Ah no, slavery is a poor hoggish thing, with which you & I have nothing to do.

I have lent the book to my friend Judge (Rockwood) Hoar, or I do not know but I should try your temper with even a longer letter. Channing & Thoreau, who are both excellent readers, agree with me in the importance of the book Its radical good sense, its reality, & its strong American flavor captivated them also. And the holding back is not to be thought of.

                                                                R. W. E.

To Ainsworth Rand Spofford, Concord, September 30, 1852[117]

                                                    Concord, Sept. 30, 1852.
My dear Sir,

I am arranging my plans to be in Cincinnati as soon as the 7th December the day on which I have written to the Mercantile Library, I can come to them. If now you think I can read a private course to begin about that time, perhaps you may think it well to arrange with Mr Huntington, that I shall come to him on the 14th, instead of the 7th, after our own course is well begun.[118] For I see clearly, that, though I leave home on the 29 Nov.r, I am not likely to reach Ohio before the

116. See *The Travels*, pp. 74–85, for Greenough on slavery, and above, September 6, for Emerson's comment.
117. MS in the Manuscript Division, DLC; ph. in NNC; envelope surcharged at Concord, September 30; printed by C. C. Hollis, *NEQ*, 38:75. The envelope is now missing.
118. H. D. Huntington of the Cincinnati Young Men's Mercantile Library Association. There was no change of date; Emerson opened the private course "The Conduct of Life" on December 9 (Charvat, p. 27).

7th; such are the perturbations caused by those jupiters of towns along the N. Y. railroad. I am in your hands. What are your commands?

R. W. Emerson.

A. R. Spofford.

To Elizabeth Dwight Sedgwick, Concord, October 1? 1852

[See below, October 13, where Emerson tells Caroline Sturgis Tappan that he has written Mrs. Sedgwick. The letter was about placing Ellen Emerson in Mrs. Sedgwick's school.]

To Henry Arthur Bright, Concord, October 2, 1852[119]

Concord
Massachusetts—
Oct. 2, 1852.

My dear Sir,

I send you, agreeably to your request, an autograph of Margaret Fuller's, and, at Mr Burder's suggestion, inclose a second.[120]

It would have given me pleasure to have seen you again, and I am not yet without hope of finding you in Boston.[121] You must not fail, on your return, to carry my kind & respectful rememberances to Mr. Martineau.[122]

Yours with much regard,
R. W. Emerson.

Henry A. Bright, Esq.

119. MS in the collection of the late Norman Holmes Pearson; now in the Beinecke Library, CtY; ph. in NNC. Listed twice by Cameron from Maggs Catalogue 741 (1941), *ESQ* (2d., 1956), 3:5, and (4th q., 1958), 13:39.

120. In a letter from Boston, (a.l.s., undated, endorsed 1852, c. October 1, RWEMA), Bright had written to ask for an autograph of the "Boston Corinne," Margaret Fuller, for his mother, Margaret Jones Bright, a collector.

121. In *Letters*, 4:335, Rusk identifies as Henry Arthur Bright, a "Mr Bright" referred to by Emerson in a letter of December 20, 1852, from Cincinnati, but on Thursday, November 18, n.y. (RWEMA) Bright writes to Emerson from Liverpool, refers to *Henry Esmond* as the newest book, and says the periodical he had told Emerson about had ceased publication while he was abroad. Bright's letter has to be of 1852, for that is the year Thackeray's novel could be called "new." The 18th of November does not fall on a Thursday again until 1858. Emerson's letters from Cincinnati and St. Louis show him to be very weary, as well he might be in this difficult lecture season. He may have given some other English traveler Bright's name. In this letter of November 18, Bright mentions Emerson's friend a Mr. Burder of Liverpool. In a letter to Hawthorne of September 21, Longfellow says that Bright and Burder are on their way to Concord to meet Emerson and Hawthorne (Longfellow, *Letters*, 3:355–356). A note identifies Burder as Thomas Henry Carr Burder.

122. James Martineau.

To Samuel Gray Ward, Concord, October 7, 1852[123]

Concord, 7 Oct. 1852

My dear friend,

Were you not to give me one Sunday before the cold weather? Can you not come next Sunday? You know I am to show you a park[124] and its leaves are already falling. You must come Saturday p m: —at 4 oclock —is best I shall depend on you.

In good hope:
R. W. Emerson.

S. G. Ward.

To George Palmer Putnam, Concord, October 11, 1852[125]

Concord, Mass., Oct. 11, 1852.

Gentlemen:

Nothing could be more agreeable to me than the establishment of an American Magazine of truly elevated and independent tone, and if you shall really and perseveringly attempt that, you shall be sure of my hearty co-operation and aid.[126] Perhaps my interest in such a project is even more serious than your own; but if I were nearer New York than I am, I should immediately seek an interview with you to name certain parties whose concurrence I think important; and now I shall esteem it a favor if you will inform me who, if any there be, in Boston is acquainted with your design, or if none there, what literary man in New York.

Respectfully,
R. W. Emerson.

123. MS in the Ward papers, Houghton Library, MH; ph. in NNC.
124. The "park" is, I believe, the region of Concord known as Eastabrook farms; see *JMN*, 10:360, for Emerson's description of it. The journal entry was used in "Country Life," *Works*, 12:146, and see below, June 6, 1859. The other possibility is Ebenezer Hubbard's woods; see *Letters*, 4:299, and *JMN*, 11:146.
125. No MS has been found; text from George Haven Putnam, 1:177; listed *Letters*, 4:318, which gives also sources for the story of the founding of *Putnam's Monthly Magazine*. Correspondence with other writers is printed by G. H. Putnam.
126. Emerson had long since recognized his hopes for a good magazine as a disease with which he and Lowell were likely to be infected.

To Caroline Sturgis Tappan, Concord, October 13, 1852[127]

> Concord, 13 October
> 1852

Dear Caroline,

When have I breathed a word concerning old papers of mine? Never. Burn them when you will. Or they may come as you propose to my fire[128] Certainly one would not in these autographic days be glad to find them in young gentlemen's albums. I am touched to be remembered so kindly in your woods, & wish I could reply worthily. Still more I wish I could come & spend a day with you. I pray you do not shut the door. For Mrs Sedgwick, I have written to her, have yet no reply.[129] I was a little astonished at your giving her my note to you, & conceived, of course, that I had made some mistake, & this was some proper rebuke.[130] All schools & any school seem to yield the least possible value; the pupil carries thither all she will get. I am only in pursuit of the best <u>alterative</u> as we say of sea voyages. I hate to lose the girl too. Ellen chatters with her mates: with me she is so quiet & intelligent as no one else is. And I, like the rest of the race of papas, to the end that she shall chatter well, give up a year of quiet reason.[131] But I will hope to take up my pen again, —since you give me leave—, with a moment more of time.

> Waldo E

To Benjamin Marston Watson, Concord, October 16? 1852

[In a letter of October 18, 1852 (RWEMA), Benjamin Marston Watson writes that he is glad that Emerson can come to Plymouth on October 24. This Sunday evening lecture is not listed in Charvat. Watson usually paid his lecturers a small fee, but there is no Account Book record of it; see January 15, above.]

127. MS in the Tappan papers, Houghton Library, MH; ph. in NNC. He is here acknowledging her long letter of the 5th, MNS.

128. Emerson later returned to her Mrs. Tappan's letter to him.

129. Emerson reckoned without Mrs. Tappan's inordinate admiration of Charles Sedgwick, of whom she had given Emerson a glowing description in 1846 (see above September 1846). In a letter to Samuel G. Ward, of April 8 [1847], she had written: ". . . tell Mr Sedgwick not to forget I am his ever loving grandchild . . the next time I come to this world I am going to make it a condition that I shall be his child" (Ward papers, Houghton Library).

130. In her reply of October 21 (MH), Mrs. Tappan explains Mrs. Sedgwick's failure to reply; she was out of town.

131. Ellen Emerson attended Mrs. Sedgwick's school for a year and a half, from May 1853 to October 1854.

To John T. Douglass, Concord, October 16, 1852 [132]

Concord ⎱ 16 October
Mass.   ⎰ 1852

Dear Sir,

I am sorry it will not be in my power to come to St. Louis on the 10 November. Some private & some public engagements will keep me at home until the 1 December.[133] I believe, I am promised [134] at Cincinnati for the 7 December; & probably I might come to St. Louis as soon as the 20th, or, perhaps better, directly after Christmas. But if your arrangements require a day as early as November, I shall lose the pleasure of a visit to your city, this season.

Respectfully,
R. W. Emerson.

John T. Douglass, Esq.

To Ainsworth Rand Spofford, Concord, October 19, 1852 [135]

Concord Mass.
19 Oct 1852

My dear Sir,

I hear nothing from you,[136] nor from the Mercantile Lib.y. since I put ⟨y⟩myself in your hands. Meantime, I am urged to this & that, by the people of St Louis,[137] & by other people. ⟨C⟩Have the goodness to tell me at once whether you or your neighbors have promised anything from me, & if so, what. Today I learn, with regret, by a letter from Clough,

132. MS in the papers of MoSM; ph. in NNC; printed by John Francis McDermott, *ESQ* (1st q., 1957), 6:7. The addressee is listed in St. Louis directories as John T. Douglass of the storage firm of Douglass & Beer.

133. Emerson changed a number of lecture engagements in expectation of Clough's arrival. He gave St. Louis seven lectures on "The Conduct of Life" beginning after Christmas, December 27 (Charvat, pp. 27–28). See *Letters*, 4:314, for the original arrangement. This letter of October 16 apparently went astray. See below, November 4 and December 7. And see October 19 for Clough's unsettling change of plans.

134. Emerson rarely uses an end-line hyphen. When he does so, he may use a double hyphen, as he does here after "prom" falling at the end of a line.

135. MS in the Manuscript Division, DLC; ph. in NNC; envelope surcharged at Concord October 14; printed by C. C. Hollis, *NEQ*, 38:75–76. The envelope is now missing.

136. Spofford, in a letter of October 17 which crossed this one, explains the delay.

137. See letters to John T. Douglass above, October 16, and, below, November 4 and December 7.

that he sails not till 30 Oct., to arrive here probably 30 Nov.;[138] just as I am departing for Ohio! So make me as late as you can.[139]

Yours,

R. W. Emerson

A. R. Spofford.

To Horatio Greenough, Concord, October 21, 1852[140]

Concord, 21 Oct. 1852.

My dear Greenough,

I am very happy that you will come to see me. I wish it were today. But I go to Plymouth, on Saturday, for two days. Then, Tuesday shall be my day. Cannot you come on Tuesday, leaving Boston at 12 noon? We will let you go down on the next day or the next after, if it prove stormy weather. Send me a line that Tuesday suits you; if not, name the day after. Here are some lines from Martial which fit you.[141] My wife depends on seeing you.

Yours

R. W. Emerson

Horatio Greenough.

138. Emerson's efforts to ensure his being home to welcome Clough and introduce him to helpful friends obliged him to cancel engagements made in Western New York and to rearrange others.

139. This season of 1852–1853 is the first of a series of strenuous programs (for others as well as Emerson); improved means of transportation opened up the Middle West to the Eastern lecturer.

140. MS owned by Mr. David Richardson; ph. in NNC; addressed, p. [4]; Horatio Greenough, Esq./ Care of Henry Greenough, Esq/ Cambridge./ Mass./; printed by Wright, *HLB*, (Winter, 1958), 12:108.

141. In a journal entry of October 14, Emerson reminds himself to send Greenough, Martial's Epigram to Faustinus, *JMN*, 13:86, and in an entry in MS journal TU (11:26) he notes that he has done so. (This entry has to be later than this letter of 1852; the editors of the journal appear to assume that all entries in TU are of 1849.) Emerson has misnumbered the epigram as Lib. I.26; it is the 25th. His enclosed version reads:

Ede tuos tandem populo, Faustine, libellos,
  Et cultum docto pectore profer opus:
Quod nec Cecropiae damnent Pandionis arces,
  Nec sileant nostri, praetereantque senes.
Ante fores stantem dubitas admittere famam?
  Teque piget curae praemia ferre tuae?
Post te victurae, per te quoque vivere, chartae
  Incipiant: cineri gloria sera venit.

To Arthur Helps, Concord, October? 25? 1852[142]

& which will make the period memorable. Your proverbs & sentences I read & remember; and, one day, somewhere, (What days & wheres are ours, God knoweth!) I shall hold you to give me more of the same sense. One effect, too, the story wrought,—I lamented, I believe, for the first time, my total ignoran[ce] of the Spanish tongue, which, I had fancied, was the least of my sins. But the book is new, & must gain a little perspective by time, before we can measure it.[143] Yet I assure myself of many a good friend, in this country, who will read it gladly. It is a little too soon (I hope only a little,) to have the benefit of copyright here.

I know not what I can tell you of interest here. We have, however, a superior man, whom I have seen much lately, Horatio Greenough, a sculptor, long in Florence, & now employed in part by our government at Washington, who threatens to use the pen better than he did his chisel, (which however he handled well,) and sends me a brochure full of good sense about Architecture, Beauty, & the dangerous topics.[144] But my men at home here are no authors,[145]—those I mean whom I should show you, & you would see with the most interest. But do you know that Oxford Clough is coming hither to spend some weeks with me? Meantime, all blessings rest on the house, on the hill [a]t Bishops Waltham.

R. W. Emerson

Mr Helps.

142. MS (defective) in the Barrett Collection, Alderman Library, ViU, ph. in NNC; listed with the conjectured date September 4, *Letters*, 4:311, from the evidence of Helps' reply of May 9, 1853 (RWMEA), and a letter of September 4, 1852, to Charles Eliot Norton. The allusion to Bishops Waltham puts the identity of the addressee beyond doubt.

Before September 4, Charles Eliot Norton sent Emerson the American reprint (from a private English printing) of Arthur Helps' article on *Uncle Tom's Cabin;* on September 4 Emerson tells Norton that the reprint gives him an occasion to write to Helps (*Letters*, 4:310–311 and n. 155). The missing first page of this letter is very likely about the article (it appeared in *Fraser's Magazine*, August 12). The letter had to be written after September 2, when Horatio Greenough sent Emerson his brochure (*Letters*, 4:312, n. 160), and before November 12, when Arthur Hugh Clough arrived in Boston (*Letters*, 4:324, no. 203). A letter to Sumner of October 16 (*Letters*, 4:319) shows that Helps was then recalled to Emerson's thought, probably by the same pamphlet. I date the letter late in October after Greenough's second visit to Emerson (see October 21 above), for two visits seem more nearly to fulfill Emerson's report of having "seen much" of Greenough.

143. Helps' *Companions in My Solitude* was published by Munroe in 1852; see above, June 13, 1851.

144. Slavery; Greenough's views were in some respects, eccentric; see above, September 25, and below, November 11, for Emerson's objections.

145. Emerson's men are probably Alcott, Ellery Channing, and Thoreau (see above, July 14, 1851, for evidence that Emerson would not expect an English correspondent to have read Thoreau's *The Week*). However much Emerson admired his "men at home," his opinion of their writing was always qualified by criticism.

To Derick Lane, Concord, October 27? 1852

[In a letter of October 25, 1852 (RWEMA), Derick Lane asks Emerson to confirm his engagement to lecture in Troy, New York, on November 25; see *Letters,* 4:316–317, for note of Lane's letter of October 5. It is to his letter of October 5 that Lane wants an answer.]

To Edward Brooks Hall, Concord? October 27? 1852

[In a letter of October 26, 1852 (RWEMA), Edward Brooks Hall asks for Emerson's recollections of Mary L. Ware whose life Hall proposes to write. Examination of the 1867 printing of the book *Memoir of Mary L. Ware* (Harding, p. 125), now in the Emerson house, shows no passages that can be attributed to Emerson. Hall mentions the recollections of correspondents but gives no names. Emerson would not, I think, have ignored Hall's letter. See, above, October 9, 1827, and December 21, 1836.]

To Ainsworth Rand Spofford, Concord, October 29, 1852 [146]

Concord⎤ 29 October
Mass. ⎦ 1852

My dear Sir,

It is unpardonable to wait so long before replying to your letter of the 17th. But, I fancied, I might hear so decisive a concurrence of my correspondents at Buffalo & elsewhere, with my petition for a new & later day, that I might wish to obtain grace of you also in the same way. At any rate, I am glad you have settled with Mr Huntington, for the 14th, which is better than the 7th.[147] My misfortune is, that, I have lately learned from Clough,[148] that he takes the packet of 30 Oct., instead of

146. MS in the Manuscript Division, DLC; ph. in NNC; envelope (now missing) postmarked at Concord October 29; printed by C. C. Hollis, *NEQ,* 38:76.

147. See Charvat, p. 27, for the final Cincinnati schedule, and see September 18, above.

148. See October 19 above, the day on which he learned of Clough's change of plan, necessitating a revision of the schedule for New York State sent him by E. Carlton Sprague of Buffalo on October 18; see *Letters,* 4:319, where, from Sprague's letter, seven towns are listed; of these Emerson was able to visit only two, Troy and Rochester. See Charvat, p. 27.

From letters to Emerson, not consulted by Charvat, it is possible to delete the questioned lecture at Lima, for Genessee College; a letter from Charles H. Peirce (Rochester) clearly rules out this engagement, for the college was closed between November 26 and December 2. From letters to Emerson of November 30 from George G. Riley (of Rochester) and Emily Mervine Drury (of Canandaigua), the dates of November 30 for Palmyra, December 1 for Penn Yan, December 2 for Elmira, and December 3 for Canandaigua are all confirmed. This final schedule is surely no more inconvenient than that originally proposed by Sprague (of Buffalo), which would have entailed backtracking from Buffalo to Auburn and Oswego.

When Emerson left for his first engagement in Troy (November 25), he still expected to go to Buffalo (see *Letters,* 4:323), but on the 29th, E. C. Sprague (who had not been noticeably accommodating) wrote that he had secured "Mr Hudson" (probably Henry N. Hudson) to take Emerson's place. (The Buffalo directory for 1851 lists E. Carlton Sprague

the 15th, as had been settled, & so may arrive here on the very days when I should depart. After making many arrangements, all ⟨to⟩ I could do, on ⟨l⟩receiving this letter, was, to ask these western N. Yorkers to excuse me until my return from Ohio. If they accede, —& they seem to say they will no[w—] I may get 3 or 4 important days, in which to assist Mr C. by making him acquainted with persons who may be useful to him.[149] It is possible that I may yet beg you to reprieve me for that first week, & let the 14th be my first appearance, though I see the disadvantage. For the particulars of the Hall, & tickets, I have no opinion; &, if you are at a loss about the first, toss up a cent for an answer: for the second, I lean, as you do, to low prices.

Ever your obliged

A. R. Spofford.   R. W. Emerson.

TO GEORGE WILLIAM CURTIS, CONCORD, NOVEMBER 1, 1852 [150]

Concord, 1 Nov. 1852

My dear Sir,

You will have inferred from my slowness to reply, that my article was not done, copied, stitched, & in the pigeon hole waiting to go. For all that I am heartily glad that you will make this experiment, which, though often made before, I ⟨never⟩ feel never to have been quite rightly made. If I were a little younger, —ten years or so, —I should volunteer to be of the direction.[151] As it is, I am quite sure to write in spring & summer, if you can hold the Journal to any thing like literature & humanity, & away from that moribund respectability, to which every thing American tends. Can you not engage Horatio Greenough in it? He is full of thoughts, & with a power of expression like Canning.[152] Weiss of New Bedford

---

of the firm of Houghton and Sprague.) See *Letters*, 4:322, for note of two telegrams relating to these New York engagements. A MS Account Book (1849–1853) entry of November, n.d., but after the 9th and before the 17th, records (p. 229) the payment of $4.79 to the telegraph office.

149. Emerson gave a dinner for Clough on November 20 at the Tremont House, where he introduced his guest of honor to the literary men of Boston and Cambridge; Clough found himself welcome in more than one circle, thanks to his own charm and Emerson's choice of guests; see Clough's letters from America in Mulhauser's edition.

150. MS in the Curtis papers, Houghton Library, MH; ph. in NNC.

151. See October 11 above. Curtis, with Charles F. Biggs and Parke Godwin, was editing George Palmer Putnam's new magazine. Emerson is being facetious in this first sentence.

152. See *Letters*, 4:312, and September 6 above, for the same comparison with George Canning. Canning was known for his sarcasm; the comparison cannot be an altogether unmixed compliment in spite of Emerson's readiness to admire wit even when, like that of Ellery Channing, it was touched with malice. Two journal entries perhaps explain a comparison which is otherwise vague. In an entry of October 30, 1835, he quotes this judgment:

ought to be engaged to go to New York, & work in it.[153] And Lowell is now [on] his way home.[154] I have several more names in my bag; but these are enough for today.

Yours,
R. W. Emerson—

C. W. Curtis, Esq.

To Horatio Greenough, Concord, November 1, 1852 [155]

Concord, 1 November 1852

My dear Greenough,

I have looked through the book again, and I do not quite find any chapter which I like to suppress. The brush with the Tribune is the one I had first marked: [156] but that contains good sense, &, with a little dropping of the compliments, on which I must insist, that may stand. The chapter on Webster's nightcap of course, cannot now stand, unless with some grave & generous preamble inserted.[157] For that on chastity, —you must judge for yourself.[158] I like it well enough. That on abolition, I have told you, is bad: if you print it, we will roast you. The Illinois bank-note, again,[159]—whether you keep these lighter craft must depend on how much solider matter you may find in your portfolio. Some or all of the Preface, I could willingly spare,—if I came to particulars,—for instance, the first page. But there is no end of this paring & chipping, when one begins, and I will stuff my cavils into my Errata. Rather than not publish, if the sponge & interpolation take too much time, print away, good & bad, with all my heart; and suddenly.

" 'Mr Canning was always great when he was jocular & always small when he was serious' " (*JMN*, 5:106). In a passage headed "Eloquence," Emerson writes: "In Brit. Parliament all the renowned speakers can go to any length on a new subject & unexpected. The extempore harangues of Canning & Mackintosh are however interlarded with elaboratt & finely turned periods that smell of the lamp ..." (*JMN*, 6:132). The ready talker was likely to win Emerson's admiration; *e.q.*, Alcott and Margaret Fuller.

Of Emerson's friendship with Greenough, Richard Henry Dana, Jr., remarked unkindly that "Emerson was friendly with Greenough only when he was crazy" (*Journal*, 2:523).

153. Early in 1852 John Weiss had written Emerson that he would like to leave the church and engage in literary work (*Letters*, 4:279).

154. See November 17 below. Lowell traveled on the same ship as Clough (and as Thackeray, bound on a lecture tour).

155. MS owned by Mr. David Richardson; ph. in NNC; printed by Wright, *HLB*, (Winter, 1958), 12:109.

156. See September 25 above.

157. See Greenough's *The Travels*, pp. 110–112; Webster is not named, but the details identify him.

158. Chapter 2, pp. 51–60, "The Virtue of Chastity."

159. Chapter 5, pp. 106–110, "Bank Note Typography."

I see /p./ good strictures on Academy Education, abroad.[160] W. H. Furness, Jr. a young artist,—crayon sketches,—son of Dr F. of Phila., told me in the street, a day or two since, he goes presently to Dusseldorf.[161] I said remembering the feats or sublime of drawing-school exercise which I had lately seen in the Dusseldorf gallery,[162]—"Do the masters say that is wisest? if Mr Greenough were in Boston, I should send you to him to ask." Or, is it best, the boys should all go somewhere, for a kind of shock & salubrious alterative in their training?

You have done me a world of good by a pair of conversations. May I often see you!

R. W. Emerson

H. Greenough.

To John T. Douglass, Concord, November 3, 1852

[Telegram repeating gist of letter of October 16, see above, which apparently went astray. The MS Account Book for 1849–1853, p. [228], entry of November 3, records the cost ($2.78) of this telegram under the date November 3.]

To John T. Douglass, Concord, November 4, 1852[163]

Concord ⎱ Nov 4 1852
Mass.   ⎰

Dear Sir,

I had yesterday a telegraphic note from you announcing that you expect me at St. Louis on the 20 November. Immediately on receiving your letter of 5 Oct. I wrote you by mail that certain engagements & mainly, the unexpected arrival of a friend from England, will detain me at home until /about/ 7 December; that, from that ⟨da⟩time I am engaged at Cincinnati, for a fortnight; & that I could not therefore hope to be at St Louis earlier than from about Christmas. This letter, it would seem you have not received.[164] I sent you, ⟨a⟩today, a telegraphic dispatch to the same purport. I am very sorry that this failure in our correspondence

---

160. Chapter 7, pp. 120–216, "Remarks on American Art."
161. Young Furness was to study in Düsseldorf, Germany.
162. The Düsseldorf Gallery in New York is referred to here.
163. MS in the papers of MoSM; ph. in NNC; printed by McDermott, *ESQ* (1st q., 1957), 6:7.
164. See October 16 above.

should have occurred. If the date of 24 or 25 December is too late for your convenience, I must postpone my visit to St. Louis for another year.

Respectfully yours,

R. W. Emerson

J. T. Douglass, Esq.

To John T. Douglass, Concord, November 5, 1852

[A second telegram to John T. Douglass is listed in the MS Account Book for 1849–1853, p. [229] under the date November 5; see *ESQ* (1st q, 1957), 6:4. The cost of the second telegram is $4.79. Which of the two telegrams is the one Emerson refers to in the letter above is not clear.]

To Edwin Percy Whipple, Concord, November 6, 1852

[MS listed in Carnegie Bookshop Catalogue (1972) 318, lot 131. See *Letters*, 4:321. Obliged to break upstate New York lecture engagements because of the expected arrival of Arthur Hugh Clough, Emerson asks Whipple to take his place. See *Letters*, 4:322.]

To J Prince, Concord, November 7, 1852

[See *Letters*, 4:317, for Emerson's original offer of January 26 as the date for a lecture in Essex, Massachusetts. Emerson entered January 26 in his tentative list in the Account Book for 1849–1853, p. [294]; he has, however, deleted it, entering Essex under February 3, the final date. See Charvat, p. 28, where the questioned entry for a second lecture on February 15 should be deleted.]

To Charles Mason, Concord, November 8, 1852

[Emerson's letter of November 8 to Charles Mason of Fitchburg seen in Altman's (December 2, 1981). Emerson is answering Mason's letter of October 29 (RWEMA) asking for a lecture. Emerson offers February 22 or 23. Presumably the dates were not acceptable, and there may have been further correspondence. Emerson does not enter Fitchburg in his tentative list in the MS Account Book for 1849–1853 (p. [294]. In the MS Pocket Diary for 1853, Fitchburg appears against the date March 1 (*JMN*, 13:476) and in Charvat, p. 28, with a question mark; no receipt from Fitchburg appears in the MS Account Book.]

To Thomas Starr King, Concord, November 10, 1852 [165]

Concord] 10 Nov.r 1852
Mass]

My dear Sir,

The necessity of waiting at home for my English friend Clough, (who has unexpectedly changed his time for sailing & so for arriving here) has made me suddenly beg to be released from an engagement to western N.Y. on certain days from Nov 24 to Dec 1.[166] The Lyceums there entreat me to supply my place. Whipple cannot go. I have seen Holmes, who cannot go. Cannot you go? I enclose the letter of the Syracuse Secretary which tells all the details. I suppose you are going, in the cause. If not, then go now, in the name of literature, mercy, & peace!

Please to send me back a favorable answer, which, I know, I have only a right to expect from that magnanimity which removes mountain. ⟨T⟩and, also please send me back the Secretary's letter.

In the best hope,
R. W. Emerson

T. Starr King.

To Horatio Greenough, Concord, November 11, 1852 [167]

Concord
11 Nov.r 1852

My dear Greenough,

I sent the book by mail this morn.g,[168] & now enclose the chapter. I am sorry that a mountain of letters which the ridiculous trade of lecturing piles up for me added to some other imperative circumstances at home, have left me no leisure to write you at once, & as I would, on this appendix. But though the piece has its merits, & may well go with its antecedent, it is very splendidly wasted powder, & all makes only more

---

165. MS in the Edward Laurence Doheny Library, CCamarSJ; ph. in NNC. Damage repaired by gauze does not affect the text. Listed *Letters*, 4:322.

166. See *Letters*, 4:319, 320, 322, for entries noting letters from the Secretary E. Carlton Sprague of Buffalo. Some of the towns were willing to accept a change of date.

167. MS owned by Mr. David Richardson; ph. in NNC; printed by N. Wright, *HLB* (Winter, 1958), 12:110–111.

168. The chapter referred to is, I infer, the "more words 'in behalf of this Falstaff,' " that Greenough had sent with his letter of November 4 and asked for in his letter of the 10th (Wright, p. 110). In the second of these letters, Greenough had asked for the whole book because he wished to use it for lectures.

flagrant this new example of genius spent in a bad cause. Indeed, the whole thing ranges itself under the dread old category of liberty & necessity, all the reason begin on one side, all experience on the other. hence, in dialectics, it is pertinent to argue for slavery, but to practical purpose tis reckoned the high absurd, as if, finding my knave disposed to steal, I should expound to him the eternal foreordination, & the irresponsibility of men

I sent you my copy, but must have it again without fail.

Yours faithfully
R. W. Emerson

Horatio Greenough.

TO EDGAR L. HIGHLY AND SAMUEL MOSLEY, CONCORD, NOVEMBER 12?, 1852

[In a letter of November 10, 1852 (RWEMA), Edgar L. Highly and Samuel Mosley of the Palmyra Young Men's Association ask Emerson to lecture on his way to or from Rochester. Emerson's Rochester correspondent Charles H. Peirce does not mention Palmyra in any of his communications; I infer that Emerson set this date, November 30, himself. It is confirmed by Emily Drury's letter of November 30 (RWEMA) saying she cannot go to Palmyra to hear him "tonight."]

TO JAMES RUSSELL LOWELL, CONCORD, NOVEMBER 17, 1852 [169]

Concord Wednesday
17 Novr

My dear Lowell,

Joy to you & yours & to us all, that you are come home again. In fault of being able to come & see you today, I write to to beg you to come & dine with me, to meet Mr Clough & a few other friends, at the Tremont House, Boston, at 3 o'clock, on Saturday; & greatly help & comfort [170]

Yours
R. W. Emerson.

J. R. Lowell, Esq.

169. MS in the Berg Collection, NN; ph. in NNC; listed in *Letters*, 4:322, from auction catalogue.
170. Lowell preserved with this letter a menu card signed by all the guests. Two other invitations follow below. The guests were, besides Lowell, Longfellow, Hawthorne, Samuel Gray Ward, James Elliot Cabot, Theodore Parker, Edward Bangs, William Ellery Channing, Horatio Greenough.

To Henry Wadsworth Longfellow, Concord, November 17, 1852 [171]

Concord 17 Novr

Dear Longfellow,

Will you not give me the pleasure to come & dine with me, to meet Mr Clough, & a few other friends, at the Tremont House, on Saturday, at 3 o'clk p.m., & greatly oblige yours faithfully,

R. W. Emerson

H. W. Longfellow, Esq.

To Henry A. Page, Concord, November 17, 1852 [172]

Concord, 17 Nov. 1852

My dear Sir,

I have been absent from home a couple of days, or your friendly note should have had an instant reply. I am very glad to be remembered by you, & so kindly at this time I have never heard & only seen once Mr Johnson,[173] but I have uniformly heard a very high ⟨opinion⟩ esteem expressed for him by our common friends I should be very glad to hear these lectures whose fame I have already heard, & it would please me heartily, & my wife also, to come to your house. But none of these things can now be. I am to go to Cincinnati, & still farther west, either next week or the following, & shall probably be gone six weeks or more with I know not how many engagements on my return.[174] My wife has tried to show me how I can accept the invitation for one of the days /& for both of us/. But it will not quite appear. So please to give my kindest remembrances to Mrs Page, & tell her, I wish to keep the door still ajar, till I have a little more leisure.

Your affectionate servant,

R. W. Emerson

Henry A. Page.

171. MS in the Longfellow papers, Houghton Library, MH; ph. in NNC. This letter escaped from Craigie House, hence its listing by Cameron in *ESQ* (1st q, 1957), 6:27; it has since been returned to the Longfellow papers. See Samuel Longfellow, *Life*, 2:244.

172. MS in the Feinberg collection, MiD; ph. in NNC; printed by White, *AL* (May 1961), 33:165–166. Henry Page of Medford, where Emerson had lectured in the 1851–1852 season; see above, April 6.

173. I infer from Lidian Emerson's apparent eagerness to hear the lectures that Mr. Johnson is Oliver Johnson, anti-slavery leader. See *Letters*, 4:476, 490, 491, for Emerson's later connection with Johnson.

174. Emerson's serenity must have been under a severe strain in this hectic season. See *Letters*, 4:323–324, and 325–326, which show him to be as weary as he had been harassed.

To Thomas Wentworth Higginson, Concord,
November 17, 1852 [175]

Concord
Nov 17 1852

My dear Sir,

I have been much indebted to you lately for two sermons first Mr Wasson's, which I read with su⟨p⟩rprise & pleasure, & which fully justifies the good opinion you expressed of him: [176] secondly, your own which I read with great satisfaction; only—I remember—one sentence with great humility. [177] Both these pieces my wife & her sister have also duly read & pondered.

I wish I knew what to say about Ellery. [178] He never shows me anything he writes nor even that he is writing anything. I am glad if he has written lectures & Biography is a very promising topic for him,—promising to avoid the sand without lime or lime without sand style of the old ones. Nobody knows better than he the genius & quality of the men he reads of. I am crowded for time with a new English friend Clough here & a mountain of letters it happens just now to write & I am going off on the instant. But if I can wile out of Ellery any account of his plans I will.

Yours gratefully,
R. W. Emerson

T. W. Higginson.

175. MS in the Feinberg collection, MiD; ph. in NNC; printed by White, *AL* (May 1961), 33:165.

176. David Wasson's *A Sermon Delivered . . . On Fast Day,* April 8, 1852 (Boston, 1852).

177. Higginson's most recent publication was his sermon of October 31, *Elegy without Fiction) (BAL,* 8210), but he may have sent Emerson his sermon on his installation as minister of the Worcester Free Church, *Things New and Old (BAL,* 8209).

178. Higginson's first wife was Ellery Channing's sister Mary; Higginson became involved in the marital difficulties of his feckless brother-in-law and assumed responsibility for advising and helping Ellen Channing and her children when the separation came. He has evidently inquired of Emerson what Ellery's prospects are for work. (There is evidence that Samuel Gray Ward was a large contributor to Channing's upkeep; Channing certainly did very little for himself.) Higginson's first wife appears to have been like her brother in temperament; Higginson was perhaps the more sympathetic to Ellen Channing.

To Horatio Greenough, Concord, November 17, 1852 [179]

Concord 17 Novr

Dear Greenough

Will you not help & oblige me by coming to dine with me to meet Clough, & a few other friends, at the Tremont House, Boston, next Saturday at 3 p.m.

Yours faithfully,
R. W. Emerson

Horatio Greenough.

To Francis B. Eaton, Concord, November ? 1852

[In a letter of September 1, 1852 (RWEMA), F. B. Eaton of Manchester, New Hampshire, asks for a lecture for the Lyceum and proposes December 4. An undated printed folder (probably of October) listing the lectures for the season has Emerson down for January 5, 1853. Eaton writes Emerson that, if that date is not convenient, he invites him for February 2. Emerson enters his Manchester engagement under the date February 2 in the tentative list, p. [294], of his MS Account Book for 1849–1853 and in his MS Pocket Diary for 1853 (*JMN*, 13:475). Since Emerson's Western trip did not begin to take shape until late October, I conjecture that he did not accept the offer of February 2 before November. It is likely that the addressee is Francis B. Eaton, librarian of the Manchester Atheneum, 1854–1863. Maurice D. Clarke, *Manchester: A Brief Record of Its Past and a Picture of Its Present*, Manchester, N. H.: John B. Clarke, 1875, p. 89.]

To Charles H. Peirce, Concord, November 19, 1852

[In a letter of November 19, 1852 (Goodspeed's, August 1977), Emerson promises Charles H. Peirce to lecture in Rochester, New York, November 29 and December 2 as Peirce had asked in his letter of November 16 (RWEMA); see *Letters*, 4:322, for a note of Emerson's telegram of that date. In the letter of the 19th, Emerson asks of Peirce can arrange for a third lecture on the 1st or 3rd of December "at not too great distance." See December 2 below for the actual schedule and corrections of Charvat.]

To James T. Fisher, Concord, November 20? 1852

[In a letter of November 19, 1852 (RWEMA), James T. Fisher encloses a letter "filled with the names of your friends" asking Emerson for an address on the character of Daniel Webster. Rusk's conjecture that Emerson refused (*Life*, p. 368) seems reasonable; yet he had something to say of Webster, see *JMN*, 13:111–112.]

179. MS owned by Mr. David Richardson, ph. in NNC; printed by Nathalia Wright, *HLB* (Winter 1958), 12:111.

To George Merrick Brooks, Troy, New York, November 26, 1852[180]

Troy, N. Y.

Nov. 26 1852

My dear Sir,

I wish to ask your professional aid in a little affair. Some time since, my brother William at the request of my mother, caused to be drawn up the enclosed Will of my mother. As he rather wished to gratify her than to keep all the forms, he allowed the children, his own & mine, to sign it as witnesses, there being no suitable witnesses, at the time, present. On his return to N. Y. he reflected, that the thing was informal, & desired me to copy the instrument & have it properly witnessed.[181] I have neglected to do this but at coming away from home for several weeks I considered it not proper to omit it; & asked my mother for the paper to leave with you to transcribe & ⟨execute⟩see signed. In leaving town, I had not time to see you & now enclose it with the request that you will copy it or make out a new instrument to the same effect, & carry it to my mother & have it properly signed & witnessed. I believe my mother intends on my brother's return to Concord to consult with him on some alternations or additions; but I advised her & you may perhaps find it best to advise her to content herself, at present, with simply establishing this much, & awaiting William's visit, in the spring, for any additions.

I shall see you on my return, & am, meantime,

Yours with great regard,

R. W. Emerson

George M. Brooks, Esq.

To Lydia Jackson Emerson, Elmira, N. Y., December 2, 1852[182]

Elmira, N. Y.

2 Dec. 1852

Dear Lidian

I trust you got safely a letter I despatched to you with money /$10.00/ & ⟨a⟩ /my/ cheque on the Atlantic Bank, dated, in advance, 8 Dec., for

180. MS in Special Collections, Mugar Library, MBU; ph. in NNC; p. [4] addressed: George M. Brooks, Esq./ Concord—/ Massachusetts./; postmarked at Troy, N.Y., November 26.

181. In a letter of November 22, 1852, Emerson acknowledges his brother's letter concerning their "mother's affairs"; he says there he hopes "to get our part done" (*Letters*, 4:324).

182. MS owned by the Raymond Emerson estate; ph. in NNC; listed *Letters*, 4:326.

$100., enclosed. If you have not had this letter, tell Mr Adams that I have sent it & he will stop the payment of the cheque I believe it was payable to the order of Mr Cheney.[183]

I have been well & kindly treated in this country with the exception that the rogue reporters systematically steal my lectures, &, if I dare read aloud a single sentence, they print it. Nor can I go where a newspaper is not printed. I have read a lecture at Penn Yan last night & shall here, tonight.[184] Tomorrow at Canandaigua again, where lives my friend Mrs Drury.[185] Thence to Cincinnati as fast as I can. I have been sorry not to sit down anywhere long enough to write you a letter & tell you many things that occurred to add to the table of memoranda I left on the mantelpiece. A lonely man here in an ampitheater of mountains by Chemung Creek, I miss my boy, I miss my girls, Let them send me word to Cincinnati, how Virgil or Aeneas wanders ⟨in⟩down to Acheron,[186] & how Long Division prospers, & whether we have got to sentences again in the Latin grammar.

Tell John to give the horse no grain when he does not work, or the horse will master the man. John must pull up all those beanpoles /in the field/, which, I forgot to tell him to carry under the shed.[187] I shall immediately send you money, probably $100. & you must pay $50. as quick as you can, on Mr Jones's bill for the furnace.[188]

Best let Aug. Adams carry it[189] I trust Mamma walks firm with her sticks. I trust Sarah & & Kate & the other girls are contented.[190] The rest of my trusts you shall read next time.

R. W. E.

183. The letter of November 26, *Letters*, 4:325–326. Abel Adams and John Milton Cheney are referred to here.

184. See Charvat, p. 27; this letter makes the Penn Yan and Elmira dates secure.

185. Emily Mervine Drury.

186. Ellen Emerson, December 20 (RWEMA), reports that Aeneas has just been landed by Charon & is bearing Cerberus' three heads back.

187. Probably John Clahan, the handyman.

188. The MS Account Book for 1849–1853, p. [233], under January records the payment of $60.00 to "E." Jones and Son; later entries give the firm name correctly as L. Jones & Son; Lewis Jones & Son, stove manufacturer, is listed in Boston directories of 1852. Other entries record payments he had directed Lidian to make in his letter of November 26. As a marginal note records, he has copied these entries from a letter to him.

189. Augustus Adams, the express man.

190. The hired girls.

To John T. Douglass, Cincinnati, December 7, 1852 [191]

Burnet House
Cincinnati
7 December 1852

Dear Sir,

I find here your note forwarded to me from Concord & thank you for your kind care to make all plain again.[192]

I ⟨&⟩ learn here that by the best arrangement my friends could make for me I shall be detained here until the morning of the 21 instant, when I shall set out for St. Louis.

Will you, then, have the goodness to arrange beforehand the best order of evenings[193] to suit the convenience of the Mercantile Library for the six Lectures, and communicate it to me. Perhaps the best order of subjects though not quite the natural order will be—

Conduct of Life

Lecture	I	Power
	II	Wealth
	III	Economy
	IV	Fate
	V	Culture
	VI	Worship

If I can stave off the threatened report in full of the Lecture I have read tonight on "the Anglosaxon." I shall like to add that as a volunteer; for as it is my newest, I fancy it. We will make it a compliment to the Mercantile Library if they can find a corner for it within the fortnight, but they shall not be bound to go & hear it.

Respectfully,
R. W. Emerson

J. T. Douglass, Esq.

To George Ware Briggs, Cincinnati? December 7? 1852

[In a letter of December 14 (RWEMA) to Lidian Emerson, George Briggs of Plymouth says he has received a letter from Emerson offering February 7 or 14

191. MS in the papers of MoSM; ph. in NNC; printed by McDermott, *ESQ* (1st q., 1957), 6:8; listed *Letters,* 4:326.

192. See above October 16 and November 4, and below December 20.

193. McDermott has "evening,"; the singular makes no sense here; Emerson's final "s" is sometimes unclear, especially if it follows a "g" or any descending or ascending letter. The "s" is clear in the manuscript.

or any date in that interval for a lecture in Plymouth. Emerson was replying to Briggs' letter of December 1 (RWEMA), asking for a date in January other than the 3rd Briggs' letter had to have been forwarded to Cincinnati (see *Letters*, 4:325, 327); an answer earlier than December 7 is unlikely. As the lecture schedule now stands (Charvat, p. 28), he could not have conveniently gone to Plymouth; the MS Account Book schedule (p. 294 of Account Book of 1849–1853) does not show a lecture for Plymouth.]

To Dwight Foster, Cincinnati, December 8, 1852

[Rusk lists this letter under the conjectured date of December 20; but the Pocket Diary for 1853, *JMN*, 13:476, shows that it was written on December 8. Under the date February 24, 1853, Emerson writes: "Worcester? if D F writes Dec. 8." See *Letters*, 4:343–344, for Foster's not writing. The MS Pocket Diary entry is crossed out in pencil and under the dates March 31 and April 7 "Worcester" is entered in pencil. There was only one lecture in Worcester.]

To Nelson Sizer, Cincinnati, December? 8? 1852

[On October 30, 1852, and again on November 24 (RWEMA), N. Sizer of New York reminds Emerson that after his lecture of February 10, he had been invited to lecture again for the People's Course at the Tabernacle (see Charvat, p. 27). In his first letter Sizer outlines the method of profit sharing to be employed and gives as his references Horace Greeley, William Cullen Bryant, and Henry J. Raymond. The second letter lists the speakers already engaged and hopes for the addition of Emerson's name. Some letter to Sizer seems to be indicated by the entry of his name and the address, 131 Nassau Street, against the date January 25 in the Pocket Diary for 1853 (*JMN*, 13:475); this entry is the source of Charvat's listing, p. 28. And as late as January 11 Emerson expected to be lecturing in New York (*Letters*, 4:343). The odd sum of $76.71 sent him by his brother (February 15 and 16, 1853; see *Letters*, 55:345), might be the money for a lecture; cf. the $83. received in 1852; the entry of February 18 (p. [234] in the Account Book for 1849–1853 describes the payment as "on a/c by draft." Since Sizer's letter of November 24 had to be forwarded to him, I conjecture that Emerson could not have answered it before he came to rest for his lectures in Cincinnati. There may have been an earlier letter, but Sizer's second letter does not imply that Emerson had answered the first one. No Sizer is listed at 131 Nassau Street, but that is the address of the Phrenological Cabinet familiar to Walt Whitman and to others who had their bumps read. nelson Sizer was well-known as a phrenologist. He is listed at 102 Nassau Street in 1851–1852 directories, his occupation given as a publisher. Sizer's references, the three newspaper owner-editors, make it likely that he is Emerson's correspondent. Moreover, Emerson's correspondent of 1851 (see above, December 24, 1851) was the phrenologist Samuel Robert Wells (future publisher of *Leaves of Grass*), with whom the lecture of February 10, 1852, had been arranged.]

To George? W. Churchill, Cincinnati, December 8, 1852

[In the MS Pocket Diary for 1853, *JMN*, 13:476, Emerson enters the town Lowell against the date March 2, 1853, and adds "if G W Churchill writes at once Dec 8." No receipt of a fee from Lowell appears in the MS Account Book for 1849–1853, from which I infer that Emerson wrote Churchill who did not reply in time, but the entry in the Pocket Diary is not deleted. A George W. Churchill, physician, is listed in a Lowell directory for 1852.]

To John T. Douglass, Telegram, Cincinnati, December 20, 1852

[This telegram reads simply "approved"; see McDermott, *ESQ* (1st q., 1957), 6:8. It cannot be, as McDermott assumes, in answer to Douglass' letter of December 13 (RWEMA). Emerson's letter of December 7 was answered by Douglass on December 13. Douglass says that he has set the 28th as the first day for the St. Louis lectures, but the *Daily Missouri Republican* gives the opening day as the 27th (*Letters*, 4:336). Moreover, Douglass' letter proposes only two lectures a week, bringing the course to a close on January 14. It is certainly not of this arrangement that Emerson "approved." There must have been another exchange between Emerson's receipt of Douglass' letter of December 13 and this telegram of the 20th to bring about the final schedule as given in Charvat (pp. 27–28); this schedule is confirmed by letters and the *Daily Missouri Republican*. McDermott locates the telegram with the letters in the St. Louis Mercantile Library, but the library cannot now (1984) find it.]

To Fred A. Moore, St. Louis, December 26? 1852

[In a letter of December 25, 1852 (RWEMA), F. A. Moore invites Emerson to lecture in Springfield, Illinois. That Emerson wrote a tentative reply is clear from Moore's letter of January 1, 1853, taken with a note from John Douglass of St. Louis; both Moore and Douglass tell him of the inaccessibility of Chicago, and Moore adds to his discouraging information the high-powered argument that Springfield wants him, the Governor and the Secretary included. I hardly think Moore would have mentioned the difficulties of getting to Chicago if Emerson had not asked him, as he evidently asked Douglass. See *Letters*, 4:342. Moore subsequently moved to La Crosse, Wisconsin (see below, note of letter of May 1853 to Cornelia Kegwin); in *History of La Crosse County, Wisconsin* (Chicago: Western Historical Company, 1881) p. 528, Moore's first name is given as "Fred" and his purchase of the *National Democrat* is recorded with a note of his "peculiar style of editing."]

1853

To Fred A. Moore, St. Louis, January 2? 1853

[In letters of December 25, 1852, and January 1, 1853 (RWEMA), F. A. Moore of Springfield, Illinois, asks Emerson to repeat all or some of his lectures in Springfield. See *Letters*, 4:340 and 341, where a letter to his brother of December 31 and one to his wife of January 7 show that he changed his plans between these dates, betrayed into the "deep mud of the prairie" (see *Letters*, 4:342) by Moore, to whom he must have written his acceptance. Moore planned the lectures to coincide with the meeting of the legislature. The MS "Journal at the West" records Emerson's meeting with Illinois politicians whom he first encountered "in the baggage car where they had a box of brandy, a box of buffalo tongues; and a box of soda biscuit" (p. [83]). The company included Senator "Breeze" (Sidney Breese), Ninian Edwards, and Timothy Roberts Young, former congressman; see *JMN*, 11:527.]

To Luther Haven, St. Louis, January 2? 1853

[In a letter of December 20, 1852 (RWEMA), Luther Haven invites Emerson to lecture before the Young Men's Association of Chicago. That Emerson had it in mind to do so is clear from his letter to his wife of December 31, 1852 (*Letters*, 4:339); Haven's name is listed at the end of the MS Pocket Diary for 1853. An undated note from John T. Douglass (RWEMA) tells him that to get from Springfield, Illinois, to Chicago, he would have to travel the whole way (150 miles) by stage; he can return from Chicago to Cincinnati via Cleveland by railroad. Douglass's note shows that Emerson had been tempted; it shows too that he has already committed himself to the invitation to lecture in Springfield, Illinois. Fred A. Moore to Emerson, January 1, 1853, extends the invitations to Springfield with similar discouraging information about travel to Chicago. I conjecture a letter or telegram of refusal to Haven. (There is evidence also of an invitation from Lockport, for the name of S. S. Pomroy of that town is entered in a list of names at the end of the MS Pocket Diary for 1853 (*JMN*, 13:481).]

To Lidian Emerson, St. Louis, January 5, 1853

[In Cabot's Index 4, no. 1664 of January 5 is listed as a letter to Lidian Emerson. What I believe to be the same letter appears in a list sent to Rusk: it is there described as the "money letter," dated from St. Louis, and given the impossible year 1857; it is only in 1853 that Emerson is in St. Louis on January 5. The letter has not turned up in the Emerson papers, Houghton.

[The MS Account Book for 1849–1853, pp. 231 and 233, carries a series of undated January 1853 entries showing the payment of a good many substantial bills. The entries are in Emerson's hand, but the first is marked in the margin: "copied from Lidian's minutes" and the second: "copied from L. E's letters." There are no entries for December 1852, and on p. 230 appears an appraisal of the Jackson property in Plymouth. This "money letter" could, I think, be about the bills, or the Jackson property or both. In the Emerson papers is a letter from Lidian to Emerson without year but dated at the end: "Wednesday eveg—Jan 19th"; the allusions to bills paid square with the second MS Account Book entry. In 1853, January 19 fell on a Wednesday.

[In Emerson's absence, it was customary for some member of the family to act as "treasurer"; laid in some Account Book are scraps in various hands, Emerson himself transferring the records so kept to his account books. In 1853, only Lidian could be the treasurer; in later years each of the children, usually Ellen, filled the role.]

TO DAVID PRINCE? ST. LOUIS, JANUARY 8? 1853

[I conjecture a letter to Dr. David Prince of Jacksonville, Illinois, on or about January 8, for Emerson lectured in Jacksonville on January 13. To the entry of Jacksonville against that date in his MS Pocket Diary for 1853 (*JMN*, 13:475); he adds the names of Dr. David Prince and "T." B. Turner; he enters Prince's name again in a list of correspondents at the end of the Pocket Diary (*ibid.*, p. 481). His first mention of the possibility of going to Jacksonville is in a letter of January 8 to his wife, *Letters*, 4:341. See *JMN*, 11:531, and n. 60 for Dr. Prince and Jonathan Baldwin Turner.]

TO FRITZ RÖLKER, OHIO RIVER, JANUARY 18, 1853 [1]

On board steamer
Telegraph, Ohio River
Tuesday, 18 Jan.y 1853

My dear Sir,

I trust I shall be able in the morning, by means of an Express, to return to your hands the two volumes of Gervinus,[2] & the one volume of Vischer,[3] you were so good as to lend me. I thank you heartily for them.

1. MS in the Whelpley papers, OCHP; ph. in NNC. See letter of January 21 below, which shows that Emerson sent this letter by express on January 20. The addressee is Dr. Frederick Christian Roelker (1809–1883?), who received his medical degree in 1841 from the Cincinnati Medical School. He is listed in Cincinnati directories first as Dr. Fred. Rolker and then as Dr. Fritz Roelker. On February 1, 1853, he would marry Catherine Ray Green (see *JMN*, 11:516, and n. 20).

2. Georg Gottfried Gervinus. There is no clue to which of Gervinus' works Roelker had lent Emerson, possibly the first two volumes of his *Geschichte der poëtischen Nationallitteratur der Deutschen.*

3. Friedrich Theodor Vischer. Possibly the work Rölker lent was the second volume of his *Aesthetik, oder Wissenschaft des Schönen;* see *JMN*, 11:511, where Emerson quotes a passage

They have been valuable travelling companions & I have read in strange places lessons from them that were all the more gratefull for their violent contrast with my company & circumstance. I have found some curious & some valuable hints in Vischer, and am sorry not to have had opportunity to look further in his book. If I have better eyes, I shall yet. Meantime I am sorry to find that it is not quite safe for me to stop at Cincinnati, as I had hoped. I am much later than I designed to be. I hope I shall have the pleasure of seeing you in Massachusetts.[4]

On board this shaking steamer, which will not let me either read or write, I am

With great regard,
Your obliged servant,
R. W. Emerson

Dr F. Rölker.

TO FRITZ RÖLKER, CLEVELAND, JANUARY 21, 1853[5]

Weddell House
Cleveland 21 Jan.y 1853

My dear Sir,

I dispatched to you yesterday, by the "American Express," your books, Gervinus & Vischer, with a note written on the steamboat. I am a little anxious that such good books should arrive safely at your proper shelves & therefore trouble you with the additional line to announce the fact, & to repeat my thanks for your goodness. When you shall be in Massachusetts, it will give me great pleasure to show you my little library at Concord.

Ever your obliged servant,
R. W. Emerson

Dr Rölker

TO ——— HARDING, CONCORD, JANUARY 31, 1853

[Swann's auction catalogue for February 10, 1949, quotes a letter to "Harding" dated January 31, 1853. The portion quoted reads: "You had better not rely on me for this season."]

---

from the second volume on the verso of the front cover of his "Journal at the West." *JMN*, 11:511.

4. Roelker's younger brother, Bernard was practicing law in Boston; Emerson assumes that the doctor may come to Boston to visit his brother. For Bernard Roelker, see Appletons' *Cyclopedia of American Biography* For Dr. Roelker, see Henry A. Ford and Mrs. Kate B. Ford, *History of Cincinnati* . . . (Cleveland, Ohio: N. A. Williams, 1881), p. 135. A later history gives no more information except the uncertain year of his death.

5. MS in the collections of OCHP; ph. in NNC. See January 18, above. Two envelopes

To Benjamin Pond, New York? January 31? 1853

[In his MS Pocket Diary for 1853 (*JMN*, 13:476), Emerson enters under the date March 3: "East Boston 7½ o'c. Send at 6 to (?)." In pencil he has added: "East Boston offered to B Pond 23 O State House 31 Jan." I take January 31 to be the date of Emerson's letter offering March 3 as the lecture date. Pond's letter of November 6, 1852, to Emerson (RWEMA) shows that the lectures for the East Boston Library Association were scheduled for Thursday; January 31 fell on a Monday; March 3, on Thursday. There was probably an earlier letter, for Pond had offered Emerson earlier dates that he would have to reject.]

To Benjamin Rodman, Concord, February 7? 1853

[In a letter of February 6, 1853 (RWEMA), Benjamin Rodman extends his customary invitation for Emerson to be his guest when he lectures in New Bedford February 16 (Charvat, p. 28).]

To Anna Barker Ward, Concord, February 15, 1853[6]

Concord
Tuesday Morn,g 15 Feby
'53

My dear Anna,

The bag of rich nuts[7] came safely to a joyful market of young people, on Saturday night; & they, & Lidian, on her part & theirs, desire special thanks to be sent to you for the kind thought & act.

For Thursday evening, —I am by no means sure that I can command the hour; for I am promised to be out of town on the same evening; — but if I find it possible to come also to your house, —I will keep the glittering invitation before me to encourage me to be so brave. Mr Clough is not here, but at Cambridge, &, I hope, will not miss your card.[8] If I do not see him at your house, I shall see him on Saturday night.[9]

---

accompany these letters to Dr. Roelker. Both are addressed to Dr F. Rölker, Cincinnati, Ohio; neither shows a postmark, the stamps being torn away. The punctuation differs.

6. MS in the Ward papers, Houghton Library, MH; ph. in CUL.

7. A note not in Emerson's hand says "pecans"; Mrs. Ward may have been visiting New Orleans, or her father may have sent them to her.

8. Clough had moved to lodgings in Cambridge; he boarded with Sally Robbins Howe, widow of Judge Samuel Howe (*EYSC*, p. 284). He was a frequent visitor at the Wards, identifying Anna Ward with the "Margaret Fuller set"; he had known Margaret Fuller in Italy (Mulhauser, 1:241).

9. Clough mentions the visit in a letter of February 18, 22 to his fiancée Blanche Smith (Mulhauser, 2:337), and comments: "I feel refreshed . . . considerably by his company."

And Thursday night, & every day & night, every muse & grace attend you!

R. W. E.

Mrs Anna H. B. Ward.

To Wendell Phillips, Concord, February 19, 1853[10]

Concord

19 February 1853

My dear Sir,

I read the Petition with attention, & with the hope that I should find myself so happy as to do what you bade me. But this is my feeling in regard to the whole matter: I wish that done for their rights which women wish done. If they wish to vote, I shall vote that they vote. If they wish to be lawyers & judges, I shall vote that those careers be opened to them But I do not think that wise & wary women wish to be electors or judges; and I will not ask that they be made such against their will If we obtain for them the ballot, I suppose the best women would not vote. By all means let their rights of property be put on the same basis as those of men, or, I should say, on a more favorable ground. And let women go to women, & bring us certain tidings what they want, & it will be imperative on me & on us all to help them get it.

I am sorry that you should have had to write twice. Though I am a slow correspondent, I should have written today, without a second urgency. Do not despair of me. I am still open to reason.

Yours gratefully,

R. W. Emerson

To Cyrus? Swan, Concord, February 23? 1853

[In a letter of February 22, 1853 (RWEMA), C. Swan of Poughkeepsie writes in dismay that the 22nd of March falls on a Tuesday; a lecture on that date will interfere with every church in the village. He asks if Emerson can come some other day that week. Emerson may have been obliging and changed the date, for his MS Account Book for 1849–1853, p. [236], records the receipt of $40.00 for

10. MS in the Phillips papers, Houghton Library, MH; ph. in NNC, with stamped envelope addressed: Wendell Phillips Esq. Florence Post Office, Hampshire Co. Massachusetts; postmarked at Concord February 19. See *Letters*, 4:345–346, where Rusk notes Phillips' original letter of January 25, his later letter of February, n.d., endorsed 1853 by Emerson, asking if Emerson has forgotten the circular about women's voting, and his reply of February 23 to this letter. Phillips asks the question: "Will it do to put off granting rights till the deprived class asked for them?" All Phillips' letters and the circular are in the Emerson papers; and a draft of the letter of February 23 is in the Phillips papers.

Poughkeepsie under the date April 1, the entry following the specifically dated entries for Hingham, Randolph, and Worcester. The date is unchanged in the Pocket Diary for 1853 (*JMN*, 13:476). A Cyrus Swan, attorney, is listed in the Poughkeepsie directory.]

To HENRY E. HERSEY, CONCORD, MARCH 5, 1853[11]

Concord
5 March.

My dear Sir:

I am sorry it should happen that I am also engaged on the 17th; so that I shall hold myself bound to you for the 29th instant.

R. W. Emerson—

H. E. Hersey, Esq.

To JOHN GREENLEAF WHITTIER, CONCORD, MARCH 14? 1853

[In a letter of March 12, (RWEMA), Whittier writes Emerson that he is expected to lecture for the Amesbury Lyceum on March 17; "of course thee will come directly to my house." Whittier writes again on the 16th to tell Emerson to take the 5 o'clock train to East Salisbury where he will find a carriage waiting. It is clear that there was at least one letter to Whittier, but the date is uncertain.]

To ELIZABETH PALMER PEABODY, CONCORD, MARCH 26, 1853[12]

Concord, 26 March, 1853.

Dear Miss Peabody,

I send you a letter for Mr Putnam, which, if you like, you shall send, if you dislike, & want another, you shall burn, & tell me so.[13] I talked

11. MS in the miscellaneous autographs, Houghton Library, MH; ph. in NNC. The date is secure from the MS Account Book for 1849–1853, p. 235, where an 1853 entry dated March 29 shows the receipt of $20. from Hingham. Henry E. Hersey, on March 1, had written Emerson (RWEMA): "We shall depend upon hearing you at Hingham on the 15th inst. . . ." This letter of March 5 suggests that there may have been an exchange of letters between the first and sixth, if Emerson's "17" is not an error for "15." The MS Pocket Diary for 1853 has a pencil entry for March 15 deleted and an ink entry for March 29 (*JMN*, 13:476, 477.)

12. MS in DFo; ph. in NNC; single sheet, addressed on verso: Miss E. P. Peabody, Care of George P. Putnam. 10 Park Place. New York.; postmarked at Concord, March 26. Printed by Theodore Bacon, p. 55. Postscript quoted by Vivian Hopkins, p. 151. Emerson reversed his sheet and wrote his postscript between his dateline and salutation; the postscript then appears upside down.

13. For the letter to Putnam enclosed, see below. It is not clear that Miss Peabody heeded Emerson's wish that Miss Bacon decide to what use his letter to Putnam should be put. Miss Peabody's inclination to take over the management of other people's affairs is amply documented. See Hopkins, pp. 166–167, for Putnam's offer which Miss Bacon refused. The

with Hawthorne who did not seem to think that he was the person;[14] but, if Miss Bacon would really come to Concord, & board with Mrs Adams, as, I doubt not, is practicable, we would make him listen, & she should make him believe. With my kindest salutations & respects to Miss Bacon you ever obliged servt.

R. W. Emerson.

I can really think of nothing that could give such eclat to a magazine, as this brilliant paradox.

To George Palmer Putnam, Concord, March 26, 1853[15]

Concord, Mass
26 March 1853

Dear Sir,

Miss Peabody writes me that you are treating with Miss Bacon for her papers on Shakspeare; and intimates that Miss Bacon persists in her design of going to England to complete & verify her discoveries; & that you are prepared, in certain contingences, to aid her in going thither.

I am happy to hear thus much; & hasten to add my testimony, as, I learn, it has been appealed to. I am only in part made acquainted with Miss Bacon's results. I by no means accepted her conclusion, which was a paradox so bold that it went to shake all one's literary faith about his ears. Yet my respect was surprised & commanded by her thorough knowledge of her subject, & her mastery of all her weapons. Two MSS, only she has sent me, & both these quite preliminary, but I have seen nothing in American in the way of literary criticism, which I thought so good. The whole treatment inspired a confidence that the writer had something worth knowing to communicate. She did not impart to me a certain secret key[16] or method, which she professed to have found; but

---

letter helped to secure for Miss Bacon the generous patronage of Charles Butler (Hopkins, pp. 164 and 327, n. 57).

14. The reluctant and skeptical Hawthorne was finally drawn into Miss Bacon's affairs. Miss Bacon acting on her own brought about what Hawthorne's sister-in-law and Emerson could not effect.

15. MS in the Phillips Library, MSaE; ph. in NNC. This is certainly the letter enclosed with that to Miss Peabody of the same date, see below. Emerson's last sentence with the complimentary close and signature is written on the first page above the dateline. There is no room for the addressee's name. This letter has recently been printed by Helen R. Deese in the *Essex Institute Historical Collections* (April 1986, 122:107–108. A typographical error gives the dateline "23 March 1853"; the date is given correctly in the text of the article which provides a good deal of useful information.

16. That Emerson does not know of Miss Bacon's "secret" method raises the question of whether he'd have supported her at all if he had known it.

so far interested me, that I wrote to urge on her the propriety of writing out a summary of her results, & ⟨ha⟩ confiding them in a dated & sealed ⟨p⟩envelope to some safe trustee, to secure the discovery, & her title to it, from accident. I had also offered my aid in finding her a proper organ in an English journal for the publication /of/ her papers as soon as they were ready. Her health & other circumstances induced her to postpone sending them. I like better that they should appear in America. & if her papers have the general ability that marked those which I saw, & if her conclusion is fortified in any manner adequate to the ability she exhibited, you would, I am sure, be amply justified in any preliminary expenses the piece required. Her discovery, if it really be one, is of the first importance not only in English, but in all literature. And after waiting /for it/ with much impatience for many months, I shall be glad to know /that/ it is to be fully unfolded & its grounds shown.

And if I can aid in the bringing it before the public, I shall not fail. Respectfully

R. W. Emerson.

To Delia Salter Bacon, Concord, April 13, 1853 [17]

Concord
13 April
1853

My dear Miss Bacon,

I was cordially gratified by the good news your note contained, that you were going forward with your studies, & really decided to prosecute them in England; and I was not a little flattered by being made however accidentally & insignificantly a party to the transaction. I am glad also that you will trust me farther with insights of your results. By all means, let it be so! And, by all means do you go forward to the speediest completion! Now let me not fail of my communication. I grieve very often,—seldom so much as now,—at the disheartening infirmities & invalidity of my wife, which makes it most part of the time quite out of question to invite any worthy mortal to visit my house. I do not know that I can come to New York,—and yet I am not sure but I shall make the time to do so, if there is no other way. But, if you are coming to Boston or Cambridge, before your departure,—have the goodness to

17. MS in DFo; ph. in NNC; printed by Theodore Bacon, pp. 57–58; listed in *Letters*, 4:349. Emerson centered his dateline; he so rarely does that remark seems called for, though in this year it appears to be a habit.

apprise me now of the fact, & when, & where.[18] In assured hope & with constant respect

Yours,

R. W. Emerson

Miss Bacon.

To Caroline Sturgis Tappan, Concord, April 14, 1853 [19]

Concord

14 April

1853

I was glad to see your autograph this morning, & wish such sunbeams often shine on me. I turned the mocking paper in & out round & round but could find no address no hint of where. I will launch this leaf on the wide air of New York & we will see if it find guidance to your door. If so, let it bring back explicit date & place, and, also, word where you will be a month hence, or at some other measurable futurity. With these foundations fixed, who knows but we may get up a little correspondence, or telegraphing from cliff to cliff a few facts that still require statement

Do not go to Europe, without advertising me of it. Do not go into the country, here, without telling me. Perhaps I wish to see you, perhaps to avoid you, certainly always to hear from you.

I am not wiser for my age,

Nor skilful by my grief;

Life loiters at the Book's first page,

Ah, could we turn the leaf!

Ever yours,

W—

To William Ellery Channing, Concord, May 5? 1853

[Emerson would have had to answer William Ellery Channing's letter of May 4; the letter sets the terms of a contract for Channing's preparing for publication a

---

18. Miss Bacon visited Concord early in May 1853; see May 12 below and Hopkins, pp. 170–171 (Miss Hopkins' account here is a fiction, for she has contrived dialogue from one questionable source and from a letter that antedates the visit).

19. MS in the Tappan papers, Houghton Library, MH; ph in NNC. Page 4 is endorsed "R W Emerson /1853/ JEC d." The Quatrain that closes the letters was later given the title "Climacteric," appropriate for his fiftieth birthday, May 25, 1853. See *Poetry Notebooks*, pp. 434, 759.

On p. 4 Mrs. Tappan has written two quatrains of her own and in the margin attempted a third. Her first makes the somewhat extravagant claim "Thy lineage is one with mine." She dates the first: "1863. Lenox—written before rereading the letter."

work to be called "Concord Walks," the matter to be culled by Channing from the journals of Emerson, the composition and writing to be Channing's. Emerson would certainly have to acknowledge at least the first page of the letter. I give the whole here as characteristic of the writer's habitual presumption of defeat.

["My dear Emerson

"if you are in earnest about the literary work of which you spake, I will be in earnest too, & give you my terms. I will undertake the MS in question, to be done by 1st of October next, in twenty chapters at $5,00 per chapter payable monthly by date.

["I should demand access to all your journals that could be used as this, and will be further responsible as to the MSS.* More than this, I would correct the proof in case (which is very unlikely) you should print it. If you desire to throw away the above sum, I will do the work, having laid down the rule, that I will not work without pay at the time. Because, having already printed so much without return, it will not do. I should not make this offer, saw I any means of finishing that business.

["I advise you as a friend (in private) not to accept that mad offer of W.E.C., on t'other page. In the first place, you may feel bound to read a few pages of the MS which will only try your eyes & in the next place you throw away your money. For, just as surely, as the said W.E.C. has anything to do with the MS aforesaid, it will be a plump squash.

["Again, your journals will get badly overhauled, for I shall not scruple to use of them what I can. Again, there are great difficulties if we come out flat-footed, & call our book C.W. as you propose, & then put in characters like yours and A's and T's etc, everyone will know (victim & all) who it is. Will this answer? Again, unless great skill is used, even if we give it another name, & call it, "Walks in Addlebury," of ⟨B⟩ "Musings or the Piddledees," & the like, the secret will out. Flat-footed C.W. would hardly go. However, it is all one to me, if you arder the MS. I will put in the names of the figures, & write as the ostrich did, under his red cat, chat gris, 'this is a Lion.'

["But I assure you, it is no joke to write a solid work in 20 Chapters for so little money, especially as you will get laughed at for your pains. Still, I meant to be fair, with even so great a jester & practical joker as yourself. I still cannot for the life of me, see, how you who dare not in your works, even call a dollar by its name, expect to write or cause to be written a book, that shall galvanize, and embalm all your next neighbors by their right names, & above all, as you calmly proposed it to me, as a serious poet. I have all along, & do regard it as part of that insufferable nonsense you are in the habit of talking, or as one of those whims that occur to gentlemen of 50, & who seem to suppose that young people of 40, are so much greener than themselves. At any rate, you have got my ultimatum above, & in that way, & in no other way, & for no less sum of money

---

["*Neither can I pay a great regard to criticisms on the same, as having been forty years in the business, I suppose myself partly learnt."

will I undertake the aforesaid C.W. And now in the name of God! let us drop the whole matter.

WEC

[Channing's letter here calls in question the statement that Channing was to provide "five monthly parts at $20. a part." On October 6, Emerson paid Channing $20, the only recorded payment. On the terms Channing lays out above, the payment is for four chapters. That, in October, Channing had given Emerson more than one chapter is evident form Emerson's letter to Caroline Tappan; see October 24 below. See *Letters*, 4:389. I see no way to reconcile the discrepancies here, even on the supposition that "part" does mean the same as "chapter."]

To CORNELIA KEGWIN, CONCORD, MAY ? 1853

[Rusk lists a letter under the conjectured date of May 12, *Letters*, 4:358, from Cornelia Kegwin's acknowledgment, dated May 19 (RWEMA). In a MS notebook entitled "Journal at the West" (the title is not in Emerson's hand), p. [104], is an entry reading: "Spfld. Ill. Cornelia Kegwin, to whom I must send one of my books; and, above all, George Herbert" (*JMN*, 11:531). Emerson evidently sent her his own *Poems* along with Herbert's; a.ll.s. (RWEMA) May 19, from Cornelia Kegwin and May 18, from Fred A. Moore whom Miss Kegwin would shortly marry. John Carroll Power, *History of the Early Settlers of Sangamon County Illinois* (Springfield, Ill.: Edwin A. Wilson, 1876), p. 423; the name is here spelled "Keigwin". According to Moore's letter of January 14, Miss Kegwin had been reprimanded by her minister for neglecting prayer meetings to attend Emerson's lectures (a.l.s., RWEMA). There may have been further correspondence after Moore and his wife moved to LaCrosse, Wisconsin, in 1845, for both are clearly serious admirers of Emerson. Cornelia Moore died in 1856 (Power, p. 423); Moore's second wife apparently heard more of Emerson than she could bear; a letter of September 10, 1860 (RWEMA), challenges him to explain the heterodox ideas she has heard from her husband.]

To GEORGE BANCROFT, CONCORD, MAY 9, 1853[20]

Concord 9 May 1853

My dear Bancroft,

Miss Delia S. Bacon sails for England from New York, next Saturday. She goes to London with purely literary objects & wishes to make some researches in the Library of the British Museum, & perhaps in some private libraries. Her studies respect some very curious literary inquiries which she has originated in regard to the age of Queen Elizabeth, & which she prosecutes with abundant talent & devotion. Of course, she appreciates the privilege of consulting the best English scholars whom

20. MS in the Bancroft papers, MHi; ph. in NNC.

she can meet,[21] and already has letters to Grote, Carlyle, &, I believe, to Milnes. I thought that if you would give her a letter to Mr Hallam, she would have the best possible counselor, not only in regard to librarians & scholars, but also to /her/ literary questions. Some writings of Miss Bacon's, which I have /lately/ seen, have impressed me with great respect for her literary ability, & with a cordial wish to see her way smoothed in this undertaking. I do not know whether you have allowed your English correspondence to drop, but I hope it will be in your power to succour a lady of eminent worth & talent, with such credentials.[22]

Ever gratefully Yours,

R. W. Emerson.

To Delia Salter Bacon, Concord, May 12, 1853[23]

Concord

12 May 1853

My dear Miss Bacon

I wrote to Sumner but have as yet no answer. Perhaps he has directed his answer, as I suggested, to Mr Butler. I enclose a letter to Mr Martineau, to whom, if you have good opportunity, I think I would rankly open the general design of your inquiries, but you will judge best on seeing him. I send a letter also for Carlyle, to find Spedding. I think I will write myself again to Carlyle, as I shall ⟨pe⟩need, perhaps, in a few days I enclose a letter to John Chapman.[24] Perhaps you will find his house a good home for you, in London. I took rooms & board there, & was well accommodated.

---

21. See above, June 12, 1852, for Emerson's first letter to Delia Bacon and the beginning of his efforts on her behalf. For other probable letters of this kind written for her, see list, *Letters*, 4:358.

22. From Charles Butler, who had also befriended Delia Bacon, Emerson learned that Bancroft had supplied a letter to Sir Henry Ellis, librarian of the British Museum, but did not write to the ailing Henry Hallam (a.l.s., May 18, 1853, RWEMA). In his letter of August 10 to Carlyle, Emerson says that (Edward?) Everett supplied her with a letter to George Grote (Slater, p. 492). For Carlyle's judgment of Miss Bacon's project, see Slater, p. 495, n. 6.

23. MS in DFo; ph. in NNC; printed by Theodore Bacon, pp. 58–59; listed *Letters*, 4:388.

24. Emerson's letters to James Martineau, Charles Sumner, Charles Butler, and John Chapman have not been found. For the letter to Carlyle, see *Letters*, 4:357–358, and Slater, pp. 487–488. (There is no evidence that he wrote a second letter to Carlyle.) For the delayed letter to Arthur Helps, see *Letters*, 4:367–368; the letter was apparently never presented; it is still in the Bacon papers, DFo. Vivian Hopkins (p. 171) lists also a letter to "Arthur" Hallam, but see May 9 above to George Bancroft and notes for the evidence that George Bancroft was to write Hallam but did not do so because of Hallam's illness. The historian Henry Hallam is meant here; his son Arthur died in 1833.

I have not yet written, /for/ want of time & a little mountain to get over to write to him, —to Helps. Leave me your London address, & I will yet write. Mrs Emerson is mortified at her heedlessness in putting you to sleep in a chamber certain to be disturbed by too-early-rising washers in the night. She never remembered it would be so, nor tho't of it till next day. But Fare well & fare gloriously!

With best hope,
R. W. Emerson

Miss Bacon.

To WILLIAM HENRY FURNESS, CONCORD, MAY 12, 1853[25]

Concord
12 May 1853

My dear friend,

This is your old malice prepense, & I know it for such,—always in conspiracy to inflict benefits & hatching good will into deeds, and, to be sure, tis none of your work, but only a sudden fortuitous concourse of lovers & & aiders, such as is, I suppose, at any time sporadic in the air of Philadelphia![26] Well, you are a wonderful man, & an honor to Dame Whitwell's a-b ab school,[27] & will make her famous to all time, though I see she was partial, & taught you something she taught no other; for I cannot remember that Sam B. or that Walter Langdon sat on the bench,[28] though I never see them now without belief that you must have given them private rehearsals, & probably showed them the red handkerchief (ah beautiful beautiful in my memory!) on which the House that Jack built, was depicted. But to all others to whom you have have not opened your & Mrs Whitwell's heresy, it is still sealed.

But for your project itself,—it is really very gratifying to me, &, if it prove feasible, I shall not be wanting to it. It will be a great advantage to me to know of it thus early, & to hold it before me. I am working just now on my little <u>English</u> Book & when that is done I will think of this.[29]

25. MS in the Furness papers, Van Pelt Library PU; ph. in NNC; printed in *Records*, [88]–89; listed in *Letters*, 4:358.

26. Furness had evidently written of the plan for a private course of lectures to be given in Philadelphia (Charvat, pp. 28–29); see December 18 below.

27. Susanna Whitwell, see Rusk, *Life*, p. 23. Furness would recall in other letters the ABC school he and Emerson had attended as children.

28. Samuel Bradford; see above, April 9, 1840, for Emerson's renewed acquaintance with these childhood friends; Langdon was of his brother William's age.

29. *English Traits*.

And yet I have often thought lately, I should leave the Lyceum to the juniors. I will write you again

Goodbye for today. Affectionately,

W. H. Furness.   R. W. E.

To John Albee, Concord, May 20, 1853 [30]

Concord 20 May 1853

My dear Sir,

I duly received your kind note, a "Herbert",[31] & was reminded at once of my negligence in failing to acknowledge an earlier letter which had interested me much. I am glad you like these old books, or rather, glad that you, (like the authors of these old things,) have

> "Eyes that the beam celestial view
> Which evermore makes all things new"[32]

There is a super-Cadmaean alphabet, which when one has once learned the characters, he will find, as it were, secretly inscribed,—look where he will,—not only in books & temples, but in all waste places, & in the dust of the earth. Happy he that can read it; for he will never be lonely or thoughtless again. And yet it is a solid pleasure to find those who know & like the same thing, the authors, namely, who have recorded their interpretation of the legend, &, better far, the living friends who read as we do, & compare notes with us. I gladly hear what you say of your new pleasures at Andover. If any thing in the way of book or thought occurs to you to write, do not fail to send it me: it may easily come to me, when I shall have somewhat to say.

J. Albee.   R. W. Emerson

To Martha Robinson, Concord, June 16, 1853

[In the MS Account Book 1849–1853, under the date June 16 (p. 261), is this entry: "Pd inclosed in a letter gift sent from Mrs R. E to Rev Lincoln Ripley — (letter mailed to Miss M. Robinson) 10.00." Lincoln Ripley is Emerson's uncle;

30. MS owned by Samuel French Morse; ph. in NNC. This is the letter Rusk lists *Letters*, 4:321, under the conjectured date October 30, 1852, where he notes that it is printed in part in the *New-York Tribune*, July 23, 1882; *Concord Lectures on Philosophy*, R. L. Bridgman, ed., p. 68, and Albee, *Remembrances of Emerson*, 1901, pp. 30–31. As the full letter shows, Emerson did not acknowledge Albee's letter of October 23, 1852 (RWEMA). Printed also (in full) by Cameron in *ESQ* (1st q., 1858), 10:38.

31. In his letter of October 23, 1852, Albee reports that he finds Herbert's poetry an antidote to the Orthodox sermons he hears in the Andover chapel, and he puts Herbert in his "calendar of saints." On Emerson's recommendation, he is also reading Adam Smith, *The Theory of Moral Sentiments* (see Harding, p. 250).

32. From John Keble's "Morning."

Mrs. R. E., his mother. In the explosion of the *Jenny Lind* in San Francisco Bay, April 11, 1853, Lincoln Ripley's adopted son, Noah Ripley, his wife and children were killed (see *Letters,* 4:359). Martha Robinson was Lincoln Ripley's adopted daughter who "took care of him through his lengthened life." Henry P., William, and Samuel Warren, *The History of Waterford* (Portland: Hoyt, Fogg, and Donham, 1879), pp. 284–285.]

To WALTER SAVAGE LANDOR, CONCORD, JUNE 25? 1853

[In a letter of June 23, n.y., but certainly of 1853 (MNS), Elizabeth Peabody asks Emerson to write to Walter Savage Landor on behalf of Delia Bacon. She has heard that Landor is in Bath. She has written Charles Butler to ask him to carry such a letter and gives Emerson Butler's Wall Street address. The greater part of this four-page letter, the first page crossed, tries to persuade Emerson to see Mrs. Caroline Wilson that the sculptress may make changes in her bust of Emerson. It does not occur to Miss Peabody that she is in effect asking Emerson to write four letters. That the letter appears in the Tappan papers in the Smith College archives suggest to me that Emerson sent it to Caroline Sturgis Tappan in hopes that she could protect him from the tasks, or some of them. I enter as questionable a letter to Landor and a letter to Butler.]

To CHARLES BUTLER, CONCORD, JUNE 25, 1853

[See above note of possible letter to Landor to be carried to England by Butler. There is no confirming evidence for either.]

To NORTH PINDER, CONCORD, JUNE 28, 1853

[A letter of June 28, n. y., addressed to N. Pinder is listed and quoted in Robert K. Black's catalogue 65, May 1959, item 59, and in James Lowe's catalogue 24, 1983, item 50. The Black catalogue entry is reproduced by Cameron, *ESQ* (2nd q., 1966), 43:144. Lowe quotes the letter, more fully than Black, as follows: "I am very happy to hear that any greeting from Miss DeQuincey is on its way to me: and I am glad to hear that yourself of whom I had already heard, will be the bearer. Meantime, it happens, for my mortification, that painters & workers are just now making a desolation of my house. Tomorrow my plight will be no better. I think, I will come to see you tomorrow afternoon, & we will consult on the best time for me to show you our Concord meadows. I will seek for you at the Revere House, tomorrow."

[In a letter of April 27, 1853 (RWEMA), Margaret De Quincey says Mr. Pinder of Trinity College, Oxford, had wanted a letter "from papa, who was prodigal of his promises to do so, but as he has never been known to write even a short note under many month's incessant persecution . . . I have ventured to offer my services as a 'medium.' . . ." North Pinder, a fellow of Trinity College, with two other young men from Oxford, visited Emerson on July 5; see below, July 4 to Carolina Tappan. The MS Account Book for 1849–1853 records the expenses of a new furnace, paper hanging, and a new mantle-piece. See *Letters,* 4:370–371, 375, for the leaking roof that required major repairs.]

To ———, CONCORD? JULY? 1853?[33]

All my fifty years have not cured me of my hope have not steeled me to patience have not won me to the majority; worst of all, have not weaponed & instructed me to an effectual soldier; so that I remain a displeased observer taught severely to adjourn my peace & kingdom to conditions & cooperations that I shall not see untied in this world. Tendencies are the best heaven now permitted. Success we must not talk of

It is curious that the new generation have no love of life. Suicide is contemplated familiarly, & in some instances is committed ⟨n⟩by young people who seemed to have all the world can offer at their feet; —by a brilliant young matron, the other day, the darling of society, & of her husband, with a child unborn in her bosom. And they that remain do not blame, but rather envy her. They do not care to live, though manliness & the imagination will keep them from using poison too. I am sometimes ready to accuse our American climate

as if it dephlogisticated or unnerved us, by force of too much stimulation. We say that our sulphuric acid is not concentrated, has only half the strength of the English article. I think that our men are not saturated with their proper quality, but have an underdose, & are not complete for their own ends. Clough was very welcome here to some of our best people, for, though gross & bald, they found or fancied a wonderful youth in his smiling eyes.

TO CAROLINE STURGIS TAPPAN, CONCORD, JULY 4, 1853[34]

Concord 4 July 1853

Dear Caroline,

I was on the point of saying to you a multitude of things which your letter suggested, when Ellery brought me the terrible story which cut off all writing.[35] I have in vain reproached myself, since, with my silence.

33. MS in "Autobiographical Miscellany," Emerson Papers (RWEMA), Houghton Library, MH; ph. in NNC. This draft is marked in green pencil, probably by Cabot: "Perhaps belongs with letter to Carlyle . . . Apr. 1853." But the clear allusion to the suicide of Susan Sturgis Bigelow and the implied departure of Clough make a date earlier than June 9 impossible and one not long after June 29 (Clough's sailing date) likely. It is not from any letter to Carlyle; see Slater, p. 491, where Emerson's letter of August 10 shows that he had not yet answered Carlyle's letter of May 13.

If this passage is from a letter at all, it was surely not in any version actually mailed. It is, however, the kind of thing that Emerson might fall into as he wrote a draft. The conclusion is evoked by his work on *English Traits*.

34. MS in the Tappan papers, MH; ph. in NNC.

35. A long letter of June 7 (MNS). Caroline Tappan's sister, Susan Sturgis Bigelow, had committed suicide June 9, 1853.

For, I know, that when we are shocked by calamity, life itself seems absurd, & everything but actions of necessity or of extraordinary vivacity looks impertinent. You have & will have your own resources. To me, that great mental activity which grief sometimes permits, as by exasperation, seems the best. But it is little we can do. Generally, we must rely on that tough fibre, which makes the substratum of all strong individuals,— whose "time & hour wear through the roughest day."[36] For the supreme resource of a tranquillity of heart too deep to be shaken,—/that/ comes or comes not as it lists,—is to be received or to be waited for; and rules or modes of approximation cannot be prescribed. Whilst I am waiting to know what I should say, I wish I could interest you with any details. I read history lately, and find great volumes of self-support in it, perhaps because it is so in contrast with our American way of speed & shifts. I do not know but the Goethean Ottilia's[37] saying that "she could never re-member anything of history but an anecdote or two,"—has done much harm, by giving a colour to our native superficiality. But what vexations must not this Bohn cause to the Hallams & Palgraves[38] & other dry as dusts of England,—men who have built a reputation on having unearthed & deciphered some one or two old books, now this new Fust[39] prints every fortnight a Saxon Chronicle, Bede, Roger de Hoveden, & so on,[40] without stint, each for a few shillings, & each a book which we could not get in America before! I believe the general impression in Engd & in America is, that we are not as patient readers as the English. Talking with Clough, the other day, he said, that the men there are great streams of tradition; that, in each family, they know certain things, & very deeply; that here the climate stimulates us, & we talk, but you soon come to the end of what we know; there, what they say rests on longer & richer accumulation.—Somewhat like this, he said; but all travellers may be said to be kleinstadtlich,[41] & to draw conclusions much too fast from few instances. Clough—do you know?—is suddenly gone from again. The

36. Emerson misquotes Macbeth I.iii.146–147.

37. The heroine of Goethe's *Die Wahlverwandtschaften*.

38. Henry Hallam and Sir Francis Palgrave.

39. Johann Fust, who took over Gutenberg's press and type in payment of debts. Henry George Bohn is the modern publisher referred to.

40. On July 2 Emerson had withdrawn from the Boston Athenaeum the Boston edition of *The Chronicle of Henry of Huntingdon* (Cameron, *ER*, p. 28). In June he had been reading John Allen Giles, *History of the Ancient Britons,* and Augustin Thierry, *History of the Conquest of England by the Normans* (Cameron, *ER*, p. 26). He owned the Bohn edition of Bede's *Ecclesiastical History* which was printed with *The Anglo-Saxon Chronicle* (Harding, p. 24). I do not find any reference to Roger de Hoveden's *Chronica* in journals or letters.

41. Provincial. The word falls at the end of the line; Emerson breaks it after "Klein" without a hyphen.

English government have offered him some place in their Board of Education or Inspection of Schools; & his friends wrote urgently for him to come & decide on the spot. He went reluctantly & sends me word he will probably return in September. He is here fully occupied with a new translation of Plutarch's Lives, which will take nearly a year to finish. Part is already printed. I have to receive tomorrow three young Oxonians, one of whom, Mr North Pinder, brings me a letter from Dequincey's daughter Margaret.[42] These young English are a pleasant race, & I like their manners, like to see their absolute ways, when by themselves,—in hotel or boat,—but, as Kurroglou[43] says of rich men—"they are all alike,"—& the chance of finding a genius seems always less.

Thanks thanks for your kind intention of seeing Ellen.[44] Her mono-syllabic letters, so young & yet so old—I am almost tempted to ⟨y⟩ inclose one to you. I am really pleased that she went—the change is so great for her.

Carlyle writes me lately a great tragic letter scared, like Dr Johnson by Old Age.[45] Arthur Helps writes to praise Alexander Smith's Poems; in which, the little I read did not please.[46] I think I am too old. I dare however believe, I shall write you presently again.[47]

Your affectionately,
Waldo E.

To Elizabeth Dwight Sedgwick, Concord, July 20, 1853

[In her letter of July 22, 1853 (RWEMA), Elizabeth Dwight Sedgwick tells Emerson that she is sorry he thought it necessary to send her the receipt. She appears

42. See June 28, above.
43. Roushan Beg.
44. Ellen Emerson at Elizabeth Dwight Sedgwick's school in Lenox; Ellen's letter of July 24 says Mrs. Tappan has invited her and two of her friends "for the third time" and they have decided "they ought to go when they have been invited so often." Ellen's letters are unaffected and forthright. The thirteen-year-old Ellen is careful of her money; she wishes she could have some oranges sent "for they are 75 cents a dozen even in Pittsfield" (July 2). She has her own opinions: "What's to be done with me next winter? Please don't send me to Mr Emerson's school. . . . I don't like schools where they let you do all kinds of things and never say anything." She is referring here to George B. Emerson's policy of no punishments for poor conduct.
45. Letter of May 13, Slater, pp. 488–491.
46. A letter of May 9, 1853; Helps wants Emerson's approval of Alexander Smith's A Life Drama; see also July 22 below.
47. In her reply of July 13 (MNS) Mrs. Tappan expresses her feelings about her sister's death with restraint. She has reread her sister's letters and sees for the first time their excessive hilarity and wonders whether in replying she "ever said anything in earnest or only laughed too." Of Emerson she says she has thought of him a good deal since she saw him in Boston. "You will never dash the cup aside—How self-possessed you looked—younger than any one, as if you had become one of the immortals" (MNS).

to be replying to a letter. The only receipt that seems likely is one for Ellen
Emerson's board bill; the MS Account Book for 1849–1853, p. 266, shows the
payment of $20.28 to Mrs. [Frank] Farley for Ellen's board under the date July 9.
Emerson had sent the money to Ellen in a letter of July 8; see *Letters*, 4:372, and
October 6 below.]

To Caroline Sturris Tappan, Concord, July 22, 1853[48]

Concord, 22 July 1853

Dear Caroline,

You say truly & wisely, we must learn from our losses not to let our
friends go; yes; one would not willingly omit one good office: and yet
when we do not speak or write, it is out of a confidence that we know our
party, & are known for our own quality, once for all. I believe, my
slowness to write letters has grown from the experience, that some of my
friends have been very impatient of my generalizings, as we weary of any
trick, whilst theirs are still sweet to me. So I hesitate to write, except to
the assessors, or to the man that is to slate my house. And my friends are
an ever narrowing troop. Yet I am incurable, &, to this day, only rightly
feel myself when I meet somebody whose habit of thought, at least, holds
the world in solution, if I cannot find one whose will does. Friends are
few, thoughts are few, facts few—only one: one only fact, now tragically,
now tenderly, now exultingly illustrated in sky, in earth, in men & women,
Fate, Fate.[49] The universe is all chemistry, with a certain hint of a magnificent Whence or Whereto gliding or opalizing every angle of the old
salt-&-acid acid-&-salt, endlessly reiterated & masqueraded through all
time & space & form. The addition of that hint everywhere, saves things.
Heavy & loathsome is the bounded world, bounded everywhere. An
immense Boston or Hanover street with mountains of ordinary women,
trains & trains of mean leathern men all immoveably bounded, no liquid-
ity of hope or genius. But they are made chemically good, like oxen. In
the absence of religion, they are polarized to decorum, which is its
blockhead;—thrown mechanically into parallelism with this high Whence
& Whither, which thus makes mountains of rubbish reflect the morning
sun & the evening star. And we are all privy-counsellors to that Hint,
which homeopathically doses the System, & can cooperate with the slow

48. MS in the Tappan papers, Houghton Library, MH; ph. in NNC.
49. See July 4 above for Susan Sturgis Bigelow's death, and Mrs. Tappan's letter of July
13. Her letter sends Emerson back to the subject of Fate, the first in the lecture series "The
Conduct of Life." She has written in such a way that he can risk the "generalizing" he
supposes his friends are weary of.

& secular escape of these oxen & semioxen from their quadruped estate, & invite them to be men, & hail them such. I do not know—now that stoicism & Christianity have for two millenniums preached liberty, somewhat fulsomely,—but it is the turn of Fatalism. And it has great conveniences for a public creed. Fatalism, foolish & flippant, is as bad as Unitarianism or Mormonism. But Fatalism held by an intelligent soul who knows how to humor & obey the infinitesimal pulses of spontaneity, is by much the truest theory in use. All the great would call their thought fatalism, or concede that ninety nine parts are nature, & one part power, though that hundredth is elastic, miraculous, and, whenever it is in energy, dissolving all the rest.

Forgive this heavy cobweb, which I did not think of spinning, & which will put you too out of all patience with my prose. But I see sun-colours over all the geometry, & am armed by thinking that our wretched interference is precluded.

Thanks for the new invitation. I very much wish to come & see you, & will use the occasion of Ellen's wants to come.[50] Did you read Van Artevelde Taylor's "Notes on Life"[51] I think he calls it? The first look of the book was sinister, but I found some things I would not have missed. Alexander Smith I have not read, my attempts were not successful.[52] "History & tradition" which you so characteristically disdain, are good in the interim, when no clarion of the muse is heard from the steeps, and are as good as bibles, when we ourselves are full of light, to read the three meanings from.[53] And so may all high & happy thoughts dwell with you!

Your friend,
W. E.

To CHARLES KING NEWCOMB, CONCORD, AUGUST 10? 1853

[Emerson refers to a letter to Newcomb in his letter of August 10 to Caroline Sturgis Tappan; he cannot be referring to the letter of July 10, *Letters,* 4:373, for he had not then received Clough's letter of July 22, the letter which prompted him to write Newcomb. A journal entry made after his visit to Lenox suggests that while there he read over letters by Newcomb; *JMN,* 13:37.]

50. Emerson visited Lenox in the following week; see *Letters,* 4:378.
51. Sir Henry Taylor; Emerson attaches the name of Taylor's hero Philip Van Artevelde to identify him. Taylor's *Philip Van Artevelde* had been extremely popular with Margaret Fuller and her friends when it first appeared (1834, with an American edition in 1835).
52. See July 4 above for Alexander Smith's *A Life Drama.*
53. Emerson is referring to the three modes of interpreting the Bible; they are the allegorical, the moral, and the anagogical.

Concord, 10 August, 1853

Dear Caroline,

Clough writes that he has reluctantly taken the offered place, "a Clerkship or Examinership in the Education department of the Council Office, ⟨at⟩ Whitehall, Salary £300 a year, work 6 hours a day." He says, if he refused it, he seemed to have no farther chance of England, & hopes he does not forfeit all chance in America.[55] So departs he whom I fancied was a real acquisition to us here so robust & capable, & with whom I had learned to live in a kind of working-friendship. To meet so shrewd a loss, it behoves us certainly to put all our old affections in good repair, that they may last as long as we; and I have, on the instant, written to Charles K. N. the penitence I felt;[56] & to Carlyle, whose *sad epistle* I had no acknlwedged.[57] But mainly I must seek you, who are steadily good to me you whom I am always fearing that marriage or New York or Italy or I know not what farther displacement or dis-timing will take from me—not you, but that fragment of you in which my shadow of a right has always been allowed. It was a great pleasure to see you, & your state, & your <u>reflections</u> (as one might say to a swan on the water) and the steadiness of the image now after so many years still deeply pleases me.

I was very happy to see William Tappan,[58] & could not help renewing some old wishes & beliefs that if the old tyrants, time & space, permitted it, we might yet grow to a real understanding: and I can hardly pacify myself by saying, "Well, if I do not find him, another will."[59] So you see that today finds me a rank sentimentalist, only, like all other days.

Yours affectionately,

R. W. E.

When Ellen's box goes up in a few days, I am to send the books.

54. MS in the Tappan papers, Houghton Library, MH; ph. in NNC.
55. Clough's letter of July 22 (*Emerson-Clough Letters*, no. 20; Mulhauser, 2:457–458).
56. The letter to Newcomb has not been located; it cannot be the letter of July 10 (*Letters*, 4:373).
57. Slater, pp. 488–493.
58. On his visit to Lenox (*Letters*, 4:378); see also *JMN*, 13:36–37.
59. Emerson uses the single quotation mark here. There can be no certainty of Emerson's intent here. He normally, but not consistently, uses double quotations marks for genuine quotations and single for imaginary ones.

To Franklin Benjamin Sanborn, Concord, August? 23? 1853

[In a letter of August 22 1853 (DLC), from Hampton Falls, New Hampshire, Frank B. Sanborn proposes a meeting with Emerson and some of his Harvard friends; he proposes September 10 as the date. Emerson enters Sanborn's name with the Hampton Falls address in MS journal DO (*JMN*, 13:6) and in the Pocket Diary for 1853, under the date October 22, enters "Sanborn & friends" (*JMN*, 13:477). See October 24 below for his comment on the meeting which shows that Emerson invited the young men to Concord. I infer that Emerson replied to Sanborn's letter, though perhaps not at once and possibly more than once since the date proposed was changed.]

To William Francis Channing, Concord, September 1, 1853[60]

Concord, 1 September, 1853.

My dear Sir,

Your kind letter would almost decide my course for the next week, if I were free, [&] draw me to your mountains. But I promised my brother William in New York, a month since, that I would make a little excursion with him in September; and it is to the Cape, I believe, he is bound.[61] But I am pleased at heart to have been so kindly remembered by you, and in the interesting spot you have chosen. I know something of the scenery, & climbed Kearsarge[62] many years ago. I hope you will keep your invitation open, and in another year I mean to claim it. With kind respects to Mrs. Channing, Your gratefully,
W. F. Channing.   R. W. Emerson

To Ellen Emerson, Concord, September 26, 1853

[Rusk prints this undated letter, 4:387, and correctly argues for the date. The MS Account Book for 1853–1859, p. [278], has the entry "Sent Ellen cash by letter."]

To Miss A———, Concord:, September 27, 1853

[In Cabot's Bluebook Calendar 5 with the key number 80, is a note of a letter of September 27, 1853, to "Miss A." The letter is not in Cabot's index. A likely "Miss A" is Abby Larkin Adams.]

60. MS in the collections of RHi; ph. in NNC; printed by Granville Hicks, "Letters to William Francis Channing," *AL* (November 1930), 9:296; listed *Letters*, 4:384.
61. See *Letters*, 4:380, and n. 170.
62. There are no allusions to Mt. Kearsarge in Emerson's letters and journals. He does not appear to have been well enough to climb mountains in 1832; he is known to have done so in 1839, but the mountain is not far from Waterford, Maine, so that he might have climbed Kearsarge on any one of a number of visits to Waterford.

To John N. Pomeroy, Concord, September ? 1853

[In a letter of September 1, 1853, John N. Pomeroy of Rochester, New York, asks Emerson to lecture for the Rochester Athenaeum in the coming season. There is no entry for Rochester even in the tentative lecture engagements listed at the end of the MS Account Book for 1853–1859. Emerson would presumably have to write at least a letter of refusal.]

To John Greenleaf Whittier, Concord, October ? 1853

[Whittier's letter of October 24, 1853 (RWEMA), tells Emerson what train to take to keep his lecture engagement of October 28 (Charvat, p. 28); there was surely at least one letter to Whittier to settle the date.]

To Frank D. Farley, Concord, October 6, 1853

[In the MS Account Book for 1849–1953 (RWEMA), p. [279], Emerson records the payment of $53.72 to F. D. Farley for Ellen's board. Emerson would, I believe, have accompanied the payment with at least a note to this admired but unstable Brook Farmer. Farley had gone to Lenox in 1845; see George William Curtis to John Sullivan Dwight, September 14, 1845, *Early Letters of George W. Curtis to John S. Dwight*, George Willis Cooke, ed. (New York: Harper's, 1898), p. 228. When Hawthorne lived in Lenox, Farley had served as his copyist. See Henry W. Sams, *Autobiography of Brook Farm* (Englewood Cliffs, N.J.: Prentice Hall, 1958), pp. 14, 15, 18, 19, 24, 31, for letters from Brook Farm mentioning Farley; see Hawthorne, *Works*, 8:447, 450–451, 455, 605, 657, for Farley in the Berkshires, and see below, February 16, 1867, for his subsequent settlement in Iowa. In a letter of October 10, 1862 (MHi), Hawthorne appealed to James T. Fields for work for Farley, "my old and valued friend."]

To Francis Hall, Concord, October 7, 1853 [63]

Concord ⎫ 7 Oct.
Mass. ⎭ 1853

My dear Sir,

It would give me much pleasure to visit Elmira, if I can this winter.[64] At present, I dare not promise it. But I think it not improbable I shall make a western visit late in the winter, & should it be so, I will try to

63. MS in the Beinecke Library, CtY; ph. in NNC; printed by Cameron, *ESQ* (1st q., 1958), 10:38.
64. Emerson got to Elmira on February 18, 1854 (Charvat, p. 29); see below, December 8, 1853, and notes for January 31, 1854, for Francis Hall's later efforts to unscramble Emerson's upstate New York engagements.

apprize you of it in such season that you may keep a space open for me
in your Course.

With great regard,
R. W. Emerson.

To Julia Griffiths, Concord, October 24, 1853[65]

Concord ⎱ Oct 24
Mass.   ⎰ 1853

Miss Julia Griffiths
    In reply to your request I venture to send you a few lines, which I
hope will not come too late for your use.[66]

Respectfully,
R. W. Emerson

To Caroline Sturgis Tappan, Concord, October 24, 1853[67]

Concord, 24 October, 1853

Dear Caroline,
    How gladly I would go to Lenox with Ellen, but I am the only person
I know who has no leisure, & can never do a happy thing.[68] I am to go to
Philadelphia presently,[69] and am not quite ready, and am to go to the
printer presently, & am not quite ready.[70] I have never heard before of
any late plan of Ellery for going to Lenox and do not believe that his wife
would listen to such a proposition.[71] Pity that you find his II chapter so
bad, for I believe it is the best of all the five: and he tells me that he has

65. MS in the Barrett Collection, Alderman Library, ViU; ph. in NNC.
66. Julia Griffiths, in a letter of August 7, n.y. (RWEMA), solicited from Emerson a
contribution for "The Autograph for Freedom" (published as *Autographs for Freedom*), asking
it to be sent by mid-September. The annual, intended for sale in December for the Rochester
(New York) Anti-Slavery Society, was published with an 1854 date (*BAL*, 5224). Miss Griffiths' letter had to have been written in 1853; Emerson has endorsed it 1852. With this note
Emerson must have enclosed the MS of "Freedom" (*Works*, 9:198); in *Autographs for Freedom*,
it has the title "On Freedom." First drafts of the verses appear in MS journal HO, pp. 72–
77, *JMN*, 13:229–239. The poem betrays Emerson's difficulty in writing to order. See *The
Poetry Notebooks*, pp. 442 and 796.
67. MS in the Tappan papers, Houghton Library, MH; ph. in NNC.
68. Ellen returned to Mrs. Sedgwick's school with her friend Ida Wheeler and Ida's
father, Samuel G. Wheeler (a.l.s., Ellen Emerson to her father, November 1, 1853 (RWEMA)).
69. For the series of lectures initiated by Furness, see May 12 above.
70. *English Traits*, but the work was long delayed, see *BAL*, 5226, "London Editions," for
its being announced in England as early as July 9, 1852.
71. The Channings were on the verge of their first separation; see *Letters*, 4:404.

done his part "conscientiously." [72] When Ellen goes, I will try to send you a book or a name of a book that you will like: but you should have told me whether you found Thorpe's Mythology good or bad. [73] Perhaps I have accidental associations with the subject, that warp me in favor of such books. If you send the Causeries to Care of Phillips, Sampson, & Co, Boston they will come safe; or, just as well, as you propose, to Abel Adams, 2 Winthrop Place,—for the dear good head grows white, but sits over the same kind heart & stout frame. There is a very promising youth at Cambridge named Frank Sanborn whom I saw here last Saturday, [74]— a Junior, I believe, though my Eddy says "he is as tall as if he were standing on a chair" A very cheerful healthy sensible fellow he seemed, and a good friend of Clough's. Were you not glad to read of a North West Passage made at last? [75] Men have made great strides to the mastery of the globe, since I have been on it. But on the other fairer side the first step to the conquest is yet to be taken.

Ever yours,

R. W. E.

72. The projected book on "Country Walking," a work undertaken by Channing at Emerson's suggestion; it was to make use of passages from the journals of Emerson, Alcott, Thoreau; to be paid for by Emerson, and eventually to be published; it was not printed until Channing used it in his *Thoreau, the Poet Naturalist*. See *Letters*, 4:389, and Rollo G. Silver, "Ellery Channing's Collaboration with Emerson," *AL* (March 1935), 7:84–86. It is in his letter of October 6, printed by Silver, that Channing says he has worked "conscientiously." It is on the sixth that Emerson pays Channing $20.00 "on a/c of MSS. of 'Concord Walks'" (MS Account Book for 1853–1859, p. [279]). See above, May 5, for Ellery Channing's letter of May 4 (not in Silver).

73. Benjamin Thorpe, *Northern Mythology* (Harding, p. 292). Charles Augustin St. Beuve, *Causeries* (Harding, p. 238); see also *ER*, pp. 28 ff., where Emerson's withdrawals from the Athenaeum of some of the volumes of *Causeries* are listed. Since he withdrew volumes 3 and 4 in December 1853, I infer that he had lent Mrs. Tappan, volumes 1 and 2. These volumes are not in Emerson's library; the concern here for where they are to be sent suggests that he had borrowed the books for her. They belonged to Henry James, Sr. (*Letters*, 4:381).

74. In a letter of August 22, Sanborn had invited Emerson for a "conversation" with him and other Harvard students, proposing the date September 10. He had already called upon Emerson in July (*Recollections*, 1:46). See *JMN*, 13:6, 477.

75. Sir Robert John Le Mesurier M'Clure. M'Clure had made the discovery in October 1850, but M'Clure and the crew of his ice-bound ship, the *Investigator*, had not been rescued until June 17, 1853; transferred to the *Resolute* also to be icebound, M'Clure did not get his despatch out until Edward Augustus Inglefield, commanding the *Phoenix*, brought out Lieutenant Samuel G. Cresswell of the *Investigator* bearing M'Clure's account of his voyage and his land explorations dated from the Bay of Mercy April 1853. The news reached the American newspapers by the *Asia* and is reported in the *New-York Daily Tribune*, October 20 (p. 6) and the *Boston Daily Advertizer*, October 21 (p. 2) where Emerson must have read it. He alludes to the discovery, if not the discoverer, in *English Traits*, *Works*, 5:91.

To Henry Stephens Randall, Concord, November 15, 1853[76]

Concord, Mass.

15 November 1853

Dear Sir,

I am very happy to learn that so rich a gift is in store for me as the Documentary History of New York.[77] It will be very highly prized not only by me, but by some good students of northern history near me. If you will have the goodness to address the volumes for me to the "Care of Phillips, Sampson & Company, Boston," they will reach me securely. I am very much bound by the munificence of the State which collects & publishes these historical treasures, & by the personal kindness which directs them to me.

Respectfully & gratefully,

R. W. Emerson.

Henry S. Randall, Esq.
Secretary of State.

To Eben Norton Horsford, Concord, November 20? 1853

[In a letter of February 1, 1853 (RWEMA), Professor Eben Horsford acknowledges a letter of January 24, 1853, and mentions two earlier letters from Emerson, both concerning the date of his lecture for the Concord Lyceum. In his MS Pocket Diary for 1854 (*JMN*, 18:485–486), Emerson lists the lecturers he has invited for the Concord Lyceum; Horsford's name appears against the date February 8. I conjecture that at least one of the letters Horsford refers to was written on or about November 20, 1853; see letter to Theodore Parker, *Letters*, 4:404. As Emerson's correspondence with the lyceums he lectured for shows, the invitation and the settling of the date often called for at the least two letters and might require three. Horsford, who did get his dates mixed, describes Emerson's "first note" as proposing a Wednesday or a Thursday and his "next" as specifying February 8. I let this entry stand for both letters.]

76. MS in the Ransom Collection of Autograph Letters (31:84), CtLHi; copy in NNC. See November 21 below for Emerson's acknowledgment of the work (Harding, p. 82).

77. New York State.

TO HENRY STEPHENS RANDALL, CONCORD, NOVEMBER 21, 1853[78]

Concord } 21 Novr
Mass.tts } 1853.

Dear Sir,

The four volumes of the Documentary History of New York[79] arrived safely & welcome at my hands on Saturday night. It is a noble work, & does great honor to the gentlemen who have cooperated in its preparation, as well as to the State Government. I renew my thanks to you & through you to the Legislature for the munificent gift. I have also, this morning, received by mail your "Decision,"[80] which I shall examine with much interest.

Respectfully & gratefully,

Henry S. Randall { Secretary
{ of State.

Your Servant,
R. W. Emerson

TO ROBERT BULKELEY EMERSON, CONCORD, NOVEMBER 23? 1853

[In the MS Account Book for 1853–1859, p. 7, is an entry detailing expenses for the case of Bulkeley Emerson; it begins with "cash [1.00] sent in letter to RBE." This is listed again, p. [48], under the date November 21, in a two-page full account of expenses for the care of Bulkeley, one half of which is William Emerson's share.]

TO JAMES RUSSELL TRUMBULL, CONCORD, NOVEMBER 23, 1853[81]

Concord } 23 Novr
Masstts } 1853

Dear Sir,

I kept your invitation long by me in the belief that I should be able to combine a visit to Northampton with other engagements. I do not

78. MS in the Manuscript Collection of the Iowa State Education Association; ph. in NNC. The letter is inlaid; it was removed from an extra-illustrated edition of Dickens (catalogue note).

79. See Harding, p. 82, for this four-volume work; and see below, March 26, 1858, for Emerson's securing from Randall a set for Thoreau.

80. Emerson appears to be referring to an article by Randall, but no such title can be found. Randall had wanted the office of Secretary of State in New York chiefly because of his interest in public instruction. His term ran only through 1853, but he secured the establishment of a separate department of public instruction before his retirement; he was the author of the bill proposing it. The law was put into effect in 1854. It seems likely that what Emerson refers to concerns this legislation.

81. MS in the papers of the Northampton Young Men's Institute, Forbes Library, Northampton, Massachusetts; ph. in NNC. James Russell Trumbull, of Amherst, had settled in Northampton in March 1853 as editor of the Hampshire Gazette. His History of Northampton

find it easy to do so & must relinquish the hope[82] going thither at present.

Respectfully,
R. W. Emerson

J. R. Trumbull, Sec.y

To George Bailey Loring, Concord, November 27, 1853[83]

Concord
27 November, 1853

My dear Sir,

I was prevented from acknowledging your kind note yesterday. I am very much obliged by your courteous & friendly invitation, but I have found the railroad hours in the morning usually so impolite that I rarely venture to sleep out of a public house when away from home.[84] But if you are at home on Tuesday evening I promise myself to come & drink tea with you.

Yours with great regard,
R. W. Emerson

Mr Geo. B. Loring

(Northampton: Press of Gazette Printing, 1898, 1902), was completed by Nancy Z. and Anna Miller, who give a sketch of Trumbull's life in their preface to the second volume.

82. Emerson omitted the preposition here.

83. MS in the Phillips Library, MSaE; ph. in NNC; printed by Helen R. Deese (see March 26 above), Essex Institute Collections, (April 1986), vol. 122, no. 2.

84. Emerson lectured for the Salem Lyceum on Tuesday the 29th, repeating the lecture "American Character" for the same institution the following day, Charvat, p. 28. Emerson's MS Account Book for 1853–1865 shows, at p. 9, that he paid for four fares to Salem; the entry is under the date November 30. Apparently he returned home on the 29th and returned on the 30th. What is puzzling is Emerson's repeating a lecture in the same town for the same lyceum. Charvat gives no source for his title (it is not in the Pocket Diary, *JMN,* 13:477). Possibly the lectures were the two given in Philadelphia, March 14 and 15; See Charvat, p. 28, for the titles "The Anglo-American" and "American Power" and see Cabot, 2:754.

To E   H. Roberts, Concord, December 8, 1853[85]

Concord, 8 Dec.
Mass.tts 1853

Dear Sir,

You shall hold me engaged to you for the 25 January next.[86]

Respectfully,
R. W. Emerson

E. H. Roberts, Esq.

To Francis Hall, Concord, December 8, 1853[87]

Concord 8 Dec.r
Mass.tts 1853

My dear Sir,

I have mislaid at this moment your newly received letter, but I had seen at once that it could not meet my plans. I am to be at Utica on the 25 /Jan/ & now at Auburn on 23 & I believe at Palmyra on 24th I am promised to be at Toledo on 31 ⟨Feb⟩Jany & at ⟨Chicago⟩ /Detroit/ at the beginning of February, having promises at Chicago about 6 Feb. and even as far as Milwaukie.[88] so that the best I can promise will be an exact account of myself to you from my western terminus that if it be not too late in your season, you may give me a space on my return, & Mr Tompkins[89] may do the like at Binghamton. I am sorry to have occasioned you this uncertainty & dislocation of plans; but I have been absent from home, & could not promptly reply to your note. I do not go to Philadelphia, until 1 January, & stay there three weeks

Respectfully,
R. W. Emerson

Francis Hall, Esq.

85. MS in Special Collections, University Library, OU. This note was originally laid in a copy of Emerson's *Essays,* 1844. The book has the name of William Russell on the flyleaf and the text is marked. The names of additional subsequent owners appear at the foot of the flyleaf with dates, the last of which is 1895.

86. See Charvat for lecture at Utica January 25, 1854, and *Letters,* 4:423, and n. 49.

87. MS in the Feinberg collection, MiD; ph. in NNC; printed by White, *AL* (May 1961), 33:166. The addressee is Francis Hall, Elmira (see October 7 above and January 31, 1854, below), who was attempting to make additional New York State engagements for Emerson. The letter to which this is a reply is not in the Emerson papers.

88. The initial "s" is clearly lower case in spite of the preceding period. The letter shows many signs of haste.

89. Possibly Phineas B. Tompkins, town clerk in 1850-51, or Edward Tompkins, lawyer. The Binghamton Young Men's Library Association was founded in 1852.

To Hannah Thomas Davis, Concord? December 9? 1853

[In the MS Account Book for 1853–1859, an entry of December 9 (p. 13) reads: "Sent to Mrs C. G. Davis subscription of Scholars of G. P. Bradford." See *Letters*, 4:410, 411, and n. 278 for the fund raised by George P. Bradford's students to give him a trip to Europe. I conjecture that Mrs. Charles Gideon Davis is meant here. A Hannah Thomas married Charles G. Davis in 1845 (William T. Davis, *Ancient Landmarks of Plymouth*, Part 2, p. 81).]

To George Barrell Emerson, Concord, December 12, 1853[90]

Concord 12 Decr 1853

Dear George,

I am much gratified by your friendly summons,[91] and I should highly enjoy the occasion, but I am promised to be in Maine, at Lewiston, on that day,—the 15th. All the more, I charge you to see that the Republic of letters receives no detriment. With joy that it is in such good hands,

Ever, your affectionate
Cousin Waldo E.

George B. Emerson, Esq.

To Benjamin Rodman, Concord, December 14? 1853

[In his letter of December 13, 1853 (RWEMA), Benjamin Rodman extends his usual invitation for Emerson to be his guest when he lectures in New Bedford December 20 (Charvat, p. 28).]

To William Henry Furness, Concord, December 18, 1853[92]

Concord, 18 Dec.r
1853

My dear friend,

I am afflicted with a fastgrowing terror lest I should fail to meet these fine fortunes you are preparing for me,[93] so you must mix a little wormwood from some quarter, that it may not turn my head. Far be it from

90. MS in the G. B. Emerson papers, MHi; ph. in NNC.
91. Emerson's cousin, in a letter of December 9 (RWEMA), invited him on behalf of the State Board of Education to speak at the dinner following the dedication of a hall for the use of the State Normal School at Framingham.
92. MS in the Furness papers, Van Pelt Library, PU; ph. in NNC; printed in *Records*, p. [90]; listed *Letters*, 4:411.
93. The course of private lectures arranged for by Furness; see above May 12, and *Letters*, 4:390–391.

me to murmur or interfere in any manner, but, on the contrary, I dispose myself to obey you & the gods with all docility. Only I hope I may have something good & fit to say to such beneficient immortals & mortals. For "tickets to the press," o certainly; as, perhaps, by sending them, they may be moved to stay away, or, if they come, may listen to good counsel & make short reports. For a boardinghouse I shall be very glad to be provided if you know one without seeking. I have uniformly gone to hotels—in Cincinnati St Louis, New York, but this would be far better.

You speak of my Mother[94] I cannot tell you how much my house has suffered by the loss of that one more room, one more home in it for me & each of us. Mamma was made to live, & her death at 85 years took us by surprise, & my wife mourns so many undone things. There was something majestic in one of those old strong frames built to live so tranquilly usefully & kindly. The later generation seem to me to spend faster. But one of these days we too shall be better than now. Then now & ever your affectionate

Waldo Emerson

W. H. Furness.

I see that your date is 12th.[95] I only got home last night from an absence of three days to find your note.[96] Perhaps I shall mend my Programme tomorrow. Meantime I shall tread securer if you can ascertain for me whether the five Lectures which I read in 1849–50 were severally these;—

1 England
2 Natural Aristocracy
3 Eloquence
4 Spirit of the Age, or XIX Century
5 Books

I read a sixth on "Instinct & Inspiration" by daylight; but I should gladly know if any youth or maid have a memory so incredibly tenacious as to verify this list. Or was there, instead of one of these topics, a Lecture called the "Superlative"[97]

94. Ruth Haskins Emerson died November 16.
95. The date of Furness' letter.
96. Lecturing in Maine.
97. For this long postscript, Emerson used the recto and verso of half a single leaf of quarto letter paper. He turned the resulting sheet so that the rough edge is on the right of the recto and the left of the verso. Henry Howard Furness prints the text as a postscript to

To David Atwood Wasson, Concord, December 21? 1853

[In a letter of November 23, 1852, David Wasson asked Emerson to bring with him to Newburyport the *Bāgvāt-Gēētā*. In a letter of May 30, 1854, Wasson enthusiastically thanks Emerson for the loan of the book and refers to a letter of "last winter" from Emerson "giving me notice of your coming," which "did not arrive until you had been there and gone." Emerson lectured in Newburyport on December 23, 1853; I conjecture that the letter Wasson refers to was sent just before the scheduled date; Emerson apparently brought the book as asked. Wasson's letters to Emerson are with the Cabot papers in the Schlesinger Library, Radcliffe.]

To Julia Ward Howe, Concrod, December 30, 1853 [98]

Concord⎱ 30 Dec,r
Masstts ⎰ 1853

Dear Mrs Howe,

I am just leaving home with much ado of hasty preparation for an absence of some weeks, but must take a few moments to thank you for the happiness your gift brings me.[99] It was very kind in you to send it to me, who had forfeited all apparent claim to such favor, by breaking all the laws of good neighborhood, in these years. But you were entirely right in sending it, because, I fancy, that among all your friends, few had so earnest a desire to know your thoughts, &, I may say, so much regret at never seeing you, as I. And the book, as I read in it, meets this curiosity, & better than curiosity of mine, by its poems of character & confidence, private lyrics, whose air & words are all your own. I have not gone so far in them as to have any criticism to offer you, & like better the pure pleasure I find in a new book of poetry so warm with life. Perhaps, when I have finished the book, I shall ask the privilege of saying

---

Emerson's letter of March 24, 1850 (see above and *Records*, 10, 76); but the text cannot possibly belong to a letter written before the lectures listed were given in Philadelphia (April 3–11; see Charvat, p. 25). In 1853, he might reasonably hope for a "youth or maid" who might recall these lectures of 1850. For the lectures of 1854, see Charvat, pp. 28–29.

98. MS in the Chapin Library, MWiW; ph. in NNC. The text fills five pages; the extra page appears now on the recto of a single leaf. Traces of gummed paper still adhere to the fourth page and to the extra leaf. Remnants of glue on the fourth page partially obscure some end-of-line letters, which can however be read in the original if not on the photocopy. Printed inaccurately by Laura Richards and Maud Howe Elliott, *Julia Ward Howe* (Boston: Houghton Mifflin, 1916), 1:139–140; listed *Letters*, 4:412.

99. Mrs. Howe's *Passion Flowers* (BAL, 9409) was published anonymously in deference to Dr. Samuel Gridley Howe's objections to his wife's appearing publicly as an author, but her authorship was no secret. The book is not now in Emerson's library.

something further.[100] At present, I content myself with thanking you.

With great regard,
R. W. Emerson

Mrs Howe.

To ? 1853

[In the *Month at Goodspeed's* (April 1966), 37(7):196, a letter of 1853 from Concord is described. The letter says that he "cannot visit Greenfield or Holyoke"; listed *ESQ* (2d q., 1967), 47:125. There is no extant letter from a Greenfield or Holyoke correspondent to provide a clue to the date; presumably the letter concerns lecturing and would refer to the 1853–1854 season.]

100. Mrs. Howe's reply of January 1, 1854 (RWEMA), seizes on this half-promise, but there is no evidence that Emerson fulfilled it.

1854

To Henry Reed, Philadelphia, January 14, 1854[1]

La Pierre House,
1, Jany, 1854.

My dear Sir,

Your little condition affixed to the Contract, namely, that I should send you my opinion of Mr. Wordsworth's Genius has checked my readiness to send you my mite for the tablet, until this time: for I have been in New York two days, & there is no time in Philadelphia, I find, for a stranger;—no time there to fit & form his obligations to the solitariest & wisest of Poets, I do not know but I must defer it altogether to a silent hour, by & by, far from cities. It is very easy to see, that to act so powerfully on this practical age, he needed, with all his oriental abstraction, the indomitable vigor rooted in animal constitution, for which his country men are marked. Otherwise he could not have resisted the deluge-streams of their opinion with success. One would say, he is the only man among them who has not in any point succumbed to their ways of thinking, & has prevailed. I mean, not consciously consented,—for his Church and State, though genuine enough in him, I look upon as the limitations & not the excellence of his genius.

Rather than not write, I will send this rude note, referring my right to communicate a more considered ballot, as soon as I find a quiet half hour to rejoice in my remembrances of this old benefactor. I hope you do not want the newspaper you were good enough to leave with me; for, though I hid it for safety, evil hands, I fear, have taken it. I enclose $15.00.

Gratefully & respectfully Yours,
R. W. Emerson.

Professor Henry Reed.

1. No MS has been found; text from a typescript in the Berg Collection; NN; printed by Reed, *Transactions of the Wordsworth Society* (1853), no. 5, p. 124, with the date January 1; the MS as listed in a catalogue of Bangs & Co., 1901, also has the date January 1. Rusk demonstrates that the probable date is January 14 (*Letters*, 4:417–418). In a letter of January 9 (RWEMA), Reed asked for a contribution and a comment; in a letter of the 16th, he

To William Henry Furness, Philadelphia, January 21, 1854[2]

LaPierre House
4 o'clock
21 Jany

My dear friend,

To my mortification, the day is proving all too short to hold what belongs to it, and am not getting to your house, nor to Sam B's,[3] nor to Mr Kanes.[4] A visit to Pennington's,[5] a call at Dr Hares,[6] notes, &c. have cut me short. Well, you must do as you are wont, namely, persuade your household & my other friends that my short comings are merits!

I send to Frank,[7] with my love, a stereoscope & photograph of a piece of sunshine which he must admire as much as I did.

Ever your bounden
Waldo E.

To Edward Bangs, Detroit, January 31, 1854[8]

Detroit Michigan
31 January 1854

My dear Sir,

I have never had the good fortune to meet you since our conversation at the Athenaeum,[9] but, as I have never heard from you, I am holding

regrets missing Emerson on Saturday (the 14th) "when you did me the favour to leave your . . . contribution" and thanks him for "the acceptable note that accompanied it." The contribution is noted in the MS Account Book for 1853–1859, p. 19, where the entry is dated only January, the date covering a cluster of entries including the payment to Elizabeth Sedgwick for Ellen's schooling; see *Letters*, 5:421, for evidence that this bill was paid on January 19.

There may be another letter to Reed or to his wife, for in his letter of the 16th Reed says his wife has written Emerson to invite him to call that evening.

2. MS in the Furness papers, Van Pelt Library, PU; ph. in NNC; the date is 1854, when Emerson gave his Philadelphia course, the last lecture was delivered on the 20th; he left Philadelphia on the afternoon of the 21st (*Letters*, 4:420).

3. Samuel Bradford. Emerson omitted the necessary "I" here.

4. In a letter to his wife (*Letters*, 4:415–416), Emerson alludes to "Mr Kane" as among his Philadelphia friends; the reference is indexed by Rusk under Elisha Kent Kane, but Dr. Kane was in the Arctic in the winter of 1853–1854. Emerson is probably referring to the explorer's brother Thomas Leiper Kane. Emerson's Pocket Diary for 1854 (*JMN*, 13:484, 499), twice lists T. L. Kane, "8" Girard St.; Philadelphia directories give his address as 38 Girard St.

5. John Pennington's bookstore; see *Letters*, 3:141.

6. Robert Hare, M.D.; see *Letters*, 4:415, n. 10. Hare's name is listed inside the front cover of the MS Pocket Diary for 1854, *JMN*, 13:484.

7. Furness' son.

8. MS in the Feinberg Collection, MiD; ph. in NNC; printed by White, *AL* (May 1961), 33:166–167; listed *Letters*, 4:426 from an auction catalogue.

9. Emerson had withdrawn books from the Boston Athenaeum more than once in December (*ER*, p. 28); it was probably on one of these occasions that he met Bangs.

you firm to your good will on that occasion. Accordingly you will find yourself booked in the registers of the Concord Lyceum as the Lecturer for the evening of the 22 February, & a full expectation from all worthy citizens & ladies of that town awaiting you. Mainly too my wife & I expect you without fail at our door. I believed I should have been at home earlier than this, & it now looks a little doubtful whether I shall return sooner than the 20th instant. If any accident in so many weeks has made the above named day inconvenient to you, (which I trust may not be the case,) I must refer you in my absence to A. G. Fay Esq or Rev B. Frost,[10] as my colleagues in the curatorship at Concord. But do not fail me.[11]

Yours affectionately,
R. W. Emerson

Edward Bangs, Esq.

To Alfred Wilkinson, Detroit, January 31, 1854[12]

Detroit, 31 Jany. 1854

Dear Sir,

I was to tell you when I should pass Syracuse on my return from these parts. I have offered the evening of 13 February to the Association at Palmyra N. Y. & mean in that week to keep some other promises at Penn Yan, Elmira, and other towns. In this distance, & the uncertainty of obtaining any reply until I arrive in your neighborhood, I will venture to offer you Friday 17 Feb.y[13] If that night, from any cause, does not suit you, I believe I must refer you to Mr Francis Hall, at Elmira, to whom I am also writing, & whom I shall authorize to make some other engagements that week for me.

Respectfully,
R. W. Emerson.

Mr Alfred Wilkinson.

10. The Reverend Addison G. Fay and the Reverend Barzillai Frost. Emerson had served as a curator of the Concord Lyceum frequently in the forties. This season was his first term of service in the fifties. Emerson's list of speakers for this season is in his MS Pocket Diary for 1854, verso of titlepage, *JMN*, 13:485–486, with Bangs down for the 22nd. The list shows a liberal choice from Emerson's friends with Thoreau leading on December 14.

11. See *Letters*, 4:424, 431.

12. MS in Special Collections, CSt; ph. in NNC.

13. See Charvat, p. 29, and, below, notes to the letter to Francis Hall for these upstate New York engagements; the Franklin Institute of Syracuse accepted the date Emerson offers here.

To Francis Hall, Detroit, January 31, 1854[14]

Detroit, 31 Jany. 1854

My dear Sir,

I do not find that my times quite fit yours, this winter. I am to be at Toledo, O. on the 11th: then, I have offered J. C. Gallup of Palmyra, to be there on the 13th Feby.;[15] and to Mr A Wilkinson of Syracuse,[16] I have offered the 17th Friday. Then, and this is the principal fact, I have taken the liberty to refer both those gentlemen to you, if these evenings do not suit them: & I wish to put myself on your goodness to make a little plan for me, even if I cannot come to Elmira,[17] that will allow me to go to those two towns, and to Penn Yan[18] & perhaps Corning or Brighamton,[19] from all which places I have invitations. I cannot come within corresponding distance of these gentlemen, until I reach N.Y. &[20] I dreamed like an Indian that you would befriend me & make a weeks programme for me. The whole fact you possess in knowing that I am to be in Toledo 11 Feb. I wish to go home on Saturday, or Monday, at farthest.

With best hope & assurance,

Yours,

R. W. Emerson

Mr. Francis Hall.

14. No MS has been located; text from a copy provided by John Olin Eidson, who printed the letter (then in a dealer's hands) in his "Two Unpublished Letters by Emerson," *AL* (November 1849), 21:335–336, with informative notes and an account of the enterprising Hall, at that time a bookseller. Listed *Letters*, 4:426, from Hall's reply. See above December 8, 1853, for initial correspondence with Hall.

15. Identified by Eidson (n. 3) as James C. Gallup. Hall's reply of February 6 (RWEMA, printed by Eidson, p. 336), gives the 14th as the date for the lecture at Palmyra; the date is confirmed by the Wayne *Sentinel* of February 15 (Eidson, n. 7). Emerson's Pocket Diary for 1854 has the correction (*JMN*, 13:490).

16. See above, letter of the same date to Alfred Wilkinson. This date is confirmed by the Syracuse *Daily Standard* of February 16 (Eidson, n. 8).

17. Emerson lectured in Elmira on the 18th as announced in the Elmira *Republican* of that date (Eidson, n. 9). Emerson's Pocket Diary entries for Elmira and Penn Yan are both in pencil (*JMN*, 13:490–491).

18. The Penn Yan date is incorrectly given as February 15 by Charvat (p. 29), although the date in the Pocket Diary (*JMN*, 13:490), is clearly the 16th confirmed by the *Yates County Whig* of February 23 (Eidson, n. 7). The subject of the lecture was "The Anglo-American."

19. No arrangements for Corning or Binghamton were made. Eidson's printed text and his copy both read "Brighamton," and I have so printed it although I question that Emerson made such an error; I believe it to be a misreading of Emerson's carelessly formed "in." There are now no letters from Corning or Binghamton in the Emerson papers.

20. Eidson's printed text has a period here instead of the ampersand that appears in his copy.

To Penn-Yan,[21] I particularly should like to go; yet I find, I have not with me the name of the gentleman who invited me;—a different person from my last year's correspondent.

To Henry James, Sr., Chicago, February 8, 1854[22]

Chicago 8 February, 1854

My dear James,

Was I not to write you a line from Detroit? Well, to your ample vista the space betwixt Detroit & Chicago is ⟨a⟩inappreciable and if it were Nebraska it would be the same. And yet the material measures in this country are very impressive to one whose habit & acquaintance, like mine, have been wholly in corners. I have been for four or five days in Wisconsin,[23] &, through a railroad accident, was forced to ride 60 or 70 miles in an open sleigh, through plots of sea like prairie & huge stretches of "Oak openings."[24] There is nothing but size, or nothing else in winter; for the only variation is from stagnant to rolling prairie, &, on the last, all the trees are oaks. I saw, in a whole day, only a few maples, a few hickories, & never a pine. Yet the farmers—a class which I always respect —have here a new interest as colonists, & the historical importance of these days & of their work here, which the traveller cannot lose sight of, they too seem to have some dignified prevision of. And the courage & selfreliance which their work has required, I find in their faces. But they are all violently preoccupied, and there is no thinking or reading in all this Siberia. Harper, Putnam, & the N. Y. Tribune, are the gentle boundaries of the wings of the Illinois & Wisconsin Muses. And yet, on Rock river, I found such warm & expectant watching of your genius, your proper opinions & career, that I was too glad to buy a welcome by sacrificing the "Letter to the Sectarian" (which you gave me for viaticum,) to the ardour of a young clergyman who promised to read it to all the

21. Eidson's printed text and his copy have a hyphen here, but Emerson frequently runs words together, the long stroke that links them should not be read as a hyphen.

22. MS in the James papers, Houghton Library, MH; ph. in NNC; printed by Perry, 1:76; listed in *Letters*, 4:428.

23. Lecturing in Janesville, Milwaukee, and Beloit (Charvat, p. 29); see below, March 14, where Emerson's allusion to the sleigh ride suggests that it carried him from Janesville, Wisconsin, to Milwaukee. The trip back to Beloit would be only slightly longer. Emerson later bought Wisconsin land; of this awkward purchase, Hubert Hoeltje gives an account in his "Emerson's Venture in Western Lane," *AL* (January 1931), 2:438–440. See also below, October 14, 1862.

24. Whether this is to be taken as an allusion to Cooper's novel is not clear.

ministers of his town.[25] I could safely praise it to him also, & mark the capital sentences, for I had read it well, though not enough. I told him what I had found,—that nobody accosted the truth so largely and adequately as this amateur writer, and with a sound humanity, too, which kept him from losing his way. Nay, it might be seen in this very tract, that he could take two or three consecutive steps in the same direction,—a feat scarce accomplished by another man in the century—and that, with so much wit, so much penetration, & so much right manly purpose he could only fail of being what we call a classic, from some apparent scorn of details & finish. I tried hard to keep my minister from too much admiration, by accusing the Scholastic dress & dialectic forms; but he was determined to be pleased, & I had to leave him. And by this time, I doubt not, all Rockford is impregnated. And here is the end of my paper & I not arrived at what I had to say.

Affectionately,

Henry James, Esq. R. W. Emerson

To Francis Hall, Palmyra, February 14, 1854[26]

Palmyra

14 Feb 1854

My Dear Sir,

I am very much bound by your persistent & efficient good offices in making & getting ratified my week's programme. I was very sensible of the liberty I took in putting it upon you, but ventured, not knowing how else to help myself. I find here your new proposition, and decide to come to Elmira on Saturday, where it only because you ask it, though I had made up my mind to go homeward that day, as, indeed, it is high time I should.

your obliged servant,

R W Emerson

Mr Francis Hall.

25. Emerson lectured in Rockford, Illinois, on February 5 (Charvat, p. 29). In his MS Pocket Diary for 1854 with his memo of the lecture, he enters the name "Rev. John M. Windsor," possibly the clergyman referred to here and, certainly the name of the man with whom he corresponded. *The Church of Christ not an Ecclesiasticism;* Letter to a Sectarian (New York: Redfield, 1854).

26. MS in the Feinberg collection, MiD; ph. in NNC; printed by White, *AL* (May 1961), 33:167, where the heading gives the correct year, but the text is given the incorrect dateline "14 Feb 1856"; the MS is correctly dated. See above, January 31, for Hall's efforts on Emerson's behalf. Emerson arrived home on the night of the 20th; he certainly did not lecture in Vernon, N. Y., on that day (Charvat, p. 29, where the entry for Vernon is

To Anna Parsons, Concord, February 22, 1854?

[A letter to Mrs. Parsons was originally in the Colson estate, its present where-abouts unknown. Emerson tells Mrs. Parsons that he will call at Winter Street on Saturday. The addressee then is the wife of the poet-dentist Thomas William Parsons, whose home and office was at 16 Winter Street until he moved to the Hotel Pelham in 1873. The earliest possible year is 1852 (the stationery requires an envelope). The earliest date with evidence of a Saturday visit to Boston is 1854, when he withdrew books from the Athenaeum on the 25th (*ER*, p. 28).

Ruled out are 1861 and 1868 when the 22nd itself was a Saturday; ruled out also are years when Emerson's lecture schedule took him out of the state: 1855, 1860, 1865, 1866, 1867; and 1873, when he was abroad. Unlikely are 1856 and 1861 when Saturday was the following day; unlikely also is 1857 when Emerson had the measles (*Letters*, 5:63, and letter of March 3, 1857, Ellen Emerson to her cousin Charlotte Haskins). A faithful member of the Saturday Club, Emerson can be placed in Boston on Saturday after February 22 in 1858, 1859, 1863, 1864, 1869–72; the latter years seem unlikely because letters from Mrs. Parsons to Emerson of December 1873 imply that she has not seen him for some time.]

To Henry David Thoreau, Concord, March 5, 1854[27]

Sunday Eve

Dear Henry,

I am off again to New York in the morning, & go leaving my Professor Horsford once more to your tender mercies. He is to come surely Wednesday Evening, & I ventured to promise him your kind conduct to the Hall. So you must come to tea, & hear the Chemistry.

Ever your bounden
R. W. E.

To William Emerson, Norwich (Conn.), March 8, 1854

[William Emerson, in an addition of March 10 to his letter of the 9th (Dr. Wortis), assures his brother that his baggage ought to be on the boat; he has made inquiries. He is obviously answering a note from Emerson, possibly more than

___

questioned); no engagement for Vernon is listed in the Pocket Diary for 1854 or in the manifestly earlier engagement list on the final pages of the Account Book for 1853–1859. Vernon does appear in listings for 1855; and Emerson had received invitations from Vernon before that year.

27. MS in the Barrett Collection, Alderman Library, ViU; ph. in NNC; p. [4] addressed: Henry D. Thoreau. | Concord. Eben M. Horsford was to have lectured for the Concord Lyceum on February 8, MS Pocket Diary for 1854 (*JMN*, 13:486), and on that occasion, too, Thoreau had been deputized to act as host (*Letters*, 4:413, and 2); the lecture was postponed to March 8. Emerson is in New York on March 7, "a prisoner" of his "papers" as he prepares to deliver that night his (second) address on the Fugitive Slave Law (*Works*, 11:217–244), for the fourth anniversary of Webster's speech of 1850. See March 14 below. Sunday in 1854 fell on the 5th. No other day or year fulfills the conditions of this letter. "Wednesday" is

one. See *Letters*, 4:432, for letter of the 10th reporting that the baggage was found.]

To Moncure Daniel Conway, Concord, March 12, 1854[28]

Concord, 12 March, 1854.

My dear Sir,

On my return I find your note. I fear I cannot exactly identify the book you want, on the egg-form in Vases. It is one of D. R. Hay's books, which I had for a few weeks several years ago and looking at the list of his works, I believe, it must be one of these two, namely,

"Proportion, or the Geometric principles of Beauty analyzed." 4to. London, 1846.

or

"First principles of Symmetrical Beauty." 12mo. 1846

The volumes which I had, belonged to Miss Peabody, & were sold by her. I had a few of the drawings copied for me by a friend, which I shall be glad to show you, whenever you will come & see me.

Yours,

R. W. Emerson

Mr Conway.

To Elizabeth Dwight Sedgwick, March 12? 1854

[In a letter of March 5, 1854 (RWEMA), Elizabeth Sedgwick asks Emerson to let her know whether Ellen Emerson is to remain at her school through the summer term. In a letter of March 20, Emerson tells his daughter that he has told Mrs. Sedgwick that she will be returning for the summer term; see *Letters*, 4:434. In n. 101, Rusk conjectures that Emerson may have visited Lenox on his way from or to New York for his anti-slavery lecture, but if he had done so, Ellen would not have to be informed by letter of the decision. Moreover, it is clear that Emerson did not visit Lenox on his return from New York, for he traveled by boat; see *Letters*, 4:432.

[Emerson may have had some difficulty in writing because of the affair of the raisins and nuts. In a birthday box, the Emersons had sent their daughter what they regarded as fruit, knowing that Mrs. Sedgwick forbade cake and candy and

---

written over an incompletely washed-out word with an opening letter having an ascender— either "Tuesday" or "Thursday."

28. MS in the John Hay Library, RPB; ph. in NNC. The letter answers Conway's query of March 3 (Conway papers, Special Collections, Butler Library, NNC); as Conway puts it, there is no reference to vases or to the eggshape. See *JMN*, 16:131–132, and 250, for allusions to Hay's theory of the form of Etruscan vases; the editors of *JMN* cite Hay's *The Science of Beauty* . . . (1856), p. 87. Emerson's statement of the theory in the journal passage cited uses the word "ellipse."

assuming that fruit was not forbidden. Ellen ate the nuts and found herself in disgrace much to the indignation of her mother who did not want her daughter's integrity questioned. "Your father," she tells Ellen, "is rather disgusted and provoked—and will not write ... to Mrs Sedgwick. ... He says 'tell Ellen to use common sense and ask Mrs. S. to do the same' " (a.l.s., Mrs. Emerson to Ellen, February 28, RWEMA). In the letter of March 5 Mrs. Sedgwick tactlessly refers to the affair "as the only wrong thing" Ellen has done "so far as I know" and says she does "not lay it up against her." Mrs. Sedgwick's letters are rarely gracious; this one could not have delighted the father.]

To WILLIAM HENRY FURNESS, CONCORD, MARCH 14, 1854[29]

> Concord ⎱ 14 March
> Masstts ⎰ 1854

My dear friend,

I carried all the kind words & deeds of Philadelphia as stock to think on in my Northwestern journey, and the wonder of them is not less, nor the blessing, unto this day.[30] I have never told you that I went as far as Milwaukee, and, fault of broken railroad, the last ⟨s⟩65 miles in an open carriage; and found true what a settler told me, that "the world was done up in large lots, in Wisconsin." I am afraid the space is the most interesting feature. And yet the farmer is also a Colonist, & draws great doses of energy from his local necessities. One looks around heedfully, too, because it is plainly the heroic age of Wisconsin, and we are spectators Anno Urbis Conditae.[31] I came home near three weeks ago, with good hope to write a plea for Freedom addressed to my set; which, of course, like a Divinity Collegian's first sermon, was to exhaust the subject & moral science generally; but I fared much as those young gentlemen do, got no answer to my passionate queries—nothing but the echo of my own cries, and had to carry to New York a makeshift instead of an oracle.[32] Yet I am still so foolish as to believe again that the thing I wished can be done,

29. MS in the Furness papers, Van Pelt Library, PU; ph. in NNC; printed in Records, p. [92]; quoted in part by Edward Waldo Emerson, *J*, 8:448; listed in *Letters*, 4:433.

30. According to Charvat (p. 28), the Philadelphia course was apparently Emerson's most successful so far; but I have been unable to find anywhere an Account Book entry for January 21, 1854. An entry on p. 8 of the Account Book for 1853–1859 gives no sum at all; an entry of March (p. 12) gives $118.00 as the balance received from Furness & Brinley Co. Among uncatalogued business papers (RWEMA) is a separate sheet headed: "Furness, Brinley & Co 1854," giving money due January 21, 1854, and a list of payments made. The gross receipts are given as $1,357.39; expenses totaling $191.05 leave the net receipts at $1,166.34 (Charvat's figure), of which $1,044.00 in four installments had been paid, leaving a balance due of $122.34. The March payment of $118.00 brings the actual net receipts to $1,162.

31. In the year of the founding of the city, i.e., Rome.

32. The New York address on the Fugitive Slave Law.

& I shall not cease to try—after a time: I have not been to Boston yet with a free hour. As soon as I do, I shall try to get my head of Carlyle copied for you, as I said. In New York I found Mr Sam Lawrence[33] the London artist, who, you will remember, had painted a head of Carlyle, which Mr Car⟨y⟩ey had copied. He had brought a letter to me from C. and is painting prosperously in N.Y. He is taking Bancroft's head, & Miss Lynch's, &c &c[34] I find myself too much in arrears to my tasks here, to think quite yet of making my hoped visit to Philadelphia. Yet I shall gladly come. Meantime I am going down to Cambridge to learn what good news I can from Horace.[35] When is it, what week, what day, that you are to come there, & here?—Did you read in Littells Living Age, a little story or novellette, called "Art, a Dramatic Sketch." by, ____ Read, Esq.[36]—I found Dr Kane's book excellent.[37]

Your affectionate
Waldo Emerson

William H. Furness.

To Richard Bentley, Concord, March 20, 1854[38]

Concord⎫ 20 March
Mass.tts. ⎭ 1854

Dear Sir,

I regretted extremely the interruption which has delayed the completion of my Book, and I have feared that you might think yourself ill used in this long delay of a ⟨boo⟩work in which you had acquired some interest.[39] But the hindrances have been unavoidable. (I ought to say, meantime, that I never authorized the advertising the book her or in England.) Nor am I yet ready to fix a day when the book shall be done, though I

33. Samuel Laurence; see Slater, p. 496, for Carlyle's letter of introduction for Laurence. As a frontispiece for the Carey and Hart edition of Carlyle's *Miscellanies;* see, above, letters to Furness of 1845.

34. Anne Charlotte Lynch, who later married Vincenzo Botta.

35. Furness' son. Furness was to speak at the Divinity College July 16; see July 15 below.

36. Charles Reade's "Art, a Dramatic Sketch," was first published in *Bentley's Miscellany* (December 1853, January 1854), from which it was reprinted in *Littell's Living Age* (February 18, 1854), 40:363–383.

37. Elisha Kent Kane, *The U.S. Grinnell Expedition in Search of Sir John Franklin: A Personal Narrative* (New York: Harper, 1853).

38. MS in NNPM; ph. in NNC. This letter is reproduced in facsimile and printed by the Thoreau Society and the Friends of the Dartmouth Library (1954) in a souvenir brochure (for *Walden*) edited by Herbert F. West (not in *BAL*); see M, A64.1.a, pp. 505–506.

39. Neither Blanck nor Myerson found any printing of *English Traits* by Bentley, although the earliest located advertisement of the book (July 9, 1853) is by Bentley (*BAL*, 5226, "London Edition"). The English edition was printed by Routledge.

am now seriously at work, again, on it ⟨&⟩with a good hope of bringing it
to some end.

I write today to bring another matter to your attention.

A friend of mine, Mr Henry D. Thoreau, is about to publish, by
Ticknor, Fields, & Co. Boston, a book he calls "Walden, a life in the
woods." It will make a volume about the size of Carlyle's "Past and
Present." Mr Thoreau is a man of rare ability: he is a good scholar, & a
good naturalist, and he is a man of genius, & writes always with force, &
sometimes with wonderful depth & beauty. This book records his solitary
life in the woods by Walden (a lake in this State,) for a couple of years.
⟨his experiences⟩ and his observations of life & nature. He has mother
wit. I have great confidence in the merit & in the success of the work.

This book Ticknor & Co begin to print this week, & will stereotype
2000 copies. I should be glad if you inclined to publish it, in London.
Will you do so? Ticknor & Co. mean to have the book ready about 1
May, and they can send you the revises as fast as they are printed, &, at
the end, might wait for you the needful time. If you incline to print it,
have the goodness to write immediately what terms you will offer Mr
Thoreau for copyright.[40]

Respectfully, your obedt serv.t

R. W. Emerson

Mr Richard Bentley

——

I forgot to say that Mr Thoreau is known here by a remarkable book
called "A week on the Concord & Merrimac Rivers."

To Arthur Hugh Clough, Concord, March 28, 1854[41]

Concord⎤ 28 March

Mass^tts ⎦1854

My dear Clough,

My friend, Mr George P. Bradford,[42] goes to London tomorrow, & I
can not let him go without a charge to call on you. I know not how it
happened, that he, whom we have the habit of looking at as if he were all

40. Bentley did not publish *Walden* either. West gives an account of James T. Fields'
efforts on Thoreau's behalf.

41. MS in the Clough papers, Bodleian Library, Oxford; ph. in CUL; printed in *Emerson-
Clough Letters*, No. 22, and in Mulhauser, 2:480; listed *Letters*, 4:435.

42. Bradford's trip to Europe was financed by a gift from his students; see above
December 9, 1853. The self-deprecatory Bradford made no great effort to see the friends to
whom Emerson introduced him; see *Letters*, 4:459, 480.

one as of our house & blood, did not meet you, when you were here. Well, he knows every body here whom I love, & is loved by every body that knows him. And you must give him a chance to repair the above-named defect of not knowing you.

I use the occasion the gladlier, because I suffer month by month the chronic remorse of my silence to you. But I have not recovered from the grief of your astonishing desertion of me. And if you had all the testimonies which I could furnish of the grief of your friends here, on the same account, I think you would yet take your household gods & goddess with you, & come again over the sea.—

Can you not put Mr Bradford into a way of seeing Oxford?

My wife sends her best regards to you, but I doubt if she will let Mr B. carry home your valise.

Yours affectionately,

R. W. Emerson

A. H. Clough, Esq.

To Caroline Sturgis Tappan, Concord? April? ? 1854[43]

and what I read in ⟨c⟩Haydon's autobiography was good anecdote also. I have asked all round me for a French book, but in Boston is no bookshop & no collector that I know. That I may not send you nothing, I shall roll up this translation of Toussenel, which I found brilliant & readable enough. I believe I have no word to tell you of any creature. But still befriend your friend.

W.

To George Lyman Emerson, Concord? April 5, 1854

[The MS Account Book for 1853–1854, p. [31], under the date April 5, has the entry: "Cash sent in a letter to George L. Emerson, gift, 10.00."]

43. MS, incomplete, in the Tappan papers, Houghton Library, MH; ph. in NNC. This is clearly part of a longer letter of four full pages; for this portion, Emerson uses the first and second pages of another four. The letter is apparently later than December 1, 1853, for this is the date Emerson enters in volume 1 of his copy of the *Life of Benjamin Robert Haydon* . . . Tom Taylor, ed. (London, 1883); see Harding, p. 129. Moreover, Emerson had lent the book to William Emerson, Jr., in late December 1853 or early January 1854 (a.l.s., January 12, 1854, William Emerson, Sr., to his brother, RWEMA). The American edition of M. Edgeworth Lazarus' translation of Alphonse Toussenel was published in 1852 (see Harding, p. 224); Emerson is quoting from it in journal entries of September 8, 1853 (MS Journal HO, pp. 3–7, *JMN*, 14:pp. 208–210). I assign the letter to April 1854 because of the allusion in the letter of August 6, (below) to a long "silence."

To Daniel Foster, Concord, April 7, 1854

[In the MS Account Book for 1853–1859, p. [33], under the date April 7, 1854, is a note: "Cash sent in letter to Rev. D. Foster 3.00." The Reverend Daniel Foster, well-known in anti-slavery circles, had served in Concord for a year (1851) as minister of the Trinitarian Church; see February 23, 1858, below. I conjecture that Emerson is contributing to one of Foster's causes.]

To Elizabeth Dwight Sedgwick, Concord, April 14, 1854

[In the MS Account Book for 1853–1860, p. [37], under the April 15, 1854, is a note: "Pd. Mrs Sedgwick's bill for Ellen's board, tuition, & sundries 51.78." Emerson enclosed this letter and the money in his letter to Ellen of April 14; see *Letters*, 4:440.]

To Eliza Buckminster Lee, Concord, April 15? 1854

[In a letter of April 14, 1854 (RWEMA), Eliza Buckminster Lee asks Emerson's help in finding a place in Concord where the eight-year-old son of a German widow may board while he attends school in Concord. See below, letter of April 21, 1854, for evidence that Emerson executed this commission. It is probable that Emerson acknowledged this letter of April 14.]

To Eliza Buckminster Lee, Concord, April 21, 1854[44]

Concord

21 April

My dear Mrs Lee,

I have been talking with Miss Emme/l/ine Barrett,[45] on the subject of your note, and I find that she is probably the person to whom you allude as having formerly taken charge of a ward of yours.

Miss Barrett would receive into her family the child of Mrs Wendte[46] any time after the 12th of May. She will charge herself with his guardianship, board, washing, & mending, ⟨at⟩for $3.00 a week. The public schools

44. MS in the Barrett Collection, Alderman Library, ViU; ph. in NNC. Emerson is carrying out the commission of Mrs. Lee (see, above, entry for April 15) to find a suitable boarding place for an eight-year-old boy that he may go to school in Concord.

45. Emmeline Barrett must be the Miss Barrett referred to in a letter of January 3, 1858, and one of October 4, 1859. In the one her prospective boarder is the son of John Murray Forbes and in the other, the son of Samuel Gray Ward (*Letters*, 5:94, 176). Her clientele appears to ensure the character Emerson gives her.

46. In her letter of the 14th Mrs. Lee had described Mrs. Wendt (the child's mother) as a widow who supported herself by teaching German. "J. Wendte" is listed in Dickinson's 1849 Almanac under Teachers; German is specified. Jane Wendte, widow, is listed in the 1850 Boston directory at 31 Pleasant Street. Mrs. Lee had reported that Mrs. Wendte could pay $150. a year.

in the town, I believe, are very good the Intermediate, & the High School /(public)/ at which he will arrive in due time, I believe, are excellent. Miss Barrett is a very fit person to take this charge, as she is a very maternal as well as efficient head. Dr Charles T. Jackson's son has been in her family quite happily last winter, and Mr Ames's sons from Cambridge.[47]

At present I do not think it necessary to inquire further (I had already, however, proposed the matter in another quarter, without effect,) but I shall be glad to make any other inquiries that you may suggest.

With great regard,
R. W. Emerson

Mrs Lee.

To Charles Loring Brace, Concord, May 17, 1854?[48]

Concord.

My dear Sir

I am glad you are coming hither. On Saturday, I am to receive a little party of collegians; but on Monday, I am free, & if you will leave Boston in the Fitchburg train, at 11 o'clock, you will be here in time for a country dinner, & I shall depend on you.

The "Four Classics" of China I have seen, but have not now. It is a pearl of a book. I can show you the Desatir & the Veish⟨o⟩noo Sarma.[49]

Yours faithfully
R. W. Emerson

17 May ⎱
Wednesday ⎰
C. ⟨G.⟩L Brace, Esq.

47. Of the sons of Dr. Jackson, either Charles Francis Jackson or John Cotton Jackson would be the right age. Frederick Lothrop Ames, son of Oliver Ames, was not from Cambridge, but he was educated in Concord and in 1854 would be eight or nine years old. Given the size of families, it is likely that he had a brother.

48. MS in Special Collections, Butler Library, NNC; ph. in NNC. The year is not likely to be earlier than 1854; Brace was born in 1822 and in 1843 would be a "collegian" himself; moreover, a letter of November 26, 1853 (RWEMA), from Brace does not imply a long acquaintance. In 1848 Emerson was in England. 1865 is not impossible, but I choose 1854 because it is in the 1850s that Emerson was entertaining collegians, particularly Frank Sanborn and his friends.

49. *The Chinese Classical Work Commonly Called the Four Books,* translated by David Collie (Malacca, 1828); Emerson's journals of 1841–1843 quote passages from this work referred to as the "Four Books"; see *JMN,* 8:146 *et passim;* 9:7, 32–34, and 403. He first mentions the work in a letter on June 7, 1843, *Letters,* 3:179. His copy of the Desatir is incomplete (Harding, p. 79); for the Vishnu Purana, see Harding, p. 288.

To Emily Mervine Drury, Concord, May 19, 1854[50]

Concord ⎱ 19 May
Masstts. ⎰ 1854

My dear Mrs Drury,

A letter of kind remembrance which came yesterday had a little sting in it for me, as it made my omissions more glaring.[51] Yes, I surely received all those kind words & deeds,—the Astor House letter, the sermon of Mr Daggett,[52] the Southerner's communication in the newspaper & lately another slip or slips from a newspaper. My hearty thanks for the goodness that sent them all. None of your benefits are quite lost on me, though I speak no word. I use them all, only I know that I deal with a magnanimous person who likes to give. Today I shall not even answer your letter, though I mean to answer it. Thank Mr Daggett with my kind regards for the two sermons, the Eulogy of Mr Willson, & the New Years'.[53] If Mr Drury is at home, remember me to him. Yours,

R. W. Emerson

To Elizabeth Dwight Sedgwick, Concord, June 6? 1854

[In the MS Account Book for 1853–1859, p. [51], under the date June 6, 1854, is a note of "Cash sent by letter to Mrs Sedgwick a/c Ellen 50.00." An entry of June 21 (p. [53]) does not explicitly mention a letter, but records an additional $30.25 sent to Mrs Sedgwick "by cheque." I let this note stand for the possibility of two letters in June to Mrs Sedgwick.]

To Ellen Tucker Emerson, Concord, June 7, 1854

[Rusk gives a plausible reason for giving this letter of "Wednesday" the date September 7, 1853 (*Letters*, 4:385), but he overlooked Ellen Emerson's endorsement: "Father/ June 7."/; the note then has to be 1854, when June 7 fell on a

50. MS in the Autograph Collection, Houghton Library, MH; ph. in NNC.
51. Mrs. Drury had evidently invited him to call when he was in New York in March (see *Letters*, 4:431–432).
52. Oliver Ellsworth Daggett, minister of the Congregational Church of Canandaigua, New York; Emerson would twice try to effect a meeting between Daggett and Alcott (*Letters*, 4:391–392; 5:89).
53. George Willson, 2d; Daggett's funeral sermon is dated January 1, 1853 (Canandaigua; Repository Office, 1853). Daggett's New Year's sermon is surely his *Anniversaries . . . preached . . . January 1, 1854* (Canandaigua: Repository Office, 1854); in 1854 the first fell on a Sunday.

Wednesday. See above June 6; Emerson may have sent the money due Mrs. Sedgwick with this note to Ellen.]

To Charles Loring Brace, Concord, June 26, 1854 [54]

Concord 26 June
1854

My dear Sir,

You have much reason to be surprised at my delay in replying to your note. But there was to be a an ⟨anti⟩Nebraska Indignation meeting here, & I—of all men—was put forward to collect the materials. [55] It has consumed a week, & I wrote no letters.

For your request,—I hardly retain any correspondents in England, & not one whom I think specially interested in the two objects to which you refer. [56] I did know a Dr Toynbee, [57] a friend of Lord Morpeth (now Ld. Carlisle) [58] & to whom I was introduced at Lord M's house, whose specialty, I think, was Sanitary Reform. If I can recover his name & address, I shall venture to write him, as he was a young active & intelligent philanthropist. I will strain a point, too, but I will venture a letter on the /European-/ Liberty—side, to Mazzini, for so well-entitled a republican as yourself. [59] But I hate to hear that you are going away, now, when

54. MS in Special Collections, NNC; ph. in NNC.
55. Emerson is referring to the preparation for the People's Convention held in Boston, July 7, and called by a Committee of Citizens of Concord. It is clear from a letter of July 5 (RWEMA) from Edward W. Gardner of Nantucket that Emerson had also the task of sending out some of the invitations for the convention. Gardner's letter acknowledges a copy of a letter from the committee as well as a note from Emerson. The occasion was the Kansas-Nebraska Act of May 30, 1854. The MS Account Book for 1853–1859, under the date June 21, shows the payment of $1.00 for "Nebraska posters." The New-York Tribune of July 10, 1854, represents the Boston occasion as largely attended by the "Free Democratic organization" and reports that the meeting resulted only in a resolution to take no action because there was already a call for a meeting in Worcester on the 20th; the Tribune implies that the Worcester meeting will draw members of all parties and "The matter is thus left to the people themselves." Listed as attending the Boston meeting are the following Concord residents: Samuel Hoar, George Frisbie Hoar, "Simeon" [Simon] Brown, and Emerson.
56. On June 14 Brace had written Emerson to ask for letters of introduction to Londoners interested in charitable institutions. Brace was an active philanthropist, founder of the Children's Aid Society of New York.
57. See Letters, 4:94, where Emerson tells Lidian he has met a "Dr Toimbly" at Lord Morpeth's (June 28, 1848). Rusk conjectures that Joseph Toynbee is meant. Toynbee sent Emerson some of the publications of philanthropies he was interested in, one of them the Samaritan Fund for the prevention of disease (idem, n. 333).
58. Lord Morpeth became the seventh Earl of Carlisle (in the Howard line) in October 1848.
59. Emerson's word "venture" recalls his difficulties in getting a reply from Mazzini when he tried to solicit a letter about Margaret Fuller.

every true hearted American abroad ought to come home & defend freedom here.[60]

Yours,
R. W. Emerson.

C. L. Brace.

To Joseph Toynbee, Concord, June 26? 1854

[There is no record of Toynbee's address in Emerson's notebooks for his English visit of 1847–1848. Unless he could lay his hand on Toynbee's letter of June 30, 1848, he might not have been able to provide a letter of introduction for Charles Brace; see above.]

To Joseph Mazzini, Concord, June 26? 1854

[See, above, letter of this date to Charles L. Brace.]

To Edward W. Gardner, Concord, July 3? 1854

[From Edward W. Gardner's letter of July 5, 1854 (RWEMA), Rusk (4:451) records a letter of July 3 from Emerson enclosing a letter of a citizens' committee in Concord announcing a convention for July 7 in Boston at the Hanover House. For Emerson's involvement in the preparations, see above letter of June 26 to Charles L. Brace. The meeting was intended to bring political leaders together to form a new party; the effort was in response to the Kansas-Nebraska Act of May 30. Gardner wrote: ". . . all honest, true-hearted men of all parties should unite and form a great party of freedom." The Whigs opposed such a convention, and the gathering was apparently ill-attended. Possibly Emerson solicited others. See *Life*, pp. 369, 405, for Emerson and the Republican Party.]

To William Henry Furness, Concord, July 15, 1854[61]

Concord,
Saturday Noon
July 15, 1854

My dear friend,

I have just learned with surprise & to me mortification that your Discourse to the College is set for tomorrow.[62] It was set in my mind a

60. This letter solves the puzzle of an illegible name in Emerson's letter of August 28, 1854, to George P. Bradford (*Letters*, 4:454–462). The name Rusk read as "Bruce" (p. 462) has to be "Brace."
61. MS in the Furness papers, Van Pelt Library, PU; ph. in NNC.
62. Furness was to address the Divinity College students. See July 24 below for Theodore

week from tomorrow; and I was to see & hear. In this blunder, I have acted for our town in getting Theodore Parker up here, who is to read his Fourth of July Discourse to us tomorrow Evening, & is to be my guest. It is an absurd <u>contretemps</u> & I the victim,—irreparable now. What remains but to beseech you, out of the greatness of your heart & mind & misericord, to come up to me Monday morning,[63] bringing Horace[64] with you, & spend Monday with me. I will try to keep Parker, in that hope: If you are engaged, Monday, then Tuesday will do; only send me some word, as soon as you pass by a Post Office, ⟨when⟩ that you will come, & when. & do not fail me, I entreat.

Ever your affectionate
Waldo E.

To Arthur Hugh Clough, Concord, July 24, 1854[65]

Concord ⎱ 24 July
Mass^tts ⎰ 1854

My dear Clough,

I was heartily glad to see your handwriting once more, & touched by the significant token which your note enclosed. Many white days & years may that little card open to you! England is immensely rich to you who have learned to live in it, socially, mentally, politically, and I suppose your skill to live there is really inability to live here, though I hoped otherwise, & hoped a brilliant benefit to myself. But England drams & drugs you with concentrated culture, & you can never be water drinkers. Fairest greetings & my happiest wishes to your wife![66] which she will admit to be the more gracious, that she stands the manifest cause of your desertion of us. I hope, a silver candlestick, which I ventured to send her through Felton's /messenger's/ hands, arrived, before the sacred day; I

Parker's importance in 1854; see Emerson's letter of invitation to Parker to open "with eclat" a series of weekly meetings "for liberty" (*Letters*, 4:452). See August 22 below for Emerson's regret that Furness could not come.

63. Breaking this word at the end of a line, Emerson provides no hyphen; it is unlikely that he intended it to be two words.

64. Furness' son.

65. MS in the Clough papers, Bodleian Library, Oxford; ph. in NNC, printed in the *Emerson-Clough Letters*, No. 24, and in Mulhauser, 2:487.

66. Clough and Blanche Smith were married May 22, 1854; his Cambridge friends Cornelius Felton, Charles E. Norton, Longfellow, and others sent a parcel of wedding presents (Mulhauser, 2:484). Emerson's MS Account Book for 1853–1859, under the date May 27, has an entry for the purchase of the silver candlestick from Bigelow, Kennard & Co.

should have had her initials engraved, if Felton could have made me sure of them. One of these years, she will come, with you, to see us, & Ellen & Edith shall show her Concord. Edith is much obliged to you for your remembrance. If you see Carlyle, give my love to him. I shall write to him soon, perhaps today. Wo worth the while, he is accustomed to my backslidings. You speak of our politics.[67] They are the most deplorable the world ever saw, and threaten to drive every decent man to give up housekeeping, to save the state. Sumner & Theodore Parker are our saints. I shall greet a letter from you gladly. Yours faithfully,

R. W. Emerson

To Caroline Sturgis Tappan, Concord, August 6, 1854[68]

Concord, 6 August 1854

Dear Caroline,

I could heartily wish to carry Lidian to your house, & show her its inmates & its landscape: but she is not well enough to go where robust health seems to be the indispensable qualification & she is, in these very days, preparing to go to Plymouth with Edith & Edward. For me, I am always happy to be invited, & mean surely to see you on my way to Williamstown,[69] whither I think to carry Ellen: but, I am sorry to say, cannot at this date give you the smallest encouragement of any entertainment at Wmstown, & will absolve you from any such youthful purposes as journeying in the hot season.

I am glad to hear from you,—though always afraid to break the silence.—I remember feeling, in Mrs R.'s[70] pictured parlor, as if I had written verses,—must of course be rich in verses: but, I suppose, I was no sooner out of the parlor, but drowsy Pan spirited poppies & poppy juice about. I had not thought of it again. And the poetry so plentiful

67. Emerson has in mind the Kansas-Nebraska Bill, signed May 20, 1854, and the case of Anthony Burns. Emerson's wish to keep Charles Brace at home, the reception in Concord of Theodore Parker's Fourth of July Address (see above June 26 and July 15), and the message to T. W. Higginson, below July 25,—all show that anti-slavery feeling is running high in Concord.

68. MS in the Tappan papers, Houghton Library, MH; ph. in NNC. Emerson is replying to Caroline's invitation of August 3, MNS, Archives.

69. Emerson was to address the Adelphi Union of Williams College on August 15. See his letter of August 8 to his daughter Ellen, *Letters*, 4:455.

70. Mrs. Russell is named in Caroline's letter. She is possibly Sarah Shaw Russell (Mrs. George R. Russell), who, by the marriage of her brother Francis George Shaw to Caroline Tappan's first cousin Sarah Blake Sturgis, was by way of being a relative, Francis Shaw and Sarah Sturgis being themselves half-first cousins.

seems shrunk to a few dry leaves. I find one or two that I think you have not seen.[71]

Ever yours,
R. W. E.

To Caroline Sturgis Tappan, Concord, August 21, 1854[72]

Concord
21 Aug
1854

Dear Caroline,

Edith came safely & easily through to her home on Saturday—Miss Minnie Washburn[73] very kindly charged herself with the duties of nurse & guardian as far as Worcester;—and today, she is quite well again, tho' a little weak & interesting. I did not fully know until Edith told her mother particulars here at home how seriously ill she had been & how important was the care & nursing at your home. Lidian has all but written to thank you—stings herself all this day (a day of much preparation for her journey) that she does not write to thank & bless you. & to thank the kind Susan who watches with her Well Lidian & Edith shall watch & nurse some other invalid—it is a class that, like kings never dies out. Rarely or never let it comprise you & your house! And Edith sends her love to Ellen & Baby Tappan.[74]

I send the two books to you for Miss Hamilton & Mrs. S. by Express.[75] You shall open & detain them if you will but for fear you may not I send them to you & you can seal again. I am always happy in your kindness.

Affectionately
R. W. E.

To Christopher Gore Ripley, Concord, August 22, 1854

[The MS Account Book for 1853–1859, p. [63], under the date August 22, records sending to C. G. Ripley a payment to Elizabeth Sedgwick for Ellen Emerson's tuition at her Lenox school.]

71. Caroline had reminded him that he had promised to send her some poetry. The poems by Emerson now in the Tappan papers are all too early; which ones were sent with this letter cannot be determined.

72. MS in the Sophia Smith Collection, MNS; ph. in NNC.

73. See *Letters*, 4:456–457, for Edith's illness in Lenox. Minnie Washburn may be of the family related to Emerson's first wife, but there is no clue to her identity.

74. Mary is Caroline Tappan's younger daughter.

75. Mrs. S. is Mrs. Charles Sedgwick who ran the school Ellen Emerson was attending.

To William Henry Furness, Concord August 22, 1854[76]

Concord 22 Augt 1854

My dear friend,
You must often have wondered where that daguerre of Carlyle loitered that was destined for you. I carried the primitive plate to Boston three times but such is my dread of having more copies, taken than I wish, that I could never trust it in the hands of the chattering operators. At last William E. offered to get it done in N.Y. & as there is security in a multitude, I consented & he tells me it is a perfect copy.[77] I hope you have already got it. That was a cruel mishap to me—that you could not come to me nor I to you lately. I was truly grieved that it was a calamity in your brother's house, I am afraid I shall never see you in mine. And you have given away Annie,[78] & sent William abroad, & now Horace; and when Frank comes to College, I think your ties must be looser, & you can come also & see your friends, & & renovate Massachusetts. I have had kind notes lately from Randolph,[79] & really thought at one time I should go to Phila. this summer, but I fear I shall not. You must not,—I had almost forgot to say,—let this particular Carlyle be duplicated again,—without extreme reasons. Your loving

R. W. E.

W. H. Furness.

To Joseph M. Edmonds, Concord? August 26, 1854

[Rusk lists a letter of August 26 from the sale catalogue of Scott & O'Shaughnessy (1917), *Letters*, 4:459; a letter of the same date is listed as item 144 in Catalogue 8 and 9 of Pearson. In Pearson's listing, the letter of this date is quoted as follows: "If I read a lecture the association will pay me 30 dollars"; the addressee is given as Mr. "Edwards." In the MS Pocket Diary for 1854 (*JMN*, 13:494), under the date November 21, is entered an engagement for Portsmouth, New Hampshire, followed by the name of the institute representative. Rusk's original (ms) note has

Miss Hamilton is Miss Mary M. Hamilton (see *Letters*, 4:462, n. 225.) The letter cited is of August 24, 1854, and thanks him for "this *precious* book," which appears to have been the Bhăgvăt-Gēētă. The other book was evidently of poetry.

76. MS in the Furness papers, Van Pelt Library, PU; ph. in NNC; printed in *Records*, pp. [95]–96; listed in *Letters*, 4:457.

77. William Emerson visited Concord July 28; it was probably then that he took the plate to New York. He reported the results in a letter of August 14; on the 21st Emerson told him to send it on to Furness (*Letters*, 4:454, 455).

78. Annie Furness had married Dr. Caspar Wister.

79. Philip Physick Randolph, who, in a letter of May 30, proposed that Emerson come to Philadelphia for a few weeks; for Randolph, see *Letters*, 4:538. Emerson had met him in 1851; it is probably through Emerson that Charles King Newcomb came to know Randolph when he lived in Philadelphia.

the name as "Edwards," with the conjecture that the name might be "Edmonds"; he later corrects his note. In other words, Emerson's writing of the name is such that it can be misread as Edwards. On September 8 Joseph M. Edmonds of Portsmouth writes Emerson to confirm the date November 21 (RWEMA). The MS Account Book for 1853–1859, p. [26], shows that Emerson was paid $30.00 for his lecture in Portsmouth (Charvat, p. 29). I conclude then that it is possible that the letter of this date listed by O'Shaughnessy is the same as that listed by Pearson. See November 19, below, where the name is clearly "Edmonds."

The letter listed with year only by Bangs & Co., 1902, is, then, as Rusk suspected, a different letter, for it concerns Emerson's honorary membership in the Everett Literary Association, *Letters*, 4:459; I therefore list it separately below.]

To Edward Waldo Emerson, Concord, August 28, 1854[80]

<E>Concord, 28 August
1854

Dear Edward,

I hope it will not be so cold but that you will go into the salt water a few times whilst you are in Plymouth. If you become acquainted with any good boy, ask him where he goes, & when, & tell him you wish to learn to swim.[81] But, unless somebody goes with with you who is bigger than you, it will not do for you to venture up to your shoulders. Tell your mother, that 'tis pity she should go so late to P.; for the school-term begins on Monday, 11 September, & that it will not do for any good scholars to be absent on the first day. She must please get you & Edith ready for your duties on that morning.[82] The sending you home on Saturday will leave her more leisure & quiet to finish her visit. Tell her that we have entertained no strangers; only, Mr. Alcott spent Sunday here, & returned home this morning. On Saturday night, we had rain for an hour,—the first rain of any consequence since the 25 July. Give my love to Edith, who, I hope, has been with you to the "Grave-yard-hill," to see the view of the harbour. Mamma ought to go with you to tell you all the stories of the old Pilgrim times. Be sure that you find your way to Mr. Hedge's wharf,[83] so that you may know where the Forefathers really landed. How far has Captain Cook sailed with you?[84]

Papa.

80. MS in the Raymond Emerson estate, MH; ph. in NNC; listed *Letters*, 4:462.

81. In a letter of August 29, continued on September 1 and 3 (RWEMA), Edward declares that he does not like salt water as well as fresh; he has tried it.

82. See *Letters*, 4:462–463, for Emerson's directions to Mrs. Emerson about sending the children (Edith and Edward) home alone; she is evidently fearful, and he is plainly irritated.

83. "Forefathers Rock," located between Hedge's Wharf and Davis Wharf.

84. Edward explains in his letter that, not having been able to find the first volume of

To Lidian Emerson, Concord? September 11? 1854

[The MS Account Book for 1853–1859 (p. [63]) enters under this date a note of cash sent to Mrs. Emerson then in Plymouth; it seems likely that he wrote a letter too. See *Letters*, 4:465; the money ($30.) he "thinks to inclose" with his letter of September 6 is entered in the Account Book on the same page.]

To Lidian Emerson, Concord, September 16? 1854

[In the MS Account Book for 1853–1859, p. [63], under the date September 16, is a note of cash sent to Mrs. Emerson, then in Plymouth. It is likely that the money was sent with a letter; see *Letters*, 4:465, and entry above of September 11.]

To Charles Chauncy Shackford, Concord, September 15, 1854[85]

Concord, 15 Sept. 1854

My dear Sir,

I will come to Lynn, with pleasure, on a Wednesday evening of Nov, Dec. or January.[86]

Yours ever
R W Emerson

Rev. C. C. Shackford[87]

To Thomas Wentworth Higginson, Concord, September 25, 1854[88]

Concord
Sept. 25, 1854.

My Dear Sir,

I shall like very well to read the Discourse that shall be written, at Worcester, on any night that suits you after it is read in Boston.[89]

The nights of the Boston Course are not yet fixed.

James Cook's *Voyages*, he did not bring the book with him. (There is no copy now in Emerson's library.)

85. MS in the Feinberg Collection, MiD; text from original; printed by White, *AL* (May 1961), 33:167.

86. Emerson lectured in Lynn November 15 (Charvat, p. 29). The engagement is listed in ink in the MS Pocket Diary for 1854 (*JMN*, 13:494).

87. Shackford was a classmate of Ebenezer Rockwood Hoar.

88. MS in the Feinberg Collection, MiD; text from original; printed by White, *AL* (May 1961), 33:167.

89. White erroneously assumes the reference here to be to the lecture "The Anglo-American" given for the Mercantile Library Association, Boston, on the 29th of January, but the reference is certainly to the lecture on "Slavery" given on the 25th in Boston and on the 26th in Worcester. Charvat (p. 30) questions the date, but the date is listed in ink in the MS Pocket Diary for 1855 (*JMN*, 13:504).

We hold your name in so high regard here, that I am happy in having a note from you.[90]

Yours,
R. W. Emerson

Rev. Mr Higginson.

To ELIZABETH DWIGHT SEDGWICK, CONCORD? OCTOBER 5? 1854

[The MS Account Book for 1853–1859 has an entry under the date October 5 (p. 69): "Pd Mrs Sedgwick by letter 25.90"; this is the last payment for Ellen Emerson's schooling at Mrs. Sedgwick's.]

To DAVID ATWOOD WASSON, OCTOBER 5? 1854

[In a letter of October 4, 1854 (MH, Schlesinger), David Wasson asks if the rumor is true that Emerson proposes to bring out an American edition of the Bhăgvăt-Gēētā. Emerson would have answered; see above December 21, 1853, for his having lent Wasson the book. See October 19, 1856, below, note 178, for Emerson's having rejected an 1853 proposal to reprint the book.]

To ELIZABETH DAVIS STURGIS, CONCORD, OCTOBER 11, 1854[91]

Concord, 11 October,
1854

My dear Mrs Sturgis,

I found on my return home from an absence of two or three days the five comely volumes of the Travels of Anacharsis[92] which Mr Whiting[93] was so good as to leave at my door from you. I recollected at once the kind assurance you gave me, two or three years ago, that this fragment of my father's library should come again to me. I can dimly remember the book in my childhood. It has gathered value & honor in my eyes from its two latest possessors, & I shall prize it dearly for this steadfast kindness in yourself, which it shows me. I shall use the first opportunity

90. Emerson alludes here to Higginson's bold action in the attempted rescue of the fugitive slave Anthony Burns; see Edelstein, pp. 155–166, for the full story of Higginson's helping to break down the Court House door and, with a black companion, being the first inside. Arrested for riot, Higginson, at the time this letter was written, was out on bail (Edelstein, p. 164).

91. MS in the Tappan papers, Houghton Library, MH; ph. in NNC.

92. See Harding, p. 22. Emerson's father's library was sold at auction after his death. Probably the purchaser of this edition of Jean Jacques Barthelemy's *The Travels of Anacharsis* was Mrs. William Sturgis' father Judge John Davis.

93. The bearer of the book was probably William Whiting.

I may have of being in Roxbury, to come & thank you personally for this remembrance.

With respect & affection,
R. W. Emerson

Mrs Sturgis.

To ———— STONE, CONCORD, OCTOBER 12, 1854

[A letter seen in Goodspeed's, 1984, addressed to "Mr Stone," is of October 12, 1854, and is evidently the letter listed by Rusk, and conjectured to be addressed to Thomas Treadwell Stone (4:472). Emerson says he is protecting January from engagements. No "Stone" is listed against any engagement recorded in the Pocket Diary for 1855. Emerson would not, I think, address the Reverend Thomas T. Stone as merely "Mr Stone" nor write so perfunctory a note to a man he knew well. In 1866 he is corresponding with a Zina Eugene Stone to arrange lecture dates in Lowell, a possible addressee here. See also November 25, 1850, for another possibility.]

To WILLIAM HENRY FURNESS, CONCORD, OCTOBER 13, 1854[94]

Concord, 13 Oct 1854

My dear friend

There was a talk between us of Lectures, this winter, on the incredible & truth-stranger-than-faction pattern of the last.[95] But I have been so drowsy & implacable, or, at all events so unsuccessful about the little book I have had in hand,[96] that it has neither got done itself, nor allowed any other thing to be done. Letting aside the natural impossibilities of the lecture-project, as being the very wax you like to mould, I beg you will allow this plea of a badly preoccupied workman, & take no step in the affair, for this winter. In the course of the summer, I will take care to ripen the best I can, various hopeful buds in my conservatory, whose growth has long been arrested, & so I shall have the better hope to justify your habitually exaggerating good opinion of your friends[97]
W. H. Furness.

---

94. MS in the Furness papers, Van Pelt Library, PU; ph. in NNC; printed in *Records*, p. [99]; listed in *Letters*, 4:473. The signature with complimentary close has been carefully cut away so as not to affect the text, which is complete.

95. The success of the Philadelphia course.

96. *English Traits*.

97. Emerson did not undertake a second Philadelphia course.

To Jeremiah L. Newton, Concord, October 13, 1854[98]

Concord
Oct 13 1854

Dear Sir,

I believe I offered you 23d February,[99] for my visit to Newburyport. On looking over my memoranda, I see that it would be safer for me to offer you the 22d December.[100] Will that day suit you as well? If not will Friday 2 March do?

Respectfully,
R. W. Emerson

I should have said that I am to be in Western New York until the 20th Feb., & may be detained longer than I allowed.

To Daniel N. Haskell, Concord, October 18, 1854[101]

Concord, 18 Oct.r 1854

Dear Sir,

I thank you for your offer, & I may be glad to use it. At this moment, I am pressed with some tasks that will not allow me to think of anything else.[102]

Respectfully,
Mr Haskell.   R. W. Emerson

To Albert T. Wheelock, Concord, October ? 1854

[In his letter of October 24, 1855, to John G. Fiske (see below), Emerson says that A. T. Wheelock of Belfast was his correspondent "last year" when he tried to arrange a series of lectures in Maine. The physician Albert T. Wheelock is the likely correspondent. Joseph Williamson, *History of . . . Belfast,* pp. 416, 419.]

98. MS in the collections of MHi; ph. in NNC; with envelope addressed to J. L. Newton-Esq. | Newburyport. | Masstts.; postmarked at Boston October 14. Newton's letters to Emerson (October 9 and 19, RWEMA) are signed with initials; a Jeremiah L. Newton, a teacher in the Putnam Free School and a founder of the Newburyport Library Association is the likely addressee. John J. Currier, *History of Newburyport,* 2:369, 176.

99. Newton's letter of October 9 implies an earlier letter; he accepts there the February 23, 1855, date.

100. The MS Pocket Diary for 1854 has a tentative list of 1855 dates; here Emerson would find the February listing crowded with engagements in upstate New York, including Hamilton for February 23. The diary in its final list has Newburyport down for December 22 with a question mark deleted. See *JMN,* 13:484–485, 495. Newton acknowledges this letter on October 19, reporting that he was able to rearrange the schedule to allow Emerson December 22.

101. MS in the Manuscript Division, NN; ph. in NNC.

102. This note is an answer to a letter of October 15 from Daniel Haskell, editor of the *Boston Evening Transcript.* In a conversation with Nathaniel Langdon Frothingham, Emerson

To WILLIAM DICKINSON M. D.? CONCORD, OCTOBER ? 1854

[In the November 1940 list of American Autograph Shop is listed (item 68) a letter described as of 1854 "about his lecture in Taunton on Dec. 21st" and as stating his fee. In the MS Pocket Diary for 1854, Emerson has entered Taunton against the date December 21 and later deleted it (see *JMN*, 13:495). I conjecture the addressee to be Dr. W. Dickinson for no better reason than that Dr. Dickinson was his correspondent in the following season (see *Letters*, 4:541, and below, February 1, 1856). William Dickinson, physician, is listed in an 1855 Taunton directory.]

To CHARLES C. TERRY, CONCORD, OCTOBER 24, 1854[103]

Concord ⎱ Oct. 24
Mass.tts. ⎰ 1854

Dear Sir,

Will it suit your plans, if I should come to Hudson, on Friday, 9 February?[104]

Respectfully,

C. C. Terry, Esq.   R. W. Emerson

To WILLIAM ORNE WHITE, CONCORD, OCTOBER 28? 1854

[In a letter of October 27, 1854 (RWEMA), Will O. White of Keene, New Hampshire, asks Emerson to send him the subject of his lecture scheduled for November 1 (Charvat, p. 29), that the subject as well as the lecturer may be advertised. The Reverend William Orne White was a classmate of James Elliot Cabot ('40) and took his Divinity School degree in 1845.]

To OLIVER JOHNSON, CONCORD, NOVEMBER 12, 1854[105]

Concord ⎱ 12 Novr.
Mass.tts ⎰ 1854

Dear Sir,

I am not very ready to come to N. Y. this winter, on the errand you offer me: but not so set against it, as to insist in a refusal. I am en-

---

had suggested that a notes & queries column might be useful; Haskell is following up the suggestion, and says he would be glad to publish such communications. One of Emerson's notebooks is entitled "Notes and Queries" ("NQ" on backstrip); it is chiefly a record of quotations he hopes to locate and sometimes does.

103. MS in the Barrett Collection, Alderman Library, ViU; ph. in CUL. Charles C. Terry appears in the Hudson directory (1856–1857) as a dealer in dry goods.

104. See *Letters*, 4:493, and note of letter to Terry of c. February 8, 1855, below, for Emerson's change of date to March 2 (Charvat, p. 30).

105. MS in COMC; ph. in NNC. See *Letters*, 4:476 and 488, 490, for Emerson's lecturing before the New York Anti-Slavery Society (Charvat, p. 30), at the request of Oliver Johnson

gaged on the 30 Jan.y, but if 6 February will serve you, you may hold me.

Respectfully

/And that is the only day I can offer you./

Mr Johnson   R. W. Emerson

To Charlotte Haskins Cleveland, Concord, November 13? 1854

[The MS Account Book for 1853–1859, p. [25], has, under the date November 13, the entry: "Sent Mrs Charlotte Cleveland, by mail, sum bequeathed her by will of Mrs Ruth Emerson 20.00." Charlotte Haskins Cleveland was Emerson's cousin; before her marriage she had lived with the Emersons to care for his mother, and she undertook later the trying task of having Aunt Mary in her neighborhood (Rusk, *Life*, pp. 363, 371; *Letters*, 4:253, 446, 450). In 1851–1852, when Emerson was having trouble with his eyes, his cousin read to him. He certainly wrote a letter to accompany the legacy.]

To C—— H—— Plummer, Concord, November 13, 1854

[A letter to C. H. Plummer of November 13, 1854, is listed twice in ABPC, 1945–1946, p. 10 and p. 619. The second entry describes the letter as of one page and "about his many engagements," lecture engagements, I infer. Plummer's name does not appear in the MS Pocket Diary for 1854 or 1855.]

To Moncure Daniel Conway, Concord, November 7? 1854

[In the Conway papers, Special Collections, Butler Library, NNC, is a letter from Conway to Emerson, dated November 6, 1854; Conway says he can't get a copy of the English version of the Bhăgvăt Gēētā; Little and Brown has sent him the Sanskrit text. He asks Emerson to give him full titles and publisher. Emerson has annotated the letter with the information for both Wilkins' translation of the Bhăgvăt Gēētā and his translation of the Puranna Vishnu. It seems likely then that he wrote Conway.]

To Joseph M. Edmonds, Concord, November 19, 1854[106]

Concord⎱ 19 Nov.r
Mass.tts. ⎰ 1854

Dear Sir,

I am sorry to be so slow,—too slow, I fear, for any use,—in answering your note. I was out of town for a couple of days, & negligent one. I shall

and the urging of Wendell Phillips. The insertion was crowded in above the addressee's name after the letter was finished. The MS is torn and water-stained; the word "very" in the first line is clear in the photostat, but not clear in the manuscript.

106. MS in the New England collection, MnM; ph. in NNC. Printed in *Nineteenth Century New England Authors* (Minneapolis, [1978]), p. 2.

take the 4 o'clock train which you advise. For my subject, I like well to be at liberty to choose my subject at the last moment; but if you wish to announce one, & if there is any time, you can say, "English Civilization," which will cover the topics of a new lecture which I think of reading.[107]

Respectfully,
R. W. Emerson

Mr Edmonds.

To Delia Salter Bacon, Concord, November 20, 1854[108]

Concord ⌉ Nov 20
Masstts ⌋ 1854

My dear Miss Bacon,

I am heartily grieved—but it is past help—at my silence & delays. There can be no forgiveness for it. I have had both your letters, & made ineffectual attempts to answer both. I was very happy to read the good news, which both contained, of your studies & enjoyments. And I heard collaterally from Carlyle,[109] of his goodwill & respect. The statements in your last letter especially engage my interest, and it seems most honorable & most useful,—that which you say, that you can live & study in England for no more than it would cost in America, & that the supplies for one summer, can be spun out to serve for two. I can hardly refrain from publishing the fact in the newspapers, for the benefit of all scholars. That your readings prosper, & that you confirm yourself in your conviction, is also good news; for, though I think your hypothesis more incredible than the improbable traditions (& unexplained) it would supplant, yet you cannot maintain any side, without shedding light on the first of all literary problems. Carlyle, too, I found, with decided interest & respect, had no faith in the paradox. I went to Phillips & Sampson the last time I was in town to engage their interest in the book. They considered it a promising enterprise but could not think of it for themselves and the better the book should be they said the worse for them. For they have several "first rate" books, as they call them, now in press, or just out of press, and are afraid of a good book as likely to damage these! do not wish to stand in their own light, or over lay their own children. I went to

---

107. See August 26, above, and Charvat, p. 29, for Emerson's Portsmouth, New Hampshire, engagement for November 21. This letter would appear to confirm the Lynn and Milford engagements, and it provides the subject for the Portsmouth lecture.

108. MS in DFo; ph. in NNC; printed by Theodore Bacon, pp. 73–74; listed *Letters*, 4:476; quoted by Vivian Hopkins, p. 186.

109. See Slater, pp. 495 and 502.

Ticknor & Fields, but with no better success. They are afraid, if I understand it, of a literary book; and answer steadily, "any time but now," as if now, nothing but Russia, Australia, & Romance,[110] would have any attraction. These two are the best here, & I hesitate a little about the next step; yet shall take another. If you are sure of the book, you may easily be sure of a publisher. I beg you will write me once more, (notwithstanding my ill deserts,) that it is ready; or that it will soon be & when & how large it will be. I think of applying to Mr J. C. Derby of New York, of whom I hear much good.[111] I meant to print my own tardy Mss Speculations on England in this month; but I doubt & delay. I am however extremely busy.[112] With all congratulation & good hope

R W Emerson.

To James Cephas Derby, Concord, November ? 1854

[See above, November 20, where Emerson tells Delia Bacon that he considers writing James C. Derby on her account. There is nothing to show that Emerson carried out this intention.]

To Francis Brown, Concord, December 9? 1854

[The MS Account Book for 1853–1859, p. [79], under the date December 9, has the entry: "Sent a gift to Frank Brown 20.00." A note probably accompanied this gift to Lidian Emerson's nephew.]

To Anna Barker Ward, Concord, December 13, 1854[113]

Concord
13 Dec. 1854

My dear friend,

I was glad to be invited. I am sorry I cannot come tonight. I am going from home on an engagement far less pleasing.[114] There is always better

110. That is, the Crimean War, the rebellion in the gold fields of Ballarat, and, for romances, possibly Emerson had in mind John Esten Cooke's *Leather-Stocking and Silk* and *Virginia Comedians*, both of 1854 and, with a local setting, Maria S. Cummins' *The Lamplighter*. See V. Hopkins, p. 190, for Miss Bacon's variation on this passage in her letter of July 5 to Phillips, Sampson & Co. Issues of *Norton's Literary Gazette* for November 1854–January 1855 show that both publishers were offering morals, medicine, and fantasy along with safe poets like Gray and Goldsmith and a few contemporaries, Paul Hamilton Hayne and Bayard Taylor.

111. The publisher James Cephas Derby had moved from Auburn, New York, to New York City in 1853.

112. *English Traits.*

113. MS in the Ward papers, Houghton Library, MH; ph. in NNC.

114. Emerson had a lecture engagement at Randolph (Charvat, p. 30).

music at your house than any stringed instruments can make, and tis that I hate to lose,[115] & beseech you, for all my absences, still to keep the door open for me.

Ever yours,
R. W. Emerson

Mrs Ward.

To the Everett Literary Association, Concord, ? 1854

[See August 26 above, where this letter accepting honorary membership in the Everett Literary Association is distinguished from a letter of that date to Joseph M. Edmonds. See *Letters*, 4:495, where, from a catalogue of Bangs & Co., 1902, this letter to Everett Literary Association is noted.]

To Anna Jackson Lowell, Concord,? 1854?

[In *Letters*, 5:129, a letter to Anna Jackson Lowell is recorded from a fragment quoted by Edward W. Emerson in both *Memoirs of the Social Circle in Concord* (2nd Ser., 2nd Pt.) and *Emerson in Concord*. Rusk conjectured 1858 as the year. I think this letter with its hope that young Charles Russell Lowell "will never get over" his dissatisfaction with society is earlier than 1858. In 1858, Charles Lowell was in Europe and Africa traveling for his health. Earlier, as a Harvard undergraduate, Lowell had been exposed to Frank Sanborn's radical views and had witnessed the effects of the Fugitive Slave Law. Lowell's address as valedictorian of his class ('54) and his active participation in the protest against the arrest of Anthony Burns suggest that the letter is of 1853 of 1854. The valedictory address is distinctly Emersonian in theme. See Edward Waldo Emerson, *The Life and Letters of Charles Russell Lowell* (Boston: Houghton, Mifflin, 1907) pp. 7–13.]

115. Anna B. Ward was a patron of musicians; Emerson implies a preference for conversation.

1 8 5 5

TO EDWIN PERCY WHIPPLE, CONCORD? JANUARY 2, 1855[1]

Tuesday 2 Jan.y 1855

My dear Whipple,

I am heartily grieved that I cannot be at home on the 4th, (Thursday) when you are due here.[2] My wife is fully expecting you at my house, where you must make your home.

Yours.

R. W. Emerson.

TO MARTHA ROBINSON? CONCORD, JANUARY 13, 1855

[In the MS Account Book for 1853–1860, p. [87], under the date January 13, 1855, is a note of $5.00 sent to the Reverend Lincoln Ripley; see above, June 16, 1853. In a letter of February 11 (RWEMA) Ellen Emerson tells her father of Lincoln Ripley's thanks. The message came from a letter to Elizabeth Hoar from Ripley's adopted daughter, Martha Robinson. The money was probably sent to Martha Robinson.]

TO DELIA SALTER BACON, CONCORD, JANUARY 15, 1855[3]

Concord Mass

15 January 1855

My dear Miss Bacon.

Your valued letter, solid with facts which I wished to know, deserves a better reply than the short one I must content myself with. I have only today time enough to convey my message, & do not see, for many days

1. MS from which the text is taken originally in the Colson estate, then in Goodspeed's; present location unknown; reproduced in facsimile in *The Month* (November–December 1965), Vol. 37; printed in Goodspeed's catalogue 1968. The illustration from *The Month* is reproduced by Cameron in *ESQ* (2d q., 1966), 43:143.

2. Whipple was scheduled to give a lecture for the Concord Lyceum; Emerson would be lecturing in Westford, Massachusetts.

3. MS in DFo; ph. in NNC. This letter makes it clear that Vivian Hopkins (p. 189) has created a ghost with her assumption of an Emerson letter of June 1855 informing Delia Bacon of Phillips & Sampson's proposal. Miss Hopkins drew her inference from Carlyle's letter to Delia Bacon of June 7 (Theodore Bacon, p. 79). Not only is there no reference to an Emerson letter of June in Carlyle's letter, but it is impossible that there should be, for no June mail from the States could have reached England by the 7th of the month.

before me, a probability of more. I talked at large with Mr. Phillips (of Phillips, Sampson, & Co.) two or three days ago, of your book. He offers to publish it on these terms. P. & S. are to take all the costs & risk and will give you ten per cent on the retail price of all sales.—i. e. if a copy sells in the shop for $2.00 you are to have 20 cents.[4] Meantime Mr P. assures me that it is now possible & expedient for you to print it contemporaneously in London, taking out copy right there, which "residence" has been allowed to authorize. Tis said Mr Prescott is going out to London simply for the purpose of taking out copyright, & then to return.[5] It is necessary that your book should be published first in England, if only by a day. Then you may have copyright in both countries. To secure copyright here, you must send home the exact title of the book as it is printed there & shall be printed here & copyright will be taken out on that.

In regard to the size of the book, I must own, Mr P.[6] & his partner spoke like booksellers, & heartily wished it might be one volume; Apollo pardon their blindness!

The offer is neither good nor bad, I suppose, but indifferent. But I think well of the house; they are energetic men, mean fairly, & will do all for the book that American publisher can.

I am very happy in the courage & vigor you express, which are the best signs. I divine something of your mind on the subject of the "Instauration" for I had occasion in the summer to read carefully the "Advancement of Learning," & to write of it.[7] You are very heartily to be congratulated. I think <you> Mr Parker, after his deliberations, owes you at least the good turn of helping you to a London Publisher. He can very well advise you & perhaps would like to print the book, if not the Article. If you please you shall not "wait a hundred years for a reader."

With assurance & hope,
Ever Yours,
R. W. Emerson

Miss Bacon.

To Theodore Parker, Concord, January? 17? 1855

[A letter from Theodore Parker to Emerson (RWEMA) is catalogued by Houghton Library as of "July" 19, 1855, and certainly Parker's handwriting allows that

4. See *Letters*, 4:521, n. 151, for Emerson's further dealings with Phillips & Sampson on Miss Bacon's behalf. He had to cope with her naive expectations of 90 percent of the profits.

5. He cites the example of William Hickling Prescott as persuasive.

6. John W. Parker, publisher of *Fraser's Magazine*.

7. For *English Traits*; see *Works*, 5:238–244. Notes for this reading are in MS journal HO.

reading, but the letter refers to Parker's expected trial for his part in the attempt
to rescue Anthony Burns from the U.S. marshall arresting Burns under the
Fugitive Slave Law. Parker had been arrested November 29, 1854, and his trial
was set for April 3, 1855. The letter cannot then be as late as July; I read the
dateline as "Jany." In it Parker says he is sorry he cannot hear Emerson "next
Thursday"; on Thursday, January 25, Emerson was to give his address on slavery.
Parker's letter thanks Emerson for the concern he has expressed and defends his
choice of counsel (Charles Ellis), about whom Emerson has apparently expressed
doubts. Clearly answering a letter from Emerson, Parker reassures him on the
ground that in any case the lawyer is to tend only to technical matters; he himself
will address the jury. This fantasy was not to be realized; the indictments against
Parker, Higginson, et al. were quashed in the Federal District Court by the
decision of Judge George Ticknor Curtis, Judge Peleg Sprague concurring (Edelstein, p. 171).]

To Theodore Parker, Concord, January 22? 1855

[In a letter catalogued as of July 21, 1855 (RWEMA), Parker asks Emerson if he
can supply two tickets for his lecture on "next Thursday." Emerson gave no
lecture in July; I read the dateline as "Jany"; see January 17 above for another
letter from Parker with a scarcely legible dateline. The lecture on Thursday,
January 25, was the lecture on slavery. Emerson would have replied.]

To Charles Hosea? Hildreth, Concord, January 23 ? 1855

[In a letter of January 24, 1855 (RWEMA), C. H. Hildreth of Gloucester, Massachusetts, is replying to a letter from Emerson asking for confirmation of his
engagement to lecture on January 31; Hildreth writes that he is expected on that
date and that it is owing to a mistake that he was not notified. The birth of
Charles Hosea Hildreth in 1825 is entered in the Vital Records of Gloucester,
Massachusetts.]

To William Henry Furness, Concord, January 26, 1855[8]

Concord
26 Jany
1855

My dear Furness,

Something was said, months ago, of my reading an Antislavery lecture
in Philadelphia. I said, I can come <6> /2/ Feb y. Friday.[9] But it was left
hanging a little loosely. Is it set down in any body's programme or

---

8. MS in the Furness papers, Van Pelt Library, PU; ph. in NNC; printed in *Records*, p.
[104]; listed *Letters*, 4:487.

9. Emerson gave his lecture on slavery in Philadelphia on February 8; see February 5
below.

intention that I shall come & on that day? If so, write me immediately, for I have a pretty good lecture this time,—good for me, or good "considering," and can come: good, you understand me, if I am engaged; but not good enough to create an occasion for, if it is not already settled. I beg you to put a strong yoke on that blessed constitutional tenderness of yours towards me, and answer officially. I should like well to come to Philadelphia before I set forth on a promised circuit in N.Y.; and yet the absence of Walter Langdon darkens the broad hospitable city for me.[10] Where has he carried all that tenderness & strength? Where shall I find him again? And for you—you draw all people unto you—but I know you must want him day by day.

I trust you have good news from your travellers.[11]

Yours affectionately,
Waldo Emerson

To James Morrison McKaye, Concord, February 4? 1855

[In a letter of February 3, 1855 (RWEMA), James McKaye writes that he hopes Emerson can lecture in Brooklyn when he comes to New York next week; he asks for a reply to his Manhattan office, 82 Broadway. He hopes Emerson will at least dine with him. There is no proof that Emerson replied, but McKaye was a friend of Henry James, Sr., not simply a lyceum secretary.]

To William Henry Furness, Concord, February 5, 1855[12]

Concord 5 Feby 1855

You dear good William, friend of me I tell you I am heartily disappointed that since I am to go to Phila. & appear before your solemn Antislavery Society, I cannot go as I had counted with advantage in having three days before me. I offered you long since 2 Feb.y with that view. Then I had not this luckless 8th day to dispose of. It was promised somewhere, & has been released. Now I am to arrive at Phila only on the p.m. of the 8, to leave it on the a.m. of the 9th to go up the Hudson river somewhere.[13] How am I to see you and your pictures? How to hear the

---

10. For Walter Langdon's illness and death, see *Records*, p. 103, and *Letters*, 4:479, 491.

11. Furness' sons William Henry, Jr., and Horace Howard were in Germany.

12. MS in the Furness papers, Van Pelt Library, PU; ph. in NNC. Apparently Emerson had no envelope. He has folded his letter and sealed it with wax; it is addressed: William H. Furness, D.D. | Philadelphia | Penn. | ; postmarked at New York, February 7. Printed in *Records*, p. [103]; listed *Letters*, 4:489.

13. Emerson is referring to the lecture scheduled for the 8th in Peekskill, New York, listed in his MS Pocket Diary for 1855 (*JMN*, 13:505). Charvat, p. 30, has Peekskill questioned down for the 9th, but that was the original date for the lecture in Hudson.

story of them? How to see Sam B[14] & weave my annual excuse for not going to his house with bag & basket, how to see Philip Randolph, & find why I did not come in summer days?[15]

Well I am glad the boys are happy in Germany, happy in the Arts. Who has better right? How so good? I am going to La Pierre.[16]

Yours, Waldo E.

To Charles C. Terry, Philadelphia?, February 9? 1855

[Listed by Harding, *ESQ* (4th q., 1958), 13:35, from Paul F. Hoag's catalogue for March 1953, with the year only suggested. Emerson missed his original date at Hudson, New York, scheduled for February 9 (see *Letters*, 4:493). This letter, proposing the new date, March 2, and offering a new lecture, "English Civilization," was written between February 9 and 11 from Philadelphia or possibly from Clinton, New York.]

To Albert Haller Tracy, Buffalo? February 14, 1855?[17]

American House
14 Feb

My dear Sir,

I find here my friend Mr Scherb[18] a scholar & gentleman very highly prized by many good men & women in our eastern region. I cannot help asking for him the privilege of that conversation which the upper Powers seem to deny me[19] and I am quite sure that you cannot hear one of his Lectures without interest.

With great regard
R. W. Emerson.

Mr Tracy.

14. Samuel Bradford.

15. Two accidents allowed him to see all his friends; a mixup in Newark permitted him to reach Philadelphia on the 7th, and on the 9th the train he was to take to Hudson, New York, was detained (*Letters*, 4:491, 493–494).

16. La Pierre House, not in directories, is described in a guidebook as a "splendid establishment" on the West side of Broad Street, below Chestnut Street. *The Stranger's Guide to Philadelphia* . . . (Philadelphia: Lindsay & Blakiston, 1860), p. 259.

17. MS in Special Collections, Butler Library, NNC; ph. in NNC. Emerson can be located in Buffalo on February 14 only in 1855; he normally stayed at the American House.

18. Emmanuel Vitalis Scherb.

19. Tracy, a Buffalo lawyer, had served in Congress with Margaret Fuller's father; a letter to him by Margaret Fuller (Overbury Collection, Woolman Library, Barnard College), implies that she had supposed him to be her father's choice of a suitor for her. Emerson found Tracy as good a talker as Alcott and hoped to have the two meet (*Letters*, 5:53, 89). See *JMN*, 14:116–117, for a report of a conversation with Tracy.

To Horatio Woodman, Rochester, February 21, 1855[20]

> Eagle Hotel
> Rochester N.Y.
> 21 Feby 1855

My dear Sir

Your kind note tantalizing me with gorgeous operas, has just arrived before my eyes, having been twice or thrice forwarded to me, from home to N. York, from N.Y. to New Jersey, & now & here contrasts somewhat violently with quite unmusical surroundings. But I am not indifferent to the persistent good will it shows, but thank you heartily therefor. I have given up this month of February to a dragon that does not sing—but roars or yelps,—let us hope that a long acoustic perspective may soften these into some kind of euphony. I shall come back with all the better will to your friendly Saturdays.

> Yours gratefully,
> R. W. Emerson

Horatio Woodman, Esq.

To Thomas Wentworth Higginson, Concord, March 6, 1855[21]

> Concord 6 March
> 1855

My dear Sir,

I enclose 20.00 which you sent me too soon from the Antislavery Society[22] It comes back slower than it should, but I hope not quite too late.

> Ever yours,
> R. W. Emerson.

T. W. Higginson

---

20. MS in the Woodman papers, MHi; ph. in NNC. This letter is misdated 1865 by MHi and in Cameron's list of MHi holdings *ESQ* (1st, 1957), 6(3):21–22. The third digit is carelessly written, but 1855 is the only year when Emerson was in Rochester on February 21. In 1855, the Italian Opera Company performed in Boston for a month, January 15–February 10 (*BET*, January 15 and February 10). To account for the journey of Woodman's letter, I infer that he wrote Emerson on February 6. Emerson found that he was not, as he had supposed, expected in Newark, New Jersey. To reach him as late as February 21 the letter must have followed him through upstate New York (see Charvat, p. 30).

21. MS in the Newport Historical Society; ph. in NNC. This is a very hastily written note. A write-over in the date looks like Mar⟨d⟩h; the signature and the addressee's name are crowded in at the foot of the page.

22. In a letter to Higginson of October 20, 1854, Emerson says he is willing to be held to a lecture in Worcester on January 26, 1855; the MS Pocket Diary has Worcester against that date. I conjecture that Emerson repeated there his anti-slavery lecture given in Boston on

To Franklin Benjamin Sanborn, Concord, March 13, 1855.[23]

Concord
13 March, 1855.

My dear Sir,

I have only succeeded thus far in obtaining from persons interested in our school a guarantee, such as they have been wont to make, namely, of twenty scholars at 10. per quarter. Judge Hoar[24] does not doubt that the school, when set well agoing will bring 25 scholars to it. But three bad quarters have hurt our reputation a little. Not to leave it quite here, however, I will venture to offer you today a guarantee of $850. a year, & the rent of the schoolhouse, that is to say, and the schoolhouse without rent, and I strongly hope we shall be able to better that security before three months are past. Miss Maynard [25] had 25, & even 29 pupils during the last year.

If you shall decide to come to us, you may rely on every endeavor on our parts to make your position good & better.

A few persons are very anxious to have the matter settled; so you shall write me soon.

Yours faithfully,
R. W. Emerson

To Charlotte Haskins Cleveland, Concord, March 16, 1855

[In the MS Account Book for 1853–1860, p. [91], under the date March 16, is a note of $5.00 sent to Charlotte H. Cleveland on account of expenses for the care of Mary Moody Emerson.]

---

the 25th, and that he is here returning a fee for it. After the 29th Emerson was on the road until the date of this letter. I have no evidence at all for this conjecture, but repeating a lecture, Emerson customarily charged less for it, and for Higginson, very much a hero in 1854–1855, he might have charged nothing.

23. MS in the Honnold Library, CCC; ph. in NNC; listed *Letters,* 4:497. The addressee is in no doubt; see Sanborn, *Recollections,* 2:441–442, where Sanborn says he accepted and would be ready to open the school on the 26th of the month.

24. Ebenezer Rockwood Hoar, Judge in the Court of Common Pleas. He would retire in this year to return to private practice. In 1859 he would be appointed to the Supreme Judicial Court of the Commonwealth of Massachusetts.

25. See August 5, 1850, for Helen Maynard, later Mrs. Joseph Keyes.

To David Mack, Concord, March 26, 1855[26]

Concord 26 March
1855

Dear Sir,

On returning home from an absence of a few days, I find your note, & one from Mrs Shilloch. I am grieved to hear that this amiable lady should have suffered, as you say.[27] I wish I knew of pupils for her to teach. Here we have just imported Mr Sanborn from Cambridge, & installed him, this day, with much self-gratulation, on our part: And out of his school, private pupils are none in Concord. Of Mrs S. I know nothing more than she told me in the half hour in which she introduced herself to me. She seemed a very kindly & worthy person, & my wife was especially interested in her. I will keep my eyes & ears open, if perchance I can discover any thing that may profit her.

With great regard to yourself & Mrs Mack,

R. W. Emerson

To Edward Lillie Pierce, Concord, March 30, 1855[28]

Concord ⎱ 30 March
Masstts ⎰ 1855

Dear Sir,

I do not know Mrs Wilson's address,[29] having had no correspondence with her since she went abroad. I have no doubt a letter addressed to the care of her banker at Paris will be forwarded to her, as that is the usual course.

Respectfully,
R. W. Emerson

Mr Pierce.

26. MS in the Treasure Room, MB; ph. in NNC. This letter was acquired by the Boston Public Library with the letter of August 16, 1858 (see below), addressed to Mrs. David Mack by members of the Adirondack Club. William J. Stillman, prime mover of the club, had married the Macks' daughter. *The Autiobiography of a Journalist* (Boston and New York: Houghton, Mifflin, 1901), 1:281.

27. There is now no letter from Mack in the Emerson papers. Mrs. Matilda Shilloch's letter of March 22 from Boston tells of hardships and illness in Texas and asks for help; she wants work teaching the piano, singing, and German, and she would like also to do some translating, all while her husband studies law. Her letter implies some earlier correspondence of which I find no trace.

28. MS in Houghton Library, MH; ph. in NNC.

29. Caroline Wilson; see *Letters*, 4:441, for her going to Europe.

To Louis Agassiz, Concord, April 1, 1855

[In a letter of April 2, 1855 (RWEMA), Louis Agassiz writes that it will give him pleasure to have Emerson's daughter attend his school and he hopes that he and Emerson may now enjoy a "personal acquaintance." The letter reads as if it were an answer to one from Emerson.]

To ———— Concord, April 12, 1855

[Item 16 in Dr. Frank Matthews' 1985 Fall Mail Sale is described as about "a lecture engagement." The only letter as early as this asking for a lecture for the 1855–1856 season is from E. P. Hill, corresponding secretary for the Friends of Freedom. Haverhill, Massachusetts. No Haverhill lecture is recorded by Charvat or listed in the Pocket Diaries.]

To Mary Howland Russell, Concord, April 17, 1855[30]

17 Apr. 1855

My dear Miss Russell,

I wish you all the joy that your two magnificent presents, sent through Lidian's hands can reflect. The children here conceive of you as some beatified person walking softly and invisibly to serve clouds of clients. Ellen read the mystic scrap of paper her mother brought her with puzzled eyes and arrived very slowly, and not unassisted, at the meaning. A little additional gravity has marked her manners; but the cloud rises.

I wrote on Sunday night to Mr Bradford what was enjoined me by Lidian; and the letter goes tomorrow if a steamer sails. The cheque for him I sent to Mr Gamaliel Bradford his banker, and have his receipt for the same. Mrs Ripley & Sophy were as much delighted as our children;[31] so that I look upon the whole design as a spell you have read out of some book of magic to add a little youth and rose-leaves to all the beholders.

Your much bounden
R. W. Emerson

30. The MS has not been located; text from a copy (apparently complete) in Ellen Emerson's hand, Emerson papers (RWEMA), Houghton Library, MH; ph. in NNC. Miss Russell had given Lidian Emerson a check for $100 for Ellen. The sum is entered in the Account Book for 1853–1859 under the date April 19 (p. [36]); the entry is a record of Emerson's promptly borrowing the money from Ellen and giving her his "note for the same." See Letters, 4:501, for the letter to George P. Bradford and the check for him; there the gift to Ellen is mentioned and Miss Russell's name given in full. The receipt and the deposit of the money for Bradford are recorded in the Account Book, p. [95], under the date April 16.
31. Bradford's sister Sarah Bradford Ripley, and his niece Sophia.

To Julius Rockwell, Concord, April 19, 1855[32]

Concord ⎱ 19, April
Mass.tts. ⎰ 1855

Dear Sir,

I am not very willing, at this time of the year, to promise lectures for the winter. And I am always meaning to leave off to read them. But Berkshire[33] is new & very attractive country to me, and I incline to accept your proposition, as you put it, without phrase.[34] Say rather, I will come to you, unless I decide to go nowhere with lectures. If I come, I shall prefer the first week in your course. I notice, you give me a title of reverend to which I have long lost all claim. You shall not advertise me so. Respectfully,

/Hon/ Mr Rockwell.   R W Emerson

To Christopher Pearse Cranch, Concord, April? 20? 1855

[From Paris on March 20, 1855, Christopher P. Cranch wrote Emerson (a.l.s., MHi). Emerson would, I think, have replied. Cranch asks for a letter and supplies a full address.]

To Eliza Buckminster Lee, Concord, April 20? 1855

[Mrs. Lee, in a letter of April 20, asks Emerson to pay Miss Emmeline Barrett the board money for Mrs. Jane Wendte's son and to accept the receipt in his name rather than hers. See April 15, 1854, above, for Emerson's acting as Mrs. Lee's agent in this charity. Emerson would certainly have acknowledged this letter and its enclosure.]

32. MS in the collections of NHi; ph. in NNC.

33. This letter, with that of February 15, 1856, below, shows that by "Berkshire" Emerson means the county and not the town of that name. The entries in the MS Pocket Diary for 1856 that list "Berkshire" for February 18, followed by "B" for February 19, 20, and 21, are tentative entries (*JMN*, 14:436). The final dates for the lectures in Great Barrington, Lee, Pittsfield, and North Adams were March 11, 12, 13, and 14 respectively (see February 15, 1856, below). From Charvat, p. 32, the questioned entry of "Berkshire" for February 19 should be deleted. When Emerson wrote his brother on February 10, these March dates had not been settled (*Letters*, 4:10).

34. The expression "without phrase" means without coaxing or wheedling; the source of this usage is probably Scott.

To CAROLINE STURGIS TAPPAN, CONCORD, APRIL 27, 1855[35]

Concord, 27 April,
1855.

Dear Caroline,

I shall not forgive myself for allowing you to leave town without the visit to Concord, which, however short in time or chained in thought mischance might make it, would yet have been a cherished memory to young & old. Lidian & the children had begged too, that your children[36] might come, & my Ellen & Edith were eager to promise for all attentions they might require. And now, this bright occasion slipped, I see no future for me at all. You will go to Europe, & easily find homes enough to appease your eyes & mind for months & years, and will have no cause to remember the great unfinished America, which, like an outline drawing, or acres of snow, has nothing for the imagination. But an American or two here at home will be the poorer for missing your presence or your neighborhood. And I, who see you less than any of your friends, shall regret your going as much as any. Yet none has gone to the old world who had better title, or to whom its pomps & riches could be less strange. I fancy already some commotion of lights & shades on reliefs & frescoes aware that a more exigent eye & insatiable wish approached, & queenlier science. Well,—see then, see happily & thoroughly, to the very gods that stand dimly behind every stone,—throw the flowers of your costlier praise on mythology & feudalism & Christendom,—but respect the poverty of America, the rough burr, the cheap energy, not yet knowing what it is strong for,—country-strength, & animal sense, yet moral as a child, and its imagination, starved hitherto, clamoring to be fed.

I went the other day to see your sister,[37] who received me with great kindness. Her manners & beauty will serve to vindicate America to you in England & Italy, and, whilst she stays at home, I shall reckon securely on your return.

Far capitals & marble courts her eye seemed still to see,
Minstrels, & dames, & highborn men, the princeliest that be.

Please give me, if you can, a little exact information as to your times—

35. MS in the Tappan papers, Houghton Library, MH; ph. in NNC.
36. The Tappans had two daughters, Ellen Sturgis and Mary Aspinwall.
37. Caroline's sister Ellen died in 1848, and her sister Susan, in 1853; the surviving sisters were Ann (Mrs. Samuel Hooper) and Sarah (Mrs. Francis George Shaw). The verses identify the sister as Ann Hooper; see *Works*, 9:291, the quatrain to "A. H." and *JMN*, 13:407, 420. The verses here appear to be the improvisation the second journal entry considers.

when at New York, when to sail. Do you wish any letter to Carlyle? or to Wilkinson,—a more gentle & scarcely less powerful person, busy lately in Scandinavian poetry, reading Icelandic, to translate the Edda.[38] Or I know Arthur Helps. Clough you will send for. If I can serve you in any matter abroad, or here at home,—even by writing to Ellery, there will be consolation in the service. I send also my best wishes to William Tappan: Europe will find him better employment for his taste & polished cosmopolitanism, but I would fain charge him to bear in mind the unpaid debt —ever-growing to America.[39]

Your affectionate R. W. E.

To Henry James, Sr., Concord, May 4, 1855[40]

Concord, 4 May, 1855.

My dear James,

Your letter was a blessing, but after your squandering way, it was loaded with double & treble weight of its own kind & of other kinds, love, Science, poetry, from the oldest old, & the newest new. May I live long enough to receive such another envelope!

Wilkinson's wealth, if he only write a letter, begets wonder.[41] His insight & his prodigal fancy advertise us of eras & revolutions close by. Things cannot go on long at their old jog, if such wings as these exist, & can be furnished to another man, to other men, revolution will be cheap, & ascension easy, if such a faculty is suffered to remain in the planet. Tis droll to remember our canting disparagements of 'the Age,' which has a man who seems large enough to furnish two or three. His totally inadequate reputation proves well enough his exceeding dimensions. However, the fame runs & grows, from London, oversea to America, & <e>vibrating back more violently to London again. They must all find him soon;—I hope, before the man is quite out of their reach.

For the poem, I found it easy to read, & helpful, & the rather, that I have long had a keen relish for the Norse genius, having Dasents "Younger

38. See below, May 4, for Emerson's comment on Wilkinson's translation.

39. Emerson evidently expected Tappan to do some writing; there's nothing to show that he did.

40. MS, defective, in the James papers, Houghton Library, MH; ph. in NNC; printed by Perry, 1:78–79; listed *Letters*, 4:505. The MS was incomplete when Perry used it; James may have lost the last portion when he sent the first part of the letter to James John Garth Wilkinson (see Perry, 1:79–81).

41. With his letter of April 24 (Perry, 1:78), James had sent Emerson letters from Wilkinson as well as Wilkinson's translation of "Hamais Heimt" (Perry, 1:77).

Edda," & the Heimskringla, & Mallet, & Thorpe, & Ker,[42] on my shelf. I
rejoice in the authoritative verdict of Wilkinson. Yet, on the first reading,
I thought it a little harsh, and, that the skeleton must be made presentable by <a>the least pulp or film of muscle & fat, even at the expense of
some strength. I wished readers, & I remembered the feeble interest I
have found in various attempts to lend the "Younger Edda." But on
reading the piece to my children three, at night, the success was surprising at a second reading to the same audience, with additions, the next
day, it was better understood & admired; and since the third reading to
increasing numbers, it is a classic. It is to be recited at school. I understand tomorrow, & without an

To Edward Kent, Concord, May 9? 1855

[In a letter from Boston of May 8 (RWEMA), Emerson's classmate Edward Kent
of Bangor, Maine, says he would like to come to Concord on Saturday (the 12th)
if it is convenient. Emerson certainly replied, for he invited Benjamin Tyler Reed
and Nathaniel Wood to come to Concord to join him and John Milton Cheney
for dinner with Kent; see Letters, 4:507]

To Charles De Berard Mills, Concord, May 9? 1855

[In a letter of May 11 1855 (RWEMA), Charles de Berard Mills of Syracuse, New
York, acknowledges books sent him by Emerson and a portrait. It is likely that
Emerson, lending the books, wrote to him. See April 30, 1856, below, for a second
likely letter to Mills.]

To Henry Wadsworth Longfellow, Concord, May 10, 1855?[43]

                                                    Concord
                                                    Thursday, 10 May.
Dear Longfellow,
    Your note, retained by I know not what envious postmaster, did not
reach Concord until last evening.—informing me of opportunities which
I could not have refused.

                                                    Ever yours,
                                                    R. W. Emerson.
H. W. Longfellow, Esq.

42. See Harding, pp. 86–87, for George Webbe Dasent's translation of the prose Edda;
pp. 251–252, for Samuel Laing's translation of *Heimskringla:* p. 181, for Paul Henri Mallet's
Northern Antiquities; p. 272, for Benjamin Thorpe's *Northern Mythology;* p. 158, for John
Bellenden Ker's *Essay on the Archeology of Our Popular Phrases and Nursery Rhymes.*
43. MS in the Longfellow papers. Houghton Library, MH; ph. in NNC. On May 7, 1855
(RWEMA), Longfellow had written to invite Emerson to dinner with George W. Curtis and

To SIDNEY E. BRIDGMAN, CONCORD, MAY 25, 1855[44]

Concord ⎱ 25 May
Mass.   ⎰ 1855

Dear Sir,

If it be not too late to reply to your letter, I will say, that, though I do not like very well to fix a date at this distance of time, I can probably come to Northampton in November.[45] If I come, <I>the Institute shall pay me thirty dollars.

Respectfully.
R. W. Emerson.

Mr Bridgman.

To T. WILLARD LEWIS, CONCORD, MAY 25? 1855

[In a letter of May 23, 1855 (RWEMA), T. Willard Lewis, chairman of the lecture committee of the Marlboro Mechanics' Institute, asks for a lecture on a Wednesday in December. See Charvat, p. 31, for the Marlboro lecture given on Friday, December 7. There is no proof that Emerson wrote Lewis at this time, but he had to have written him to settle the date, for the MS Pocket Diary for 1855 shows Marlboro entered as of (Wednesday) December 5, and then deleted in favor of Clinton (*JMN,* See 13:510). below, November 22?, to John Ring for the failure of the Clinton course arranged by Artemas G. Bigelow. See also, below, October ? 1855, for a second likely letter to Lewis.]

To MARY PRESTON STEARNS, CONCORD, MAY 28, 1855[46]

Concord, 28 May
1855.

My dear Mrs Stearns,

What a long memory for any beneficent purpose you have! My little boy is highly pleased with his invitation, but unhappily his vacation does

---

William H. Prescott on Wednesday, May 9. This note of Thursday, May 10, is certainly of 1855.

44. MS at p. 165 in a grangerized copy of *Out of the Heart* . . . Selected by John White Chadwick . . . and Annie Chadwick, Boston, Joseph Knight Company [1891], MNF; ph. in NNC. Emerson's "Friendship" is printed at p. 165. The volume was prepared by Sidney Bridgman and presented to his daughter on her birthday, May 6, 1902. Listed by B. Simison, *MLN* (June 1940), 55:427.

45. The date settled upon was December 12. The visit to Northampton was combined with letters at Greenfield and Shelburne Falls; see *Letters,* 4:524.

46. MS in the Barrett Collection, Alderman Library, ViU; ph. in NNC; printed, with the wrong date and with errors, by Frank Preston Stearns, *The Life and Public Services of George Luther Stearns* (Philadelphia & London: Lippincott, 1907), p. 95; listed *Letters,* 4:511. See *Letters,* 4:482, n. 1, for Emerson's first acquaintance with the family of George Luther Stearns.

not square with Frank's.[47] Next Saturday, however, is a full holiday; and if you are willing to take the trouble of him, & Frank will run the risks of a new acquaintance Edward shall go down in the morning train from Concord at 7 o'clock, & be at Porter's[48] at 7.50 a.m. if Frank will meet him there. and if you will be so good as to see that he is at Porter's again at 6.40 in the evening, he will have all the privilege & happiness of the day,—"no duty left, no calling broke."[49] My wife is very sensible of your kind thoughts but is more than usually an invalid in these days. With kindest regards to Mr Stearns, & to the young people

Yours faithfully,
R. W. Emerson.

Mrs Stearns.

To Azariah? Smith, Concord, May 29, 1855[50]

Concord ⎫ 29 May
Mass.tts. ⎭ 1855

Dear Sir,

The invitation you send me from the Library Society of N.Y. Central College is very kind & very attractive to me. But, on looking at my tasks & engagements for the summer, I see no option left for me but to decline it. Please to express to the members my thanks, & my regret.

Respectfully,
R. W. Emerson

Mr Smith.

47. In her letter of May 24 Mrs. Stearns recalls Emerson's letter of January 8; she now proposes that Edward Emerson visit her boy Frank in Medford, if he has already had whooping cough.

48. Porter's Landing, the stop closest to Medford.

49. Emerson has conflated the opening phrases of ll. 129–130 of Pope's "Epistle to Dr. Arbuthnot." Pope's couplet reads:

> "I left no Calling for this idle trade,
> No Duty broke, no Father dis-obeyed."

50. MS in the Barrett Collection, Alderman Library, ViU; ph. in NNC. In the Gerrit Smith collection, Ernest S. Bird Library, University of Syracuse, is an invitation to the 1855 "Literary Anniversaries" of New York Central College. The invitation was issued by Azariah Smith of the Union Society and J. Metcalfe Smith of the Dialexian Society. There is no way of knowing which of the two Smiths wrote to Emerson. The speaker on the actual occasion was Gerrit Smith, who took a special interest in the short-lived Baptist institution in Mc-Grawville (now McGraw). See Ralph Volney Harlow, *Gerrit Smith* (New York: Henry Holt, 1930), pp. 231–232. Professor Joseph Slater kindly provided the information identifying the college referred to and the Smiths.

To Elizabeth Palmer Peabody, Concord, May 31, 1855 [51]

Concord, 31 May 1855

My dear Miss Peabody,

I had last night your kind letter which interested me much. I cannot believe but that many families in town & country will be quickly open to this young governess you describe. It is precisely what I have so long wished for my children & for myself—and still wish—But Lidian's health is so miserable—She is much of the time in a nervous prostrate condition —as to quite forbid my adding to her thoughts any thing which she would feel a serious care. Ellen & Edith are both at school, very well provided in that particular now, as formerly not, and Ellen goes in September to Agassiz.

So I relinquish very sorrowfully any thought of inviting the young teacher. The more's the pity! I will go & name the opportunity to other people, & see if I cannot find an offerer.

Your obliged
R. W. Emerson

To William Williamson, Concord, June? 2? 1855

[In a letter of June 1, 1855 (RWEMA), William Williamson of Amesbury invites Emerson to lecture on November 15 for the Washington Lyceum in Amesbury. This unquestioned engagement with Williamson's name is entered in the MS Pocket Diary for 1855 (*JMN*, 13:509), under the date November 15. See Charvat, p. 31. When Emerson accepted the invitation is uncertain, but he had to have written Williamson at least once.]

To Mrs. _____Wagner, Concord, June 5, 1855 [52]

Concord
June 5 1855

Mrs Wagner [53]
Madam,

I am sorry that today & tomorrow find my afternoons engaged hopelessly. I shall probably be in Boston, in the course of two or three days,

51. MS in the New England Collection, MnM; ph. in NNC. Miss Peabody's letter to Emerson does not survive, so the young lady must remain unidentified.

52. The MS (pasted into a volume of *English Traits*) was owned in 1939 by Una Mirrielees Bernard Sait who lent it to Rusk; ph. in NNC; text from the photostat which Rusk had checked against the original.

53. Only two Wagners are listed in the 1855 Boston directories: Antony Wagner, laborer; and Charles Wagner, coppersmith. Neither seems likely. Moreover, it is possible that the lady was a visitor to the city.

when I shall not fail to call on you. If, meantime, we shall not meet, I will
be at home on Tuesday p.m.

> With great respect,
> R. W. Emerson.

To Adam Knight Spence, June ? 1855

[See below, January 7, 1856, for evidence of a letter to Adam Knight Spence in
the "summer" of 1855 saying that if he came West he would try to give a lecture
for the "Students' Lecture Association" of the University of Michigan.]

To M_____ C_____ Maynard, Concord, June 10? 1855

[In a letter of June 6, 1855 (RWEMA), M. C. Maynard asks Emerson to lecture
for the Cleveland Library Association in the coming season. See Charvat for
Emerson's lecture engagement of January 23, 1856. There must have been one
letter at least to Maynard.]

To Charles Hazeltine Goddard, Concord, June 10? 1855

[In a letter of June 4, 1855 (RWEMA), C. H. Goddard asks if he may use
Emerson's name as a reference on a card he intends to circulate to offer himself
as a lecturer; he hopes to secure his friends' help in circulating the cards. In
Emerson's MS Pocket Diary for 1855 (*JMN*, 13:503), second flyleaf, is a note
"Letter to C. Goddard." The entry is a reminder to write, but is not surely related
to Goddard's request. See *Letters*, 4:495, n. 57, for Goddard's having lectured in
Boston in February and March 1855 on *Paradise Lost*, and see *Letters*, 4:204, for
Emerson's meeting Goddard in 1850.]

To James Morrison McKaye, Concord, June 11, 1855[54]

> Concord 11 June 1855

My dear Sir,

I have been exceedingly busy for an idle man, & very little at home, &
then with company, since your note came to me, or you should have had
an earlier reply. Yet I have so little to communicate.—I am almost scared
to observe that almost all the people I know are hurrying to Europe—
ten, within a few weeks, I have counted,[55]—and, for the most part, I

54. MS in the Barrett Collection, Alderman Library, ViU; ph. in NNC.
55. Colonel James McKaye had written Emerson on June 4 from Newport asking for
advice and letters for his trip to Europe. McKaye had earlier in the year (February 4)
proposed that Emerson lecture in Brooklyn and invited Emerson to be his guest. See *Letters*,
4:243, for what may be an allusion to the same McKaye, a parishioner of Samuel Longfellow
(*Letters*, 4:40); and see below June 4. For an account of McKaye's friendship with Henry
James, Sr., see Perry, 1:83, n. 2. James reports to Emerson, McKaye's meeting with Carlyle
in 1856 (Perry, 1:83–84).

would far rather hold them fast at home. But you have your duties &
enterprises drawing you thither, & will enjoy so keenly England & Paris,
—that, I suppose, I must give you joy, on the occasion. Not a word of
counsel, not a line of introduction have I to pester you with, though you
flatter me in asking these. The travelling has grown now to be a huge &
perfect institution: Murrays ⟨guide⟩ /hand/ books are so perfect, & written by the most competent persons,—that nothing is to be added to them
which the valet-de-place who is waiting for you at each hotel to show you
the lions, cannot supply. I have suffered, one by one, all my English
acquaintances who once were many,—to leave me without a letter; and,
as they do not send travellers to me, I decided early that it was not fit
that I should send travellers to them. Even Carlyle, who has a long lived
good will, I rarely hear from,—more rarely write to him. The right way
is, wherever you find yourself in the neighborhood of any person to
whom you know your own affinities,—to send him a note, saying this, &
asking an interview.[56]

In London, the two chief things to be seen are certainly Parliament,—
which will probably be still sitting after your arrival; and the British
Museum. The American Minister will always give you cards admitting
you to both ⟨h⟩Houses of P. to your heart's content. And the ⟨P⟩Museum
has now a Hand-Book, which is an immense improvement over the book
we had a few years ago. You must go thither to see the Elgin Marbles,
once & again, & again, until suddenly their beauty comes to you. I think
it would be money well paid if one could hear of some skilful young man
who would show the antiques for a stipulated fee. The whole Museum is
open, you know, to all the world three days in the week. Coventry
Patmore is a good hearted youth, a sublibrarian—when I knew him—in
the Library there. I was under great obligations to his knowledge as well
as his courtesy. If he is still there, say so to him from me, & ask him to
show you some of the fine things he showed me. But I am scribbling at a
dangerous rate to you, who have trunks to pack for sea. So, the best
voyage, & the satisfying journey, & the happiest return, to you! prays
Yours faithfully,
Col. McKaye. R. W. Emerson.

56. The "way" he had used on his first trip to Europe.

To Elizabeth Palmer Peabody, Concord, June 13, 1855[57]

Concord 13 June 1855

My dear Miss Peabody,

I hate to hear that the Essay was not crowned.[58] I thought its chances very good; that, in Scotland, they were not very likely to know things told or implied in your paper; nor to have experience of a bolder treatment, than, I think, the beginning of your Essay showed. For present employment I must think the journals or monthl⟨y⟩ies ought to give you scope, & they be thankful. They can have no more facile writer; &, if you will compromise so far as to give them short papers, I am sure you have reading & knowledge that will be new & spicy to them,—the two qualities magazines require. Write a little article on one of your books you showed me, & call it, "Bed of the Mediterranean;" and do not take but three pages or four. Write "an Evening with Allston"[59] & collate in it half a dozen sayings of his, the best you can recall from your interviews with him. "A day in Boston," how easily you could fill with a little arrangement of anecdotes of conversations with Kirkland, Channing, Spurzheim, Follen & even Jonathan Phillips,[60]—with a little dexterity & heed to the proprieties,—all out of your private diaries. Make them short, & you make them striking. There is a very knowing public that peeps into Putnam as well as the careless crowd, and their value for an original anecdote of a good head will teach the ⟨pu⟩editors to value your contributions. You can say to the Boston of 1855, "I knew your father"—"I mind the bigging on't"—and Father Taylor, Brownson, & Parker, of ten years ago, so public as they are, might sit for a short crayon sketch without offense, so they sit together.[61] You know I have your journal of Margaret Fuller, which waits your order. I say this, because I think you have real records that would furnish a few good points on each of these, at small cost to yourself. I suspend all judgment on whatever deeper funds you may command. For the Foreign journals, I have never tried my hand at propitiating their ⟨notice⟩ /reception/ of any paper. In the

57. MS in the James Duncan Phillips Library, MSaE; ph. in NNC.
58. Emerson is referring here, I believe, to Miss Peabody's essay on "Primeval History," which he later would try to get into the *Atlantic*.
59. Moncure Conway recalls Emerson's saying that Miss Peabody's "recollections and correspondence would comprise the spiritual history of her Times" (*Emerson at Home and Abroad*, p. 261).
60. John Thornton Kirkland, the Reverend William Ellery Channing, Dr. Johann Christoph Spurzheim (the phrenologist died in Boston), Charles Follen.
61. Edward Taylor of the Seamen's Bethel, Orestes Brownson, Theodore Parker.
62. Delia Bacon.

case of Miss Bacon,[62] who had a remarkable subject, which she thought ought first to appear in England, I remember I told her I thought it would be easy, & I would write to England in her behalf. But ⟨t⟩she decided to go herself thither, & means, I believe, to publish there & here simultaneously. I have no correspondent in any foreign journal, but, in the like case, where a commanding fitness existed, I might try my intervention. Ever yours,

R W Emerson

To Paulina W. Davis, Concord, June 13, 1855[63]

Concord, Mass. June 13, 1875

Dear Madam:—I think I may venture to promise you what aid I can, at your meeting in September. So many fine days as should occur between now and then, must suggest something good, we may hope, to the dullest soul. At all events, if I understand you, the meeting is to be beholden, and others are to take their part whether I do or not. So I think I shall keep it before me, and will bring you what I find.

With great respect.
R. W. Emerson.

Mrs. P. W. Davis.

To John O. Fiske, Concord, June 21, 1855

[In a letter of June 18 (?) 1855 (RWEMA), John O. Fiske of Bath, Maine, asks for a lecture for the coming season and wants Emerson to name a date and fee. In catalogue 12 (1980) of Lowe, item 58, Emerson's reply of June 21, 1855, to Mr. Fiske is quoted: ". . . It will give me pleasure to come to Bath next winter, if I can. This is not the first invitation I have received, nor the first expression of willingness to go I have returned . . . early in the season I think I may combine several proposed visits to your region. If that can be done, the Lyceum shall pay me thirty dollars." See October 24 below for a second letter to Fiske. This is possibly the same letter listed *Letters*, 4:512.]

To Edward Boltwood, Concord, June 25? 1855

[See *Letters*, 4:513, for Emerson's having asked his young relative to visit him; unable to accept Emerson's invitation for the 9th, Boltwood wrote again proposing June 29 and 30 for his visit; he asks for a reply. Boltwood was a first cousin once removed, the grandson of Deborah Haskins Shepard.]

63. No MS has been found; text from *The Una*, (August 15, 1855), 3:126. Emerson is answering Mrs. Davis' letter of June 7 (RWEMA) asking him to speak at the Convention for Women's Rights to be held in Boston in September. Emerson gave a speech on "Woman" on September 20. See also October 1 below.

To HENRY JAMES, SR., CONCORD, JUNE 25, 1855[64]

$$\text{Concord} \left.\begin{matrix} \\ \\ \end{matrix}\right\} \begin{matrix} \text{25 June} \\ \text{1855} \end{matrix}$$
$$\text{Mass}$$

My dear Henry James,

I began a letter to you four days ago, immediately on receiving your farewells;[65] but have since been flitting between Boston & Cambridge, & must take a new date, & speedily too, lest it come too late. I had already heard, with a certain terror, from Anna Ward, of this resolved departure, & was holding back my speech from you that it should not be too full of patriotic anger & dirges of personal disappointment. When I was cool, I was to have written at large. But your letter disarms me with your radiant bonhommie, & would make old me young again with your loving romances. Of course, I dared not bring home to myself one drop of the beautiful poison. I remembered your phosphoric chromatizing ways. But reading on, I found you had quietly jumped the whole argument, namely, the causes of this astonishing exodus, & dexterously alighted on the interesting episode of your sister's accompanying you. O yes, reason enough for sisters

To CHARLOTTE HASKINS CLEVELAND, CONCORD, JUNE 30, 1855[66]

$$\text{Concord} \left.\begin{matrix} \\ \\ \end{matrix}\right\} \begin{matrix} \text{30 June} \\ \text{1855} \end{matrix}$$
$$\text{Masstts.}$$

My dear Cousin,

I enclose $10.00 agreeably to your letter, for Aunt's board. I am sorry that my affairs, which have kept me busy, have delayed this reply which should have been prompt. I have not even seen Elizabeth H.[67] or heard of the contingency in Auntie's boarding affairs, which you have written her.[68] So much the more shame to me, who should have seen dear E. oftener, & inquired more exactly about Aunt Mary.

You see it makes us all careless when we know that there is a careful

64. MS (defective) in the James papers, Houghton Library, MH; ph. in NNC; printed by Perry, 1:81–82; listed *Letters,* 4:513. The MS was defective when Perry used it.

65. Emerson is answering James' letter of June 25 (Perry, 1:80–81), which announces his departure for the 27th and extravagantly regrets leaving Emerson's vicinity.

66. MS in the Abernethy Library, VtMiM; ph. in NNC.

67. Elizabeth Hoar.

68. See above, November 13, 1854, for Mrs. Cleveland; her care of Mary Moody Emerson is referred to in letters of 1854 (*Letters,* 4:446, 450), and above. The MS Account Book for 1854–1859, under the date June 30 (p. [102]), has a note of this letter and the money sent for Miss Emerson's board "to be divided between W. E. & R. W. E."

loving Cousin there on the spot, who will not let things go wrong. Well, so much the more do you continue to heed & befriend both her & us. But Elizabeth has lately been three weeks away. We are as well & as ill as usual here, but all your friends.

affectionately,

Mrs Cleveland.   R. W. Emerson

To Anna W. Bardwell, Concord, June 30? 1855

[In a letter of June 28, 1855 (RWEMA), Mrs. Anna W. Bardwell tells Emerson that the president of the Adelphi Society of Williams College has refused to pay the Mansion House bill incurred when Emerson lectured for the society August 15, 1854. She wishes a statement from Emerson about whether he was alone or accompanied. Emerson may have obliged. His daughter Ellen had gone with him to Williamstown, but she had not stayed at the hotel (see Letters, 4:456).]

To Benjamin Marston Watson, Concord, July 6, 1855 [69]

Concord ⎫ July 6
Mass ⎰ 1855

My dear Sir,

I believe I ought to have written you before, to explain our small plan for the benefit of Mr Alcott; & all the more, because I believe you are proposing or executing some design of your own in the same direction.[70] He proposed as he has probably told you, to go to England; & Mr Davis & Mr Barker of Providence gave him together 150. for that purpose.[71] When he came to me, I said, not a penny for England, shall I, nor with my good will shall Davis give; but we will make of this an occasion for making up a little fund to stay at home upon. Mr. Davis consented readily on my application to have this new direction to his $100. Mr

69. MS in the Watson papers, Hillside Collection, MPlPS; ph. in NNC; the signature and complimentary close have been cut away, shaving the lower portion of the last line on page three and cutting off the conclusion, here conjectured, of the final question. Printed in part by Lawrence D. Geller, Between Concord and Plymouth, p. 39. The letter is listed as of "1853" (pp. 138, 157).

70. See Letters, 4:504, 514, for Emerson's continued resolution to prevent Alcott's going to Europe.

71. Joseph A. Barker and Thomas Davis had both contributed to the fund for Alcott's first trip to Europe. Davis' name, but not Barker's, appears in Emerson's MS Ledger for 1849–1872 (p. 143) in the list of contributors to the "Alcott Fund" (the record is dated 1858) and is a MS "Statement of monies received by Samuel G. Ward from sundry persons, and held by him for the benefit of A. Bronson Alcott, Esq." (RWEMA). This account is dated October 20, 1863. Emerson's ledger figures are in round numbers; the 1863 document is more precise. Not in the 1863 document, but in Emerson's Ledger appears the name of Thoreau as donating $10.00. See Letters, 5:159–160, n. 105.

Longfellow at Cambridge ⟨ga⟩ promised me a Poem, or $50. Starr King a Lecture or $50. Whipple & Parker each a lecture. Mr Woodman, Mr Apthorp, Mr Fisher, promised contributions. Mr Beck sent me 20.00; &c &c.[72] Now we had already, long since, 500. secured to him, & bearing interest; we propose to get $1000. more, &, with $1500. we think we shall have $150. a year in some safe form. I have kind replies from those I have seen & several names in my mind of persons from whom I anticipate kind replies. I think, there are many persons who will like to give small sums, after I have exhausted the list of those who will give round ones. But what is important is to concentrate, &, if possible, save & turn every particular & temporary aid into this permanent one. Can you not, in whatever you are doing for him, join with us: Do you know any persons at Plymouth[73] who would like to aid [in this design?]

To Samuel Gray Ward, Concord, July 10, 1855[74]

Concord
10 July 1855

My dear friend,

Here is Abel Adam's note, which only came last night, though I wrote him from Boston immediately after seeing you. Do you persist in your opinion, notwithstanding his objections? If so, I think I shall be guided by it, though I shall grieve to act against A. A.'s[75] who has been generally a wise & always the kindest adviser.

I have one more new book so extraordinary for its oriental largeness of generalization, an American Buddh,—that I must send it to

72. Longfellow, Frederick Beck, and Thomas Starr King contributed to the fund; I find no record of contributions from Whipple, Parker, Apthorp, or Fisher. Not named here are Seth Cheney and Mrs. Cheney, Wendell Phillips, and C. F. Hovey. I believe Fisher to be James T. Fisher of the defunct Town and Country Club. R. E. Apthorp is possibly Robert E. Apthorp, Boston attorney. C. F. Hovey is possibly Charles F. Hovey, head of a dry goods company in Boston. In the MS Account Book for 1853–1859, contributions are recorded as follows: p. [38], June 30, 1855, from Frederick Beck, $20.00 and p. [58], June 9, 1856, an additional $20; p. [40], September 24, 1855, from Ednah Dow Cheney, $50.00; p. [56], May 9, 1856, from Thomas Davis, $106; p. [58], May 31, 1856, from C. F. Hovey, $10.00; p. [80], July 25, 1857, from Horatio Woodman, $50.00.

73. When the notion of a fund for Alcott was first broached in 1842, Mrs. Emerson's sister wrote from Plymouth (March 25, 1842, RWEMA) that she doubted that any help would come from Plymouth, for "there is such a prejudice against him on account of his unwillingness to work for a living; even among his friends."

74. MS in the Ward papers, Houghton Library, MH; ph. in NNC; quoted by Rusk, Life, p. 372.

75. A. A. is Abel Adams; the subject of the letter is the Vermont and Canada Railroad shares Emerson held; see Letters, 4:515, and n. 140.

you, & pray you to look it over, if you have it not? It is called "Leaves of Grass."

Yours,
R. W. E.

S. G. Ward.

TO RALPH FARNSWORTH, CONCORD, JULY 12, 1855 [76]

Concord ⎱ 12 July
Mass.tts ⎰ 1855

My dear Sir,

The Class of 1821 have engaged a room for the whole of Commencement day, 18th instant, at the Lyceum Building, next the Episcopal Church, Cambridge.

For fear that the printed notification of the Committee, forwarded to you, may have miscarried, I have been requested to send you this second summons; which I do very gladly from my personal wish to see you. I heartily hope it may be in your power to come to the meeting W [77]

With great regard,
Your classmate & next man, [78]
R. W. Emerson—

Dr R. Farnsworth.

Cheney joins me in kind salutations. [79]

TO HENRY JAMES, SR., CONCORD, JULY 17, 1855

[As the letter to Clough below shows, Emerson must have written to James as well, enclosing with his letter that to Clough.]

To Arthur Hugh Clough, Concord, July 17, 1855 [80]

Concord ⎱ 17 July
Mass ⎰ 1855

My dear Clough,

I have suffered Mr Henry James to ⟨r⟩go to Liverpool without a letter to you. And knowing you both to be curious in men, & both inestimable,

---

76. MS in the Palmer Library, CtNIC; ph. in NNC; listed in *Letters*, 4:518, from Farnsworth's reply of July 16 (RWEMA).

77. A false start of the complimentary close, Emerson miscalculated his space.

78. I take this to mean in the alphabetical list of the class.

79. John Milton Cheney.

80. MS in the Clough papers, Bodleian Library, Oxford; ph. in NNC; printed *Emerson-Clough Letters*, no. 26, and Mulhauser, 2:503; listed in *Letters*, 4:518, with the Clough letter referred to here.

& he the best man in New York, I send after him /this/ note, praying him to deliver it to you without fail. For, as it was foreordained that you two should meet, I should be chagrined if I were not in some sort a party to your congress. I keep your letter of last month lying on my table, for a good sign, & to provoke me to good works in your direction.

Yours faithfully,
R. W. Emerson

A. H. Clough, Esq.

To Arthur Helps, Concord, July 17, 1855[81]

Concord, Masstts.,
17 July 1855.

My dear Mr. Helps,

Mr. Henry James, a valued friend of mine, and as I am wont to think, the best man in the city of New York, for all its millions of bodies, goes to London and to France, and though he hinted a wish for letters to "souls in prison," I think he might also go to enfranchised and palatial souls.[82] You will find him well versed in what is good in America, and with a compass in his thought and his love of men that is rare here. He is meaning, I believe, to put his boys in school in Switzerland. I think I cannot do either of you a greater kindness than to present you to each other, I wish he may add motives to the inclination you professed to visit your friends and readers in this country.

With kindest regards,
Yours faithfully,
R. W. Emerson.

To Caroline Sturgis Tappan, Concord, July 17, 1855[83]

Concord, 17 July—

Dear Caroline,

I have been checked in my repeated wishes to send you a message, by rumours that you had sailed,—were sailing,—were at New York;—& other confused echoes, which my stay-at-home-habits had no means of

81. No MS has been found; text from *Correspondence of Sir Arthur Helps*, E. A. Helps, ed. (London: John Lane, 1917), p. 177; printed also by Perry, 1:82.

82. For Henry James, Sr., on Helps, see Perry, 1:84.

83. MS in the Sophia Smith Collection, MNS. The year is certain from Emerson's expectation that the Tappans are going to Europe. The original plan had been to sail on June 1st; an undated letter (MNS) to Emerson gives the plans; the letter is apparently late April; see *Letters*, 4:504, where Emerson tells George Bradford of the Tappans' plans.

rectifying. But Mrs Lowell[84] told my brother William, in his way hither, that you were at Lenox still. I had heard already with joy that the children were safe & sound again.[85] But I suppose no delays, & no Rachel,[86] & no new discoveries of genius at home, will keep you long from the old appointed Pinacothecas and Gylptothecas of educated eyes, & you must find the ⟨wat⟩baths out of which the eastern stars converge. I have made up my mind to resignation, & even to sympathy with your career as ever, so now.

Twice or trice lately in turning over my portfolios I have found with penitence ⟨N⟩Charles K. Newcomb's Swedenborg notes which you lent me. I had partly copied them & had desisted. I did not like to set my young people on copying what they had no love for & meant to end it myself. Do you want them abroad? I suppose not, for unless you carry a lumber wagon with you you cannot verify these in the tomes of the dear old mystagogue. But if you have the least wish, tis but an hour's work to transfer them & send them. One strange book you ought to see before you go, or carry with you,—a thin quarto called "Leaves of Grass," printed at Brooklyn N.Y., apparently not published, & sent to me thru the Post office. Tis the best piece of American ⟨philosophy⟩ Buddhism that any one has had strength to write, American to the bone, & with large discourse before & after, &, infinite of some crudeness, & strange weary catalogues of things like a warehouse inventory, & in spite of an unpromising portrait on the frontispiece, contains fine stories of genius & unforgettable things. Brooklyn too & Walter Whitman, perhaps you know more of it than I do. I have sent mine to Sam Ward. And if when you are well over the salt sea, & pitching a rover's tent from land to land, one of your sometime gossips should be ambitious to say a word to you you should leave some bye-way not likely to be choked up through which it could pass.[87] Yet, I suppose, Mrs Hooper[88] & your father will always know your address. With kind salutations to William Tappan, Ever yours,

R. W. E.

Mrs Tappan.

Emerson knew of the postponement by July 9 (*Letters*, 4:517). See below, October 3, for note of the new sailing date, October 10.

84. Probably Anna Cabot Jackson Lowell.

85. I find nothing to explain this passage; probably the children had fallen ill. Since the Tappans intended to take the children with them, their illness would account for postponing the journey.

86. The famous French actress was on tour in this country in 1855.

87. Emerson would write her two letters, neither mailed; see below Oct. 13, 1857, and May 13, 1859.

88. Caroline's sister Ann, Mrs. Samuel Hooper.

To Walter Whitman, Concord, July 21, 1855[89]

Concord ⎤ 21 July
Masstts. ⎦ 1855

Dear Sir,

I am not blind to the worth of the wonderful gift of "Leaves of Grass." I find it the most extraordinary piece of wit & wisdom that America has yet contributed. I am very happy in reading it, as great power makes /us/ happy. It meets the demand I am always making of what seemed the sterile & stingy Nature, as if too much handiwits fat & mean. I give you joy of your free & brave thought. I have great joy in it. I find incomparable things said incomparably well, as they must be. I find the courage of <u>treatment</u>, which so delights us, & which large perception only can inspire.

I greet you at the beginning of a great career, which yet must have had a long foreground somewhere for such a start. I rubbed my eyes a little to see if this sunbeam were no illusion; but the solid sense of the book is a sober certainty. It has the best merits, namely, of fortifying & encouraging.

I did not know until I, last night, saw the book advertised in a newspaper, that I could trust the name as real & available for a post-office. I wish to see my benefactor, & have felt much like striking my tasks, & visiting New York to pay you my respects.

R. W. Emerson.

Mr. Walter Whitman.

To Frederic Dan Huntington, Concord, July 24? 1855

[In a letter of July 25, 1855 (RWEMA), the Reverend Frederic D. Huntington of Hadley, Massachusetts, hopes to secure a visit from Emerson after the Amherst College commencement August 8 (Charvat, p. 32). He wants Emerson to meet his father, the Reverend Dan Huntington, "so complete an instance of serene age that a look at him is worth a little turning out of one's way." See below, October 1? 1855, for Emerson's invitation to Huntington.]

89. MS in the Feinberg collection, Manuscript Division, DLC; text checked against the original, with envelope addressed: Walter Whitman, Esq. | Care of Fowlers & Wells. | 308 Broadway. | New York. | ; postmark blurred. The letter has been frequently reprinted, first by Whitman himself, and reproduced in facsimile; listed *Letters*, 4:520. See October 24 below for Emerson's response to Whitman's printing of this letter in the *New-York Daily Tribune* of October 10. For comment by Emerson antedating this letter, see above, July 10 to Ward, and July 17 to Caroline Tappan.

To Cyrus Augustus Bartol, Concord, July 25, 1855[90]

Concord
25 July 1855

My dear Sir,

Kindest thanks for your faithful memory of my wants & longings. I should be so glad to go to P⟨ae?⟩igeon Cove, that I am much tempted by this opportunity with which you have so smoothly bridged my way[91] My brother⟨'s⟩ & /his/ family from New York are at Concord & I am to go to Amherst on the ⟨9⟩8th Aug.t to read a discourse. Yet, if I dare, I shall come to you on that 31st night of July, & learn at least the way to the place with friendly guides

Yours faithfully,
R. W. Emerson

C. A. Bartol.

To Delia Salter Bacon, Concord, August 5, 1855[92]

Concord Aug 5 1855

My dear Miss Bacon,

I give you joy on the good news you send me of the ending of your work. What if it is only the beginning of another, it is also the pledge of power to do it. I hope & trust it is good news for us & all people also. And to this end I sent your two letters at once to both the Publishers; & enclose to you Mr Putnam's reply, which, indeed, I anticipated, as knowing he had been long embarrassed in his trade, though retaining, I am told, the respect of his community.[93]

In the shortness of the time we have to act in, I think it best also to send you Phillips & Sampsons letter; of which, otherwise, I should only

90. MS in MWelC; ph. in NNC.

91. See in *Letters*, 4:524, for Emerson's having spent two days with Bartol at Pigeon Cove; presumably on July 31 and August 1. If he went swimming, as he liked to do, he'd have found the North Shore water cold. Pigeon Cove is on Cape Ann.

92. MS in DFo; ph. in NNC; printed by Theodore Bacon, pp. 82–84; listed *Letters*, 4:523; quoted by Vivian Hopkins, p. 191.

93. That is, to Phillips & Sampson and to George Putnam. Emerson had commissioned his brother William to see Putnam and to carry a letter to him. In a letter of August 2 (RWEMA), William Emerson reports that Putnam on his own account could do nothing but would appeal to Appleton's and, with a letter of the 3rd, he encloses Putnam's letters of August 2 to Emerson and to Miss Bacon. Putnam has had no success with Appleton who was not inclined to buy a pig in a poke. For the response of Phillips & Sampson, see *Letters*, 4:521–522, n. 151.

send a summary. I failed to see them, though I went to their compting-room. If you go on with them, you had better preserve their letter. They may seem to you timid, but they are as brave as their experience will allow them to be. Such is the advertising system under which they live, & the giving away of copies to every newspaper, that it costs them $150, I think they showed me,—before a single copy is sold,—for that expense alone. And they have been losers by many books.

You will see that P. & S. object to the title. I do not know but I put it in their heads. I think you can easily give the book a simpler name, simply descriptive, the plainer the better, with or without a motto, & let that not be italicized, as, the "Authorship of the Shakspeare Plays," or the like. I who do not know the book, cannot tell the title,—but wish it to be of stone.[94]

I am just running up to a country college[95] to read a discourse to the Alumni, & therefore hasten to put these two notes together, lest they lose a steamer, & to cut short my billet. The best hap which ever awaits truth await you! And let me hear & convey your decisions, to these men.

Yours faithfully,
R. W. Emerson.

Miss D. S. Bacon.

To David Atwood Wasson, Concord, August 15, 1855[96]

Concord—
August 15,
1855.

My dear Sir,

I am a little mortified to refuse your kind request,—which is attractive to me. But I am under vows to stay at home, just now,—though much of the time to little purpose,—until one or two pieces of work come to some end.[97] But I will keep your invitation before me, & sooner or later, will hope to obey it.

Yours with respect
R. W. Emerson

Mr Wasson.

94. See Hopkins, p. 188, for Miss Bacon's notion of a title; Emerson is clearly referring to her elaborate concoction.
95. Amherst College; see Charvat, p. 31.
96. MS in the Barrett Collection, Alderman Library, ViU; ph. in NNC.
97. Emerson is answering Wasson's letter of August 13 inviting him to lecture (a.l.s., Schlesinger Library, Radcliffe). Emerson was struggling with the long-delayed manuscript

To Dexter? S. Burnham, Concord, August 19? 1855

[In a letter of August 17, 1855 (RWEMA), D. S. Burnham of Milford, New Hampshire, asks Emerson to lecture for the Lyceum and offers him several dates, of which November 21 is the first. Emerson presumably wrote, choosing the first date; see *Letters*, 5:534, where a second letter of November 2 is recorded from Burnham's letter of November 3. Emerson's correspondent is probably Dexter S. Burnham, described as a "man of scholarly tastes" who served the town on the school board and as a trustee of the public library. George A. Ramsdell and William P. Colburn, *The History of Milford* (Concord, N.H.: Rumford Press, 1901), p. 445.]

To Richard Bentley, Concord, September 6, 1855[98]

Concord, Mass.tts.
6 September, 1855

Mr Richard Bentley.
Dear Sir,

When my publishers, Messrs Phillips, Sampson, & Co. closed a copyright contract with you for my "English Notes," it was my intention to have gone to press in a short time. It happened that the work was necessarily interrupted, & is only ready now. In the meantime, a ruling in your courts has made it impossible to protect you or me in the copyright. This, of course, cancels the contract referred to, & makes it proper that I should ask what you can now do?[99]

My book will fill, say, 250 to 300 pp. 12mo. The proofsheets might be mailed by each steamer, as we proceed; giving you an opportunity of being twelve or fifteen days in advance of the possible reception of the American edition. Would such sheets be of value to you? If so, an early reply stating what compensation, & in what time,—you incline to offer, will greatly oblige

Yours respectfully,
R. W. Emerson

---

of *English Traits;* see *Letters*, 4:528, for his hope of having his "copy" ready by October 1. And see September 6 below, where he refers to his work as "English Notes." Although the book was not published until August 1856, his MS journal RO, p. [109] (*JMN*, 14:31), shows that he sent the MS of the first chapter to Phillips and Sampson on October 4, 1855, and his letter of December 26 below asks Thoreau to read proof.

98. MS in the Treasure Room, MBU; ph. in NNC; printed by Cameron, *EE*, 2:217; listed from Bentley's reply of October 5, *Letters*, 4:528.

99. See *Letters*, 4:528, for the substance of Bentley's reply of October 5 and also for a note of an unlocated letter to George Routledge and Company who subsequently printed the book (*BAL*, 5226, London editions). Rusk gives the substance of Routledge's reply of October 5.

To Luther L. White, Concord, September 8? 1855

[In a letter of September 7, 1855 (RWEMA), J. F. G. Baxter invites Emerson to lecture before the Mattapan (South Boston) Literary Association on November 14. He asks for the lecture on Anglo-American character. He wants Emerson to write an early reply to Luther L. White, care of Wm. Minot, Jr., Court Street, Boston. I assume Emerson replied, for he did lecture in South Boston on that date; see Charvat, p. 31, where the subject is not given nor the lyceum identified. James F. G. Baxter is listed in the 1855 Boston directory with his business address as the Columbian Bank.]

To Susan T. Hillard, Concord, September 16? 1855

[In a letter dated September 15, n.y. (RWEMA), Susan T. Hillard reminds Emerson that he had talked in the spring of Ellen Emerson's living with the Hillards during the winter. She needs to know whether to expect Ellen, having other applicants to consider. Emerson had already heard from Agassiz that his school was to open on September 26 (a.l.s., August 28, 1855, RWEMA). And on that day he bought a season railroad ticket for his daughter according to the MS Account Book for 1853–1859, p. 107. The Account Book later shows payments to Mrs. Hillard for Ellen's board. I think Emerson would have notified Mrs. Hillard to expect Ellen in the winter. Ellen's letters from Boston begin on November 1; she apparently commuted during October and on weekends. Mr. and Mrs. George Stillman Hillard lived at 62 Pinckney Street.]

To Sarah Ann Clarke, Concord, September 17, 1855 [100]

Concord, 17 Sept. 1855

My dear Friend,

We shall all be home on Saturday to welcome you. Edith is to carry this note, to make her own requests touching Lily Clarke,[101] and, if the sun shines on Sunday, we will show you our fields in the afternoon. So fail not yours,

R.W.E.

Miss Clarke

100. MS seen in Goodspeed's Book Shop (December 9, 1969); copy in NNC.
101. Lily Clarke, daughter of James Freeman Clarke, niece of the addressee.

To William Howland, Concord, September 17, 1855[102]

Concord, Mass.tts

Dear Sir,

It will give me pleasure to come to Lynn, Wednesday, 7 November, if that night suits your convenience.[103]

Respectfully,

R. W. Emerson.

Mr. Howland.

To The New York Publishers' Association, Concord, September 19, 1855[104]

Concord, Mass., 19th Sept., 1855.

Gentlemen,—

An occasion of much local interest to this town, and on which I have duties to perform, falling nearly at the same time with the festival, puts it out of my power to accept your invitation.[105] I am sorry for the accident, for it is easy to see the brilliant promise of your meeting. I know the power and enterprise of your association, which is pushing across the continent the most civilizing of all trades. I am well acquainted with the high personal worth of many of its members, and I have just learned what a rare circle of guests you have summoned to grace the day. I am truly sorry that I cannot use the privilege you so courteously offer me. May every happy and cordial feeling brighten the day! The friendliest meeting of the authors and publishers of good books, I must think one of the fairest omens for mankind.

Respectfully, your obliged servant,

R. W. Emerson

102. MS in the Pierpont Morgan Library; ph. in NNC. The MS is tipped in a copy of *Parnassus*, opposite the copyright page.

103. The date, the place, and Howland's name are entered in the MS Pocket Diary for 1855 (*JMN*, 13:509). The MS Account Book for 1853–1859, p. 42, has, under the date November 7, the receipt of $25 from the Lynn Lyceum.

104. No MS has been found, text from the *American Publishers' Circular and Literary Gazette* (September 29, 1855), 1:75; listed *Letters*, 4:528. Emerson is refusing an invitation to the "Fruit Festival" held at the Crystal Palace, in New York, September 27.

105. Emerson was to give an address September 29 for the dedication of Sleepy Hollow Cemetery (*Works*, 11:429–436). See also *Letters*, 4:530, where Emerson tells his brother he is "content to allow this home engagement to detain him from the Crystal Palace Banquet."

TO CHARLES HOSEA HILDRETH, CONCORD, SEPTEMBER 20? 1855

[In a letter of September 13, 1855 (RWEMA), C. H. Hildreth of Gloucester, Massachusetts, offers Emerson a choice of eleven dates for a possible lecture. Emerson apparently accepted February 6; Gloucester is so entered in both the tentative list in his MS Pocket Diary for 1855 (*JMN*, 13:512), and the final list in that of 1856 (*JMN*, 14:455).]

TO MARTIN P. KENNARD, CONCORD, SEPTEMBER 21, 1855 [106]

Concord, Mass.
Sept 21 1855

Will Mr Kennard please send by the Express, who will call for it this p.m., a silver table spoon of a handsome pattern, to be marked A.T.S.,[107] —not exceeding the value of two dollars;—and charge the same to his obedt. servant,

R. W. Emerson.

TO JULIUS ROCKWELL, CONCORD, SEPTEMBER 22, 1855 [108]

Concord, 22 Sept. 1855

Dear Sir,

Are the towns for which you wrote, still meaning to have their lectures?[109] In that expectation, I have been keeping one or two weeks unbroken by any single engagements. If the design is given up, will you be good enough to to say so? If not, I should like to have the last week of November, or the last but one.

Respectfully,
R. W. Emerson

Hon Julius Rockwell.

---

106. MS in the Manuscript Division, DLC; ph. in NNC; p. [4] addressed: Mr Kennard.| Bigelow, Brothers, & Kennard| Jewellers| By Adams Express Boston|.

107. The MS Account Book for 1853–1859, p. [111], under the date October 15, records the payment of 2.00 to Kennard, Bigelow & Co. "for a spoon for A. Small." See *Letters*, 5:155, for mention of an "Elmira Flint, of Concord, now a widow by name of Mrs Small." In the *Concord Births, Marriages, and Deaths*, p. 301, appears an "Almira Flint"; possibly the spoon was for a daughter. Mrs. Almira Small appears frequently in this Account Book as the recipient of small sums paid her for various services and also as having lent Emerson money.

108. MS in NHi; ph. in NNC.

109. See above April 19, and below, October 25, 1855, and February 15, 1856, for Emerson's arrangements to lecture in the Berkshire County towns of Great Barrington, Lee, Pittsfield, and North Adams; listed in the MS Pocket Diary for 1856 (*JMN*, 14:437) under the respective dates of March 11, 12, 13, 14 (see Charvat, p. 32).

To William Henry Furness, Concord, October 1, 1855[110]

Concord Oct. 1 1855

My dear friend,

It is my part always to meet your worth with unworthiness, and so now. I believe I make the worst antislavery discourses that are made in this country. They are only less bad than slavery. I incline this winter to promise none.[111] And have not dared to accept any new invitation. Besides, I could not come to Phila.—I know not when. I am to keep by the printers for six weeks or more; then I am to go to Illinois, once more, & for many weeks, in December and before I go & after I return my days are mostly promised. Pity me & forgive, Each of us is in a prison house whose secrets it were a new crime to afflict his brothers with.

I should have answered your kindest note at once, but I had an address on my hands for the ⟨ded⟩ Consecration of our Cemetery[112] here in this town which I made ⟨yes⟩ /on/ Saturday . . . You should have added one line of the welfare of Annie Wistar, & of the boys away & at home.[113] My eldest girl Ellen goes daily to school to Agassiz.[114]

Your loving
Waldo Emerson.

W. H. Furness.

Sidney Smith's memoirs though so feebly edited,[115]—they should have applied to you, instead,—must yet have rejoiced your heart. Have you read that wonderful book—with all its formlessness & faults "Leaves of Grass"?—

110. MS in the Furness papers, Van Pelt Library, PU; ph. in NNC; printed *Records*, pp. [106]–107; listed *Letters*, 4:531.

111. See Furness' reply of October 3 (*Records*, p. 108) and, below, Emerson's weakened refusal October 10.

112. Sleepy Hollow; Emerson had served on the town committee, and in this year he and his brother purchased the lots where they are now buried (*Letters*, 4:530, a.l.s., William Emerson to his brother, September 27, 1855, and MS Account Book for 1853–1860, entry of December 8). Nothing is omitted here; the elision marks are Emerson's.

113. Furness' daughter and the sons in Europe. Emerson's spelling of Wistar, the family was spelling it Wister in 1855.

114. In the MS Account Book for 1853–1860, Emerson records his first payment of $37.50 to Louis Agassiz under the date December 3, 1855, p. [114].

115. *A Memoir of the Reverend Sydney Smith*, by his daughter Lady Holland, with a selection from his letters edited by Mrs. Austin. An American edition was published in 1855. Emerson's MS journals have Smith's first name spelled both ways.

To Oliver Johnson, Concord, October 1? 1855

[In a letter of September 29, 1855 (RWEMA), Oliver Johnson, from the Anti-Slavery Office in New York, asks Emerson for a lecture; he has heard that Emerson is to speak in Philadelphia; the same lecture would do for both. There is no sign that Emerson answered this letter, but see October 1 above to Furness for the certainty that he would have refused.]

To Paulina W. Davis, Concord, October 1? 1855

[In a letter of September, 29 n.y. (RWEMA), Paulina Davis thanks Emerson for his address at the Convention on Women's Rights, September 20, 1855, and asks his permission to print it. Emerson would have to reply. It was not printed until 1881 when it appeared in *Woman's Journal* for March 26. Emerson had prepared for publication in 1862 something very much like this address, but the periodical for which it was then intended did not come into existence (see *Works*, 11:403, 426, and 627–630).

[Writing Emerson on October 7, 1855 (RWEMA), Caroline H. Dall hopes that he has been officially thanked for his "beautiful address" and that he has been asked to provide a copy for publication. Since, as she observes, the newspapers could not tell whether Emerson was for or against women's rights, one wonders that the ladies should want it.]

To Frederic Dan Huntington, Concord, October 1? 1855

[In a letter of October 9, 1855 (RWEMA), the Reverend Frederic Dan Huntington says that an injury prevents his accepting Emerson's invitation to Concord. Huntington had just become Professor of Christian Morals at the Harvard Divinity School. A second letter to Huntington is a possibility.]

To Alfred Amos Abbott, Concord, October 2? 1855

[In a letter of October 1, 1855 (RWEMA), A. A. Abbott of South Danvers (now Peabody), Massachusetts, invites Emerson to lecture in the coming season. See Charvat, p. 32. The lecture was for the Peabody Institute set up in 1852 and named for the benefactor, the banker George Peabody, on a motion made by Alfred Amos Abbott. William C. Endicott, *History of the Peabody Institute* (Danvers, Mass., Boston: Thomas Todd, 1912), p. 16.]

To Reuben Atwater Chapman, Concord, October 3, 1855

[Always cautious, Rusk allows for the possibility of this letter only in a footnote, 4:532 and 186, but the evidence for the letter noted seems firm enough. Emerson tells Abel Adams that he has sent Chapman a copy of an account book entry of December 11, 1850, recording his payment through Adams for the purchase of a $1,000 bond of the Rutland & Burlington Railroad. See *Letters*, 4:528–529 and n. 171 for the difficulty that led Adams to suggest that Emerson ask the attorney

Reuben Atwater Chapman to act for him. For Chapman, see Mason A. Green, *Springfield 1636–1886* (Springfield: C. A. Nichols, 1888), pp. 399, 541, 522.]

To CAROLINE STURGIS TAPPAN, CONCORD, OCTOBER 3, 1855[116]

Concord, 3 Oct.r 1855

Dear Caroline,

Send me word where you are in town, & if you know, when you are likely to be at home, & I will come to town too glad to see you once more. I will bring with me the strange book,[117]—into which I have not looked again,—if I believe you have leisure & fancy for it. I walked about with my great secret of your approach, until Ellen came home from Mrs Lowell publishing the news.[118] And you speak of Europe with a cool air of adoption, and ready to the honours of it. Well, I will not quarrel with you that you have two continents, and I doubt not, each will recommend the other. Happily the bridge is shorter than once from one to the other. For Hegel,[119] if you do not carry it, I shall be glad to be the depository, having just returned Cabot's, after keeping it too long unread.

Faithfully,
Waldo E.

To WILLIAM HENRY FURNESS, CONCORD, OCTOBER 10, 1855[120]

Concord, 10 Oct.r 1855

Ah if you knew how puny & unproductive I am! The pain of slavery & detestation of our politics only working the wrong way to make me more dumb & sterile.[121] I see at this moment neither arguments nor days to

116. MS in the Sophia Smith Collection, MNS; ph. in NNC.
117. Probably *Leaves of Grass;* see Emerson's letter of July 17 above. In her letter of September 26, MNS, she wishes he had sent her the "unforgettable things to read" while she was in Lenox. Whitman certainly qualifies as "unforgetable." Her letter, however, begins: "I have seen some extracts from your new ascendant but they were not of great magnitude." She is certainly referring to Whitman here.
118. In the letter of the 26th, Caroline Tappan had told him that the Tappans had taken passage to Liverpool for October 10th and that they expected to be in Boston "nearly a week beforehand." She tells him too that his cousin George Barrell Emerson sails on the same ship. Anna Jackson Lowell was Ellen Emerson's informant.
119. She had offered to leave her three new volumes of Hegel with him, if he wishes. In the letter of the 26th of September, she had written "Breathe it not in Concord that we are to be in Boston, or to be 'on board.' " She then expected to be in Boston "next week." In the letter telling him of the original plan to sail in July, she had enjoined Emerson not to tell Ellery Channing of the plans. She does not want him to travel with them. She explicitly says that Ellery would wish to join "William" (i.e., her husband).
120. MS in the Furness papers, Van Pelt Library, PU; ph. in NNC; printed in *Records*, p. [109]; listed, *Letters*, 4:533.
121. See October 1 above and *Records*, p. 108.

say them in. I am pinned to a printer probably till 1 December. and thence onward I have a long western journey to the Missisippi back & forth for a month or 6 weeks more.[122] The places only are fixed, the dates not. After that, new engagements follow here, tis ignominious to think of. I wait & moan and if in the mean time any word of the [123] should come into me like a sharp sword as it came aforetime to good men I shall be as swift as now I am slow to carry it to Philadelphia. Indeed, it lies in my heart to ⟨re⟩bring something solidly good to that city, before I die: as I have said & done nothing there that was contenting to me. You deserve well of all, best of me. I rejoice in the volley of good news you send of the boys. Ellen is to tell Agassiz of Horace's finding, today.[124]

Your affectionate
Waldo E

William H. F.

To James Livermore, Concord, October 10, 1855

[Rusk lists this letter from the reply to it, but he has misread the first name as "Jane"; see *Letters*, 4:533.]

To T. Willard Lewis, Concord, October ? 1855

[It is likely that Emerson wrote at least two letters to T. Willard Lewis of Marlboro to settle the date of his lecture there on Friday, December 7. Lewis had originally asked for a Wednesday date (see May 25? above). The MS pocket Diary for 1855 (*JMN*, 13:510, with slightly different reading) has against the date the complicated entry: "⟨⟨Marlboro⟩⟩ Clinton ⟨T Willard Lewis $15 Hanover J T Thomson⟩." This entry leaves only Clinton undeleted. On the letter of invitation from Artemas Bigelow of Clinton, September 25 (see *Letters*, 4:531), Emerson wrote: "Offered him 6 Feb.y / Say 5 Dec/ omit Marlboro/⟨21 Nov to Dartsmouth⟩"/. This annotation parallels the diary entry. Emerson was juggling three invitations; he decided in favor of Clinton and must have written Lewis who, I conjecture, replied with an offer of the Friday date. See below, November 22? for the later failure of the Clinton course and correction of Charvat and Rusk. In *JMN*, 13:510, the Pocket Diary entry has the misreading "7." for Lewis' first initial "T" and omits what looks like the superior sign for dollars before "15." Thomson's middle initial is uncertain, but Rusk's note gives a questioned "T" and that is what it looks like to me.]

---

122. See Charvat, pp. 31–32, for the strenuous Western tour.
123. Emerson left this article without its noun. Omitting "of the" leaves sense.
124. The good news referred to is omitted from *Records*, which gives only the anecdote of Horace Furness' finding Agassiz's name and the date "1838" incised in a rock near the Rosenlaui Glacier (*Records*, n. pp. 109–110). The MS of this letter of Emerson's has also an initialed note of this anecdote in Horace Furness hand.

To Joseph H. Bragdon, Concord, October 13? 1855

[In a letter of October 12, 1855 (RWEMA), Joseph H. Bragdon tells Emerson that his lecture in Newburyport on November 27 has been announced; he needs to have Emerson's assurance that he will come on that date. See Charvat, p. 31. Bragdon was an attorney; he had been a founding member of the Mechanic Library Association. John J. Currier, *History of Newburyport,* 2:177, 287.]

To George Palmer Putnam, Concord, October 19, 1855[125]

Concord⎱ 19 Oct.
Mass. ⎰ 1855

Dear Sir,

I send you Miss Bacon's Preliminary Chapter for Putnam's Magazine; and her note to you, enclosed.[126] I have kept the Chapter a few days, as ⟨t⟩she desired me to read it, & correct it, if I thought fit. I have read it, but, on the whole, decided to let well alone; partly, because I have not, in these days, the time to correct anything so important; & chiefly, because it reads well as it is. I think it will commend itself to your Editors, as a strong preliminary statement, and presenting the negative argument.

I have from her a long letter describing the terror of the several London publishers, when they were successively made acquainted with her main design.[127] All that makes it formidable there, should make it popular here. But I do not think well of her plan of publishing it in parts; and ⟨should⟩ shall advise her to print it here in ⟨twe⟩12 mo volumes.[128]

If anything occurs to you that can aid her here or in London, pray advise her. She believes so heartily in her theory, & works so nobly, that she cannot fail to interest.

Mr. Longfellow said one day to me, that the "Magazine" wanted more literature," That want this paper will go to supply.

Respectfully,
R. W. Emerson

Mr. Putnam.

125. MS in the Dix papers, Houghton Library, MH; ph. in NNC; printed by Vivian C. Hopkins in "Two Unpublished Emerson Letters," *NEQ* (December 1960), 33:503.

126. Miss Hopkins cites Putnam's letter of August 1 to Miss Bacon suggesting that she submit an article to *Putnam's Monthly Magazine.* The article was published in the January 1856 number as "William Shakespeare and His Plays: An Inquiry Concerning Them" (7:1–19).

127. This letter is printed by Miss Hopkins in her *Prodigal Puritan,* pp. 189–190.

128. Emerson's objections to Miss Bacon's publishing her work piecemeal involved him in difficulties with her (see Miss Hopkins' account, pp. 503–504, of *NEQ* article).

To Alfred Macy, Concord, October 23, 1855

[In a letter of October 22, 1855 (RWEMA), Alfred Macy of Nantucket tells Emerson that November 13 is now free and offers him that date for a lecture. In his MS Pocket Diary for 1855 (*JMN*, 13:509) Emerson had entered Nantucket with a question mark against the date November 13; the question mark is crossed out. Presumably there was an earlier letter to Macy whose name is entered in the Pocket Diary. Emerson did lecture in Nantucket on that date; see Charvat, p. 31.]

To Samuel Longfellow, Concord, October 24, 1855 [129]

Concord] Oct. 24
Mass.tts. ∫ 1855

My dear Sir,

I am slow to answer, because I hate to say No, to an invitation so agreeable. I am due at the Brooklyn Athenaeum on the 11 Dec.r. I believe: [130] cannot well go before, & immediately after, am the victim of distant Sarmatia [131] or Illinois. nor do I see any day when I could certainly come to Brooklyn, earlier than the second or third week in February; which is a little late for prospering Courses. Another winter, I ⟨am⟩do not mean to go west; &, tis possible, you may command me for more seasonable service.

I am very glad that you are in communication with Whitman; of whom I have already heard something. He has done a strange rude thing in printing in the Tribune, I am told, my letter of thanks for his book. [132]

Yours, with great regard,
R. W. Emerson

Rev. Mr Longfellow.

129. MS in Craigie House; ph. in NNC.
130. Emerson did not go west until December 27 (*Letters*, 4:539, 540), but his final schedule left him no extra days in Brooklyn.
131. Pomponius Mila, classical topographer, gave the name Sarmatia to what is now, roughly speaking, eastern Poland and western Russia, lying outside the Roman empire, therefore remote and alien territory.
132. The letter of July 21, see above. It is not clear whether Emerson ever saw the flyer Whitman had printed (*BAL*, 5225), but he must have seen the printings in the 1856 and 1860 editions of *Leaves of Grass*. The letter appeared in the *New York Daily Tribune* on October 10.

To John O. Fiske, Concord, October 24, 1855[133]

Concord ⎤ Oct. ⟨1⟩24
Mass.tts. ⎦ 1855

Dear Sir,

I find the same difficulty occurring in regard to invitations from Bath, & from towns in your neighborhood, every winter.[134] It would give me pleasure to go to several towns which have invited me. But when I am invited by one, I am not yet invited by others, and it seems not well to go so far to read a single lecture. Last year, I was at different times invited by Bath, Belfast, Augusta, Gardiner, &, I think, Wiscasset. but never so, that the Lyceums could be combined in one visit.[135] Nor can I propose a visit, of course, to any who do not invite me. If any gentleman in one of these towns would take on himself the trouble of a little correspondence with th⟨a⟩e neighboring Lyceums, so far as to learn that a lecture from me was desired in them, nearly at the same time, I would come to Bath & its neighborhood, say, in the week beginning 10 February. and visit the towns on successive nights, on any practicable arrangement. Mr A. T. Wheelock from Belfast,[136] was my correspondent, last year.

Respectfully,
R. W. Emerson

Mr Fiske.

To Julius Rockwell, Concord, October 25, 1855[137]

Concord ⎤ 25 Oct
Mass.tts. ⎦ 1855

Dear Sir,

I am sorry to say that I cannot take the week you offer me.[138] I kept the last week of November & first of December open for some time for a

133. MS in NcD; ph. in NNC.
134. See *Letters*, 4:535–536, for a letter from Fiske settling the date of February 13, 1856, for a lecture at Bath (Maine) and nn. 197–198 for other engagements in Maine evidently initiated by Fiske in response to this letter. See also, above, June 21.
135. The MS Pocket Diary for 1856 (*JMN*, 14:435–436) lists for February 11, 12, 13, 14, and 15 the towns of Hallowell, Gardiner, Bath, Bangor, and Belfast (the last with a question mark deleted). He was unable to keep the Bangor date on the 14th, being detained on the train. The *Bangor Daily Whig and Courier* of February 15 announced him for the 15th, but the Account Books record no payment from Bangor or from Belfast, showing instead the receipt of $35 from Augusta; see *Letters*, 4:535, where he mentions the possibility of an invitation from Augusta for Friday (February 16). Charvat here requires correction (p. 32).
136. Albert T. Wheelock, M.D.
137. MS in NHi; ph. in NNO.
138. See above, April 9 and September 22, for early correspondence with Rockwell to

summons to Berkshire, but I inferred too hastily, it seems, from receiving no second message, that your plan had been given up,—and I gave away the days. At present, I have no unbroken week before 15 December, when I am promised to a chain of towns & cities in Ohio & Illinois, probably for six weeks: nor do I see room to go to Berkshire, until, say 16 February, which is probably too late for you. I am very sorry; and, if anything breaks up my western journey,—which is not yet settled in detail, I shall report myself at once to you.

Respectfully,

Hon. Mr. Rockwell. R. W. Emerson

To George W. Frost, Concord, October 29? 1855

[In a letter of October 29, 1855 (RWEMA), the Reverend George W. Frost of Waltham writes that the hall is not available for Thursday night (31st) and offers Emerson a choice of three days in the following week. He asks for an "express" reply by the bearer of his letter. According to the MS Pocket Diary for 1855 (*JMN*, 13:509), Emerson was originally to have lectured in Waltham on October 24: the entry is cancelled and Waltham entered again against the date November 8, when he did in fact lecture for the Rumford Institute. In addition to his obligatory letter here, Emerson must have written at least two earlier letters to Frost.]

To Samuel H. Dale, Concord, November 3, 1855

[In a letter of November 2, 1855 (RWEMA), Samuel H. Dale of Bangor, Maine, asks for a lecture on February 14, 1856, for the Mercantile Association. Bangor is entered against that date in the MS Pocket Diary for 1856 (*JMN*, 14:435) with Dale's name. Dale's letter suggests that Emerson had already settled the date for his lecture in Bath (February 13). His correspondent in Bath, according to the Pocket Diary, was T. O. Fisher, but there is no trace of this correspondence; see Charvat, p. 32.]

---

arrange lectures in four Berkshire County towns. The dates were not settled until February 2, 1856; see below.

To A. B. Wiggin, Concord, November 9, 1855[139]

Concord ⎱ Nov. 9
Mass.tts ⎰ 1855

Dear Sir,

I can come to Yarmouth on Monday, 11 February, if that day suits you.[140] If I come, the Lyceum shall pay me Twenty dollars.

Respectfully,

Mr. Wiggin. R. W. Emerson

To Lydia Maria Child, Concord, November 11, 1855[141]

Concord, 11 Nov.r 1855.

My dear Mrs Child,

It is a very slow acknowledgment of your great gift[142] to say that it has only come to me on Friday night, and I have only taken a survey & a few soundings here & there. But, as neither now, nor tomorrow, nor for three days, to come, during which I am to be a traveller, can I take any right possession of it,[143] I will not wait longer to say that the Books are here, with all the wealth that their "Contents" & my dipping into the Indian portion assure me, and that I am deeply beholden to you for a present which, I see plainly, was not made in a month or a year, but which cost many summers to ripen. Well, it is a noble piece of work to spend summers on, and I shall see Wayland, as often I do see it from our hills, with new esteem & reverence I give you joy & honor on your high tasks, which cannot but bring a present reward with them in advance of the good fame, which, I doubt not, is to bring you its glad certificates.

I do not see before me presently any free days. I am absurdly enslaved

---

139. MS in the Miller Library, MeWC; ph. in NNC; printed by Arthur J. Roberts, "Emerson's Visits to Waterville College," *Colby Mercury* (April 1, 1934), 5:44, n. 29.

140. In a tentative list for 1856 Emerson has entered Yarmouth (Maine) with a question mark in his MS Pocket Diary for 1855 against the date February 11; he adds the name of A. B. Wiggin (*JMN*, 13:512). In the Pocket Diary for 1856, the entry for Yarmouth against the same date is deleted and "Hallowell?" substituted; the MS Account Book for 1853–1859, p. 50, shows the receipt of $30 from Hallowell, but no receipt from Yarmouth (see Charvat, p. 32).

141. MS in the Beinecke Library, CtY; ph. in NNC; with envelope addressed: Mrs L. M. Child.| Wayland.| Massachusetts.|; postmarked at Boston November 12. Printed by Stanley Williams, *JEGP* (October 1927), 26:482; listed *Letters*, 4:536.

142. The books are the three volumes of Mrs. Child's *The Progress of Religious Ideas, Through Successive Ages*, New York: 1855 (*BAL*, 3180), still in Emerson's library (Harding, p. 59).

143. Emerson had a heavy lecture schedule ahead of him and he had also "copy" for *English Traits* to get in.

for days & weeks to come, but I shall use my earliest leisure to study this book, whose topics have the strongest attraction for me. And I shall not fail to write you what fortunes I shall find. Meantime, accept my serious thanks for a noble gift.[144]

With great respect,
& best wishes, Yours,
R. W. Emerson

Mrs Child.

To George Partridge Bradford, Concord, November 19? 1855

[In a letter of November 20, 1855 (RWEMA), George P. Bradford accepts Emerson's customary invitation for Thanksgiving dinner. See *Letters*, 4:537.]

To John Ring, Concord, November 22? 1855

[In a letter of November 21, 1855 (RWEMA), John Ring of Clinton writes Emerson of the "failure of the course of lectures for which you were engaged in this place" and asks him to "transfer his engagement" to the Clinton Rhetorical Society which he represents. He wants Emerson to lecture on a Wednesday after December 5. Ring's letter clears up some puzzles. First, the entry of Clinton in Charvat under the questioned date of December 5 can be deleted. Second, Emerson's annotations on the letter of September 25, 1855, from Artemas E. Bigelow (*Letters*, 4:531), become intelligible. Emerson offered Bigelow December 5, and it is this engagement that fell through owing to the failure of the course.]

To Edward Everett, Concord, November 24, 1855 [145]

Concord
Novr 24
1855

My dear Sir,

I was interrupted yesterday just as I went to acknowledge your kind note.[146] I certainly can have no objection to this generous bestowal of

---

144. Emerson may have written Mrs. Child again about her book, but there is no evidence of it. He uses half-promises of this sort in other letters to authors who have given him their books.

145. MS in the Everett papers, MHi; ph. in NNC; printed by Paul Revere Frothingham, *Edward Everett* (Boston: Houghton Mifflin, 1925), p. 369; listed *Letters*, 4:537.

146. Everett, on November 22, had written to ask Emerson's permission to include in his third volume of orations his remarks on Emerson's brothers Edward Bliss and Charles Chauncy from his Phi Beta Kappa dinner speech of August 31, 1837 (Frothingham prints the remarks, pp. 367–368). With his letter Everett encloses a copy of the passages for Emerson.

your praise on friends so dear to me and must thankfully accept it passing the all unmerited compliment to myself, with which it is inextricably connected. I well remember the joy & pride of heart with which, so long ago, I drew from each of those youths in turn the account of your marked notice & growing kindness,—believing that they could not win a surer certificate of literary merit than your approving regards; & they well knew how warmly I shared their admiration of their friend. You will forgive me, if I add, that when I recall the zeal of praise & delight which your eloquence in those days kindled in many & many a household of educated young men & women,—what a literature, glory, & hope it was, —I doubt could you have seen those interiors,—whether any or all your manifold tasks & triumphs since could yield so deep a pleasure;—so rare, costly, & not to be divided with any other, is that influence of the Muse.

I once attempted in a lecture at Philadelphia some sketch of the influences working on us from your quarter of the heavens, say from 1820 to 1825, and if I should have an hour of leisure & of courage presently, I may venture to extract something from it that may amuse you.[147] Your genius, like all genius, has done many benefits when it meant them, & many which it knew not of.

Ever gratefully,
Your obliged servant,
R. W. Emerson.

Hon. Edward Everett.

147. Emerson is apparently referring to his Philadelphia lectures of 1852, but he had long since, in 1843, given an extended account of Everett in his New York lectures on New England. A passage in the MS of lecture 3, "Manners," was later transferred to the essay "Historic Notes of Life and Letters in New England" (*Works*, 10:330–335). As reported in New York newspapers, the lecture of 1843 decidedly did not amuse Everett, who recalled it seven years later in a letter of 1852 (August 23 to Samuel Osgood, MHi). Everett was piqued particularly by Emerson's references to his "nasal" voice and his coldness (see *Works*, 10:331, 332), which to his mind marred the generally complimentary character of Emerson's comments, and he was the more hurt because at the time the news came to him, he was "across the Atlantic" as Minister to the Court of St. James's.

Plaintively, in 1852 Everett tells his correspondent that when he had spoken in public of Emerson, he had combined praise of Emerson with praise of two of Emerson's brothers whom he had loved with "a love passing the love of women." If Emerson repeated in Philadelphia his remarks of 1843, they would scarcely have pleased Everett. The evidence of Emerson's journals and Everett's letters show that in the eyes of neither had the other lived up to youthful expectations, and by the time this letter was written, Everett's support of Webster's stand on the Fugitive Slave Law had deepened Emerson's disillusionment with the hero of his youth.

To Henry Wadsworth Longfellow, Concord,
November 25, 1855 [148]

Concord
25 November
1855

My dear Longfellow,

Sanborn brought me your good gift of Hiawatha, but I have not read it without many interruptions nor finished it till yesterday.[149] I have always one foremost satisfaction in reading your books that I am safe—I am in variously skilful hands but first of all they are safe hands.[150] However, I find this Indian poem very wholesome, sweet & wholesome as maize very proper & pertinent to us to read, & showing a kind of manly sense of duty in the poet to write. The dangers of the Indians are, that they are really savage, have poor small sterile heads,—no thoughts, & you must deal very roundly with them, & find them in brains; and I blamed your tenderness now & then, as I read, in accepting a legend or a song, when they had so little to give.)[151] I should hold you to your creative function on such occasions. But the costume & machinery, on the whole, is sweet & melancholy, & agrees with the American landscape. And you have the distinction of opening your own road. You may well call it an Indian Edda. My boy Edward finds it "like the story of Thor," meaning the "Hammersheimt," which he admires.[152] I found in the last cantos a pure gleam or two of blue sky, and learned thence to tax the rest of the poem as too abstemious. So with thanks & greeting

Yours affectionately,
R. W. Emerson.

148. MS in the Longfellow papers, on deposit, Houghton Library, MH; ph. in NNC; printed by Samuel Longfellow, 2:265–266; listed *Letters*, 4:538.

149. Sanborn had begun teaching in Concord; the American edition of the book was published on November 10 (*BAL*, 12112); Emerson's copy uninscribed is still in his library (Harding, p. 172).

150. That Emerson preferred not to be safe his letter to Whitman of July 21 shows.

151. Emerson knew nothing about Indians. Caroline Sturgis' father could have told him a good deal that might have enlightened him.

152. See May 4, 1855, above.

To James E. Wharton, Concord, November 26, 1855.[153]

Concord ⎫ Nov. 26
Mass.tts. ⎭ 1855

Dear Sir,

My engagement with a series of towns near the Mississippi River has been pushed a fortnight later than was at first arranged. I do not begin my lectures in that region till 31 December, at Davenport, Iowa. I shall not then be ready to begin my lectures in Ohio, till quite three weeks later, say about 21/22 January. And now I dare not fix the day with certainty. If however you need to fix your days, if you will arrange me ten (is it not ten?) on nights beginning say 22 or 23 Jany, I will try to bend my plans to them. There are two or three places in Ohio, where I am bound to lecture,—Columbus, Cleveland, & Yellow Springs,[154] (the last not so binding.)[155] Perhaps a space might be left in your programme for the two first.

I shall be glad to hear if you are still proposing to make good our design.[156]

Respectfully,

Mr Wharton.   R. W. Emerson.

To Delia Salter Bacon, Concord, December 3, 1855[157]

Concord 3 December 1855

Dear Miss Bacon,

I have only a few minutes, & perhaps no intelligence for you, & yet cannot let another steamer go in silence. I received your first chapter &

153. MS in the Harkness Collection, Manuscript Division, NN; ; ph. in NNC. The MS is mounted in an album in such a way as to obscure partially an endorsement and note on the final page. The note reads: Begin at Mansfield Jan 2 ?22| Notify towns.| The endorsement reads: Answered| There to| be named| in letters| to towns.| In his MS Pocket Diary for 1856 (*JMN*, 14:435), Emerson enters J. E. Wharton's name with "Massillon O"; Wharton, I infer, is acting for the Massillon Association, See Carl Bode, *The American Lyceum* (New York: Oxford University Press, 1956), pp. 169, 193–194; and David Mead, *Yankee Eloquence in the Middle West*, pp. 191–192. James E. Wharton owned and edited the *Massillon News* for a brief period, selling out early in 1858. See William Henry Perrin, *History of Stark County* (Chicago: Baskin & Battey, 1881), p. 420.

154. The MS Pocket Diary lists six possible other engagements, but the MS Account Book for 1853–1860 records receipts from only four: Cleveland, Columbus, Akron, and Hudson. There is no evidence that he lectured in Sandusky or Ravenna (see Charvat, pp. 31–32).

155. Horace Mann had invited Emerson to lecture in Yellow Springs (MHi, Mann Papers III).

156. Emerson apparently heard from Wharton before December 19; see below.

157. MS in DFo; ph. in NNC; printed by Theodore Bacon, pp. 93–95; listed *Letters*, 4:538.

read it, & sent it immediately to Putnam, with all the Imprimatur I could add. I did not write you, for I have been uncomfortably, nay ridiculously busy with printing, writing, & a correspondence of absurd extent, which my practice of lecturing creates. I delayed your letter day by day, until now comes your second parcel,[158] & enclosed letter, giving so much to think of—really so much to think of; that I heartily wish the right man were here to think & counsel. Immediately on its arrival, comes at last a letter from Putnam's editor, signing himself Dix Edwards,[159] saying, that he did duly receive the First Chapter, will print it at last as leading article on 1 January, & wishes Miss Bacon will follow it up, in their Monthly, as fast as she can. Meantime, I hoped that you would yet decide to print by Phillips & Sampson, & make the book at once. I ought to have explained to you, whilst their statement was fresh in my mind, that you are not holden to them by publishing by them any longer than you please. At the end of the first, or of the second, or whatever edition, you can take your copyright to a new publisher. Still, there is a reason for holding on by them, namely that they say, they spend a great deal of money on each of their books, before any remuneration comes. Also, they reply to your feeling of the injustices of receiving only a tenth part of the price of the book to yourself, that they receive still less, unless & until the book is very successful; for it costs no more to produce a book that sells fifty thousand copies that the one that sells one thousand.[160]

Now you leave me in your last letter quite too much liberty. You have not said what I shall do. I am going to the Mississippi, as soon as, or before my little book is out; & am to read lectures in that country for six weeks perhaps,—through dire necessity, & not from any desire to that work. You must choose then whether to print the Book by P. & S., as the only offer in that form we have; or, in Articles by Putnam. I much prefer the first mode. If I had my freedom, I should go to Boston or New York & read your letters & chapters to good men, & found a new Shakspeare Society to print the Book, & install the Author. But the mud of the Missisippi forbids: and though you suggest several good journals &c.

158. In October, Emerson had sent the first chapter of Miss Bacon's book to George Putnam (see above, October 19). What he refers to here is the manuscript of chapters 2–4 which Miss Bacon had sent on November 1 via her brother Leonard (Theodore Bacon, p. 88).

159. Putnam, in financial straits, had sold *Putnam's Monthly Magazine* to Dix and Edwards who would publish Miss Bacon's first chapter in the January issue (7:1–19) as "William Shakespeare and His Plays; an Inquiry Concerning Them."

160. On Miss Bacon's irrational expectations, see Hopkins, pp. 191–192 *et passim*.

which ought to exist here for us, they do not yet exist. The first Chapter was excellent. So is the Second. These are all that I have read. I have the other two, & when I leave home, shall leave my wife charged to obey exactly the instructions you shall send,[161] in case they arrive before my return, which perhaps will not be till 1 February. Still, what you write will be sent to me in the west. I have not time for another line, & only write this that I may not be heinously negligent where your genius & the high Fate that seem to accompany you have right to demand instant service. I shall strive to find a breathing time to say so much to your friends.

Respectfully & gratefully

Miss D. S. Bacon   R. W. Emerson

To James E. Wharton, Concord, December 19, 1855

[A letter to J. E. Wharton of December 19, 1855, is listed in *ESQ*, (2d q., 1956), 3:4, from catalogue 46 (item 80) of Robert K. Black, 1956. See above, November 26 and below, January 9, 1856.]

161. The chapters referred to here are those that were subsequently lost. See below, June 23, 1856, for Emerson's letter of explanation and apology; in that letter Emerson naturally does not go into detail not immediately relevant, but what happened in late December and early January is misleadingly represented in *Prodigal Puritan*. On the point of leaving for the West, Emerson did not turn over "the negotiations with Putnam's to his brother William," as Miss Hopkins assumes (p. 197), though he apparently informed his brother that Miss Bacon had sent additional chapters (he may have done so on December 11 when he lectured in Brooklyn). He is explicit here when he tells Miss Bacon he will not act without her expressed wish. See also his letter of December 30 to his wife (4:540), where he directs her to follow any instructions from Miss Bacon. His brother meanwhile had written on December 21 (RWEMA), reporting that the editor of *Putnam's* doubted the wisdom of printing Miss Bacon's work, but "Still the editor is willing to receive and examine the additional matter, if you think it expedient to submit it to him; and if it is thought favourably of, he will publish some of it in February." It is from this letter that Emerson learns that Miss Bacon is to be paid $55.00 for the first chapter. By December 30 he had received also a letter from Mr. Olmsted probably to the same import. Neither William Emerson nor Olmsted had heard from Emerson by December 30, as William Emerson tells Ellen Emerson in a letter (RWEMA), undated but probably of December 31, in which he asks if her father had said anything about his letter of December 21 and inquires "when and where to address him by telegraph within the next fortnight." As Emerson would later explain (January 14, 1856, *Letters*, 5:8), he had thought the sum of $55.00 "totally inadequate" when he had a copy of the January number in hand and could count the pages; he had waited to reply to Olmsted until he could do so. The magazine had offered $5.00 a page (Theodore Bacon, p. 96). The article ran to seventeen pages by Emerson's reckoning. I conjecture that he got hold of a copy in Chicago on his arrival there on December 29. It is in Chicago too that he met Parke Godwin and consulted him on the question of whether magazine publication was to Miss Bacon's advantage. What Emerson wrote to Olmsted we do not know, but he apparently wrote him before the first of January. He could not have known of William Emerson's letter

To Henry David Thoreau, Boston, December 26, 1855[162]

American House
Boston
26 Dec 1855

Dear Henry,

It is so easy at distance, or when going to a distance, to ask a great favor, which one would boggle[163] at near by. I have been ridiculously hindered, & my book is not out, & I must go westward. There is one chapter yet to go to the printer, perhaps two, if I decide to send[164] the second. I must ask you to correct the proofs of this or these chapters I hope you can & will, if you are not going away. The printer will send you the copy with the proof, and yet tis very likely you will see good cause to correct copy as well as proof. The chapter ⟨that⟩is "Stonehenge"; & I may not send it to the printer for a week yet; for I am very tender about the personalities in it, and of course you need not think of it till it comes. As we have been so unlucky as to overstay the market day, that is, New Years, it is not important a week or a fortnight now. If any thing puts it out of your power to help me at this pinch you must dig up Channing

to Ellen, and the only forwarding address Ellen could give her uncle would be for Chicago to which Emerson would not return until late on January 12. It is surely the urgency implied in William Emerson's letter to Ellen that prompted Mrs. Emerson to violate her husband's injunction not to act until a letter from Miss Bacon gave the order. See *Letters*, 5:7, for Emerson's reproof when he learned by January 13 that she had sent the MSS to his brother; to this rebuke Mrs. Emerson turned the other cheek in a letter remarkable for its sweetness and the absence of any mention whatsoever of the Bacon MSS (a.l.s., January 19, 1856, RWEMA). By January 14, Emerson knows that the first of the three chapters has been set up in type. By January 20 Dix & Edwards had changed their minds and rejected the second chapter and withdrawn consideration of the third and fourth. In a letter of that date (RWEMA) the publisher reports to Emerson that the MSS have been turned over to William Emerson, and enclosed to Emerson is a copy of their letter of January 24 to Delia Bacon (see Hopkins, pp. 197–198). Miss Bacon certainly had a genuine grievance against Dix & Edwards as the editor George William Curtis acknowledged (see Hopkins, p. 211); it is not clear that she had any against the Emersons. She did not, after all, answer this letter; she wrote instead directly to Dix & Edwards (see below April 25, 1856, and Theodore Bacon, p. 157). Rusk does not hazard an identification of "Olmstead" as Emerson spells it in his letter of January 14, 1856, to his brother (*Letters*, 5:8 and n. 27). Frederick Law Olmsted was managing editor of Putnam's 1855–1857.

162. MS formerly on deposit, Mugar Library, MBU; MS copy by Cabot (RWEMA); ph. in NNC. Printed by Sanborn, *AM* (June 1892), 69:751, and. from Sanborn, by Harding and Bode, pp. 403–404; printed incompletely by Richardson in his catalogue All printings contain alterations of punctuation and spelling and each has a misreading. Cabot's copy is correct. Listed *Letters*, 4:539.

163. Sanborn, and Harding and Bode after him, have "haggle" here; the word is clearly "boggle," which makes sense.

164. Richardson has "find" here; the word is clearly "send."

out of his earths, & hold him steady to this beneficence.[165] Send the proof, if they come, to Phillips, ⟨&⟩ Sampson, & Co.

Winter St

We may well go away, if one of these days we shall really come home.

Yours,
R. W. Emerson

Mr. Thoreau.

165. Emerson did not finish *English Traits,* prevented by the extreme cold; see letter of January 13 and 14 to Lidian Emerson, *Letters,* 5:7. See JM, p. 242, for publishing history.

1856

To George H. Wyman, LaSalle, Illinois, January 2, 1856

[In his MS Pocket Diary for 1856, under the entry for his lecture engagement January 2 in LaSalle, Illinois, Emerson enters a note reading: "G. H. Wyman, Cleveland 10 or 15 Jan"; I believe this note indicates a letter to Wyman offering him January 10 or 15 for a lecture in Cleveland. The lecture engagement was finally set for January 23 (see *JMN*, 14:434, 435, and Charvat, p. 31). See below, January 7, for a recorded second letter to Wyman.]

To Adam Knight Spence, Belvidere, Illinois, January 7, 1856[1]

Belvidere Illinois
7 January 1856

Dear Sir

I had a note from you, last summer, inviting me to read a lecture to the "Students' Lecture Association" at the Michigan University. I replied, that I would endeavor to do so, if I came westward,—which then seemed improbable. I write now to say that it will be in my power to come to Ann Arbor, Saturday, 19 January.[2] If that day suits your convenience, will you write me a line to Care of J. C. Vaughan,[3] Tribune Office, Chicago. You ask me to name a price—I do not know the condition of your treasury, but the Association shall pay me twenty five dollars, if they are easily able.

Respectfully,
R. W. Emerson

Mr. A. K.. Spence.

1. MS in the Bentley Historical Library, MiU; ph. in NNC. The second and third leaves of the MS are reproduced in facsimile as a frontispiece for the *Michigan Alumnus*, October 1901. Emerson spells Belvidere correctly in the MS Pocket Diary for 1856 (*JMN*, 14:434), so that, although he has not dotted the "i" here, I take it as correctly spelled. Spence, in 1856 a sophomore, ultimately became a professor of Greek and French, and then served Fisk University as Acting President, 1870–1877, and as Dean of the Faculty thereafter.
2. The MS Pocket Diary for 1856 has Ann Arbor with a question mark for January 19, but the MS Account Book for 1853–1859, p. [46], records the receipt of $25.00 (Charvat, p. 31).
3. John C. Vaughan.

To George H. Wyman, Belvidere, Illinois, January 7, 1856

[From Swann's catalogue 98, October 26, 1944, Cameron twice lists a letter of this date, *ESQ* (2d q., 1956), 3:5; and (4th q., 1958), 13:40. The letter concerns a date for Emerson's lecture in Cleveland. See above, January 2, for conjectured letter offering January 10 or 15 for the Cleveland lecture. The actual date is January 23; to settle it at least two letters would be needed. In a letter to his brother of January 14 he asks that letters to Cleveland be sent in care of G. H. Wyman, identified by Rusk as a Cleveland lawyer; see *Letters*, 5:9, and n. 31, and also 5:8. In his letter Emerson tells his brother that he will be in Cleveland on the 23d.]

To James E. Wharton? Belvidere, Illinois, January 9, 1856[4]

Belvidere Illinois
9 January, 1856

My Dear Sir,

I am extremely mortified to find that after troubling you with so much correspondence, I am not likely to be a very faithful servant to your association. My letter to you accepting a later day than that first proposed was not sufficiently considered; and on a careful review of my engagements at the eastward, I do not think it will be safe for me to visit more than the first two towns named by you, namely, Akron, on the 25 Jan. and Hudson on the 26th.[5] For I have an engagement at home on

4. MS in the Edward Laurence Doheny Memorial Library when first gathered, present location unknown. Ph. in NNC. Because this letter is about Ohio engagements, I conjecture the correspondent to be J. E. Wharton, to whom Emerson wrote on November 26 and on December 19, 1855; see above. Wharton of the Massillon Association was acting as agent for a group of Ohio towns. The postscript is written along the margin of page [3].

5. The MS Pocket Diary for 1856 is not so clear as one could wish. There are double entries for four dates: 25 Jan. Mansfield. O. . . . Akron; 29 Jan. Harvard [Mass.] Salem [Ohio]; 30 Jan. Exeter [N.H.] Canton; 31 Jan. Worcester [Mass.] Massillon. The entries for Salem, Canton, and Massillon are in pencil; the eastern towns are in ink (see *JMN*, 14:425). I infer that Wharton, in the letter Emerson is here answering, had proposed, in addition to Akron and Hudson, the towns of Salem, Canton, and Massillon, and possibly Ravenna, all in Ohio. (Charvat's entry for Salem, "Mass.," p. 32, is clearly wrong; the format of the Pocket Diary list shows that Salem, Ohio, is meant.)

The eastern date that is troubling Emerson is the date for Exeter, New Hampshire; it is for the names of his correspondents from Harvard (Mass.) and Exeter (N. H.) that he asks his wife in his letter of January 5 (*Letters*, 5:5). He was apparently able to postpone Harvard to February 27 and Exeter to March 6 or 7 (the Pocket Diary had "6"; the Account Book for 1853–1859, p. [59] has "7.")

Charvat here requires corrections (p. 32): the deletion of the entries for January 28 and 29; the transposition of the Salem entry of February 10 to February 5 in place of Danvers (see *Letters*, 5:9–10); the deletion of the question mark for Hallowell; the deletion of Berkshire; the change of "Mass" to "N. H." and the addition of the title "Beauty" for Exeter, March 6. the *Exeter News-Letter*, a weekly, of March 10, briefly notices the lecture and gives the title. The tentative Pocket Diary, *JMN*, 14:436, entries are for the Berkshire County dates, not for the town of Berkshire; the editors of *JMN* repeat Charvat's error here, indexing "Berkshire" as the town, not the county; see February 15 below.

Wednesday 30 Jany, which I hoped to stave off, but which proves imperative; and I do not see how I can meet it, unless I take the Eastern train on Monday morning.

You must make the best apology for me both to yourself, & to the towns in the association which I hoped to visit.

Respectfully,
R W Emerson

My present address is Tremont House, Chicago, Illinois.

TO ELLEN EMERSON, COLUMBUS? OHIO, JANUARY 24? 1856

[Emerson may not have answered his daughter's letter of January 21, 1856 (Gregg, 1:109), but she asks anxiously if she is returning to Agassiz's school and reminds him that Agassiz needs to know by February 15. See February 14 below for the decision to let Ellen return.]

TO WILLIAM DICKINSON, CONCORD, FEBRUARY 1, 1856[6]

Concord, 1 Feb. 1856

Dear Sir,

You shall announce "Beauty" for the topic of my lecture, if you please.[7]

Respectfully,
R. W. Emerson

⟨Mr⟩ Dr Dickinson.

TO GEORGE LYMAN EMERSON, CONCORD, FEBRUARY 6, 1856

[The MS Account Book for 1853–1860, p. [121], has an entry of 1856, February 6; it records sending $5.00 to George L. Emerson as a gift from Lidian Emerson. It is not clear that there was a letter too, but he would certainly wish to make it known that the gift was from Mrs. Emerson.]

TO GEORGE STILLMAN HILLARD, CONCORD, FEBRUARY 7, 1856

[In a letter of February 6, 1856 (RWEMA), George S. Hillard sends his bill for Ellen Emerson's board; the MS Account Book for 1853-1859, under the date February 7, p. [121], shows the payment of $63.00 to Hillard; the top of Hillard's

6. MS in the Firestone Library, NjP; ph. in NNC. Emerson's correspondent is William Dickinson, M.D., with whom Emerson corresponded in October 1854; see above, *Letters*, 4:541, and *JMN*, 14:435.

7. See Charvat, p. 32, for the engagement in Taunton on February 4; see *JMN*, 14:435, for the Pocket Diary entry.

letter where the bill appeared has been torn away. In his letter, Hillard writes: "We like Ellen very much."]

To Moses G. Thomas, Concord, February 9, 1856[8]

Concord, 9 Feb. 1856

My dear Sir,

I have strangely mislaid a little note which I received, from you, & read hastily in a heap of notes & letters &c, on coming home, two nights ago. It invited me to lecture at New Bedford, as I think, about the 27th, —but I am not sure of the date. If that is it, I am engaged 27th, & the next week, March 5, but free on the following Wed.y, March 12. I am also free 28 Feby Thursday;[9] & the next week, 6th March, if that were the day. I fear, I must give you the trouble to write once more,—after much searching. I shall like very well to come to N. B., if I can. I was glad to hear the best news of you from Miss Arnold,[10] who spoke very warmly as your friend.

With great regard,
R. W. Emerson

Rev. Mr. Thomas.

I am in Maine next week, & may not reply so promptly, but a letter to me care of S. H. Dale, Bangor, would find me on Thursday night, probably, there.[11]

8. MS in NhHi; ph. in NNC. In 1856 Moses G. Thomas was living in New Bedford (see *Letters*, 5:95). Emerson had known Thomas twenty-eight years earlier. Thomas was the first minister of the Unitarian church established in Concord, New Hampshire, partly through the agency of Colonel William Austin Kent (the first Mrs. Emerson's stepfather) and his son. Thomas married Mary Jane Kent, Kent's daughter by his first wife. There are several allusions to Thomas and his courtship in Ellen Tucker's letters; see, *passim, One First Love*, Edith W. Gregg, ed., and pp. 32, 178, 187 (Mrs. Gregg is, I think, mistaken in her interpretation of Ellen Tucker's comment on the engagement of Thomas and her half-sister; she takes Ellen to imply that Thomas had once been her suitor, but I believe her to be drawing a teasing analogy between one courtship and another.)

9. The 28th of February is the date finally settled on. There may have been a second letter.

10. The daughter of James and Sarah (Rotch) Arnold of New Bedford; see *Letters*, 5:12.

11. The postscript here suggests that the date of the Bangor lecture was February 14 (see Charvat, p. 32); and that is the date in the Pocket Diary for 1856 (*JMN*, 14:435), where the entry for Bangor is followed by the name of S. H. Dale, but the Account Book (1853–1860, p. [50]), does not show the receipt of any payment from Bangor, Emerson having been detained on the train from Portland. Samuel H. Dale was a Bangor merchant and late the mayor of the city.

To Emily Mervine Drury, Concord, February 10, 1856[12]

Concord, 10 Feb. 1856.

My dear friend,

Do not blot my name out of your books because I have been very slow to answer your letter. I tried hard to come to Canandaigua, but could not.[13] I had even a faint hope that I might come back thither from home, but it is fast fading away. Tis plain that I am no free agent yet; that my liberty is still postponed. But you said in your letter, that you would visit Mrs Thayer in Boston.[14] If you do so, you must add to your goodnesses, this, of sending me word that you are there, and I will come, & perhaps bring my wife, to agree with you for a peaceful hour which you shall give us at Concord. I have great need of reasonable conversation, whatever you may think of my seeming omissions to secure it.

Mrs. Drury.

To Louis Agassiz, Concord, February 12? 1856

[I conjecture that Emerson wrote Agassiz to let him know that Ellen Emerson was to continue at Agassiz's school. In a letter of January 21 (RWEMA) Ellen had told her father that Agassiz expected to be notified by February 15, and on February 12 Emerson told his daughter she was to have another year.]

To Ellen Emerson, Concord, February 14, 1856

[In a letter of February 15 to her brother and sister Ellen says she had a letter yesterday from her father telling her that Anna Barker Ward had persuaded him that she should have another year at Agassiz's school (Gregg, 1:111–112). Ellen was boarding at George S. Hillard's in Boston; her letters show that Mrs. Ward was very hospitable to her.]

12. MS in the Feinberg Collection, MiD; ph. in NNC; the signature and complimentary close have been cut away; the text is unaffected. An incomplete copy is in the Marietta College Library; ph. in NNC (see *Letters*, 5:25, n. 94).

13. The MS Pocket Diary for 1856 (*JMN*, 14:440) does not show any prospective engagements in upstate New York; Mrs. Drury had written him November 30 [1855] that she had hoped to see him but that she had heard that his coming (to Canandaigua) was uncertain.

14. In her letter, Mrs. Drury had reported Canandaigua's loss of Miss Granger to Boston's Mr. Thayer; Cornelia Adelaide Granger had become the second wife of John E. Thayer. James A. Granger, *Launcelot Granger of Newbury, Mass. and Suffield, Conn. A Genealogical History* (Hartford, 1893), p. 305. John Elliot Thayer and his brother Nathaniel ran a brokerage firm, which by the 1850s was contributing to the building of western railroads.

To Julius Rockwell, Augusta, Maine, February 15, 1856[15]

Feb. 15.
1856

Dear Sir,

I have just received your letter forwarded to me from home. I am content with the new days you have assigned me, say, Tuesday March 11, 12, 13, 14;[16] and the order you propose, namely,

G. Barrington   Tues.
Lee   Wed.
Pittsfield   Thurs.
N. Adams   Friday

I presume you have made a series which ⟨will⟩ will facilitate my arrival, & departure homeward. So we will understand this matter to be settled.[17]

With great regard,
R. W. Emerson.

Hon. Mr Rockwell.

To Benjamin Rodman, Concord, February 24, 1856

[In a letter of February 20, 1856 (RWEMA), Rodman offers his customary hospitality for the evening Emerson is to lecture in New Bedford (February 28). Rodman wrote again on the 22nd to correct his error in the date of Emerson's lecture. See note, February 23 above, of letter to Ricketson. I simply guess that the note to Ricketson falls between the two letters from Rodman with whom Emerson usually stayed.]

To Daniel Ricketson, Concord? February 25? 1856

[Daniel Ricketson, in a letter of February 26, 1856, to Thoreau, refers to a note from Emerson in reply to his invitation to Brooklawn. See Harding and Bode, p. 409, from Anna and Walton Ricketson, *Daniel Ricketson and His Friends* (Boston: Houghton Mifflin, 1902), p. 55. Ricketson seems uncertain that Emerson will

15. MS in the collections of NHi; ph. in NNC.
16. See April 19, September 22, and October 25, 1855, for earlier letters to Senator Rockwell about his proposal that Emerson lecture in Berkshire County. Emerson had originally held February 18–21 for "Berkshire," by which he meant the county (MS Pocket Diary for 1856; *JMN*, 14:436). The days of the week here appear to be added later with a finer pen.
17. He reached home Saturday night (See below, March 17); he could not have traveled from North Adams the whole way by railroad, for the Hoosac tunnel, begun in 1855, was not finished until 1874, so long in construction that it became a local joke. By returning to Pittsfield, he could get to Boston by railroad and out to Concord by the Fitchburg line. By 1855 the Fitchburg line had been extended to Greenfield; he might then have traveled from North Adams to Greenfield by stage, returning to Concord by train.

lecture in New Bedford "tomorrow" although he is expected. See below, February 9, where, among other dates, Emerson offers February 28, not 27, the date originally proposed. He did in fact lecture in New Bedford on the 28th.]

To Horatio Woodman, Concord, March 4, 1856[18]

Concord

4 March

My dear Sir,

No man is to be holden to "promises of conversation," and yet, last night, I fancied that I found not only honesty, but ⟨even⟩ some social & even some aesthetic advantages in the general clearance of my portfolio which your pretty scheme of Boston Lectures flattered me with, eight days ago.[19] So you shall not be holden, if you have forgotten it, or if any of twenty things shall have made it less plausible. But if you or Mr. Alger[20] wish to burn your hands in this fire, I will furnish kindlings on my side: and am ready, on any day or days after 20th March, to read. It might be said, Mr E having read six or seven lectures that were never read in Boston has been requested, &c.

The ⟨topics⟩ subjects will be 1. English civilization

2. France

3. Signs of the Times

4. Beauty

5. Poetry

6. The Scholar[21]

[or, in lieu of the last, which was an oration at Amherst College, I can read "Stonehenge," which describes an excursion with Mr Carlyle.][22] Ordinarily, when I advertise a course, I do not name the topics, except in the special notice of the evening.—Is it still feasible?

Yours,

Mr. Woodman.   R. W. Emerson—.

To Lidian Emerson, Concord, March 9? 1856

[In the MS Account Book for 1853–1859, p. [123], under the date March 9, is an entry: "Cash to L. E. at New Bedford 5.00"]

18. MS in the Woodman papers, MHi; ph. in NNC. The year is certain; see below, March 18, *Letters*, 5:15, and n. 59, and Charvat, p. 32.

19. Probably nine days ago, February 23, at a club meeting.

20. The Reverend Rounseville Alger; see *Letters*, 5:19–20.

21. For the changed order of the lectures here listed, see below, April 7, and *Letters*, 5:19–20.

22. The brackets here are Emerson's.

To Anna Cabot Jackson Lowell, March 10? 1856

[Emerson certainly answered Anna Cabot Jackson Lowell's letter of March 9, 1856; Emerson adds the year in his endorsement. Mrs. Lowell tells him that she hopes to publish the extracts "relating to life and character" which she had read to her class. She writes for Emerson's permission to print several selections from Emerson's essays. Emerson gave her permission. Her book, *Seed-Grain for Thought and Discussion* in two volumes, was published later in the year.

Her volumes have no index and all selections are identified only by their authors' surnames. Emerson is represented by ten passages in volume 1 and sixteen in volume 2. In volume 1, see pp. 42–43, 120, 171, 198, 229, 237, 238–239, 259, 260, 266. In volume 2, see pp. 77, 78, 84, 85, 86, 87, 96–97, 106, 123, 126–127, 135–140, 173, 176–177, 203, 214.]

To Horatio Woodman, Concord, March 17, 1856[23]

Concord 17 March
1856

My dear Sir,

I have been gone, in Berkshire, the last week & only had your letter on Saturday night.[24] I ought to have foreseen & arranged for its reaching me. I go to Dartmouth College,[25] next Thursday, and, after that, am free. Twice a week would be quite possible for the lectures.[26] I have no choice of days. The only request that occurs to me is the old one of all the tribe how to choke off the reporters. Cannot the two or three reporting newspapers[27] like the "Traveller," be personally requested to consign us to neglect Tell them how young & modest we are, & that if they will not report we will give them an abstract of the lecture. I do not know that I care to defend any lecture so much as "Stonehenge",[28] if I read that, since, in the form I gave it at Cambridge, it was full of personalities. But my mail waits

Yours gratefully,
R. W. Emerson

Mr Woodman.

23. MS in the Woodman papers, MHi; ph. in NNC.
24. Lecturing, see above, February 15.
25. The Account Book for 1853–1859, p. [54], shows the receipt of $40.00 from the "Hanover Lyceum," not from Dartmouth College.
26. Except for the third lecture, the schedule was for successive Thursdays; for the third lecture date, see below, March 24.
27. See below, March 26.
28. He had proposed "Stonehenge" as an alternative to "The Scholar"; see above, March 4. To Charvat's entry for Cambridge, March 5 (p. 32), the title can be added.

To Horatio Woodman, Concord, March 18, 1856[29]

Concord—
March 18.
1856—

My dear Sir,

Tis plain I have fallen into good hands, & may go to sleep & be cared for. I dont know but the interval of a week, at this time of year, is a little long, & the class may forget the rare-recurring day.[30] I shall probably be too glad to join you at dinner, on Thursday, 27th, and, if not, will send you word. I am ignorant of Mr Ames's picture till now,[31] & shall see it with sharpened eyes.

Yours faithfully,
R. W. Emerson

Mr Woodman.

To Arthur Hugh Clough, Concord, March 18, 1856[32]

Concord ⎱ 18 March
Masstts ⎰ 1856

My dear Clough,

Mr William Goodwin who I believe read a little Greek with you in Cambridge,[33] has since taken his degree of Doctor of Philosophy at Bonn, and, (as I learn from some of his compatriots there) with special distinction. He is now returning home, & passes through London. You must give him the comfort & honor of seeing your face, & bringing us tidings of you. I saw Thackeray the other day, and gladly; and have not seen another Englishman for long. But we read good books from y⟨?⟩our country, & last, "the Angel in the House."[34] Several of your friends

29. MS in the Woodman papers, MHi; ph. in NNC.

30. See above, March 17, where he had worried about spreading the lectures over so long a period so late in the season; according to a note in *BDA*, April 24 (the date of the fourth lecture), the chapel at Freeman Place was "entirely filled each evening."

31. Joseph Alexander Ames had done a portrait of Emerson without, however, Emerson's sitting for it.

32. MS in the Clough papers, Bodeleian Library; ph. in NNC; printed in the *Emerson-Clough Letters*, No. 27, and in Mulhauser, 2:517.

33. William Watson Goodwin's name is not in the list of the students Clough gives Miss Smith (March 22, 1853), Mulhauser, 2:399.

34. Coventry Patmore's book was published anonymously; see Harding, p. 209, and below, May 5.

believe, in spite of contradiction, that the poem is yours: and we shall ascribe good things to you, until you send us better.

Yours affectionately,
R. W. Emerson

A. H. Clough, Esq.

To Horatio Woodman, Concord, March 24, 1856[35]

Concord
24 March

My dear Sir,

Do you know how to send ⟨these⟩ /this note, containing/ ⟨tickets⟩[36] to Mr Alcott, who, I learn, is in Boston, though I have not seen him? Please say to the doorkeeper that he shall honor my written cards, like the one I enclose. What shall we do for the second Thursday night, which is Fast-Day Eveg? Can we not have the hall, Wednesday or Friday of that week? I am meaning to see you Thursday at dinner.[37]

Do not take any trouble about Mr Alcott. If he do not come to you, I will leave word for him at the Athenaeum. In which Expectation.

Yours,
R. W. Emerson

Mr Woodman.

To Horatio Woodman, Concord? March 26, 1856[38]

26 March

My dear Sir,

I enclose a synopsis which, I trust I have made sufficiently jejune to satisfy the Journal. With all my heart I compassionate the labors your goodness has brought upon you

R. W. E.

Mr Woodman.

35. MS in the Woodman papers, MHi; ph. in NNC. The year is certain; the third lecture of the Boston course of 1856 was given on Wednesday, April 9, Fast-Day in that year falling on Thursday, the 10th. The Emersons regularly observed this Puritan holiday.

36. Crossing out "ticket," Emerson failed to supply a word to replace it. What he enclosed with this letter was a note to Alcott and a "written card" for his admission to the lectures; see *Letters*, 5:16. There may have been a second note to Alcott left at the Athenaeum.

37. Before the first lecture; see above, March 18, to Woodman.

38. MS in the Woodman papers, MHi; ph. in NNC. See above, letter of March 17, 1856, where Emerson proposes supplying the newspapers with abstracts of his lectures in order to

To BENNET H. NASH, CONCORD, MARCH 27? 1856

[In a letter of March 25, 1856, Bennett Nash wrote Emerson to ask his judgment of the poetry of Coventry Patmore and Walt Whitman. The young man's mother was Paulina Tucker Nash, sister of Emerson's first wife. Bennett Nash and his brother Francis had already visited Emerson; see *Letters*, 4:475. I think Emerson would have answered the young man's letter. For the text of Nash's letter, see Tilton, *"Leaves of Grass:* Four Letters to Emerson," *HLB* (July 1979), 27(3):337.)]

To GUGLIEMO GAJANI, CONCORD, APRIL 1, 1856[39]

Concord ⎱ 1 April
Masstts ⎰ 1856

Signor Gajani.
Dear Sir,

I hasten to thank you for the interesting gift which I received last night, under cover from Mrs. Jackson.[40] Though I do not often read by night, I managed to read a good many Chapters before I went to bed, which it was easy to do. I am very glad to see these painful matters treated with a mastery & lightness which will give the book, I doubt not, a wider publicity and it is very desireable that these facts of Italy should be known. But I have been forced to stop my readings today, &, when I resume them, shall perhaps have somewhat to say to you of them. At present, with my thanks I wish the book the widest & heartiest welcome.

Respectfully,
R. W. Emerson

forestall full reporting. I found no "abstracts" of the first lecture in the major Boston dailies. There is no record of such abstracts in Rusk's notes; nor have I found any in the Emerson papers. None are recorded by Myerson.

39. MS in the Barrett Collection, Alderman Library, ViU; ph. in NNC.

40. Gugliemo Gajani's book *The Roman Exile (ER*, p. 112), was sent at the author's request to Emerson March 31 by Susan Bridge Jackson, Lidian Emerson's sister-in-law, who, in her covering letter, had suggested that Albert Stacy, Concord stationer, take a few copies for sale. The MS Account Book for 1853–1859, p. [131], under the date April 6, shows the receipt of $1.00 for Gajani, and see May 6 below for another $1.00. An entry of February 28, p. [52], recording the receipt of $10.50 from Stacy and of an additional fifty cents from another source is not, I think, for sales of the book, but for tickets for Gajani's lecture in Concord on March 15. (The Concord Lyceum had just determined to use the method of advance sale of tickets; Emerson was a curator for this year.) An entry of March 9, p. [123], shows the payment of $12.00 to Gajani "for lecture." See also *Letters*, 5:14 and no. 52. Gajani had been a member of Mazzini's short-lived Constituent Assembly; his lecture was about the failure of the republican movement in Italy (1848–1849).

To Louis Agassiz, Concord, April 2, 1856[41]

Concord, 2 April.

My dear Sir,

I keep before me with great pleasure your kind invitation for to-morrow.

Yours with constant regard,
R. W. Emerson

Professor Agassiz.

To Ellen Emerson, Concord, April? 2? 1856

[The MS Account book for 1853–1860, p. [125], under the date April 2, has an entry for $2.00 sent to Ellen "in a letter." Under April 7, he enters his payment of $91.00 to George S. Hillard for Ellen's board to April 1. This letter was presumably addressed to Ellen at Hillard's in Boston where she lived while attending Agassiz's classes.]

To Horatio Woodman, Concord, April 7, 1856[42]

Concord
7 April
1856

My dear Sir,

I find that my "Signs of the Times" is a little old, & needs both suppression & enlargement to bring it to any fitness: So I must read, this week, /on Wednesday,/ the lecture on "Beauty,"[43] which is newer & safer. I hope this notice comes in time to prevent any error in advertising.[44]

Ever your obliged.
R. W. Emerson

Mr Woodman
P.S. I have written to Mr Alger.[45]

41. MS in the Autograph Collection, Houghton Library, MH; ph. in NNC. Longfellow refers to this dinner as of 1856, *Life*, 2:308.

42. MS in the Woodman papers, MHi; ph. in NNC.

43. "Beauty" was apparently first given in 1855, March 29, for the Concord Lyceum; "Signs of the Times" I believe to have been the second lecture in the Philadelphia series of 1854 from which Emerson also took "Poetry," "France," and, I think, "English Civilization." In Glasgow in 1848 he gave a lecture called "The Genius of the Present Age" (see above entry for February 1, 1848).

44. *BDA*, April 3, announcing the second lecture listed the others in the original order (see above, March 4); the announcement for April 9 gives the correct subject for this third lecture.

45. See *Letters*, 5:19–20.

To Anna Barker Ward, April 14, 1856[46]

Concord, 14 April.

My dear friend,

You shall not wait for me an instant by day or night, next Thursday; & I hasten to say so, because the expecting people is odious when one is not strong. Before I met you the other night, I had promised to go somewhere to meet Henry Hedge, if he should be in town next Thursday evening;—which was then doubtful, & I supposed he would not come. Now I am told he is expected; so I shall find ten other minutes in one other of your precious days to hear how bright the voyage opens, & what else you will tell me, and to thank you for your goodness to Ellen, who esteems you as little less than one of the Olympian figures, & also as much more & better than they.

Yours affectionately,
R. W. Emerson

Mrs Anna Ward.

To William Rounseville Alger, Concord, April 21, 1856

[In a letter of April 21, 1856 (RWEMA), William R. Alger asks Emerson to join him and Frederic Henry Hedge for "a social hour" after the lecture to be given April 24. Alger was acting with Horatio Woodman in arranging the Boston series of lectures that began March 27. See above, April 14, for Hedge's being expected in town.]

To Horatio Woodman, Concord, April 22, 1856[47]

Concord, 22 April.

Yes, "Poetry," by all means for Thursday: and may the much-offended muses be placable.

Yours,
R. W. E.

46. MS in the Ward papers, Houghton Library, MH; ph. in NNC. The year I conjecture to be 1856 when Anna Barker Ward sailed for Europe on May 9; Emerson was lecturing in Boston on Thursdays, and Mrs. Ward had been particularly kind to Ellen Emerson who had been boarding in Boston while she attended Agassiz's school. See February 14 above, for a note of Mrs. Ward's good offices in securing Ellen another year at the school. Finally, in 1856 Hedge was expected in town and did appear on Thursday, April 24, (a.l.s., of William R. Alger, April 21, RWEMA).

47. MS in the Woodman papers, MHi; ph. in NNC. The date is secure from the earlier

To LEONARD BACON, CONCORD, APRIL 25, 1856[48]

Concord, 25 April, 1856.

Dear Sir,

I received your note last night. I am sorry to say that I have not had any letter directly from Miss Bacon, since last December. Her publishers have a letter dated 28 February last. Her address, at her last writing, was still 12 Spring Street, Hyde Park Gardens, London. I had no right to expect a letter after December, as I had told her that I was going to Illinois, about Christmas, to be absent six weeks or more;[49] & she accordingly wrote directly to Dix & Edwards of Putnams' Magazine. I have regretted much my tasks & preoccupations that forbade my keeping up an active correspondance with her, & reproached myself lately with omissions, which, after a few weeks I am hoping to repair: And I hear with the more concern that you have no recent news of her. Her letters are full of confidence & devotion to her task, heroic devotion to it, & repeated expressions of indifference as to what becomes of herself, if only she accomplishes her task. Her latest letters had also some sad allusions, I thought, to disappointment in not receiving expected letters, & some misgivings as to her means for remaining in England to prosecute her studies.

Her arrangements for publication had not turned out to my wish. I advised her not to print in Putnam, but to publish her results in a book; & I communicated to her a proposition from Phillips, Sampson, & Co. which, well-explained, was fair & even generous.[50] But she decided to print in Putnam, and the editors, after the first article was printed, refused to print the following ones; and assigned their reasons. This refusal left me in no proper plight to carry the book to Phillips & Sampson again, after it was thus used & rejected.

I have not written to her, as indeed I have laid my whole correspondence on the shelf, until certain imperative tasks of my own are ended, which should soon be.[51] Meantime, I shall await with great interest your

---

letters to Woodman; for example, see above March 4, 17, and 18; "Poetry" is the fourth lecture (April 24) in the Boston series managed by Woodman and Alger.

48. MS in DFo; ph. in NNC; printed by Theodore Bacon, pp. 162–163; listed *Letters*, 5:20.

49. See December 3, 1855, above.

50. See January 15, 1855, above.

51. See *Letters*, 5:18–19, for a letter of April 5 where Emerson tells his brother of lectures and the still-delayed book *English Traits*.

news about her, & shall be entirely at your service to obtain information respecting her address, &c. if she has changed her place.

With great respect,
R. W. Emerson

Rev. Dr Bacon—

To Charles De Berard Mills, Concord, April 30? 1856

[In a letter of April 28, 1856 (RWEMA), Charles de Berard Mills of Syracuse asks Emerson if he would like to have the books he has lent Mills returned immediately (for the loan, see note of letter of May 9? 1855, above). Mills mentions volumes of Giardano Bruno in Italian (see Harding, p. 43). Since Mills does not return the volumes until October 16 (a.l.s., RWEMA), I infer that Emerson wrote to say that he had no immediate need of the books. See *Letters*, 5:220, for note of a later letter to Mills, again on the subject of Giardano Bruno.]

To Cyrus Augustus Bartol, May? 1? 1856

[A series of letters by Bartol to Emerson (Cabot papers, Schlesinger Library, Radcliffe), concerns arrangements for the Emersons to join the Bartols at Pigeon Cove (Cape Ann) in July. The proposal made by Bartol in a letter of April 29, 1856, is followed up in a letter of May 19 giving information about lodgings and costs. A letter of July 8 announces that he and his family go to Pigeon cove "Tuesday next," and a letter of July 25 expresses dismay that Emerson should have paid for the accommodations for both families. Emerson may then have written Bartol between April 29 and May 19. See also below, May 21, *Letters*, 5:23–24, and *JMN*, 14:100–101, 108. See also Edward Emerson's note, *J*, 9:55–56, where he tells of Emerson's discovery that the first passage in his journal SO is almost blank verse.]

To Horatio Woodman, Concord, May 1, 1856 [52]

Concord, 1 May

My dear Sir,

Thanks for the good action you have set on foot for the philosopher. Count me for a subscriber, &, though I am sorry I cannot come tonight I depend on taking a part in the class on Tuesday.

Yours,
R. W. Emerson

Mr Woodman.

52. MS in the Woodman papers, MHi; ph. in NNC. The year is derived from Alcott's letter to his wife of April 26, 1856, *Letters of A. Bronson Alcott*, Richard L. Herrnstadt, ed. (Ames: Iowa State University Press, 1969), pp. 191–192. Alcott credits William Henry Channing with initiating the series of Tuesday evening conversations, but this letter of Emerson's makes Woodman the "angel." Alcott's letter mentions Woodman's invitation to

To Arthur Hugh Clough, Concord, May 5, 1856[53]

Concord, 5 May, 1856.

My dear Clough,

Mrs Ward's visit to London makes an important gap in my little 'great world,' & I am only consoled by believing, that she will see & bring home good tidings of you, & other good friends. I wish she might bring home you & other good friends.[54]

Is Tennyson in Italy? I heard or read, the other day, a piece of a letter from Browning, in Paris, which spoke of Tennyson passing through,— but which way I know not. If he is in or about London, Mrs Ward should not fail to see him, nor he her.[55] I have dreams lately that I have found or am finding my pen for writing letters, which has been long lost.

Ever your friend,
R. W. Emerson.

A. H. Clough, Esq.

To Jane Welsh Carlyle, Concord, May 5, 1856

[MS in the National Library of Scotland, Edinburgh; ph. in NNC; printed by Howard Fish, Jr., *AL* (March 1955), 27:29, with the wrong date of May 6 and the erroneous reading "goodness" for "good nerves"; printed correctly by Slater, p. 508. Listed, *Letters,* 5:20, from letter to T. Carlyle.]

To Coventry Patmore, Concord, May 5, 1856[56]

Concord ⎱ 5 May
Mass.tts. ⎰ 1856.

My dear Sir,

I think there never was so sudden a public formed for itself by any poem as here exists for "the Angel in the House,"—which was read & published by acclamation of a few, before yet any one had heard or

---

dine on "Thursday" with Agassiz and Emerson; the first Thursday after April 26, 1856, was May 1, the date of Emerson's letter.

53. MS in the Clough papers, Bodleian Library; ph. in NNC; printed in the *Emerson-Clough Letters,* no. 28; and in Mulhauser, 2:517.

54. See letters of the same date to Coventry Patmore (below) and Jane Welsh Carlyle (Slater, p. 508).

55. Clough was already acquainted with Anna Barker Ward; he had been a frequent visitor at her house during his visit to America in 1852–1853.

56. MS in the Bapst Library, MChB; ph. in NNC. Listed in *Letters,* 2:20, where Rusk prints Patmore's reply of September 30; Mrs. Ward did not deliver this letter until September 29.

guessed the name of the author; & since our edition was out,[57] is known & loved & recited by young & old, an ever enlarging company. I give you joy & thanks as the maker of this beautiful poem, & pray you to make no delay to print the promised "Espousals."[58] I try to give myself importance among my friends as one who has known the author, & has owed to him valued attentions.

I use the occasion to say, that there is a lady in London, a friend of mine, Mrs Ward of Boston,[59] who likes the book as well as I do, & who can tell you how much the Americans value it: and Mrs Ward is a lady prized by her friends at that rate, that, I am sure you will thank me if your leisure give you the opportunity of seeing her. So I have begged her to send you her address, if she stay in London any number of days.

Yours, with kindest remembrance,
R. W. Emerson.

Coventry Patmore, Esq.

TO ANNA BARKER WARD, CONCORD? MAY 5? 1856[60]

But it makes little difference what you see or even whom You will still have the secret of drawing a glory out of dull hours & dull men. And happy are they that are with you, and they that have been. And if I shall not be in town tomorrow to see you again, that is my parting advice; for the heavens have been very kind to thee, & to us, thou dear child!

Ever Yours,
R. W. Emerson

Mrs Ward.

57. The American edition of *The Angel in the House* was published by Ticknor and Fields.
58. The American edition of *Espousals*, published by Ticknor and Fields in 1856, is in Emerson's library (Harding, p. 209).
59. Anna Barker Ward left on the *Arabia* on the 9th (see *Letters*, 5:21). For other letters for Mrs. Ward, see Emerson to Jane Carlyle, Slater, p. 508, and, above, to Clough. Patmore was delighted with Anna Ward; see *Letters*, 5:20–21.
60. MS in the Ward papers, Houghton Library, MH; ph. in NNC. I believe this note to have accompanied the letters of introduction Emerson gave Mrs. Ward in 1856; these are dated May 5; see above for letters to Arthur Hugh Clough and Coventry Patmore; and for a letter to Jane Welsh Carlyle, see Slater, p. 508. For Emerson's glowing description of her for Carlyle, see *ibid.*, p. 510. (The letter to Carlyle went by mail.) This note is, I think, complete as it stands.

To Charles Thomas Jackson, Concord, May 6, 1856[61]

Concord 6 May 1856

My dear brother,

I enclose $11.00 whereof $10. were kindly lent me by you on Friday last, & 1.00 was received by me today for one of Mr. Gajani's books;[62] & will you please give it to Susan[63] for him.

Yours affectionately,
R. W. Emerson.

To Wendell Phillips, Concord, May 7? 1856

[In a letter of May 6, n. y., endorsed 1856 by Emerson (RWEMA), Wendell Phillips asks for Carlyle's address. Emerson would have answered.]

To Wendell Phillips, Concord, May 14, 1856[64]

Concord ⎱ 14 May
Mass.tts ⎰ 1856

My dear Sir,

I do not know whether you have not quite as much good to do as belongs to one pair of hands, nor do I know whether my friend Mr Alcott falls within or without the class to whom you would think your aid & comfort first & foremost due; but I am quite sure you will like to know that any efforts are made for his benefit. Last summer I talked with several of his friends in turn, with a view to learn whether anything could be done to obtain for him by joint contribution the purchase of any the smallest annuity which he could not alienate whilst he lived. Thomas Davis of Providence promised me $100. Longfellow $50. Starr King $50. Mr & Mrs S. Cheney 50. H. Woodman 50. /Mr Beck 20./ and other gentlemen as Whipple, Parker, Fisher, Apthorp, & others, promised eventual aid. Two subscriptions are paid; the others are to be paid, say, as soon as 1 June; and as there exists a fund for his benefit worth $500. I am not without hope that by adding /the above named subscriptions/ smaller & & the smallest aids, which any friends who /can/ only give such,

61. MS owned by Kenneth W. Cameron who prints it twice, in *ER*, p. 129 and *ESQ* (4th q., 1858), 13:37; listed *Letters*, 5:21, from booksellers' catalogue. Emerson customarily addressed his brother-in-law this way.

62. For Gugliano Gajani's book *The Roman Exile*, see above, April 1, 1856.

63. Susan Bridge Jackson.

64. MS in the Phillips papers, Houghton Library, MH; ph. in NNC; with envelope addressed: Wendell Phillips, Esq | Boston. | Mass.tts |; postmarked at Concord May 14. See below, May 21, for Emerson's acknowledgment of Phillips' contribution.

will give gladly, we may obtain an annuity, or other safe investment, which will yield him $150. per annum, which will pay a philosopher's board in the country.[65]

I give you these details, that you may judge of the whole design. If it suits you to aid in it directly, you shall pay any sum you can spare for this purpose, to Sam.l G. Ward, State Street, who will act as our treasurer. If you know any friends who you think would favor the design, I wish you would represent ⟨th⟩ it favorably to them. I am sure you will feel that Mr Alcott's whole genius & influence are in harmony with your own philanthropies. And I do not think it necessary to enter with you into the reasons which make his case exceptional, whilst we hold every other healthy man bound to get his own living. Forgive me this long story, which I must seek an occasion to make longer, by word of mouth. With greatest respect,

Wendell Phillips, Esq.   R. W. Emerson.

To HORATIO WOODMAN, CONCORD, MAY 15, 1856[66]

Concord 15 May
1856

I enclose the signed papers & your due-bill with a full degree of that wonder & delight which I presume all laymen feel in seeing their affairs prospering in skilful hands.[67]

Yours,
R. W. Emerson.

H. Woodman, Esq.

To WENDELL PHILLIPS, CONCORD, MAY 21, 1856[68]

Concord, 21 May
1856.

My dear Sir,

I heartily thank you for your ready & efficient action on my request. With all your solid claims to our praise & gratitude, I must needs reckon

65. See July 6, 1855, above, for citation of the records for this fund and identification of the contributors and those solicited for contributions.

66. MS in the Woodman papers, MHi; ph. in NNC.

67. I take this letter to refer to Woodman's management of the Boston lectures. the MS Account Book for 1853–1860, p. [56], records the receipt of $772.36 as the "net proceeds" of the lectures under the date May 5. I assume the "due-bill" is for the expenses of the hall, advertizing, and tickets, expenses Woodman had withheld from the gross receipts.

68. MS in the Phillips papers, Houghton Library, MH; ph. in NNC; with envelope addressed: Wendell Phillips, Esq. | Boston. | Mass.tts |; postmarked at Concord, May 22.

this last a very high one, because I know to what a minority of a minority Alcott appeals, & his superlative inefficiency as a worker very naturally makes those who act directly & with terrible force on society impatient of his pretensions.

All the more honor to your noble & charitable interpretations! They also have made the "long talk" you allude to quite unnecessary, though I sometimes fancy that my better acquaintance with A. enables me to make out for him to others a better exceptional case.[69]

Gratefully Yours,
R. W. Emerson

Wendell Phillips, Esq.

To Cyrus Augustus Bartol, Concord, May 21, 1856[70]

Concord 21 May 1856

My dear Sir

I am happy to hear what you say of the friendly probabilities at Pigeon Cove. I find the middle of July meets all the several conveniences of my little party & I shall rejoice if this seaside visit can be made under your auspices without giving you too much trouble in the preliminaries.

Yours gratefully
R. W. Emerson

Rev. Mr Bartol

To David Atwood Wasson, Concord? June? 11? 1856

[In the Schlesinger Library, Radcliffe, is a letter to Emerson from David A. Wasson dated plainly June 9, "1857." The letter asks for letters of introduction to Carlyle and Wilkinson. Since Wasson's trip to England was made in 1856, the year is impossible. Emerson presumably answered, though possibly to refuse.]

To Thomas Ridgeway Gould, Concord, June 12? 1856

[In a letter of June 11, 1856 (RWEMA), Frederick Beck suggests that Emerson propose to the artist Thomas R. Gould that he contribute to the Alcott fund

---

Emerson is acknowledging Phillips' letter of May 20 (draft in Phillips papers) reporting that he has taken to Ward his $50 contribution to the Alcott fund as Emerson had asked in his letter of the 14th (above).

69. See Emerson's letter of the 14th where he hopes to talk to Phillips on Alcott's behalf; in his reply, Phillips professed to value Alcott but says also that he could not say no to any request of Emerson's "unless it were just long enough to secure that 'long talk' you promise."

70. MS owned by Mrs. William Pierson; ph. in NCC; Emerson is answering Bartol's letter of May 19 (Schlesinger Library) describing the accommodation available at Pigeon Cove (Cape Ann).

$50.00 in two installments. He describes Gould as a staunch believer in Alcott. There is no record that Gould contributed; a list of the contributions and sums given is in Emerson's Ledger for 1859–1872, p. 143. There is no evidence then that Emerson acted on Beck's suggestion, but I think he might have done so in his eagerness to provide for his improvident friend.]

To Delia Salter Bacon, Concord, June 23, 1856[71]

Concord, 23 June
1856

My dear Miss Bacon,

I am heartily sorry that after so long a space I should not be able to send you some good news. But this time none at all, & indeed much worse than no good news, namely, the most vexatious. There is nothing for it but the kind of earnest that many serious drawbacks & disasters give to the brave & well deserving, of new & better turns that must befall. On my going west in December I left the three (?) mss chapters with my wife. Putnam already had the first. As I had dissuaded the printing in the Magazine, they were not to have the rest without your express ⟨w⟩advice. They printed the first & then sent to my brother W. E. in N. Y. demanding the rest to go on at once. He sent to my wife for it & she supposing that this was the contingency I had told her of sent the 3 (?) chapters. After reading them, they refused to go on, & returned them to W. E. Lately on receiving your letter of May, I received soon afterwards what mss you sent in May to Dix & Edwards from them with word that they did not find them suited to their purpose. Then I wrote to W. E. to restore the 3 (?) Chapters.[72] He wrote me back that he was pained to say that they were lost. Just before my letter came, he had given them to Sophy Ripley who was coming home to Concord via Springfield to bring to me. Miss Ripley had been on a visit at his house in Staten Island for a day or two her trunk was in N. Y. City. She took the sealed parcel in her hands & came down to the S. I. ferry with my brother in his carriage /1½ mile,/ & just before reaching the boat perceived that she had not the parcel. W. E. was needed at his office /&/ he sent back the driver instantly from the boat to find the parcel, informed the collec-

71. MS in DFo; ph. in NNC; printed by Theodore Bacon, pp. 191–195; listed *Letters*, 5:24.

72. William Emerson had asked in a letter of March 30 whether he should keep the MSS; Emerson had replied that "they had better come back to me by the first safe means" (*Letters*, 5:19, no. 72). See notes, December 3, 1855, above.

tor at the boat office, & advertised it with a /reward/[73] at once, the chances seemed all for recovering it at once, but it has never appeared! Sophy Ripley has returned home & dared not come to see me until her mother Mrs Ripley had come to tell me her consternation. They inquire ⟨if⟩ first of all if you have a duplicate? Of which I am not sure. I assure you, all the parties to this misfortune are very miserable at present.

I wish I could relieve this disaster with some better face of the whole affair But it does not yet show its best side. I could not carry the Mss if I had them thus far complete to Phillips & Sampson (or to another publisher) & ask as favorable terms as they had offered me at first for the éclat & what publishers would esteem the promise of the work was seriously diminished by Putnams publishing & then rejecting. That is a damage which one would say can only be properly met & overcame by publishing the book at your own risk, in its mature form.

I have now been trying to read the papers ⟨ret⟩ sent to me by Dix & Edwards & which they decline to print. It is very difficult for me to read them, so small & crowded is the writing, & so much interlined & corrected. My eyes are very failing servants in these days, & with glasses I do not much help them. I have set my daughter & my wife also to help me, & at last I have mainly surmounted the difficulty. I hesitate a little that I think the magazine men judged rightly in asking still another form. The moment your proposition is stated that Shakspeare was only a player whom ⟨a⟩ certain superior person or persons could use, & did use as a mouthpiece for their poetry it is perfectly understood. It does not need to be stated twice. The proposition is immensely improbable, and against the single testimony of Ben Jonson "for I loved the man & do honor his memory on this side idolatry as much as any,"[74] cannot stand. Ben Jonson must be answered, first. Of course we instantly require your proofs. But instead of hastening to these, you expatiate on the absurdity of the accepted biography. Perfectly right to say once, but not necessary to say twice, and unpardonable after telling us that you have proof that this is not the man, & we are waiting for that proof—to say it thrice. There is great incidental worth in these expatiatings; but it is all at disadvantage because we have been summoned to hear an extraordinary announcement of facts & impatient of any episodes. I am sure you

73. The word "reward" is inserted on the facing leaf, the first, appearing above the salutation.

74. See *ER*, frontispiece and p. 45, for Emerson's borrowing of Jonson's *Works*, vol. 7, where this well-known passage in *Timber* appears at p. 91.

cannot be aware how voluminously you have cuffed & pounded the poor pretender, & then again, & still again, & no end. I think too but this I say with less assurance that you lean much harder than they can bear on many passages you cite from the plays as if they contained very pointed allusions which admitted of only one application.

Once more, I am a little shocked by the signature "Discoverer of the Authorship of Shakspeares Plays" which should not be used one moment in advance. Yes, & welcome, & forevermore, wear the crown, from the instant your fact is made to appear, not before. Certain great merits which appeared in your first papers, mark these last also,—a healthy perception, & natural rectitude, which give immense advantage in criticism, where they are so rare. The account of Englishmen, & what is servile in them, & the prophetic American relations of this poetry, struck me much, & your steadfast loyalty to cause & effect, in mental history.[75]

What practically should be or can be done, I cannot see today. There is no publisher, because there is not yet the ready book. If you are to be anticipated, I think you should write a short letter announcing exactly your propositions, the points you are prepared to prove, send it to Fraser, or any other English journal, tho' it were the lowest that will print it; print it also in Putnam, or the Tribune, or the Crayon, here; & then publish your book containing the full exposition, whenever you can have it ready. I have been a much worse agent lately than you might have found me earlier,—tho' never a good one,—but worse now thro many ⟨re⟩ causes weary to tell of,—perhaps another year will set me on my feet again, & then!—

With entire respect,
Yours,
R. W. Emerson.

Miss Bacon.

To Horatio Woodman, Concord, June 30, 1856[76]

Concord
30 June 1856

My dear Sir,

Mrs Ripley[77] infers from her letters that you have come home & brought them. I have this special interest in the question today;—that

---

75. See Theodore Bacon, pp. 198–201, for Miss Bacon's response to Emerson's criticism (in a letter to Hawthorne).

76. MS in the Woodman papers, MHi; ph. in NNC.

77. Probably Mrs. Samuel Ripley.

Agassiz & Pierce[78] asked me on Friday if we should hold a club on Saturday next, 5 July.[79] I answered, Yes, if our President returned; I promised to advise them. So write me word that you shall be at the head of the table at Parker's next Saturday, at 2.30, and so it shall be.

Yours constantly,
R. W. Emerson

H. Woodman, Esq.

TO HENRY J. GARDNER, JULY 4, 1856

[In the Manuscript Department, Lilly Library, InU, is a letter addressed "To His Excellency the Governor of our Commonwealth"; the letter is in the hand of Frank B. Sanborn; Emerson's signature is the second of twelve that include those of Thoreau and his father, and Lieutenant-Governor Simon Brown. The letter protests the abuse of citizens of the commonwealth of Massachusetts by citizens of Missouri and calls upon the governor to take "immediate action . . . to protect our fellow citizens and the rights of Massachusetts." The text plainly specifies Missouri, but a note (in a tremulous hand) on the letter describes it as about the "outrages on Mass. people in Kansas." The date suggests that the occasion referred to is the attack by Missourians on an armed band of men from Worcester, Massachusetts, led by Dr. Calvin Cutter, who instead of traveling to Kansas through Iowa made the mistake (?) of going to St. Louis and then traveling by a Missouri River steamboat. See Edelstein, pp. 183–185. The party with its weapons must have been released; scarcely two months later, Cutter led his company to capture at Palmyra (Kansas) a nine-wagon freight en route from Santa Fe to Samuel L. McKinney, merchant, Westport, Missouri. For this exploit, John Brown was at first to get the credit. Sanborn has certainly misrepresented the character and purpose of Cutter and his company. See James C. Malin, *John Brown and the Legend of Fifty-Six* (Philadelphia: American Philisophical Society, 1942), pp. 499, 626.]

TO ELIZA BUCKMINSTER LEE, CONCORD, JULY 5? 1856

[In a letter of July 4, 1856 (RWEMA), Eliza Buckminster Lee asks to borrow for an interested friend Delia Bacon's letters to Emerson. The friend has reported to her Miss Bacon's financial straits, and Mrs. Lee hopes that she may anonymously send her some money. Emerson clearly volunteered to see to it (*Letters*, 5:27). From a second letter of July 30 from Mrs. Lee, it can be inferred that he asked her to confirm her wish for secrecy. There may have been more than one letter

78. Emerson had dined on Friday, June 27, with Benjamin Peirce; see *Letters*, 5:25, where, as here and elsewhere, Emerson misspells the name.

79. The Saturday Club has not yet settled to its regular meeting on the last Saturday of the month; see below, October 4, to Lowell. The MS Account Book for 1853–1859, pp. [132] and [140], records payments to Woodman for club dinners: on May 9 for four dinners, and on July 23 for two. If there was no June meeting, then the July payment is for Emerson and a guest.

before he sent the gift on July 28. Emerson records the receipt of the money in his MS Account Book for 1853–1859, p. [60], under the date July 10, and in the same Account Book, p. [131], under the date July 26, records the purchase from S. G. Ward & Co. of a "bill of exchange on London to credit of Miss D. S. Bacon."]

To Cyrus Augustus Bartol, Concord, July 11, 1856[80]

11 July 1856

My dear Sir,

Thanks for your constant attention to our little adventure by the seashore. You may be sure the hours are carefully counted here to the 15th. If the sun shines I doubt not we shall try to make our journey on that day. If I find that my class keep their quinquennial anniversary or more rightly their quinquanniversary I may stay a day or two behind them but my hope & purpose are as fixed as the young peoples and to write. Thanks & affection

Yours
R. W. Emerson

Mr Bartol

To Elizabeth Hoar, Concord, July 14, 1856[81]

Concord
July 14, 1856.

Dear Elizabeth,

I return Mr Randalls poems[82] which I have kept longer than was right, from liking & because one is always expecting a better day & mood to read these pastoral verses. I find them always pleasing, with a solid honesty quite free from prettiness or showiness, and, if they do not rise to any great heights, never balking the sense with whim or folly. They are manly & right minded, & inspire a respect for the poet, and whilst they particularly please me that he praises our own stream & hills, they make me wish his farm & walks were a few miles nearer mine, that I could see his /chimney/ smoke, & hope sometimes to encounter him in

80. MS owned by Mrs. William Pierson; ph. in NNC. Emerson is replying to Bartol's letter of July 8 (Schlesinger Library). Bartol had written that the day of departure for Pigeon Cove was "Tuesday next," which is July 15.

81. MS in Goodspeed's 1941; ph. in NNC.

82. John Witt Randall, whose *Consolations of Solitude* was published anonymously by John P. Jewett of Boston in 1856. See September 11 below. Randall and his sister Belinda were close friends of Elizabeth Hoar; and in 1840–1842, Margaret Fuller was often a guest in the Winter Street home of their father Dr. John Randall (see *Letters*, 2:448). There are other allusions to the Randall family in the *Letters*.

his walk, or even to venture on him in his house. These are well named Consolations of Solitude & one must wish the full sweetness of his verse to the poet.

Ever thankfully,
Your brother
Waldo.

To J—— C—— Hobbs, Concord, July 22? 1856

[In a letter of July 21, 1856 (RWEMA), J. C. Hobbs of Blackstone, Massachusetts, asks Emerson to lecture for the Blackstone Literary Association. I conjecture Emerson answered to keep the offer open; see *Letters*, 5:37, for record of a later letter to a Blackstone correspondent. The town is entered under the date December 18 in the MS Pocket Diary for 1856 (*JMN*, 14:439), but no correspondent's name is given, nor is it given in the MS Account Book for 1853–1859, p. 72, where the receipt of $20.00 is recorded under the date December 12.]

To Mary Eliot Dwight Parkman, Concord, July 25, 1856[83]

My dear Mrs Parkman,

Paul Ferroll[84] came safely, & proved an easy task for two or three hot hours. He is a sad sentimentalist, however, and quite an impossible hero. I think he will do no harm. Yet the action of the book is carried on with so much force, as to make it very easy reading, in spite of this Chinese management of the hearts in the piece. I am sure you will forgive me that I ventured to lend the pretty book to Mr Bartol, & to Miss Cabot,[85] at Pigeon Cove, Mr B. taking your address,[86] & promising to send it faithfully to Tremont Street.

Your obliged servant,
R. W. Emerson

Concord, 25 July, 1856.[87]

To Cyrus Augustus Bartol, Concord, August 1? 1856

[Three letters by Bartol to Emerson (Cabot papers, Schlesinger Library, Radcliffe) suggest the likelihood of a letter between July 27 and August 12. Bartol

83. MS in the collections of the Hagley Museum and Library; Wilmington, Delaware, ph. in NNC. An envelope addressed to Mrs. Parkman at 270 Tremont Street has a July postmark, the numerals blurred. It goes with no letter in the Parkman papers. I take it to belong to this letter.

84. Caroline Clive's novel was published in 1855; in 1856 it was published in New York by Redfield. In 1860, Mrs. Clive would publish the sequel: *Why Paul Ferroll Killed His Wife*.

85. Possibly Elliot Cabot's sister Sarah Perkins Cabot.

86. See July 11 above.

87. Emerson wrote this date across the contiguous Leaves.

writes on July 25, 1856, in distress at the discovery that Emerson had paid for the accommodations (his own and Bartol's) at Pigeon Cove (Cape Ann) for the week of the Emersons' visit (see *Letters,* 5:23–24, and *JMN,* 14:100–101, 108). In the MS Account Book for 1853–1859, p. [139], under the date July 12, 1856, the payment of $43.66 for "Mrs. Babson's bill" is recorded. The Babson family owned a two-hundred-year-old house, according to Ellen Emerson, which they kept for summer visitors; Edith and William Forbes spent a week there after their marriage (Gregg, 1:350). On the 14th of August, Bartol writes: "As you throw in the *Divine* values with the human, as what you were to pay for here, I shall not controvert your idea of the moderateness of the charge—Not for this I write again, but to beg you take no pains to send me your book, as Whipple has brought me his copy ..." Emerson plainly had replied to Bartol's letter of July 25. The book referred to is *English Traits.* The copy Emerson presented to Bartol is acknowledged by him on August 24. See below, September 16.]

To George Bancroft, Concord, August 7, 1856[88]

Concord—
7 August, 1856

My dear friend,

Your letter, which miscarried to new Hampshire, through no fault of yours, came to me last night.[89] I hardly know how to resist you when you add the calling of the sea to your own & your wife's society. But no such good thing is for me today or tomorrow, & I cannot come. Perhaps before the twenty days are gone, I shall have more liberty, then I shall send to ask if there is still a corner for me. Meantime, with kindest remembrances to Mrs Bancroft, I am always your debtor,

R. W. Emerson.

George Bancroft, Esq.

To Phillips, Sampson & Co.?, Concord, August 12, 1856[90]

⟨Mr⟩Gentlemen,

Will Mr. Loring[91] please add to his "presentation list, From the Author"

Dr O. W. Holmes
Mr J. T. Fields

88. MS in the Bancroft papers, MHi; ph. in NNC.
89. Bancroft's invitation to Newport (R.I.) is dated August 3 (RWEMA).
90. MS in the Perkins Library, NCD; ph. in NNC; printed incompletely in Carroll A. Wilson, *Thirteen Author Collections,* D. A. Randall and S. Wilson, eds. (New York: Scribner's, 1950), 1:29. Single leaf, the second cut away.
91. An Aaron K. Loring, clerk, is listed in Boston directories with a business address at 13 Winter Street, the address also of the publishing firm. The book is *English Traits.* The

and send the copy marked for Mr A. B. Alcott <u>to the care of Samuel E. Sewall, Esq.</u> whose office is in Washington St, near State St. Will he please look & see if a copy went to William E. Channing, Esq. New Bedford, (Office of the Mercury) from the author. If not, send it,

& oblige yours
R. W. Emerson

Concord.

12 Aug. 1856.

To Samuel Joseph May, Concord, August 15? 1856

[Writing Emerson on August 13, 1856 (RWEMA), Samuel J. May opened with "Dear Doctor"; May's letter of August 20 shows that Emerson promptly assumed that the letter was not for him and sent it back to May without reading it. If he had, he'd have known it was for him, for it is a pleasant letter of praise for *English Traits*. See August 26, below.]

To Octavius Brooks Frothingham, Concord, August 23? 1856

[In a letter (from Burlington, Mass) of August 22, n. y., endorsed 1856 by Emerson (RWEMA), O. B. Frothingham asks Emerson to lecture at his church in Jersey City. He asks Emerson to write him at the Neptune Insurance office in Boston. An undated letter from Frothingham endorsed 1856 (RWEMA) is, I believe, an acknowledgment of Emerson's reply to his letter of August 22. He says Wednesday is the day; but any evening will do, and he proposes the last week in November or the second week in December. Emerson endorses the letter "25 Nov? or 10 Dec?", the first a Tuesday and the second a Wednesday. Rusk, using this undated letter, conjectures that it is an acknowledgment of a letter from Emerson of October 27 (*Letters,* 5:41). But see below, September 12, where Emerson engages himself to Lynn for December 10. Frothingham's undated letter with its annotation cannot be later than September 12, for by that date Emerson no longer had December 10 free. See also, below, letter of November 1 to Samuel Longfellow.]

To Thomas Carlyle, Concord, August 22, 1856

[The MS of this letter is in the Humanities Research Center, University of Texas, Austin. The text differs slightly from Moncure D. Conway's copy (Slater, pp. 512–513). Conway changed Emerson's "or" to "nor" and omitted "the other day" from the last sentence. There are changes in punctuation and spelling; ampersands are expanded to "and."]

---

names of Holmes and Fields and the line with Channing's name are checked in the margin. The check marks appear to have been made with the same pen and at the same time as the letter was written.

To Francis Underwood, Concord, August 26, 1856[92]

Concord, 26 August,
1856.

My dear Sir,

I did not receive your note until the Boston train had already gone on Saturday. I am well contented that the Club should be solidly organized, & grow.[93] I am so irregularly in town, that I dare not promise myself as a constant member, yet I live so much alone that I set a high value on my social privileges, & I wish by all means to retain the right of an occasional seat.

So, with thanks, & best wishes,

Yours,
R. W. Emerson

Mr. Underwood.

To Charles Sumner, Concord, August 26, 1856[94]

Concord, 26 Aug.t 1856

My dear Sumner,

I read with joy the good news you sent me of your better health,[95] & hastened to impart it to Mr ⟨C⟩Hoar, Senior,[96] who received it, with his piety, like a good providence. and then to some younger friends who deserved to know it. Deeply as I grieve that Massachusetts should be crippled in these days in the Senate, I trust that your physician will not suffer any haste or impatience to risk the permanent cure of his patient. Your suffering has been a strange manifest benefit to the country; your

92. MS in the Barrett Collection, Alderman Library ViU; ph. in NNC; printed by Bliss Perry, *Park-Street Papers* (Boston: Houghton, Miflin, 1908), p. 232.

93. The club in this case is not the Saturday Club but the informal group known as "The Magazinists" or "The Atlantic Club"; Underwood is engaged in promoting a new magazine to be established in 1857 as *The Atlantic Monthly*. Membership in the two groups overlapped, but the clubs were essentially different in conception and purpose. See below October 4.

94. MS in the R. M. S. Jackson papers, Pattee Library, PSt; ph. in NNC; printed by Emil Freniere, *ESQ* (1st q., 1961), 22:47. With this is a mounted clipping from the envelope; addressed: Hon Charles Sumner | Cresson—|Allegheny Mts | Pennsylvania; postmarked at Concord, August 26.

95. Emerson is answering Sumner's letter of August 16 written from Cresson, Pennsylvania (RWEMA). Sumner describes his physician as treasuring his book (*English Tracts*) by Emerson, reports that Furness had visited too, and refers to Emerson's beautiful speech "here." There is no evidence that Emerson had lectured in Cresson or in the cities (Altoona, Johnstown) near it. Sumner is probably referring to Emerson's speech of May 26, 1856 (*Works*, 11:247–252), at a public meeting in Concord held four days after Congressman Preston Brooks' attack on Sumner.

96. Samuel Hoar.

health, I confide, will be a pure & splendid benefit to it. Bad times are bitter when passing; but, if well used, how glorious forever afterward! The approach & fusion of sensible & forcible people of all shades of party was never so swift as now. And many good signs appear. Who is your physician & friend? Is it Dr Robert Jackson,[97] once of Bairsville? I infer so much from what you say. If so, I desire the kindest remembrances to him, as to an old friend. The love of all good men & all good spirits keep you!

R. W. Emerson

To Samuel Joseph May, Concord, August 26, 1856 [98]

Concord ⎤ 26 August
Mass.   ⎦ 1856

Dear Sir,

Forgive me, if you can, my heavy head, which blundered so badly at the first lines of your letter & gave you all this trouble.[99] And now my hearty thanks follow it, for the hospitable reception you gave to the poor little book. Certainly I ought to hold myself prearranged to come to Syracuse, when you please to call me. And yet I dare not say I will come on the holiday you so honorably keep; for, though it looks fair & gay at this interval, I know by much experience that, when it draws nigh, it will find me in the thick of my tasks,—which, I know, look like a game, to all serious people, but are peremptory to me. I should like well to hear your Tyrtaean speeches of that rare quality, that—non resistant as you are— drives men to break heads.[100] I should like well to hear Gerrit Smith, of whose renown I have happened lately to hear more & better than ever.

97. Dr. Jackson is listed by Emerson as an honorary member of the Town and Country Club (*JMH*, 11:237); Freniere gives an account of him.

98. MS in Rare Book Department, NIC; ph. in NNC. The letter is complete; Emerson simply breaks his postscript with "but."

99. See above, August 15, for note of Emerson's returning unread Samuel May's letter of August 13 (RWEMA) because he assumed that addressed "Dear Doctor" it was not for him, as it was; being praise of *English Traits*, a request for a bill, and an invitation to attend a celebration, October 1, of the rescue of the fugitive slave "Jerry." Gerrit Smith is to preside. Emerson answers both May's original letter and a second letter of August 20 (RWEMA). Since Emerson ignores the request for a bill, I conjecture that he had given a free lecture in Syracuse, but he did not visit Syracuse in the 1855–1856 season. He did speak on slavery in Syracuse on February 25, 1855. The 25th was a Sunday, and he may well have spoken also in May's church.

100. In his *Some Recollections of our Antislavery Conflict* (Boston: Fields, Osgood, 1869), pp. 372–383, May gives an account of the rescue (1851) of the fugitive slave William Henry, known as "Jerry." See also Stanley W. Campbell, *The Slave-Catcher 1850–1860*, pp. 154–157. The arrest of "Jerry" had taken place when there was a large gathering of abolitionists in Syracuse: a prime mover among them was Gerrit Smith (see also above, May 29, 1855).

But such things, I see plainly, are not very likely to be in store for me, on the 1 October. I will keep the day in mind, & try to write you a letter.[101] Honor evermore to your love of freedom & of man![102] And with my private thanks,

Yours,
R. W. Emerson

Rev. Mr May.

Thanks specially for the Oration,[103] which was sent me—by you? I have read it well, & have somewhat to say of one particular, but—

To Austin Adams, Concord, August 26, 1856[104]

Concord ⎱ 26 August
Mass.tts. ⎰ 1856

Dear Sir,

I should be very glad to come to Dubuque, but at present I dare not promise it. I shall probably go west, a little way, in the winter, but perhaps not farther than B[u]ffalo; but probably to Chicago. I am not ready now to say that I can go farther. If I find, hereafter, that I can make a longer excursion, I will write you to give me any vacancy that may occur in your programme.

Respectfully,

Mr Adams.　　　　　　　　　　　　　　　　　　　　R. W. Emerson

101. Emerson apparently means that he will try to write a public letter suitable for the celebration on October 1. I find no record of such a letter.

102. Emerson has so written his exclamation point that only the period is visible when the letter is folded. The vertical falls in the margin of the first page.

103. May had delivered a Fourth of July oration in Jamestown, New York; it was printed with the title *Liberty or Slavery, the Only Question*. Possibly it is this oration Emerson refers to, although the wording of this postscript leaves the matter in doubt. If a speech by Gerrit Smith is meant, then the only 1856 printing recorded in *NUC* is his Albany speech on suffrage (February 28, 1856). No separate printing of his March 15 speech at the Albany Kansas meeting is listed.

104. MS in the Iowa Archives, State Department of Archives; ph. in NNC. Single sheet, the right-hand corner is damaged affecting the divided word Buffalo on the verso. Printed in the *Iowa Journal of History and Politics* (April 1927), 25:240–241; listed *Letters*, 5:33. Emerson did not get to Dubuque until 1866. The MS Pocket Diary for 1857 (*JMN*, 14:454), has on the rear flyleaf a list of correspondents with the towns they represent. Adams' name appears on the list.

To SARAH ANN CLARKE, CONCORD, SEPTEMBER 2, 1856[105]

> Concord, 2 September,
> 1856.

My dear friend,

You find me the slowest of all your correspondents, & yet none of your friends was more glad to hear of your return. I have all manner of debts to you, & I accept my indebtedness as the good will of God toward me. You will admire my Turkish piety, and ask whether my resignation extends also to the bounties of your Roman friends, who sent me their poems, & had no tidings even of their arrival. On seeing Lowell a few days ago, I found he knew Torlonia, & when I mentioned my purpose of writing to him, he told me it was entirely needless, for he had made every apology for me, & that Torlonia was satisfied.[106] So you see I have reason to fold my hands, & thank the gods. But I wish to see you, and to hear all you will please to tell me. When shall it be? We are entirely free in this house & sit listening for your wheels. When will you come?[107] My wife sends you her cordial greeting, & prays for your earliest leisure. Ellen, Edith, & Edward, my children three, are old enough, to the youngest, to fell a warm interest in the matter and so I entreat you to come, & we will try to make this cold house ⟨w⟩comfortable to you for as many days as you can give us. Elizabeth Hoar returns tonight or tomorrow from New Haven.[108]

> Yours affectionately,
> R. W. Emerson

Miss Sarah Clarke.

To MOSES DRESSER PHILLIPS, CONCORD, SEPTEMBER 4, 1856

[A letter of September 4, 1856, to Moses Dresser Phillips is twice listed by Cameron from an unspecified English catalogue: *ESQ* (2dq., 1956), 3:5; and (4th q., 1958), 13:40. The letter is described as asking Phillips for an account. There must have been other letters to Phillips in this year, written by Emerson on Carlyle's behalf as well as his own.]

105. MS in the Clarke papers, Houghton Library, MH; ph. in NNC.
106. Lowell had spent the spring of 1856 in Italy, returning to this country in mid-August. Emerson had probably seen him at a Saturday Club dinner. The poet is Giovanni Torlonia (1831–1858); his *Poesie* was published in Rome in 1856 by Bertinello.
107. I find no reference to this visit in the letters or journals.
108. For Elizabeth Hoar's expected return, see *Letters*, 5:34.

To John Winship, Concord, September 11, 1856[109]

Concord, 11 Sept. 1856

Dear Sir,

If Thursday 13, Nov.r suit your Lyceum, you may hold me engaged for that day.

Respectfully,
R. W. Emerson.

Mr Winship.

To William Howland, Concord, September 12, 1856[110]

Concord, 12 Sept. 1856

Dear Sir,

You shall then hold me engaged to you for Wednesday, 1⟨2⟩0 December.

Respectfully,
R. W. Emerson

Mr Howland.

To Samuel Gray Ward, Concord, September 12, 1856[111]

Concord, 12 Sept. 1856.

My dear friend,

By all means, & do not forget tis the last Saturday of each month. For the Scot,—I always pay through Woodman. I was in town Wednesday,

109. MS in Special Collections, Butler Library, NNC; ph. in NNC. Listed *Letters*, 5:38, under the conjectured date of October 1 from Winship's reply, which is dated only "Oct." Winship accepts the date proposed here for a lecture in South Reading, and the engagement is so listed in the MS Pocket Diary for 1856, *JMN*, 14:438. The receipt of $20.00 is listed in the MS Account Book for 1853–1859, p. [68] in an entry dated only November (listed Charvat, p. 32).

110. MS in the Feinberg Collection, MiD; ph. in NNC; printed by Harding from Carnegie Book Shop Catalogue no. 223, February 1958, in *ESQ* (4th Q., 1958), 13:35 and also by Cameron, *ibid.*, p. 41; reprinted by White, *AL* (May 1961), 33:168. See *Letters*, 5:35, and n. 121, for earlier letters about this lecture engagement in Lynn. Emerson is here replying to Howland's letter of September 5 (RWEMA). The receipt of $25.00 from Lynn is entered under the date December 10 in the MS Account Book for 1853–1859, p. [72].

111. MS in the Ward papers, Houghton Library, MS; ph. in NNC; incompletely printed in *EYSC*, p. 16; listed *Letters*, 5:36.

but not with time enough to see your portfolio of the School of Design,[112] which I hope is not yet gone.

Always yours,
R. W. E.

S. G. Ward.

To Joseph Hutcheson, Concord, September 15, 1856[113]

Concord 15 Sept
Mass.tts. 1856

My dear Sir,

You have mentioned in your note 22 & 23 January for lectures.[114] It will please me well to come to Columbus again, but Monday 19th, & Tuesday 20th January will suit me better /then the days you name/. If I go to you, I suppose I must accept invitations at Chicago, & I write now to my correspondents there to name the same week for my visit.[115] I shall presume, in writing to them, that you will let me keep these days I name, and if they are content to receive me in the same week to their two societies, I shall settle it so. If anything makes the days impracticable for you, perhaps a little more writing may fix another day.

Yours, with kind remembrances,[116]
R. W. Emerson

Jos. Hutcheson, Esq.

112. The Boston School of Design is meant; in a diary entry of March 24, 1852, Anna Ward notes "Sam gone to School of Design meeting" (MS copy of portion of Mrs. Ward's diary, MH).

113. MS in Autograph File, Houghton Library, MH; ph. in NNC; p. [4] endorsed by recipient R. W. Emerson | Sept. 15, 56 |.

114. Emerson is answering Hutcheson's letter of September 5 (RWEMA) requesting two lectures for the Athenaeum in Columbus, Ohio, for which Emerson had lectured on January 24. Hutcheson writes as Secretary of the Lecture Committee. The 1857 dates Emerson proposes here were accepted. (Charvat, pp. 32, 33).

115. Only one Chicago lecture, on January 22, 1857, is recorded (Charvat, p. 33). See Letters, 5:36, where the letter to Edwin S. Wells and W. T. Helm of the Metropolitan Literary Union is recorded; see below for note of letter to John Howland Thompson of the Young Men's Association. It is for the latter that the one Chicago lecture was arranged. See Letters, 5:38, for second letters to these Chicago correspondents.

116. This complimentary close suggests that on his earlier visit to Columbus, Emerson had been Hutcheson's guest.

To John Witt Randall, Concord, September 15, 1856[117]

Concord, 15 Sept. 1856.

My dear Sir,

I thank you heartily for your kind gift of the Poems,[118] so truly named, & so truly written. I had borrowed them of Elizabeth Hoar, read them with much interest, as celebrating places & experiences which are mine also; and I pleased myself that, some day, our walks might meet[119] —you at the extreme of your ramble & I at the extreme of mine, I sent E. H. some note of what I found in the book. Now I shall keep it by me for the weather & mood that require it. I have no verses to send you in return, but shall ask my publisher to send you a copy of my "English Notes,"[120] and, if the prose is extreme, I hope you will lay it to the necessities of the theme. With great regard,

yours,

R. W. Emerson

Mr Randall.

To John Howland Thompson, Concord, September 15, 1856

[See above, September 15, where Emerson tells Hutcheson that he is writing to his Chicago correspondents to accommodate these dates to the one he proposes for Columbus, Ohio.]

To Cyrus Augustus Bartol, Concord, September 16, 1856[121]

Concord, 16 Sept
1856

My dear Bartol,

I am deeply in your debt, & over & over again for steady friendliness always shown in word & deed, & now lately for these fine sayings about my poor little book, which fine sayings shall not turn my old head if I can

117. MS in MH-AH; ph. in NNC, with envelope addressed: J. W. Randall Harrison Avenue Boston. Printed by John Witt Randall, *Poems of Nature and Life*, F. E. Abbot, ed. (Boston: George H. Ellis, 1899), p. 12. The printed version is dated September 11.

118. See Eli, p. 224, for Emerson's copy of Randall's *Consolations of Solitude*, corrected in ms. by the author. See also above, July 14, for Emerson's letter to Elizabeth Hoar.

119. Randall, with his sister Belinda, lived in Roxbury.

120. *English Traits*, finally published, *BAL*, 5226; M. A24.1.a, pp. 242–243.

121. MS in the Providence Athenaeum, ph. in NNC; printed in the *Athenaeum Bulletin* (March 1934), Vol. 6, where the letter is conjectured to be a reply to a letter by Bartol acknowledging his presentation copy of *English Traits*. Emerson is answering two letters by Bartol, one of August 14 and the other of August 24 (in the Cabot papers, Schlesinger Library, Radcliffe). In the first (ph. in NNC), Bartol praises the book which he had already

help it. But I have been very sorry I could not come down & spend another day with you by the sea, & gaze at one of your great storms. As it is, I carry my week of sunshiny sea in my memory as the East Indian sews into his clothes the diamond which is to be his estate.[122] I look to draw on it in many a cloudy day & year. I & mine remember the bright peaceful week; and the young people are very well pleased to be remembered by you in your invitation to come & compare notes with Lizzie, & learn of her all that befel.[123] They promise themselves to come & see her by & by, & learn the immutable conditions of term time & holiday, and, I doubt not, they will be able to win her to our pastures & boat-rides, one day. My wife has claimed & seized the book of the West Church as her own. I read sometimes in the European Pictures, &, last Sunday, the two chapters of History & Destiny,[124] full of culture & thought & tenderness. Yours constantly,

R W Emerson

To ALBERT HALLER TRACY, CONCORD, SEPTEMBER 17, 1856[125]

Concord⎱ 17 Sept.
Mass.tts ⎰ 1856

My dear Sir,

Your note gave me true pleasure, for I know well the value of your suffrage—I am heartily contented too with the promise it flatters me with, that, I shall have new opportunity of conversing with you once & again in the coming days. Well, I shall not come to Buffalo again, without seeing to it, that neither your affairs nor my affairs shall be suffered to be pleaded in bar of my having a solid sitting, or a set-to, if you please, wherein I may ask all the questions & win all the answers I can. In which good hope, I rest, yours, with great respect,

R. W. Emerson.

A. H. Tracy, Esq.

---

read, having borrowed Edwin Percy Whipple's copy; he tells Emerson not to send him a copy; see August 1 above. The letter of August 24 acknowledges the book and invites Emerson's daughters to spend a week in Boston.

122. See above, May 1, for the week with the Bartols at Pigeon Cove, Cape Ann.

123. Ellen Emerson, in a letter from Pigeon Cove of July 18, gives a lively description of the visit, mentioning "Lizzie," Elizabeth Bartol, the Bartols' daughter.

124. Although there are a number of works by Bartol in Emerson's library, these two are not among them. The books are probably *Pictures of Europe* (Boston: Crosby, Nichols, 1855), and *The West Church and Its Ministers* (Boston: Crosby, Nichols, 1856).

125. MS in Special Collections, NNC; ph. in NNC. Emerson is replying to Tracy's letter of September 10 (RWEMA) in praise of *English Traits*. See *Letters*, 5:53, n. 10, where Rusk identifies Tracy and refers to his letter giving the date as 18 (or 10?). This reply from

To Phebe Farnham Cobb, Concord, September 29? 1856

[In a letter of September 29, n.y., endorsed 1856 by Emerson (RWEMA), Emerson's cousin Phebe Cobb invites the Emersons to dine with the Reverend Orville Dewey and his wife on Wednesday, October 1. Louisa Dewey was a Farnham and therefore also a cousin. Emerson would certainly have to answer.]

To Louis Agassiz et al., Concord, October 2? 1856

[Emerson's letters of October 4 and October 8 below show that he wrote invitations for his dinner party of October 11 to Louis Agassiz, Hammatt? Billings, Benjamin Peirce, Samuel Gray Ward, Edwin Percy Whipple, and Horatio Woodman. The dinner originally to be given in Concord had to be changed to the Parker House in Boston because of Ellen Emerson's illness. Letters to Ebenezer Rockwood Hoar and Thoreau are possible. The letter of October 8 below lists the guests, and see notes.]

To Francis H. Underwood, Concord, October 4? 1856

[In the November 1940 list of the American Autograph Shop is listed (item 66) a quarto letter to Francis Underwood of one page dated "Saturday, 3d October" and described as "dealing with a note for Mr. Lowell." See the fully, though incorrectly, dated letter to Lowell above. I believe that the letter here described is the cover to Underwood Emerson there refers to and that he has again misdated his note.]

To James Russell Lowell, Concord, October 4 1856 [126]

Concord 3 Oct. 1856
Saturday.

Dear Lowell,

Do not let any of the new Clubbists [127] hold you for Saturday next; for I wish to put you on your goodness to come & dine with me then. Agassiz has promised to come, & we will bring you some more friends who wish to behold you. [128]

Emerson shows that Tracy's letter must be of the 10th. See also February 14, 1855, above. Emerson would lecture in Buffalo on January 13, 1857.

126. MS in the Barrett Collection, Alderman Library, ViU; ph. in NNC; listed in *Letters*, 5:38, from a booksellers' catalogue. Saturday fell on the 4th in 1856.

127. This letter helps to clear up the confusion of the club. The "new Clubbists" are apparently the group known as "The Magazinists"; Emerson does not want Underwood, zealous promoter of the magazine that will come into being in 1857, to get hold of Lowell for a dinner on Saturday (October 11), hence his tactic of sending the letter in Underwood's care. See also August 26 above.

128. See *Letters*, 5:38 and 39, for additional letters to Lowell about this dinner which had to be transferred to Parker's in Boston because of Ellen Emerson's illness.

I send this to Mr Underwood, hearing that you will come to town today, & fearing the "entangling alliances."

Yours constantly,
R. W. Emerson

Mr Lowell.

To Melusina Fay, Concord, October 7? 1856

[See below, August 22, 1859, for a letter to Zina Fay; the letter reads as if there had been earlier correspondence. Together with Emerson's mention of Miss Fay's sister Laura in his letter of January 17, 1857, to his wife (*Letters*, 5:56), it allows the conjecture that Emerson answered Zina Fay's first letter to him, October 5, 1856 (RWEMA). Miss Fay takes him to task for a passage in *English Traits* which she was then reading. Quoting his account of a talk with Carlyle and "Mr. H." (Arthur Helps) on the subject of "the dogma of no government and non-resistance" (*Works*, 5:287), she refers him and Carlyle to the Bible, where irreligious moralists will learn that their so-called dogma is by Christians called the millennium. She regrets that she finds "no Christianity" in his book "from one end of it to the other." Since he is no Christian, he cannot alleviate "the wounds & sores & anguish of humanity." Rebuking him as a mere "Theorist," she writes: "when you die someone else will succeed you with new theories, & you will not be like Latimer or Herbert, or Milton, or Luther, or Calvin or Zwingli, but like Hobbes & Voltaire or any other proud visionary." The letter is the kind of letter Emerson would answer, I think, even if his wife did not urge him to.]

To Martha Robinson, Concord, October 7? 1856

[The MS Account Book for 1853–1869, p. [146], under the date October 7, 1856, has a record of $10.00 in cash sent the Reverend Lincoln Ripley "in a letter to Miss Robinson." Martha Robinson was Ripley's adopted daughter; see, above, June 16, 1853. A letter from Mary Moody Emerson, September 23, n. y. (endorsed by Emerson 1856, RWEMA), reported that "Uncle Ripley" had not received any help recently from Emerson. I think Miss Emerson's letter prompted this gift. Possibly Emerson wrote also to his aunt, but there is no evidence.]

To Horatio Woodman, Concord, October 8, 1856[129]

Concord
Wednesday, 8 Oct.r

My dear Sir,

I am not in good plight for my little party on Saturday. My daughter remains quite weak, though not otherwise attacked, & my wife is ill. I

129. MS in the Woodman papers, MHi; ph. in NNC. The year is secure from a series of letters to James Russell Lowell; October 4 above, and see *Letters*, 5:38, 39.

hope they may both be right again directly, but think it prudent to change to place of my little party to Parker's, at the same hour, 2½ clock Saturday. And now I must pray you to help me out with it. I shall invite Agassiz, Pierce, Judge Hoar, Billings, Lowell, Whipple, /Ward,/[130] & yourself;—and perhaps one or two more. Thoreau I suppose will refuse to go there, though you should have had him here. Will you not secure the room for me & aid me with some good advices necessary. I shall come to your rooms in a day or two to be set right.

Yours with great regard
R. W. Emerson

Mr Woodman.

To Louis Agassiz, et al., Concord, October 8, 1856

[Changing the place of his October 11 dinner party, Emerson would have to notify his guests. See above, October 8, where the guests are listed and *Letters*, 5:38, 39, where letters to Lowell of October 7 and 8, show that Emerson decides to make the change on October 8. I let this entry stand for these likely letters.]

To Samuel Longfellow, Concord, October 10, 1856[131]

Concord, 10 October,
1856.

My dear Sir,

I was surprised & vexed not a little, when, this evening, on returning from Boston, my wife showed me a couple of letters, received a fortnight ago, which a careless girl had mislaid, & ⟨h⟩which had never been shown me. I hasten to say that if it is not too late I should like very well to come to Brooklyn & do as you bid me.[132] It looks to me at the first glance as if

---

130. Before the insertion of "Ward," a name is heavily marked out; no letter is legible; the name appears to have nine or ten letters and to include in it one letter with an ascender and one with a descender. Louis Agassiz, Benjamin Peirce (Emerson usually misspells the name), Ebenezer Rockwood Hoar, Hammatt (?) Billings, Edwin Percy Whipple, James Russell Lowell, Samuel Gray Ward. According to a letter of Ellen Emerson (see above, notes for October 4), Sanborn was invited. The MS Account Book for 1853–1859, p. [146], under the date October 17, shows the payment of $34.00 to Parker's for dinner for "10 persons"; Sanborn would make ten.

131. MS in the Feinberg Collection, MiD; ph. in NNC; printed by White, *AL* (May 1961), 33:168–169.

132. See *Letters*, 5:39–40 and n. 135, where William Emerson's letter reporting Samuel Longfellow's concern at not hearing from Emerson is quoted. The letter of October 14 printed there is the "more definite answer" referred to here; it proposes that the series begin on November 24. The plans for Brooklyn fell through because the governors of New York and Massachusetts proclaimed different days for Thanksgiving, an important holiday for

I might arrange a short Course of 5 or 6 Lectures to read to you between 25 Oct. & 10 Nov.r; but, tomorrow or Monday, I will try to send you a more definite answer. I write now merely to explain my silence.

Yours faithfully,
R. W. Emerson.

Rev. S. Longfellow.

To William Francis Channing, October 11, 1856 [133]

Concord, 11 Oct.r 1856

My dear Sir,

I shall be glad to obey you if I can. [134] I have no lecture written which I can think of offering you, but I have something in preparation [135] which I will try to get ripe, or at least presentable by the beginning of November. It would heartily gratify me if I thought I could so give a couple of hundred dollars to Kansas.

Yours faithfully
R. W. Emerson

Dr W. F. Channing

To Hannah E. Stevenson, Concord, October 14? 1856

[In a letter of October 13, n.y., endorsed 1856 by Emerson (RWEMA), Hannah E. Stevenson asks Emerson to supply Theodore Parker's pulpit. A fully dated letter (RWEMA) of the same day from the Reverend John Turner Sargent gives the date "next" Sunday (19th) and Parker's going west as the reason; Sargent refers to Miss Stevenson as Parker's "right hand man." Sargent is anxious to let Emerson know that he will not take the devotional part of the services, for he is as unwilling to do Emerson's praying as he is Parker's preaching. There is nothing to show whether Emerson obliged Parker, but he would have to answer Miss Stevenson.]

---

the Emersons (see *Letters*, 5:46, n. 153), and for Emerson's attempt to work out new dates, see below, November 1.

133. MS privately owned; ph. in NNC.

134. The letter implies that Dr. Channing had asked Emerson to give a lecture (in Boston?), the proceeds of which would go to the Kansas Relief Fund for which he had already spoken in Cambridge on September 10 (see Charvat, p. 32). There is no record of his giving a second lecture for this purpose. Without a record and Channing's letter, there is no clue for conjecture. And see below, the letter of November 27 to Edward Atkinson, in which he refuses to give a lecture for the benefit of Kansas.

135. The lecture referred to is "The Conduct of Life"; see *Letters*, 5:40, where he gives this title to "a new lecture not quite ready." The lecture, "Works & Days," was apparently not ready until January.

TO MONCURE DANIEL CONWAY, CONCORD, OCTOBER 16, 1856[136]

Concord, October 16, 1856.

My dear sir,—I remember well your pleas for the "Church of Freedom" in Washington, made in our town hall last June.[137] On that occasion, after your discourse, and after a statement made by one of your friends, Lieutenant-Governor Brown,[138] touching the wants of the church, in which most of the champions of freedom worshipped,—and I think he said the only one in Washington where the civil freedom of all men was vindicated,—one of our citizens, W. S. Robinson,[139] rose and put the question to you, what security had we that any moneys now to be contributed by us would go to a "Church of Freedom" (in the sense in which the term was used that night, that is, Antislavery). You answered that you would see that this money went to no other; or somewhat to that effect. So Mr. Robinson tells me, and so other gentlemen say.[140]

We cannot recall the words, but all agree that the answer was satisfactory, and the contribution was made.

The amount was small, but it was demanded and paid on the claim of Anti-slavery.

Many years ago I had the happiness of obtaining from my old church, the "Second Church" in Boston, $300 for the benefit of this same religious society in Washington.

I entreat you and them not to make us ashamed of our spending, by perverting the church to the support of slavery.

136. The MS has not been located; text from Moncure Daniel Conway, *Autobiography*, 1:243. Listed *Letters*, 5:40.

137. Conway had raised $1,699.90 for the First Unitarian Church of Washington, but the church had dismissed him for his political activities; see Mary E. Burtis, *Moncure Conway* (New Brunswick: Rutgers University Press, 1952), p. 57. In a letter to Emerson of October 7, endorsed 1856 (Conway papers, NNC.), Conway tells Emerson of his dismissal and his hope to start a new church. It is to secure the sum for the new church that he appeals to Emerson for a "certificate" testifying to what had gone on at the Concord meeting. He wants Emerson to say "that before any collection was taken up in the meeting on that evening the question was distinctly propounded by some one as to whether I was to remain at Washington, & if there was any danger that their money should go to the church for the suppression of free speech & I pledged them that their money would be safe in that regard and that only then did I obtain it."

138. Simon Brown, a Concord resident, was lieutenant-governor 1855–1856; he later edited the *New England Farmer*.

139. Probably William Stevens Robinson, born in Concord, and living there again 1854–1857, free-soil journalist and editor, well-known in 1856 for his "Warrington" letters to the *Springfield Republican*.

140. Emerson's MS Account Book for 1853–1859, p. [135], shows that he paid, June 9, James Tolman twice for "posters for Rev Mr Conway" and on June 14, 1856, he paid George Brooks, selectman $3.00 "for use of Town Hall for benefit of Washington Church."

To Samuel Gray Ward, Concord, October 16, 1856 [141]

Concord, 16 Oct.r 1856

My dear friend,

You were born under the best star, & your shadow is health giving. Ellen gets well & thrives under the delicious sense of being cherished. [142] Anne, & Ida Agassiz have written to her, [143] Mrs Lowell [144] nursed her at Cambridge, & she is haughty with your fostering & concern. The departure absence & return of Mrs Ward are days & weeks in her calendar from which time & life are measured & dated; [145] and she will count the hours to her coming, like one of your own children. The happiest winds fill her homeward sails!

Your promised box I found in my hall last night. [146] I have not opened it, nor shall, for the present, but it shall lie there for a good omen, bearing your name.

Ever yours,
R. W. E.

S. G. Ward.

To William Rounseville Alger, Concord, October 19, 1856 [147]

Concord, 19 Oct.r 1856

My dear Sir,

I have delayed thanking you for the gift of your book, [148] till I could look a little into it: and though I have not yet nearly done with it, I have made some eager search into the heart of it. The enterprize is very welcome to me, this brave sally into orientalism, & the attempt to popularize some of its richest secrets. And yet I own to some caprices or alternation of feeling on that subject. When it was proposed to me once to reprint "the Bhagvat" in Boston, [149] I shrunk back & asked time,

141. MS in the Ward papers, Houghton Library, MH; ph. in NNC.
142. For Ellen's illness, see above October 2 and 8.
143. Anna Ward, Ward's daughter; Ida, daughter of Louis Agassiz.
144. Possibly Anna Jackson Lowell.
145. Anna Barker Ward returned from Europe in later September. See February 14 and April 14 above.
146. See February 14 and April 14 above.
147. MS in the Beinecke Library, CtY; ph. in NNC; printed by Stanley Williams in *JEGP* (October 1927), 26:483–484; listed *Letters*, 5:40.
148. *The Poetry of the East* (Harding, p. 9).
149. In April 1853, the Reverend Luther F. Dimmick of Newburyport, to whom Emerson had lent his much battered copy of Charles Wilkins' translation (acquired in September 1845 and from then on generously circulated), asked if Emerson intended to get out an American edition and proposed to do so himself from Emerson's copy, if he agreed (a.l.s.,

thinking it not only some desecration to publish our prayers in the "Daily Herald," but also that those students who were ripe for it would rather take a little pains, & search for it, than find it on the pavement. It would however be as neglected a book, if the Harpers published it, as it is now in the libraries. Well, now we shall see the result of this middle course of yours, of collecting gems from so many mines & exhibiting them in the public Square. In the universal reading of our people, I have no doubt some extraordinary passages will go to extraordinary readers; and I think the carrying a poem to an imaginative mind in the right moment is worth living for. Your introductory chapter is rich & interesting, & every taste will find something to thank you for in your collections. For the new versions you have more courage than I and value fidelity far above music. I am terribly severe on this head with other people, and if I can meet with you at leisure mean to call you to strict account for the carelessness of your verse. But today I have only to send my thanks.

Yours with great regard.
R W Emerson

Rev. Mr Alger.

To ELLEN EMERSON, CONCORD? OCTOBER 21, 1856

[The MS Account Book for 1853–1859, p. [147], under the date October 21 records $10.00 "sent to Ellen."]

To ———, CONCORD, OCTOBER 27, 1856

[In *Letters*, 5:41, Rusk lists an inferred letter to Octavius Brooks Frothingham and suggests that a letter of October 27, 1856, listed by C. F. Libbie and Co. (May 9–10, 1911) may be the same. The Libbie catalogue shows that there was a letter of October 27, but see above, August 23, for the evidence that Frothingham's undated letter from which Rusk drew his inference cannot be later than September 12. This letter of October 27 might be to Frothingham, but it could be to Dwight H. Olmstead: see November 1 below for evidence that Emerson had recently written both of them.]

Dimmick to Emerson, April 9, 1853, RWEMA). In a letter as yet undiscovered, Emerson expressed his objections (a.l.s., Dimmick to Emerson, April 26, RWEMA; see *Letters*, 4:350–351); presumably the objections were those expressed here.

See *Letters*, 3:288 and 303, for Emerson's ordering and acquiring the Wilkins text, and *ibid.*, pp. 290, 293, 399, for his first acquaintance with it through a copy borrowed from Cabot. By the time he lent his own copy to Dimmick, it was so badly damaged that Dimmick took the liberty of sending it to his binder. See *Letters*, 4:479, for the difficulty of getting a copy. In 1873 Emerson is still counting the book among those that matter to him; see *Letters*, 6:246.

To Samuel Longfellow, Concord, November 1, 1856[150]

Concord, 1 Nov.n 1856

My dear Sir,

I am sorry to spin out my little affair to your annoyance.[151] I must modify again. I can take the ⟨da⟩four days you offer me, only reading 9th for 10th. Thus; December 1st, 5th, 8th, & 9th. On the 10 Dec. , I am engaged at home, &, I suppose, cannot easily be disengaged. If you think it better, I shall be well content ⟨for⟩to wait for some future fortnight, more propitious, when the words & the days shall run more to our minds. I find, too, that neither of the off days in this programme will serve either Mr Frothingham, or D H. Olmstead, to both of whom I have some debts. So let any trifle decide you to adjourn our plan for the present.

Ever yours,
R. W. Emerson

Mr Longfellow.

To Ellen Emerson, Concord? November 5? 1856

[In a letter to her sister Edith, Ellen Emerson says she has received her father's letter "with the hundred dollars from Miss Russell." Ellen's letter is dated from Cambridge "Thursday Nov. 7th 1856." The 7th of November did not fall on a Thursday in 1856; Ellen was boarding in Cambridge that year, but in no year in which the 7th was a Thursday, Ellen meant, I think, either November 6 or Friday, November 7. Mary Howland Russell had sent Ellen a hundred dollars in 1855 (see above April 17, 1855) and may well have done so again, though I find no record of it in the Account Book, unless the entry of November 17 is relevant; it reads: "Rec.d of Ellen T. E. on deposit 50.00" (MS Account Book 1853–1859, p. [68].

150. MS in the Longfellow papers, Houghton Library, MH; ph. in NNC. The MS has a note, in an unidentified hand, on p. [3] below Emerson's signature: "This letter was given me by my friend Samuel⸗Longfellow—brother of Henry W. Longfellow—this letter is written to ⟨Samuel⟩ H W—Longfellow." The erasure of the name Samuel and the substitution of the better known initials "H W" could perhaps have been an innocent act. The addressee is Samuel Longfellow; see above, October 10, and *Letters*, 5:39–40, 44–45, for Emerson's effort to find suitable dates for a series of lectures in Brooklyn where Samuel Longfellow was minister of the Second Unitarian Society.

151. Emerson is trying to work out a schedule that will allow him to lecture in Jersey City for Octavius Brooks Frothingham and in New York City for Dwight H. Olmstead; see *Letters*, 5:41, 46. These engagements he was finally able to fulfill on February 12 (New York) and February 13 (Jersey City); see Charvat, p. 33; both are listed in the Pocket Diary for 1857.

To George Sewall Boutwell, Concord, November 12, 1856

[In a letter of November 13, 1856 (RWEMA), George S. Boutwell says he is holding December 17 as the day for his lecture for the Concord Lyceum. Emerson has entered Governor Boutwell's name with that date in his schedule for the Concord Lyceum, MS Account Book for 1853–1859, p. [291]. According to the MS records of the Concord Lyceum (MCo), Edwin Percy Whipple gave his lecture on "Courage" on December 17; see *Letters*, 5:42, for a note of Whipple's original acceptance of December 10 and his later request for a change of date. Further correspondence with Boutwell is likely.]

To William Orne White? Concord? 1856?

[The Seven Gables Bookshop had, in 1960, a MS fragment cut from a letter (probably for the signature). The recto reads: "Keene strongly recommends to my acquaintance [word cut away] which he represent[s] [word cut away]. The verso reads: "but your obedient servant R. Waldo Emerson." Emerson had lectured in Keene, New Hampshire, on November 1, 1854, on the invitation of the Reverend William Orne White, to whom in 1856 he sent a copy of *English Traits* (a.ll.s. from White Oct. 27, 1854, and August 22, 1856). I simply guess that White (classmate and friend of Cabot) had made the recommendation referred to in the fragment. Other associations with Keene, New Hampshire, appear to have been transitory (see *Letters*, 1:144, 2:200 and n. 75, and 4:222).]

To James Freeman Clarke, Concord, November 18? 1856

[In Brian Kathenes' Catalogue 9, item 64 lists a letter of 1856 to James Freeman Clarke. It is quoted in part as saying that he will be returning "... from a promised meeting [?] in New Haven ... So if that day is still free to you for a meeting, I shall like very much to come. Wednesday is is still open too, of [if?] that suits you better." In 1856, Emerson's New Haven lecture was given on November 20, a Thursday. Emerson was free from lecture engagements the rest of the month. The Wednesday he refers to in the passage quoted would be the 26th; what day Clarke had proposed is not clear.

[The meeting proposed is, I believe, the first effort to revive the Transcendental Club of the 1830s and '40s. See below December 8 and 10; Cyrus Bartol's letters show that there had been an earlier meeting at Clarke's. The Radical Club of a later date may reasonably be regarded as a revival of the Transcendental Club.]

To Frederick Dan Huntington, Concord, November 25? 1856

[Frederick Dan Huntington wrote Emerson on November 26, 1856. The letter reads as if he were replying to a letter in which Emerson had tentatively promised some "words ... about your Concord patriarch Mr. Hoar. ..." Emerson may also have invited Huntington to give a lecture for the Concord Lyceum; the lyceum records show that Huntington did lecture on December 26. See *JMN*, 14:442, where Theodore Parker is down for the 24th, but apparently did not lecture that week; Huntington replacing him. See M, p. 673, entry E 128.]

To Edward Atkinson, Concord, November 27, 1856 [152]

Concord, 27 Nov. 1856

Dear Sir,

I am very sorry to be wanting to what seems so beneficent a plan in its aim & conduct as that you have communicated: [153] but my time for the next weeks & months even is quite as fully promised as I think is safe or prudent to public lectures. I dare not add one more, and am trying how I may make them fewer. Well, I shall feel my debt to Kansas a little increased by this refusal. In the best hope for the success of all efforts in its behalf, yours

respectfully,
R. W. Emerson

Mr Atkinson.

To Edwin Percy Whipple, Concord, December 1? 1856

[Emerson would have to answer Edwin P. Whipple's letter of November 30 asking to change the date of his lecture for the Concord Lyceum from Wednesday the 10th of December to Monday, Thursday, or Friday. The records of the Concord Lyceum show that Emerson obliged; Whipple lectured on Thursday, the 11th. See *Letters*, 6:42, and *JMN*, 14:442 and n. 40.]

To Samuel Gray Ward, Concord, December 4, 1856? [154]

Concord, 4 Decr

My dear Friend,

Forgive me the egotism of sending Henry James's fine long scolding of me, which yet Anna asked to see, as it held his Castilian courtesies for her. [155] I am safe, for she cannot find time to read it in the short days, and I will punctually demand it back. I enclose also Patmore's letter

152. MS in the Atkinson papers, MHi; ph. in NNC.
153. Atkinson had probably asked Emerson to lecture in the cause of raising funds for the relief of Kansas; see Harold Francis Williamson, *Edward Atkinson* (Boston: Old Corner Book Store, 1934), p. 4.
154. MS in the Ward papers, Houghton Library, MH; ph. in NNC. The year is secure from the allusion to Coventry Patmore's letter.
155. I find no letter from Henry James, Sr., that answers this description; an undated letter from London, printed by Perry, 1:83–84, does not seem to deserve the epithet "scolding."

which she brought me,[156] but which she has not seen.—Ticknor & Fields have already sent him money,—I so understood them,—& offers for his Book. Thanks for H. J.'s speculations, which I return. H. J. possesses with much finer things that talent of voluminous expression, which made the fortune of Dugald Stewart. Ellery C. made me laugh very heartily one day with equivocal compliments to Hawthorne, that he had the undeniable test faculty of narration, one event to every 140 pages, a cough took up ten pages, & sitting down in a chair six more.[157] I shall come to you on the 20th, as always, with gladness.

R. W. E.

To William Lloyd Garrison, Concord, December 5, 1856[158]

Concord Dec. 5 1856

My dear Sir,

I am heartily vexed that a note from you should remain so long unanswered. My correspondence happens to be in this month of Lyceums ridiculously large & complicated, & I have been absent from home, to make it worse.[159] For the proposition you convey to me & so kindly I hardly know what to say. My claims to sit with such high company, I see well are none but pure good will, faith without works. Then I have no tolerable print or drawing of any kind to send. I shall be in town on Monday,[160] &, if I am not better instructed in the mean time, will perhaps call on Mr Brainerd, & take advice on the possibilities of a sitting though I am a very bad sitter to the Daguerre artists.

Respectfully, & always gratefully
Yours,

Mr. Garrison.   R. W. Emerson

156. See *Letters*, 5:20–21, where Rusk prints Patmore's letter in full. Patmore there complains that Ticknor and Fields, American publishers of *The Angel in the House,* have not paid him.

157. See Hawthorne's *American Notebooks,* Centenary Edition, 8:357–358, for Hawthorne on Channing.

158. MS in the Montague Collection, Manuscript Division (Annex), NN; ph. in NNC.

159. Garrison's letter asking Emerson's cooperation in Charles Henry Brainard's project to get out a set of pictures of anti-slavery men is dated November 20; see Rusk, *Life,* p. 390. The volume was called *Heralds of Freedom* and was a companion for the earlier *Champions of Freedom* got out by the same publisher. The picture of Emerson is misleadingly described as a "bust" and misdated 1855 by Frank B. Sanborn in his "The Portraits of Emerson," in *The New England Magazine* (December 1897), 15(n.s.): 453, where it is reproduced, and p. 466 where it is described.

160. He has to be referring to his engagement in New Haven, Charvat, p. 32, on November 20. Although Danbury is entered in the Pocket Diary for 1856 (*JMN,* 14:438), there is no confirming entry in the Account Book for 1853–1860.

To Cyrus Augustus Bartol, Concord, December 8, 1856[161]

Concord, 8 Dec.r 1856

My dear Bartol,

I ought to have written you already to tell you what you already know, how much my girls enjoyed their visit, & how rich they have come home in experience and hope. Of course, their hope is to have Lizzie for their guest, when May days come again & before sea days arrive. My wife sends her kindest gratefullest regards to Mrs Bartol. Ellen tells me that you wish to hold a meeting of the Club, on one of these two Saturdays.[162] The next Saturday I shall be free, & I think Sanborn will. He shall know of the design, if you persist. The following Saturday, & the next after,, I shall not be free. I hoped, before we met again, Mr Alcott would return, & he may yet. The last I have heard of him was /that he was/ at Philadelphia. The only real barrier that I know to meetings now, ⟨is⟩besides the absences which the Lecture season must occasion, is, that the winter trains carry out the countrymen too early. Thus our /latest/ train is 5:30. Yet we must return, for it is Saturday night. If, in spite of these deductions, the meeting is called, I shall surely come. And will you please remember to write George P. Bradford, from Salem, who heard with great interest of the revival of the club after its sleep like a Seventeen-Years-Locust. Emanuel V. Scherb, too, should come, I think.

Ever yours,
R W Emerson

To Cyrus Augustus Bartol, Concord, December 10, 1856

[In a letter of December 10, 1856 (Cabot papers, Schlesinger Library, Radcliffe), replying to Emerson's letter of the 8th, above, Cyrus Bartol attempts to arrange the meeting at his house at a time that will permit Emerson to stay overnight. Regarding Emerson as the "sine qua non" for the meeting, Bartol makes several proposals and then in a postscript suggests Friday, December 19, when Edwin Percy Whipple can surely come. I conjecture that Emerson accepted the Friday date. See his letter of November 16 (*Letters*, 5:47), where he writes John Murray Forbes: "Friday, there is a kind of Club, which I am bound to attend." Bartol's letter invites Sanborn too, refers to an earlier meeting at James Freeman Clarke's, and, expecting a delay, hopes for Alcott's presence.]

161. MS in the New England Collection, MnM; ph. in NNC.
162. See December 10 below for Bartol's reply and the probability that this revived Transcendental Club met on Friday, December 19. There had been a meeting at James Freeman Clarke's, apparently before this correspondence of December 10.

To Samuel G.? Wheeler, Concord, December 20, 1856 [163]

Concord, 20 Dec. 1856

My dear Sir,

Your prompt & providing goodness makes me always your debtor. I am very much obliged by it, & shall accept your kind invitation with much pleasure.

Yours gratefully
R W Emerson

Mr Wheeler.

To Martha Robinson, Concord, December 25? 1856

[In the MS Account Book for 1853–1859, p. 152, under the date December 25, is a note of a "gift" of $10.00 to Lincoln Ripley. It probably went addressed to Martha Robinson, as earlier gifts did.]

To Wendell Phillips, Concord, December 31, 1856

[Listed in *ESQ* (2d q., 1956), 3:5, and again twice in (2d q., 1958), 13:40, from *The Collector;* quoted as reading in part: "You said in the street that you come to us next week. I find on my calendar your name marked for 14 January. . . . Mr Gilman is coming for the 7th. . . . he was engaged since you were & on the belief that you came on the 14th. I hope it is right." In 1856 Emerson was serving one of several terms as a curator of the Concord Lyceum. His MS Pocket Diary for 1857 lists Concord Lyceum lectureres on the last page; the list has Gilman down for the 7th and Phillips for the 14th (*JMN*, 14:454; the editors' pp. [173–174] refer to the flyleaf.) The MS records of the lyceum show that Arthur Gilman lectured on January 7.]

To William H. Fish, Concord, December 31, 1856

[A letter of December 31, 1856, is listed in item 296 of the catalogue of the American Art Association of December 1936. It is described as listing lecture engagements for January 1857. Emerson lectured in Cortland, New York, on January 14, 1857, and again on January 15, 1859 (see Charvat, pp. 33, 35). See *Letters*, 5:123–124 and 131, for note of letters to Emerson from the Reverend William H. Fish of McLean, New York. In a letter of September 23, 1856, Fish tells Emerson that he has formed an association for "Independent Lectures" to

163. MS in IaMc; ph. in NNC. The language of the letter implies an invitation given and accepted more than once. I conjecture that Wheeler has offered Emerson a ride home from Boston. On this day, a Saturday, Emerson was to dine with the Wards (*Letters*, 5:47). On Saturday the train service was poor (see December 8 above). Offered a ride, Emerson need not hurry away from his friends. Samuel G. Wheeler, father of Ellen Emerson's schoolmate (see October 24, 1853, above) had his business in Boston and his home in Concord. He might then be the Wheeler to whom the letter is addressed.

be given at Cortlandville. He tells Emerson that "We want every speaker to be himself—as of course you would be & give us his highest thought." He suggests one of the "Lectures for the Times" published in the *Dial*, "nobody perhaps in the neighborhood having heard of the Dial. They would get some of your peculiarities from one of them & some practical & useful." See *JMN*, 14:448, where a deleted entry for "MacLean," New York, appears. Charvat's record is derived from p. [74] of the MS Account Book for 1853–1859, where the receipts for January lectures are listed.]

1857

To Margaret Perkins Forbes, Concord, January 4, 1857[1]

Concord, ⟨3⟩4 Jany.

My dear friend,

I am very sorry I cannot come. How absurd & how mean it is to be promised elsewhere, when we are invited where we wish to go. What spite in the Powers, or what Sin it is of mine, that Mr Hunt could choose the days for his visit when I am going to Philadelphia & to Cincinnati & cannot meet him.[2] I had just been admiring his two pictures in Balch's picture shop with disinterestedness,[3] for I did not dream of seeing him & now y[ou] h⟨ave⟩ all things. and I can only say my farewells. But I shall come to Milton, on my return, to hear what you shall say.[4]

To William Mathews, Concord, January 5? 1857

[In the MS Account Book for 1853–1859, p. [154], under the date January 5, is the note: Pd. W. Mathews, Esq for 'London Leader' by E. L. Pierce 5.00." On February 14, 1856, William Mathews had written to Emerson from Chicago apologizing for the erratic delivery of the periodical, announcing the demise of the periodical, and asking for $5.00 for the 1866 numbers. Emerson is apparently

1. MS in Special Collections, Butler Library, NNC; ph. in NNC. One of a group of letters to Margaret P. Forbes from some of which the signatures have been carelessly cut away, as here, destroying part of the texts. Correspondence of 1859 (see below May 12, 1859, and *Letters,* 5:141) is about William Morris Hunt and would suggest that year, but in 1859 Emerson did not lecture in Philadelphia and Cincinnati, and by January 4 he was already in Baltimore. The letter had to be after 1855 (Hunt returned from Europe that year) and cannot be 1856. I choose the earliest possible year, the only one that satisfies the conditions; see Charvat, p. 33, for the lecture schedule of January and February 1857.

2. Margaret Forbes' brother John Murray Forbes admired Hunt's work; he could be said to have been Hunt's patron. Hunt's wife, Louisa D. Perkins, was a cousin of the Forbes.

3. See *EYSC,* for Edward Waldo Emerson's recollection of a visit to Hunt's Newport studio (p. 467) and his account of Hunt's unfinished portrait of Emerson, destroyed in the Boston fire of 1872 (p. 468).

4. Emerson was never a whole-hearted lover of art in spite of the tutelage of Samuel Gray Ward and Sarah Ann Clarke. A journal entry of 1858 (MS journal WA, p. 23) is revealing: "Blackbirds in hundreds; swallows in scores or tens, sitting on the telegraph lines, assisted, & one heron (ardea minor). Before these perfect pictures, what weary nonsense is the dreary collecting of rubbish canvas of rubbish masters, in the neglect of a lovely river-valley where the multitudinous life & grace makes their pictures ridiculous cold chalk & ochre." William T. Balch was a picture-framer; his shop was on Tremont Row.

sending the money via Edward L. Pierce. The Account Books show earlier payments without specifying means of delivery. The William Mathews named here is not Emerson's Swedenborgian friend from Birmingham (see 1848 *passim*), as the handwriting of his letter shows. I assume Emerson accompanied this belated payment with a note.]

To Susan Bridge Jackson? Syracuse? New York,
January? 16? 1857?

[In her letter of January 11, n. y., endorsed 1857 by Emerson (RWEMA), Edith Emerson reminds her father to thank "Aunt Susan" for the slippers she gave him. Edith has evidently been prompted by her mother to give Emerson this nudge. I conjecture that he obeyed. The donor of the slippers could have been Susan Haven Emerson, but I chose Lidian's sister-in-law as the more likely.]

To Horace Mann, Cincinnati, February 2, 1857[5]

Burnet House
Cincinnati, 2 Feb.y
1857

My dear Sir,

I own I was much ashamed when your telegraph⟨y⟩ic despatch came to me just now, that your letter, which I have carried with me for days, should remain unanswered, & need to add the spur of electricity to its urging.[6] But I am not so bad as I seem, having been on the road much of the time since I first had your note, & the least possible command of

5. MS in the Mann papers, MHi; ph. in NNC; printed by Louise Hastings, "Emerson in Cincinnati," *NEQ* (September 1938), 11:456.

6. Emerson is replying to a letter of January 22 from Horace and Mary Mann inviting him to visit Yellow Springs (Mann papers, MHi). Jogged by the telegram, Emerson now answers the letter. But Yellow Springs is entered in pencil against the date February 5 in MS Pocket Diary for 1857 (*JMN*, 14:449) and the records of the Antioch Adelphian Union record a lecture by Emerson on that day (Hastings, "Emerson in Cincinnati," n. 37). There is no record of any payment for a lecture. That Emerson did visit the college is clear from a letter of November 2, 1858 (see below), where he says it would give him "great pleasure to . . . see again the college, which received me once so kindly. . . ." In that letter of 1858 he has to be referring to a visit in 1857; from this letter to Mann it is clear that Emerson had not seen Antioch before then. The letter of 1858 is addressed to a student, Cyrus W. Christy, of the class of '60.

What evidently changed Emerson's mind is his receiving at noon on February 3 the MS of "A Plea for The Scholar," which he had telegraphed for on January 29 (see *Letters*, 5:61 and 62). He had then in hand a lecture appropriate for delivery to a college audience and, with February 5 free and Antioch accessible within a day, he could finally accept Mann's invitation. He was also saved the necessity of trying to write a new lecture for Conway's private course. Very likely he welcomed the chance to rehearse the reading of the lecture before repeating it in Cincinnati on February 6. As for Mary and Horace Mann, they were no doubt happy to produce Emerson at last; the first invitation is of 1854.

time here in C., <u>writing</u> as well as reading lectures & having many friends! But I suppose the effective cause of delay was the unwillingness to say what your telegraph forced out of me, that I could not come though so near. I read here on Friday night, & set out for home on Saturday morning, as I am bound to be in Boston on Tuesday. If the propositions which had been early made to me to add private lectures to that before the M. Library[7] had not been pressed on my arrival, I should gladly have found or sought opportunity to make you the visit you have repeatedly proposed, which my curiosity in /regard to/ the College, & my personal respect to you & yours urged. Well, the day is not yet done,[8] Yours gratefully,

R. W. Emerson.

To Marcus Spring, Cincinnati, February 2? 1857

[In a letter of January 25, 1857 (RWEMA), Marcus Spring invites Emerson to lecture for the community at Eagleswood. Spring sent his letter to Philadelphia in care of Furness who forwarded it to Concord. On the assumption that the letter then went to Cincinnati, I conjecture that Emerson could not have answered it much before February 2 (see Charvat, p. 33, for Emerson's lecture schedule). There is no evidence that he lectured for the Eagleswood community (near Perth Amboy, New Jersey), but I doubt that Emerson would have ignored a letter from Margaret Fuller's old friend.]

To Horace Mann, Cincinnati, February 3? 1857

[Having written Mann on February 2 (see above) that he could not visit Antioch, Emerson would have to notify Mann by letter or telegram that he could after all visit the Manns and the college.]

To Horace Mann, Cincinnati, February 3? 1857

[Emerson must have wired or written Horace Mann to tell him that he could come to Antioch after all. See above.]

7. Young Men's Mercantile Library Association, January 27. See Charvat (p. 33).
8. This sentence suggests that Emerson had hopes that the lecture telegraphed for would come.

TO CHARLES F. SMITH, CONCORD, FEBRUARY 17, 1857[9]

Concord
Tuesday 17 Feb

Dear Sir,

I am sorry to find that I am engaged at Roxbury on Tuesday, 3 March; and at Wrentham Tuesday, 24 Feb.y. I have no other Tuesday, or scarce any other day for a month to come, that is not now free.[10]

Respectfully,
R. W. Emerson

Mr Smith.

TO FREDERIC AUGUSTUS TENNEY, CONCORD, FEBRUARY 19? 1857

[The MS Account Book for 1853–1859, p. [155], between entries dated February 16 and 24, 1857, shows the payment of 65 cents for a telegram. Emerson's MS Pocket Diary for 1857 has under the date February 19 a deleted note of a lecture engagement in Newport and gives F. A. Tenney as the name of his correspondent; the same Pocket Diary shows a questioned Newport engagement for March 27 (*JMN*, 14:449, 450). In the Account Book entry the receipt of $20.00 from Newport is under the March date (Charvat, p. 33, requires correction). I conjecture that the measles which afflicted Emerson for three days, as he tells his brother (*Letters*, 4:63), obliged him to change the date of the Newport lecture and that this telegram asks for the change of date, though there is no proof. In a letter of March 3 Ellen Emerson reports her father recovered from the measles and "away again."

The Reverend F. A. Tenney is listed in the Newport directory for 1856–1857. A Frederic Augustus Tenney is listed in the class of 1853, Harvard Divinity School.]

TO STEPHEN HIGGINSON, CONCORD, FEBRUARY? 25? 1857

[See *Letters*, 5:63, for Higginson's letter of March 11 (RWEMA) which implies a letter to Higginson as well as the letter of recommendation for Higginson's son, Francis John Higginson.]

9. MS in the Houghton Mifflin papers, Houghton Library, MH; ph. in NNC. The MS Pocket Diary for 1857 shows these engagements at Wrentham and Roxbury (*JMN*, 14:450), and in 1857 the 17th of February fell on a Tuesday. See *Letters*, 5:43, for evidence of a letter of November 27, 1856, to Mr. Smith concerning a lecture date for 1857; Rusk reasonably conjectures the addressee to be Charles F. Smith of Charlestown. It is with Charles F. Smith, secretary of the Mishawum Literary Association, Charlestown, that Emerson corresponds in 1853 and 1862 (*Letters*, 4:394; 5:291). The Pocket Diary shows a deleted Charlestown engagement for February 10 and two entries for March: one for Friday, the 6th, and one for Tuesday, the 10th, deleted (*JMN*, 14:449, 450).

10. The MS Account Book for 1853–1859, p. [76], shows the receipt in March of $25.00 from Charlestown.

To Evert August Duyckinck, Concord, March 5, 1857 [11]

Concord

5 March 1857

My dear Sir,

I can have no objection to your use of the verses you wish to republish; only I wish they were better.[12]

Respectfully,

R. W. Emerson

Mr Duyckinck.

To ———, Concord, March 9, 1857

[In his letter of March 7, 1857, to John Murray Forbes (*Letters,* 5:66), Emerson promises to try to free himself from his engagement for March 18 at Gloucester; on the 12th he writes Forbes again that his correspondents are "slow and intractable" (5:67). Pretty clearly he wrote his Gloucester correspondent, not named in the MS Pocket Diary for 1857 or in the MS Account Book.]

To Franklin Benjamin Sanborn, Concord, March 30, 1857 [13]

30 March,

1857

My dear Sir

You are quite too careful a curator. I designed to make my subscription of $15., if that was it, to the Lyceum; but if you see how that is not needed by the Lyceum, ⟨ca⟩pray appropriate it to Mr B. of Kansas. Yours ever,

R. W. Emerson

To Fritz Rölker? Concord, April 7, 1857

[Twice listed by Cameron in *ESQ* from Percy J. Dobell's catalogue 97 (1947) is a letter of April 7, 1857, described as about a list of books on art and as addressed

11. MS in the Duyckinck papers, Manuscript Division, NN; ph. in NNC; with envelope addressed: Evert A. Duyckinck, Esq| New York|; postmarked at Boston March 6. Facsimile of letter and envelope in *The Bookman* (New York) (June 1903), 17:331; listed *Letters,* 6:65.

12. Duyckinck was selecting his "Additions" to the Reverend Robert Aries Willmott's *The Poets of the Nineteenth Century* (New York: Harper 1858), *BAL,* 1663, m. G34, p. 712. The poem, at p. 406, is "The Humble-Bee."

13. MS in the Abernethy Library, VtMiM; ph. in NNC; listed in *Letters,* 5:69; cited Rusk, *Life,* p. 397. In 1857, Emerson's fellow curators of the Concord Lyceum were the Reverend Grindall Reynolds and Frank Sanborn. Since "Mr B of Kansas" is surely John Brown, I take the "careful" curator to be Sanborn. I find no appropriate entry in the MS Account Book for 1853–1859. An entry of March 19 p. [160] records the payment of $10.00 to Sanborn

to "Dr Rother" (2d q., 1956, 3:5; 4th q., 1958, 13:40.). See above, letters of January 18 and 21, 1853, to Dr. Fritz Rölker of Cincinnati. Emerson's script could easily lead to mistaking "lk" for "th"; and more often than not he omits diacritical marks. I think it possible that this letter is to Dr. Rölker.]

To JOHN R. MANLEY, CONCORD, APRIL 22? 1857

[See below, April 24, to Manley.]

To JOHN R. MANLEY, CONCORD, APRIL 24, 1857?[14]

Concord
Friday, 24 April

Dear Sir,

You were kind enough to invite me to visit you on Sunday. I neglected in replying to your note to thank you for your hospitable offer, & to say that whenever I come into the city with errands of this nature, I find it mo⟨re⟩st convenient to stay at the "American House," Hanover Street.

Respectfully,
R. W. Emerson

Mr Manley.

To THE CORPORATION OF HARVARD UNIVERSITY, CONCORD, MAY 9, 1857[15]

Concord, May 9, 1857.

Gentlemen,

I learn with pleasure that Rev. Martin W. Willis of Nashua is a candidate for a Master's degree in Harvard University.[16] I think that if the

---

for John Brown, who had lectured in Concord in February and visited Emerson (*JMN*, 14:125–126), but this entry leaves $5.00 unaccounted for.

Pasted to the recto of the second leaf was a slip bearing four lines from Emerson's "Two Rivers," signed and dated Concord, Massachusetts—December 10, 1878. The poem is now filed separately.

14. MS in Special Collections, Butler Library, NNC; ph. in NNC. An "errand of this nature" can only be a public speech; Emerson did speak at the Music Hall, Sunday, April 26, 1857; see *Letters*, 5:72 and n. 99, for Emerson's letter of April 20 to Theodore Parker and Parker's letter of April 25, 1857. Parker's letter, dictated and unsigned, tells Emerson that "Mr. Cabot" is to call for him at the American House on Sunday morning and will escort him to the Music Hall. Since it is Manley who, in 1860, secured Emerson to speak at the exercises in honor of Parker (*Letters*, 5:220), I infer that he has here acted for Parker. Clearly there is an earlier letter to Manley. (Other possible years for this letter are ruled out.)

15. MS in the College Papers, 2nd Series, 24:177–178, Archives, MH; ph. in NNC; printed by Kenneth W. Cameron in "New Emerson Letters," *ESQ* (4th q., 1958), 13:96.

16. Martin Wyman Willis was graduated from the Harvard Divinity School in 1843; Emerson had known him at least since 1841 when he presented to him a copy of *Essays*

diploma honors the man, it will also in this instance honor the College. I
have known the history of Mr Willis, from his early youth, when he was
an excellent son, and very fond of books,—with some knowledge of his
successive homes & labors,—from all which a good report has come to
me, up to his present responsible position in Nashua. I have seen some
printed sermons & other matter from his pen: And I draw from what I
have heard & seen a belief that Mr Willis has earned by his own diligence
in good letter & arts, at least an equal title to honors from the University
to that which is derived from completing within its walls the course of
studies.

Respectfully,
R. W. Emerson

To the Corporation of
Harvard University.

To Thomas Carlyle, Concord, May 17? 1857

[Emerson encloses a letter to Carlyle with his letter of May 17 to his cousin George
Barrell Emerson; see below. George Emerson visited Carlyle on June 18.]

To George Barrell Emerson, Concord, May 17, 1857[17]

Concord
17 May, 1857

Dear George,

Thanks for your welcome letter, which came, I dare not say how many
days ago, & made me remember that I was to write you a note to Carlyle.
I trust this enclosed one will not be too late to find him in London, where
Parliament will keep people in town still. I give you joy on all the good
grand leisures you have been as I learn, employing so happily & well.
Botany[18] in Italy, to be sure, holds of semi-divine worlds traces, filled
with poetry & mythology, as it is. And so many other ties, too, as you
have to all that has been around you,—so much & various discipline &
preparation as you carry to the men & things!—I desire to be in the

---

(*JMN*, 7:546). There is no work by Willis in Emerson's library. The Andover-Harvard
Theological Library has his *Discourse on Christian Doctrine* (Bath: printed by Haines & Freeman, 1853). Willis received his honorary M.A. at Commencement.

    17. MS in the George Barrell Emerson papers, MHi; ph. in NNC.

    18. Emerson's cousin is the unnamed author of *A Report on the Trees and Shrubs Growing
Naturally in the Forests of Massachusetts . . .* (Boston: Dutton and Wentworth, State Printers,
1846).

favored company that shall have the early hearing of your story, when you come back. Give affectionate remembrances & congratulations from me & mine also to Mrs Emerson.[19] She also will see & hear for us all. We are living as usual in our dull industrious idleness here in Concord,— wife, Ellen, Edith, Edward & I,—the three younkers filled to the lips with schooling,—better far, as I think, than in my time: but the old ones cannot hug themselves much on their performings. With kindest remembrances & hopes, yours,

Waldo E.

To William Emerson, Jr., Concord., May 24? 1857

[Emerson's letter of May 26 below implies a letter to his nephew advising him about his western trip.]

To Elihu Burritt, Concord, May 25? 1857

[In a letter of May 21, 1857 (RWEMA), Elihu Burritt asks Emerson to endorse, attend, and address a national convention to advocate compensated emancipation. Some answer is likely. A letter of the same date from Theodore Parker encloses a letter from a "Mr B" and asks Emerson how to answer it; I simply guess that Parker refers to Burritt here. Burritt held his first convention in Cleveland in August 1856; Emerson had been invited to attend that one; there is no record of his attending either; see Merle Curti, *The Learned Blacksmith* (New York: Wilson-Erickson, Inc., 1937), p. 120.]

To Rebecca Vose Stetson, Concord, May 26, 1857[20]

Concord, 26 May,
1857

Dear Mrs Stetson,

My nephew, William Emerson, jr. Esq., late of the Cambridge Law School, & now a practitioner in New York, takes his holidays with the railroad excursionists to St Louis, & means to look about him in your

19. Rusk records the second marriage of Emerson's cousin, *Letters*, 1:418, n. 46. By an oversight, the index has only the name of the first wife, Olivia Buckminster Emerson, who died in 1832. The second marriage was of 1834; all references in the index (6:426) to pages in vols. 2, 3, and 5 are to the second wife. The *Boston Daily Advertizer*, cited by Rusk, identifies her as the daughter of William Rotch of New Bedford and gives her name as Mary Rotch Fleeming; Emerson in the letter annotated has it "Fleming"; her first husband's name was Flemming.
20. MS in Special Collections, Butler Library, NNC; ph. in NNC.

beautiful city.[21] I have charged him to pay his respects to you, in passing, if his time permits it. With kindest regards to Mr Stetson, & to Miss Vose,

Your friend & servant,
R. W. Emerson.

Mrs Stetson.

To Amos Bronson Alcott, Concord, June 9, 1857

[Printed from a copy by Alcott, *Letters*, 5:79. The original, privately owned, does not differ substantively from the copy. Emerson writes "⟨day⟩ year"; "New York" has no hyphen, and the last two sentences are a separate paragraph.]

To William Henry Furness, Concord, June 9, 1857[22]

Concord 9 June
1857

My dear friend,

I have been slow in writing, for I did not find my /bibliopolic/ friends, Phillips & Sampson, at all courageous about Heine. They have the usual terror of book-sellers at any new name, & Heine s[23] is totally new to them. Tis very sad, & often wakens my sympathy for the craft in this country,—their total unacquaintance with the wares they deal in, & the makers of the wares. They know only those of their own shop, & those which come to them from known shops. These particular men,—P. & S. —are much less acquainted with books than is usual; for, though bold & able business men, they were not bred, I believe, to this business, &, having printed one or two books which advertising,—their cheval de bataille,—could not ⟨sell⟩ /carry/, they have resolved to believe hencefor- ward in nothing but Mr Prescott & Mrs Stowe;[24] who were both proved, before they engaged with them. They told me, they had printed no new book, but Jackwood,[25] I think, this year. But let not Horace halt a moment.[26] If he gets ready a book of thoughts & pictures which interest him, he can rely that they will interest others, and he will readily find a

21. Rebecca Vose Stetson (Mrs. Charles Stetson) was a schoolmate of Mrs. Emerson's; see *Letters*, 4:206. The Stetsons entertained Emerson at dinner during his 1857 visit to Cincinnati (*Letters*, 5:55, and n. 19).

22. MS in the Furness papers, Van Pelt Library, PU; ph. in NNC; printed in *Records*, p. [113]; listed in *Letters*, 5:79.

23. Emerson omits the apostrophe, though leaving space for it.

24. William Hickling Prescott and Harriet Beecher Stowe.

25. *Neighbor Jackwood*, by John T. Trowbridge.

26. Furness' son.

publisher, a month sooner or later. Perhaps these very men of ours[27] be eager for the book after a little while.

I have been shut up at home for days & only got a chance to /go/ speak to Phillips, the other day. Munroe I do not now go to; and Field[28] of F. & Ticknor, was away. But I shall be in town again, perhaps tomorrow, & will make further inquiries. Have you taken your Bible oath never to come to Massachusetts, or never with time enough to see my little village & my girls & boy? My house, to which I am making some important addition of convenience,[29] lacks one of the best titles to my love & respect, so long as it has not held you. Tell me when you will come & I will have Hedge & more good men to meet you. Yours affectionately

R. Waldo E.

William Furness.

To Horatio Woodman, Concord, June 13, 1857

[In his MS Account Book for 1853–1859, p. [177], under the date June 11 (1857), Emerson enters calculations of what is "due to H. Woodman" for Saturday Club dinners and "Alcott ticket." Under the date June 13, he enters "Enclosed to him today $21.00."]

To Arthur Buckminster Fuller, Concord, July 5, 1857

[In a letter of July 4, 1857 (RWEMA), Arthur Fuller offers Emerson a plaster copy of the medallion portrait of his sister Margaret on her monument in Mt. Auburn Cemetery. I think Emerson would have acknowledged the letter.]

To Edwin Percy Whipple, Concord, July 7? 1857[30]

My dear Whipple,

You shall not praise my poor little ode[31] so unmercifully. Even the merits of the praiser cannot save it from sinking under such a big

---

27. Emerson omits "will" here.

28. James T. Fields; Emerson has omitted the final *s*.

29. A new roof chiefly, see *Letters*, 5:74, 76.

30. MS in the Barrett Collection, Alderman Library, ViU; ph. in NNC. I date this letter 1857 because it was certainly written early in the history of the Saturday Club. According to Richard Henry Dana, Jr., the rules for election were first put into effect in that year with the election of Dr. Oliver Wendell Holmes and Cornelius C. Felton (*Journal of Richard Henry Dana*, 2:830). Dana's journal entry is dated August 6, 1857. The first meeting Holmes attended as a duly elected member was that of October 31; see my *Amiable Autocrat*, p. 239 and p. 419, n. 14.

31. With the year surely 1857, the "ode" referred to has to be "The Ode Sung in the Town Hall, Concord July 4, 1857" (*Works*, 9:199–200). See *BAL*, 5227; M, A25, for a leaflet printing apparently distributed on the occasion.

bouquet. And yet I am very happy in Mrs Whipple's good will, & very proud of yours.

Next Club day I think we must set apart ten minutes for the settlement of our only scrap of business, namely, the two or three rules touching the election of members. Can we not?

Yours faithfully,
R. W. Emerson

To Charles Wesley Slack, Concord, July 8, 1857[32]

Concord
8 July 1857

Dear Sir,

I received, a few days ago, your friendly invitation, which much honors me, to join the holiday excursion of the Twenty eighth Cong. Society on the 14th instant.[33] I have kept your note before me a little while, thinking it might be in my power to go. I find now that it will not be. A necessary absence of three preceeding days will make it necessary that I should be at home ⟨?⟩on that day.[34] I am sorry, for I know I shall lose much good company, &, in particular, some few friends whom I should rejoice to see & hear. You may be sure, I heartily share the interest of all that company in Mr Parker's health & welfare,—a property to his city & his country, which I deem inestimable. Respectfully, your obliged servant,

R W Emerson.

Mr C. W. Slack.

To _____, Concord, July 23, 1857

[A letter of July 23, 1857, is advertised in Carnegie Bookshop catalogue 194. Possibly this is the same letter listed in the Feinberg sale catalogue, lot 295, and described as in a copy of *Nature*.]

32. MS in MH-AH; ph. in NNC. Emerson enters the addressee's name across the fold of his opened sheet, drawing a diagonal rule to separate it from the last two words of his complimentary close. He crowds his own signature in at the bottom edge of the third page.

33. See July 8, 1858, below, which gives the place of this annual festival as Watertown.

34. I find nothing to show what would take Emerson away July 11–13. A letter of July 18 from Ellen to her mother shows that she is visiting the Washburn family in Middleboro. She writes ". . . if I could only walk I should be very well." Possibly her father had escorted her to Middleboro the week before. The dates Emerson mentions are for the weekend; he would probably have to stay over.

To WILLIAM H. FULLER, CONCORD, JULY 25? 1857

[In a letter of July 24, 1857 (RWEMA), William H. Fuller (Cambridge, Mass.) asks Emerson to write a letter to Hawthorne for Major William F. Johnson, a state senator from Ohio. I doubt that Emerson obliged Mr. Fuller, but he probably answered the letter if only to refuse. Hawthorne's letter to Emerson of September 24 (RWEMA) does not mention a Major Johnson.]

To THE NATIONAL LITERARY INSTITUTE, CONCORD, JULY 27, 1857

[B. Altman & Co., c. 1960, had a note of thanks for an honorary membership in the National Literary Institute.]

To GEORGE FRISBIE HOAR, CONCORD, AUGUST 4, 1857[35]

                                        Concord
                                        Tuesday, 4 Augt
My dear Sir,

I thank you for your kind care & trouble about Mr Loudon. It is certainly a great economy to buy as you do, & the lesson shall not be lost on us. Albert Stacy[36] promises to go to N.Y., in September, to these Trade Sales,[37] & we are to send orders.

But for the book in hand, it is a little too late for us, as we took possession of Reynolds's copy[38] & put it into the Library, on Saturday night, at 17.60 I believe. I looked over the work on Saturday & think it cheap even at our price.

                                        Your obliged servant,
                                        R. W. Emerson.
Mr. Hoar.

To CARL MEYER, CONCORD, SEPTEMBER ? 1857

[In a letter of August 12, 1857 (RWEMA), the German publisher Carl Meyer asks permission to print a translation of *English Traits*. See George Willis Cooke, *A Bibliography of Ralph Waldo Emerson* (Boston: Houghton Mifflin, 1908), p. 113, for

35. MS in the George Frisbie Hoar papers, MHi; ph. in NNC. The date is established by George F. Hoar's fully dated letter of August 1 from Worcester (RWEMA). For the Concord Free Public Library, Hoar offers Emerson the 1844 edition of John Claudius Loudon's *Arboretum et Fruticetum Britannicum*, 8 volumes (London, 1844), for $15.00. The 4th of August fell on a Tuesday in 1857.

36. Concord postmaster, bookseller, and stationer.

37. Hoar had reported the advantages of buying books at the trade sales directed by the New York Book-Publishers' Association. In 1857 one more such sale was to be held September 8. The sales were regularly advertised in the *American Publishers' Circular*.

38. Probably the Boston bookseller William S. Reynolds.

Friedrich Spielhagen's translation published (Hannover) by Meyer in 1857. See also M. A 24.3, p 251. A reply from Emerson is possible if uncertain.]

To Mattie Griffith, Concord, September 22, 1857[39]

Concord, 22 Sept.
1857.

My dear Miss Griffith,

Is it quite out of the question that you should spend a day with us here in the meadows? Our house has been beset with so many needs & infirmities, that I have hardly ventured to risk its sombre influence on a presence so brilliant & glad, and whilst I knew, too, that I should be drawing you from so many welcoming friends. But I hoped yet by dint of age & the faithful Furness, to claim to be one of your tutors, & to persuade you to come to me in my turn for a lesson, when I meant to wear the cowl with great dignity, and to wile all your beautiful stories out of you. You are to impute to me the wisdom, & I am to be really wise through sympathy with your expectation. Tis a magic that has often been & may be again. I will read Browning, or Goethe or Ruskin or "Margaret"[40] to know them better so. or talk with you of those problems you allude to in our times. Next Tuesday /29th/ is a kind of holiday here,[41] & will force us all to lay aside out tasks & open our doors. Is it not possible for you to come then & give us a day or two, with fresh opportunity of beneficence opened to you? And you loving so well to serve your race! My wife sends you her kindest respects & invitation.

Your affectionate servant,
R. W. Emerson

To Francis Underwood, Concord, September 24, 1857[42]

Concord, Sept. 24, 1857.

Dear Sir,

I return the proof in which I have no correction to make. Mr. Lowell showed a bad rhythm, but I do not quite like the new word he offered me—

39. MS in the collections of CtLHi; ph. in NNC. See below, December 16, 1858, and *Letters*, 5:83–84.

40. Possibly Emerson means the novel by Sylvester Judd.

41. Emerson is inviting Miss Griffith to the Middlesex County Cattle Show. She had already left Brookline for Philadelphia before this invitation arrived.

42. No MS has been located; text from Bliss Perry, *Park-Street Papers*, p. 245; listed *Letters*, 5:85.

beneath the moon,"[43]

where the new cacophony troubles my ears as much as the old one; and for the second suggestion about the word "hypocritical," he is right again,[44] but I cannot mend it to-day. If he will alter them, as he proposed before, or otherwise, he has my thankful consent.

Yours,
R. W. Emerson.

Mr. Underwood.

To _____, CONCORD, SEPTEMBER 24, 1857

[As an inference from a letter of September 24, 1857, Rusk lists two letters to correspondents "west of Cleveland" (*Letters*, 5:84). On the last page of his MS Pocket Diary for 1857, in a list of correspondents, are five names for towns west of Cleveland (*JMN*, 4:454–455).]

To JOHN WILLIAMSON PALMER, CONCORD, OCTOBER 3, 1857[45]

Concord
Oct. 3, 1857

Dear Sir,

I am sorry to have kept the papers you enclosed to me /so long./ But I am the worst person to apply to in cases of this kind, & was slow to find out what was asked of me by Mr Hurlbut.[46] Then I had no copy of my poems near me, & did not know how to select for you. I think it safest, in this ignorance, & after so much delay, to copy precisely the verses you indicate. With the best wishes for the success of your literary enterprize, I am yours respectfully,

R. W. Emerson.

⟨M⟩Dr Palmer.

I should have said also that an accumulated correspondence at this season makes me more dilatory.

---

43. The opening line of the fourth stanza of "The Romany Girl" (*Works*, 9:227), originally read: "If, on the heath, under the moon"; Emerson finally arrived at "If on the heath, below the moon," but not for the printing in the first number of the *Atlantic Monthly* (November 1857), 1:46–47, where the title is spelled "Rommany," as it appears in the copy sent to the *Atlantic*.

44. For the familiar first line of "Days"; Emerson accepted Lowell's suggestion (*ibid*, p. 47, *Works*, 9:228). The error must have been in the "copy"; Emerson's original version has "hypocritic"; see *The Poetry Notebooks*, p. 295; he would restore this word for later printings.

45. MS in the Barrett Collection, Alderman Library, ViU; ph. in NNC.

46. In a letter of September 11 William Henry Hurlburt had asked Emerson to provide a manuscript of the first eight or ten lines of "The Problem" for reproduction in facsimile in John Williamson Palmer's *Folk Songs* (*BAL*, 1:72 and 3:62), published by Scribner in 1861,

To ANNA JACKSON LOWELL, CONCORD, OCTOBER ? 1857

[From Algiers on November 24, 1857, Charles Russell Lowell writes his mother of her "proposal for the 'Atlantic,'" and in a letter of December 5 he tells his friend John C. Bancroft that his mother "has been twice asked, by Mr. Emerson by the Editor independently of each other to get some letters from Algiers out of me" (Edward W. Emerson, *The Life and Letters of Charles Russell Lowell*, pp. 149, 150). A letter from Emerson to Mrs. Lowell seems inferrable here. (The "Editor," James Russell Lowell, was the young man's uncle.)]

To FRANCIS? H? UNDERWOOD, CONCORD, OCTOBER 11, 1857?[47]

Concord
11 Oct.r

My dear Sir,

I fear it is quite out of my power to join your pleasant party on Saturday, when I am particularly engaged at home.

With great regard,
R. W. Emerson.

Mr Underwood.

To CAROLINE STURGIS TAPPAN, CONCORD, OCTOBER 13, 1857[48]

Concord, October 13,
1857.

Dear Caroline,

You will never write me a⟨no⟩gain, I have been so ungrateful, I who value every line & word from you,[49] or about you. Perhaps tis my too

---

reissued, enlarged, in 1867 and 1871. The poem actually reproduced is "The Humblebee," p. 259, with facsimile opposite; Emerson's "Rhodora" appears at p. 124.

47. MS in the Abernethy Library, VtMiM; single sheet; ph. in NNC. If the assumption that Mr. Underwood is Francis H. Underwood is correct, then it is likely that this letter belongs to the early years of the *Atlantic Monthly* and that it was written before the failure of its first publisher, Phillips & Sampson Co. The year cannot be 1856, for in that year October 11 was a Saturday; only 1857 and 1858 are left on the assumption made.

48. MS in the Tappan papers, Houghton Library, MH; ph. in NNC; endorsed (not by Emerson), p. [6] "Letter to Caroline Tappan/October, 1857"; and below, in Emerson's hand, "unsent." Since the letter is now in the Tappan papers, the letter must have been given to her at some time. Printed in part from Cabot's copy, *Letters,* 5:86–87; Cabot copied the entire letter, but the last portion of his copy (beginning with "Ward") must have become separated from the first part; it appears on the verso of a copy of Emerson's letter of September 3, 1838, to Lowell. Finally, in MS Journal *BL*, pp. 111–112, appears a slightly different version of the passage on American authors, at the end labeled by Emerson "To C. T. 1856."

49. There are two letters to Emerson, both of 1857, from Italy and one of them mentions an earlier "affectionate" letter written from Switzerland (MNS). A letter of May 28, 1857, from Rome, begins: "Do you not envy me that yesterday I read yr poems on the

much writing in youth that makes it so repulsive now in these old days. What to tell you now that I have begun, you that are in the land of wine & oil, of us in the land of meal? Italy cannot excel the banks of glory which sun & mist paint in these very days on the forest by lake & river. But the Muses are as reticent, as nature is flamboyant, & no fire-eyed child has yet been born: Tis strange that the relations of your old friends here remain unchanged to the world of letters & society. I mean, that those who held of the imagination, & believed that the necessities of the New World would presently evoke the Mystic Power, & we should not pass away without hearing the Choral Hymns of a new Age & adequate to nature, still find colleges & books as cramp & sterile as ever, & our discontent keeps us in the selfsame suspicious relation to beauties & elegant society. We are all the worse that you, & those who are like you, if any such there be, as there are not,—but persons of positive quality, & capacious of beauty,—desert us, & abdicate their power at home. Why not a mind as wise & deep & subtle as your Browning, with his trained talent? Why can we not breed a lyric man as exquisite as Tennyson; or such a Burke-like <u>longanimity</u> as E. Browning (whom you mention in interesting positions, but do not describe to me-)? Our wild Whitman, with real inspiration but choked by Titanic abdomen, & Delia Bacon, with genius, but mad, & clinging like a tortoise to English soil, are the sole producers that America has yielded in ten years. Is all this granite & forest & prairie & superfoetation of millions to no richer result? If I were writing to any other than you, I should render my wonted homage to the gods for my two gossips, Alcott & Henry T., whose existence I impute to America for righteousness, though they miss the fame of your praise. Charles Newcomb, too, proves the rich possibilities in the soil, though his result is zero. /So does Ellery./ But who cares? As soon as we walk out of doors, Nature transcends all poets so far, that a little more or less skill in whistling is of no account. Out of doors, we lose the lust of performance,

---

beautiful Campagna to the music of the lark—I have wanted no book so much as these poems,—in Paris, last winter & in Florence this winter where I again met Mr. Browning & talked about them with him—he searched his book-shelves in vain but said he had the book somewhere wandering about. He is a most eager admirer of the poems, & I wish I could remember all that so fine a critic said—one thing was that he would have given his heart's blood (you know he is a little exaggerated in his forms of speech) if he could have seen the poems for one half hour before they were published, there are so many little things in them that only needed a word changed to be exactly right—that was why I wanted the book so much. He says no other American poet can be mentioned in the same year with you. He knew nothing about Ellery and would not believe there had once been genius there, upon my simple assurance. He says the melody in your verses is often delicious. He quoted the last verse of the Dirge & said that alone would prove the poet. He liked also the Threnody & the Snow storm particularly, but exclaimed, that without the book he could say nothing."

and are content to pass silent, & see others pass silent, into the depths of a Universe so resonant & beaming. But you will dispense with my whims, which you know, for a few grains of history. There is nothing very marked in our neighborhood, which keeps its old routinary trot. I suffered Anna Ward—I am sorry for it—to go again, without so much as a note to you, & she could have carried the books you ask for, & the pretty copy in red & gold of my "English Traits," which has slept in my drawer for you.

Our club is an agreeable innovation,[50] holding Sam G.W.; Agassiz, Pierce, Lowell, Longfellow, Dana, Whipple, Dwight, Hoar, Motley, & Holmes, & dining once a month; Agassiz is my chief gain from it,—I have seen him to very good purpose during the last year. Ellery comes to Concord occasionally, & hides for a fortnight in a chamber of his house, which is rented to Sanborn He will dine & walk with me a few times, & suddenly disappears for months again. I think he never writes. He loves dearly to hear any scrap of news of you, if he can get it without asking for it, & will plot to elicit it, affecting supreme indifference.[51]

To James Jackson Jarves, Concord, October 23, 1857[52]

Concord
23 October, 1857

My dear Sir,

I received, soon after meeting you at the Athenaeum,[53] the three attractive-looking volumes you were kind enough to send me. My reading lately has been so confined to certain narrow specialities, that these books were wholly new to me, and a very agreeable surprise. The very accosting of this topic of fine art bespeaks elevation & generosity,[54] &, before all reading we are engaged on your side. I have only found time,

---

50. Samuel Gray Ward, Louis Agassiz, Benjamin Peirce (Emerson habitually misspells the mathematician's name), James Russell Lowell, Henry Wadsworth Longfellow (recently elected), Richard Henry Dana, Jr., Edwin Percy Whipple, John Sullivan Dwight, Ebenezer Rockwood Hoar, John Lothrop Motley, and Oliver Wendell Holmes (just elected). Emerson omits Horatio Woodman and the recently elected Cornelius Conway Felton.

51. In the letter quoted, Mrs. Tappan chides him for not writing her. He would try again in 1859, but that letter too was not sent. See, below, May 13, 1859.

52. MS in Beinecke Library, CtY; ph. in NNC.

53. Emerson had withdrawn books from the Athenaeum on the 6th and 16th of October, Cameron, *ER*, p. 31.

54. Jarves had sent Emerson his *Art-Hints* (London: Sampson, Low, 1855) inscribed: "Ralph Waldo Emerson from James J. Jarves Boston, Sept 30/57"; see Harding, p. 151, where the inscription and date are given incorrectly.

as yet, to run through the books, & seize the fine names & facts, here & there; but hope to give you some day a good account of them. And yet, such is our curiosity about those famed savages,[55] that, I confess, I begun with the romance, inferring that you were entitled by opportunities & experience to write it. In my present haste, you will please accept my entire thanks for this brave package, pending my later opportunity to make a close acquaintance with the same. I should have gladly found a day to spare to come & see, under your guidance, the picture you promised to show me; but I have had no time when I could come. I regret it the more, because I think you said that you stay at home now but for a few days. Well, the later day will, I trust, arrive.

Respectfully, your obliged serv.t

Mr Jarves.   R. W. Emerson

To Elizabeth Palmer Peabody, Concord, October 23, 1857[56]

Concord
Oct 23.

Dear Miss Peabody,

If you will send me the Chapter on History,[57] or the one you elect as best for this popular audience, I will offer it to the "Atlantic" men with what confirming suggestions I may draw from seeing the manuscript.[58] I have found in all the past year the publishers very timorous & averse to any experiment. With better times their courage & liberality may return. But I will say to P. & S. anything you wish on the subject.[59] I wish the other Mr Phillips[60] ⟨were⟩ /would be/ the patron of your book.

I fear I cannot come to Dorchester now being as busy as a schoolboy

55. No other work by Jarves is now in Emerson's library, but "the famed savages" must be those of the Hawaiian and Sandwich islands and the book, Jarves' *Kiana* (Boston: J. Munroe, 1857).

56. MS in the Horace Mann (II) papers, MHi; ph. in NNC. The date is established by Emerson's fully dated letter of November 24 to Miss Peabody on the same subject.

57. Miss Peabody's work on "Primeval History," part of her *Universal History* (New York: Sheldon, 1859).

58. The *Atlantic* did not take the manuscript; Emerson's letter of February 27, 1859, asking for its return is in *Letters*, 5:134–135. Among Cabot's "Extracts" is a sheet containing a passage from Emerson's letter of November 24 and a fragment from a letter of September 27, 1858 (see below). It is clear that Emerson was reluctant to submit the MS, certain of its rejection.

59. Phillips and Sampson, publishers of the *Atlantic Monthly*.

60. Emerson may here be referring to Charles H. Phillips, listed as a printer, 36 Joy Street, in Boston directories.

for weeks & weeks before me. But I hope to send you a less sombre note
than this sometime.

With thanks & hopes, Yours,

R. W. Emerson

Miss Peabody.

To Helen Maynard Keyes, Concord, October 25, 1857[61]

Concord

Sunday Evening

My dear Mrs Keyes,

Ellen brought me this morning your very kind invitation to spend
Wednesday night with E & E[62] at your house. I am sorry I must lose for
them & me this pleasant visit, as it is necessary for me to go to Boston
that night, having promised to go to Nantucket the next day. But I shall
endeavour to reach Watertown in season to drink tea with you.

Yours, with kind regards,

R. W. Emerson.

Mrs Keyes.

To Albert Haller Tracy, Concord, November 2, 1857[63]

Concord

2 November, 1857.

My dear Sir,

My friend Mr Alcott[64] is on his way westward, & means to pass
through Buffalo. I think there was already once some movement towards
inviting him to hold one of his "Classes" or Series of Conversations, in
⟨B⟩your city. Whether this can be now or not, I do not know; but I much
desire that you should see him, & he should see you, as he passes. He is a
man of singular reach & subtlety of thought, and in every way deserving
the best reception from the best minds. He is a person of the purest &

61. MS in Houghton Library; MH; ph. in NNC. This letter was accessioned by Hough-
ton Library with the date 1856, but it has to have been written on October 25, 1857, the
Sunday before Emerson went to Nantucket. It is only in October 1857 that Emerson was in
Watertown on a Wednesday, October 28, and in Nantucket the next day (October 29)
(Charvat, p. 33). See August 7, 1850, above, for Mrs. Joseph Keyes.

62. Ellen and Edith, who had been Mrs. Keyes' students.

63. MS in Special Collections, Butler Library, NNC; ph in NNC.

64. See *Letters*, 5:55, for Emerson's characterization of Tracy as "almost as rare a talker
as Alcott," reason enough for his closing wish.

most elevated character It is his practice, in cities, to propose five or six subjects for the discussion of as many evenings, in the parlor of any house that is opened for him, and, at the close of the Course, each of the company pays him one, or two, or three dollars. But he is too glad to have any intelligent person brought to the circle /though/ without money. It is easy & simple to collect a few friends to converse with him, I hope it may be done; but, at all events, I trust you will give him the opportunity to meet you,⁶⁵ & I could heartily wish I might be of the party. With respectful & affectionate remembrances, Yours,

Mr Tracy.   R. W. Emerson

To K. E. Bemis, Concord, November 19? 1857

[Laid in the Account Book for 1853–1860, between pages having entries for October and November, is an envelope addressed: K. E. Bemis. Chicopee. Mass. Emerson lectured in Chicopee February 9, 1858. Charvat, p. 34, has "Chicopee Falls" for that date, but both the Account Book (1853–1859) p. [200], and the Pocket Diary for 1858 (*JMN*, 19:458) have Chicopee. In 1848, the villages of Cabotville, Chicopee Falls, Chicopee Street, and Willimansett were separated from Springfield and incorporated as a new town called Chicopee. Clifton Johnson, *Hampden County* (New York, 1936), 2:636. The names Chicopee Falls and Willimansett are still in use.]

To Charles O. Whitmore, Concord, November 20, 1857⁶⁶

Concord

20 November, 1857

C. O. Whitmore, Esq.

Dear Sir,

As I am told there is to be a meeting of the stockholders of the Vermont & Canada R. R. Company,⁶⁷ at some time soon, I take the liberty of requesting you to dispose of my votes on any business that may come before them, at your own discretion, in which I have the highest

65. See Alcott's letter of December 14 (*Letters of . . . Alcott*, p. 269) to his wife, where he describes his meeting with Tracy, who evidently secured Millard Fillmore as one of Alcott's company (*ibid.*, pp. 268, 271). Emerson had written also to his friend Emily Drury (*Letters*, 5:88–89), who joined forces with Tracy to assure Alcott a good group.

66. MS in the Barrett Collection, Alderman Library, ViU; ph. in NNC. This is, I believe, the same letter listed in *Letters*, 5:90, from C. F. Libbie & Co.'s catalogue of January 27 and 28, 1914. It is there described as a "business letter." Whitmore was a director of the Central Vermont Railroad.

67. See *Letters*, 5:11–12, for one of Emerson's many anxious moments about his holdings in the Vermont and Canada Railroad Company, shares he bought and held on Abel Adams' advice, selling them finally in 1868 (*Letters*, 5:28).

confidence. You will be good enough to fill up the blanks in the enclosed power of attorney. I hold sixty eight shares.[68]

> Respectfully,
> Your obed.t servant,
> R. W. Emerson

To George Sumner, Concord, November 20, 1857

[In a letter of November 21, endorsed 1857 by Emerson, George Sumner reports that Wendell Phillips will go to Taunton on December 1 and Emerson's engagement will then be for February 9 as Mr. (Abijah) Ide has it on his program. Emerson had apparently written to ask. The tentative schedule, p. 290, of the MS Account Book for 1853–1859 and the Pocket Diary show that the Taunton date was never certain. In the Account Book it appears as January 26 and is deleted for February 9 with Chicopee replacing it. The Pocket Diary for 1857 has it in pencil under December 1 with a question mark (*JMN,* 14:451), and on the inside of the back cover "1858 Feb. 9 Taunton" (*JMN,* 14:455). In the diary for 1858 it appears under January 26 in pencil, and under February 9 also in pencil, deleted, with Chicopee replacing it (*JMN,* 14:458). Since there is no record of payment, Taunton should be deleted from Charvat's list, p. 54, where it appears with a question mark under January 26.]

To Francis H. Underwood, Concord, November 21, 1857[69]

> Concord
> 21 Novr.

Dear Sir,

I am sorry I cannot come to town today, & join your strong party at dinner.[70] I shall be in town on Tuesday, probably, & will not fail to come to your Compting-Room and I will think in the meantime what I can do. For what you say of the club dinner, I have no dream of any such self-denying ordinance as you intimate. There is always a good deal of luck goes to a dinner, and if ours was a heavy one, as you say it was, there is the more reason to believe the luck will turn & be with us next time. But I was in the dark about it, & only regretted that I could not stay longer to hear the stories out. I can send you nothing for the Atlantic

---

68. In 1856 Emerson had begun to feel the pinch of the nationwide depression which became acute in 1857.

69. MS in Special Collections, Butler Library, NNC; ph. in NNC; printed by Bliss Perry, *Park-Street Papers,* pp. 253–254; listed *Letters,* 5:90.

70. An "Atlantic Club" dinner evidently, for Underwood was not a member of the Saturday Club.

sooner than the end of the month;[71]—but of this I will speak when I see you.

Respectfully,

Mr Underwood.   R. W. Emerson

To Daniel Ricketson, Concord, November 21, 1857[72]

Concord
21 November
1857

My dear Sir,

I have been unpardonably slow in acknowledging your kindest invitation. I thank you for your care & thoughtfulness in my behalf. I do not know but I shall go this time to Mrs Ben Rodman, who took care, when I was at New Bedford the last time, to say that she engaged me to her house for the next year.[73] Yet I have a very good will to read the inscriptions that have gathered on your shanty wall, and on its master's mind.[74] And, as usual, I do not know but it may be necessary for me to come & go by the short way that gave you so much amusement already.[75] So we will let all this lie for the present; for the 21 December is still a whole lunation ahead.[76]

With kindest regards to all your household from all of mine,

Your obliged servant,
R. W. Emerson.

Mr Ricketson.

71. Emerson provided "Books" for the third number of the *Atlantic;* see below, December 2, and *Letters,* 5:90–91.

72. MS in the Barrett Collection, Alderman Library, ViU; ph. in NNC; printed by Anna and Walton Ricketson, *Daniel Ricketson, Autobiographic and Miscellaneous* (New Bedford: E. Anthony, 1910, p. 115; reprinted by Cameron, *ESQ* (4th q., 1956), 13:36. Possibly this is the letter to Ricketson listed with year only in a catalogue of Goodspeed's Book Shop, October 1920 (*Letters,* 5:93).

73. Benjamin Rodman regularly invited Emerson to be his guest when he lectured in New Bedford; Rodman's letter of this year is of December 9 (RWEMA). See January 18, 1858, below, for evidence that Emerson did stay with the Rodmans.

74. Ricketson's "shanty," complete with Aeolian harp, allowed him to live picturesquely in his own backyard.

75. I believe this to be an allusion to the winter of 1854 when Emerson's lecture schedule inconveniently obliged him to traverse the same ground twice. See Charvat, p. 29, entries for December 4–7, where New Bedford is sandwiched between Weymouth and Hingham; and Pawtucket, Rhode Island, follows Hingham. Weymouth and Hingham are adjacent towns south of Boston but close to it, New Bedford lies well to the south and is closer to Pawtucket than Hingham is. Emerson was apparently willing to oblige New Bedford at considerable inconvenience to himself; see schedules for other years.

76. See *Letters,* 5:94, 95, for Emerson's appeal to Ricketson to secure his fee for the New Bedford lecture, a generous one of $50.00, but slow in coming.

To George Barrell Emerson, Concord, November 22, 1857[77]

Concord

22 Nov.r 1857

Dear George,

You were born to be magnificent. Here came, last night, these beautiful Raffaelles,[78] announcing your arrival, as noble men like to be announced by great benefits. Tis quite in character with all my experience of my cousin, of whom I am so proud. I give you joy, you & Mrs Emerson, that you are safely home again with all your new experiences & honors, whereof at intervals a flying report penetrates our woods. I wish before the history is all told, to hear a part. I wish to hear the botany, yes, & the <u>personal</u>, too. My wife & children three all send to you & Mrs Emerson their kind congratulations. I shall bring my own in the first hours that I can command.

Yours affectionately,

Waldo E.

To Cyrus Augustus Bartol, Concord? November? 22? 1857

[In a letter of November 21, 1857 (Cabot papers, Schlesinger Library, Radcliffe), Cyrus Bartol invites Emerson to dine "Tuesday next" with Agassiz and Henry Whitney Bellows. Emerson would have to reply.]

To Elizabeth Palmer Peabody, Concord, November 24, 1857[79]

Concord

24 Novr 1857

My dear Miss Peabody,

My wife instructs me to enclose to you a pair of Concord tickets.[80] I ought to have written you about the Manuscript you sent me. I read it with care twice, & have not yet sent it to the Atlantic people.[81] I wish I had time, which I have not. I should summon you to a rhetorical class, which I have always intended to open, & we would anatomize this essay for the first day on our dissecting-table. There are things in it. Well, I

77. MS in the G. B. Emerson papers, MHi; ph. in NNC.
78. Emerson's customary spelling of Raphael. The prints now hang in the Emerson house, Concord. See above, May 17, for George B. Emerson's trip to Europe.
79. MS in the James Duncan Phillips Library, MSaE; ph. in NNC. A portion of this letter was twice copied by Cabot for his "Extracts"; one copy is now misfiled among copies of letters to Emerson.
80. Probably for Emerson's lecture of December 12 (Charvat, p. 30).
81. See October 23, 1857, above and September 27, 1858, below.

wish them to be extracted from all the nebulosity, & counted & weighed, 1, 2, 3, 4, and then put back in order of number & weight, No 1, No 2 No 3, & 4, in a square & positive manner, omitting periphrasis & nebulosity, putting them as assertions, & not by implication or sidewise. This you will think is very ill gratitude for your fine chapter on Primeval History. But I wish it not to be rejected, but eagerly received, and I have been told that they have already rejected 260 articles. So I am resolved to keep it by me till I have /found/ that it can be mended, or till, on later examination, I shall find out that the fault is mine, & not yours. So you must be patient a little longer with your Loilus.[82]

With great regard,

R. W. Emerson

To Francis H. Underwood, Concord, December 2, 1857

[Listed as item 42 in James Lowe's catalogue 14, 1980, is Emerson's letter to Francis Underwood, listed *Letters*, 5:90, from Goodspeed's catalogue 169, where only the year is given. Lowe quotes: "I send you the first installment of 'Books.' The whole article will be, I suppose, more than three times as much matter. Do you prefer to divide it? More today or tomorrow; & probably the whole on the 3rd day . . ." The letter is described as "one-page . . . ideal for display"; probably this is the full text. "Books" (Works, 7:187–221), appeared in the third number of the *Atlantic* (January 1858), 1:343–353. See *Letters*, 5:90–91, and above, November 21.]

To Caroline Healey Dall, Concord, December 10, 1857[83]

Concord,

Dec 10, 1857

Dear Madam,

I shall have great pleasure in sending you Mr Smith's book, but not quite yet.[84] It is held, at present, with some other books & papers, as means or materials to some notice of Miss Bacon's work, though who will write it is not quite yet certain.

I am sorry that I cannot give you the information you ask concerning

---

82. Emerson had served as Miss Peabody's "Loilus" on another occasion; see below June 12, 1835.

83. MS in MHi; ph. in NNC; printed by Vivian Hopkins, *NEQ* (December 1860), 33:505.

84. In a letter of December 6, Mrs. Dall had asked to borrow Emerson's copy of William Henry Smith's *Bacon and Shakespeare* (Harding, p. 251; the markings are not extensive), of which she has heard from Elizabeth Peabody. See *Letters*, 5:85, for Emerson's acquisition of this pamphlet, which appeared to Delia Bacon's friends (e.g., Emerson and Hawthorne) to be a plagiarism of her work. Mrs. Dall wishes to see for herself.

Miss Bacon.[85] If you have seen Miss Peabody, I had my last tidings from her. Tis very tragic to have such extraordinary abilities made unavailable by some disproportion,[86] or by a want of somewhat which everybody else has. But if one could forget that there is a suffering woman behind it, her book, as it is, is a literary feast. More ability, & of a rare kind, goes to it, than to a score of successful works.

With much respect, Yours,

R. W. Emerson

Mrs Dall.

To Benjamin Rodman, Concord, December 10? 1857

[In a letter of December 9, 1857 (RWEMA), Benjamin Rodman offers his customary invitation to Emerson to be his guest when he comes to New Bedford to lecture, December 22. Emerson expected this invitation; see above, November 21, to Daniel Ricketson. That he accepted is clear from his letter of January 18, 1858, below, thanking Rodman for returning the rubbers he had left behind.]

To George William Curtis, Concord, December 14, 1857[87]

Concord

Dec. 14, Monday.

My dear Sir,

I am very sorry to lose your vist, from which I had promised myself much pleasure of every kind,—and to lose it by my own fault. A few weeks after you had promised to come, I was offered certain days from New Haven, & other towns in Connecticu,[88] which days, finding to be free on my working day list, I at once accepted, without a remembrance of any impediment, When I presently afterwards discovered that it was the very week you should come, I was extremely vexed, but there were four towns implicated, & it was quite too late to get my head out of the trap. Mr Thoreau & Mr Sanbo⟨n⟩rn have agreed to meet you at my

85. Mrs. Dall had asked for Miss Bacon's address.

86. See below, February 18 and 25, 1858, for Emerson's letters to Miss Bacon's brother, Leonard Bacon, on learning of her insanity.

87. MS owned by Norman Brauer; ph. in NNC. Since Sanborn did not come to Concord until 1855, the letter cannot be earlier than 1857. It cannot be later than 1863, for Thoreau died in 1864. In his tentative lists of lecture engagments, Emerson enters no Connecticut engagements in either of the two possible years, 1857 and 1863. His final records show one Connecticut engagement in 1857; see Charvat, p. 34, for the New Haven lecture on December 17. On December 17, 1857, George W. Curtis gave the Concord Lyceum a lecture on Sir Philip Sidney (Cameron, *Transcendental Climate*, 3:713).

88. The name of the state falls at the end of the line; Emerson failed to write the final "t"; the comma is clear and cannot possibly be read as an aborted letter.

house, & do all that is needful to smooth your way with the Lyceum, but my disappointment & loss are not less. My wife & children rely on the privilege of keeping you comfortable on Thursday night, and you must give me my revenge in another visit. Ever yours,

R. W. Emerson

To Francis H. Underwood, Concord, December 18, 1857[89]

Concord
Friday Evening
18 Dec

Dear Sir,

I have been out of town for a few days & find your messages only now on my return tonight.[90] I am sorry you should have deferred the good meeting on my account, for, though I cannot help a feast, I hate to hinder one. But if Mr Lowell & you have chosen that I shall come,[91] I will not stay away on Monday at 5. You say at Porters, which I suppose to be Porters at Cambridge. If not send me word. You are very kind to offer me a bed; but I shall have to go to my old haunts. So with thanks, Yours,

R. W. Emerson

Mr Underwood.

To Cyrus Augustus Bartol, Concord?, December 19? 1857

[In a letter of December 21, 1857, Cyrus Bartol (Cabot papers, Schlesinger Library, Radcliffe), is clearly answering a letter from Emerson written to settle the time he is expected at Bartol's on December 24, where he is to spend the night before giving a lecture December 25 for the Parker Fraternity. From Charvat, p. 34, the mythical town of "Bartol" should be deleted; Emerson entered Bartol's name in his Pocket Diary for 1857 under the date December 24, JMN, 14:543; the editors enter "Bartol, Mass." in the index. To Charvat should be added the lecture for the Parker Fraternity, Boston. This lecture was given in the morning, so that there is no conflict here: he could still get to Newburyport for an evening lecture there on the same day.]

89. MS in Special Collections, Butler Library, NNC; ph. in NNC; printed by Bliss Perry, *Park-Street Papers*, p. 254; listed *Letters*, 4:92. The 18th of December fell on a Friday in 1857; on December 21, at Porter's in Cambridge, there was a gathering of contributors to the new magazine the *Atlantic Monthly*.
90. In Amherst and New Haven (Charvat, p. 34).
91. James Russell Lowell, the editor.

To Anson Burlingame, Concord, ? 1857? 1858?[92]

Italy. He is master of the Italian & French languages, & at home in the society & manners of Italy. Since he left Cambridge, he has been reading law. With his character & accomplishments, I have great confidence that, if appointed, he would fully j⟨?⟩ustify his claims to the post.[93] If there is a better man, by all means let him be preferred. If not, here is a good one.

Yours, with great regard,
R. W. Emerson

Hon. Mr Burlingame,
House of Representatives.

92. MS owned by Timothy H. Bakken; ph. in NNC. The MS is incomplete. Because it is the last two pages of a four-page letter, it lacks two pages of text and therefore has no dateline. The letter has to have been written during Burlingame's term of office, 1855–1861.

93. Emerson is manifestly recommending a young man for a consular post in Italy. Of the young men who were graduated from Harvard in the possible years and who went on to study law, the most likely candidate for Emerson's support is Francis Philip Nash, son of Paulina Tucker Nash, the only surviving sister of Emerson's first wife. In 1852, Mrs. Nash brought her two surviving sons, Bennett and Francis, back to the States to live in Cambridge while the boys attended Harvard. Francis Nash, A.B. 1856 and LL. B. 1858, fits the details here. He was born in Florence, December 5, 1836. Emerson is here, I think, seizing the opportunity to do something for Mrs. Nash; the difficulties over the settlement of the Beza Tucker estate had brought about some coolness among the claimants (see January 19, 1834, below, and *Letters*, 1:349). I assign the letter to 1857, though 1858 is possible.

There is no evidence that Nash was offered the post. By 1860 he is writing Emerson from 4 Court Street, Boston; the address suggests that he is practicing law, the street being known for its numerous law offices. (See *Letters*, 5:192, and n. 27.) If the age bracket for consuls was already established, Nash would not be eligible until his 25th birthday. Nash would subsequently practice law in New York City, marry the daughter of the Episcopal Bishop of western New York, and become a professor of Latin at Hobart College. In a memorial of him, Joseph Alexander Leighton, Professor of Philosophy, would list the many languages Nash had acquired and note that his accomplishments and his experience as a lawyer together with his knowledge of European politics "fitted him for the duties of a foreign minister." The *Hobart Herald*, June 15, 1911.)

1858

To Mattie Griffith, Concord, January 3? 1858

[In a letter of December 28, 1857 (RWEMA), Mattie Griffith reminds Emerson of his promise to write her. See *Letters,* 5:83, 84, for the "brilliant young lady from Kentucky." It is possible that he answered her letter of December 28, but not certain. See December 16, 1858, below, for Miss Griffith's later difficulties.]

To Collins, Concord, January 5, 1858

[Listed by Cameron, *ESQ* (2d q., 1956), 3:6, from *The Collector,* May 1955, catalogue 747, lot 475, as about lecturing in Philadelphia and dated January 5, 1858. The quoted passage reads: "I am sorry you do not fancy my title for my lecture, as I do. I please myself that when, one of these days, I get out a fine book to persuade all mankind that they are losers in as far as they have let go their holdings on the land or on the sea, & have become mere cockneys, without science & without poetry, I shall wish to say that I carried this doctrine first to Philadelphia, & convinced a whole Society of young men, or the best of them, that they must go as fast as they could, to West Chester County, or back to the Alleganies & plant orchards & recover their privileges!" The letter offers as a new title "City Life & Country Life," described as his newest lecture. He is referring to his prospective Philadelphia lecture of February 2, 1858, for the People's Literary Institute (see Charvat, p. 34, where no title is given); the MS Pocket Diary for 1858 gives no names of correspondents.]

To Horace Day, Concord, January 15, 1858[1]

Concord 15 ⟨D⟩Jan.y
1858.

Dear Sir,

I have no strong belief that Mr Longfellow will gratify your friends in this particular, as he uniformly declines to read lectures; but there is no harm in asking him, & perhaps your invitation may make the turning point with him. So I enclose a note to him, if you choose to call upon him.[2] He is always well worth seeing. I am sorry you should have chanced

1. MS in MdBJ; ph. in NNC.
2. See *Letters,* 5:96, where Emerson introduces Day, librarian of the Young Men's Institute of New Haven, to Longfellow.

to come to Concord on the first day for a fortnight that I had been out of it.[3]

With kind regards
& respect,

H. Day, Esq.

R. W. Emerson.

To William Henry Furness, Concord, January 15, 1858[4]

Concord, 15 Jan.y 1858

My dear friend,

I am to be in Philadelphia on the 2 February, and certainly shall be glad to obey Mrs Furness in anything she shall command on the following day or days. and without reward if she will take the night of the 3d.[5] I am glad if you like the Atlantic. We hope when it shall be better. Clough's Autobiography begins in the next number.[6] One would think it would be easy to find good criticism; but this department it is hard to fill Then what I call the Zoroastrian element,[7] & which I think essential to a good American journal, Lord Bacon would "note as deficient." And I believe further that we have not had a single correspondent from Philadelphia. I hope we shall yet supply all these deficiencies.[8]

Ever yours affectionately,
R. Waldo E.

3. Probably January 12, when Emerson lectured in Littleton. Charvat, p. 34, has Littleton, Massachusetts, but neither to Account Book for 1853–1859, p. [196], nor the Pocket Diary for 1858 (*JMN*, 4:458) specifies the state, nor do I find anywhere a note of the topic. The neighboring Massachusetts town is likely, considering the small fee of $10.00, but lecturing there would not take him away from Concord all day.

4. MS in the Furness papers, Van Pelt Library PU; ph. in NNC; printed in *Records*, p. [115].

5. On February 3 Emerson gave his lecture "Works and Days" for the benefit of the Union Temporary Home. See Charvat, p. 34. The lecture for the People's Literary Institute for the 2nd was "City Life and Country Life"; see above, January 5.

6. Arthur Hugh Clough's poem "Amours de Voyage" had been held up by Lowell until he had ample copy in hand (see his letter to Clough of December 21, 1857, Mulhauser, 2:536). It ran for four numbers: February, March, April, and May 1858 (1:419–426, 536–543, 667–673, 784–790). See below, May 17, for Emerson's comment.

7. Considering the reception of "Brahma" (November 1857, 1:58), others may have supposed the "Zoroastrian element" excessive.

8. A sputtering pen makes the word appear to be "dificiencies."

To Benjamin Rodman, Concord, January 18, 1858[9]

Concord, 18 Jany. 1858

My dear friend,

It was kind of you to take so much trouble as to find me my rubbers, which safely arrived here two nights ago. I hoped they might fit some good man's feet in New Bedford,[10] if somewhat too large for anybody in your house.

Well, I am glad to have them, as they fit me; and I shall try to be as good in my turn to some other party, since you never allow me the comfort of serving you or yours.

In the warm winter, I think with some alarm of your icehouses, and hope they will be miraculously supplied.

Yours affectionately,
R. W. Emerson

Benjamin Rodman

To George Ripley, Concord, February ? 1858

[In a letter of February 12, 1858, to Richard Henry Dana, Jr. (MHi), George Ripley acknowledges Dana's comments on the article on anesthesia in the *New American Cyclopedia:* He admits that the article may have errors of detail and "perhaps deviates from the rigid standard of historical impartiality which we are pledged to adhere to." He sees no reason to remove the article or any part of it, "although Dr. C. T. Jackson & Mr. R. W. Emerson vehemently insist upon it." A letter from Emerson to Ripley seems clearly to be implied here. See below, March 1, 1863, to Charles Sumner. See Appendix C, 5.]

9. The MS has not been located (in 1932 it was owned by the Reverend Alfred Hussey); text from a typescript copy. Emerson probably used an ampersand where "and" appears in the copy. Hussey was a Unitarian minister; he had a church in Billerica at one time and visited Concord; in her letters Ellen Emerson refers to him as her friend; see Gregg, 2:323, for meeting him at the Saratoga conference of 1878. This letter and the other he had in 1932 may have come from the family.

10. See above, November 21, 1857, and *Letters*, 5:94, 95, for Emerson's trip to New Bedford to lecture on December 22.

To Leonard Bacon, Concord, February 18, 1858[11]

Concord Mass
18 February 1858

Dr Leonard Bacon.
Dear Sir,

I have just received from Mrs Flower ⟨a⟩of Stratford on Avon the enclosed note, which I hasten to forward to you.[12]

I ~~would heartily wish that I~~ had very different news to send you of a person who has high claims on me & on all of us who love genius & elevation of character. These qualities have so shone in Miss Bacon, that, whilst their present eclipse is the greater calamity, it seems as if the care of her in these present distressing circumstances ought to be not at private, but at ⟨a⟩the public charge of scholars & friends of learning & truth. If I can serve you in any manner in relation to her, you will please to command me.

With great respect,
R. W. Emerson.

To Horatio Woodman, Concord, February 21, 1858[13]

Concord, 21 Feby 1858

My dear Sir,

Besides the two lectures which I call "Country Life," and "Works & Days," and which have not been read in Boston, I wish to read new lectures on philosophy, which I might call

1. Powers of the mind.
2. The Natural system of mental philosophy.
3. Memory.
4. Health & Exercise of the mind.

Mr Phillips (Englishman) who was here this week, & read a good lecture on Ebenezer Elliot[14] said that Mr Field of F. & Ticknor, told him

11. MS in DFo; ph. in NNC; printed by Theodore Bacon, p. 312; listed *Letters*, 5:100; printed in part by Vivian Hopkins, p. 257.
12. Celina Greaves Flower. Miss Bacon was under the care of George Fayrer in his sanitarium in Henley-in-Arden near Stratford where Mr. and Mrs. Edward Fordham Flower lived. In 1853 Emerson had sent Miss Bacon a letter of introduction to Flower (*Letters*, 4:368); the letter to Flower is listed, *ibid.*, p. 367.
13. MS in the Phillips Library, MSaE; ph. in NNC. The letter is attached by a strip of opaque gauze on the last leaf; possibly the addressee's name is concealed by it. That Emerson is writing Horatio Woodman is clear from letters to Woodman printed below.
14. George Searle Phillips lectured on the Corn-Law Rhymer (Ebenezer Elliot) for the Concord Lyceum on February 17.

some gentlemen were about to make a proposition to me to read a
Course So do you please to know who they are and if there be any good
man who can relieve you of trouble in the matter—why then you shall
not be entirely released, I cannot afford that. I flatter myself that I have
a goodly quantity of material that ought to interest goodly heads. I am
not yet content with my titles, & hope to send you better, perhaps before
/to/night.[15]

Yours gratefully,
R. W. Emerson.

To Samuel Gray Ward, Concord, February 22, 1858 [16]

Concord
22 February

Thanks for the least ray of light upon Mad River & Lake Erie! I shall
have to wait until I can get a description of my bonds, which Mr Adams
has always kept for me.

You shall be sure of my vigilance in regard to a home & guardian for
Tom,[17] when he is ready to come to Mr S. I should have gone at once to
the matron whom I think the best, to bespeak a chamber for him, but for
a circumstance which raised some doubts for the time.[18] I hope surely to
find you at the Club on Saturday,[19] & will tell you what I find. It is good
that Anna is at Rome,[20] where there seems even an unusual concentration of good people.

Ever yours
R. W. Emerson

S. G. Ward.

15. See Charvat, p. 34, for the final titles for the lectures given at the Freeman Place
Chapel.
16. MS in the Ward Papers, Houghton Library, MH; ph. in NNC. See *Letters*, 5:100, n.
34, where Abel Adams' fully dated letter of February 25 secures the year for this letter to
Ward as well as that of Emerson's letter to Abel Adams of February 24 making the inquiries
here referred to.
17. Thomas Wren Ward, named for his grandfather, was Ward's only son; he had long
been deaf from a childhood illness, but apparently overroad the handicap; see below, letter
of July 2 to Ward. For young Ward's close friendship with William James, see Perry, 1:39,
159, 209, 229–230, *et passim.* He was to attend Franklin B. Sanborn's school.
18. Tom Ward would be boarded with Miss Emmeline Barrett.
19. The "Club" unnamed is, here and hereafter, the Saturday Club.
20. Emerson would soon regret Mrs. Ward's exposure to Rome. See below, May 17, and
also October 26, 1859, and notes.

To Henry Whitney Bellows, Concord, February 23, 1858[21]

Concord

23 February 1858

My dear Sir,

I have heard with regret that some party,—I know not who or why, attacks the character of Rev. Daniel Foster.[22] He was formerly a resident clergyman in this town settled as I think for a year. During that time I became a good deal acquainted with him. He was a good preacher, & I still remember a Fast Day Sermon which I thought admirable. He was a brave good pastor, & took care of the outcast & forgotten. I respected certain heroic traits which appeared in him, still more than his good sermons. His leaving of his parish was in like manner more honorable to him than his staying would have been. And afterwards, being employed as an agent by the Anti-slavery society, he offended his employers by an independent course which I thought right;[23] of his subsequent history I know less but I esteem him as a man of excellent virtues, who ought by no means to be left idle, but abundantly used & honored. With his courage & spirit of adventure, I heard with interest & pleasure that he

21. MS in the Bellows papers, MHi; ph. in NNC.

22. The Reverend Daniel Foster had addressed Bellows' New York parish on January 17, 1858, on the subject of the "religious wants of Kansas." He was soliciting funds to establish "unsectarian anti-slavery churches" on the model of one he had already set up in Emporium. His appeal received Bellows' blessing (*National Anti-Slavery Standard*, January 23, 1858, 18:3). Neither the *Anti-Slavery Standard* nor the *Liberator* report any recent attacks on Foster, and apparently Mary Merrick Brooks had not been explicit.

23. Foster had been pastor of the Trinitarian Church in Concord in 1851. See Thoreau on Foster, *Journals*, B. Torrey and F. H. Allen, eds. (Boston: Houghton, Mifflin, 1949), 3:176–177, 225, 229–230, entries of April 20? 1851, and January 25 and 26, 1852. On the verso of a printed leaflet distributed April 4, 1851, by the Vigilance Committee of Boston, a Concord citizen has written a pencil note reading: "Rev Mr Foster of Concord has made a speech worthy of the heart of a Christian minister, as one who felt that he should meet his fugitive brother at the bar of God, and was willing to suffer the odium which is cast around the path of the abolitionist for the sake of being an honest man" (MCo). The writer perhaps refers to a speech made at the Liberty meeting of the Middlesex Anti-Slavery Society, April 3, 1851; the MS records of the society (MCo) show that Foster opened the Trinitarian church for the meeting. Another possibility is his Fast Day Sermon of April 10, 1851, *Our Nation's Sins and the Christian's Duty*, printed in Concord. He distinguished himself on April 12, 1851, by his prayer on the Boston wharf as the ship carrying the runaway slave Thomas Sims was about to depart. An entry in Emerson's MS journal CO reads: "No answer could be better to most of the proslavery eloquence than our unscrupulous Mr Foster's to Cheney at the Post Office, 'Fiddlestick.'" The editors of *JMN* (11:369–370, n. 11) identify Foster as the anti-slavery lecturer Stephen Symonds Foster, but I believe that the year, 1851; the place, the post office; and the word "our" make Mr. Foster, Daniel Foster who, as Thoreau's journal entries show, had the town in a turmoil during his one year in residence. Furthermore, it seems unlikely that a transient would so address John Milton Cheney, local banker.

was planting in Kansas. My wife, who is still better acquainted with Mr Foster as a preacher & pastor, than I, holds him also in high respect.

I learn from my friend Mrs Brooks, that Mr Foster is assailed, but I know nothing more, & hasten to send you my testimony.

With affectionate regards,
Yours,

Rev Dr Bellows.   R. W. Emerson.

To Cyrus Augustus Bartol, Concord, February 25, 1858[24]

Concord
25 February

My dear Bartol,

Easy as it ought to be, easy as it probably is, if we only could get the least <u>proprio</u> <u>motu</u> push, to get out of our chalk circle into the blessed rhythmical one, yet the petty barrier or illusion of a barrier is as insurmountable as Andes.[25] I would so gladly ⟨p⟩have rendered this little service to you who never require any.—and I am a deaf-mute on the occasion. Partly, no doubt, tis distracted studies; for I am writing lectures, & printing something for the Atlantic,[26] & have had just now an onerous correspondence but mainly tis in the slow brain, which does not seem to have the properties of the Cremona violin, & become more impressionable, but less, with use & age. If any gracious /air/ of the oldest time, air of th⟨e⟩ose times that are old <u>and</u> new, shall hereafter cheer me; I mean to s⟨i⟩e⟨e⟩ize & save it for your second edition. I confess to the lectures. Mr Woodman & other gentlemen have kindly charged themselves with finding me a company in the worst of times. My household is all absent in Boston or at school. The best of this fine day to yours!

R. W. Emerson

24. MS in Special Collections, Butler Library, NNC; ph. in NNC. The "worst of times" in conjunction with the *Atlantic Monthly* suggests 1858 as the year, and in March of that year Emerson gave a series of lectures at the Freeman Place Chapel arranged for by Horatio Woodman; see Letters of March 1 and 2 below to Woodman. Rusk lists this letter, 5:268, with the conjectured year 1862; he had only a quotation in an auction catalogue to go by.

25. I have no clue to Bartol's request beyond what is inferrable from the letter that he wants a hymn. There is no record of a second edition of *Hymns for the Sanctuary* (Boston: Wm. Crosby & H. P. Nichols, 1849), itself a "new edition" prepared by Bartol and others of "the West Church Collections" (*NUC*). Emerson's Latin phrase implies that he has no appropriate impulse to write verse.

26. "Persion Poetry" was printed in the April issue (1:724–734).

To Leonard Bacon, Concord, February 25, 1858[27]

Concord
25 February

Dear Sir,

I received this morning your note, and I think it proper to forward to you also this second note from Mrs Flower, because it seems as if the apology it offers were meant to you. It also gives you perhaps later notices, if you have not yourself letters by the same arrival.

With great respect, yours,
R. W. Emerson

Rev. Dr Bacon.

To Francis Parkman, Concord, February 26, 1858[28]

Concord, 26 Feby
1858.

Dear Sir,

I send you the little MS. which I mentioned to you long ago. It was given to me a few years since, by—Hosmer, Esq. of Toledo, Ohio;[29] and when I asked, if I should restore it to him, he said that he had had thoughts of sending it to you, and that he should like to have me transmit it to you. This I should have done much sooner, but that some extraordinary lubricity seems to belong to the document: it has been lost & found & lost again, and I am keeping, this day, a keen eye on it, until I shall have it securely sealed to your address.

I am sorry I cannot tell you the very little that Mr H. told me of the history of this Ms. in his hands. I found it badly paged, but I think it is complete, though it appeared not to be.[30]

Yours, with great regard,
R. W. Emerson

Mr. Parkman.

27. MS in DFo; ph. in NNC; printed by Theodore Bacon, p. 313; listed *Letters,* 5:100. For Mrs. Flower, see above, February 18; this letter is clearly of the same year.

28. MS in the Parkman papers, MHi; ph. in NNC. On the the first page a note in Parkman's hand reads: "Ottoway Indians," apparently the subject of the document Emerson encloses.

29. On his western trip of 1854 Emerson had met a number of Hosmers (transplanted from Concord) in Detroit (*Letters,* 5:426. He does not mention a Hosmer in Toledo, but the city directory was issued by Hosmer and Harris.

30. If Parkman made any use of the document, he could not have done so before the fourth edition (1867) and might not have done so until the two-volume edition of 1870. See

To Abraham Jackson, Concord, February 28? 1858

[In a letter of February 26, 1858 (RWEMA), Abraham Jackson asks Emerson for an acknowledgment of a letter he had written on February 10. Jackson refers to bills he has sent as well as money due to Lidian Emerson and her sister. I find no entries in the Account Book for 1853–1859 that would explain Jackson's reference to bills or provide evidence that Emerson replied. At p. [198], under the date January 20, Emerson records the receipt of rents from the Plymouth and Boston properties belonging to Mrs. Emerson and her sister.]

To Horatio Woodman, Concord, March 1, 1858 [31]

Concord 1 March

My dear Sir,

On reflection I am quite of your opinion that it is better to dispose of the two miscellaneous topics at the beginning of the Course, & then proceed to the connected Lectures; And I incline to write the Programme as follows;

Mr Emerson's Six Lectures.

1. Country Life.
2. Works & Days
3. Powers of the Mind.
4. Natural Method of Mental Philosophy.
5. Memory.
6. Self-Possession.

giving notice that the subject for Wednesday Evening is Country Life. I really wish to win the attention of good heads to the attractive side of intellectual science whose very name now repels, and mainly as I think, because the professors pretend & attempt much more than they ought, whilst if they simply gave their own experiences, & stopped when these were out, they would interest everybody.

Yours faithfully,
R. W. Emerson

Mr Woodman.

Howard H. Peckham, "The Sources and Revisions of Parkman's *Pontiac*," *Papers of the Bibliographical Society of America* (1943), 37:293–307.

31. MS in the Beinecke Library, CtY; ph. in NNC. The letter is accompanied by the envelope addressed: Horatio Woodman, Esq. | Court Square. | Boston. | , postmarked at Concord March 1. The year is 1858; see Charvat, p. 34, and March 2, below. Listed *Letters*, 5:101, from the Wakeman catalogue.

To Horatio Woodman, Concord, March 2, 1858[32]

Concord

Tuesday Eve

My dear Sir

I doubt not you received my note of yesterday which went to Boston in last nights mail but as the Evening Traveller of tonight does not contain the new advertisement I think it safe to send you this duplicate. I think your arrangement best, & set the Programme in this order.

Yours ever,

R. W. E.

Mr Emersons Six Lectures.
> I. Country Life.
> II. Works and Days.
> III. Powers of the Mind.
> IV. Natural Method of Mental Philosophy.
> V. Memory
> VI. Self-Possession.

To Sarah Ann Clarke, Concord, March 2, 1858?[33]

Concord

Tuesday, 2 March

My dear friend,

My wife & I thank you for your Arabian invitation, which for tomorrow we cannot accept. But I shall come presently to find where is your new abode. I made, in the summer, some vain attempts to find you in the Temple.

Yours affectionately,

R. W. Emerson

Miss Sarah Clarke.

32. MS in the Woodman papers, MHi; ph. in NNC. The lecture titles establish the year. The letter cannot be later than Tuesday, March 2; see above, the letter to Woodman of March 1 accepting Woodman's order for the lectures is surely the "note of yesterday" referred to here. The lectures began on March 3. Emerson's Pocket Diary for 1858 lists the lectures by the titles and in this order (*JMN*, 14:459).

33. MS in the Clarke papers, Houghton Library, MH; ph. in NNC. I can make no strong case for assigning this letter to 1858, but the note cannot be of 1869 when Miss Clarke was in Rome; by 1875 Emerson's memory left him dependent on his daughter Ellen for making engagements of this kind; in 1852 Emerson was in Portland, Maine. The stationery, as well as the easy tone, rules out 1841. There is nothing against the year 1847, but I choose 1858 because I believe Miss Clarke has invited the Emersons to visit her before or after his

To Horatio Woodman, Concord, March 9, 1858[34]

Concord,
March 9

My dear Sir,

What to say Mr Rowse? I could so gladly give him these days at any time when I am not actually preparing lectures. But these new ones I have much at heart.[35] I could give him the whole of Thursday, but dare not add Friday & Saturday. Of the next week too, the lecture is to be new, and I could only offer him the Thursday. In the following week, I might offer him Thursday, Friday, & Saturday, & the better if he would go to my house.

What to do?

Some one has sent me a slip from the Transcript of Tuesday, 2 March, containing a model eulogy to pave the way to our Course;[36] & which could come from no hand but that which constitutes itself again my Tutelar Angel. I shall think the better of myself, & best of him, all my days,

Yours gratefully,
R. W. Emerson

Mr. Woodman.

---

opening lecture (March 3) in the Boston course of that year. (See *Letters*, 5:101, for a similar letter.) Moreover, the "new abode" referred to is, I think, the recently built (1857) Pelham Hotel where Miss Clarke had for many years what was known as a "French flat." In the Clarke papers is an envelope addressed in Emerson's hand to her there, the postmark is blurred but the numeral "2" and an initial *M* in the month are clear.

34. MS in the Woodman papers, MHi; ph. in NNC. Samuel W. Rowse came to Concord May 1858 to do his crayon sketch of Emerson; see *Letters*, 5:114, for his temporary abandonment of the picture. The Freeman Place Chapel lectures arranged for by Woodman were announced in *BET*, March 2, 1858.

35. Ellen Emerson, in a letter of May 7 and 11 (to her cousin Haven), gives an account of the sittings. On May 7 all was going well, the portrait being "the best that was ever made," but continuing her account on the 11th, she reports that the artist "has spoilt his picture. . . . On Thursday night it was very good and Lizzie was pleased with it, as well as father and all of us. But before breakfast on Friday Mr Rouse did something to it which changed it from father to another man. . . ." (Gregg, 1:142; the misspelling of the artist's name is Ellen's error.) Ellen's tale can't be accurate. Rowse obviously made two different sketches, each of which was photographed. Mrs. Emerson evidently liked the first sketch, a print of it is so marked by Edward Waldo Emerson. The MS Account Book for 1853–1859, under the date November 12, p. [229], records the payment of $5.00 to Rowse for three photographs from "his first sketch."

According to Ellen's letter, Emerson was at the same time sitting in Boston for an oil portrait by Moses Wright. This painting, on which Ellen had set her heart, Emerson described as " 'swinish-looking.' "

36. Emerson is alluding to the lecture series of 1856 (March 27–May 1, Charvat, p. 32), which Woodman had arranged.

To Henry Stephens Randall, Concord, March 26, 1858 [37]

Concord—
26 March, 1858.

Dear Sir,

You were kind enough to say in a note to me, long ago, that you could still command a copy of the "Documentary History of New York," if I knew a party proper to receive so good a gift. [38] I have let the the proposition lie by, not wishing to waste a rich opportunity on any unfit receiver. Lately, a friend of mind comes occasionally to my library to explore the four Volumes, and finds them to contain much valuable matter to his purpose. His estimation is the more valuable, that he under estimated them when he first looked at them, a good while since; & he is a very curious & very instructed scholar in early American History, especially in all that concerns the Indians. Is it now too late to ask that you will give the offered volumes a direction in favor of my friend? He is Henry D. Thoreau, a land-surveyor in this town, a good scholar, and though far less known than he ought to be, very well-known in this region as the author of a book called "A Week on the Concord & Merrimack Rivers," and "Walden, or Life in the Woods." If you have still a copy of the work to spare I think you will not easily find s⟨u⟩o worthy a receiver. If you have not a copy remaining, perhaps you can tell me, at what cost, I can procure it. If /the book is giveable, &/ the book be sent through a booksellers box to /care of/ Phillips, Sampson, & Co, Boston, to my address, I will cheerfully pay the cost of transportation. If not, I think I shall I shall [39] make up my mind to give Mr. T. my own.

I congratulate you on the interest with which as I judge from the journals the public receives the "Life of Jefferson", [40] & which, I doubt not, will go on increasing. My own readings in it as yet have been very partial, as it lies out of my ordinary beat, & my studies lately have been more than usually confined, [41] but my day of freedom is always coming. Mr Quincy the elder, whom I saw soon after I saw you, [42] was keenly

37. MS in the Department of Special Collections, Regenstein Library, ICU; ph. in NNC.
38. See Harding, p. 82, for the book, still in Emerson's library, and *Letters,* 5:105, for Rusk's note of a letter to Randall of April 28 showing that Thoreau had received the four volumes as Emerson here asks.
39. Turning his leaf, Emerson repeated "I shall."
40. Randall's *The Life of Thomas Jefferson* is not now in Emerson's library; this letter suggests he had perhaps received it from the author.
41. Emerson probably refers to his Boston lectures to be concluded April 7; see Charvat, p. 34.
42. I find no record of the meeting with Randall or the meeting with Josiah Quincy.

curious to know all that I could tell him of what you had told me; but I have not seen him since.

With very kind regards,
Your obliged servant

Henry S. Randall, Esq.   R. W. Emerson

To Ellis Gray Loring, Concord, March 27, 1858[43]

Concord
27 March 1858

My dear Sir

I found yesterday at Phillips & Sampson's the engraved head of Coleridge, which, I believe, had been waiting for me some days. I brought it home with due care, & ⟨s⟩unrolled it with hope, which was more than fulfilled Tis a noble copy of a master's picture of a master.[44] I wonder that I see it for the first time; so many lovers of Coleridge as are in this country, tis strange this excellent print should not be known & multiplied here. I heartily thank you for giving this trusted treasure a direction to me. I shall have it properly mounted & hung in my library, as a perpetual memorial of the English seer, and also of yourself, With great respect & kindest regards I remain your debter,

R. W. Emerson

Ellis Gray Loring, Esq.

To Edward Everett Hale, Concord, March 30, 1858

[In a letter of March 30, 1858 (RWEMA), Edward Everett Hale invites Emerson to dine the next day (before his lecture) with him; Samuel Longfellow will be there, and he hopes for Frederic Henry Hedge as well. The letter requires an answer.]

43. MS in the Barrett Collection, Alderman Library, ViU; ph. in NNC.
44. This engraving of 1854 by Samuel Cousins is from Washington Allston's painting, itself adapted from Thomas Phillips' portrait of Coleridge. The engraving is in Emerson's study as reconstructed in the Concord Antiquarian Society.

To Samuel Gray Ward, Concord, April? 1? 1858?[45]

Concord
Thursday Eve.

My dear friend,

I tried to find you this morning half resolved to repent & ask a new invitation to dine with you & Mr Probyn, and also wishing to learn what you hinted about memory. There are plenty of wonders about it,—this remembering that we remember, & the remembering that we forget, and, oddest of all, /quasi-/remembering what we never knew. Nothing strikes me more in the approaches of the subject than the apathy with which we look at the power itself & the astonishment with which we see any increased degree of the power. But before you go, if you go,—as you will,—I have other questions to ask, & must seek a time.

Will you please to have a fire made in Ellen's chamber. I have just intercepted a note to her mother asking for Mercurius, & I know not what, because she was increasing a cold. But if she has a cold, please to send her home by the first train. Ever yours,

R. W. Emerson

S. G. Ward.

To Harrison Gray Otis Blake, Concord, April 15, 1858[46]

Concord—
15 April, 1858.

My dear Sir,

I have your note today, with Mr Higginson's postscript. I learn with surprise,—& an interest which dates from college days,—Dr Blood's death.[47]

---

45. MS in the Ward papers, Houghton Library, MH; ph. in NNC. Probyn visited Boston in the early spring of 1858 bringing an introduction from Carlyle; see draft letter of May 15 to Carlyle (*Letters*, 5:108). Since in the draft Emerson tells Carlyle that he has taken Probyn to the Saturday Club, I conjecture that the dinner of March 27 is referred to; I select the March date because the Account Book for 1853–1860, p. [221], shows the payment (April 24) of $9.37 for two dinners at the Club in March and for only one in February, p. [215], I arbitrarily assign this letter to April 1. The Emerson children frequently visited the Wards, but I find no letter from Ellen Emerson to date this visit. I conjecture that Probyn was John Webb Probyn. His article "The United States Constitution and the Secessionists," makes it clear that he had visited the States (*Westminister Review*, April 1, 1866, n.s. 29:422–451). Emerson's letter to Carlyle (May 17) as actually sent does not mention Probyn (Slater, pp. 520–521), probably because he was not known to Carlyle personally.

46. MS in the Denison Library, CCC; ph. in NNC. Listed *Letters*, 5:104.

47. Oliver Hunter Blood, Harvard, B.A., '21, and M.D., '26; d. 1858 (Quinquennial Catalogue). There is one letter by Dr. Blood in the Emerson papers; the letter shows him to have been a man of spirit and humor.

I shall accept your renewed kind invitation, uncertain now whether this be that occasion on which I had promised to come, or, no,—I mean Miss Buttman's party. Mr Higginson's postscript put me in some doubt as to his wish. I had supposed that he asked me to come, ⟨s⟩out of some desire he had to try my metaphysical Lectures on the nerves of Worcester,[48] since he is a brave man;[49] and I thought I would meet much desperate courage, with my desperation: so I sent him one of my titles; but, though bullets & bayonets cannot scare him, the title does, & he pleads for "Country Life." I telegraphed to him, just now, that I would bring the last tomorrow, & also the others already named; and, if he have not advertised a title, we can choose at the last moment.

Meantime, lecture or not, I will come gladly to your house.

R. W. Emerson

Mr Blake.

To Edwin Percy Whipple, Concord, April 22, 1858[50]

Concord

22 April, 1958.

My dear Whipple,

I found at home today a rare compliment, a letter from the Greek Professor in Harvard University, perhaps the first letter I ever had from him, full of praises of something of mine;—you may well suppose my old eyes were a little dazzled, & could not make out anything distinctly, but that I had written something singularly good, to extort such commendation.[51] But pride must come down, & as soon as my eyes cleared a little from this glory, & could make out the words clearly, it was all an

48. Emerson had offered the "Natural Method of Mental Philosophy" (*Letters*, 5:102). See Cabot, 11, 763–765, for the second of Emerson's two lectures for which Higginson paid; the title announced in the *Worcester Spy* was "The Analogies of Nature to the Processes of the Mind." It is not easy to tell whether this title applies to "The Powers of Mind" or to the "Natural Method," both given in the Freeman Place series (see Charvat, p. 34). Clearly Higginson was not so timid as Emerson here supposes. The topic of the first lecture is not clear, but possibly it was "Domestic Life." See notes to May 21 below for corrections of Charvat and for Miss Butman's party.

49. Emerson's allusion here is to Higginson's attempted rescue of the fugitive slave Anthony Burns (see above, September 29, 1854). In 1859 Higginson would show himself to have as much moral courage as physical when he did not flee the country or burn his papers after the capture of John Brown.

50. MS in the Berg Collection, NN; ph. in NNC; listed *Letters,* 5:104 from dealer's catalogue; printed by Lilian Whiting, *Boston Days,* p. 231, with Cornelius C. Felton's letter of April 21 mistakenly written to Emerson (pp. 230–231), that occasioned this letter.

51. Felton names the title of Whipple's essay "Intellectual Character" (*AM*, May 1858, 1:791–800), in his first sentence. Whipple's article is a review of *The American Cyclopaedia.* All articles being anonymous, Felton might mistake Whipple's ideas for Emerson's, but it is hard

eulogy,—very just & true, be sure,—but of your article, not mine. So I send you the letter, and if your eyes are dim, Mrs Whipple shall read it to you. Not to lose all the benefit, I hastened to get the Atlantic, which I had not read, and have read the paper myself, and I think the Professor's admiration is honorable to him & to you, and when you have done as he bids you,[52] I will subscribe for twenty five copies.

Yours faithfully,

E. P. Whipple.   R. W. Emerson

To Henry David Thoreau, Concord, May 11, 1858[53]

My dear Henry,

A frog was made to live in a swamp, but a man was not made to live in a swamp. Yours ever. R.

To Arthur Hugh Clough, Concord, May 17, 1858[54]

Concord
17 May, 1858

Dear Clough,

I believe I only write to you to ask favors.[55] I wish to engage your attention to a couple of interesting friends of mine, the Longworths of Cincinnati, who are shortly going to London. You must have heard of their father, old Nicholas Longworth, who introduced the wine-grape planting & manufacture on the Ohio, where he is now a sort of agricultural duke.

Mr Joseph L. is his only son, who now goes to London with his wife, a

---

to understand how he could have mistaken the style. (Emerson had had earlier letters from Felton.)

52. Felton had suggested that the essay be issued as a handbook to be placed "in the hands of every student in every college, and in that of every man and woman—the great college of society."

53. Text from MS journal VO, p. 289 (RWEMA); probably not to be taken as a genuine letter. Printed *JMN*, 14:204. The salutation and the complimentary close are in a darker ink; the former is crowded in above the text. This text is the third version. The first is crowded in on p. 286 and reads: "I tell him that a man was not made to live in a swamp, but a frog." The footnote version is at the foot of p. 287 and reads: "If God meant him to live in a swamp, he would have made him a frog." Emerson composes this squib after a walk with Thoreau, *JMN*, 14:203.

54. MS in the Clough papers, Bodleian Library; ph. in NNC; printed in *Emerson-Clough Letters*, No. 28, and in Mulhauser, 2:548–549.

55. Cf. letter of the same date to Carlyle, Slater, p. 521; and for a draft of May 15, see *Letters*, 5:107–108. Note that there was a draft, also of May 15, of this letter to Clough. My guess is that the occasion of providing the Longworths with introductions enabled him to get on with these letters. He alludes more than once to his inability to write to distant friends.

lovely & refined woman, who, by the bye, paints landscapes with genius. They ought to see what is best abroad, and I wish that they should not lack any facilities or good advice. So I shall certainly send Mr L. to you.

I cannot forgive you for the baulking end or no end of the "Amours de Voyage." I esteemed the "Atlantic Monthly" worth the founding, when I heard that you would write.[56] I read the first livraison of your poem with joy, & said, Behold that is what cannot be written here. Tis the sincerity of British culture. Here is a man tremulous all over with sensibility, and he holds a fine pen that delicately finds the right word,— gift that brings with it all other gifts. We watched from month to month our beloved star. The hexameters frightened some citizens. But all the good readers I know gave this poem every advantage over all the rest. And when we began to build securely on the triumph of our poet over all gainsayers, suddenly his wing flags, or his whim appears, & he plunges to a conclusion, like the ending of the Chancery suit in "Bleak House," or like the denouement of Tennyson's "Princess." How can you waste such power on a broken dream? Why lead us up the tower to tumble us down? There is a statute of Parnassus, that the author shall keep faith with the reader; but you choose to trifle with him. It is true a few persons compassionately tell me, that the piece is all right, and that they like this veracity of much preparation to no result. But I hold tis bad enough in life, & inadmissible in poetry. And I think you owe us a retribution of music, & to a musical argument. As I wish now to give due emphasis to my objection, I shall say nothing of all the merits that shine in the poem.

You will have seen Mrs S. G. Ward, ere this, & probably also Sam. W. too. I grieve that she has flung herself into the Church of Rome, suddenly.[57] She was born for social grace, & that faith makes such carnage of social relations! But I confide that her happy fortunate nature cannot be thwarted by any accidents, & will certainly bring her into harmony quickly again, from whatever extremest notes. Have you seen Agassiz's "Contributions to Nat. History of America"?[58] I have come to know him a good deal in the last years, & to be proud of his knowledge & talent.

56. Lowell had secured Clough's promises of a contribution in June 1857; see Mulhauser, 2:527–528.

57. Emerson's shocked response to Anna Barker Ward's conversion to Catholicism is described below; see notes, October 26, 1859. Clough, who had known Mrs. Ward since his visit to the States, was also distressed; see Mulhauser, 2:551, 556.

58. Louis Agassiz, Contributions to the Natural History of America (Boston: Little Brown, 1858). This work is not now in Emerson's library, but the MS Account Book (1853–1860), under the date January 14, records the payment of $24.00 as "my subscription to Agassiz's vols. I & II." In 1858, Louis Napoleon offered Agassiz the directorship of the Jardin des Plantes at $20,000 a year.

The book with its merits I doubt has not the poetic scope which the first-class Naturalist must use. I fear we shall lose him, as the French Emperor is bidding high on him. But when is that promised return of yours to be to us? not always are we to be baulked by you. Affectionately Yours,

R. W. Emerson.[59]

To Charlotte Haskins Cleveland, Concord, May 17? 1858

[In the MS Account Book for 1853–1859, p. [223], under the date May 17, is an entry reading: "Cash to Mrs Charlotte Cleveland, on a/c of expenses by Rev. Mr C. for Miss M. M. Emerson—5.00." A note to Mrs. Cleveland is likely.]

To Harrison Gray Otis Blake, Concord, May 21, 1858[60]

Concord

21 May

1858

My dear Blake,

Nothing can be little which comes from such a great heart of kindness, &, since you choose to send me the odd mills, I esteem it the sacred gift of you & yours.[61] The French rule, <u>quand on paye, on s'excuse d'aimer,</u> is plainly not your rule, & so you have added praises. I can only say, my experience is, 'tis good hearing that makes the good speech; so that I will guarantee beforehand the worth of any chapter that shall be read to your company, especially in your house.

---

59. Emerson wrote the last five words, the complimentary close, and signature along the margin of the first page.

60. MS in the Rush Reis Memorial Library, NRU; ph. in NNC; listed without addressee from dealer's catalogue, *Letters,* 5:109.

61. Emerson's MS Account Book for 1853–1860, p. [210], shows under the date May 12 the receipt of $20.00 from Blake ($16.00 crossed out). Charvat, p. 34, interprets this entry as supplementary to the payment of $15.00 each made by Thomas Wentworth Higginson for two lectures given in Worcester on April 16 and 23. Only one of the lectures (for the 16th) is listed in the Pocket Diary for 1858 (*JMN,* 14:;459). See *Letters,* 5:102, for the casual arrangement (April 8) Emerson made with Thomas Wentworth Higginson for one, possibly two, public lectures and for a private reading at Blake's house. This letter, taken with that to Higginson and with a letter to Blake of July 27 (*Letters,* 5:116), shows that Emerson did give a private reading as well as the two public lectures (see Rusk's n. 43, 5:103) and that he is here promising a second private reading to be given when the "Pond party" takes place. The letter of July 27 reneges on the Pond party. Emerson in the letter here is clearly taking the $20.00 as in part payment for the first private reading and advance payment for the promised second reading. The tone of this letter implies that Emerson thinks he is overpaid. Blake's letter remitting the money does not survive, but it may have occasioned the jesting allusion to the monetary unit of "mills."

In the letter here Emerson does not mention "Miss Butnam," but she appears in the letter of April 8 to Higginson and that of July 27 to Blake. She is possibly the daughter of Asa O. Butnam, the United States Deputy Marshall whom Higginson had helped to save from an angry Worcester mob on October 30, 1854 (Edelstein, pp. 167–170), and she is

In the good hope of that Pond party,—which I am not yet in condition positively to promise myself,—I remain Yours faithfully,

R. W. Emerson

H. G. O. Blake.

To George Bancroft, Concord, May 24, 1858[62]

Concord

24 May 1858

My dear Sir,

It was very good of you to send me the history of Concord, Lexington & Bunker Hill. I have read the volume with great attention,—which it was quite easy to do—& much of it twice.[63] The history is richer not only in anecdotes of great men, but of the great heart /of/ towns & provinces than I dared believe; and,—what surprised & charmed me,—it starts tears, & almost makes them overflow on many & many a page. I must confide in your wisdom in selection, & try to believe that you have omitted nothing that I want, yet you seem to be drawing your single sentence or phrase from ⟨ri⟩such masses of materials around you, that I grow very curious & hungry as I read. It is noble matter, & I am heartily glad to have it nobly treated. My son Edward, who was once your guest for a week, read the Battle of Concord through, with eager pleasure on the night of its arrival. It will find very loving readers here for a thousand years.

I cannot tell you how much pleasure your advocacy of the cause of Kansas lately gave to us north country people.[64]

My wife is out of town these two days or would send with mine dear regards & affection to Mrs Bancroft,[65]

Yours faithfully,

George Bancroft, Esq.   R. W. Emerson

apparently the prime mover in the proposed "Pond party" or, as Emerson calls it on July 27 "lily- or lake-party." See Higginson's article "Water-lilies" in the *Atlantic* for September 1858.

62. MS in the Bancroft papers, MHi; ph. in NNC; partly printed by M. A. DeWolfe Howe, *Life and Letters of George Bancroft* (New York: Scribner's, 1908), 2:107; listed *Letters*, 5:106, under the conjectured date of May 10.

63. Volume 7 of Bancroft's *A History of the United States* (*BAL*, 590; Emerson's copy, Harding, p. 21); "From the author" appears on the flyleaf in Bancroft's hand; the title page inscription is in Emerson's hand. A note on the rear cover is in Edward Waldo Emerson's hand.

64. Emerson is referring to Bancroft's speech for the New York Democratic Anti-Lecompton Meeting, New York, February 17, opposing the constitution drawn up in Lecompton, Kansas, by the pro-slavery faction; see *BAL*, 651, for the printing of the speech.

65. See below, July 2, and *Letters*, 5:111 and 114, for a visit to the Bancrofts in July of this year.

To Mary Russell Watson, Concord, May 26, 1858[66]

Concord
26 May 1858.

My dear friend,

It is a piece of character, &, as every piece of charact⟨he⟩er in writing is, a stroke of genius also, to praise Channing's poems in this cordial way. And I read the manuscript with thankful sympathy. But you will print it. It is by no means character & genius that are good to print, but something quite different,—namely,—tact, talent, sparkle, wit, humor, select anecdote and Birmingham lacker,[67] and I have kept the paper so many days, meaning to read it later & find whether it had the glass buttons required.

On looking into it today I hesitate to send it to that sad Bench where two judges or three judges are believed to sit & read with red eyes every scrap of paper that is addressed to the "Atlantic Monthly." I know that they read 400 papers to admit ten, one time. I am not of their counsel, but some of their cruelties have transpired. Yet who but must pity those red eyed men?[68]

I can easily believe that you have the materials of a good literary article. If I had the journal in which you have at any time set down detached thoughts on these poems, it might easily furnish the needed details & variety of criticism. I am not even sure that this piece, as it is, will /not/ presently appear presentable to me. Nothing can be acuter criticism than what you say of "the art to say how little, not how much, belonging to this fatal poet." Think a moment, & tell me, if you can say another word as descriptive of his genius. The selections, too, all have good reason. But I must have a few more good points. "So saith the Grand Mufti."

Yours faithfully,
R. W. Emerson.

Mrs. Watson.

66. MS in the New Jersey Historical Society; ph. in NNC; printed without indication of addressee and with minor errors in "The Contributors' Club," AM (July 1902), 90:139. Listed in Letters, 5:109, from dealers' catalogues, one having the addressee's name as "Miss Watson," and the other having the wrong date of 1855. See Rusk's sound reasons for identifying Mrs. Watson as Mary Russell Watson. See also Letters, 5:153 and 219–220.

67. This catalogue suggests to me that Emerson has in mind Oliver Wendell Holmes' "The Autocrat of the Breakfast Table" then running in the Atlantic. "Birmingham lacker" is an allusion to decorated glass buttons manufactured in Birmingham, England.

68. James Russell Lowell, Francis Underwood, and George Nichols. See Horace E.

To Brantz Mayer, Concord, June 2, 1858[69]

Concord

2 June 1858

My dear Sir,

I make haste to obey your request, & with the most becoming gravity. Nor shall I mistrust that any neighbor of yours wishes to advertise a lotion or pearl powder.[70]

I am very glad of this token of your health & of your good will. And for the journey of five & twenty years ago, I have no doubt we should both make it over again now, with equal zest, & much more benefit! Perhaps tis well for our families that we have not much opportunity of comparing notes, & planning new journeys & castles in Spain.[71]

Thanks for your friendly invitation, which I should accept at once if I found myself in your neighborhood. But it may easily happen that you will be in Boston, & then please remember that I am only an hour from it.

With kind regards,

Yours,

Brantz Mayer, Esq.   R. W. Emerson

To Gisela Von Arnim, Concord, June 29, 1858[72]

I have received—it is already some months since,—the welcome gift of your "Dramatic Works"[73] in two volumes. I cannot tell you how pleasant was to me this token from one of your name, and, since I have become acquainted with your thoughts, this token from yourself. I had

---

Scudder, *James Russell Lowell* (Boston: Houghton Mifflin, 1901), pp. [405]–455 *passim*. See Martin Duberman, *James Russell Lowell* (Boston: Houghton Mifflin, 1966), pp. 169–170, for Lowell's unwelcome editing of Thoreau, and see Harding and Bode, pp. 515–516, for Thoreau's angry letter.

69. MS in the Barrett Collection, Alderman Library, ViU; ph. in NNC.

70. Emerson was not easily caught by requests for testimonials; Mayer has apparently asked for an autograph for someone else and given assurances of its respectful use.

71. Emerson met Mayer in Rome, April 1833, and traveled with him and others to Florence (*Letters*, 1:274, 280; *JMN*, 4:166. He renewed the acquaintance in Baltimore in 1843 (*Letters*, 3:118, 127).

72. MS in the Goethe-und Schiller-Archiv, Weimar; ph. in NNC; printed by Frederick William Holls, "Emerson's Correspondence with Herman Grimm," *AM* (April 1903), 91:470–471; and in *Correspondence Between Ralph Waldo Emerson and Herman Grimm* (Boston: Houghton Mifflin, 1903), pp. 27–28; listed *Letters*, 5:111.

73. Harding does not list Gisela von Arnim's *Dramatische Werke*, vol. 1 (Bonn: 1857); vol. 2 (Berlin: 1857). The third volume was not published until 1865.

been now for fifteen years, an admirer of your mother's genius.[74] All her books, I believe, are on my shelves and I had eagerly learned what now and then a rare traveller could tell me of her happy personal and family relations. But no traveller could tell me so much good as this little pair of books you send me has told,—of noblest culture still found in her house, and that best kind of genius which springs from inspirations of the heart. I am charmed with the "Trost in Thränen" above all; for the choice of subject indicates high sympathies, and it is almost a test by which the finest people I have ever known might be selected,—their interest in Michel Angelo and his friend, Vittoria Colonna[75] in chief, so that I dare to believe myself already acquainted with you, and very heartily your friend. You shall not let your muse sleep, but continue to draw pictures provoking a legitimate interest, by showing a heart of more refinement than any other.

Lest I should make quite no return for your goodness, I have confided to Mr. Thayer for you a few numbers of our Boston Magazine, in which I sometimes write a chapter.[76]

May I ask of you the favor to offer my respects to your mother, the Frau von Arnim, and to thank her in my name for many happy hours she has formerly given to friends of mine and to me, through her writings

With renewed thanks for your goodness, I am, with the best hope, and with great respect,

Your friend,
R. W. Emerson.

Concord, Massachusetts.
29 June 1858.

74. Bettina Brentano von Arnim; see Harding, pp. 14–15. Harding does not note that the 1839 edition of *Goethe's Correspondence With a Child* has many marginal notes; it should be recorded that these notes are by Sophia Hawthorne (a.l.s., Ellen Emerson to her sister Edith, April 22, 1859).

75. See below, October 1, 1865, to Rebecca Duncan for Emerson's interest in their relationship.

76. Alexander W. Thayer had been the bearer of Herman Grimm's letter and gifts of 1856; see *Correspondence*, p. 17.

To Herman Grimm, Concord, June 29, 1858[77]

Concord June 29,
Massachusetts 1858.

Dear Sir,—

When Mr. Thayer long since brought me your letter,[78] with "Arnim" and "Demetrius,"[79] and the pieces contributed by you to the Morgenblatt, I should have at once expressed to you the surprise and pleasure I felt,—but that Mr. Thayer assured me that he should soon return to Germany, and would carry my letters of acknowledgment. And ever since, from time to time, I have heard again, that he was on the point of going. This fact is the only palliating circumstance I can offer on this tardiest reply to your goodness. The delay has also made the few critical words I once thought of writing down impertinent, and I can only now recall how happy I was in the preferred sympathy of a scholar bearing your honored name, and well proved by what I read worthy to bear it. It was an easy work of love to read the dramas, the poems, & the Essays in the Morgenblatt. I found special interest,—perhaps somewhat accidental, in the Demetrius. For the translated "Essay on Shakspeare,"— [80] I am proud to be introduced to Berlin under conditions of so good omen, and not a little proud to read myself in German at all. It is cheering to know that our fellow students,—lovers of the same muses,—work in one will, though so widely sundered,—and the more, because facilitated intercourse suggests to each the hope of seeing the other. I am grown to the stationary age; but who knows but the westward tendency, which seems to be impressed on the whole Teutonic family, will one day bring you to us!

As Mr. Thayer generously offers me room in his trunk, I gladly use the opportunity to send you a copy of all my books in the corrected edition.[81] By and by, I hope to send you a chapter or two of more permanent interest.

With all kind & grateful regards
R. W. Emerson.

Herman Grimm Esq.

77. MS in the Goethe-und Schiller-Archiv, Weimar; printed by Holls, *AM* (April 1903), 91:470–471, and *Correspondence*, pp. 27–28; listed *Letters*, 5:111.

78. A lapse of more than two years; Grimm's letter is dated April 5, 1856 (*Correspondence*, p. 17).

79. See Harding, p. 120, for the play *Arnim* (1851). *Demetrius*, a verse play, published in Berlin, 1853.

80. *Ralph Waldo Emerson über Goethe und Shakespeare.* Aus dem Englischen nebst einer Critik der Schriften Emersons von Herman Grimm (Hannover: Carl Rümpler, 1857).

81. Emerson probably sent Grimm a set of his books as reprinted by Phillips, Sampson, and Company.

To George Bancroft, Concord, July 1, 1858[82]

Concord, 1 July, 1858

My dear Bancroft,

Why do you & Mrs Bancroft tantalize me with delicious invitations to Newport & to your house, when I am bound, in all honesty & scholarly duty, to stay at home, & mind my task? Please to consider that it is not every one that can read libraries & write adequate continental histories, & yet have boundless leisure for hospitality & the joys of the sea. It argues great power of work somewhere to do thus.

My kindest salutations to Mrs Bancroft, & thanks for her letter to Lidian, who is in & about Boston, yesterday & today, & therefore all unconscious till tonight of the fine proposal.[83] I fear she must manage to go without me, much as I deplore the savage ⟨de⟩self-denial of staying away. I am promised to go to the Adirondac country in August, with a party,[84] which will cost some weeks, and, after that, I am to have some printing done.[85] Yet the wish to go to you is very strong, & perhaps will overcome all obstacles. Lidian will return tonight, and I will send you an exact answer tomorrow.

With kindest regards
R. W. Emerson

To Samuel Gray Ward, Concord, July 2, 1858[86]

Concord, 2 July. 1858

My dear S.

The Sanborn school closes with an Examination on the 13th, & some sort of pic-nic or school-festival on the 14th. I think you had better come out a little earlier, say Friday 9th instant,[87] for possibly on Saturday, Lidian & I may go to Newport to the Bancrofts for a pair of days.[88] Thursday is an Ordination day of the new minister, which does not

82. MS in the Bancroft papers, MHi; ph. in NNC. See above, May 24, where Emerson acknowledges the seventh volume of Bancroft's *History of the United States.*

83. See below, July 2, for Emerson's willing acquiescence to his wife's persuasion. See also *Letters,* 5:110, 111, and 114.

84. Emerson did not give up the Adirondack trip; on July 30 he bought a rifle, MS Account Book 1853–1860, p. [232].

85. Emerson is evidently already at work on the copy for *The Conduct of Life.*

86. MS in the Ward papers, Houghton Library, MH; ph. in NNC.

87. See February 22, above, for Emerson's part in finding lodgings for Thomas W. Ward II while he attended Franklin B. Sanborn's school.

88. See July 1 and 2 here to Bancroft.

happen in Concord oftener than once in 20, 30, or 50 years[89] But all the other days of the week are free to you. Come & spend Monday the Fourth, we will carry you to the Battle-Field: or Tuesday, or Wednesday. Only come on one. The ⟨1⟩11⟨15⟩/o'c/ train will bring you best. I hear from young people the best account of Tom.

Yours faithfully,
R. W. Emerson

S. G. Ward—

Ellery has just printed a poem,[90] which he does not publish, & which he has not sent me, but I will show it to you.

To GEORGE BANCROFT, CONCORD, JULY 2, 1858[91]

Concord
2 July, 1858.

Dear Bancroft,

Will you say to Mrs Bancroft that my wife is as contented with her letter as I anticipated, & means to go to Newport, next Saturday, and is bent on persuading me to go with her. As I am already very much inclined in the same direction, I think we shall try to spend a pair of days with you.[92]

Yours,
R. W. Emerson

We shall take, if all goes well, the boat which, Mrs. B. says, reaches Newport at 8 p.m.

To AINSWORTH RAND SPOFFORD, CONCORD, JULY 6, 1858[93]

Concord
6 July 1858

My dear Sir,

I received duly the MS. addressed to me many weeks ago, & read it with care. I readily decided that it was "righteous," which was the question submitted to me, & accordingly I forwarded it to the Atlantic people,

89. The Reverend Grindall Reynolds was ordained July 8, succeeding Barzillai Frost, who had been the minister for twenty-one years when he resigned September 13, 1857 (*Letters,* 5:11, n. 42).

90. *Near Home. A Poem,* printed anonymously, *BAL,* 3065; Harding, p. 56.

91. MS in the Bancroft papers, MH; ph. in NNC.

92. See above, July 1, for the invitation to Newport. The expenses of the trip are entered in the MS Account Book for 1853–1889, p. [229], under the date July 10 (Saturday).

93. MS in the Spofford papers, Manuscript Division, LC; ph. in NNC. Printed by Hollis, *NEQ* (March 1965), 38:83.

telling them no more of the Author, than, that it came to me from Cincinnati.[94] Yesterday I received a note from the sub-editor, saying, that "the piece is respectfully declined," and inquiring "what disposition shall be made of it?" They keep their mouths close shut, & do not give us a hint of the reason. Perhaps, it was impossible to print it at once, & it might grow quickly out of season. I gave them no name, for I know they do not wish to know the names of their authors, but prefer to try every paper on its merit, & subject, etc. I did not think I found in the manuscript the high merit of "Higher Law," though sharing the like moral dignity as that pamphlet. Well, we have offered to utter a piece of wholesome truth to the people, & if they would not hear, we have at least cleared our skirts. It is a solid comfort to me to know that you are always there fast abiding in convictions, & inevitably a power for good in that important community.

Yours faithfully,

Mr Spofford.   R. W. Emerson

To Charles Wesley Slack, Concord, July 8, 1858 [95]

Concord 8 July 1858

Dear Sir

I am heartily obliged to the Committee of the Twenty Eighth Society for their honoring invitation to the rural festival at Watertown, and the more that it repeats a former courtesy.[96] It will give me I doubt not great pleasure to ⟨co⟩join you, if I shall be ⟨fr⟩ at home & free at that time. But I am leaving home /with my wife,/ on the 10th, to pass a few days at Newport with some old friends on an engagement of some standing, and I am not sure that I shall return so soon.[97] You must keep a corner of room for me in the afternoon. With my best wishes for the happiest day to all your company,[98] I remain

Your friend & servant

Mr Slack.   R. W. Emerson

94. "Napoleon's Nemesis," which Emerson submitted to Francis Underwood, June 3; see *Letters*, 5:109. Hollis conjectures that the article was by Charles H. Goddard (n. 60). That the article is Spofford's own seems to me suggested, though not made certain, by the allusion to his pamphlet *The Higher Law*. See above, May 23, 1851, and March 15, 1852, for Emerson's admiration of and debt to Spofford's pamphlet protest against the Fugitive Slave Law.

95. MS in MH-AH; ph. in NNC.

96. See July 8, 1857, for the invitation of that year.

97. To visit George Bancroft and his wife, Lidian Emerson's friend of many years.

98. In his letter of July 15 (*Letters*, 5:114), Emerson tells John Murray Forbes that he returned from Newport "last night," so there is no certainty that he got to the festival on the afternoon of the 14th.

To William J. Stillman, Concord, July 20? 1858

[In a letter of July 22, n.y. (endorsed by Emerson 1858, RWEMA), William J. Stillman says he agrees with Emerson that there should be no dinner party before the trip to the Adirondacks; see Rusk, *Life*, p. 398, for the trip. A letter seems to be implied and more than one is likely. Stillman tells Emerson he need not trouble to take a gun; but see above, July 1, and notes, for Emerson's purchase of a rifle. The full expenses and an itinerary are entered in the MS Account Book for 1853–1859 (pp. [234–235]) under the date August 18. There is no connection between the Saturday Club and the Adirondac Club save the accident of overlapping membership; in this year only half the group belonged to the Saturday Club; *JMN*, 14: 270, n. 165, gives misleading information here.]

To ———, Concord, August 1, 1858

[A three-page letter of August 1, 1858, was advertised in 1929 in the catalogue (p. 231, lot 1538) of Von K. Gregg-Hagenbach of Basel. See *Letters*, 5:117, for two letters of this date; this letter may be the one to Henry Whitney Bellows.]

To Mrs. David Mack, Saranac Lake, August 16, 1858

[Emerson is a signer of a note written on birch bark in Louis Agassiz's hand and dated "Camp Maple Aug 16 '58," Treasure Room, MB. The note reads: "Voted that the thanks of the company be tendered to Mrs. Mack for her contribution of ginger-snaps." The other signers are Horatio Woodman, Jeffries Wyman, James Russell Lowell, John Holmes, Estes Howe, William J. Stillman, Ebenezer Rockwood Hoar, and Amos Binney. See Rusk, *Life*, p. 398, for the Adirondac trip.]

To Mary Moody Emerson, Concord, August? 23? 1858?[99]

We are talkative but Heaven is silent. I have puzzled myself like a mob of writers before me in trying to state the doctrine of Fate for the printer.

99. No MS has been found; text from MS journal EO Fate, pp. 174–176, Emerson papers (RWEMA), Houghton Library, MH; ph. in NNC. In the MS journal, it is headed: "I write to Aunt Mary." Printed in part in *J*, 10:472–473, with no indication of its being part of a letter. A portion omitted from *J* appears as the conclusion of "Powers and Laws of Thought," *Works*, 12:64. Listed *Letters*, 4:249, as possibly from a letter acknowledged by Miss Emerson in hers of April 19 [1851].

For several reasons, I think 1851 too early. First, there is the allusion to the printer. The lecture "Fate" was given on December 22, 1851, but Emerson does not begin to speak of publishing until a letter to his brother of October 18, 1858 (*Letters*, 5:122), and even there declares the book "not yet ready." (See also, above, July 1.) The essay as finally printed in *The Conduct of Life* draws on material of 1851–1859 from several journals as well as EO Fate. There are very few dates in this journal; three periodical quotations are of 1851 (p. 40), 1854 (p. 115), and 1856 (p. 147), all entered before the letter. After it, p. 214, appears an entry dated June 1859.

A second reason for thinking 1858 more likely than 1851 is a letter from Miss Emerson of August 25, n.y. (endorsed 1858 by Emerson, RWEMA). In part a meditation on her 84th birthday, the letter seems to refer to Emerson's essay; she writes: "Who could better (once!)

I wish to sum the conflicting impressions by saying that all point at last to an unity which inspires all, but disdains words /& passes understanding./. Our poetry, our religions, are its skirts & penumbra. Yet the charm of life is the hint we derive from this:[100] they overcome us, like perfumes from a far off shore of sweetness: & their meaning is, that no tongue shall syllable it without leave; that only itself can name it; that by casting ourselves on it, & being its voice, it rushes each moment to positive commands, creating men & methods, & ties the will of a child to the love of the first /Cause./ As soon as it is uttered, it is profaned. The thinker denies personality out of piety, not out of pride. It refuses a personality which is instantly imprisoned in human measures.

To Gisela Von Arnim, Concord, September 3, 1858[101]

Concord, Mass.
September 3, 1858

To Fraulein Gisela von Arnim,

Will you allow me to press the slight claim to your acquaintance which your valued gift created.[102] So far as that I should present to you an intimate and honored friend of mine, Miss Elizabeth Hoar, who goes to pass a year in Europe and means to visit Berlin. She was, many years

---

give original ideas of natural religion than him who is responsible for her: The sublime idea of necessity wh gives our existence to be connected by its' nature to the only source of life and joy & virtue." My conjecture is that Emerson had written her a birthday letter of which the journal entry is a part.

Not, I think, against this dating is the probability that Miss Emerson was already living in Concord, boarding with a Miss Wright (see *Letters*, 5:122, and, for her proposal to live in Concord, 5:106). Her letter gives no place, but must have been written in Concord, for on September 2 Emerson takes over the burden of paying the bills and continuing the deception Elizabeth Hoar had already set up. The MS Account Book for 1853–1860, pp. [224] and [235], shows that the beleaguered landlady added to her charges $2.29 "for extra trouble." If Miss Emerson and her nephew might find it difficult to meet in Lidian Emerson's parlor, they could meet on the plane of metaphysics and renew in writing something of the uneasy rapport of thirty years ago.

Admittedly, these "reasons" do not constitute hard evidence, the less so because he was working on the essay in 1852 (*Letters*, 4:330), and in 1853 (Slater, p. 485). That he was still working on the essay after 1857 is clear from the allusion to the earthquake in Naples of that year (*Works*, 6:7).

100. Here the word "assurance" is inserted above the line; the word is not in Emerson's hand. The sentence is clearly from Emerson's recollection of the response to the Divinity School Address.

101. No MS has been located; text from a copy (from the MS) provided by Goodspeed's Book Shop; listed in *Letters*, 5:20, under the conjectured date of October 5.

102. Gisela Von Arnim had sent Emerson her *Dramatische Werke* (Bonn, 1857), of which only vol. 2 is inscribed on the outside cover: "Herrn R. W. Emerson . . . von de Verfasserin," dated at Berlin, November 1857. Harding does not list this work. The first two volumes have an 1857 title page; the third volume, also in Emerson's library, but unlisted, is of 1865.

since a faithful reader, with me, of the books of Frau von Arnim, and I wish to ask for Miss H. an introduction to her, if she is in Berlin and in good health. Miss Hoar travels with her brother Mr Hoar, and her friend, Miss Pritchard.[103] I am very sure that any acquaintance you shall make with my friend will be self-rewarding.

With great respect and
regard, yours,
R. W. Emerson.

TO ARTHUR HUGH CLOUGH, CONCORD, SEPTEMBER 5, 1858[104]

Concord
5 September
1858

My dear Clough,

A very dear & honored friend of mine, Miss Elizabeth Hoar, goes to spend her year in Europe. This custom of my countrymen is rarely so much honored as by this act of my friend. Who now will stay at home, when she has given them leave to go?

We do not often send you a traveller who has so much penetration or correct taste, or so much goodness, and I am naturally ambitious that she should see the best. You must give her any advice that occurs to you for her better direction, in the short time that she stays in London. Miss Hoar is well acquainted with some of your old friends here, with Mrs Lowell[105] & Miss Sturgis (Mrs Tappan) and with your new friends, that is, those who heartily thank you for verses.

I am afraid that Madame Bodichon,[106] whom I saw, forgot on her

103. Edward Sherman Hoar and Elizabeth Hollett Prichard were married in Florence, December 28. See *Letters,* 5:121, no. 114, for the date of their sailing with Elizabeth Hoar. The copy here reads Pritchard and Emerson may have misspelled it, for he does so elsewhere.

104. MS in the Abernethy Library, VtMiM; ph. in NNC., with envelope addressed: A. H. Clough, Esq. | Downing Street, | London. |, without stamp or postmark. Emerson has clearly written September; see Emerson's similar letters of October to Charles Bray, Arthur Helps, Coventry Patmore (below), and Carlyle (Slater, p. 525); all are of October 5. See below April 16, 1861, for a second letter introducing Miss Hoar to Clough; I conjecture that on this journey of 1858 Elizabeth Hoar did not present this letter. If she had, one would expect to find it with the others in the Bodleian Library. Clough did meet her in 1861; see his letter of July 4, 1861, where there is no mention of an earlier meeting (*Emerson-Clough Letters,* No. 33; Mulhauser, 2:586).

105. Anna Jackson Lowell. By the time Clough came to America in 1852, Caroline Sturgis had been Mrs. Tappan for five years.

106. Barbara Leigh Smith Bodichon was a cousin of Clough's wife; she had recently married Dr. Eugene Bodichon.

return to advise you to come to America; and I am afraid if she did, that you have forgotten it. It is only when you English are just out of Oxford, that there in any plasticity in you. Any colors must be laid fast on surfaces that harden so quickly. We would have made a great man of you by the immensity of the demand in this vacant country; whilst, in London, you will proudly say, see the crowd of competitors, what need of my straining my self? Are there not enough already? Charge Mrs Clough, whom I wish I knew, not to let you slumber nor sleep. Yours affectionately,

R. W. Emerson

To James Morrison McKaye, Concord, September 10, 1858

[Catalogue Thirty-Seven of M & S Rare Books, Inc., lists as item 64, a letter to Colonel "McKaye" replying to a query about Frank Sanborn's school to which he considers sending his sixteen-year-old son. Emerson provides costs and other information about the school which his children attended. The catalogue entry correctly identifies the son in question who later changed the spelling of his surname to MacKaye; his father followed the change. The surname was originally McKay; the colonel having added the final "e." See above, February 17, 1852.]

To William Stevens Robinson? Concord, September 12, 1858

[A one-page note dated September 12, n.y., is listed by Cedric Robinson in Catalogue 142, Fall 1982, item 44. It is described as addressed to Mr. Robinson and quoted as follows: "Do not promise my speech in todays paper, but leave me a chance for the 'Previous Question' today." The addressee is very likely William Stevens Robinson (see *Letters*, 5:118, n. 101). It is not at all certain that this note of September 12 follows that of September 9 (5:117–118), but there is no record of any September speech in other years when Robinson might have importuned him.]

To William Henry Furness, Concord, September 22, 1858 [107]

Concord
22 September, 1858

My dear friend,

Thanks for the verses of Chamisso,[108] which yet Lowell will not print. He has not seen them; but I explained to him their origin, and he

---

107. MS in the Furness papers, Van Pelt Library, PU; ph. in NNC. The MS is defective; the signature and complimentary close have been cut away. As the final sentence here shows, no part of the text is missing. Furness has added "from R. W. E." below "a fault," probably at the time the signature was cut off.

108. Probably the translations are by Furness' son or his daughter; see above June 9, 1857.

declared at once that they had made up their minds not to admit translations into the Atlantic.[109] I think he has a pride about it as thinking to
favor the American laurel, by forbidding the foreign. And, I understood
him, he had received many proffers of German translation.

I have kept back this note a couple of days, because I have mislaid
your letter unaccountably, & it does not come up today; otherwise, I
should offer you a varior⟨a⟩um or two on ⟨the⟩ lines that I marked.
Perhaps it is well that I should not hazard the new reading & should
strut off with the arrogance of finding a fault.

To David Greene Haskins, Concord, September 22, 1858[110]

Concord

Sept. 22

1858

My dear Cousin,

I am gratified by your kind proposition, but I fear it will not be
prudent for me to take any part in your plan for this season. I have
already allowed my self to be coaxed into one course of Boston lectures
/for/ this winter, Mr Parker's, which embarrasses me when I come to read
a course of my own, as I am solicited to do.[111] ⟨If⟩When I see you, which
I must try to do, I wish to know more of your plans, & see whether
perhaps I may not aid you in some similar way hereafter,

Yours affectionately,

R. W. Emerson

Rev. D. G. Haskins.

To James Russell Lowell? Concord? September 27, 1858

[On the same sheet on which he has copied a part of Emerson's letter to Elizabeth
Peabody of November 24, 1857 (see above), Cabot has entered a fragment dated
as above. The fragment reads: "But the religion of the piece seems to me borrowed of a period forever passed. . . ." while it is possible that this fragment is

109. Including the original poem by William D. Howells that Lowell held onto so long
to be certain that it was not a translation of Heine. *Life in Letters of William Dean Howells*,
Mildred Howells, ed. (New York: Doubleday, Doran, 1928), 1:24.

110. MS in the Barrett Collection, Alderman Library, ViU; ph. in NNC. Emerson is
answering a letter of September 21, 1858 (RWEMA), from his cousin the Reverend David
Greene Haskins of Roxbury. The manuscript is glued to a backing concealing the apostrophe *s* in Parker's and the comma following it; a mirror image is visible through the paper.

111. He is referring here to his six lectures for the Parker Fraternity and his Freeman
Place lectures (see Charvat, p. 35). I take him to mean that the combination of a series of six
lectures in the course of his own with six for the Parker Fraternity, all in Boston, strained his
resources.

from a letter to Miss Peabody, I conjecture that it is from a letter to Lowell, a letter either accompanying the manuscript of Miss Peabody's "Primeval History" or acknowledging the rejection of the manuscript, a rejection for which Emerson's letter of November 24, 1858 (above), had prepared the author. That the manuscript was sent by Emerson and rejected by the *Atlantic Monthly* is clear from Emerson's letter to Lowell of February 27, 1859 (*Letters*, 5:134–135). Cabot copied this passage twice, in one version writing "from" changed to "of."]

To HENRIETTA CROSBY INGERSOLL, CONCORD, SEPTEMBER 30, 1858 [112]

Concord
Sept. 30, 1858

Dear Madam,

I have been so busy with some new duties, during the past week, that I have been forced to leave my correspondence in arrears, and, with the rest, your letter.

I willingly accept the new day you offer me, 28th October; & note what you say of the cars. [113]

I had not any thought when I wrote you of declining any invitation that had been given me but I remember that I took the impression that I should meet at Mrs Appleton's house the ladies interested in ⟨m⟩your present design, but I did not know that a further invitation was made. Between a hospitality which I never intended to refuse, & that which you now offer me, I think you must in your goodness decide which I ⟨must⟩ shall share.

For the "subject",—perhaps of the lectures I now have in my portfolio, it will be safest at this moment, to choose the one which you indicate, & which I call "Works & Days." If I shall have something newer & better, I will tell you so.

I am with great respect,

Yours,
R. W. Emerson

Mrs Ingersoll.

To DAVID ATWOOD WASSON, CONCORD? OCTOBER 1? 1858

[In a letter to Emerson of April 19, 1861 (Schlesinger Library, Radcliffe), Wasson recalls a letter to him from Emerson written shortly after Wasson's essay "The

112. MS in the Berg Collection, NN; ph. in NNC.
113. See the letter of May 11 to Mrs. Ingersoll, *Letters*, 5:106–107, and nn. 54 and 55. See October 29, below, for the cancellation of the October 28 date for Bangor, Maine, and the proposal of the last Thursday in February 1859. Charvat, p. 34, requires correction here.

New World and the New Man" had appeared. The essay was printed October 1858 in the *Atlantic Monthly*, 2:513–531. Since the October issue would be available in late September, I conjecture October 1 for the date. Wasson writes that Emerson's "words of rcecognition" were "invaluable" to him. Emerson's letter also included words of "censure": "Especially you accused me of betraying 'an evil influence of Carlyle,' and so explained your meaning that I at once saw its truth, though without this explanation it was puzzling & thwarting to me."]

TO CHARLES BRAY, CONCORD, OCTOBER 5, 1858[114]

Concord, Mass.

5 October 1858

My dear Sir:

A dear friend of mine who is just going to Europe told me today that she was to pass through Coventry on her way to London. It occurred to me, as often before, that I once spent a very happy day in Coventry and its neighborhood under your auspices, and that, since, I have been seriously interested and indebted to a book and tracts which I received from you.[115] It cannot be that as bright sunshine always rests on Coventry and on Stratford and the lands between, as on that day did rest for me. But I thought I would give my friend this note in her hand to present my greetings to you, if she found opportunity. My friend is Miss Elizabeth Hoar,[116] for many years a sort of sister of mine, and on whom I and all her friends set the highest value. She goes to spend a year in Europe, she and her brother, Mr. Hoar, and her friend, Miss Pritchard.[117] And if your goodness and your health abound as they did when I saw you, you shall put my friends in the way to see the old church, which I remember with great respect, and give them any good advice that may occur to you for their guidance on their onward road.

With kindest remembrances and benedictions to you and yours. From your obliged servant.

R. W. Emerson

114. The MS has not been located; text from a copy provided by Goodspeed's Book Shop. Emerson probably used ampersands. The addressee is pretty surely Charles Bray (see *Letters*, 4:98, n. 352).

115. The only books by Bray now in Emerson's library are too late to be those referred to here. Bray had recently published a fifteen-page tract, *The Income of the Kingdom* (London: Longman, 1857), and an eighteen-page tract, *The Industrial Employment of Women* (London: Longman, [1857]). Neither was likely to have given Emerson delight.

116. See, below, the letters to Helps and Patmore of the same date.

117. See, above, letter to Clough of September 5; Emerson frequently misspells Miss Prichard's name. Edward Hoar and Elizabeth Hallett Prichard would be married in Florence on December 28.

To COVENTRY PATMORE, CONCORD, OCTOBER 5, 1858 [118]

Concord,
October 5, 1858.

My Dear Sir,

I have once [and] again strained my slender claim to your acquaintance, for the benefit of my friends, when they were lovers of your genius,[119] and now am emboldened by my regards for the traveller to do the like again.

My friend Miss Elizabeth Hoar (who should have been these many years my sister), desires to see you, as few have read your poems better, and I could not easily send you a more discerning and more cultivated person. Miss Hoar travels in Europe for a year with her brother and her friend Miss Pritchard,[120] and, though they stay in London but a short time, mean, of course, to see the Museum;[121] and I must rely on your kindness to point out to them precisely those things which you value most. Miss Hoar will give you at least the satisfaction of a clear intelligence and a correct taste.

I confide that you will find your acquaintance with my friend self-rewarding. And I hope you will impart to her some good news of yourself and your literary designs, which may arrive at last at me.

With grateful regards,
Yours

Mr. Patmore.   R. W. Emerson

---

118. No MS has been found; text from Basil Champneys, *Memoirs and Correspondence of Coventry Patmore* (London: George Bell, 1900) 2:382–383. There is no way of knowing whether the bracketed "and" is Emerson's. A manifest typographical error, *descerning* for *discerning*, has been corrected.

119. See March 18 and May 5, 1856, for the American edition "The Angel in the House."

120. See notes on letter of the same date to Charles Bray above.

121. Patmore worked in the British Museum; in 1848, he had been Emerson's guide to its resources.

To Arthur Helps, Concord, October 5, 1858 [122]

Concord
5 October 1858

My dear Sir,

An intimate & honored friend of mine, Miss Elizabeth Hoar, goes to England on her way to the continent,[123] and, as she is a reader & lover of your books, and as I think you will not often find a more discerning one, or one whose regard ⟨was⟩is more seriously valuable, I thought I would send you this token, if my friend should come into your neighborhood. Miss Hoar travels with her brother, and her friend Miss Prichard,[124] & means to spend a year in Europe.

If any good advice occurs to you for the guidance of very intelligent persons on their journey, I pray you to impart it to them. In the meantime, I hope the echoes of Bishops Waltham are as busy & as joyful as they were when the voices were younger which I heard there.

Ever your obliged servt.
R. W. Emerson

To Bryan Waller Procter, Concord, October? 5? 1858?

[In a letter of introduction of July 25, 1860 (see below), Emerson speaks of kindness owed to Bryan Proctor "not only in London but once and again since." I conjecture here that he provided Elizabeth Hoar with an introduction to "Barry Cornwall."]

To George William Curtis, Concord, October 7, 1858 [125]

Concord
7 Oct 1858

My dear Sir,

I am doubly grieved, first, that I have not answered your note of 30 Sept.r; and, secondly, that I cannot gratify you, if you are still looking to me. I have happened to have a shower of letters in the last ten days, and an incapacity of writing, at the same time, growing out of combined impediments, and I did not observe at once, as I ought, the peremptory

---

122. MS in Special Collections, Butler Library, NNC; ph. in NNC. with envelope addressed: Arthur Helps, Esq. | London. There is no postmark or stamp.

123. See, above, the letters to Bray and Patmore of the same date; and see letter of September 5 to Clough.

124. This time Emerson spells the name Prichard correctly.

125. MS owned by Nicholas B. Scheet; ph. in NNC.

nearness of your day. But now that I see the whole, I cannot help you.[126]
I have been drawn into this engagement, without any readiness for it,
simply by the debt we all owe, & I most, to Mr Parker.[127] But I know not
yet how to meet it, & cannot be ready this month. They have set down
my name for an old lecture which I do not wish to read. But I console
myself that you can never be at a loss, & have already settled what to do.

Your tardy servant,
R. W. Emerson

Mr Curtis.

To Mary Anne Devereux Silsbee, Concord, October 11, 1858[128]

Concord
11 October
1858

Dear Mrs Silsbee,

I heard with much pleasure from Mr Bradford,[129] that you had interested yourself in my lectures, & wished me to read them, at Salem, &, on
Saturday, I received your kind note on the subject. Certainly, it would
give me a much better & more agreeable audience, if I bring my portfolio
to Salem than I would probably find elsewhere. And I shall value the
opportunity of reading my Boston Course again, as the four last lectures
still interest me as studies & gain much by repetition.

The time you propose, the month of November, is also free to me, so
that I am entirely ready to come, if you shall hereafter think the design
still looks feasible. I have but one objection, namely, that I am sure that
this beneficent good nature of yours will probably give you a good deal
of trouble. Will you not, then, be advised by me to put the whole matter
into the hands of one of your booksellers, who can easily, after a few

126. See September 22, above, where Emerson more lucidly refuses to give a lecture in
a local course because he is to offer a course of his own in Boston. In that letter, as in this
one, he mentions his commitment to the Parker Fraternity as an embarrassment.

127. His "debt" to Parker is effectively described in Journal CL (*JMN*, 14:352–353,
354).

128. MS in the New England Collection, MnM; ph. in NNC. This letter initiates the
series given in Salem on November 4, 9, 11, 16, 18. It is the first of five letters listed 1940 in
Parke-Bernet's catalogue of February 28 and 29, lot 93, where three of the letters are
described as having to do with the Salem lectures. Four of the letters fall between October
11 and November 22; the fifth is undated. All five letters have to do with the 1858 Salem
lectures; see below, letter conjectured to be of November 1, and letters of November 16 and
22.

129. George Partridge Bradford was then living with his sister Margaret Bradford Ames
(Mrs. Seth Ames).

days' advertising, ascertain whether it is worth while to push the subject, & I will come or not, as he shall find the sense of the city is. Twice a week, for three weeks—is a good course, & you shall elect the days.

I heartily thank you for your kind interest in the affair; and again for your hospitable invitation.[130] If I come, I shall esteem it a privilege that I am to see you.

With great respect
⟨am⟩Your affectionate servant,

Mrs. Silsbee.   R. W. Emerson

To Messrs. Sauers [?] Howland, and King, Concord,
October 22, 1858 [131]

Concord Masstts
⟨20⟩22 October 1858

Dear Sirs,

I have your friendly invitation to Port Byron,[132] which comes to me in good time, as it enables me to combine a little series of visits in your region. I have been invited to visit Cortland [133] & my wish is to be in that town on Saturday, & Sunday, 15 & 16 January. Will you let me offer you the ⟨e⟩following evening, Monday 17 January, at Port Byron? Then I can go to Batavia on the 18 & thence to Cleveland, Ohio, which is my remotest point. I can only accept these invitations on the condition that all of them can be combined, and if the evening I offer you is convenient to your Association, I shall be glad to know it If I come, the Lyceum shall pay me Thirty dollars.

The subject I shall probably wish to bring you, is "Country Life;" or

130. Mrs Silsbee invited Emerson and Mrs. Emerson to be her guests when the lectures were given. See November 22 below.

131. MS in the Barrett Collection, Alderman Library, ViU; ph. in NNC Howland is apparently Horace V. Howland; King, Finlay A. King, both lawyers; *History of Cayuga County, New York*, compiled from papers in the archives of the Cayuga County Historical Society . . . (Rochester, N.Y., 1908), pp. 327–328, 345, 347. The first name is not decipherable with any certainty.

132. Emerson's MS Pocket Diary for 1858 lists Port Byron with a question mark (*JMN*, 14:462); the more accurate Pocket Diary for 1859 lists "PTB" crossed out (*ibid.*, 466, with the "t" read as &). The MB of the letter is endorsed above the dateline with an arrow pointing to "Terms: $30 -" twice underlined. Possibly Port Byron could not afford him, although his terms were considered by other lecturers to be damagingly low.

133. See letter of same date to William H. Fish, *Letters*, 5:123–124. Charvat does not list the unprofessional Sunday engagement in Cortland (evidently Emerson preached without charge). He leaves Batavia with a question mark; it appears in the 1859 Pocket Diary without a question mark (*JMN, idem*); but there is not record of a fee in the Account Book for 1853–1860.

"Town & Country Life." But before that day I may wish to substitute another.

Respectfully,
R. W. Emerson.

Messieurs Sauers[?]
   Howland Committee
   King

To Henrietta Crosby Ingersoll, Concord, October 29, 1858[134]

Concord
29 October 1858

Dear Madam,

I am heartily sorry that the enterprize of the ladies has suffered any check. I am sorry on my own account, that a visit to Bangor ⟨wh⟩from which I could promise myself only pleasure,—so much goodness had marked all your arrangements,—should be made uncertain.[135] If, as you intimate, the ladies mean to persist in their design, I shall gladly cooperate with them somewhat later.—Perhaps about the last Thursday of February. But let this proposition depend entirely on what you shall find expedient on the whole. With great respect, yours,

R. W. Emerson

Mrs Ingersoll.

To Henry Ames Blood, Concord, October 29, 1858

[A letter of October 29, 1858, is listed in Robert T. Batchelder's catalogue 37, item 46. It is described as with envelope addressed to H. Ames Blood of East Jaffrey, New Hampshire. The letter is quoted as follows: "I find nothing exceptional in the phrase to which you call attention. It is an expression of true vivacity, but is descriptive, and sufficiently correct. I am very happy to hear that I have found a friend, hitherto unknown to me, in the region of Monadnoc, whose top I often see in my walks. I shall see it now with more kindness." The addressee is certainly Henry Ames Blood, born in Temple, New Hampshire, in 1836 and graduated from Dartmouth in 1858. On October 7, 1958, he gave the address at the ceremonies in celebration of the 100th anniversary of the town and also wrote *The History of Temple, N.H.* (Boston: Rand & Avery, 1860). The style of the address printed in *The History* is decidedly unconventional; it may have been a sentence of his own that Blood asked Emerson about.]

134. MS in the Feinberg Collection, MiD, ph. in NNC.
135. See above, September 30. There is no evidence that Emerson went to Bangor, though he lists this new date, February 24, 1859, in the Pocket Diary for 1859, *JMN*, 14:467,

To Mary Anne Devereux Silsbee, Concord, November? 1? 1858

[The Parke-Bernet catalogue of February 28 and 29, 1940, lot 93, describes one of the five letters to Mrs. Silsbee as listing the topics of the lectures to be given in Salem (see October 11, above, for Emerson's advice to have a bookseller advertise the lectures in advance). The topics listed are "Powers of the Mind," "Natural Method of Mental Philosophy," "Memory," "Self-Possession," "Poetry and Imagination." Charvat, p. 34, is then mistaken in supposing the Salem lectures to be from the series on "The Conduct of Life"; these are topics from the Freeman Place lectures of March 1858 (p. 34). For a sixth Salem lecture of 1858, December 29, Emerson does use "The Conduct of Life," but this lecture was not part of the series Mrs. Silsbee arranged. November 1 seems to me the latest likely date for this still unlocated letter.]

To Cyrus W———— Christy, Concord, November 2, 1858[136]

Concord Mass.
2 Nov.r 1858

Dear Sir,

It would give me great pleasure to come to Yellow Springs, & see again the College, which received me once so kindly, but I do not think it will be in my power this winter.[137] I have strained my plan a little to meet an old engagement at Cleveland, where I am holden for the 20 January; but I doubt much if I can penetrate farther west or southwest, as my duties bring me home again on the 25th. I hear with much interest of the brave exertions & brave successes of the college & its friends, to which I wish the best issue.[138]

Respectfully
R. W. Emerson

Mr Christy.

---

with a question mark. Since the Saturday Club met in the afternoon and he did attend the meeting on the 26th (see *Letters,* 5:134), he would have had to leave Bangor on Friday.

136. MS in private hands; ph. in NNC; with envelope addressed: Mr C. W. Christy. | Antioch College. | Yellow Springs. | Ohio. | ; envelope endorsed "Rec.d Nov. 8th."

137. The sentence proves that the Emersons visited Antioch in 1857 though not before that year. See above, February 2, 1857, for Emerson's refusal to visit and n. 6 for his being unexpectedly able to do so.

138. The financial troubles of Antioch were well known.

To Henry James, Sr., Concord, November 15, 1858[139]

> Concord
> 15 Nov.r 1858

My blessed Henry James,

I do not know what mortal sin I have done late or early, for which I should be tormented by these three sufferings, namely, the tantalization of three welcomest invitations from you all made of none effect by contretemps. The first letter reached me on my return home on Saturday night from Boston,—no cars thereafter, & none on Sunday. The second was verbal & through Fisher[140] & I went to Boston armed & eager to stay through Sunday, having been assured you would arrive on Friday. But the weather was bad, & you had not arrived, & I came sadly home again. And now, on Saturday, as I hastened at noon to Boston to a certain business-meeting, in spite of a disgraceful cold wheezing through my head & lungs, I found your letter at the Post Office, too late to turn back even for a shirt, & with absurd & quite unnecessary engagements drawing me home for Sunday, & new ones again on Monday morning;—it was with bitter vexation that I read your cordial & head- & heart-assuring invitations for this Sunday—now passed by me in quite less dignified & exhilarating[141] company. I have told this long specification only to acquit me to you by showing you my Penal Fate which stood between & held me from you; & to entreat you, for the next occasion, to put your letter for me one post earlier into the mail bags, because I live in the country. I said when we parted, "Remember Saturday," because I had invited you to our Saturday Club, for that last Saturday of October.

To Mary Anne C. Devereux Silsbee, Boston, November 16, 1858[142]

> American House
> Boston, 16 Novr

Dear Mrs Silsbee,

I trust to be in Salem this evening at 6 o'clock; but I shall not have the happiness of coming to your house. I have just discovered that an incon-

---

139. MS, incomplete, in the James papers, Houghton Library, MH; ph. in NNC; printed by Perry, 1:86; listed *Letters*, 5:125. The text fills all four pages; I think there cannot be much missing.

140. Fisher is probably James T. Fisher; see above, March 12, 1850.

141. The "h" is written over an undecipherable and unimaginable letter.

142. MS in the Abernethy Library, VtMiM; ph. in NNC. The date is established by Emerson's lecture schedule of 1858; a series of five lectures at Salem (see October 11 below) is interrupted by one at Peterboro, New Hampshire, on November 17 (Charvat, p. 34). The

siderate engagement made long since to go to Peterboro tomorrow, requires that I should spend the night in Boston; & so I shall return hither, in a private carriage, directly after my lecture. And a foolish cold that made me question, till this morning's sunshine, whether to come to Salem at all, will make me a quiddle,[143] & keep me close to the Lyceum Hall. So forgive me according to your great kindness.

Yours ever,
R. W. Emerson

Mrs Silsbee.

To Mary Anne Devereux Silsbee, Concord, November 22, 1858[144]

Concord
22 Novr. 1858

Dear Mrs Silsbee,

I received on Saturday night your letter, & its enclosure, with much pride & gratitude in obtaining my accounts through such distinguished stewardship.[145] You have my best thanks for all your care & counsel. The rehearsal of the lectures to so good a company was by no means useless to me.[146] If it were now to be done again, you would find them wonderfully mended. My wife joins her thanks to mine for your kindest hospitality; and we believe that we have established a claim on you & your family to make an inn of our house, whenever you should come into Middlesex. I have told my children so much of Mary's drawings,[147] that they, who are very curious in these things, are plotting how to allure her to Concord. With my best regards to Mr Silsbee,

Your affectionate servant
R. W. Emerson

Mrs. Silsbee.

MS Pocket Diary for 1858 shows that the Peterboro date was originally scheduled for December 2; the entry for that date is crossed out and the town appears under November 17 (*JMN*, 14:460).

143. That is, a fussbudget; Emerson uses this uncommon word also in *English Traits;* see *Works,* 5:104. Emerson uses the the adjective "quiddling" also; see *Works,* 6:154.

144. MS in the New England Collection, MnM; ph. in NNC.

145. The MS Account Book for 1853–1860 records without date, p. [247], the receipt of $151.00 from Mrs. Silsbee for five lectures.

146. This is a very clear statement of Emerson's use of lecturing in order to hear his own work, the better to revise it.

147. Mrs. Silsbee's daughter.

To Robert Carter? Concord, November 23, 1858

[This letter is listed by Rusk, *Letters*, 5:125, as addressed to "McCarter." I believe that his source, a catalogue of the Newark Galleries, misprints Emerson's "Mr Carter"; Emerson's "Mr," which he habitually writes without a period, could easily be read as "Mc." The letter is described as an offer to sell some recently purchased land. It is Robert Carter who, in 1859, bought the Asabet pasture that Emerson had purchased in 1855 from Edmund Hosmer. See below August 4, 10, and 29, 1859.]

To Charles Wesley Slack, Concord, December 3, 1858[148]

Concord
Friday, 3 Decr

Dear Sir,

I shall be at the American House on Tuesday, p.m.

You were kind enough to say, when we had some conversation in reference to this Lecture, that you thought you could obtain the favor of the Newspapers to abstain from any report of it. I shall be glad to have that request made. The "Courier', the "Advertiser," "Journal" & "Traveller" are the only papers that are likely to attempt it. The Courier lately did me great disservice by what is called an able report.

Thanks for your kind sending of cards for Mr Beecher's Lecture; & for the friendly directions you send me.

Respectfully,
R. W. Emerson

Mr Slack.

To Samuel Gray Ward, Concord? December 6, 1858?[149]

Monday 6 Dec.r

I am very tender about Alcott, & could have well wished you should have heard his happiest thoughts. He has now & then a plume from an

148. MS in Special Collections, CV-SB; ph. in NNC. The only year that fits the content of this letter is 1858 when on Tuesday December 7, Emerson gave a lecture for the Parker Fraternity (Charvat, p. 34). Ordinarily his lectures for the Fraternity were given on Sundays as they were in 1864 when he also tried to prevent the papers from reporting them (*Letters*, 5:389, n. 172, and 394). The reference to tickets for Beecher's lecture clinches the date. That Henry Ward Beecher should lecture for the (Unitarian) Parker Fraternity was a sensational event. He gave two lectures in December 1858, reported in the *New York Independent* of January 6.

149. MS in the Ward papers, Houghton Library, MH; ph. in NNC. The 6th of December fell on Monday in 1858, and in that year, on November 29, Alcott, Henry James, Sr.,

archangel, and higher hints than you shall elsewhere find. And when I vexed myself to think you should suffer such heavy entertainment for so many hours at my house, I was glad to remember that you had proposed it & not I. Not the less but the more thanks to you for coming. Stillman [150] seems still to have had the laboring oar at the Hills. I shall be at home on Friday night, & if he means to report on Saturday, I shall be glad to be kept informed. —Yours ever,

R. W. E.

To William H. Fish, Concord, December 9? 1858

[In a letter of December 7, 1858 (RWEMA), William H. Fish of Cortland, New York, hopes for Emerson's assurance that he will come to lecture on January 15 and 16. He says he has answered Emerson's letter of October 22 (*Letters*, 5:123–124) telling him that the itinerary there proposed is feasible. For the January 16 engagement, see notes, October 22 above.]

To Thomas P. Haviland, Concord, December 11, 1858 [151]

Concord
Dec. 11, 1858

Dear Sir,

I might come to Auburndale, if you wish it, on Tuesday 28 December or on the day preceding.[152] The Lyceum shall pay me Twenty dollars.

Respectfully
R. W. Emerson

Mr Haviland

Mary Moody Emerson, and others, including Ward, were gathered at Emerson's house; Alcott, *Journals,* p. 310. It is, I think, this occasion that Henry James, Sr., recalls in a letter of January 27, 1862, to Mrs. Robert Carter (a.l.s., Knox College Archives). He writes: "I remember very gratefully your merciful demeanour in that confabulation at Mr Emersons a couple of years ago, wherein I was 'shamefully treated' by the old Lady from Maine, as Mr E puts it; but really to my own sense soothed and delighted. The old lady had the flavour to me of primitive woods wherein the wolf howls, and the owl has never been dislodged; and I enjoyed the novelty of her apparition in these days too much to mind the scratches I got in making her better acquaintance."

150. William J. Stillman, a prime mover of the Adirondac Club; see *Letters,* 5:110, and nn. 62, 116, and 92.

151. MS owned by Philip H. Burn (I have not seen the original); text from printing by Thomas P. Haviland, "Two Emerson Letters," *AL* (March 1951), 23:127.

152. Emerson enters this date for Auburndale in his Pocket Diary with a question mark; *JMN,* 14:461. There is no Account Book entry for the receipt of payment from Auburndale in December 1858. See January 29, 1859, below, for the new date of February 3 and for the likelihood of another letter between this one and that.

To Hannah Shepard Terry, Hartford, December 15, 1858.[153]

Allyn House
15 Dec

My dear Cousin,

I am very sorry to find that my Aunt Mary's packing of trunks & some other petty accidents have deprived me of the pleasure on which I depended much of coming to see you. The visits of friends too have shortened my short morning. I shall yet hope for another opportunity.

With great regard,
Your affectionate cousin,
R. W. Emerson.

Mrs Terry.

To William Henry Furness, Philadelphia, December 16, 1858[154]

LaPierre House
Thursday Dec 16

My dear friend,

I enclose my mite for the Christmas box you spoke of, of our friend; and am, as ever, yours thankfully & affectionately.[155]

R. W. E.

W. M. Furness.

153. MS in the Redwood Library, Newport, R.I.; ph. in NNC. The year is secure from Emerson's letter of November 26, 1858, to his brother William (*Letters*, 5:125–126). He tells his brother that he will bring Mary Moody Emerson to New York on December 15; he will travel via Hartford where he is to lecture on December 14. He writes this letter to his cousin, Mrs. Seth Terry, from his Hartford hotel. The expenses of the trip are listed in the MS Account Book for 1853–1860, p. [249], under the date December 13.

154. MS in the Furness papers, Van Pelt Library, PU; ph. in NNC; the address places Emerson in Philadelphia; Emerson lectured in Philadelphia on December 16, 1858, a Thursday.

155. This note is explained by an entry of the same date in the MS Account Book for 1853–1859 p. [253], "Pd W. H. Furness, as my subscription to fund of Mattie G.—10.00." Mattie Griffith (originally of Kentucky), who, in 1857, had been staying with Eliza Cabot Follen in Brookline and had moved to Philadelphia in late September of that year (*Letters*, 5:83, 84, and, above, September 22, 1857). Her letter to Emerson of December 28, 1857, is, however, dated from Boston; she is disappointed at not having her visit to Emerson; she returns to Philadelphia in the morning; she hopes for letters from Emerson.

To Christian Nestell Bovee, New York, December 17, 1858 [156]

My dear Sir,

I hoped to find you if only to thank you for your magnanimous care of me & to say that I go in the Stonington boat this afternoon. My brother tells me that you advise tomorrows boat; but that would throw me into Boston for the Sunday. Can you not arrange your next visit to Boston so as to include the last Saturday of some month, say January, or February, and let me introduce you to our club? & we will ⟨cele-brate⟩elaborate a high treaty between your metropolitan & our provincial ⟨s⟩circle. [157] Say January—29th,—Shall you not have an instalment of marging [?] to carry to the "Atlantic" for February on that day? [158] Be it when it will, after this month (whose Saturday falling on Christmas will ⟨o⟩probably be passed over,) you are to send me word of your Boston address, & it will give me great joy to carry you.

                                                    With kindest regards,
Mr Bovee.   R. W. Emerson

To George L. Duyckinck et al., Concord, December 26, 1858 [159]

                                                    Concord 26 Decr
                                                    Mass 1858
Gentlemen,

My absence from home prevented me from receiving your letter on its arrival, or it should have been acknowledged at once.

156. MS in the New England Collection, MnM; ph. in NNC. The date of this letter has to be December 17, 1858. Emerson had lectured on December 15 at the Brooklyn College Hospital at Bovee's invitation; see above, October 12. On the following day, he lectured in Philadelphia; by Sunday the 18th he was at home in Concord. See *Letters*, 5:165, 168. It is only on December 17 that he could have taken the boat from New York to Stonington, Connecticut; thence (by train) to Boston so that he could get to Concord on Saturday. Neither the Saturday Club nor the *Atlantic Monthly* existed in 1852; in 1880, Emerson could not have written this letter, and in 1869 he was at home. The letter is written, manifestly in haste, on lightly ruled quarto paper; evidently Emerson used whatever was available; by 1858, envelopes with stamps were required.

157. Emerson is referring to his Saturday Club and Bovee's Athenaeum Club.

158. Bovee's article "Suggestions" had appeared in the December *Atlantic* (2:816–824); the December issue would have been available in November. The word Emerson writes here is not clear; it plainly begins "ma" and ends "ing"; the second of two intervening letters appears to have a descender, but Emerson is crowding the word down the margin. I conjecture "marging." *OED* has an example of "marge" as a verb, citing *Fraser's Magazine*, 1856; Emerson read this periodical, though he could easily have invented it himself. The article, already published, is a series of brief entries arranged alphabetically by topics as if culled from a commonplace book; they have also the character of marginalia, and one of them is about reading Emerson (p. 819).

159. MS in NHi; ph. in NNC. In addition to George L. Duyckinck, the addresses are

It would give me great pleasure, certainly, to meet the Historical Society & to obey their wishes, but I do not find myself prepared at this moment to bring them any paper such as I should like to offer them, nor can I command for some weeks to come the time to supply the want; so that, I am compelled, for the present, to decline the invitation with which you have honored me.

Respectfully,
R. W. Emerson

Messieurs Brown
    Hansen
    Mayo
    Hicks
    Duyckinck Committee.

To Daniel Coit Gilman, Concord, December 27, 1858 [160]

Concord ⎱ 27 Dec
Masstts ⎰ 1858

Dear Sir,

I have to ask your forgiveness for neglecting, for some weeks, I fear, to acknowledge your note. I enclose five dollars, as my annual assessment in the Oriental Society. [161]

Respectfully,
R. W. Emerson

Mr Gilman, Treas.r

To Mary Anne Devereux Silsbee, Concord, December 28, 1858? [162]

Concord
28 Decr

My dear Mrs Silsbee,

Thanks always to your goodness, with its exact memory! I promise myself the pleasure of drinking tea with you tomorrow evening, & Edith insists that she is asked, & she shall go.

Edwin J. Brown, Jacob Hansen, William S. Mayo, and Thomas Hicks, constituting the lecture committee in 1858; R. W. G. Vail, *Knickerbocker Birthday* (New York: The New-York Historical Society, 1954), p. 114, where a letter of December 27 from Oliver Wendell Holmes to the same committee is printed. The Emerson letter is catalogued as addressed to E. A. Duyckinck, but the MS minutes of the society confirm Vail (2:152, entry of November 2, 1858).

160. MS in MdBJ; ph. in NNC.

161. Entered in the Account Book for 1853–1859, p. [255], under this date as "my first assessment"; see Rusk, *Life*, p. 397, for the recent visit to Concord of the Brahmin, Philip Jobut Sangooly.

162. MS in the New England Collection, MnM; ph. in NNC. The date assigned is not secure. Emerson lectured in Salem on December 29, 1858 (Charvat, p. 34); 1858 is the only

I shall be very glad to see Mr Peabody's pictures, if the hour permits; but the next day is quite too near the new year to allow country papas & daughters any enjoyment but of shopping.[163]

Yours faithfully,

Mrs Silsbee.   R. W. Emerson

To ——— BARTLETT, CONCORD,? 1858?[164]

Concord—

Thursday Morning

Dear Mrs. Bartlett,

My wife & I are highly flattered by the persevering kindness which send us this brave invitation to your house, next Friday. and though I have no hope that we shall be able to go to town that night,[165] yet I mean to avail myself of the liberty this card gives me of re-claiming the right to come & see you, which, I feared, my multiplied omissions had forfeited. May best stars light the brilliant occasion!

Your obliged faithful servant,

R. W. Emerson

Mrs Bartlett

———

year when he was certainly in Salem on December 29. The letter is pretty clearly written before Edith's marriage in 1865.

163. That the Emerson girls were anxious about presents is evident from Ellen's letter to Edith of December 22, 1858 (Gregg 1:160–161). The family custom was to exchange presents on New Year's Day.

164. MS in the Abernethy Library, VtMiM. This very carefully written letter is manifestly to a Mrs. Bartlett Emerson had known for some time. I conjecture Mrs. Sidney Bartlett; see *Letters,* 5:157, and 6:78, 79. The letter provides no clue to its date, except that the stationery shows it to be after 1852, and the handwriting suggests the 1850s. The years 1854, '55, '60, '66, '67, and '73 are impossible; a date in the years after '72 is unlikely. I arbitrarily assign it to 1858.

165. Beginning his second page, Emerson forgets that he has closed the preceding sentence.

1 8 5 9

TO SARAH ANN CLARKE, CONCORD, JANUARY 8, 1859[1]

Concord
8 January 1859

My dear friend,

On coming home, I have found your immortalization of my summer-house,[2] which E. & E. & E., my children three, had impatiently watched, nor untied a know of, & now made haste to deliver & reveal. Tis a brave piece of work, and far more suggestive than the decaying original, and it will make a fine curiosity fifty years hence, what was the design of the building it portrays; the more, that no means of a scale are given and the eye is left free to magnify it infinitely. Mr Alcott is gone to St Louis,[3] but, you may be sure, will gladly & critically study it when he comes back.

But what shall I do for you who do so much for me? I have no book nor poem nor thoughts nor cheer to bring you, but sit solitary here, & ever the more as penalty of having been solitary already. Yet you are ever one of the benign Powers whom I see, absent or present, & from whom I expect influence & healing.

Well, I must try to come where the fire is. Yet the days of freedom I am always promising myself loiter tediously, and, my unreadiness is wonderful.

At the same time with your gift, I received a letter, which, if you read, as I cannot, the German script, I must bring you. It comes from Gisela von Arnim, Bettine's daughter. She had sent me her Dramas, and I had written my thanks;[4] and now she sends me a letter Bettine might almost have written, and which Ellen, who is skilful, has not yet quite translated for me.[5] It is of many sheets. But it opens a good picture of a circle of

1. MS in the Clarke papers, Houghton Library, MH; ph. in NNC.
2. See *Letters*, 4:411, 413, and 445, for Alcott's building of this summer house, more picturesque than sound. Miss Clarke's picture of it now hangs in the Red Room of the Emerson house. Emerson's account of the effect of magnitude is accurate.
3. In St. Louis, Bronson Alcott would make important friends among the Hegelians there.
4. See above, June 29 and September 3, 1858.
5. See *Letters*, 5:157–158, for Ellen Emerson's answer to Gisela von Arnim's letter.

friends in Berlin, of whom the Arnims & Hermann Grimm form the centre, & where Boston experiences appear to be repeated.

Has Caroline Tappan seen Berlin?[6] I think not; but this lady is precisely the person she should see, & I must bestir myself at once to that end. Alas, Alas! our wonderful Bettine is a dying woman of 74!

I have much to say to you, but shall not come yet to your house. I go westward on Monday or Tuesday, for a pair of weeks, but I am ever your friend

R. W. Emerson

Miss Sarah Clarke.

To CHARLES S. FARLEY, CONCORD, JANUARY 8? 1859

[Sending Emerson the printed schedule of lectures for the Brooklyn Mercantile Library Association (RWEMA) Charles S. Farley appended a note, October 25, 1858, asking Emerson to confirm his January 11 engagement a few days before the day. I assume Emerson complied. (He had gone back to Concord after his Baltimore lecture in order to escort his daughter Edith to New York; see *Letters*, 5:130, 132.)]

To ELBRIDGE GERRY DUDLEY, CONCORD? JANUARY 19?, 1859?

[In the Slack papers, OKentU, is a letter from John R. Manley to Charles W. Slack, dated January 19, n.y., reporting that Emerson has written to Elbridge Dudley to announce that the topic of his next Sunday lecture for the Parker Fraternity will be "Works and Days." The lecture was first given in February 1856 (Charvat, p. 32). Emerson's correspondence with Dudley falls between 1859 and 1863; he gave a Parker Fraternity lecture on January 30, 1859. There is no record of the topic, but he charged only $35.00, as he was likely to do if the lecture was not a new one. There are no January lectures for the Fraternity in 1860–1863.]

To THOMAS P. HAVILAND, CONCORD, JANUARY 29, 1859[7]

Concord
29 Jan

Dear Sir,

I mean to be at Auburndale, on 3 February, as was agreed between us. I shall bring more than one lecture in my portfolio, but, at this moment, I incline to read one which I call "Conduct of Life."

Letters of 1838–1839 attest to the vogue for Elizabeth von Arnim's largely spurious *Goethe's Conversations with a Child*.

6. See May 13 below.

7. MS owned by Thomas P. Haviland; ph. in NNC. printed by Haviland, *AL* (March 1951), 23:128, with "to read" misread as "toward." See above, December 11, 1858, for initial

I shall probably come to you by the train from Boston which you name, leaving Boston at 6.30

Respectfully,
R W Emerson

T. P. Haviland, Esq

To Margaret Perkins Forbes, Concord, February 2, 1859[8]

Concord
2 February

What to say to an a⟨O⟩dmirable Margaret Forbes, who persists in feeding me with the bread I like best, who includes me among her "eleven friends," and, if I come only at the eleventh hour, I am enriched by ⟨en⟩believing that there exist ten men and women as good as the two or three members of your 'Round Table' whom I surely know.—Ah, if you have a second comparable to this child of genius,[9] who wrote the letters you send me! But no, she was born to make poets of all who beheld her, just so long as they beheld her, & to expiate their ecstasies by living in their memories for the remainder of their term. Tis wonderful her own persistency, and justifies all her lovers that we did not overrate her genius & her charm, when we lived, by dint of sympathising with her, on skies, seas, flowers, statues, & drawings; and,—when the enchantress departed,—fell souse into cold Massachusetts air & water, & began to rub our eyes & suspect we had been philtered. Very likely, but she is guiltless, for there she is, still true to her old tastes, & with the same magnetic selection as ever. I had some fresh recollections of her last

negotiations for a lecture at Auburndale and confirmation of the year assigned to this letter. The date for the lecture is less certain. Emerson runs his figure into the F in February; it looks like "30" but Emerson would not need to settle a date so far in advance. I read the figure as "3".

8. MS in the Sophia Smith Collection, MNS. Unsigned. The last verse of the poem falls at the foot of the fourth page. Given Margaret Forbes' inclination to keep her friends supplied with autographs, I think she gave away the rest of the letter which may have had no more than the complimentary close and the signature. The letter and the verses certainly refer to Caroline Sturgis and the verses are appropriate only to her trip abroad (1855–1859). Moreover, the letter is part of a collection given to the Smith College Archives by a descendant of Mrs. Tappan. I assign the letter to 1859 because what is manifestly an earlier version of the poem appears in MS Journal VO of 1857–1858. For this letter 1858 is impossible, Emerson being in Philadelphia on February 2. Since the letter itself refers to the poem as written last summer, the year can't be 1857, which in any case would also be impossible, Emerson being in Cincinnati.

9. An asterisk after "child of genius" refers to a marginal note not in Emerson's hand identifying the allusion as to Caroline Tappan. The letters Miss Forbes sent Emerson are then from Mrs. Tappan, long a close friend of Miss Forbes. The details in the letter are applicable to her as they are not to any other friend of both Emerson and Miss Forbes.

summer, in the woods, & actually began to send her the lament of Musketaquit—Nature, as I had overheard it.

> She had wealth of mornings in her year,[10]
> And planets in her sky,
> She chose the best thy heart to cheer,
> Thy beauty to supply.
> Now, younger lovers find the stream,
> The willows & the vine,
> But aye t⟨he⟩o me the happiest seem
> To draw the dregs of wine.

To GEORGE B. COALE, CONCORD, FEBRUARY 14, 1859[11]

Concord
14 February, 1859.

My dear Sir,

I am heartily obliged to you for your goodness in sending me this Chant, to which, it seems, by preordained harmony our saint's inspiration was modulated. I have shown it already to a virtuosi, but am to meet Dwight, next week, & he shall sit upon it.[12] When I understand it a little better, I shall communicate with Saint Jones himself. Meantime, I send you the most inward & spiritual of all his poems, which has never been published except in a newspaper.[13]

'Tis a very odd return this for the wonderful comedy you give me in "Father Tom," &c which really deserves all your praise & is incomparable in its kind.[14] I carried it to Lowell, but found that he knew it well already, as he has sure affinity for everything good in this vein.

10. See *JMN*, 14:183, for an earlier version of these lines. The version here is better in all respects but one; the journal reads "willow"; the singular is certainly preferable here to the plural.

11. MS in MdB-J; ph. in NNC; with envelope addressed George B Coale, Esq. | Baltimore. | Maryland. | ; the stamp, and with it, the surcharge, has been removed.

12. Coale's letter to Emerson of January 27 says he is enclosing lines of a poem by Jones Very that he has fitted to the tones of a Gregorian chant. John Sullivan Dwight was a member of the Saturday Club; Emerson would see him on the 26th.

13. The poem by Very is probably "The Stranger," published in the *Salem Observer*, February 15, 1840, too late for inclusion in Very's *Essays and Poems*, published under Emerson's auspices in 1839. Emerson three times copied out this poem by Very (e.g. *JMN.* 7,485), and he included it in *Parnassus* (p. 159). See *J*, 5:383, for Edward Waldo Emerson's note of his father's admiration for this poem. Emerson lists the poem among those he should have read in his public reading at Chickering Hall in 1869. See *J*, 10:285; William Irving Bartlett, in his *Jones Very* (Durham: Duke University Press, 1942), p. 126, misreads this journal entry.

14. The Irish comic story "Father Tom and the Pope; or a Night at the Vatican," from

I shall carefully guard these tokens of the bright evening & brightest friends you gave me at Baltimore.[15]

In good hope of seeing you one day here in Massachusetts

Your obliged friend,
R. W. Emerson

Mr Coale.

To Cyrus Augustus Bartol, Concord, February 14? 1859

[In a letter of February 17, 1859 (Cabot papers, Schlesinger Library, Radcliffe), Cyrus Bartol answers a query from Emerson. He refers Emerson to a Miss Mary Otis. See, below, February 19.]

To Margaret Perkins Forbes, Concord, February 15, 1859?[16]

Concord
15 February

My dear friend,

I send you back the Counterparts, a talismanic book full of secrets, guarded too that no profaner eye can read: for the gem will be taken by people for a dull pebble, whilst you are here you have seen it shoot rays of green blue & rosy fire.[17]

I do not know what novel (English) has contained so many searching glances into the house of life. None that has given the reader this joy of sincere conversation, rightly made the culmination of interest. Genius always treats us well, and we are not rudely turned out of doors at the end of the story by a prosperity exclusively the hero's, but are delighted to find he means us. What a discovery to know that there is an author of "Counterparts" hidden so near, among those slow British people! [Shall

---

Blackwood's Edinburgh Magazine (May 1838), 43:607–619, attributed to Samuel Ferguson (*Wellesley Index*).

15. Emerson lectured in Baltimore on January 4 (Charvat, p. 35).

16. MS in Special Collections, Butler Library; ph. in NNC. The signature and complimentary close have been cut away. The damage leaves the tops of the words in the last line on the third leaf visible; the missing final syllable on the fourth leaf in inferrable. It is clear that nothing more is missing. The letter is one of a group of letters similarly damaged; all are addressed to Margaret Forbes. Part of this letter is printed in *J*, 9:170–171, and in *JMN*, 14:223–224, over the date February 14, 1859; listed *Letters*, 5:134.

17. Emerson's admiration of the novels of Elizabeth Sara Sheppard (at least of *Counterparts* and *Charles Auchester*; he had reservations about *Rumour*) is disconcerting. See *Letters*, 4:459; 5:273, and, below, August 3 and December 4. In his MS journal VA, p. 72 (*JMN*, 15:255), he speaks of her with Harriet Prescott as having "the courage of genius" and names her with Bettina von Arnim and George Borrow was "our romantic writers," His general topic is "Romance"; his test is that works of Romance "move me precisely as true poets do" (*JMN*, 15:255). And he quotes from her *Counterparts* in *Letters and Social Aims* (*Works*, 8:66).

you not go to] London in May to find her or him? Send to Caroline T. to meet you at an evening with the author of C——.[18]

I have not marked the book with pencil, as you permitted,—thank me for it,—and am already sorry that I did not fix a few passages that had a boundless musical mean[ing]

To Henry Stephens Randall? Concord, February 19, 1859[19]

Concord
February 19 1859

My dear Sir,

Do not think me negligent of your request that I do not yet send you the name you ask for. A year ago, I should at once have communi-/cated/[20] with William Foster Otis, third son of Harrison Gray Otis, a man of much worth, and my classmate in College. He has lately died abroad. And I was in town yesterday, & made some inquiries, and think I have now in view the right person, and, when I am in Boston again, a few days hence, I shall finish my quest, & will send you the best name.[21]

Yours, with great regard,
R. W. Emerson

Mr Randall.

To Horatio Woodman, Concord, March 24, 1859

[See April 1, below, where, asking Woodman to look for spectacles left behind in Freeeman Place Chapel, he refers to his earlier having left manuscripts behind. He has to be referring to the occasion of his first Freeman Place lecture March 23 (Charvat, p. 35).]

To James Marius Macrum, Concord, March ? 1859

[In a letter of December 26, 1871 (RWEMA), James Marius Macrum speaks of "that 'Fasciculus of Juvenilia' " he had given Emerson "a dozen years ago. You then kindly (or unkindly, if the Destinies were cruel) said 'Try again.' " See Harding, p. 180, for Macrum's 1846 book *Solitary House of Fancy and Feeling*

18. See May 13, below, for Emerson's having at first supposed the novels written by Charles King Newcomb.

19. MS in Houghton Library, MH; ph. in NNC. I conjecture the addressee to be Henry Stephens Randall, for no better reason than that Emerson had corresponded with him (see November 15 and 21, 1853, March 26, 1853, and *Letters*, 5:105) and that he had read Randall's biography of Jefferson.

20. Ending his first page with the first three syllables, Emerson forgot to finish the word when he turned the sheet. The final syllables are a marginal insert on the second page.

21. See, above, note of letter of c. February 14 to Bartol, who gives Emerson the name of Miss Mary Otis. Mary Alleyne Otis was the daughter of William Foster Otis.

inscribed "9 March 1859." The 1871 letter shows that Emerson acknowledged the 1859 gift.]

To Horatio Woodman, Concord, April 1, 1859 [22]

Concord
Friday 1 April

My dear Sir,

Do not suspect my message, because of this date. I did not leave mss. this time in the Chapel, but I did insert my spectacle-case, including spectacles under the desk, which, I found, sloped a little too much to hold my sheets. Last night I missed them, in attempting to read some fine print, &, today, it occurred to me, that I had left them there. Will you not mercifully send once more to the sexton, &, if they come to you, keep them for me? I do not need them this week. [23]

Yours penitently,
R. W. Emerson

H. Woodman, Esq.

To Mary Eliot Dwight Parkman, Concord, April 11, 1859? [24]

Concord—
11 April.

My dear Mrs Parkman,

Nothing could be more agreeable to me than your kind invitation. I am sorry that I cannot claim your hospitality next Thursday; but if you will let me name so distant a day as the following Thursday, at 2 1/2 o'clock, I shall not fail to keep it, unless advised that any thing makes you wish to change the day.

With great regard,
R. W. Emerson,

---

22. MS in the Woodman papers, MHi; ph. in NNC. A pencil date 1856 added in an unknown hand cannot be correct, for April 1 fell on a Tuesday in 1856. It did fall on a Friday in 1859 when Emerson gave a series of lectures in Freeman Place Chapel, of which the second was given on March 30. In no other year after Emerson acquired his first spectacles (see March 15, 1851, and note), did Emerson lecture in the Freeman Place Chapel just before an April Fool's Day that fell on a Friday.

23. The letter implies an earlier letter to Woodman about lost manuscripts.

24. MS in the Mary E. Parkman papers, Houghton Library, MH; ph. in NNC; dated 1862 by Houghton, but I believe the letter to be of 1859. In that year Emerson did dine with Mrs, Parkman on the second Thursday after April 11 (a.l.s, Ellen Emerson to her sister

To Edwin Percy Whipple, Concord, April 18, 1859[25]

Concord, April 18.

Dear Whipple,—

I am too well pleased to know that I have fallen into your good hands, and I took up my pen on Saturday to tell you so when I was called away peremptorily. I did not return home in time for the mail. In ten or twelve days I will attend to the matter of dates, and will make out a list of such as I may think you may want with all the gravity which the occupation demands.

Ever yours,
Ralph Waldo Emerson.

To Edwin Percy Whipple, Concord, April 22, 1859[26]

Concord, April 22, 1859

Dear Whipple,

I have with too much pains notched out my calendar of two little events, but as I had begun to fix the year of each work, thought I would wade through. What is curious I have omitted; namely, that by paternal or maternal lines I am the eighth consecutive clergyman. Otherwise, for eight generations we are a consecutive line of clergymen on one or the other side, reaching back to Peter Bulkeley, the founder of Concord, who is my ancestor. Was it not time I should vote for the necessity of change? The rest of all this detail is for your article,[27] but I thought you should have it in manuscript for public reference. Make the shortest article, for I grudge you here to the cyclopedia, which I have not looked

---

Edith, April 22) and a Thursday was a reasonable day in that year when his Boston lectures were given on Wednesdays obliging him to spend the night in town. According to Ellen's letter, he described Mrs. Parkman's house as he would not need to do if she had seen it, as she had by 1862. The year 1859 is likely if not secure.

25. No MS has been located; text from Lilian Whiting, *Boston Days*, p. 125; listed in *Letters*, 5:140, under the date April 16, from the catalogue of C. F. Libbie & Co. (April 7–8, 1903). A second listing by the Anderson Galleries (March 31,–April 2, 1919) gives the date as April 18. The text in *Boston Days* and the description in the Anderson catalogue make it clear that these are one and the same. It is possible that the actual manuscript is dated April 16 (a Saturday) emended to 18. The year is established by Emerson's dated letter of April 22, 1859. Both letters are concerned with Whipple's article on Emerson in *The New American Cyclopaedia*, edited by George Ripley and Charles A. Dana (New York: Appleton, 1858–1863). The full signature is supplied by Miss Whiting.

26. No MS has been found; text from Lilian Whiting, *Boston Days*, pp. 124–125. Miss Whiting has "Bulkley"; Emerson is not likely to have misspelled the name, nor is he likely to have used his full signature.

27. See above, April 18.

into, but believe is to have nothing good but what you and Lowell have put into it.[28] I gave you already the ground of my life.

Yours ever,
Ralph Waldo Emerson.

To Elbridge Gerry Dudley: Concord, April 28, 1859[29]

Concord Thursday
28 April

Dear Sir,

You shall, if you please, announce my subject of 1 May, at the Music Hall, "Wealth."

Respectfully,
R. W. Emerson

To Samuel Gray Ward, Concord, April 29, 1859[30]

Concord
Friday, 29 April.

My dear friend,

The goodly bunch of a hundred larches arrived safely at my door ⟨Thur⟩ /Wedne/sday night, & are now all growing in the new woodlot, with might & main, under bright sun & east wind. Many thanks to you for your thoughtful care! I have put some acorns in the garden to be transplanted when they sprout, & have set out 250 pines; am collecting walnuts & chestnuts; but the main planting will be next autumn.

You will not fail, I hope, to come to the Club tomorrow. Yours,[31]
S. G. Ward.   R. W. E.

28. Lowell contributed the article on Dante to the *New American Cyclopaedia*.

29. Text from facsimile in List 59 (1979) of Joseph Rubinfine, item 44; the letter is quoted in full in Catalogue 20 of Robert F. Batchelder, item 30. In neither does the addressee's name appear, but it is with Dudley that Emerson corresponded about lectures for the Parker Fraternity; see *Letters*, 5:138. See Charvat, p. 35, and for Emerson's Pocket Diary (1859) entry, see *JMN*, 14:468. In 1859, April 28 fell on a Thursday.

30. MS in the Ward papers, Houghton Library, MH; ph. in NNC. The 29th of April fell on Friday in 1859; the letter is so endorsed. The MS Account Book for 1853–1859, p. [260], shows, under the date April 21, 1859, the payment of $7.50 to Thoreau for two and a half days in planting Wyman's field. In the MS Account Book for 1853–1859, p. [269], under the date May 21, Emerson describes his treatment of the lot, including: "set a hundred little birch trees," dated May 2; "set a hundred little larches by HDT," and "set out 240 pine trees by HDT," these dated April 20, 21. The Wyman lot on Walden Pond was purchased in 1844 from Cyrus Stowe, administrator; the deed was recorded on October 3 (Middlesex County Registry of Deeds, MS Vol. 449, p. 515). It is on this lot that Thoreau's cottage was built.

31. The "Club" is the Saturday Club. Someone has appended a note "Town & Country?" to which is added a correction signed "E W E" and reading: "Probably the Saturday Club."

To Margaret Perkins Forbes, Concord, May 12, 1859?[32]

> Concord
> Thursday 12 May

My dear friend,

I hate to refuse an invitation that promises me so much that I want. But young people here in the house, as guests, today & tomorrow, & a necessity of being in the city, on Saturday, hold me fast tomorrow. Yet your note sorely tempts me to snap all my threads. I should come fast enough, if so I could reach the conversation that always flies us, & which neither you nor William Hunt will give me,—though all of us be willing, —& yet it is only postponed.

> Yours gratefully,
> R. W. Emerson

Miss Margaret Forbes.

to Caroline Sturgis Tappan, Concord, May 13, 1859[33]

> Concord, May 13, 1859

Please, dear C., not to embark for home until I have dispatched these lines, which I will hasten to finish. Louis Napoleon will not bayonet you the while,—keep him at the door. So long I have promised to write! so long have I thanked your long suffering! I have let pass the unreturning opportunity your visit to Germany gave to acquaint you with Gisela von Arnim (Bettina's daughter), and Joachim the violinist, and Hermann

32. MS in Special Collections, Butler Library, NNC; ph in NNC. The year is not secure, but the letter is certainly later than that of January 4, 1857, above, since it implies earlier missed opportunities to talk with William Morris Hunt. See also *Letters*, 5:141, for a letter of April 27, 1859, where the painter's gift of pictures is mentioned, but no meeting implied. In 1864, the next possible year when May 12 fell on a Thursday, Emerson is corresponding with Hunt, and by 1870 Hunt had been a member of the Saturday Club for ten years.

33. No MS has been located; text (incomplete) from Oliver Wendell Holmes, *Ralph Waldo Emerson*, pp. 225–227. In MS Journal LN, p. 17 (*J*, 10:142) appears an entry that identifies the name, Charles K. Newcomb, Holmes omitted from Emerson's speculations about the authorship of *Counterparts*. The entry shows also that the letter may have contained comment on Holmes himself. The matter of Journal LN is largely of 1866, a fact which accounts for oddities of the text that follows. The journal entry reads:

"I copy a scrap copy of ⟨a⟩ /my/ letter sent to Mrs C. T., when in Europe, ⟨⟨e⟩perhaps never sent) which I pick up today. ⟨")I have let go the unreturning opportunity ⟨of⟩ /which/ your visit to Germany gave /me/ to acquaint you with Gisela Von Arnim, & Herman Grimm her husband, & Joachim the violinist A and I who prize myself only on my endurance, that I am as good as new when the others āre gone,—I to be slow, derelict, & dumb to you in all your absence! I shall regret this as long as I live. How palsy creeps over us with gossamer first, & ropes afterwards! And you have the prisoner when you have once put your eye on him, as securely as after the bolts are drawn.—How strange that C.K.N., whose secret you & I alone have, shd. come to write novels. Holmes's genius is all that is new,—nor that to you.

Grimm, the scholar, her friends. Neither has E.[34]—wandering in Europe
with hope of meeting you—yet met. This contumacy of mine I shall
regret as long as I live. How palsy creeps over us, with gossamer first,
and ropes afterwards! and the witch has the prisoner when she has put
her eye on him, as securely as after the bolts are drawn. —Yet I and all
my little company watch every token from you, and coax Mrs. H.[35] to
read us letters. I learned with satisfaction that you did not like Germany.
Where then did Goethe find his lovers? Do all the women have bad noses
and bad mouths? And will you stop in England, and bring home the
author of "Counterparts" with you?[36] Or did . . .[37] write the novels and
send them to London, as I fancied when I read them? How strange that
you and I alone to this day should have his secret! I think our people will

---

The worst is that we can do without it. Grand behavior is better, if it rest on the axis of the world."

It is Newcomb whom Emerson considered "paralyzed by his whims"; I conjecture that in the original letter the allusion to Holmes followed upon the sentence about Newcomb. A puzzling fact about the journal entry is the allusion to the marriage of Gisela von Arnim and Grimm; they were not married until October 24, 1859; and it was another year before Emerson learned of the marriage from Grimm's letter of October 25, 1860. If the "scrap copy" was a draft, Emerson must have "corrected" this passage as he copied it, sufficiently long after the marriage for him to have forgotten the exact date.

Making for further confusion here is a folded letter sheet laid in MS Journal OP Gulistan at p. 30. This is headed: "To A.H.B.W.?" (Anna Hazard Barker Ward); the text is printed by Rusk, Letters, 5:143, in n. 58. The paragraph begins: "The faults of youth . . ." and is clearly a draft of the last portion of this letter to Mrs. Tappan, not, as Rusk conjectured, a draft of a letter to Anna Barker Ward. Emerson's questioned identification of the addressee apparently derives from the fact that on the folded sheet reversed appears "My dear Anna"; that is, the draft of this part of the letter to Caroline Tappan is written on what was to have been a letter to Anna Ward. I reprint this text here that it may accompany the text above:

"The faults of youth will not wash out, nor ⟨m⟩ the merits, & creeping time convinces ever the more of the insignificance of us & the irresistible bias. Still this is only science We must forever hold our companions responsible, or they are not companions, but stall-fed I think as we grow older, we decrease as individuals & ⟨only,⟩ like an audience who hear stirring music, & only join emphatically in the chorus. So we volunteer no opinions, despair of guiding people, but are confirmed in our perception that Nature is all right, & that we have a good understanding with it We must shine to a few brothers as ⟨palm Trees or roses⟩ palms, or pines or roses do, from their convenient nature, but tis almost chemistry at last, though a metachemistry. Here comes out around me at this moment the new June—the leaves say June, though the calendar says May—and we must needs hail our young relatives again, tho' with something of the gravity ⟨with which⟩ /of/ adult sons & daughters receiving a late-born brother or sister. Nature herself seems a little ashamed of a law so monotonous, billions of summers & now the old game again without a new bract or sepal."

34. Elizabeth Hoar.
35. Anne Sturgis Hooper.
36. By August 3 Emerson knows that the author is a woman; see February 15 above for his first allusion to the book. He had read Charles Auchester earlier (Letters, 4:499 and note). See March 9, 1860, below, for comments on other books by Elizabeth Sheppard.
37. The omitted name here has to be Charles King Newcomb. An entry in MS journal AC, p. 261 (repeated p. no.) makes clear that the secret is Newcomb's "original genius," his mind "far richer" than Emerson's (JMN, 14:279).

never allow genius, without it is alloyed by talent. But . . . is paralyzed by his whims, that I have ceased to hope from him I could wish your experience of your friends were more animating than mine, and that there were any horoscope you could not cast from the first day. The faults of youth are never shed, no, nor the merits, and creeping time convinces ever the more of our impotence, and of the irritability of our bias. Our praxis is never altered for that. We must forever hold our companions responsible, or they are not companions but stall-fed.

I think, as we grow older, we decrease as individuals, and as if in an immense audience who hear stirring music, none essays to offer a new stave, but we only join emphatically in the chorus. We volunteer no opinion, we despair of guiding people, but are confirmed in our perception that Nature is all right, and that we have a good understanding with it. We must shine to a few brothers, as palms or pines or roses among common weeds, not from greater absolute value, but from a more convenient nature. But 'tis almost chemistry at last, though a meta-chemistry. I remember you were such an impatient blasphemer, however musically, against the adamantine identities, in your youth, that you should take your turn of resignation now, and be a preacher of peace. But there is a little raising of the eyebrow, now and then, in the most passive acceptance,—if of an intellectual turn. Here comes around me at this moment the new June,—the leaves say June, though the calendar says May,—and we must needs hail our young relatives again, though with something of the gravity of adult sons and daughters receiving a late-born brother or sister. Nature herself seems a little ashamed of a law so monstrous, billions of summers, and now the old game again without a new bract or sepal. But you will think me incorrigible with my generalities, and you so near, and will be here again this summer; perhaps with A. W.[38] and the other travellers. My children scan curiously your E.'s[39] drawings, as they have seen them.

The happiest winds fill the sails of you and yours!

R. W. Emerson

38. Anna ward.
39. Mrs. Tappan's daughter Ellen.

To Louis Agassiz, Cambridge, May 18, 1859[40]

May 18
Thursday

Dear Agassiz,

I am very sorry to find you gone, as I came loaded with books, & was to show you the places. First, I ⟨came⟩am to call to your mind that you promised to give an hour to this tedious question, before you went abroad; and I fancied myself in condition to shorten your inquiry. I think our Doctor Jackson has been cruelly wronged in the matter; so think your friends, the younger Cabots;[41] so thinks Elie de Beaumont; so Whewell; & so Humboldt,[42] who has lately examined the whole affair, & sent him the Prussian Eagle[43]

Will you please to look at Dr Mortons own book, Anaesthesia, herewith sent, and at his witness, Dr Gould's, testimony. What is most material is, I believe, marked with pencil on the margin. I have asked the Doctor J. to put the principal heads of his plea on paper, which you will find within the covers of "Anaesthesia."[44]

May I ask the kind attention of my friend, Mrs Agassiz, to this particular Volume, as I am to restore it to the Doctor J., to whom it is important, Ever Yours,

R. W. Emerson

40. MS in the Jackson papers, Ether volume, MHi; ph. in NNC; reproduced in facsimile in William Barber's "Dr. Jackson's Discovery of Ether," *National Magazine* (October 1896), 5:46–58. Listed *Letters* 5:93 as of 1857. Over the first syllable of "Thursday" in a hand not certainly Emerson's and with a sputtering pen, someone has written "Wednes"; May 18 was a Wednesday, not a Thursday, in 1859. That the year was 1859 is certain; see, below, the fully dated letter of June 13 on the same subject. This letter was manifestly written at Agassiz's house.

41. James Elliot Cabot and his brother were cousins of Mrs. Agassiz (née Elizabeth Cabot Cary). Samuel Cabot, Jr., M.D., is a signer of the February 1852 Memorial presented to Congress in support of Jackson's claim.

42. Élie de Beaumont, William Whewell, and Alexander von Humboldt are the naturalists cited here.

43. The Cross of the Red Eagle.

44. There is no book by Morton with the title *Anaesthesia* and with Gould's testimony. Emerson may mean *Statements Supported by Evidence of Wm. T. G. Morton, M.D. on his Claim to the Discovery of the Anaesthetic Properties of Ether* . . . (Washington, D.C.: 1853). Gould's testimony appears, with replies on cross-examination, at pp. 265–286. The statements were submitted to the Select Committee appointed by the Senate, 32d Congress, 2d Session, January 21, 1853. See Appendix C, 4, for additional notes.

To Charles Wesley Slack, Concord, May 19, 1859[45]

Concord
19 May 1859

Dear Sir,

I was absent from home yesterday when your note arrived. In Boston, I met Mr Dudley,[46] who asked me for my subject for Sunday. I told him he might call it, "Mental Temperance." It is substantially the same discourse as I once read in Boston, under the name of "The Superlative," to a class.

I will look at the Lecture on "Criticism," to which you allude, & will see if it can be offered to you at any time hereafter.[47]

With great regard,
R. W. Emerson

Mr Slack.

To James Thomas Fields, Concord, May 21, 1859[48]

Concord
21 May
1859

My dear Sir,

Under such friendly auspices, & on terms so liberal, it would be quite out of question to refuse the service you ask, and you shall put my name on the list, if the design is carried into effect.

Yours, with great regard,
R. W. Emerson.

Mr Fields.

45. MS in Special Collections, OKentU; ph. in NNC.
46. Elbridge G. Dudley. See Charvat, p. 35, May 22. The MS is so dated; see *Works*, 10:163–179. I find no record of a Boston delivery. In 1847–1848, he gave a lecture on "The Superlative in Literature, Manners, etc." in England (see *Letters*, 3:431 and 4:103). It is evidently the same lecture that he gave in Concord, April 4, 1849 (Charvat, p. 24).
47. See Charvat, p. 35, June 12 and July 3, where no titles are recorded for the Parker Fraternity engagements; possibly Emerson provided "Criticism" for one of them. The lecture "Art and Criticism" had been prepared for the Freeman Place Chapel series; see Charvat, p. 35, April 13, and *Works*, 12:283–305.
48. MS in the Fields papers, CSmH; ph. in NNC. The letter provides no solid clue to the precise nature of the "service." Fields has asked for. In 1861 Ticknor and Fields published *Favorite Authors*, which includes Emerson's "Threnody," along with prose and poetry by others: e.g., Hawthorne, Holmes, Longfellow, and Lowell. The volume was edited by Fields (*BAL*, 5943, deposited for copyright December 12, 1860). Arrangements for the volume would have to have been made well ahead of time. This letter may be in answer to a request

To Horatio Woodman, Concord, May 24, 1859[49]

Concord
24 May 1859

My dear Woodman,

In looking over my accounts in these last two days, I see that you have paid me nearly seven hundred dollars, or exactly six hundred eighty seven $\frac{85}{100}$ dollars, as net proceeds from my Boston Course of Lectures.[50] Now though I suppose the drafts & checques certified the receipt by me of this money, yet the circumstance of seeing you once & again all the days when you were making me payments ought not to have hindered me from making a specific & full acknowledgment of the amount, &, beyond the cash, of the amount of generous service bestowed by yourself now for the second & third time on my enterprizes. You are pleased to make light of your cares & attentions but I cannot let your generous disclaimers hide from me the deal of annoying details which you have faced & mastered. And easy or not easy to you, I know how /essential/ your kindliest direction has been to the whole affair. Please to know, then, that I & mine look on you as a capital benefactor of us in these years.

Ever yours gratefully,
R. W. Emerson

Horatio Woodman, Esq.

To L. MacFarland and Others, Concord, May 26, 1859[51]

Mr & Mrs R. W. Emerson acknowledge the honor of the invitation to the Social Levee & Promenade supper of the Massachusetts & of the Boston Homoeopathic Medical Societies, on Thursday next, at Faneuil Hall; & return their thanks to the Committee of Arrangements for this polite attention. Mr & Mrs Emerson regret that private engagements at

---

from Fields for a poem to be included. The reference to a "list" implies that others are being written to; and the "liberal" terms implies that the "service" is to be paid for. The conjecture is reasonable, but there is no proof.

49. MS in the Woodman papers, MHi; ph. in NNC.

50. The MS Account Book for 1853–1859, pp. [250] and [254], shows that Woodman paid him in three installments: $200 on April 29, $100 on April 30, and the balance of $387.85 on May 5. See Charvat, p. 35, for the dates and titles of this series. The series of 1858 had been more lucrative. These were depression years, a fact that accounts for Emerson's language here.

51. MS in the Barrett Collection, Alderman Library, ViU; ph. in NNC.

home will deprive them of the pleasure of being present at this attractive festival.[52]

Concord
26 May, 1859

Dr Macfarland,
Dr Fuller,
Dr Thayer,
Dr Geist,
Dr Talbot.—Committee

To Samuel Gray Ward, Concord, June 6, 1859?[53]

Monday, 6 June.
Concord—

Dear S.

Would you not like to see Tom & his boys at school? The fortnight's declamation falls on Wednesday, P.M. at 2 o'c. and if it is not a steamer day,[54] you had better come up /at 11 o'c/ & dine with me at 1. o'clock and go to school at 2. We will gladly keep you all night, & show you the Park[55] you have never seen. Yours.

R. W. E.

S. G. Ward.

52. See *Letters*, 5:147–148, for Emerson's informal reply to an invitation to the dinner given on the same occasion. The addressees are the same, Emerson giving full names for all but the first. The others are Milton Fuller, David Thayer, Christian F. Geist, and I. Tisdale Talbot. I. is correct, but Emerson here, as in the informal letter, writes the initial so that it looks like J.

Israel Tisdale Talbot was the president of the Boston Homeopathic Medical Society and a leader in the struggle to get homeopathic physicians recognized. He had taken his 1853 medical degree at the Pennsylvania Homeopathic Hospital and then added a Harvard M.D. in 1854. He was Professor of Surgery at the Boston University Medical School.

53. MS in the Houghton Library, MH; ph. in NNC. The 6th of June fell on a Monday in 1859; the other letters of that year show that Ward's son Tom was still going to school in Concord; see above February 22 and July 2, 1858, for his attending Sanborn's school.

54. Probably an allusion to the mail boat; as a representative of Baring Brothers, Ward would probably have to stay in town for the London mail.

55. The "Park" is probably the area of Concord known as Estabrook Farm; see above, October 7, 1852, for an earlier invitation.

To LOUIS AGASSIZ, BOSTON, JUNE 13, 1859[56]

American House,
Boston 13 June 1859

Dear Agassiz,

I saw Dr Jackson, last evening, & catechized him on the questions you put to me.

I asked him what was his discovery? He answers, that sulphuric ether paralyzes the sensations of pain.

Then remembering what you said about the good fortune, or the instinct which led him to select Ether, I asked, What led him to select Ether as an anesthetic agent? He replied; his great familiarity with ether as an antidote to Chlorine, he having first discovered the effect of it, in 1837.

Following up the hint from Davy,[57] with respect to his supposed anaesthetic effects of protoxide of nitrogen, he had repeatedly tried Davy's method, with a direct view to this discovery, but without success, he finally fixed on ether, in 1842, & proved its anesthetic effects on himself, & prescribed it to Joseph Peabody, & to Dr W. F. Channing.[58]

Then I asked, Why did you not try the experiment on animals? He answered, Not being in the habit of experimenting on animals, the idea did not occur to him. He has never tried an experiment on an animal in his life.

2. He presumed an experiment on himself would be satisfactory.

It was his intention to bring out this discovery first in the French hospitals; but being constantly in the field, at that time, with his geologic Surveys, he could not go to France, as he had intended.

For your Second Question—Did he impart the idea of anaesthesis. prior to the Hospital experiments? he answers:[59]

56. MS in the Jackson papers, Ether volume, MHi; ph. in NNC.
57. Sir Humphrey Davy.
58. William Francis Channing, M. D.
59. An undated MS list in Jackson's hand (Jackson Ether papers, MHi), does not exactly square with this list. The MS lists names including those given here by Emerson, followed by dates, and concludes with the note: "To all of the above I fully communicated the fact that by the inhalation of the [illegible word] of Sal Ether the nerves of sensation are paralyzed temporarily & safely & that surg. op. could be done without pain."
For Blake, Jackson gives "1842 Spring in my office"; for Augustus A. Gould, "1846 Oct at his house—"; for William Francis Channing, "1842 all Summer on Govt Survey"; for Samuel A. Bemis, "1842 Sept 30th 3 P.M Crawford White Mts"; for William P. Dexter, "1842 Oct 5 or 6th betn Lancaster & Whitefield N H"; for Henry D. Fowle, "1842–3 in my office Somerset Str"; for George Darracott, "1842–3 in my office Somerset Str"; for D. Jay Browne, "1845 in my Laby & office"; for Joseph Peabody "1846 Feby—in my office—"; for Morton "Sept 30th in my Laby—in presence of George O. Barnes & Ja's M'cIntire—" I have

He communicated it to George Darracott on the day he made it

2. To John H. Blake a few days afterwards, March 1842

3. In 1842, to Dr A. A. Gould, then one of his most intimate friends: (See Dr Gould's sworn deposition, called out by Dr W. T. G. Morton).

4. To ⟨M⟩Dr W. F Channing, in 1842.

5. To S. A. Bemis, in presence of Dr W F Channing in 1842, with authority to use it in dental practice.

6. To Henry D. Fowle, druggist, in 1842.

7. To Dr Dexter of Lancaster, N. H. 1842

8. To D H Browne of U. S. Patent office, in 1845.

9. To Joseph Peabody, Feb. 1845.

10. To W. T. G. Morton, then Dr Jackson's pupil in medicine, 1846. To Morton he gave it in trust for practical trial, & Morton agreed to pay Dr Jackson $500. for the right to use it in dental surgery. (See Dr Bowditch's Hospital Report.)

Dr Jackson took upon himself, before witnesses, the entire responsibility, & warranted the method to be safe & efficient (See the testimony of Barnes & MacIntyre.)

To this point, by the way, the Doctor remembers with pleasure, & has before cited it to me, a remark once made by you, in a conversation with him & Dr Gould, "Oh, if ⟨the⟩ Doctor Jackson took the responsibility of the device, then the discovery is his."

It seems to me I make an answer only too abundant to your queries. What strikes me most favorably is the clear & assured tone of all Doctor's conversation with me on this matter. He has run the gauntlet so often, & has come at last to see that there is a power in facts against all opposition, that he has become perfectly peaceable & amiable on the subject, & quite

---

supplied full names here from other documents in Jackson's Ether papers. The papers include copies of some of the sworn depositions of Jackson's supporters (e.g., that of George O. Barnes, a pupil in dentistry, witnessed by Joseph Peabody) and a copy of Jackson's printed "Memorial" of 1864 addressed to Congress; this memorial reprints the memorial of 1852: among the signers of the letter are the dentist Samuel A. Bemis, and Drs. William P. Dexter and William Francis Channing. A copy of the deposition (December 19, 1851) by D. Jay (?) Browne in Jackson's hand leaves his name in doubt, but the first letter of the middle name is clearly not "H." Browne testifies that according to his diary of 1845, he had called at Jackson's Somerset Street laboratory and there heard from Jackson of the discovery that "arose from an accident that happened to you while hastily preparing some chlorine gas for one of your lectures. . . . You confided it to me as one of your pupils, and I . . . never divulged the secret before it was made public by yourself the next year." A John B. Brown is listed in Dickinson's 1847 almanac (see Appendix C, 4), and J. B. Brown is listed by Morton in his advertisement; "Browne" is likely to be Daniel Jay Browne, who was appointed a clerk in the Patent office in 1853.

Nathaniel Ingersoll Bowditch, *A History of the Massachusetts General Hospital* (Boston: John Wilson, 1851), p. 234.

willing to say nothing, & let his claim rest on the very testimony offered by his opponents.

I am however weak enough to think it of high importance to him that you should be accurately informed of the facts he rests upon.

Yours affectionately,
R. W. Emerson.

TO ANNA CABOT LOWELL, CONCORD, JUNE ? 1859

[Anna Lowell's letter of June n.y., endorsed 1859 by Emerson (RWEMA), reads as if she were replying to a letter from Emerson asking for a bill for Edith Emerson's board. Edith had been attending Agassiz's school. Mrs. Lowell says she must be excused "from making any charge for . . . the last few weeks"; Edith has been so infrequently there. The MS Account Book for 1853–1860 shows a payment to Mrs. Lowell on February 7, 1859 (p. [260]). No further payment is recorded.]

TO HORATIO WOODMAN, CONCORD, JUNE 13, 1859

[In the MS Account Book for 1853–1859, p. [177], under the date June 11, Emerson enters a record of what he owes Horatio Woodman for Saturday Club dinners and "Alcott ticket." His calculations give the sum of $21.33. The entry of June 13 reads "Enclosed to him today 21.00." See also *JMN*, 14:452, for a Pocket Diary entry of the same payment under the date June 12.]

TO CYRUS AUGUSTUS BARTOL, CONCORD, JULY 1, 1859

[Rusk's dating of this letter, *Letters*, 5:155–156, is confirmed by Bartol's fully dated letter of acceptance, July 2, 1859, Schlesinger Library, Radcliffe.]

TO SAMUEL GRAY WARD, CONCORD, JULY 6, 1859[60]

Concord
Wednesday Eve
6 July

My dear friend,

I return About, with thanks. He makes a bad case against Rome But the bad position of France in the matter, & his false praise of her, makes

---

60. MS in the Ward papers, Houghton Library, MH; ph. in NNC. The 6th of July fell on Wednesday in 1859. Edmond About's *La Question romaine* was published in that year (Brussels: Meline); and in Boston, J. R. Tilton published in the same year a translation by Mrs. Annie T. Wood. There is also a London translation by H. C. Corpe reprinted in New York by Appleton in 1859. Which version Ward had lent Emerson there is no way of knowing. The subject would have been of particular concern because of Mrs. Ward's conversion to Catholicism; see *Letters*, 5:142–144, and below, August 6.

the weakness of the book. I think of an absurd conversation I once heard, where one party cried, "Well hove, but you're not the man to heave it."

I fancy you have not heard from my wife of her pleasure in her beautiful picture.[61] She thinks it a dream. And it certainly is a poetic picture. The color is so lovely, & so essential, that one would say, there can be no engraving of Turner. I know that Lidian is wishing hard to write to you, but I doubt,—we shall see.

Tom tells me he is to be one of the "speakers" at the Examination. And Ellen is intent on bringing Lily & Bessie[62] with you, to hear him & see him. But I suppose she has written her own message. Confiding to see you on Saturday—

Yours,
R. W. E.

S. G. Ward.

To Samuel Gray Ward, Concord, July 9, 1859[63]

Concord—
9 July 1859

My dear friend,

I got a sprain yesterday in coming down Wachusett in Princeton, which has actually bro't me to[64] crutches today though I hope for my feet again tomorrow or Monday.[65] Meantime, will you be so good as to give my vote at the Adirondac meeting as you give your own For J. M. Forbes,[66] of course, first then, if there be another vacancy for Edward Bangs or for Theo Lyman[67] as you see best.

Yours
R. W. Emerson

61. Just what Ward gave Mrs. Emerson is a puzzle. In the Emerson house is a Turner engraving, untinted, of the second in his English river series; in Ellen Emerson's room are two chromolithographs which certainly have the look of Turner watercolors. All of the Turners given to the Fogg Museum by Edward Waldo Forbes were acquired by purchase; and Mrs. Gregg told me she knew of no Turner in the possession of the family. That Ward was himself a painter and might have made a copy leaves the puzzle open.
62. Ward's children.
63. MS in the Ward papers, Houghton Library, MH; ph. in NNC.
64. A blot obscures the word "to" here; it can't be any other word.
65. As later letters show, the "sprain" was more serious than Emerson supposed; it gave him discomfort for the rest of the year; see *Letters*, 5:171, for differing doctors.
66. John Murray Forbes.
67. Theodore Lyman.

To Herman Grimm, Concord, July 9, 1859[68]

Concord   ⎱ 9 July
Massachusetts ⎰ 1859

My dear Sir,

I have been too much & too long your debtor. But I will not tire you
with excuses which fate made, & which words could not help or adorn.
It is much that I have felt that I was dealing with one who could well
afford me as much time as I wanted. Now I have been reading over your
letter, & your Morgenblatts, & your Essays,[69] & I am warmed with such
thankful kindness, that the time more or less seems not important. I have
read the first Canto of the Cimbri & Teutons, which gives high assurances of power. The only question I ask, and, in this case, with impatience, is, How many years does my part count? For, if you are still
young, you will carry it very far,—With such aplomb, such reserves, &
such mastery of your means. But, in our distracting times, the writers
falling abroad with too much information amassed upon them, it needs
the irresistible drive-wheel of early manhood to overcome the forces of
dispersion. But I will allow you more years than you have, as I choose to
ascribe to you the rare felicity of carrying into maturity the heat of youth,
and so I augur "a new morn risen on mid noon"[70] to your people. I have
just been reading, with great content, the paper on Michel Angelo in the
"Essays" The views taken are all wise and generous; and to me also the
contribution from Raczynsky is new & most welcome.[71] But I give you
fair warning, that, as I alone in America, at this day, possess this book of
yours, I intend to use my advantage. I advise you to watch me narrowly.
I think I shall reproduce you in lectures, poems, essays,—whatever I

---

68. MS in the Goethe-und Schiller-Archiv, Weimar; printed by Holls, *AM* (Apr. 1903),
91:471–472; *Correspondence*, pp. 31–35; listed *Letters*, 5:157.

69. Grimm's Essays 1859 (see Harding, p. 121) is dedicated to Emerson "in herzlicher
Verehrung."

70. Milton, *Paradise Lost* V.1.310.

71. Grimm tells the story of Raczýnski's discovery in his essay on "Rafael and Michelangelo," *Essays*, p. 235. Count Atanazy Raczýnski had printed (from a French translation) the
"diaries" of the Portuguese painter and architect Francisco de Hollanda in his *Les Art en
Portugal*, lettres addressées à la société artistique et scientifique de Berlin et accompagnées
de documens (Paris: Jules Renouard, 1846), pp. 5–74. In the so-called diaries, Hollanda
describes meetings with Michelangelo. To Emerson's dismay the authenticity of these documents was questioned (see *JMN*, 15:6), but they were later authenticated and published from
the original MSS by Joaquin de Vasconcellos, *Quatro Dialogos sobre a Pintura* (Porto: 1896),
who credits Raczýnski as the first printer, though of a poor text. What appears to interest
Emerson is the relationship between Michelangelo and Vittoria Colonna (see below, July 10,
to Fraulein von Arnim, June 27, 1860, to Grimm, and June 27, 1861, to Rebecca Duncan).

may in these months be called to write. I have already been quoting you a good many times, within a few days, and, it was plain, nobody knew where I became so suddenly learned and discerning.

I like well what you say, that, when you are at liberty, you will come and see us. After the fine compliment you pay me,[72] I might well think twice of allowing you to undeceive yourself. I shall pay you the higher compliment of entire trust. I shall not run away. You and I shall not fear to meet, or to be silent, or to prize each other's love of letters less, because we can be modest nobodies at home. Come & see our quiet river, & its skiffs, our woods & meadows, in this little town, whose chief contribution to the public good is, that every farmer sends milk and wood to Boston. A few friends I have here, who are well worth knowing, if you will stay long enough to let the affinities play. I have found that this personality is the daintiest ware with which we deal, & almost no ability is any guarantee of sympathy, unless fortune also aid in the luck of counterparts. I have a hope as of earliest youth, since your friend Gisela von Arnim has written me such welcome sketches of her friends, and taught me to thank & prize them as mine also. Another person sent me the "Morgenblatt" containing your friendliest critique on "Emerson". I must say in all frankness, that your words about me seem strangely overcharged. That such freedom of thought as I use, should impress or shock an Englishman, or a churchman in America, is to be expected. But this same freedom I ascribe habitually to you Germans. It belongs to Goethe, Schiller, & Novalis, throughout, and I impute it to your writers whom I do not know: and I know not what whim of rhetoric I may have to thank that leads you to overprize my papers. Well, I suppose I must wish your illusions will last, until I can justify them by some real performing.

I was sad to read in the, in the Journal you sent me, the death of one of those who should never die,[73]—and untimely for me, who was just coming into relations with her nearest friends, which, could they have been earlier, would have strangely mixed dreams and realities.

I pray you to persevere, in spite of my silences & shortcomings, in sending me, now & then, a leaf written or printed. I hope I shall not be always ungrateful. My little book long delayed, which I call "Conduct of

72. "Emerson . . . Ein Brief," *Das Morgenblatt*, January 2, 1859, pp. 1–9; reprinted twice: *Neue Essays* (1865) and *Fünfzehn Essays* (1874).

73. Grimm's obituary of Elizabeth von Arnim ("Bettina") appeared in *Berlinischer Zeitung*, January 25, 1859; a clipping with envelope addressed to Emerson and postmarked January 31 is in the Emerson papers (RWEMA), Houghton Library.

Life," I mean to send you in the autumn and an enlarged, &, I hope, enriched edition of Poems. Yet it is not books, but sense and sympathy, which I wise to offer you.

Yours affectionately,
R. W. Emerson.

Herman Grimm

To Gisela Von Arnim, Concord, July 10, 1859 [74]

Concord 10 July
Massachusetts 1859

My dear friend,

You must have long ago believed that your letter had failed to reach me—no; there is more providence in the world that that so much and so precious good will can miss of its mark. Thanks for the frankness and bravery, as well as the wisdom, of these pages. They call me out, and are such a surprise, that I shrink a little before so much sincerity. In reading your letter, I felt as when I read rarely a good novel, rebuked that I do not use in my life these delicious relations; or that I accept anything inferior and ugly. I owe you, therefore, a high debt, as exiles ever do to those who speak their native language, and think, for a time, we will never speak the speech of the streets again. But you must repeat and continue your good deed, to keep me in my good resolutions.

There is much to think of, much to speak of in your letter, and, though you have been frank, you make more curiosity than you satisfy. I am piqued by your account of your habits of thought, and when I try to translate your into mine, I am not sure they correspond. In what you say of your habits of creation, I listen warily; but perhaps I do not know the like. You would rather know something of your friends' life, than what thought occupies him. I hope it is no language of despair, grown out of the failures of our fellows. One hears so much called "thought," which is not thought but only the memories of a torpid mind, that we say; Tell us rather of your own corn barn or your shoestring. But I confide, that, if my friend could give me his thought, it is the only gift, and carries all others with it. No life, no experience makes the hunger less. I have the same craving, and the same worship for a new thought as when my first

74. MS in the Goethe-und Schiller-Archiv, Weimar; printed by Holls, *AM* (April 1903), 91:472–474 and in *Correspondence*, pp. 39–44; listed *Letters*, 5:157, with the text of Ellen Emerson's letter in German and a note of a draft of this letter of Emerson's. The draft shows many false starts but does not differ essentially from the letter as sent (ph. in NNC).

intellectual friendships gave wings to my head and feet and new heavens and earth. Yet I could well believe, as I read "Queen Ingeborge," that you do not like ghosts, but real men and women, and that you think with such forms, and not with counters. That you make so much of your friends, is also the habit of a noble soul; and, since life admits of friendship, why should ever suffer it to be cheap and apathized. Thanks again that you have confided to me tidings of your companions. Berlin shall be to me henceforth a noble and cordial city. And the invitation you send me to visit it gives me new rights in Europe. I am a bad traveller, and, every year, am a little faster tied to my own nook and cell, by tasks unperformed, and by solitary habits, and, especially as regards Germany, by a despair of talking in a language which I can only read, and not pronounce, and much less, speak. But your challenge makes a kind of daily possibility to my dream. I too could heartily wish to send you friends of mind who deserve to see you. I gave a letter long since to Elizabeth Hoar, a dear friend of mine, and who should have been, had he lived, the wife of my brother Charles, but he died many years ago. She is now in Italy, or in Switzerland, and the war may prevent her reaching Berlin. Should she come, you will find her a woman in whom much culture from books has not weakened the strength or the delicacy of her native sentiment. She shares my love for your mother's genius. There was lately also in Germany a friend of mine, whom I could dearly have wished you to see, Mrs. Caroline Tappan.[75] These two would give you two styles of New England women, that might suggest to you better than almost any others, the range of our scale. But I fear she is in Paris, and already perhaps meditating a return home, though I had written to her not to leave Germany, without seeking to see you. She did not go to Berlin.

I read your plays,[76] and find them interesting,—which is to say much, for I lack, I believe, a true taste for that form, and wish always that it were a tale instead, which seems to me the form that is always in season, —whilst the drama, though it was once the right form, and then was again right, yet seems to die out from time to time; and, in these days, to labor with much that is old convention, and is so much deduction of power. Certainly it requires great health and wealth of power to ventriloquize (shall I say?) through so many bodies; whilst, in the novel, only that need be said which we are inspired to say, and the reliefs and

75. See May 13 above.
76. See above, June 29, 1858, to Fraulein von Arnim for two volumes of plays she had sent Emerson.

oppositions take care of themselves. But, in Germany, I can well see, the drama seems to cling about the intellectual heart, as if it were one of the "prime liete creature"[77] that Dante speaks of, and could not be ignored.

You must thank my young translator,[78] of whom you speak, for her labor of love, though the "glued book" you seem to have sent me, never arrived. Neither did the Hungarian poems, Petofi's,[79] which you praise. Herman Grimm's obituary notice of your mother reached me from him, and was every way important. I mourned that I could not earlier have established my alliance with your circle, that I might have told her how much I and my friends owed her. Who had such mother-wit? such sallies? such portraits? such suppression of commonplace?

Continue to befriend me, nor let my slowness to write, which I will not make worse by explanation, chill your flowing generosity, which I love like sunshine. If you will write me such another letter as you have written, perhaps all my ice will go, and I shall suddenly grow genial and affable. Ah! how many secrets sleep in each, which only need invitation from the other, to come forth to mutual benefit.

With the highest respect and
regard, yours,
R. Waldo Emerson

To William Watson Goodwin, Concord, July 11, 1859[80]

Concord
11 July, 1859

My dear Sir,

Allow me to introduce to you my nephew, Charles Emerson, of Columbia College, New York. He has just ended his Freshman year, in that College, & proposes to enter the Sophomore Class in Cambridge.[81] He professes, however, to have some doubts of his competency to do this, which, I trust, you & your colleagues will not share when he comes to you for examination. Meantime, will you have the goodness to give him

---

77. Emerson misquotes "con l'altre prime creature lieta," *Inferno* VII.95.
78. His daughter Ellen.
79. Alexander Petöfi, called the Hungarian Byron.
80. MS in Houghton Library, MH; ph. in NNC; with envelope addressed: Mr W. W. Goodwin | Harvard University | Mr Charles Emerson
81. See *Letters*, 5:162, 163–164, for Charles Emerson's reasons for transferring from Columbia to Harvard and his final arrangements.

such information as he needs as to the details of the examination, that he may the better judge whether some special reviewing will be useful to him beforehand. He will also be glad of advice as to a good room, & a boardinghouse, which direction I know you can readily give him.

Hoping to see you here during the vacation, your friend,[82]

R. W. Emerson

Mr. Goodwin.

To CHARLES COFFIN JEWETT, CONCORD, JULY 15, 1859[83]

Concord
15 July 1859
Friday Evening

Dear Sir,

I received your note this evening, & will try to meet the wishes of Mr Gilbert[84] at once; but I am not sure that I can on Monday. The bond /or note/ which I hold, is in the keeping of my friend Mr Abel Adams, & I do not know whether it is in Boston or Brookline. I write tonight to Mr Adams, & request him to send it to me on Monday, in Boston, & I ⟨will⟩ hope to go there, & receive it on that day; in which event, I will bring it to you.[85]

I am sorry, for my part, that Mr Gilbert does not let it remain as it is; since I do not know how to place the money as well[86] without mentioning the occasion it gives me twice a year of seeing you.[87]

Mr Adams may not be at home, or may not be able to send it at once, &, I ought to add, I am suffering from a sprain, & cannot be quite secure of my own locomotion. But I will do the best I can.

Yours faithfully,

Mr Jewett.   R. W. Emerson

82. The Harvard Hellenist was Concord-born.

83. MS in the Bancroft Library, CU; ph. in NNC.

84. Timothy Gilbert wishes to pay the principal of a note held by Emerson and his brother William and arranged for in 1850 on the sale of the La Fayette Estate (see *Letters*, 1:158–159 and n. 5); Emerson explains the transaction in a letter of July 1, 1850, to his brother (*Letters*, 4:215–216).

85. See *Letters*, 5:160–161, and for further correspondence, pp. 162–165, 167–168, and 189.

86. The money was subsequently loaned to Samuel Coverly on the advice of Samuel Gray Ward; see below, August 13.

87. Charles C. Jewett was the husband of one of Emerson's cousins, a daughter of Ralph Haskins (*Letters*, 4:335, n. 257).

To George Field, Concord, July 25, 1859[88]

Concord, 25 July, 1859

Dear Sir,

I have been a little surcharged with correspondence lately, or should have acknowledged your friendly note.

I am laid up in my chair with a sprained foot, which is only annoying by confining me, & therefore I cannot at present go to town though I have much need so to do. When I do, I shall watch for any opportunity to have a half hour with you at the Atheneum perhaps. You could not have done better than to have gone home with me on "that Sunday" to my chamber at the American House.[89]

I suppose when we meet, I shall concede all the weight you will claim to the needs of the day. But I hold, that, if the great laws are seen & honored, there works an incessant tendency to rectify our lot, & bring our genius & our labors at one. All labor is very <u>porous</u> to moral infusions, and it looks as if a strong character might dignify any chores.

With thanks & best wishes,

yours,
R. W. Emerson.

Dr. Field.

To Cyrus Augustus Bartol, Concord, July 26, 1859[90]

My dear Bartol,

No such blessing is in store for me in just these days as the waters of your Cove. My foolish foot will not yet let me think of such things, & when I come, as I presently must, to insist on its return to duty, it will no doubt find that it has a plenty of steps to take over due & postponed. It is not the less kind in you to offer us this freedom of your sunny terraces of rock, & waters whose electric touch I still remember,—many touches they have, but a healthful electric shock, I recall with grateful preference.[91]

88. No MS has been found, text from Stearns Morse, "An Emerson Letter," *Harvard Alumni Bulletin* (January 15, 1931), 33:480. Listed *Letters*, 5:165. See also n. 125, pp. 124–125, for Dr. Field. The lame foot, long in healing, is mentioned in many letters of 1859 and 1860; for the accident, see *Letters*, 5:161.

89. The MS Account Book for 1853–1859, p. [274], shows a two-day stay at the American House, paid for on Monday, June 13. I take "that Sunday" to refer to June 12.

90. MS in Houghton Library, MH; ph. in NNC.

91. Pigeon Cove, Cape Ann, Massachusetts; see, above, letters to Bartol of 1856 and *Letters*, 5:24, for the visit of that year. The water off Pigeon Cove can be extremely cold.

My wife joins her thanks & salutations with mine to you & to Mrs Bartol. She has already promised a week at Naushon in the beginning of August, & means, I believe, to add a week or more of Plymouth to that, so that she is likely to indemnify herself for the loss[92] the Flumebrook at Waterford.[93] This note, I hope, is not too late for the mail.

Ever yours,
R. W. Emerson

Concord, 26 July, 1859

TO ELIZABETH PALMER PEABODY, AUGUST 1? 1859

[See August 10, 1859, below, for evidence of a letter to Miss Peabody.]

TO ELIZABETH HOAR, CONCORD, AUGUST 3, 1859[94]

Concord, 3 August, 1859

May that will which is done, dear Elizabeth, keep you fast in Liverpool, or in England, till this sheet reaches you, that I may not be remembered only for the crime of not having written you one word. The amount of inertia in timorous & susceptible souls astonishes one as a practical contradiction. I look on it as a scarlet sin, & explaining jails & penitentiaries. I live in a squalid contentment with my boy & girls, and lose a great deal of time in sympathizing with their householdish & social plans which drift like clouds over every day & week. I read or write to any purpose so seldom that I cannot think of any other shoulders whereon to lay my load—yet the worst fault of the writing class, is, that there is more antechamber waste to them than to courtiers. Nine hours of expecting to one of council. But you cannot, with all your magnanimity, /understand/ such imbecility; for the doers of duty waste no time. And now you are seconded by the heaps of facts agreeable or fruitful to you. We are all the better for your searching eyes & flowing pen. And the Peace will at

92. Emerson omitted the necessary "of" here.
93. Emerson and his daughter Ellen had made a short visit to Waterford in June (the expenses recorded in the MS Account Book, 1853–1859, p. [273], under the date June 13). The Emersons had planned to spend six weeks in Waterford, Maine, later in the year, but were kept at home by Emerson's having hurt his foot in a fall on Mount Wachusett; see above, July 6, and see *Letters*, 5:152, 154, 156, 161, 162.
94. MS in NNPM; ph. in NNC; privately printed by Edward P. Hill (Yselta, Tex.: 1942, *BAL*, 5335, M. A6o, p. 497). The last two sentences are a postscript written in the left-hand margin of the first page. The signature and complimentary close have been cut away damaging three words on p. [3]; Elizabeth Hoar filled the words in before she cut off the signature.

least keep the countries open to travellers.[95] I hoped & even hope that Berlin might be in the map you had made for yourself. Since you have been abroad, I have had the best letters from Herman Grimm, Gisela Von Arnim. They are both persons of character & of mind that must attract us; Bettine died in the Spring.[96] I read Grimm's book of "Essays" with great respect. And I have told Gisela that you would come to her. We have a good book here from the senior Grimms, the first volume of their German Dictionary.[97] Other books we have had none of mark, except the two grand English books, which, coming in one year, vindicate the soundness & self equality & superiority to all Europe still, of the old island,—I mean, of course, Carlyle's & Tennyson's.[98] Ellery C. finds a prose tone running through Tennyson's Poem, though he knows its merit. I hope in England you will find who wrote "Counterparts" & "Charles Auchester,"[99] & visit her. Tis wonderful, & "the English are a singular people," as Carlyle says, that such a writer should be unknown there. But you will pass Paris now, & not see Caroline T., to my great disappointment. I suppose I can tell you nothing of home that is new. Ellen & Edith have had a good growing year in schools that are schools.[100] Edward has been at the Adirondacs 7 days with Mr Ward & Tom.[101] Mr Alcott magnifies his office of "Superintendent of Schools". Henry T. occupies himself with the history of the river, measure it, weighs it, & strains it through a colander to all eternity, I may say of such an immortal. Ellery C., to pass the time, goes with H. to the river; and is fond of making elegant presents. Rockwood who was born for greatness, as well as to achieve it himself is the best man in the state; yet, what is best, his

95. Emerson appears to be referring to the meeting of the emperors Napoleon III and Francis Joseph in Villafranca, July 11. The meeting ended the war (in Italy) between France and Austria. The aggressive action of Napoleon III had alarmed the Prussians who had mobilized on the Rhine. Emerson apparently supposes that travel in Germany will now not be restricted. While it is not clear from this letter just what Emerson knows of Miss Hoar's travels, his "hoped & even hope" suggests that he now knows that she has already been in Germany, as she had, but not in Berlin, (His letter of July 10, above, to Gisela Von Arnim shows that then he knew only of her being in Italy and perhaps en route to Switzerland.)

96. In a letter of April 25 to her sister, Edith reports a talk about Hermann Grimm's letter. See also above, Emerson's letter of July 9 to Hermann Grimm for note of Grimm's obituary of Elizabeth von Arnim.

97. The MS Account Book for 1854–1860, p. [279], in an entry for July 18, shows the purchase of vol. 1 of Jakob Grimm's *Deutsches Worterbuch*. Other volumes were added as they came out. The set now in the library runs only through vol. 5 of 1873 (Harding, p. 122).

98. *The History of Frederick II* (Harding, p. 51) and *Idylls of the King* (Harding, p. 269).

99. See above, February 15, 1859, to Margaret Forbes.

100. The Account Book shows payments to both Frank Sanborn and Louis Agassiz for Ellen and Edith and to Ida Agassiz for special tuition of Edith.

101. Samuel Gray Ward and his son Thomas. See below, August 5.

performances cost him no more than Sammy's.[102] Besides a whole [armory of] t[ale]nts, he has presence of mind. You may well go to Europe that can leave such a brother at home. Charles Emerson /is/ preparing at Cambridge to enter Freshman after the vacation, a purpose which I urge.[103] ⟨W⟩His father was here a few days ago, & gives very good accounts of Aunt Mary's comfort with Hannah P.,[104] yet she writes that she shall go up the river to board during the summer—Lidian & Edith go to Naushon, next week, to Prospero's Island.[105] Have I not told you all my tidings? It were a vice to know more. Yet Mr Billings is coming this week to Concord to make local sketches for an edition of my poems, the publishers say.[106] Was it Gibbon said, "the mediocre writers /speakers/ filled him with disgust, the great ones with despair."[107] I have scarcely made a new acquaintance since you departed, but have reinforced a few old ones. I was sorry to lose the Waterford visit, which, though projected by Ellen, had some fine prospective values for me.[108] If you do not come home, &, when you come home, let me see you sometimes. I think I may go live there.

You have heard that Mr Wasson lives in Concord.[109] Lidian warmly sends her love & remembrances.

102. Ebenezer Rockwood Hoar and his brother Samuel.

103. See July 11, above, to William Watson Goodwin.

104. Hannah Haskins Parsons.

105. As the guests of John Murray Forbes; see *Letters*, 5:168.

106. Hammatt Billings. This plan came to nothing—not surprisingly; a style of illustration suitable for Whittier's poems would scarcely be so for Emerson's. For Emerson's recollection, see notes for March 19, 1872, below.

107. Emerson here adapts Gibbon who, lamenting his own inability to speak in public, wrote a friend: "I am still a mute; it is more tremendous than I imagined; the great speakers fill me with despair; the bad ones with terror." Gibbon's letter of February 8, 1775, was written to his friend John Baker Holyrood, first Earl of Sheffield, who printed it in the first (1796) and all subsequent editions of his *Miscellaneous Works* of Gibbon (see Harding, p. 115, for the edition Emerson owned). Strictly speaking, the word "speakers" is a gloss not an insert; it is added above the word "writers."

108. For the Maine vacation, see *Letters*, 5:152, 154, 156, 162, and above, July 26, to Bartol. Emerson alludes here to more than the vacation plan frustrated by his damaged foot. In a letter of June 13 to her sister Edith, Ellen Emerson describes her father's feelings when they found a delightful brook ("mother's river") near Elm Vale and reports her father's notion of selling the Concord house, buying the brook, and moving permanently to Waterford. This daydream is not revealed in his letters to his brother, but it is here.

109. David Atwood Wasson; see *Letters*, 5:391.

Concord
4 August, 1859

Dear Sir

Mr Carter may have the piece of land on the river, if he wishes. It contains 3 acres, 25 rods, more or less; and the price is three hundred and twenty dollars. It is now rented /till October,/ to Mr Newton, as a cow-pasture. If Mr Carter wishes to build, or otherwise improve it, before 1 October, I can, doubtless, easily obtain a release or a <u>dislease</u> from Mr Newton.[111]

Respectfully,
R. W. Emerson.

H. Ware, Esq.

To Samuel Gray Ward, Concord, August 5, 1859[112]

Concord 5 Augt
1859

But Anna's letter? You have not sent it. Surely by the p.m. mail.[113]

I was heartily glad to see the boys back, for though no harm could befall such a company, I fancied you must have overstayed your design. But Edward gives the best accounts of his fortnight & would not have missed his new experiences for anything at home; though he was never from his family before. He is very sensible of ⟨his⟩your kindness to him, & so am I.[114]

I enclose my Adirondac Club assessment, which I should have sent

110. MS in the Barrett Collection, Alderman Library; ViU; ph. in NNC; with envelope addressed: H. Ware, Esq. | 34 School St. | Boston. | The addressee is a Boston attorney acting for Robert Carter. See August 10, below, to Ware and August 29 to Carter. Carter's initial move is of November 23, 1858, see above. The property was known as Asabet pasture, purchased in 1855 from Edmund Hosmer, and surveyed by Thoreau.

111. The MS Account Book for 1859–1865, p. [24], under the date April 16, 1860, records the receipt of $14.00 from H. Newton for "rent for pasture since Apr. 1859." An entry of June 15, 1861, p. [104], shows the payment of $2.47 to Herman Newton "for entertainment of certain travellers" (i.e., tramps), presumably this is the same Newton, who appears also in the Account Book of 1853–1859.

112. MS in the Ward papers, Houghton Library, MH; ph. in NNC.

113. See below 6, August and Letters 5:169.

114. Ward had taken his son and Emerson's on a trip to the Adirondacs; see Letters, 5:163 and 168.

weeks ago. /$50.00/ I add $10.00 for E's blanket, & because $25. did not cover his road expenses.[115]

My foolish foot will, I hope, grow wiser soon. But, I fear, not in season to climb Mount Ambersand.[116] The travellers loiter; smoothest seas to them![117]

Ever Yours,

S. G. Ward.   R W Emerson

To ANNA BARKER WARD, CONCORD? AUGUST? 6? 1859?

[Two letters to Samuel G. Ward, one of August 5 (above) and the other of August 10, 1859 (*Letters*, 5:169), show that Emerson received a letter from Anna Barker Ward, then in Europe, on the 5th or 6th. The letter of the 5th to S. G. Ward demands the letter from Anna "surely by the p.m. mail"; the letter of August 10 comments on its matter and manner. Emerson's concern for Mrs. Ward's health, physical and spiritual, is indicated in his letter to her of May 5 (*Letters*, 5: 142–144); it is clear too from a draft of part of that letter (*idem*, p. 144, no. 58, the first paragraph only, the second not being to Mrs. Ward) that Emerson found Mrs. Ward's conversion to Catholicism a stimulant to reflection and grounds for increasing dismay. I think he would have answered the letter he was so anxious to receive. What may be a draft of such a reply is in a small gathering of MSS labeled "Autobiographical Miscellany" (RWEMA). It is on stationery of the kind he was using in the late fifties. It is headed: "To A. W." and reads as follows: "Thanks for your spontaneous sympathy & expression You are of those who are ⟨made for⟩ torches not lights for themselves I suppose with all your wakeful perception you know the least of your history of ⟨your⟩ what rays or beams you have innocently shed on surrounding friends ⟨This Your morbid⟩ Sickness & your taste for antiquity have not carried you so far out of my reach as my own incapacities to carry rightly the simple lesson which refuses additions. I suppose it will never be given to me to talk with you here; it is a foolish reminiscence of youth to think it,—but in some long day of God. ⟨it is grateful⟩ by pleasanter hills & more enduring cities we may see what is ridiculous in life made types if explained by their sources."

An occasion for Mrs. Ward's expressing sympathy would be the sprain Emerson incurred July 8 on Mount Wachusett, an injury he reported to Ward (see July 9, above). The allusions to the recipient's sickness (Mrs, Ward suffered from trigeminal neuralgia) and taste for antiquity fit Mrs. Ward as does the allusion to "a foolish reminiscence of youth"; i.e., the confidence and intimacies of 1840. Even the allusion to "pleasanter hills" recalls the standing protests of his friends of that time that he should live in a landscape so lacking in picturesque charm as Concord.

115. These payments are entered in the MS Account Book for 1853–1859, p. [485], under the dates August 4 and 5, where Ward is labeled the treasurer of the Adirondac Club.
116. Ambersand between Lake Placid and Follenby Pond.
117. Mrs. Ward and her daughter on their way home.

See, below, for a journal passage entered under October 26 that may also be a portion of an August letter.

Not reproduced in the text above is a cryptic "C & C" entered diagonally just before the first word "Thanks"; I can offer no interpretation.]

To Eliza Thayer Clapp, Concord, August 10, 1859[118]

Concord
10 August, 1859.

My dear Miss Clapp,

I have kept by me for many days the enclosed note to Miss Peabody, which was written after receiving your note & hers, and am now more than ever at a loss how to address it to her. As it is also my only reply to your note, I think it best to send it to you, lest you should fancy I made none. Mr Sanborn is still absent nor do I know his address. —though I ought presently to inquire it, having received another piece of information that concerned him.[119]

I hope you find your old joy in books, and, in these days, in Tennyson's poem.[120] What benefits still come to us from the old island! and when shall we begin to repay them? With kindest regard

R. W. Emerson

To Henry Ware, Concord, August 10, 1859[121]

Concord 10 Augt
1859

My dear Sir,

It was heedless, but I did not find until tonight when I prepared to send my deed to Mr Brooks,[122] to be the basis of the new one, that it could not be finished now, as my wife is at Naushon, & then to be a few days at Plymouth. I will have the paper drawn at once, &, if it appear

118. MS in the Manuscript Division, DLC; with envelope addressed: Miss Eliza T. Clapp. | Dorchester. | Massachusetts | ; ph. in NNC; quoted briefly by Rusk, *Life*, p. 539.

119. Sanborn's absences were due to his deep involvement with John Brown and the raising of funds for him; how much Emerson knew of the affair and of the use to which the funds were put is a puzzle; see October 23, below. The letters Emerson refers to have not survived; what the ladies asked is obscure.

120. See August 3, above; Emerson purchased the American edition of *Idylls of the King*, Harding, p. 269.

121. MS in the Barrett Collection, Alderman Library, ViU; ph. in NNC; with envelope addressed: Henry Ware, Esq. | 34 School Street. | Boston. |

122. See August 4, above, and August 29, below. George Merrick Brooks, attorney, acted for Emerson in local matters.

that she is to remain in one place for any time, I will send the deed to her for her signature. She will not, I think, overstay ten days.

Respectfully, & with
Kind regards,

H. Ware, Esq.   R. W. Emerson

To Lidian Emerson, Concord, August 11, 1859

[In the MS Account Book for 1853–1859 (p. [225]), under the date August 11, is a record of "Cash sent to L. E. at Naushon"; a note at least probably accompanied the money—$2.00.]

To Samuel Gray Ward, Concord, August 13, 1859?[123]

Concord, 13 August,

My dear friend,

I have had a mortgage note which has,[124] for years, paid me a semiannual interest with a perfect punctuality. Unhappily, the party wished to take up his note, & has paid the amount. How can I invest this again, say $3000. securely, and have 6 per cent?[125]

I shall try to enclose again the $1. which dropt from my last note.

Yours,
R. W. E.

S. G. Ward

To Mary Howland Russell, Concord, August 17, 1859[126]

Concord, 17 Aug. 1859

My dear Miss Russell,

Lidian has just returned from Naushon having missed your letter forwarded thither, & it has arrived at her eyes today.[127] She was very

123. MS in the Ward papers, Houghton Library, MH; ph. in NNC. Catalogued as of the 1840s, this letter clearly follows the letter of August 10, 1859 (*Letters*, 5:169); the last sentence here refers to the dollar Emerson supposed he had returned with the letter of the 10th. A fragment that appears to be a false start for this letter is laid in the MS journal Orientalist.

124. See *Letters*, 5:161, 162–163, 164, and July 15, above, for the source of the money to be reinvested; "the party" is Timothy Gilbert.

125. Emerson's MS Ledger for 1849–1872 shows, under August 27, 1859 (p. 146), the loan of $3,000. to Samuel Coverly "on his mortgage note." The principal was paid April 14, 1865 (Ledger, p. 166). The MS Account Book for 1853–1859 records at pp. [280] and [282] the receipt of $4,036.68 and the deduction from this of $608.26, "⟨the⟩ /our/ note to the Haskins estate which ⟨was⟩is now paid. . . ."

126. No MS has been found; text from a copy made by Ellen Emerson, RWEMA; ph. in NNC.

127. Ellen Emerson, August 13, writes her sister Edith, still at Naushon with Mrs.

happy in your invitation but fears were in the way and Ellen who finds no benefit to her Mother like driving her from home has seconded it with her persuasions. I fancied however that Lidian was three quarters persuaded from the first and heartily pleased with the freedom of talking with you by the sea We have now just put her to bed to compensate for very rough yachting yesterday and vigils last night and I am to signify to you that she will come. Ellen is making faithful experiments in house-keeping, almost too faithful, and I think I must send her to you, if only to bring her Mother home though she thinks herself bound to stay at home. Edith is still at Naushon and returns on Saturday to help Ellen, and to supply her place. I am using my sprained foot lately as an apology for making visits to LeBaron [128] who chooses to be good angel to me. I suppose it is in the blood. Will you not send Lidian one line more to say when & how you go?

Yours affectionately
R. W. Emerson.

To Melusina Fay, Concord, August 22, 1859 [129]

Concord
Augt 22, 1859

My dear Miss Fay,

I am seriously pleased with your letter. You can know & feel, & are welcome to call your thoughts by such names as you will. I like your respect for the dear old eastern teachers, for it is sincere; & I share it, though I confine it a little less. I give them all the advantage that you do. I hear & dearly prize every word of the blessed Soul in east or west, & know how miraculous that is, but my piety will not let me soil it with the nonsense of the receivers. Your own discernment will not fail to make you as severe, & to make you deaf to the bad names people give it. Character & sense are the grand results:—a will that is filled with heaven, & constant therefore to its poles, and a perception on which no horizon falls,—these are of no country or sect, & therefore of all, & bring home

---

Emerson, that Miss Russell has written to invite her and Mrs. Emerson to visit her at Seaconett after a week at Plymouth.

128. He evidently saw Dr. LeBaron Russell, the addressee's brother, on Monday August 15; Ellen, in her letter of the 13th, says of her father's damaged foot that he intends to take "it" to Boston Monday. Her letters of July 27 and August 24 show that he habitually talked of the injured ankle in the third person.

129. MS privately owned; ph. in NNC. See above, October 7?, 1856, for note of Miss Fay's first letter to Emerson; it is likely that there was other correspondence between them.

the Godhead to the lowest duty & the most opprobious repute. No doubt, Margaret Fuller's life makes a just impression on you, & the defects you feel exist, however we call them.[130] I do not recall after so many years the letters or papers to which you allude. But all the passages are in every experience. There is a "dark quality"[131] as Behmen called it, identical though it nimbly take a thousand forms, now egotism, now wrath, now frivolity, which almost pervades humanity, & hence the transcendent wrath of the pure souls. Nay that compensation principle on which we make watches & thermometers, seems to hide in very saints & angels, and there is one somewhere who knows how much their virtue costs.

But I did not mean to weary you with homilies in my bad writing, for I am cripple in these days in hand & foot.[132] I wish I could come to St Albans, but can not yet reach my own orchard.

Yes, by all means, come to Cambridge, if that is made easy to you. My ⟨two daughters in⟩ two daughters in succession have attended & have now left the school. Ellen, the eldest, thought it had every advantage for those who would learn. Edith did not esteem it so highly as our Concord School. And indeed Ellen prizes the last so much, that she has gone thither the last year to learn Greek & will now in September begin the new.[133] Mr Sanborn is a teacher such as there are few. I have called my wife & Ellen to counsel, & they would fain urge you to come to the Concord School. But in Concord or in Cambridge, I shall not fail to see you, & you will come & visit me, & shall see my wife & children, & I can show you in my neighborhood one or two rare persons whom a good soul would not willingly leave unseen.[134]

Your friend,

R. W. Emerson

Miss Zina Fay.

130. Miss Fay had apparently read the *Memoirs*.

131. The phrase "dark quality" appears in Emerson's quotations from Sir William Jones' translations from the Vedas (*JMN*, 6:394).

132. See July 9, above, for this injury.

133. Ellen Emerson had found inadequate the instruction in Greek at Agassiz's school (a.1.s., December 15, 1855, to Haven Emerson); Professor Cornelius Felton held "a recitation only once a week."

134. Alcott, Thoreau, and Channing.

To Benjamin Marston Watson, Concord, August 25, 1859[135]

Concord—

25 August, 1859

My dear Sir,

Our supper-table showed a su⟨p⟩prise party, last night, through the arrival of your beautiful box of "herbs."[136] Is it partly owing to their miraculous efficacy that I am walking on two feet today without a staff? When I think of your art, your grounds, & of what your house holds, I count the days lost in which I have not gone to Plymouth. But this secret of the garden too is the secret of genius again: All the land & trees & rules in the world will never help, till the man makes the opportunity. But I like to hear what Channing & what Alcott have to say of you & yours.[137]

With kindest regards to Mrs Watson,[138] & to Ben,[139] Your gratefully,

R. W. Emerson

Mr. Watson.

To Calvin G. Child, Concord, August 26, 1859[140]

Aug 25. 1859

Concord, Mass.

Dear Sir,

Early in December does not promise to be as free a time to me as a /Wednesday or/ Friday in January. Nor am I quite ready even to offer you a fixed day. If you wish, I will do so later. The Association shall pay me Forty dollars for a Lecture.

Respectfully,

R. W. Emerson

Mr Child.

135. MS in the Clark papers, CtHi; ph. in NNC.

136. The word "supper" falls at the end of the line and is clearly followed by a hyphen. What Watson sent was a box of grapes and pears; in his letter Watson had said he was sending "herbs" for Emerson's "wound" (Ellen Emerson, a.1.s., to her mother, August 24).

137. Channing, Alcott, as well as Thoreau, took part in Watson's Sunday evening lecture series (see January 15, 1852, above).

138. Mrs. Watson was Mary Russell, who had been the Emerson children's teacher.

139. The Watson's son; Emerson has written the name over his first writing of it.

140. MS in the Beinecke Library, CtY; ph. in NNC. The letter is endorsed, presumably by the recipient, with Emerson's name and the date August 26, 1859. In the 1859–1860 season, Emerson had only two lecture engagements that satisfy the conditions here: one in Norwich, Connecticut, on Wednesday, December 28, and the other in Saratoga, New York,

[In the Colson estate there was a letter to a Mr. Butts, dated August 28, 1859; the letter was about Tyngsboro, Massachusetts. There is no record of Emerson's lecturing there in any year. The present whereabouts of the letter is unknown.]

To ROBERT CARTER, CONCORD, AUGUST 29, 1859[141]

Concord, 29 Augt 1859

My dear Sir,

I have been through many causes much in arrears in my correspondence lately & your letter has lain with the rest. I forwarded however Mrs Carter's very pleasing River Sketches to Mrs Hunt as you desired.[142] I asked Mr Heywood, Town Clerk, what was the tax assessed on the Asabet pasture[143] He showed me a minute for 1858 & 1859. It was $2.25 for one year, and $2.28 for the other, but I am not now sure to which year belonged the larger rate. I rented the pasture for successive years for $16.00, and, I have been trying to believe, the first year for $18.— but am not sure. In the last year, it rented only for $14. & it is now rented for the same. for it is an unknown period since it was ploughed & tilled,—which it sorely needs. Mr Hosmer would have persuaded me to retrieve it, but I found it a little too far from my house to carry manure & labor to, & harvest from, with promise & advantage.[144] Mr Hosmer is the most judicious adviser, & I esteem it a considerable value of the field, at present, that is can be worked under his eye & counsel. You will find ⟨his⟩ obedience to his counsel, in field matters, the best economy. The field has great attractions for me, &, if I were younger, I should be very

on Wednesday, January 18, 1860 (Charvat, p. 36). A Calvin G. Child, lawyer, is listed in the Norwich directory for 1861.

141. MS in Special Collections, Butler Library, NNC; ph. in NNC.

142. Possibly Louisa Perkins Hunt, wife of the painter William Morris Hunt. The first Mrs. Carter, Anna Augusta Gray.

143. Emerson had bought the Asabet pasture (3 acres and 25 rods on the river) from Edmund Hosmer on June 17, 1855, for $315.63. He sold it to Carter on August 27, 1859, for $320.00 (MS ledger for 1849–1872, pp. 139, 140; and MS Account Book for 1859–1865, entry of September 6, p. 4). Carter paid $237.00 in cash and took a five-month note for $83.00 (including interest). On September 12, Emerson paid off his note to Edmund Hosmer, $320.16. (See also Middlesex County Registry of Deeds, MS Vol. 737, p. 114, and Vol. 847, p. 258). Thoreau had surveyed the lot for Emerson, June 20, 1855 (not listed by Mrs. Moss). Emerson paid him $1.50 for the job (MS Account Book for 1853–1859, p.[101]). (Assessors' records for 1850–1860 are missing.) See above, August 4 and 10. to Henry Ware.

144. Possibly John Hosmer, but the tenor of the letter suggests that Edmund Hosmer is meant.

loth to part with it. I hope you will find all the good & none of the harm of fields.[145]

Yours with great regard,
R. W. Emerson.

To Benjamin Marston Watson, Concord, August 31, 1859[146]

Concord, August 31, 1859.

My Dear Friend:—Ever since you were here, on days when the wonderful herbs came and on other days, I designed to send you the books you desired.[147] But my absences,—of body, I mean,—my tasks, my trifles, and my epilepsies I think I must call them,—that scattering and effacing power,—have hitherto made my purpose void. . . . But if you sprain your foot, you shall find your head is sprained, and in a few weeks, all feet of all things seem to be sprained also. I hesitate much to send this volume of Landor, it pleases so few.[148] I fancy sometimes it is an accidental taste of mine to like so well an author whom good readers find so dull. But Mr. Bradford said you named Landor, so I send the strange and offensive Richelieu Dialogue, which contains some of his best things. . . . On my return home I found my wife and children were in a state of very pleasant excitement under a large surprise party of pear-trees, apple-trees and rose bushes, which had burst in upon us from Plymouth.[149] The visitors had already taken ground by the heel, in the garden, so that I could only hear the fame, but I have just now made an accurate inspection of the strangers, and find six pears of fame for me

145. It could be said that Emerson had all of the harm and none of the good of this particular field.

146. No MS has been located; text from the printing, incomplete, with signature in facsimile, in "Three Concord Letters," *Old Colony Naturalist,* Special Midsummer Number, 1904, pp. 10–11 (M. E248, p. 686); transcript in NNC. The other two letters are also to Watson, one from Thoreau and the other from Alcott. The publication was copyrighted by Ellen Watson, Marston Watson's daughter; I infer that she was the owner of the MSS. The periodical was the publication of the Old Colony Natural History Society; the first president of the group was Watson's son; see August 25, above.

147. There is no record of Watson's visit to Concord, but Ellen Emerson's letter, cited above, August 25, shows that he knew of Emerson's injured foot for which the "herbs" (fruit, in fact), had been sent out as a "cure."

148. Landor's *Imaginary Conversations of Literary Men and Statesmen;* the Richelieu conversation is in the third volume, published in 1828; see Harding, p. 162, where the 1828 date is not indicated. Emerson's admiration for Landor is attested in several journal entries; see especially, *JMN,* 13:392; note that he has borrowed from the Richelieu conversation a few entries earlier (*ibid.,* b.390, and n. 56). See also *Letters,* 1:385; 2:102; 3:296–297, 301–302, and *Works,* 12:337–349.

149. Mrs. Emerson had returned from Naushon by the 20th (*Letters,* 5:171) Watson had evidently sent pear trees for Emerson and rose bushes for Mrs. Emerson; Emerson had earlier purchased fruit trees from Watson.

with the roses that delight my wife's heart;—and withal a cornucopia of seeds whose names might serve for so many poems. I send you my hearty thanks for these elegant gifts. I shall take immediate order that the new comers shall have a fair start beside their elder brothers in my orchard, and shall try the principle of emulation in pears. . . . Meantime life wears on, and ministers to you, no doubt, its undelaying and grand lessons, its uncontainable, endless poetry, its short, dry prose of skepticism, like veins of cold air in the evening woods, quickly followed by the wide warmth of June;—its steady correction of the weakness and short sight of youthful judgments, and its sure repairs of all the rents and seeming ruin it operates in what it gave—although we love the first gift so well that we cling long to the ruin and think we will be cold to the new, if new shall come;—but the new steals on us like a star which rises behind our back as we walk, and we are borrowing gladly its light before we know the benefactor. So be it with you, with me, and with all. . . . What pleases me best in the letters is the generous trust they repose in me, and another's religion always makes me religious.

Your friend,
R. Waldo Emerson

TO WILLIAM HENRY FURNESS, CONCORD, SEPTEMBER 22, 1859 [150]

Concord—
Sept. 22, 1859

My dear friend,

May you live always, as you will; but may you live on the earth to keep it bright & warm as long as I have part here: I always think better of myself when I see your letters & that your kindness endures. And you have taken, as you must, the right part in this Unitarian brawl, & have said better what I tried to say yesterday to Bartol about Bellows & Parker.[151] I met Bellows the other day, & told him how wrong I tho't him

150. MS in the Furness papers, Van Pelt Library, PU; ph. in NNC; printed in *Records*, p. [119]; listed *Letters*, 5:175. The text here fills four pages; Furness evidently gave away the new sheet with the close and signature; Furness' reply of September 26 does not suggest that there was much more. Emerson is replying to Furness' letter of September 16, *Records*, pp. [116]–118.

151. Theodore Parker, at this time in Europe, a dying man, was still the subject of mixed judgments and debate. At the annual meeting of the Harvard Divinity School alumni, Moncure Conway had proposed a resolution of sympathy for Parker. Opponents of Conway and Parker prevented a vote. Henry Whitney Bellows had published an attack on Conway charging him with attempting "to make Boston endorse . . . radical politics under a cloak of sympathy" (Mary E. Burtis, *Moncure Conway*, p.68).

about Parker. He said, he tho't less of men, more of institutions, Certainly, I said, you must prefer the putty to the painter, But he could not even see that Horace Mann & Parker trained in the same Company.[152]

I am heartily glad to see the good gravitation, & that you & Hunt have joined.[153] I have owed many happy days to him when he was but an overgrown boy. and I have ever regretted that he was whirled out of my vicinage, & I have ⟨meet⟩met too rarely to restore our relations. It warms my heart to think that you have him.

How dare you ask me again for lectures?[154] Could ever a singer learn to say No, when invited to warble? Certainly I should come to you

To Charles Francis Simmons, Concord, September 25? 1859

[Emerson's lawyer, Charles Francis Simmons, wrote him on September 26 and again on September 28, 1859 (RWEMA), about the bankruptcy of the publishing firm of Phillips, Sampson & Co.; the letters imply letters from Emerson; in the first, Simmons reports that he has inquired about where Emerson is to apply to get his stereotype plates (it was Emerson's practice to retain ownership of the plates and to issue orders for any printings from them). Simmons reports further that 1,000 unbound copies (each) of *English Traits* (Myerson, A24. 1. e) and *Miscellanies* (Myerson, A21. 1. d. *Note*) are still in the store. I conjecture that Emerson had instructed Simmons to inquire about the plates in a letter of September 24 or 25. The second letter is a reply to Emerson's letter of September 26, below. It reports on the creditors' naming of Alexander H. Rice and Harvey Jewell as assignees of the estate of Samuel C. Perkins, surviving partner.

[Moses D. Phillips and Charles Sampson died within a few weeks of each other (August 1859) and the surviving partner, Samuel C. Perkins, with the full burden of the firm's debts, had been obliged to declare the firm bankrupt (*BET*, August 22, 1859, p. 2). The assignees were announced on September 28 (*BET*, p. 2).]

152. The coupling of the names of Mann and Parker is made the more lucid by May 24, 1860, below, and June 6, 1860, in *Letters*, 5:220–221, the first about Horace Mann and the second about Theodore Parker. Read together, they show that Emerson respected the principles of Mann and Parker, but had his doubts of the "methods" of both.

153. Benjamin P. Hunt; see Emerson's letter to Furness of October 24, 1837; this letter Furness recalls and quotes in his letter of September 16, 1859.

154. See below, October 6, 1859, and January 18, 1860; projected finally for March, the plan for lectures in Philadelphia in 1860 fell through because of Emerson's known sympathy with John Brown; see *Letters*, 5:206, and n. 102.

To Cyrus W⸻ Christy, Concord, September 26, 1859[155]

Concord ⎱ 26 Sept
Masstts ⎰ 1859

Dear Sir,

I am gratified by your invitation to Yellow Springs. I shall be at Toronto, Canada West on the 27 January, & mean to go thence Westward probably as far as Chicago. I have already some correspondence with Zanesville, & am told there is an invitation on the way to me from Cincinnati. A few days, I suppose, will enable me to fix with some precision engagements in that region, &, if I can offer you a Saturday night, I will write you on the earliest day when it can be determined.

Respectfully,
R. W. Emerson

Mr. Christy.

To Samuel Raymond Putnam? Concord, September 26, 1859[156]

Concord
26 Septr 1859

Dear Sir,

Miss E P Peabody (who may be heard of at N. Peabody's shop in Bedford Street)[157] has many copies of certain numbers of the "Dial", Mr Alcott of this town has copies of, I think, the two last numbers, XV & XVI. I have none. I believe they are hard to be found elsewhere

Respectfully,
R. W. Emerson

Mr Putnam.

To Charles Francis Simmons, Concord, September 26, 1859

[Taken with Emerson's letter of September 29, below, Charles Francis Simmons' letter of "Monday P.M. September 26, 1859," appears to have crossed a note from Emerson written on the morning of the 26th, asking additional questions. In his letter, below, of September 29 Emerson thanks Simmons for the "details" the lawyer has furnished. It is in his letter of Monday afternoon that Simmons

155. MS privately owned; ph. in NNC. See Charvat, p. 36, for the 1860 schedule.
156. MS in the Berg Collection, NN; ph. in NNC. I conjecture Samuel Raymond Putnam as addressee for no reason other than his being James Russell Lowell's brother-in-law. Lowell's sister Mary was an accomplished and learned woman who might have had an interest in finding copies of the Dial to which her brother had contributed. There is no real evidence, however, and Putnams were numerous in Boston.
157. The Peabodys had moved from West Street to Bedford Street in 1856.

gives a very detailed account of what he has learned from Mr. Wyman and Mr. Broaders about the plates, unbound copies of his books still in the store, and the claim of $400 Emerson has against the firm. Simmons' letter of the 28th is brief, merely noting the names of the assignees and reporting that Mr Wyman has repeated the assurance reported in the letter of the 26th.]

To Charles Francis Simmons, Concord, September 29, 1859 [158]

Concord

Sept. 29, 1859

My dear Sir,

Thanks for the details you have so carefully furnished me as a creditor of P. S. & Co, I have heard nothing from Mr Wyman, & nothing from Mr Lowell,[159] who, last Saturday, volun- a promise to keep me informed on their affairs. Nothing occurs to me to suggest to you except that if you see Mr Broaders[160] books I should like to have the exact information I spoke of in my ⟨S⟩Monday's note to you[161] Is it Vol 1 or Vol II of the Essays which they had printed in August? Their "Account" rendered omitted to say.[162]

I hope Mr Jewell may let us have the books. ⟨Then we shall be indebted to the firm for paper & printing.⟩[163]

Yours

R. W. Emerson

To William Davis Ticknor? September? ? 1859

[On the verso of p. 65 of the MS of the essay "Beauty" (Berg collection, NN), appears the pencil note: "The rest of this essay will be sent in a few days"; other correspondence concerning *The Conduct of Life* is written to Ticknor. The verso of the title page of this MS has a list of the contents of the book.]

158. MS owned by Joel Myerson; ph. in NNC. Since this letter concerns the affairs of the bankrupt firm of Phillips & Sampson, I believe the addressee is Emerson's lawyer, Charles F. Simmons, who had written him on the 28th and 27th. Emerson appears to be acknowledging both letters. Turning his leaf, Emerson failed to finish "volunteering."

159. See *Letters*, 5:177, for acknowledgment of a letter from James Russell Lowell. Presumably the affairs of the firm had been discussed at the Saturday Club on the 24th.

160. Frederick Broaders, bookbinder.

161. Emerson apparently started to write Saturday or Sunday here; see September 25, above, for note of Simmons' detailed letter of September 26 which, written in the afternoon, must have crossed "Monday's note" referred to here.

162. In a letter of October 28, Simmons will refer to "discrepancies" between two statements as "numerous"; one of the statements is the "account" referred to here. The unbound copies of *English Traits* and of *Miscellanies* (1,000 each) Simmons had reported in his letter of September 26.

163. This sentence is crossed out with two vertical strokes; apparently the deletion is Emerson's.

To Cyrus W. Christy, Concord, October? 1? 1859

[Emerson, in his letter of September 26, 1859, promised Christy to write soon again to settle a date for a lecture at Antioch. The date settled upon was February 1 (Charvat, p. 36).]

To Joseph Mason, Concord, October 5, 1859

[A MS fragment in the Emerson papers (RWEMA), Houghton Library, MH reads: "J. Mason,/Hamilton/Madison Co. 1859 answered 5 Oct that I wd. write again by the 13th Oct." Emerson lectured in Hamilton, New York, January 19, 1860, Charvat, p. 36. For Mason, see L. M. Hammond, *History of Madison County* (Syracuse: Truair, Smith, 1872), p. 457.]

To Kinnicutt, Concord? October 5, 1859

[The catalogue of The Rendells, Inc. (List 9), 1978, and the catalogue of Diana T. Rendell (4), 1985, list a letter of October 5, 1859, to Mr. Kinnicutt. As quoted in the more recent listing, it reads: "It would give me a great pleasure to visit Warren if I should have . . . other engagements in your neighborhood. I do not find however at present that I have any promises in your region. If . . . I find the opportunity opened, I may take the liberty to re-open our correspondence." The only "Warren" in which Emerson ever lectured is Warren, Ohio (January 18, 1865). The invitation here referred to may have come from this Trumbull County town not far from Youngstown, but there is a Warren in Massachusetts, Worcester County; a Francis H. Kinnicutt is listed in an 1866–67 county directory as president of the Citizens' National Bank and a director of the Bay State Fire Insurance Company. No entry for either Warren appears in the tentative list for 1859–1860 (MS Account Book for 1853–1859, p. 286) or in the Pocket Diary for 1859 (*JMN*, 14:469 ff.).]

To Horatio Woodman, Concord, October 6, 1859[164]

Concord
6 October, 1859.

My dear Sir,

Thanks for notice of the meeting of Saturday.[165] I am not sure I can come. My locomotive powers are very modest. And the Fitchburg gods have shortened the hours. But I like to keep the door ajar. But you have never been to Concord, &, since Saturday is the free day in usage, why will you not come up & make that promised call on Mrs Ripley,[166] next

164. MS in the Woodman papers, MHi; ph. in NNC.
165. It is unlikely that Woodman has sent a notice of the meeting of the Saturday Club, October 29; I find no clue to the meeting referred to. Emerson was still handicapped by his injured foot.
166. Sarah Bradford Ripley.

Saturday, 15th instant, dine with me at 2, & we will show you our
crimson-leaved meadows. Let it be so. Later, our woods will not be so
gay.

Yours,
R. W. Emerson

Mr. Woodman.

To William Henry Furness, Concord, October 6, 1859 [167]

Concord
6 October 1859

My dear William,— [168]

And if I called you so two & fifty years ago, tell your wife that /her/
rights to the name are recent beside mine. Tell her, too, what she believes
already, that your heart is no older now than it was then. And I find that
this affectionate memory of yours which spans so vigorously the whole
term from Mrs Whitwells to 1859, makes & keeps the blood warmer in
all your company. I feel, indeed, in looking at this long stretch, what
Jonathan Phillips once said to me, "Sir, I have lived a very long time."
But I also feel that Philadelphia is /a/ large town, chiefly distinguished as
the residence of William Furness & Sam Bradford. /These are the golden;
in the silver class are ⟨R⟩Hunt & Randolph/ [169]

But let me not forget the instant occasion of my writing. You say I
shall come to Phila. in January. [170] It is pleasant to think of. But if I were
really thinking to come & read,—is January the best time? In Boston, I
have found, of late years, March, & April, & even May, quite as good.
The people are pleased to fancy somewhat exceptional in my Course,
which the previous excess of lectures does not affect, I ask because it is
not easy at this time, in my correspondence, to keep January sacred.
Already it is mortgaged from 23d to 31st. But I could hold the first 20
days.—Another point; I have already an application for a lecture in

167. MS in the Furness papers, Van Pelt Library, NNC; ph. in NNC; printed in *Records*,
p. [123]; listed *Letters*, 5:176.
168. Furness' letter of September 26 (*Records*, pp. 121–123) opens "Dear Ralph" and
reminds Emerson that so he had called his friend in their boyhood, naming their teachers,
including Susanna Whitwell.
169. Benjamin P. Hunt and Phillip Physick Randolph; Furness had recently become
acquainted with Hunt; see above, October 24, 1837, and September 22, 1859, and *Records*,
pp. 117, 122. This crowded insert may have been added after the letter was finished.
170. See above, September 22 and note.

Phila. It is not comity, is it? to come to singulars when one is coming to the Public? But neither of these questions can you [171] answer, & therefore I shall probably decide to refuse the Phila. applicants, & on the other hand invade the sacred January.

Yours affectionately

Ralph.

TO DANIEL RICKETSON, CONCORD, OCTOBER 11, 1859 [172]

Concord, 11 October,

1859.

My dear Sir,

I received through Mr Channing[173] your gift of the History of New Bedford, for which I have delayed to thank you. I have not yet read it through, but have read a good deal in it, & with much content. It is written with good sense, & with selection, and with affection. Interesting traits have been preserved, so that you will have this plesure in mind that every year will be making your book more valuable & more valued, and distant men will heartily thank you.

I was sorry that when your son came to Concord, I should be a cripple forced to think of myself alone,[174] &, I believe, I went away the next day. When he comes again, we shall be better acquainted.

⟨G⟩With great regard,

R. W. Emerson

Mr. Ricketson.

We were all concerned that Mr Thoreau should prosper at the Music Hall on Sunday. From private reports I infer that he made a just impression.[175]

---

171. From this word on, Emerson finishes the letter by using the left margin of the first page.

172. MS in CU-SB; ph. in NNC. Printed in *Daniel Ricketson, Autobiographic and Miscellaneous*, p. 117, where it is misdated 1869 and is without the postscript, which is printed separately. Listed *Letters*, 5:176–177 with correct date. Reprinted by Walter Harding, *ESQ* (4th, 1958), 13:36.

173. William Ellery Channing. See Harding, p. 228; Ricketson's presentation inscription is dated September 9, 1859.

174. Ricketson had two sons, Arthur and Walton; there seems to be no way of knowing which was the visitor on this occasion. Emerson is referring to his injured foot.

175. Thoreau lectured for the Parker Fraternity on October 9; see Harding and Bode, p. 357, for his arrangements with Elbridge Dudley. Ricketson's letter to Thoreau of October 14, is, I think, prompted by Emerson's postscript here (Harding and Bode, pp. 560–561).

To Joseph Mason, Concord, October 13, 1859

[See note above, under October 5.]

To Franklin Benjamin Sanborn, Concord, October? 23? 1859 [176]

By all means return at the first hour wheels or steam will permit. I assure everyone that you will be here Wednesday or Thursday.

Sunday night

Yours ever, R. W. E.

To Ticknor and Fields, Concord, October 24, 1859 [177]

Concord
Oct. 24, 1859.

Messrs Ticknor & Fields.

Gentlemen,

You expressed to me, a few days ago, through Mr Ticknor, your wish to become the publishers of my books. The proposition was very agreeable to me, &, at Mr Ticknor's request, I will set down the few principal points which I wish to be considered in the agreement.

The six works in which I hold copyright as author, & of which Phillips, Sampson, & Co. were, until recently, the publishers, are;

1. Essays, Vol. I.
2. Essays, Vol. II.

176. The MS has not been found; text from Sanborn, *Recollections*, 1:196; listed *Letters*, 5:179. The 23rd is the likely date; see Emerson's letter of October 26, *Letters*, 5:179, and his letter of the same date below. Sanborn had written Emerson on October 22 from Boston. Acknowledging that his "conduct must seem . . . inexcusable," he gives "the good of others as well as my own" as the excuse for his flight and hopes for the day when he can "stand up in Concord and vindicate" himself. See Edelstein, p. 223, for Sanborn's letter of October 21 to Thomas Wentworth Higginson; Sanborn's intent to flee the country because of his involvement with John Brown appears to have been temporarily at least deflected by Emerson's note. Although Sanborn introduces this note with the epithet "laconic" implying that the text he gives is complete, his letter to Higginson, taken with Emerson's observation to Ward (below, October 26): "he should not have been absent an hour of these days," suggests that Emerson had, so to speak, ordered his return. Brown's admission of correspondence with Northerners privy to his plans had driven more than one to burning papers and to flight; moreover letters were found on his person, one from Concord signed "F. B. S." (unidentified clipping in the Emerson papers, RWEMA).

177. MS owned by Houghton, Mifflin Co.; ph. in NNC. The letter is endorsed: Sketch of contract | Oct. 24/ 1859 | R. W. Emerson | See contract—dated | Nov. 21/59 |. A draft of this letter is laid in the MS ledger for 1849–1873 between pp. 256–257 (ph. in NNC). There are no substantive differences except in the added qualification in the postscript here. Emerson evidently sent this "sketch" first to his lawyer; see October 25, below.

3. Miscellanies.

4. Poems.

5. Representative Men.

6. English Traits

Of these books I own the stereotype plates. I wish to deposit these with a printer, and whenever, from time to time, Ticknor & Fields think it expedient to publish an edition of any or all of them ⟨I wish to⟩Mr. E. will give a written order for the printing of so many copies.[178] And no copies shall be taken from the plates without such written order from him.

Ticknor & Fields shall pay for printing, paper, & binding, & shall sell the books.

And shall pay Mr E, 20 percent on the retail price of each book, on the day of publication.

Mr E. shall relinquish this copyright on all copies sent gratuitously to authors & Editors.

Mr E. proposes to put into the hands of Messrs Ticknor & Fields a new work, entitled "Conduct of Life," ⟨t⟩for publication, to which work the same terms shall apply.*

These are all the points that occur to me, of importance; and I shall be glad to have your opinion concerning them.

Respectfully

Messrs Ticknor & Fields.   R. W. Emerson/*over/[179]

---

*In regard to a new ⟨edition⟩ /work/ I am content if Ticknor & Fields *wish* it, that for the *first* payment of copyright after its issue, it shall be six months after the day of publication. But subsequent payments on it shall follow the rule stated above.

To WILLIAM W. WELLINGTON, CONCORD, OCTOBER ? 1859

[The following letter to Wendell Phillips, October 24, implies more than one letter to W. W. Wellington of Cambridgeport. I let this entry stand for these letters. William W. Wellington is listed as a physician in the Cambridge directory of 1859.]

178. A few such orders signed by Emerson, though not always in his mind, have survived; others are noted in the Account Books.

179. The word *over* and its asterisk appear lengthwise in the right-hand margin next to the signature, which, with the name of the addressee, is crowded into the foot of the page.

To Wendell Phillips, Concord, October 24, 1859[180]

Concord
24 Oct. 1859

My dear Sir,

I am vexed to find that the 28th February which I offered to promise to Cambridgeport instead of the 21st, has long been promised to New Bedford so that if I go to C-port, at all it must be the 21st I have written Mr Wellington that I may be forced to withdraw from the 14th (14 & 21, being now my days for him) because my western correspondent seems unable to arrange my visit to Chicago, & its dependencies without encroaching on February to the 15th.[181]

I am very sorry to have annoyed you with this mistake.

Every hour makes it more important for Sanborn to be at home. Yet the only message that has come from him is long farewells![182] Yours
Mr Phillips.   R W Emerson

To Charles Francis Simmons, Concord, October 25, 1859

[Listed in Charles Hamilton's catalogue 17 of January 2, 1967, as item 174 is a letter of October 25, n. y., to Charles Francis Simmons, Emerson's lawyer, concerning the contract between Emerson and his new publisher. The catalogue quotes the following: "I enclose a sketch of what I suppose should be a formal agreement with Ticknor & Fields. Please to look it over, & send it or withhold it, as you judge best. I do not know whether I or they should initiate the matter, but Ticknor said, you write us something & we will make it a basis . . ." Quoted also from Hamilton's catalogue in *ESQ* (2d q., 1967), 47:126. What Emerson enclosed is the letter of October 24 above; Simmons obviously sent it on.]

180. MS in the Phillips papers, Houghton, MH; ph. in NNC; with envelope addressed: Wendell Phillips, Esq. | Boston. | Mass.tts | ; postmarked at Concord, date blurred. In the upper right corner Emerson has written R. W. E.

181. See Charvat, p. 36, for the final schedule, and *JMN*, 14:470–472, 475–477, for successive changes in the schedule in the MS Pocket Diaries for 1859 and 1860 season. (The tentative schedules in the MS Account Book for 1859–1865 is of no use here.) The New Bedford date holds; the Western dates run through February 22. Emerson's Cambridgeport correspondent was Dr. William W. Wellington, but no letters survive.

182. Sanborn's flight after the capture of John Brown occupied a good deal of Emerson's time; see *Letters*, 5:178, and here, October 23, and notes where Sanborn's letter of October 22 is quoted; see also November 9, below. Emerson's esteem for Sanborn was somewhat chilled by his behavior and his specious defense of it.

To LUCY CAROLINE CLARK MAYO, CONCORD, OCTOBER 25, 1859[183]

Concord
25 October, 1859

Dear Madam,

I received your kind note, & the invitation with which you honored me, and it should have received an earlier reply, if it had not found me already in arears with many correspondents. I fear it will be quite out of my power to attempt to take any part in your Society's Series of tracts. I have no manuscripts in my old collections which would seem to have any fitness to the present hour, & I never disturb them. And none I have none more recent, with any suitableness, which have not already another destination,—like a piece which I am printing on "Worship".[184]

I thank you for the copies of tracts you have sent me, and I am glad to see such able coadjutors in the list.[185] You must forgive me if I cannot add one more to it.

With great regard,
Mrs Mayo.   R. W. Emerson

To SAMUEL GRAY WARD, CONCORD, OCTOBER 26, 1859[186]

Concord, 26 Octr
1859

My dear friend,

Ellen keeps us up with a belief that Anna will shine on us this week.[187] By all means let her come. Our spirits had been a little dashed this

183. MS in MdHi; ph in NNC. In 1859, Amory Dwight Mayo and his second wife, Lucy Caroline Clarke, were living in Albany. In a letter of October 3, 1859 (MH-AH), Mayo describes enthusiastically the character of "our Tract Society" which attempts "to circulate large numbers of tracts by our best men." The National Union Catalogue lists twelve *Tracts for the Times*, 1858–1859, printed in Albany (Weed, Parsons & Co.). The writers named besides Mayo himself are Octavips Brooks Frothingham, Samuel Longfellow, Moncure Daniel Conway, William Henry Furness, Thomas Starr King, James Freeman Clarke, Samuel Osgood, and Edward W. Keyes, all Unitarian or Universalist ministers. Emerson, though no longer a minister, certainly would appear in Mayo's eyes as one of "our best men." That Emerson mentions "Worship" implies that the tracts he is asked to contribute to are religious. When Mayo lived in Gloucester, Emerson corresponded with him and was his guest in 1853 (a.1.s., Mayo to Emerson, March 4, 1853, RWEMA). He may have met Lucy Clarke who, in July 1853, would marry Mayo. See Henry Miller Foote, in Samuel Atkins Eliot, *Heralds of a Liberal Faith* (Boston, 1952), 4:90–91.

184. In *The Conduct of Life*.

185. None of the twelve tracts is now in Emerson's library.

186. MS in the Ward papers, Houghton Library, MH; ph. in NNC. Quoted in a note, *J*, 9:242; listed *Letters*, 5:179.

187. In his MS Journal OP Gulistan, p. 30, Emerson enters a cross-reference to his MS

week,—that Aunt Elizabeth (Eliz. Hoar,) had gone to New Haven, & Sanborn is gone for a few days,—that Ellen wished to put her off to the end of the week for the chance of returns. But I have news today that Sanborn is on his way home, &, I trust, will return tonight, (he should not have been absent an hour /of/ these days.).[188] So I think you had better persuade Anna to keep her brave purpose, & come tomorrow, Thursday, at 11 o'clock, & do you come with her, & excuse yourself for missing two club days, which are my only days for seeing you. And if this letter should be too late to quicken this purpose, Friday is the next best, ⟨though⟩and will allow us to see Anna, & to show her Tom & his house, and, as I believe, Mr. S., whom she should surely know.

Our Kansas Cid[189] is hard bested, but a lion to the last. I keep a hope for him yet. How so wise a soldier got into this corner, I know not, but he is a true saint, and miracles wait on such.

Do not forget Saturday's club. Come & go down with me. Yours,

R. W. E.

———

Journal CL, pp. 142–143, and pp. 147–149, describing the matter on these pages as a letter. The description is open to doubt because the second of these entries begins (CL, p. 147): "Anna Ward was at a loss in talking with me. . . ."; the entry indicates a conversation rather than a letter. Both passages appear in the midst of entries of October 1859 concerning John Brown. I take them to refer to conversations with Mrs. Ward while she was a guest in Concord. Both passages are printed in *J*, 9:242–243, 244 (with proper names suppressed and other modifications) and in *JMN*, 14:330, 331. In the MS the first entry reads: "Here was happiest example of the best blood, which, in meeting the best born & best bred people of Europe speaks with their speech, & deals with their own weapons. Ah I should have been so glad, if it could have said to them, Look, I do without your rococo, You have heard much ill of America, I know its good, ⟨&⟩ its blessed simplicity, nor shall I make the mistake of baptising the daylight & time & space by the name of Jones or Jenkins, in whose shop I chance to behold daylight & space & time. Least of all will I call sacraments /those/ legendary quips of yours which break the sacraments which are most my own, my duty to my wife, husband, son, friend, country, nor can I suffer a nasty monk to whisper to me, to whom God has given such a person as ⟨S. G. W.⟩ & such children, for my confessors & absolvers."
In the MS, the initials S. G. W. are written twice, one set over the other, and twice crossed out; some attempt has been made to wash out the word "priest" and over it is written monk; and the names "Jones or Jenkins" are crossed out and encircled. It is not clear that these deletions are Emerson's. At the top of p. 142, in Edward Waldo Emerson's hand, appears the note: "R. W. E.'s Reflections on a valued friend lately turned Romanist. E. W. E." In the printed *Journal*, 9:242–243, Edward Emerson has retained "Jones or Jenkins," deleted "nasty," retained "monk," used Roman type where Emerson's underlining signifies italic, and inserted "my huband" in place of Ward's initials.
There are parallels of thought, if not of language, between this passage and Emerson's letter of August 10 to Samuel G. Ward (*Letters*, 5:189). Emerson would not have written to Mrs. Ward in this vein but he might have said something with this purport in conversation.
In the second passage, Edward Emerson makes no substantive change except in the opening phrase quoted above.
188. For Frank Sanborn's flight, see August 23, above. Emerson wants Mrs. Ward to meet her son's teacher as well as to see where the boy lives.
189. John Brown; see *JMN*, 14:329–330. Emerson certainly appears to know very little

To CHARLES FRANCIS SIMMONS, CONCORD, OCTOBER 26? 1859

[In his letter of October 28, 1859 (RWEMA), Emerson's lawyer reports on his comparison of Emerson's statement about his books and the statement in the records of Phillips, Sampson and Co., the discrepancies are such that he wishes to see Emerson the following day.]

To CHARLES J. WATKINS, JR., CONCORD, OCTOBER 28? 1859

[On a half-sheet of notepaper (RWEMA), Emerson has written: C. J. Watkins Jr | Davenport, Ia | 1859 | Fort Lee | Bergen Co | N. J I am to write again | when it is settled that | I go to Chicago. | Since a prospective Fort Lee engagement could scarcely be contingent on a Chicago date, I infer that the note refers to letters to Watkins of Davenport, Iowa. Emerson had offered February 6 to Chicago in a letter of October 27 and the date was confirmed by a letter to him of November 3 (*Letters*, 5:180); I infer then that Emerson's first letter to Watkins falls between these dates. In 1866-1867, a Charles J. Watkins represented Davenport on the Scott County board of supervisors. Harry E. Downer, *History of Davenport and Scott County* (Chicago: S. J. Clarke Publishing, 1910), 1:552.]

To HENRY ALEXANDER WISE, CONCORD? OCTOBER 28? 1859

[A draft of what was clearly intended to be a letter to Governor Henry Wise of Virginia appears in MS journal CL, pp. 159–162; see *JMN*, 14:334 (printed only in part in *J*, 9:248–249). The editors of *JMN* note the termini for a likely date. But since Emerson used a portion of the passage in his speech of November 18 for the relief of John Brown's family (*Works*, 11:266–273), a speech he did not know he was to make until November 17 (see below), I conjecture the draft to have been written before that date. The letter, which follows here, November 9, to Sanborn suggests to me that Emerson had thought of writing a letter to Wise after reading the newspaper accounts of Wise's opinion of Brown (see *JMN*, 14:331). Wise had commented on Brown in a speech given in Richmond October 21 on his return from Harper's Ferry. According to an excerpt from the *Richmond Whig* of October 22 printed in the *New-York Tribune* of October 26 (pp. 6–7), Wise had given Brown "credit for bravery, fortitude, and humanity toward his prisoners" (p. 7). It is surely to Wise's speech of October 21 that Emerson refers when, in his draft letter, he says: "You have pronounced his first eulogy." There is no evidence that Emerson ever finished and mailed his letter.]

---

about John Brown's life; see James C. Malin, *John Brown and the Legend of Fifty-Six*, pp. 289, 291.

To Joseph Gilbert, Concord, November 3, 1859[190]

Concord, Massachusetts
3 November, 1859

Dear Sir,

I am by no means sure that I can visit Terre Haute. Mr. P. L. Sherman of Chicago has kindly charged himself with the general arrangement of my visits in the West, and has probably filled the limited time of my stay.[191] I must hear from him before I can definitely answer you.

Respectfully,
R. W. Emerson

Mr. Gilbert

To William Allen Wall, Concord, November 3, 1859[192]

Concord
3 November, 1859

My dear⟨s⟩ Sir,

I have your note, with its hospitable invitation, for which I heartily thank you. It would give me great pleasure to come to your house, but I am not quite sure that I am free from some pre-engagements in your city, where one or two friends pretend claims or half-claims on me.[193] And perhaps I shall keep my whim, which I use almost everywhere, of going to the tavern.

At all events, I am bound to see you at what leisure I can, when I come, & I will therefore write you again, by & by, where I will be.

Your obliged servant,
R. W. Emerson

W. A. Wall.

190. The MS has not been located; in 1933 it belonged to Miss Margaret Gillum; text from printing by Leslie H. Meeks in the *Indiana Magazine of History* (June 1933), 29:90; listed *Letters*, 5:180. Meeks identifies the addressee as the secretary of the Ulyssean Society.

191. See *Letters*, 5:180, for Penoyer L. Sherman. Emerson does not enter Terre Haute in his MS Pocket Diary for 1859 or 1860, even as a questioned possibility.

192. MS in MoSHi ; ph. in NNC. The letter is repaired at the fold; it shows signs of having once been mounted. The salutation looks as if Emerson wrote in haste. That this letter is to the painter William Allen Wall of New Bedford is likely; his name appears against the entry of February 28 for New Bedford in Emerson's MS Pocket Diary for 1860 (*JMN*, 14:478). See *Letters*, 1:378, for Emerson's meeting Wall in Italy and 6:322, for Wall's gift to him of a copy of a painting of "The Three Fates," attributed in 1833 to Michelangelo; the painting is in the reconstruction of Emerson's study in the Concord Antiquarian Society. See *JMN*, 4:157, *passim* for Wall.

193. The Rodmans, the Arnolds, and the Ricketsons.

To Franklin Benjamin Sanborn, Boston, November 9, 1859[194]

American House—
Boston 9 Novr '59

My dear Sir,

Would it not be better that you should take legal counsel at this time, by explicitly stating your liabilities, if any exist, to a counsellor? I was talking this morning with Mr Forbes, who looked with some uneasiness at the telegraphic despatch of this morn.g, and afterwards I had a little conversation with Judge Hoar. The Judge does not overestimate the U. S. power, yet could answer no question in the dark. And it is only on the contingency, that there may be any thing in your case not known or probable to them, that the suggestion can have any importance.[195]

I have been talking with a few persons on the possibility of finding any gentleman here who might have private influence with Gov. Wise, / for Capt. B.,/ and am to see others in the morning.[196]

Yours ever,
R. W. Emerson

Mr. Sanborn.

To Charles J. Watkins, Jr., Concord, November? 10? 1859

[See above, October 28, for note of Emerson's promising Watkins of Davenport, Iowa, to write again after he heard from Chicago. See *Letters*, 5:180, for note of letter of November 3 from Chicago. See Charvat, p. 36, for the final schedule for the western trip of 1860; there is clearly no room for a trip to Davenport, and the city is not entered in the tentative or final lists for 1860 in the MS Pocket Diaries for 1859, 1860.]

194. MS in the Aronheim collection, Alderman Library, ViU; ph. in NNC. Printed by Sanborn in *Recollections*, 1:199–200; listed *Letters*, 5:181.

195. Sanborn's involvement with John Brown was sufficient to send him to Canada. See Edelstein, pp. 223, 226, for the panic of Sanborn and others when the news of Brown's capture broke. The news on the morning of November 9 was of the conviction on November 5 of the free black John Anthony Copeland, found guilty of murder and conspiracy and of the opening on November 8 of the trial of John E. Cook, which included the reading of his confession. Emerson is referring here to John Murray Forbes and Rockwood Hoar.

196. Henry Alexander Wise, Governor of Virginia. In his reply of November 10 (Sanborn papers, DLC) Sanborn questions the efficacy of a letter from any "private gentleman" and declares Governor Wise powerless in the case. He thinks Brown's best chance lies in escape and imagines that a "rescue would not be so hard to manage," but Brown, he says, "does not *wish* to escape." One of the "Secret Six," Sanborn is not being entirely candid here; see Tilden G. Edelstein, "John Brown and Friends" in *The Abolitionists*, Hugh Hawkins, ed. (Boston, 1974), pp. 75–76.

To Charles Wesley Slack, Concord, November 11, 1859 [197]

Concord, 11 Nov.r
1859

Dear Sir,

You shall, if you please, announce my subject for Sunday, at the Music Hall, as "Domestic Life." [198]

Respectfully,
R W Emerson

Mr Slack.

To Charles Wesley Slack, Concord, November 17, 1859 [199]

Concord
Thursday, 17 Novr

Dear Sir,

Certainly I will come to such a meeting if held; and will speak; though what I have to say will probably not take half the time you offer.

Yours faithfully,
R. W. Emerson

Mr Slack.

To Rebecca Duncan, Boston, December 4, 1859? [200]

American House.
4 December

My dear Miss Duncan,

I was mortified to find that you should have come so far in the bad weather in vain for the books, & that I should miss your visit. I will now

197. MS in Special Collections, OKentU; ph. in NNC.

198. See Charvat, p. 35, entry for November 13.

199. MS in Special Collections, OKentU; ph. in NNC. The manuscript shows signs of having once been mounted at the corners. The year "'59" is added to the date in pencil, not in Emerson's hand. The year is certainly correct; Emerson is agreeing to speak in Tremont Temple at a meeting November 18 for the relief of John Brown's family. See *Works*, 11:266–273, and Charvat, p. 35.

200. MS in Houghton Library, MN; ph. in NNC; with envelope addressed: Miss Rebecca Duncan. Care of E. G. Dudley, Esq. ⟨3⟩20 Court Street Boston. ; it is postmarked at Boston December 5 and bears a one-cent stamp. The letter must have been written sometime between 1857 and 1861. The year is not secure, but Emerson lectured in that year on December 4 for the Parker Fraternity. Miss Duncan was the sister-in-law of Elbridge Dudley from whom Emerson received payments for his Parker Fraternity lectures (MS Account Book for 1859–1865, p. [14].

leave them with Mr Dudley, only cautioning you that the pencil marks along the pages are none of mine.[201]

With great regard,
R. W. Emerson

Miss Duncan.

To Thaddeus Hyatt, Telegram, Concord, December 12, 1859

[In his letter of December 12 to his brother (*Letters*, 5:183) and his letter of the same day to Wendell Phillips (below), Emerson says he has telegraphed Hyatt that he will not come to New York.]

To Wendell Phillips, Boston, December 12, 1859[202]

American House.
Monday P.m.
12 Dec.

My dear Sir,

I have telegraphed Mr Hyatt that I will not go to N.Y.

I insisted in my acceptance that it should be only in the strict condition of being joined with the three names he offered me, namely Phillips Beecher & Cheever.[203] He has withdrawn Beecher substituting no one and it looks to me a partial & locally unauthoritative programme for New York.[204]

I should however sink my objection & my diffidence in Mr Hyatt's judgment, if I had any ability at the moment to justify myself to a public

201. I have no clue to the books Emerson sent to Miss Duncan. One of them may have been Goethe's *Correspondence with a Child* (London, 1839) which, to Emerson's dismay, had been marked up by Sophia Hawthorne (see Ellen Emerson's letter of April 22, 1859, to her sister, Gregg, 1:181–182). Emerson normally listed page references at the back of a book; markings in a text cannot be assumed to be his. Alcott has marked up some of them.

202. MS in the Phillips papers, Houghton Library, MH; ph. in NNC; with envelope addressed: Wendell Phillips, Esq. | Boston. | Boston, | ; postmarked at Boston December 13. See *Letters*, 5:183, and n. 213, and 5:214, for Emerson's letters of December 12 and 14 about Thaddeus Hyatt's solicitation of his presence at a meeting for the relief of John Brown's family. Rusk had not seen Emerson's letters to Phillips and so could not know that this letter of the 12th crossed the first of two undated letters from Phillips. This letter brought Phillips to Concord after Emerson mailed his second letter; see below.

203. The Reverend George B. Cheever of the Church of the Puritans, New York; see Malin, p. 289, and for Thaddeus Hyatt, *ibid.*, pp. 124, 176, 268, 650. For the distrust of Hyatt, see December 13, below.

204. Henry Ward Beecher. On Wednesday the 7th, Emerson lectured in Danbury; he may have met Beecher on the train. The Account Book for 1859–1865, p. 25, shows only the total expenses of the trip from Lynn to Danbury to Greenfield and home.

meeting in N.Y. But I am just now overlaid with tasks & though I could add my weakness to the three will not to the two which I suppose is really only me,—yourself, as it would require more force than I could command to give you any real aid. I shall be at home tomorrow.

Ever gratefully Yours,
R. W. Emerson

Wendell Phillips, Esq.

Beecher told me on Wed morning that he would attend the meeting on Saturday, but Hyatt says he will not[205]

To Wendell Phillips, Concord, December 13, 1859[206]

Concord
13 Decr 1859

My dear Sir,

I feel very penitential this morn.g in reading your note which you were writing when I was writing mine,—and after reading your Elba doings & sayings, ⟨i⟩ on my way home. With this urgency yesterday, I should have said, 'What if I have nothing to say, & New York nothing,—yet Phillips has enough & to spare, & I will go to swell his train?[207] But Redpath & Sanborn gave me an ill opinion of Hyatt—as to common sense & conduct,[208] I mean—and two other fellow-travellers an ill opinion of Cheever, and whilst I knew nothing of either, I saw I was right in guarding myself at first by stipulating for exact performance of the promise of "the four,"—only on that condition would I go.

In the present state of the thing I will say that if you have somewhat to say in N. Y. which can be inwardly & outwardly helped by my going, I

<hr>

205. This postscript is crowded in at the foot of the fourth and first pages. Beecher had in fact refused.

206. MS in the Phillips papers, Houghton Library, MH; ph. in NNC; with envelope addressed: Wendell Phillips, Esq. | Boston. | Mass.tts. | ; postmarked at Concord December 13. Emerson is repenting his letter of the 12th above which crossed a letter from Phillips (n.d., endorsed 1859 by Emerson, RWEMA), describing with touching details his visit to John Brown's grieving family in North Elba. Phillips followed his letter with a visit to Concord (see *Letters*, 5:214). According to Phillips' letter, Thaddeus Hyatt expected Emerson to lead at the proposed New York meeting, but as Phillips' second letter, postmarked at Boston December 14, shows, Hyatt could not change the date, leaving Phillips to be the main speaker.

207. Emerson presumably meant to close this imaginary quotation at the interrogation point, but he omits the closing single quotation mark.

208. James Redpath and Franklin B. Sanborn; for Cheever see December 12. This distrust of Hyatt may be owing to his management of the National Kansas Committee. In April 1856 the committee had been obliged to liquidate and to refuse funds to Kansas; it had earlier supplied money and arms (Malin, p. 271). See *Letters*, 5:183.

will smother my dislikes to the big town & go, & you may promise me to any Brown Relief meeting there from 17 to 30 Dec.r, except 21s, 22d, & 28th days.

This to be sure on the presumption that Mr Hyatt does not go with his 15th meeting—But he will, & then I am wasting your time.

Ever Yours,
R. W Emerson

W. Phillips, Esq—

To George Barrell Emerson, Concord, December 14, 1859?[209]

Concord, 14 Decr
Dear George,

A letter seems to have strayed hither, which should have stopped at your door. I greet it as giving me an occasion to send you my love.

Yours affectionately
R. Waldo E.

To Mary Lowell Putnam, Concord, December 22? 1859

[In a letter from 13 Pemberton Sq., dated Thursday, December 22, endorsed 1859 by Emerson (RWEMA), Mrs. Samuel R. Putnam, James Russell Lowell's sister, invites Emerson to dinner to meet, with her brother, a visitor from France. She names her guest; Rusk read the name as "Seibert"; I read it as Tribert, for the initial letter looks to me like the *T* in "Thursday," not like the *S* in "Sq." Mrs. Putnam indidates that Emerson had already met the gentleman. He is, I believe, Louis Tribert, acquaintance of Marie de Flavigny, la Comtesse D'Agoult ("Daniel Stern"), whom Emerson had met in 1848 (see *Letters*, 4:78, and *JMN*, 10:277). Tribert was evidently an ardent traveler (Jacques Vier, *La Comtesse D'Agoult et son temps* . . . Paris; Armand Colin, 1955–1963, 2:238, 3:154). See also below, November 4 [1867]. See below, December 23, for the fact that Emerson accepted the invitation.]

To William Henry Furness, Concord, December 23, 1859[210]

Concord
23 Dec 1859
My dear friend,

Certainly I will come to the Revere House on Thursday 29th at noon, and with joy. That day I am promised to dine with Mrs /Lowell/ Putnam

209. MS in the George B. Emerson papers, MHi; ph. in NNC; endorsed 1859 by George Emerson.
210. MS in the Furness papers, Van Pelt Library, PU; ph. in NNC; printed in *Records*, p. [127]; listed in *Letters*, 5:185.

in town.[211] But if irresistible magnetism of Phila. can be intercepted on these last days of the year, I will bring you to my house the next morning, & keep you tenderly, and all Concord shall ring with joy, and you shall dine on Saturday with our Club that I have bragged to you, Lowell, Agassiz, Longfellow, & the rest.[212]

Be good, & bring your mind to it; my dear William.

Affectionately,
Waldo E

To Messrs Ticknor & Fields, Boston, December 24, 1859[213]

Messrs Ticknor & Fields
Boston:
Gentlemen:

You are hereby notified that in case you shall publish the fifteen hundred and twenty eight volumes of printed sheets of my works pur-

211. See December 22, above.

212. Furness could not come to Concord or to the Saturday Club; see *Records,* pp. 128–129. Emerson has no definite article before "irresistible."

213. MS in the files of Houghton, Mifflin Co.; ph in NNC. Like the letter of September 19, 1860, below, this letter and its enclosure are entirely in the hand of Emerson's attorney, Charles Francis Simmons. See September 19 for Perkins, the assignees, and Emerson's account book entries.

The enclosed statements is as follows:

Statement of the condition of the publications of R. W. Emerson, as returned to his Assignee by clerks &c

Emersons poems	88 copies cloth. 35 do hf cf.		123
Rep. Men	2 hf cf.	9 hf. cf 450 sheets	461
Eng. Traits		12 hf cf. 700 sheets	712
Miscellanies	48 clo.	11 hf cf. 4 f. cf. 1000 sheets	1063
Essays. vol. 1.	31 clo.	15 hf. cf. 1 f f. 3(5)75 sheets	422
7 Setts complete works f. cf.			

1839 Settlement Aug. 29. $230. bal. fo gl.
Printed Since.—

English Traits Sept. printed	1000.
Miscellanies Sept.	1000.
	2000. @ 20% 400.

Mr Emerson settled Aug 29 & was paid balance then due—$91.—Since Aug 29. there have been printed

1000 copies English Traits.
1000 copies Miscellanies.

for these there became due according to the terms of the contract 20 cents per copy—on the day of printing. in all $400. which is the amount provable by Mr Emerson against the estate.

The abbreviations in the statement above are for bindings: "clo." for cloth; "hf cf" for half calf; "f cf" for full calf. There is clearly an error in line 7 for Essays. "1 f f" should read 1 f cf. Simmons either miscopied the original or the original has the error.

chased by you of the assignees of the late firm of Phillips Sampson & Co., or of Perkins the surviving partner of said firm, insolvent debtors, on the 15th day of November last, or at other times, I shall hold you liable to pay me a sum equal to twenty percentum on the retail price of each volume so published to you, on the day of the publication of the same, in accordance with the terms of the contract made by me with said firm, and subsisting at the date of their insolvency.

Yr obedt Servt
R. W. Emerson

Boston Dec. 24. 1859. by his attorney C. F. Simmons

To Wendell Phillips, Concord, December 30, 1859[214]

Concord
30 Decr 1859

My dear Sir,

I am in no humor for disputing with you, but had a strong hope you would see I was quite unnecessary. If you persist, I can go,—either next Thursday or Friday. I told Rantoul[215] I thought Wednesday was free; but on coming home today, I find I have long been engaged to Waltham for Wednesday next.[216] I write the like of this today to him.

Ever Yours,
R W Emerson

Mr Phillips.

To Robert Samuel Rantoul, Concord, December 30, 1859

[In his letter to Wendell Phillips of the same day, Emerson says he will write Rantoul about the proposed Salem meeting for the relief of John Brown's family. To accommodate Emerson the meeting was postponed from January 4 to Friday the 6th.]

---

214. MS in the Phillips papers, Houghton Library, MH; ph. in NNC; with envelope addressed: Wendell Phillips, Esq. | Boston—| Mass.tts. | ; postmarked at Concord December 30. Emerson is answering an undated letter (RWEMA) from Phillips who wants him to speak at a Brown Relief meeting in Salem on Wednesday, January 4.

215. Robert Samuel Rantoul; see *Letters*, 5:188 and n. 5. See *JMN*, 11:251, for a comment on Rantoul.

216. See Charvat, p. 36, for the Waltham engagement.